CARMEL COLLE __
in the KOPUL ERA

CARMEL COLLEGE
in the KOPUL ERA

A History of
CARMEL COLLEGE
September 1948–March 1962

CHAIM SIMONS
(Alumnus 1953–1960)

URIM PUBLICATIONS
Jerusalem • New York

Carmel College in the Kopul Era:
A History of Carmel College,
September 1948 – March 1962

by Chaim Simons

Copyright © 2016 Chaim Simons

Typeset by Ariel Walden

Printed in Israel

First Edition

ISBN 978-965-524-236-2

Urim Publications
P.O. Box 52287
Jerusalem 9152102
Israel

www.UrimPublications.com

Library of Congress Cataloging-in-Publication Data

Names: Simons, Chaim, author.
Title: Carmel College in the Kopul era : a history of Carmel College,
   September 1948-March 1962 / Chaim Simons.
Description: First edition. | New York : Urim Publications, 2016. |
   Includes bibliographical references.
Identifiers: LCCN 2016025467 | ISBN 9789655242362 (paperback)
Subjects: LCSH: Carmel College (Oxfordshire, England)—History.
   | Rosen, Kopul, 1913–1962. | BISAC: HISTORY / General. |
   EDUCATION / Philosophy & Social Aspects.
Classification: LCC LF795.O97 S56 2016 | DDC 373.22/2094257—dc23
   LC record available at https://lccn.loc.gov/2016025467

This book is dedicated to the memory of
Rabbi Dr. KOPUL ROSEN and his wife BELLA

"I AM CALLED the founder of Carmel but the real truth is that I am the co-founder: Bella is at least an equal partner. Had we not been united by the deepest of bonds we could not have faced all our problems together and triumphed."

Letter written by Kopul
to his father-in-law
shortly before he died.

Contents

Preface

FOR FORTY-NINE YEARS, there was an important Anglo-Jewish institution in the south of England, for the first five years near to Newbury and in the following forty-four years adjacent to Wallingford. This was Carmel College, which unfortunately came to the end of its existence in 1997. Carmel College was founded in 1948 by Rabbi Kopul Rosen and there were about 800 pupils who joined Carmel College during the Kopul era (September 1948 – March 1962).

If its history is not recorded, Carmel College will disappear from the annals of history. What is more, this needs to be done speedily, since as time progresses, documentary evidence will cease to exist and those who can give evidence will have left this World.

In order that my personal recollections of Carmel College should not be forgotten, in 2004, I wrote them down and I also made a revised edition in 2006. It was a very detailed account occupying well over 100 pages. But it needs to be stressed that these were my own personal recollections. A history of Carmel College needs to be on a far wider base, and for this reason on 15 November 2004, I put the following message on the Carmel Message Board (which at that time was on the internet), which included the following, "A history of Carmel College [needs to] be written. I would suggest it be divided into 4 parts corresponding to the 4 Headmasters (or Principals). Since it is easy to suggest that others (but not oneself!) do the work, I am prepared to volunteer to do the era of Rabbi Kopul Rosen."

It would seem that the number of Old Carmelis who saw this Message Board was not large and I got virtually no response to my message. However, the opportunity came in a reunion in Jerusalem to mark Kopul's

50th Yahrzeit. This was held on 1 March 2012 at Yakar in Jerusalem with a video link to a reunion held in London at precisely the same time. At this reunion, which in Jerusalem and London together was attended by about 100 Old Carmelis of the Kopul era, I put forward my suggestion. A few days later I sent an e-mail to the 200 Old Carmelis of the Kopul era, whose e-mails I knew, with details of how I proposed to write this history of Carmel College during the Kopul era.

After over two years of work, the book is ready. It is divided into two sections. The first is a history of Carmel College during the Kopul era, and the second is biographies of the teachers who were at Carmel during the Kopul era. (This will be elaborated on in the Introductions to these two sections.)

I decided that the book would be meticulously documented, but in order to encourage people to read beyond the third page, I have tried to utilise a lighter style than is normally found in scholarly works. I have also included some humour – as with all humour some people will like it, whilst others won't!

Just a word about the numerous quotes to be found in the book. Strictly speaking, if one wants to replace a capital letter in a quote by a small letter, or vice versa, the letter should be enclosed in square brackets. I have not done this, since it is less aesthetic and also makes it harder to read. Within a quote, round brackets ( ) mean that the words included in the brackets are words found in brackets within the original quote; words contained within square brackets [ ] indicate that these words do not appear in the original but have been added by myself for the sake of clarity. If a direct quote was more than about four lines long, I inset the quote on the left-hand side and omitted the quotation marks at both the beginning and the end of the quote.

There are "Manuals of Style" which rule, for example, whether a full stop should come before or after inverted commas, or before or after the number of the footnote. I have not followed any of these "Manuals of Style" but have made my criterion that the text should look aesthetic, and thus it could well be that the position, for example, of a full stop will not necessarily be consistent throughout the book.

There are often several ways to transliterate the same word from Hebrew to English, and the authors of the various quotes brought in this book indeed used different transliterations. The original transliterations have been retained.

Since today with the "Google" search engine, it is easy to find things on the internet, I have not, for sites referred to on the Internet, included the URL, but have just written the word "Internet."

On a number of occasions I have used material from Wikipedia. It is true that in some scholarly circles Wikipedia is frowned on, but almost all the Wikipedia references used are for background material and not directly for material on Carmel College.

I have tried to make the references user-friendly. Thus I have often repeated in full a reference which occurs on several occasions, rather than in an abbreviated form. In addition, in order to prevent the reader from having to search through earlier quoted references in order to understand an abbreviation, here is a list in alphabetical order of the abbreviations appearing in the references:

Auction Crookham = Auction catalogue used for the sale of the Crookham House Estate on 22 September 1939, Lot 15, (West Berkshire Museum).

Auction Greenham = Auction catalogue used for the sale of Greenham Lodge on 20 September 1938. Lot 20, (West Berkshire Museum).

Biography of KR = the online book by Jeremy Rosen, *Kopul Rosen 1913–1962*, (published in 2011).

CCLtd = the company "Carmel College Limited."

CCPE OSA Magazine = Chelsea College of Physical Education, Old Students' Association Magazine.

Conveyance Mongewell = Deed of Conveyance for the Mongewell Estate dated 7 August 1953.

FMF = the book *In memory of F.M. Friedmann*, (Oxford, 1978).

Founding Days = G. P. Warner, "The Founding Days of Eversley College," (Kent County Council, 1973).

Gertner = the book *Meir Gertner – An Anthology*, ed. A.H. Friedlander and Fred S. Worms (B'nai Brith: London, 1978).

Inspectors' Report = Ministry of Education, Report by H.M. Inspectors on Carmel College, issued 8 June 1955.

KR = Kopul Rosen

Memories of KR = the book *Memories of Kopul Rosen*, ed. Cyril Domb, (London, 1970).

OCA = Old Carmeli Association.

Pedgley = the book by Berenice and David Pedgley, *Crowmarsh, A history of Crowmarsh Gifford, Newnham Murren, Mongewell and North Stoke*, (Crowmarsh: Crowmarsh History Group, 1990).

Purchase Mongewell = Contract for sale and purchase of the Freehold Mansion House and premises known as Mongewell Park situated in the Parish of Crowmarsh (formerly Mongewell) in the County of Oxford, dated 26 January 1953.

Rau letters = Anthony Rau, Letters written home from Carmel College between 1950–1955.

Reflections = the book *Reflections: Carmel College 1948–1988.*

Review by Governors = Review of the Year 1955/56 by the Chairman of the Board of Governors of Carmel College, 6 December 1956.

7 years = the book by Chaim Simons, *Seven Years at Carmel College,* (published in 2006); (the page numbers refer to the revised edition of 2006). Some stylistic changes have been made.

In addition, three Latin expressions, commonly used when quoting references, appear in the footnotes. They are:

ibid. = this refers to a work cited in the immediately proceeding footnote.

op. cit. = this refers to a previously cited work. (To make the footnotes more user friendly, the term "op. cit." has only been used when it is in reasonably close proximity to the full reference.)

passim = this is used when there are a number of scattered references in the work.

A very large number of the references are from the various Carmel magazines. The word "Carmel" refers to the annual magazine brought out each summer, and it is followed by the year it was published. The magazines "Badad," "The Young Carmelonian," "The Phoenix," the "Carmel Fanfare," and the Junior Biology magazine, only had one issue and so no further identifying details are given. The "Carmel Clarion" and the various Prep School magazines both of which had more than one issue, are followed by identifying details.

A number of references are followed by the words "name withheld." This is used when the reference refers to pupils' school reports, bills for fees sent to parents, and the amount of the fees paid for individual pupils. Needless to say, this is done to preserve privacy.

At the Reunion, I requested that Old Carmelis from the Kopul era send me their recollections of Carmel College during the Kopul era, and I received such material, of varying length from about fifty of them. There were a few who sent me such material on several occasions, in some cases new material and in others revised material. The names of those who sent such recollections (whether prior or after the Reunion) together with the dates that I received them are:

Ackerman, Melvyn, 10 September 2012.
Alton, Neil, 4 July 2012.
Batiste, Spencer, 7 March 2012.
Benaim, Moshe, 13 February 2013.
Berwin, Harold, 8 October 2012.
Bharier, Michael, 2 February 2012, March and April 2012, 15 May 2012.
Blackstone, Michael, 1 February 2012, 13 July 2012.
Coleman, Jack, 31 January 2012.
Dell, Anton, 1 February 2012.
Dwek, Joe, 1 February 2012.
Dwek, Raymond, 11 June 2012.
Ellman, Michael, 8 January 2012, 18 May 2012.
Fachler, Jacob, 2 February 2012.
Fischer, John, 14 August 2012.
Fisher, Jeffrey, 8 January 2014.
Frome, David, 2 February 2012.
Gandz, Jeffrey, 6 January 2012, March 2012.
Goitein, Michael, family history, chapter on Carmel, 2011.
Gold, Alan, 31 January 2012.
Gold, Stephen, 30 January 2012.
Grodzinski, Emanuel, 30 January 2012.
Isserlin, Jonathan, 8 January 2012, 25 May 2012, 25 August 2013.
Katz, Elliot, 8 January 2012.
Law, Henry, autobiography 2012.
Levy, Solomon (Momy), 25 May 2012.
Lew, Julian, 6 January 2012.
Mandell, George, 4 March 2013.
Marks, David, 11 January 2012.
Miller, Joe, 5 March 2012, 9 March 2012.
Mond, David, 30 January 2012.
Morris, Stephen, 2 February 2012.
Myeroff, Neil, 24 July 2012.
Nehorai, Julius, 10 January 2012, 7 June 2012.
Odze, Harvey, 9 February 2012.
Panto, Ian, 20 March 2012.

Paradise, Geoffrey, 2 February 2012.
Rabinowitz, Ian, February 2012.
Robbins, David, 14 March 2013.
Robson, David, 15 September 2013.
Rosen, Jeremy, History and Memoir on Carmel chapter 1; personal
　　recollections 28 March 2012.
Saville, David, undated.
Shaw, David, 20 September 2012.
Sheldon, David, 8 January 2012.
Simons, Nigel, 21 May 2012.
Slater, Martin, 17 February 2012.
Waldman. David, 9 January 2012.

Thanks to all those who sent me recollections. They have made an important contribution to the book.

The relevant portions of the films and audio recordings were extracted by my son-in-law Baruch Mizrahi hy'd. On Erev Pesach 2014 he was murdered in a terrorist attack near Kiryat Arba, Israel.

*

This printed copy of the book includes many documents and photographs. Some of the photographs were taken by Michael Bharier and David Shaw and many of the others are from the Carmel archives "Carmelismus." Furthermore, in 2012, during his visit to the Mongewell campus, David Shaw took a large number of colour photographs. The scenes in some of them are substantially the same as during the Kopul era – namely those of the grounds and the exterior and interior of the Main Building – and these photographs appear in the book. My thanks to all these photographers.

Acknowledgment

I gratefully acknowledge DAVID DANGOOR's financing of the publication of this book in its entirety. David was a pupil at Carmel College between the years 1960 and 1967, and thereafter maintained an interest in the school. When Carmel College suddenly closed in 1997, the Exilarch's Foundation, set up by David's late father and whose trustees are David and his brothers, purchased the Carmel estate and this enabled the staff and other employees of Carmel College to receive suitable compensation for loss of employment. When I came to write this book in a voluntary capacity in 2012, David paid for my out of pocket expenses. In 2014 I finished writing the book, and I then sent copies as an attachment to an e-mail to all the Old Carmelis of the Kopul era whose e-mails I knew. A number of these alumni suggested that I bring out this book in a printed hard copy. I therefore again contacted David and he readily agreed to cover the entire cost of publication. I feel sure that the Carmeli alumni, the public at large and educational historians will forever be very grateful to David for having made this publication possible.

SECTION ONE

OVERDRAFTS
AND THEIR RESULTS

"Can you not consider it [loan to Carmel]
please within the next few minutes instead
of weeks?"

—from letter written by Kopul Rosen

Introduction

(Unless stated to the contrary, names mentioned in this introduction are Old Carmelis, and almost all are from the Kopul era.)

This section consists of nine chapters, which deal with different aspects of Carmel College during the Kopul era. It has been called "Overdrafts and their Results," since despite the fact that Carmel had a constant overdraft, Kopul managed to overcome this problem and worked wonders in running and developing the School.

To write any research work, one has to assemble material, usually from numerous sources and this book is not an exception. I shall now briefly describe how I assembled this information, with the appropriate acknowledgements to all those who provided me with this material. All those who provided me with information (even if they replied that they had no information to give me) immediately received an e-mail from me thanking them for their replies.

Carmel College was run by a Limited Company, known as Carmel College Ltd. Every such company has a file at the Companies Registration Office, which is open to inspection by the general public. I remember that in the 1960s, I myself went to inspect the file of this Company. It includes the incorporation document, the Memorandum and the Articles of Association, the Annual Accounts, Annual Returns, the appointment and resignation of the Directors, and various resolutions passed by the Company.

Anyone can order copies of any document from a Company's file – at a cost. The Companies Registration Office indeed knows how to charge! They informed me that to order all the material from the file of the Kopul era would cost about £300. One of the Directors of the Carmel College

Limited Company, which still continued to function well after the demise of Carmel College, was David Dangoor. I contacted him and asked whether he would be prepared to cover this cost. He immediately wrote back with a positive answer, indeed more than this. He realised that there would be many other out-of-pocket expenses and he accordingly arranged for the Exilarch's Foundation (of which he is a Director) to send me a cheque for £1,000. Indeed there have been numerous other out-of-pocket expenses. These include ordering documents from the National Archives (also not cheap!), photocopying of many thousands of pages, travelling expenses to visit archives and libraries, numerous telephone calls to all over the world (including within Israel, England, Ireland, USA, Gibraltar, Australia, and South Africa), shipment of a very large box of documents from England to Israel, and after scanning and photocopying the material, returning it to England. My sincere thanks to David Dangoor and the Exilarch's Foundation.

An indispensable source of information for such a book are past Carmel school magazines. At the reunion in Jerusalem, David Duke brought along to put on display almost a complete set of the Carmel annual summer magazines during the Kopul era. He kindly loaned them to me and I scanned them and also made a photocopy of each of them. David Shaw had a number of Carmel magazines, which included "The Young Carmelonian," "Badad," and "The Phoenix," each of which only brought out one issue. He also had one issue of a Prep School magazine "Alpha," and three issues of the "Carmel Clarion." Here also I scanned and photocopied them (together with other miscellaneous material which he sent me). At that stage I was still missing the Prep School magazines for the remaining years and in a letter I sent to the Old Carmelis of the Kopul era I asked if anyone had copies of them. David Sheldon replied that he had two further "Alpha" magazines which he loaned me for scanning and photocopying. The remaining two Prep School magazines were included in the material which I received from London (see below). I also received a scan of a further "Carmel Clarion" from Spencer Batiste. My thanks to all those who loaned me these magazines. I might add that, before I obtained these magazines from the Old Carmelis, I found from the catalogue of the British Library in London, that they had many of the Carmel magazines. However, when I contacted them, they could not find the magazines!

I had heard that there were Carmel archives in existence, but the question was where they were. I learned that Jeff Serlin had collected together from various sources, archival material on Carmel. On contacting him, he said that he had passed them on to Jill Kenton, and she informed me that they were stored in a warehouse, but the person who had the key was out of town for several months. Eventually she received the key, and was on the point of moving the material to a different location, which was closer to London. The material in this archive was not limited to just the Kopul era and thus someone was needed to go through it and extract the relevant material. (I obvious could not do so since I live in Israel.) This was done by Neil Myeroff and Jill Kenton, and Neil then had the material crated and sent to me in Israel. As with all the other materials, I scanned and photocopied it, and then returned it to them. One of the main items of this material was the correspondence by Kopul to countless hopefully potential donors during the years 1947 and 1948. It also included the two Prep School magazines which I did not yet have, numerous photographs, some news clippings, the Government Inspectors' Report on Carmel, a few (and I mean only a few) Governors' and Development Fund Minutes, a Carmel Prospectus from the 1950s, material on social and sportive activities at Carmel, and much other miscellaneous material. My thanks to Jeff, Neil, and Jill.

David Dangoor also had in his possession some archival material which he scanned and sent to me. This included the Contract for Sale and Purchase of the Mongewell Estate (which contained a detailed description of the Main Building), and also a number of news cuttings and some miscellaneous material up to 1955, which from the numbering on it could well have been part of "Carmelismus," the Carmel archives put together by Malcolm Shifrin ("Shif"). My thanks to David.

One of the books I used for the history of Mongewell was a book entitled "Crowmarsh" written by Berenice and David Pedgley. I wanted to reproduce several pages from this book and so I wrote to David Pedgley to ask permission, which he readily gave. As a result of our correspondence I learned that he had a copy of the Deed of Conveyance of the Mongewell Estate to Carmel, and he sent me a scan of the entire document. He had received this document from Carmel College's solicitors in 1981 when he was preparing his book. My thanks to David Pedgley.

There was also some audio material. This included speeches by Kopul which had been transferred to a DVD, and in Raymond Dwek's possession there was a recording of the entire 1960 Carmel Speech Day (with the exception of the actual distribution of the prizes) and he sent me a copy. My thanks to Raymond. A gramophone record of the Carmel choir under Dudley Cohen had been produced in the late 1950s, and Michael Bharier, who had a copy, sent me the recording by e-mail. My thanks to Michael. The families of both Spencer Batiste and Jacques Koppel had filmed on their cine cameras short extracts of Sports Days at Carmel (which included "little" David Rosen aged about 4 competing in the running against "big" Senior School boys!). They transferred them to a DVD and sent me a copy. My thanks to Spencer and Jacques.

I was informed that there was Carmel archival material still in the basement of the Main Building at Mongewell. After having obtained permission from the present owners of the former Carmel estate, David Shaw travelled all the way to Mongewell (taking with him a torch, since there was no electricity in the basement!) and searched the basement, but the only material he could see was from the 1980s which was not relevant to this book. My thanks to David.

An important source of material for those doing Anglo-Jewish historical research is the past issues of the "Jewish Chronicle." On their website, one can find where Carmel College is mentioned. During the Kopul era, it appeared about 600 times. I spent several days in the Central Zionist Archives and the Jewish National Library, both of them situated in Jerusalem, going through these 600 references (a large number were just advertisements for Carmel), extracting the relevant ones and having them photocopied. My thanks to these two institutions.

I wanted to include in this book a brief history of Greenham, Crookham, and Mongewell, from Norman times and for this I obtained material from the internet. I also found on the internet "Auction Catalogues" from the end of the 1930s of Greenham Lodge and Crookham House (the first two locations where Carmel was situated), which gave a detailed description of the rooms in the buildings and of the surrounding grounds.

I needed some material from two books/booklets which were not available in Israel nor on the internet and I received scans of the appropriate pages from the Bodleian Library in Oxford, and from the Hebrew Union College Library in Cincinnati. My thanks to these places.

I wanted to integrate the recollections of Old Carmelis from the Kopul era into the documentary material, and I thus requested that they send me such material. About fifty of them sent in their recollections. In most cases, they were written following my request, but some had sent in very brief recollections on being informed of the Reunion. In a few cases, the material was of a much greater length and had been written at an even earlier date, generally as their autobiographies, and they included their recollections of Carmel. In the references quoted at the bottom of each page, I have described all this material under the generic term of "Recollections," for this is indeed what they are. In addition, there were Old Carmelis who sent me scans of photographs which they possessed or had taken themselves, and there were those who identified pupils and teachers who appeared in photographs. I hereby thank all of them.

On a number of occasions when I needed certain bits of information, I wrote to various Old Carmelis of the Kopul era to see if they could provide the answers. In some of the cases they were able to help, and my thanks to them.

I received a very important piece of material from Anthony Rau. He had kept the letters he had written home when he was in Carmel from 1950 to 1955, and he extracted all the passages which could be relevant for my book, and gave me permission to reproduce them. These are of particular importance, since this was material, written almost like a diary, on a day to day basis, and it is therefore more reliable than recollections of events which occurred in the distant past. My thanks to Anthony.

Some other Carmel publications which were used are the book "Memories of Kopul Rosen" edited by Cyril Domb and published in 1970, and a book brought out in 1988 entitled "Reflections 1948–1988" which contains recollections (many of which are from the Kopul era), of staff members, workers, and Old Carmelis.

In conclusion, if I have failed to mention anyone who sent me material, I hereby apologise.

Chapter 1

Cash and Carmel

Kopul loved to teach Pirkei Avot and then make the boys learn it by heart. Included in Pirkei Avot is the axiom, "Where there is no flour, there is no Torah."[1] From this we can deduce that if one wants to establish a school such as Carmel College one needs cash and plenty of it! Hence one needs supporters who have large bank balances, and one must set up some sort of official Company with a Board of Governors who will administer this money. This is how Kopul accomplished this. . . .

LETTERS WITHOUT END!

In the summer of 1947, Kopul was already actively planning the opening of Carmel College. In a letter written on 5 June 1947, which he sent to numerous, what he hoped would be supporters, he began:

> For a number of years, much has been spoken and written about the need for a first-rate Jewish boarding school in Anglo-Jewry, to be run on public school lines and to reach a very high level both in secular and Jewish religious education. The dream of establishing such an institution which would ultimately become one of the greatest educational forces in our community is one which I have cherished for many years, and I feel certain that it is an idea which meets with your enthusiastic approval.[2]

---

1. Pirkei Avot, chap.3, mishnah 21.
2. Letter from Kopul Rosen [henceforth: KR] to numerous addressees, 5 June 1947.

From the continuation of his letter, we can see that Kopul was not talking in the abstract. He had already utilised his time to explore the hills and dales of the picturesque British countryside, and as a result had found an estate for his proposed school:

> Within recent weeks, I have taken the first steps to realise this project, and I am happy to inform you that a contract is about to be signed whereby a magnificent building with 60 acres of ground, on the outskirts of Newbury, Berks, will be acquired. I feel it would be detrimental to the tone and future development of such [an] institution if it were established by means of an appeal for funds, whether public or private, and it is not my intention to finance this project by means of an appeal. I feel however that responsible men in the community who approve of this great plan which is being envisaged should be made aware of what is being done and should be associated in some way with this venture.[3]

It is not clear whether Kopul had "wandered lonely as a cloud" in his meandering of the countryside to find this building or that he already had supporters to accompany him.

Kopul realised that it was essential that potential supporters meet together to advance his project and he thus concluded his letter:

> The whole scheme cannot of course be elaborated in all its details in a letter, and I am therefore inviting a number of prominent communal personalities from London and the provinces to meet in my house (50, Farm Avenue, London N.W.2.) on Wednesday, 18th June, at 8.30 p.m. when I shall be glad to outline the project and its methods of realisation, and to give an account of what has been done up to date. I shall be grateful if you will make an effort to be present at this meeting, and I shall be glad to hear that I may expect you.[4]

The letter was sent off. . . . Some RSVPs were quick to arrive – polite, but obviously a disappointment to Kopul! "Nothing would have given me greater pleasure than to have accepted your invitation for Wednesday, June 18th had it only been possible – but it is not . . . I have a previous

---

3. Ibid.
4. Ibid.

Carmel College Main Building at Greenham in 1949

engagement on that date,"[5] "I am sorry I cannot be present in London on the date on which the meeting is being convened,"[6] "I am afraid I will not be able to attend. I am devoting my time and resources to the East and West library, at present, and this seems to leave nothing over for other communal work,"[7] "I regret that I shall not be able to be present"[8] – no excuse offered!; "I have every sympathy for the project but cannot undertake any more work at the moment."[9] There were also many others who wrote likewise.

However, in contrast, there were a few acceptances. "I suppose there is no need for me to send you a formal acknowledgement of your invitation because you know how keen I am on this scheme, with certain minor reservations. I am looking forward to the meeting on the 18th instant,"[10]

5. Letter from Ivan Shortt to KR, 6 June 1947.
6. Letter from Maurice Bloch to KR, 6 June 1947.
7. Letter with illegible signature on "East and West Library" notepaper to KR, 9 June 1947.
8. Letter from Israel Sieff to KR, 9 June 1947.
9. Letter from Sidney (remainder illegible) to KR, 12 June 1947.
10. Letter from J.C. Gilbert to KR, 6 June 1947.

5th June, 1947/5707.

Dear

For a number of years, much has been spoken and written about the need for a first-rate Jewish boarding school in Anglo-Jewry, to be run on public school lines and to reach a very high level both in secular and Jewish religious education. The dream of establishing such an institution which would ultimately become one of the greatest educational forces in our community is one which I have cherished for many years, and I feel certain that it is an idea which meets with your enthusiastic approval.

Within recent weeks, I have taken the first steps to realise this project, and I am happy to inform you that a contract is about to be signed whereby a magnificent building with 60 acres of ground, on the outskirts of Newbury, Berks, will be acquired. I feel it would be detrimental to the tone and future development of such institution if it were established by means of an appeal for funds, whether public or private, and it is not my intention to finance this project by means of an appeal. I feel however that responsible men in the community who approve of this great plan which is being envisaged should be made aware of what is being done and should be associated in some way with this venture.

The whole scheme cannot of course be elaborated in all its details in a letter, and I am therefore inviting a number of prominent communal personalities from London and the provinces to meet in my house (50, Farm Avenue, London, N.W.2.) on Wednesday, 18th June, at 8.30 p.m., when I shall be glad to outline the project and its methods of realisation, and to give an account of what has been done up to date.

I shall be grateful if you will make an effort to be present at this meeting, and I shall be glad to hear that I may expect you.

With kind regards,

Yours sincerely,

The Initial Letter Written by Kopul Rosen Requesting Financial Assistance to Establish Carmel College

"I shall be pleased to attend the Meeting."[11] Both these gentlemen were to become members of the original Governing Body.

This meeting indeed took place, and in a letter to Cyril Ross written during the following week, Kopul gave him a report of the proceedings:

> A meeting was held in my house the following evening, which was attended by a number of business men and others interested in the establishment of this Jewish school. After going into the figures carefully, it was found that we would require the following sums: Property £16,000; Repairs and decorations £3,500; Equipment and Furniture etc. £5,000; Total Capital Expenditure £24.500.
>
> We made a careful examination of the money which would be required for teaching staff, administrative staff, domestic and gardening staff, food and other expenses, and it was felt that £15,000 a year would cover all our outgoings.
>
> It was the opinion of the meeting that we should try to raise £50,000 by loan, which would pay for all capital expenditure and also guarantee our expenses for more than a year. There will also have to be the capital expenditure of equipping a laboratory and a gymnasium (premises are available for such installations), but this would be covered by our budget of £50,000.
>
> I suggested that the fees should be £200 a year, but the majority of the people thought that we could ask for slightly more. It was pointed out that the ordinary Jewish boarding school, by including quite a variety of extras, charges more than £200 per annum. This means that our income from 100 pupils should be not less than £20,000 a year, and our annual expenditure will be £15,000. This will leave us a fair margin to repay interest in such cases where people desire interest on their loans.
>
> The committee was very glad to hear that you had assured me of your support. I should be pleased if you could arrange for me to meet a number of your friends, that I can outline this scheme to them. We hope to complete the deal in the very near future.[12]

However, in this detailed report of the meeting, Kopul did not state how many people attended, nor did he give any of the names of the attendees.

---

11. Letter from Oscar Philipp to KR, 10 June 1947.
12. Letter from KR to Cyril Ross, 25 June 1947.

From the content of the replies to Kopul's original letters, one might deduce that the Rosen family did not require a large budget for the tea and cake provided that evening!

A month later Kopul tried to interest Simon Marks and Israel Sieff (of Marks and Spencer's fame!) in the project[13] but received a negative reply, "I think I ought to tell you in advance that, with all the best will in the world, we do not think we can be of much assistance to you at this present moment. We have so much on our plate that to assume any other responsibility would be merely to fill our cup to overflowing, and other needs of our people would suffer." The letter ended with the oft quoted cliché, "Perhaps we can have a talk about it later on, when the time will be more propitious."[14] Harry Sacher was also a member of the Marks and Spencer's clan, and towards the beginning of 1948, Kopul met with him to obtain a loan, and he later wrote to him:

> Whenever I approach people in the community, one of the first questions they ask, perhaps unfairly, is 'have you seen Marks, Sieff and Sacher?' If I were able to state that you had helped in some measure, no matter how small, the moral effect would be far greater than you imagine. This is no flattery, it is a plain statement of fact. I would even add that it is an unfortunate fact, because I regard it as unfortunate that people are incapable of judging an educational project on its merits but always insist on knowing who are the 'big shots' who approve of the scheme. But such is the situation, and I want your help.[15]

At the same period, Kopul sent a very similar letter (namely, the 5 June letter) to two Anglo-Jewish academics, Dr. Cecil Roth and Professor Selig Brodetsky. However, in place of inviting them to the meeting he wrote, "The purpose of my writing to you is to learn your views on the scheme and to receive any suggestions which you may care to make."[16]

About a week later, Brodetsky replied, "I need hardly say that I am very much interested in the development of such a scheme and would very much like to have a talk with you about it." He went on to invite Kopul

---

13. Letter from KR to Simon Marks, 7 July 1947.
14. Letter from Israel Sieff to KR, 23 July 1947.
15. Letter from KR to Harry Sacher, 25 February 1948.
16. Letters from KR to Cecil Roth and Selig Brodetsky, 9 June 1947.

to lunch at the Kedassia Restaurant in London for this purpose,[17] which invitation Kopul accepted.[18]

At that time, what were Kopul's plans for the day-to-day running of the school? Did he plan to continue as the Principal Rabbi of the Federation of Synagogues, directing the school from afar, and making periodical Shabbat visits to the school? Or did he intend resigning from his position in the Federation of Synagogues, moving to Newbury and becoming the active Headmaster of the school?

At least a partial answer this question can be found in a letter that Kopul wrote to Isaac Wolfson in October 1947. In it he wrote, "We disagreed as to whether I should be resident in Newbury or not, but you will be glad to know that on the advice of a number of friends, including Dr. Brodetsky, I have dropped the idea of being the active Principal of the College."[19] When the school opened in September 1948, Kopul was still the Federation's Principal Rabbi and continued living in London. In fact, during much of the school's first term, he was neither in London nor Newbury. Cyril Domb reports, "In November and December 1948 Kopul visited Australia to conduct the Mizrachi Israel appeal. The War of Independence had cost heavily in money and lives. Several Mizrachi kibbutzim in the front line had been destroyed. The Mizrachi chain of schools was desperately in need of financial support." Although many were impressed by his visit to Australia, not so were the lay leaders of the Federation. "There was even talk of stopping his salary for the period when he had been 'off duty'."[20] Towards the beginning of 1949, he resigned from the Federation, sold his London house, and invested the proceeds and all his possessions in Carmel and moved to Newbury.[21]

Since, already in 1947, Kopul had decided that he would not be the active Headmaster, nor even resident at Newbury, this meant searching for a suitable Headmaster, and Cecil Roth was assigned this task.[22] It would seem that he at first searched for a Jewish Headmaster, and on this he reported to Kopul, "I did not fail to make enquiries about the potential headmaster. It turns out he is affiliated to Berkeley Street [a Reform Congregation], so that he definitely will not do. I'm afraid that I do not know

---

17. Letter from Selig Brodetsky to KR, 17 June 1947.
18. Letter from KR to Selig Brodetsky, 17 June 1947.
19. Letter from KR to Isaac Wolfson, 17 Oct 1947.
20. *Memories of Kopul Rosen*, ed. Cyril Domb, (London, 1970) [henceforth: Memories of KR], p.23.
21. Ibid., pp.23–24.
22. Letter from KR to Cecil Roth, 14 July 1947.

The Search for a Headmaster for Carmel College

of anyone else." However, Roth then went on to put forward a general suggestion. "You may recall that the greatest of all headmasters, Arnold [of Rugby School], was taken on when he had just come down from the University. It's a dangerous experiment, but the present crop of young men, especially I think in Cambridge, is promising."[23] By mid-February

23. Letter from Cecil Roth to KR, 23 June 1947.

1948, James Ewart, a non-Jew and Cambridge graduate, already experienced in education, had been appointed as headmaster.[24]

Needless to say, to run a school, one needs more than just a headmaster, and in an interview that Kopul gave to the "Jewish Chronicle" in January 1948, he said that "our problem at the moment is to get an adequate teaching staff, and we are eager to hear from Jewish teachers who feel they can be useful in this venture."[25] On 23 May 1948 a number of potential teachers, Jewish and non-Jewish, some of whom were accepted, were interviewed in London. The candidates had come for the interview from various places in England, such as Wolverhampton, Leamington Spa and Pontefract. Their travelling expenses for the interview were refunded to them at a total of £15 7s 6d.[26]

In those days one could not open a new independent school without the approval of the Ministry of Education and they only granted this in "highly exceptional cases." However, Kopul succeeded in getting this approval which he described as a "feat."[27]

From no later than October 1947, Kopul's typewriter did not rest! Indeed, one could jokingly say that the profits of the typewriter ribbon manufacturers soared! He began writing to numerous members of Anglo-Jewry in order to interest them in the project, in his words, "to support the noble undertaking,"[28] and thus to raise loans for the establishment of Carmel College. One of the first people Kopul approached was Isaac Wolfson, with presumably great expectations. In a letter which he wrote to him in October 1947, Kopul said:

> In order to make this College a first-rate institution which shall be a source of real pride to Anglo-Jewry, we need £40,000 – £50,000. I feel confident that I shall be able to raise about £15,000 to £20,000, but I need your assistance very much indeed. You have in the course of your life given away tens of thousands of pounds. I ask you now not to give, but to loan a sum of money which is perfectly secure. It will be returned within a specified period and will help in one of the most

---

24. Letter from KR to I. J. Burston, 18 February 1948.
25. Jewish Chronicle (London), 23 January 1948, p.6.
26. List of travelling expenses for interviews of potential teachers, 23 May 1948.
27. Letter from KR to Alec Stone, 17 October 1947.
28. Letters from KR to e.g. M. Berlin, I. J. Burston, F. Frohwein and M. Williams, 19 November 1947.

constructive efforts in Jewish religious education which this country has ever seen.[29]

In a postscript to this letter Kopul added, "This matter is urgent, because I must close the deal in the middle of November."[30]

On the same day that Kopul wrote to Isaac Wolfson, he also sent a copy of this letter to Alex Stone, and in an accompanying letter wrote:

> I assure you it would be useful for I.W's [Isaac Wolfson's] sake that he should be the main lender in this scheme. There will be terrific publicity in the Jewish Press, and honestly, Alec, I am interested in I.W. as a person as well as in his ability to help me, because, to be perfectly frank, even if I.W. does not help me, the scheme will not fall down. We will go on just the same, but some other person or persons will be the favoured instruments of G-d.[31]

The next extant item concerns an "At Home" meeting which was called to take place on the evening of 26 October 1947. Oscar Rabinowicz[32] was in charge of the invitations. The purpose of the meeting was not a "social tea-party," but as Kopul explained in a letter to Brodetsky, "[The meeting] will be attended by a number of people from whom I hope I shall be able to obtain substantial sums of money for my school project." He then went on to request of Brodetsky, "I think it would be helpful if I had a letter from you stating that you regard such a school, run not for private profit but for the benefit of the community, as a valuable institution in Anglo-Jewry."[33]

Brodetsky replied, "I hope that you will be able to go ahead with setting up a school for Jewish pupils in the manner that you suggested. . . . I think it is important to have schools which are essentially institutions of the Anglo-Jewish community, run by governors who have as their main object the provision of the needs of the community."[34]

There is no record of what took place at the "At Home," nor who at-

29. Letter from KR to Isaac Wolfson, 17 October 1947.
30. Ibid., postscript.
31. Letter from KR to Alec Stone, 17 October 1947.
32. Oscar Rabinowicz had been unable to attend the meeting in June, since he had just come back from the U.S.A. and in fact he only saw the invitation when he returned, and he hoped that the "deliberations were successful"; letter from Oscar Rabinowicz to KR, 20 June 1947.
33. Letter KR to Selig Brodetsky, 22 October 1947.
34. Letter from Selig Brodetsky to KR, 23 October 1947.

tended, nor indeed, how many attended. From a letter sent by Rabinowicz to Kopul, it would seem that even Kopul did not know who had been invited! Thus, following Kopul's request, Rabinowicz sent him a list of about forty people who had been invited to this "At Home." This list included, amongst many others, the men who were to be the original governors; the Labour M.P. for Bolton, John Lewis, who lived in Finchley; and Harry Grodzinki, of the famous Jewish bakery shops.[35]

Just over a week later, another meeting was called but at Kopul's home. This time only six people were invited and Kopul wrote in the invitation that "[at this meeting] the matter of Trustees, Governors, and policy of the Jewish school at Newbury will be discussed and settled. This meeting is an urgent one, as developments have reached that stage where final decisions must be made."[36] Whether or not this meeting took place is not known, but a further meeting just over two weeks later was called with the same invitees, this time planned to be at Rabinowicz' office,[37] However, the location had to be changed, since on that very day Rabinowicz' office building was closed due to the Royal Wedding (of the future Queen Elizabeth and Prince Philip).[38]

As was to be expected, Kopul received negative replies to many of his letters requesting loans, with the usual round of excuses: "It is quite impossible for me to make any financial contribution to this cause just now,"[39] "I have now decided that for the moment I cannot support this or any other similar undertaking . . . efforts must be directed in the upbuilding and fortifying of Palestine and its Institutions,"[40] "We, unfortunately, find that our position at the moment is such as not to allow us to give an appreciable help in this proposition,"[41] "I have all my capital so tied up for me that I cannot realize a sum of any interest to you. I feel sure you will be able to obtain all you need in other quarters, and I wish you all possible success."[42] There were also other letters with the same message!

---

35. Letters from Oscar Rabinowicz to KR, together with the list of invitees, 27 October 1947.
36. Letter from KR to A. Bornstein, J.C. Gilbert, B. Homa, A. Margulies, Oscar Philipp, Oscar E. Rabinowicz, 29 October 1947.
37. Letters from KR to Bornstein, Gilbert, Homa, Margulies, Philipp, 17 November 1947; letter from KR to Oscar Rabinowicz, 17 November 1947.
38. Letter from Rabinowicz to KR, 18 November 1947.
39. Letter from Councillor E. Snowman to KR, 14 November 1947.
40. Letter from M. Williams to KR, 28 November 1947.
41. Letter from brother of Clarica Davidson (signature illegible) to KR, 1 December 1947. There is also a similarly worded handwritten letter from Clarica Davidson dated 1 or 7 (date not clear) December 1947.
42. Letter from S. Myers to KR, 17 December 1947.

It was at this period that Kopul also wrote numerous letters in order to arrange meetings with potential donors. He obviously hoped that he had been successful at these meetings in persuading his potential donors to give loans, and he would thus follow up these meetings with letters. One such letter written on 9 December 1947 said, "I would be very glad if you could let me have a cheque at your earliest convenience, as the latest date for the settlement of our purchase is at the end of December."[43]

Another, which was written the same day to S. Goldstein gave this gentleman even less time for payment! "I would be very glad indeed if you would let me have your cheque during the course of the week."[44] However, in this case Kopul had been over optimistic, since he received a reply from Goldstein, "I thank you for your letter but was rather surprised to note the contents, as I said that I would consider the matter at the end of January next, and I did not agree to do anything about it immediately."[45] In fact a couple of months later he wrote to Kopul that because he had given large sums to the J.P.A. [Joint Palestine Appeal], he could not help him at that period.[46] Kopul, who was not in the habit of accepting excuses lightly replied, "All the people who have helped me are men whom you know quite well and who have also given to the J.P.A., although perhaps not to the same extent as you have done. Nevertheless they are people with great commitments, and whenever I have approached any one of them, they have asked what has Mr. Sam Goldstein lent to you."[47] However, this letter had no effect and Goldstein replied, "I very much regret that I am unable to alter my decision."[48]

There was one person, Major Edmund de Rothschild, who openly admitted to Kopul, "I am not altogether in favour of a public school such as you envisaged . . . it is only fair to tell you that I am not very happy about the scheme."[49] Kopul did not accept this answer as final but wrote back to him, "I am sure that if I had an opportunity of explaining the situation to you, you might view the project from a different angle."[50]

In contrast to the refusals, there were a few speedy promises for loans.

---

43. Letter from KR to N. Frost, 9 December 1947; similar letter written to M. Rosin, 12 December 1947.
44. Letter from KR to Sam Goldstein, 9 December 1947.
45. Letter from Sam Goldstein to KR, 11 December 1947.
46. Letter from Sam Goldstein to KR, 2 February 1948.
47. Letter from KR to Sam Goldstein, 3 February 1948.
48. Letter from Sam Goldstein to KR, 4 February 1948.
49. Letter from Edmund de Rothschild to KR, 27 February 1948.
50. Letter from KR to Edmund de Rothschild, 1 March 1948.

Charles Clore promised a loan of £1,000[51] and it would seem that S. Beckman made a similar undertaking.[52] However, a week later, Clore, with his business instincts, wrote to Kopul, "Before definitely loaning the Company the amount in question in respect of a Jewish Public School, I should like to see the agreement to be entered into."[53] Kopul immediately sent him a copy of the loan agreement, together with some technical clarifications, and concluded his letter, "I do hope that after reading through the agreement you will kindly let us have your loan as soon as possible, for we wish to complete this purchase this month."[54] A couple of weeks later, Clore's loan was received.[55]

Kopul continuously stressed that he didn't want donations but loans. But loans must have conditions attached for their repayment and in letters written in mid-December 1947, Kopul was more specific regarding details of the loans that he hoped to receive, "The average sum of money which is being loaned is between £500 and £2,000, and we are prepared to pay an interest not exceeding 4 per cent. I would like to emphasise the fact that these are loans and not donations and the Company enters into a loan agreement with every lender."[56] There were some people who were prepared to loan less than £500, but at first Kopul was not happy with this, as he write to one potential loaner, "The reason for my not having written to you before is that hitherto the minimum loan which has been given to us has been £500, and I am very reluctant to go below that figure."[57] It seems Kopul had no choice and he started to accept loans of lower sums. Indeed amongst the loans were two for just £250.[58]

Letters which were sent to potential donors from about March onwards, included the Memorandum and Articles of Association of Carmel College Limited, and a copy of the Loan Guarantee,[59] and from no later than 7 April 1948, also the Provisional Prospectus for Carmel College.[60] These Prospectuses were not donated and thus had to be paid for! There is a bill dated 12 April 1948 (and paid on 8 May 1948) which includes

51. Letter from KR to Charles Clore, 3 December 1947.
52. Letter from KR to S. Beckman, 3 December 1947.
53. Letter from Charles Clore to KR, 11 December 1947.
54. Letter from KR to Charles Clore, 16 December 1947.
55. Letter from Charles Clore to KR, 31 December 1947.
56. Letter from KR to P. Wootliffe, 15 December 1947; similar letter on same date to A. Sturm.
57. Letter from KR to F. Frohwein, 23 December 1947.
58. Letters from KR to I. Skolnick, 20 February 1948 and to Harry Grodzinski, 29 December 1947.
59. Letter from KR to J. Morgenstern, 18 March 1948.
60. Letter from KR to Julius Skrek, 7 April 1948.

500 Prospectuses at a cost of £19 10s, and 250 Application Forms for Carmel (Kopul was very optimistic!) at a cost of £2 15s, not including purchase tax.[61]

By 23 March 1948, fifteen people had loaned money to Carmel College,[62] it would seem from sums ranging from £250 to £1,000.[63] Following this date there were loans from amongst others, Kopul's father-in-law,[64] and Harold Poster[65] (who a decade later became chairman of the Carmel Development Fund). Although the minimum loan had been fixed at £250, in May 1948, a loan of just £100 was received, which was accepted, but with Kopul replying, not mincing his words, "I must be frank however and say that I had expected substantially more, especially as you are loaning this money for so short a period."[66]

A luxury Jewish hotel in Bournemouth at that period was the Green Park, where it would seem that the rich did their holidaymaking. Kopul, not missing an opportunity, wrote a letter to its proprietor Reuben Marriott:

> Because of the unique position in which you find yourself, as well as your keen interest in the whole problem of traditional Jewish training in this country, I would be glad if you would associate yourself actively with our project. This can be done in three ways: (i) By suggesting names of people who can lend money (sums from £250 upwards) to Carmel College. Among these people you can of course include yourself, if you wish. (ii) By speaking to people about this project. (iii) By joining our Board of Governors after September, when the school is opened.[67]

A few days later Reuben Marriott replied, "The moneys donated are coming in and I hope to be able to forward you a substantial cheque during the next few days."[68]

A fundamental question when asking people for loans, is what security there is for repayment of such loans. In a letter sent on 25 November

---

61. Bill from Superior Printers, New Road, London E.1, 12 April 1948.
62. List of people to whom receipts were sent, 23 March 1948.
63. Letter KR to J. Morgenstern, 18 March 1948.
64. Letter from Secretary of Company to M. J. Cohen, 14 April 1948.
65. Letter from Secretary of Company to Harold Poster, 6 May 1948.
66. Letter from KR to Julius Skrek, 12 May 1948.
67. Letter from KR to Reuben Marriott, 28 April 1948.
68. Letter from Reuben Marriott to KR, 3 May 1948.

1947[69] to Miss Clarica Davidson, Kopul wrote, "These loans are doubly secure. Firstly because the company [Carmel College Limited] is a solid one as a financial venture, and secondly because the property and the equipment will not be mortgaged to any bank or building society, but will be security to the lenders who will enter into a loan arrangement with the company."[70]

Understandably, lenders did not give their money blindly, but wanted specific details regarding their loans. One of them was I. G. Woolf who, although he had "no liquid cash at present" was prepared to "guarantee" the sum of £2,000 at Kopul's bank and Woolf would pay the interest."[71] Kopul answered:

> We have already an advance of £10,000 from the Bank. The loans are unsecured, but it is clear to all of us who are putting money into this project that the venture is so secure that there is not the slightest danger of the money not being repaid within five to six years. I would point out, and this is very important from your point of view, that in the Loan Agreement people can stipulate precisely for how long they are loaning their money and when they want it back.[72]

One can immediately see that what was written to Woolf was not the same as written to Davidson. To Davidson he wrote that "the property and the equipment will not be mortgaged to any bank." However, to Woolf he wrote that the Bank had advanced £10,000 – namely there was a bank mortgage! Obviously, Kopul was not getting the response to requests for loans which he had hoped for!

Woolf must have had second thoughts since during the following month he changed, much to Kopul's anger, the terms of his offer. As a result, it was on 20 January 1948 that Kopul wrote to him:

> In your last two letters, you have brought forward an entirely different proposal. You now offer to guarantee in the Bank £2,000, provided that the Trustees will guarantee the £2,000. Your kind offer to pay the interest for two years means in effect that you are prepared to donate a

---

69. Similar letters were also sent by KR to Mrs. S. Landau and to Alfred Cope, both on 8 December 1947.
70. Letter from KR to Miss Clarica Davidson, 25 November 1947.
71. Letter from I. G. Woolf to KR, 17 December 1947.
72. Letter from KR to I. G. Woolf, 23 December 1947.

sum of £160 to the school. Such generosity I am happily in a position to be able to decline.

I thought that your sympathy with Jewish education was such that when a really first-rate educational institution would be established, one to which you would feel privileged to be able to send your own grandchildren, your interest would be aroused. Unfortunately I was mistaken. Again let me express my disappointment, not in the absence of your help which is not of a decisive nature, but in the manner in which you have approached this plan, and above all in the fact that you have broken your promise and gone back on your word.[73]

THE LIMITED COMPANY OF CARMEL

Meanwhile, whilst all this letter writing was going on, on 3 December 1947 George Francis Shipman, who was a solicitor in Slaughter and May, signed a "declaration of compliance with the requirements of the Companies Act, 1929 on application for registration of a Company [named] Carmel College Limited."[74] (Slaughter and May was not a meat producing factory as the name might indicate, but a very large international law firm founded in 1889 by William Capel Slaughter and William May.) Submitted with this declaration was a "Memorandum of Association" and "Articles of Association."

The Memorandum included the "objects for which the Company is established" and in the course of the 23 sub-paragraphs of paragraph 3, gave a whole range of activities. The first sub-paragraph read:

> To establish, provide and carry on, whether in the United Kingdom or elsewhere, a school or schools where pupils may obtain a sound education of the highest order, and to provide religious instruction and training therein in accordance with the doctrines and principles of traditional Judaism, and generally to foster education and moral and religious training in accordance with the said principles.[75]

A school requires adequate buildings (parents would not agree to their sons living in tents!), and the next sub-paragraph dealt with this question:

---

73. Letter from KR to I. G. Woolf, 20 January 1948.
74. Carmel College Limited, Incorporation document, first two pages.
75. Carmel College Limited, Memorandum of Association, [henceforth: CCLtd Memorandum], par.3 (1).

To provide any accommodation which may be deemed desirable for pupils attending and persons employed at any school or schools carried on by the Company, including assembly halls, class rooms, sitting rooms, dormitories, studios, laboratories, libraries, music rooms, sanatoria, swimming and other baths and gymnasia, and to afford to such pupils and persons facilities and conveniences for religious instruction and reading, writing and exercise of all descriptions, and to provide board, lodging and attendance for such pupils and persons.[76]

The Jewish ethos of the school was very important and sub-paragraph 5 stated "to provide for, support and aid the performance of religious services and the delivery of religious instruction in accordance with the doctrines and principles of traditional Judaism . . ."[77]

All the above requires plenty of money and thus many paragraphs dealt with this question: "procuring contributions by way of donations, subscriptions, devises, bequests or in any other manner . . . ,"[78] "to solicit and procure by any lawful means and to accept and receive any donation of property of any nature . . . ,"[79] "to purchase, take on lease or in exchange, hire or otherwise acquire any real or personal property or any estate . . . ,"[80] "to borrow and raise money in such manner as may be considered expedient. . . ."[81]

The "Articles of Association" which comprised 77 paragraphs, dealt with the technical details of running the Company and included such headings as the "General Meetings," "Proceedings at the General Meetings," "Votes of Members," "Disqualification of Governors," keeping of Minutes of Meeting, use of the "Seal" of the Company, keeping of Accounts and Auditing of them, and how the Company could be wound up.[82]

All the seven original governors signed this document, their signatures being witnessed by a solicitor. These governors were (in the order they signed the document): Joseph Gilbert who was a merchant shipper; Alexander Margulies, a clock manufacturer; Abraham Bornstein, a director of estates companies; Bernard Homa, a medical practitioner; Oscar Philipp,

---

76. Ibid., par.3.(2).
77. Ibid., par.3 (5).
78. Ibid., par.3 (6).
79. Ibid., par.3 (9).
80. Ibid., par.3 (13).
81. Ibid., par.3 (15).
82. Carmel College Limited, Articles of Association [henceforth: CCLtd Articles].

DUPLICATE FOR THE FILE

No. 446445

Certificate of Incorporation

I Hereby Certify, That

CARMEL COLLEGE LIMITED

and 1947,
is this day Incorporated under the Companies Act, 1929, and that the Company is Limited.

Given under my hand at London this   Eleventh   day of
December   One Thousand Nine Hundred and Forty-seven.

Registrar of Companies.

Certificate received by

Date

Certificate of Incorporation of Carmel College Limited

a metal merchant; Kopul Rosen; and George Shipman, a solicitor.[83] At that period Kopul was President of the British Mizrachi and most of these governors were members of the Mizrachi.[84]

---

83. Ibid., p.23.
84. Recollections – Jeremy Rosen, chap.1.

The first meeting of Carmel College Limited took place at the offices of Slaughter and May on 17 December 1947. In his letter convening the meeting, Kopul wrote, "It is of absolute importance that we should all be present at this meeting, because it is only then that we shall become formally established as a Company and shall be able to proceed further."[85]

Draft minutes for this meeting were written up, before this meeting actually took place! This can be seen from the heading "Draft Minutes of First Council Meeting *to be held* . . . on 17th December 1947" *(emphasis added)*. Spaces which were left in these minutes to be filled in later, were for the names of those present at the meeting, for the names of those appointed to be the first Governors, and for the name of the person to be appointed as Chairman of the Council. The remainder of the planned agenda was to put before those present at the meeting, the various official documents of Carmel College Limited.[86] Carmel College Limited thus became a fact, although Carmel College School was still nine months into the future – an eagerly awaited birth!

£. s. d.

As stated above, by the beginning of the summer of the year 1947, Kopul had already found premises for Carmel, but he did not receive them on a "silver platter" – on the contrary he had to pay "silver" for them – or in modern language "hard cash!"[87] The £.s.d. that was required to purchase Greenham Lodge was £16,528 7s 6d. In addition there were developments and improvements which had to be made on the property and they came to £12,604 11s 3d. Needless to say a school requires furniture, fittings, cutlery linen, and bedding, and this was at a cost of £4,478 19s 5d. This was not the end of the story! Up to the end of March 1949 (the end of the second term of Carmel), whereas the income from school fees came to £4,006 2s 10d, the expenditure for education, administration, domestic and establishment matters exceeded this income about by nearly £8,000.

---

85. Letter from KR to B. Homa, A. Bornstein, J. C. Gilbert, A. Margulies and Oscar Philipp, 15 December 1947.
86. CCLtd, Draft Minutes of First Council Meeting.
87. Cyril Domb wrote (Memories of KR, p.22) that "Mr. S. London advanced £500 as a deposit" for the purchase of Greenham Lodge. Amongst the list of lenders there is S. London for £500; however Domb did not state a source that S. London's £500 was specifically for the deposit. Who was this S. London? He never became a Governor and his name does not appear in any other Carmel records. At that period, there was a Solomon London who was active in charitable organisations and was Treasurer of the London Board of Jewish Religious Education, although there is no evidence that this was the S. London who loaned money to Carmel.

All this came to total liabilities of over £42,000 (which was a very large sum towards the end of the 1940s). How were these liabilities secured? Loans on "borrowed money not currently repayable" was £14,850 0s 0d; the "bank overdraft, secured on title deeds of property" was £21,287 9s 10d; "sundry trade and expense creditors" was £5,543 14s 11d and there was also a "temporary loan" of £589 17s 0d.[88] Cyril Domb comments:

> One might perhaps dwell for the moment on the enormous responsibility which Kopul was shouldering. Besides the capital expenditure required for the building, a large and steady subsidy would be needed for salaries and maintenance during the first few years . . . Early in 1949 he [Kopul] sold his London home and invested the proceeds and all his possessions in Carmel.[89]

Kopul, of course, realised the grave financial problems, and even after the school had opened he continued writing letters asking for loans. In January 1949, one recipient of Kopul's letters replied that he would consider the matter in "another few weeks,"[90] but Kopul was not prepared to accept this dilatoriness and he replied, "I am a little disturbed however by the fact that you say that you will consider it within the next few weeks. The school is growing rapidly and certain necessities are so pressing that we must borrow money immediately to deal with these vital capital outlays. Can you not consider it please within the next few minutes instead of weeks?"[91]

When Carmel opened, Kopul was the Principal Rabbi of the Federation of Synagogues, where, needless to say, he received a salary. He was therefore able to be the Honorary Principal[92] of Carmel and not draw a salary. As a result, he was qualified to be a member of the Board of Governors of Carmel College Ltd. However, after he resigned his position from the Federation of Synagogues, and started taking a salary from Carmel, a problem arose. According to the "Articles of Association," "The Governors shall not be entitled to any remuneration for their services"[93] and

---

88. Income and Expenditure Account for the period 11 December 1947 to 31 March 1949 and Balance Sheet, as at 31 March 1949, [henceforth: Auditors' Report with appropriate date].
89. Memories of KR, pp.22–23.
90. Letter from Joseph Green to KR, 26 January 1949. It would seem that the expression "another few weeks" (or a similar one) had been used in a previous letter which has not been traced.
91. Letter from KR to Joseph Green, 25 January 1949.
92. e.g. Jewish Chronicle advertisements for Carmel College during 1948.
93. CCLtd Articles, par.48.

CARMEL COLLEGE LTD. (Limited by Guarantee)		REG.OFFICE: 46a FINSBURY SQUARE,E.C.2.	
INCOME & EXPENDITURE ACCOUNT.		FOR THE PERIOD 11th DECEMBER 1947 to 31st MARCH 1949.	
EXPENDITURE.		INCOME.	
To Educational, Domestic,Administration & Establishment Expenses.	11404 15 3	By Fees Receivable.	4006 2 10
Audit Fee.	105 - -	Excess of Expenditure over Income.	7851 7 11
Preliminary Expenses written off.	347 15 6		
	£ 11857 10 9		£ 11857 10 9

The First Income and Expenditure Account of Carmel College Limited

furthermore, one of the reasons for "Disqualification of the Governors" was "If he shall hold any place of profit under the Company.[94] It was also stated in the "Memorandum of Association" that ". . . no member of the Council or other Governing Body for the time being of the Company shall be appointed to any salaried office of the Company . . ."[95] On 30 April 1950, Kopul resigned as a Governor.[96]

Two weeks later, five new Governors were appointed. These included Leslie Paisner who was a solicitor, and Armin Krausz who was a cutlery manufacturer from Sheffield.[97]

Everything concerning Carmel was not only expenditure! There was also a major item of income, namely the school fees paid by parents. During every school holiday, the parents would receive a bill for the next term's fees and for the "extras" from the previous term. At the top of this bill was a reference which was the pupil's name and his school number. (At least some use was made of a pupil's school number!)

The bill began with the fees for a particular term "payable in advance." For the Winter Term 1949 it was £83 6s 8d, namely two hundred and fifty pounds per year. Then followed "Books and stationery" with a "detailed

---

94. Ibid., par.49(3).
95. CCLtd Memorandum, par.4.
96. Carmel College Limited, Notification of Change of Directors or Secretary or in their Particulars, [henceforth: CCLtd Notification], registered 17 November 1950.
97. Ibid.

account below." These details included exercise and note books, pencils, rubbers, and even postage stamps. The next item was "Clothing and Sundries" and again here, details were given below. They included tie, scarf, belt, shoe repairs, and even toothpaste. Other extras on this bill included music lessons, railway fares, breakages, and repairs to watch/bicycle/ fountain pen. Cheques had to be "crossed and made payable to Carmel College Ltd."[98] A sticker was attached to each bill which stated "Parents and guardians are kindly requested to settle the school's account before the commencement of the next term."[99]

One of the "extras" charged each term, from about 1953 onwards, was the sum of 16 shillings per term for "Medical Inspection."[100] The reason for this charge, as explained by the school, was that when a pupil was taken ill, instead of the pupil going to the medical doctor, the doctor would hold a regular surgery at the school. This was a standard charge, irrespective of whether or not that pupil was actually ill that term.[101] To get value for your money, it was worth being ill!

Despite all these fees and extras, by the end of March 1950, the liabilities of Carmel had escalated to £57,106. To provide cover for this large amount, someone (or more than one person) had given an additional loan, "not currently payable" of £5,000. Martin's Bank gave a loan of nearly £20,000, which was "secured on Buildings and Estate." There was also a bank overdraft of over £7,000 of which nearly £5,000 was secured by Guarantee. On the income side, school fees paid by parents had increased to £12,455, but at the same time the expenditure had almost doubled to £21,581. This included, "Education" to the sum of £7,513 and "Household" to the sum of £9,845. After allowing for a few other receipts, the excess of expenditure over income was over £8,000.[102]

During the course of the following months, the school purchased Crookham House for the Preparatory School and, as a result, under "Fixed Assets," the value of the Buildings and Estate increased from £32,101 to £47,767. The "excess of current liabilities over current assets" was £25,552.[103] It can be clearly seen that when not allowing for the value of

98. Carmel College, sample school fees bill, Winter Term 1949, bill for Charles Gale (since this bill was reproduced in "Reflections," the name is not withheld here).
99. Carmel College, sticker attached to each bill.
100. Carmel College, sample school fees bill, dated August 1955 (name withheld).
101. Unwritten recollections of author.
102. Auditors' Reports, 31 March 1950 and 31 March 1951; (from now on, figures will be given to the nearest pound).
103. Ibid., 31 March 1951.

the buildings and fixtures and fittings, the cash liability was much higher.

The school needed to find ways to raise money, and quickly too! On this Anthony Rau, who was a pupil at the school, wrote in the summer of 1952, "Lots of trees in the grounds are being cut down, because the school is short of money. There is a rumour that the school will get £10,000 for the trees."[104] Was it a rumour or was there in fact money for trees?! The School's financial accounts don't mention it! However, there is further support for "money for trees" from a report on the recollections of Charles Gale, "He [Gale] remembers well that trees were sold from the Greenham Common Site, where the school started, to help meet the inaugural costs."[105]

THE CARMEL WAR

The school's financial problems were exacerbated when the lenders, soon after, took back their money. This was the period of the "war" between Kopul and the Governors. Cyril Domb writes:

> Kopul's relations with the Board of Governors of Carmel College about this time were none too happy. He had very definite ideas about how the school should be run, whereas the Governors felt that Kopul was taking too many decisions himself without adequate reference to them. Matters came to a head early in 1953 when the Governors made it clear that unless he resigned his position they would no longer be willing to support the school. Kopul declared his intention of carrying on and the Board of Governors resigned en bloc withdrawing the money which they had invested in the college.[106]

A few months earlier, a Committee of Inquiry had been set up by the Governors and following its Report, a letter dated 4 September 1953 and signed by eight Governors and marked "Private" was sent to the Parents:

> Dear Sir or Madam,
>   At a meeting of the Board of Governors of Carmel College held on the 18th August, we, the undersigned, announced our intention to

---

104. Anthony Rau, Letters written home from Carmel College, [henceforth: Rau letters], 21 May 1952.
105. Communication from Old Carmeli Association to fellow Old Carmelis, February 1997.
106. Memories of KR, p.25.

resign from the Board of Governors. In the course of a statement, Mr. J. C. Gilbert, the retiring Chairman of the Board of Governors said:

Some five years ago on Rabbi Rosen's initiative, a Committee was formed consisting of myself and most of the present Governors (later transformed into the Board of Governors) with the object of creating a school run on the principle of English Public Schools and simultaneously based on Jewish tradition and Hebraic culture. Carmel College was to become a Jewish national establishment, eliminating any profit making motive and concentrating solely on the first attempt in Anglo-Jewry at a synthesis of what is best in English education and Judaism. Without having any model or precedent on which to work, the Governors during the experimental years had to surmount many obstacles and the school had to adapt itself to changing conditions as and when they arose. At long last the time became ripe for putting Carmel College on a permanent basis.

The school having reached a certain grade of development and having acquired new and more suitable premises, it was felt that this was the right moment for forging ahead to that degree of permanency to which we had all been looking forward. This, however, coincided with a controversy within the body of the teaching staff and between some of the masters and Rabbi Rosen, the Principal. With the formal approval of the Board of Governors, the Principal and the teaching staff, a fact-finding special Committee was set up, consisting of Mr. L. Paisner, Dr. J. Braude, Dr. O. K. Rabinowicz and Rabbi M. Sperber, to investigate and to enquire into the various suggestions, grievances and proposals relating to all aspects of the school.

On the basis of the special Committee's report, and of the experience accumulated during the experimental years, the Board of Governors unanimously agreed upon a number of basic principles and clearly defined rules which seemed to them indispensable for attaining the aim they had set themselves for establishing the desired permanency of the school. Their decisions, however, were not acceptable to the Principal. The fundamental differences regarding structure, administration and object of the school then became obvious and proved to be insurmountable. There remained for the Governors only two alternatives, either to begin a fight with all that this implied, or to resign. The Governors unanimously came to the conclusion that an open fight would cause unspeakable harm to the school and they decided to avoid this under all circumstances. Their conscience forbids them to bear responsibility for what they believe is not the establishment they set out years ago to build and they have therefore taken the grave decision to resign.

Yours truly,

A Bornstein, J. Braude, J. C. Gilbert, B. Homa, Alex Margulies, L. Paisner, Oscar Philipp, O. K. Rabinowicz.[107]

As was to be expected, Kopul did not let this letter pass in silence, but a few days later on 14 September, he also sent a letter headed "Private" to parents:[108]

Dear Sir or Madam,

You have in all probability received a letter signed by a number of the retiring Governors stating why they have resigned from the Governing Body of Carmel College. I can well understand that you are disturbed by it.

It is not my intention to engage in a debate by correspondence. I shall convene a meeting at Wallingford early next term where I shall gave a full and frank statement and *substantiate it with documentary evidence and the recorded minutes of the Governors meetings.*

I shall content myself at this stage with a few observations:-

1. The letter which you have received from ex-Governors contains some statements which are false and others which are tendentiously expressed and therefore misleading.

2. Since I established the school five years ago and invited these gentlemen to become Governors, *not a single Governor has spent a single educational day at the School.* Apart from a fleeting visit by three Governors to a class in Talmud during the very first term of the School's existence, five years ago, *no Governor has visited a class or has had any personal knowledge or direct experience of the education, routine, conduct and character of Carmel College.* Any statement, therefore which suggests that there is an educational and ideological basis for a friction is a mere pretext to conceal the real and unworthy issues underlying this unpleasantness

New Governors have been appointed whom I shall introduce to you at this meeting. The majority of them, I am pleased to state, have

---

107. Letter from Governors to Sir or Madam [i.e. Parents], 4 September 1953.
108. The underlined words are underlined in the original.

attended English schools and English Universities and are familiar with English educational life.

Meanwhile I wish to express with clear heart and mind and complete conviction that Carmel College is more stable both in the material and spiritual sense than ever before and that its standard and character far from suffering from this passing upheaval will develop unhampered more healthily and rapidly.

Yours truly,
Kopul Rosen
Founder and Principal[109]

Over three weeks later on 7 October 1953, the eight Governors who had resigned sent out a further letter, again headed "Private":

Dear Sir or Madam,

You have received a communication dated 14th September 1953, containing Rabbi Kopul Rosen's observations on our letter of 4th September, in which we informed you about our resignation from the Board of Governors of Carmel College.

In his observations, Rabbi Rosen says that our letter 'contains statements which are false and others which are tendentiously expressed and therefore misleading'. We should like to inform you that the text of our statement was dealt with at the Governors' Meeting on 18th August 1953, at which Rabbi Rosen was present. He read the draft, made certain suggestions for alterations and corrections, which we readily accepted. He finally agreed that our statement as amended was a fair one.

Rabbi Rosen, at the same meeting, undertook to submit to us the draft of his own communication to the parents before despatching it. He did not do so.

These facts speak for themselves.

Yours truly.
A Bornstein, J. Braude, J. C. Gilbert, Bernard Homa, Alexander Margulies, Leslie L. Paisner, Oscar Philipp, Oscar K. Rabinowicz.[110]

---

109. Letter from KR to Sir or Madam [i.e. Parents], 14 September 1953.
110. Letter from Governors to Sir or Madam [i.e. Parents], 7 October 1953.

A few days later, these resignations were reported in the "Jewish Chronicle" with the comment "No reasons have been announced for these resignations which took effect on August 18." In this report, despite the background for the resignations, Kopul magnanimously stated:

> I should like to publicly express my deep gratitude and warm appreciation to those of the retiring Governors who have given so much of their time and energy for Carmel College. I must single out Mr. J. C. Gilbert, whose zeal and devotion to this cause has been remarkable and beyond all praise.
>
> The differences of attitude which led to the resignations constitute both a challenge and an opportunity to the new Governors, the teaching staff, and myself. I am certain we shall succeed and lead Carmel College to even greater successes. I am sure Carmel College has the good will and good wishes of the retiring Governors for its future success.[111]

The author recollects the meeting with parents that Kopul referred to in his letter. "For the first term at Mongewell, there was no travelling home for half-term. That half-term was all in all, a Sunday visiting day at the school. This was during November 1953, and in the letter telling the parents about half-term, was an invitation to go to a meeting that afternoon in Rabbi Rosen's study to hear a statement from him. (I have often wondered whether this was the reason for having half-term at the school rather than the pupils going home.) I asked my father what was said at the meeting and he said something about the Governors resigning."[112]

"It is clear from Kopul's diary," writes Cyril Domb, "that he looked upon this as the greatest challenge he ever had to face in his life. He felt that failure at this juncture would destroy him completely . . . He then set about reconstituting the governing body."[113] In fact, on the very same day that the eight Governors resigned, five new governors were appointed, They were: Henry Shaw[114] who was Kopul's brother;[115] Isaac Noah Cohen, who was Kopul's brother-in-law; Samuel Stamler, who was David

---

111. Jewish Chronicle, 9 October 1953, p.9.
112. Chaim Simons, *Seven Years at Carmel College*, (Kiryat Arba, Israel, 2006), [henceforth: 7 years], pp.23–24.
113. Memories of KR, p.25.
114. A very short period later, Henry Shaw handed in his resignation as a Governor (CCLtd Notification. Registered 20 October 1953).
115. At an earlier date Henry Shaw had changed his surname from Rosen to Shaw.

Stamler's brother; a young solicitor Irvin Goldstein, (who was tragically killed a few years later in a motor accident in Sicily[116]); and Berl Wober, a businessman and Jewish communal leader in Glasgow.[117] A few months later, in December 1953, Joseph Collier was also appointed as a Member of the Board of Governors.[118] There was still the serious problem of the £14,000 which the previous governors had withdrawn. Kopul turned to Isaac Wolfson who agreed to supply this money.[119] On this Jeremy Rosen writes, "The School was a charitable trust and so long as he [Isaac Wolfson] was satisfied that a reasonable board of new trustees, Governors, would accept responsibility he would be happy to pay up and leave the rest to them. Kopul never forgot that debt."[120] One might add that Isaac Wolfson was never a Governor of Carmel.

Kopul was of course human and all this worry and aggravation had an effect on him. David Stamler writes, "For most of this period Kopul Rosen's mood was of the blackest, and on occasions he came near to a mood of despair. Serious as this was, it was doubly so in that with the whole school revolving around him, his mood coloured everyone's outlook.[121]

DRIVEN OUT OF GREENHAM

At the same period, Carmel had an entirely different serious problem. Bella Rosen reports:

> Around 1952, we suffered a setback since the U.S. Air Force decided to take over Greenham Common, which lay between the Senior School and the Junior School, as their headquarters. As they intended to erect buildings of their own, they were not forcing us to leave and so were not obliged to recompense us. This put us in a grave financial situation because we felt it was imperative to move. The noise alone would have seriously interfered with the running of the School.[122]

After an extensive search for new premises, the Mongewell estate was found and purchased. The Auditors' Report for 1953 states that Carmel

---

116. Jewish Chronicle, 5 April 1957, obituary, p.27.
117. CCLtd Notification, registered 5 October 1953.
118. Ibid., 2 February 1954.
119. Memories of KR, p.25.
120. Jeremy Rosen, *Kopul Rosen 1913–1962*, (2011), [henceforth: Biography of KR], p.41.
121. Memories of KR, p.106.
122. *Reflections: Carmel College 1948–1988* [henceforth: Reflections] – Bella Censor (Rosen).

Carmel College Campus at Mongewell in 1953

had agreed to buy the estate for £19,000.[123] In addition to this £19,000, a further £300 was paid for "the Tenant's fixtures and other Chattels" in these premises[124] (which in those days was a considerable sum of money!). The Contract of Sale and Purchase did not include the playing fields of Carmel College. However, in the Deed of Conveyance dated 7 August 1953, the amount paid was £20,750.[125] A comparison of the description of the property purchased in the Contract of Purchase[126] and in the Deed of Conveyance[127] shows that, in the latter document, the extensive playing

123. CCLtd Note to Auditors' Report, 31 March 1953, p.2.
124. Contract for sale and purchase of the Freehold Mansion House and premises known as Mongewell Park situate in the Parish of Crowmarsh (formerly Mongewell) in the County of Oxford, dated 26 January 1953, [henceforth: Purchase Mongewell], par.1.
125. Deed of Conveyance for the Mongewell Estate dated 7 August 1953, [henceforth: Conveyance Mongewell], p.1.
126. Purchase Mongewell, The First Schedule, p.4.
127. Conveyance Mongewell, The First Schedule, p.4.

fields were included, thus explaining the increase in the amount paid. For some reason, the Auditors' Report gives a different figure, namely, "Purchase Price of School, Premises and Grounds in January 1953, £21,459."[128] Could the difference be due to estate agent's or lawyer's fees?

At that period, Greenham Lodge and Crookham House together with their estates were valued at £46,833.[129] As was to be expected, under these circumstances (who wants to be woken up every night by the sound of aeroplanes?!), the sale value of Greenham Lodge and Crookham House plummeted and they were sold for only £36,000.[130] The following year's Auditors' Report thus states that the "loss on sale of freehold properties" was £10,883.[131]

RE-ENTRY OF KOPUL AS GOVERNOR

According to the then terms of the Memorandum and Articles of Association, since Kopul was receiving a salary from Carmel College, he was precluded for several years from being a Governor. To rectify this, in January 1954 a Special Resolution was passed by Carmel College Limited, in which small changes were made in these Memorandum and Articles, which would allow Kopul to be a Governor. It may be noted that even though Kopul had not yet officially been reappointed as a Governor, this Resolution was signed "Kopul Rosen, Chairman."[132] It would seem that the reason that this amendment had not been passed years earlier was that the tension between Kopul and the previous Governors, would have precluded their agreement to such an amendment. Now that they had resigned, it was possible to have such a resolution passed. However, government offices act amazingly slowly and it was nearly two years later that the Ministry of Education confirmed this resolution and sent a letter stating "in this particular case there seems to be every reason why Rabbi Rosen should be a member of the Governing Board." This letter was read out to the Governors on 26 February 1956[133] and on that same day Kopul once again became a Governor of the school.[134]

---

128. CCLtd Auditors' Report, 31 August 1956, p.2.
129. CCLtd Auditors' Report, 31 March 1953, p.3.
130. CCLtd Note to Auditors' Report, 31 March 1953, p.2.
131. In the Auditors' report for 1954, this loss increased by £50; it is not clear why.
132. CCLtd, Special resolution dated 24 January 1954, received by Companies Registration Office 21 April 1954.
133. CCLtd, Special resolution read out on 26 February 1956.
134. CCLtd Notification, registered 17 July 1956.

Returning to the events at the end of 1953, Cyril Domb writes:

> Joseph Collier agreed to serve as Acting Chairman of the [Governing] Board. Kopul then drew on his exceptional knowledge of the Anglo-Jewish Community to build up from scratch an effective and capable team. Most of the new Governors did not come from the religious section of the Community. They were personally devoted to Kopul and whatever their own standards of Jewish observance felt that the new generation of Anglo-Jewish youngsters should be given the chance to experience traditional Judaism.[135]

Amongst the Governors appointed during 1954 were Leonard Wolfson,[136] (the son of Isaac Wolfson), who was a Director of Great Universal Stores; Charles Sebag-Montefiore; Michael Sieff, who was a Director of Marks and Spencer; and Sir Maurice Bloch, who a decade earlier had proposed Kopul to be the Communal Rabbi of Glasgow.[137]

Governors appointed over the course of the years, were generally from the upper economic strata of Anglo-Jewry. Most of the Guests of Honour at the Annual Speech Days were already Governors (namely, Joseph Collier and Bernard Lyons), or were appointed to this office, usually soon after the Speech Day (namely, Alderman Moss, Israel Sieff and Leonard Wolfson).

Under the terms of The Companies Act, 1948, every Company "not having a Share Capital" had to file an "Annual Return" which gave the "Particulars of the persons who are Directors of the Company at the date of this return." These particulars included, in addition to the names of the Directors, their "Usual residential address" and "Business occupation and particulars of other directorships." The Directors in the case of Carmel College were known as its Governors. Carmel College Ltd. thus filed such an Annual Return from 1949 onwards. However, it is perhaps significant that the Company file has no record of such a Return for the year 1953, the year of the "revolution" of the Governors. Companies House reported on this absence "Missing or not filed." During the Kopul era the number of Governors steadily increased. In 1949, it was just eight

---

135. Memories of KR, p.25.
136. Leonard Wolfson resigned as a Governor in 1955. CCLtd Notification, registered 12 March 1955.
137. CCLtd Notifications. There were several during the course of that period.

directors; by 1954 it had increased to twelve; in 1958 it was eighteen; and in 1962 it had reached twenty-five.[138]

In addition to Governors, Carmel College had (as is common with many other organisations), very prominent personages, who were known as "Patrons." The Patrons of Carmel included The Very Rev. The Chief Rabbi Israel Brodie, Professor Sir Isaiah Berlin, Lord Cohen of Birkenhead, and The Hon. Sir Seymour Karminski.[139] Having such Patrons adds to the status of an organisation, and, even more important for Carmel, might attract additional donors.

Indeed, Kopul would utilize every possible opportunity to try and obtain money for Carmel. The author describes one of these attempts:

> Whilst I was in Carmel, Cecil B. DeMille produced his film, 'The Ten Commandments.' He pledged that the proceeds would go to worthy causes. Rabbi Rosen told us that he took this opportunity to write and ask that some of the proceeds should go towards building a Synagogue in Carmel College, saying that surely this is a worthy cause. He told us that he got a vague reply that they had not yet decided and so on. I never heard of Carmel receiving money from that source. It would be interesting to know who received this money.[140]

As another means of obtaining donations, towards the end of 1953, Carmel set up a "Life Associate Scheme." A duplicated sheet which was distributed said:

> Parents and well-wishers of Carmel College will wish to learn of this scheme whereby they can be of considerable help to the School and have their names permanently associated with this great educational undertaking.
>
> By donating £100 you will become a Life Associate of Carmel College and will receive the following privileges:
>
> (a) Your name will be inscribed on the notice board in the entrance hall.

---

138. CCLtd, various Annual Returns, giving Particulars of the Directors and Secretaries of Carmel College Limited, [henceforth: CCLtd Annual Returns], and note pointing out absence of 1953 Annual Return.
139. Carmel College Prospectus, undated (about 1959).
140. 7 years, p.74.

(b) You will be invited to all Carmel College social functions and will receive all school publications.

(c) You will receive a plaque of the Carmel College crest which can be fixed to the wall of your office or home.

(d) You will be invited to an Annual meeting at which a comprehensive report of the progress and development of the School will be given.[141]

A very large board was affixed at the entrance to the Main Building and periodically a sign painter would come and add in black paint the names of the latest Life Associates.[142]

ENTER ACCOUNTANT NORMAN COHEN

After the "changing of the guard" on the Governing body in 1953, Norman Cohen, a Chartered Accountant, became the Company Secretary of Carmel College Ltd.[143] He explains how this arose:

> I first met Kopul when he was associated with the Mizrachi and then lost contact as he gave more and more of his energies to Carmel. Then one day his Secretary telephoned and made an appointment for him to call on me. He failed to arrive. A second appointment was made and, this time at least, it was cancelled in good time. The third appointment – *mirabile dictu* – was kept and I was invited to come down to the College to discuss professional matters there. He arranged to meet me at Wallingford station, but I was glad, after half an hour's wait, to avail myself of the local taximan (called, very aptly, if I remember correctly, Mr. Messenger). But all beginnings are difficult, as the rabbinical dictum states, and afterwards, when I had learnt to anticipate Kopul's aberrations, we got on very well.[144]

Despite his "aberrations" Kopul had grandiose plans for buildings. Having such plans was not a sign that the financial situation of Carmel had become rosy! On the contrary, there was a very large overdraft with the bank which was rising from year to year, with only part of it being secured

---

141. Life Associate Scheme, Duplicated Circular, undated (1953).
142. Unwritten recollections of author.
143. CCLtd Notification, registered 24 November 1954.
144. Memories of KR, p.111.

by Carmel's assets. For example, in 1953 it was £28,825, in 1954 £38,662, in 1955 £50,763, and in 1956 £53,279.[145] On this overdraft, Norman Cohen writes:

> I recall how, at one time, the Bank Manager became increasingly restive as the overdraft steadily increased. As there was little chance of arresting, much less reversing, the trend, every pretext was used to avoid the interview that the bank was demanding. Finally it could be avoided no longer; I met Kopul at lunch and we discussed every point that might be raised and every possible answer that could be provided. We then went to the interview, the magnetism was turned on, everything connected with Carmel (except the overdraft) was discussed, and we departed in an atmosphere of absolutely unjustified bonhomie.[146]

Despite this "success" with the bank manager, the school lived "from hand to mouth." In his biography of Kopul Rosen, his son Jeremy writes, "[Kopul] was burdened by the constant need to find funds to keep the school alive. On many occasions tradesmen refused to deliver because bills were not paid. Too often he had to beg and just as often he was humiliated by refusals. . . . Things were often so desperate that on one occasion Bella's engagement ring went to a tradesman as security to provide the pupils with breakfast . . . Kopul would spend more and more time in London trying to raise funds and often returned to Carmel dispirited and depressed. . . . He was very successful raising large sums for other causes, not his."[147]

The accounts of the school show that, even by the end of March 1949, namely after just two terms of Carmel, the debts to the "Sundry Trade and Expense Creditors" had reached £5,544,[148] and five years later (1954) they had jumped to £27,435.[149] The poor payment record of Carmel to the local tradesman even had an effect on the family of Morris Ellman, who was a teacher at the school. His son Michael writes on "Carmel's poor credit-rating at Newbury." "I remember that my father, when working at Greenham, once requested a credit account with a Newbury shop. They

---

145. CCLtd, Auditors' reports: 31 March 1954, 31 August 1955, 31 August 1956.
146. Memories of KR, p.113.
147. Biography of KR, pp.37, 39, 47.
148. CCLtd Auditors' Report, 31 March 1949.
149. CCLtd Auditors' Report, 31 March 1954.

were very skeptical when he said that he worked at Carmel. This must have reflected late payment of bills by Carmel, which in turn must have resulted from its precarious financial position."[150]

Joseph Collier, the businessman and Chairman of the Governors, had ideas, at least theoretical ones, on how to improve Carmel's precarious financial position. Norman Cohen explains:

> Collier and Estrin[151] knew all about stores and suchlike, but a College run on a continuous deficit by a dedicated enthusiast was absolutely unfamiliar to them. Estrin devised a highly complicated form of monthly financial statement which was to pin-point the administrative weaknesses. But however useful such a statement might have been in a department store, it was of very limited value for a College. Mr. Collier fretted himself monthly over minor variations in the milk bill, but Carmel approached no nearer to solvency.[152]

Despite all the serious financial problems, Kopul Rosen always had plans for Carmel, without worrying how much it would cost, as can been seen from the following real estate purchase:

> In 1956 he had negotiated the acquisition for the College of an adjacent estate of some 200 acres [at Newnham Murren, about quarter of a mile from Carmel in the direction of Wallingford]. Many of the Governors were opposed to the purchase since the College was still heavily in debt. Kopul with his usual disregard for conventional finance maintained 'We simply cannot afford *not* to buy it.' The estate was bought for £30,000. It possessed a farm which brought in an annual income, but Kopul had different plans for its use.
>
> Firstly he envisaged a Girls' School to parallel the Boys' School. Secondly he contemplated the establishment of a Teachers' Training College. He discussed the project with the Director of Education for Berkshire; students would be sent to the Reading Institute of Education for lectures daily and would carry out their teacher practice at Carmel. More remotely he dreamed of a 'garden village' which would

---

150. Recollections – Michael Ellman.
151. Maurice Estrin was the Chief Accountant of Colliers' United Drapery Stores Group.
152. Memories of KR, p.112.

serve as a cultural centre of Jewish learning radiating from the Carmel Synagogue.[153]

SOME PARENTS PAID LESS!

Had the parents of all the pupils at Carmel paid full fees, the income would have been greater, but the policy of the school was to provide reduced fees for suitable pupils whose parents could not afford the full payment. There were annual scholarship examinations from 1953 onwards to select such pupils. For example, in 1953 the full school fees were £280 per annum. The value of the scholarships ranged from £80 to £130.[154] There were cases where Kopul completely remitted the school fees. One such case was with the three Rabinowitz brothers, as Ian Rabinowitz reports:

> I do not know my school number. My reports do not show one. I think that the only place one could have appeared would have been on my bills. I have to say that, because of the "Mir network," my father did not pay any school fees for me (or for my younger brother Lionel who joined in October 1955, or for my youngest brother Benny who joined in October 1956, before they both left in December 1956). My bills were for books and pocket-money only, so small that no bill was ever kept.[155]

A similar case was that of Michael Ellman, the son of the Maths teacher, Morris Ellman, after Michael returned to Carmel in about 1956. On this Michael writes, "He [Morris Ellman] and Kopul got on well (they were both orthodox, had both been to Yeshiva, and both had some non-Jewish interests). It was this that got me my free place [at Carmel] when Moishe [Morris Ellman] moved back to London."[156]

On Kopul giving reductions in fees, Norman Cohen writes, "Kopul was more interested in building up the school than in acquiring financial caution and, especially in the early days, he sometimes made arrangements regarding fees that were scarcely advantageous to the College."[157]

---

153. Ibid., p.27.
154. Unwritten recollections of author.
155. Recollections – Ian Rabinowitz.
156. E-mail from Michael Ellman, 13 May 2012.
157. Memories of KR, p.113.

This, a few years earlier, had been one of the objections of the founding governors before they resigned en masse in 1953. As Jeremy Rosen writes, "In particular they [the Governors] objected to the cavalier way my father handed out scholarships and gave reductions in the fees when there were no endowments to cover them."[158] An example of this (recollected by her son), was of a mother who told Kopul that she

> couldn't afford to pay full fees and KR [Kopul] said something to her like 'Pay whatever you can.' I don't know what he said to the school bursar, whose job it actually was to collect the money from parents, but I think it was either nothing or something vague – he was terrible at day-to-day organisation and couldn't be bothered with it. I think the result was that my mother sometimes felt pressured by the bursar to make payments that she couldn't afford. Naturally it was a bit difficult for her, as a recipient of the school's charity, to object, but at some point she did apparently feel the need to protest in some way, or ask for more information.[159]

Clearly, the bursar did not get any message from Kopul, since the arrears noted in the boy's bill reached £428.[160]

There was one boy who, as the result of an illness, was left with a physical handicap. His Local County sent him to Carmel paying (at least part of) his school fees. The County Education Committee were pleased with their decision to send him to Carmel, and they accordingly wrote the school a letter which contained a "very favourable report on the progress of a 'handicapped child' they had sent to Carmel College for his education."[161] In addition, several other pupils' fees were paid (or perhaps partly paid) by various Local Councils.[162]

There is a Jewish school in London called the Solomon Wolfson School. The Wolfson family offered to pay the full fees at Carmel for a boy chosen by the school.[163] The boy who was chosen was invariably top of his class in that school and was likewise so when he attended Carmel.[164]

---

158. Biography of KR, p.40.
159. E-mail from (name withheld), 5 March 2013.
160. Carmel College school fees bill from August 1955, (name withheld).
161. Minutes of Carmel College Board of Governors Meeting, 6 November 1957.
162. List of pupils, headed "Covenants."
163. Related by the boy to the author, December 2013, (name withheld).
164. Unwritten recollections of author.

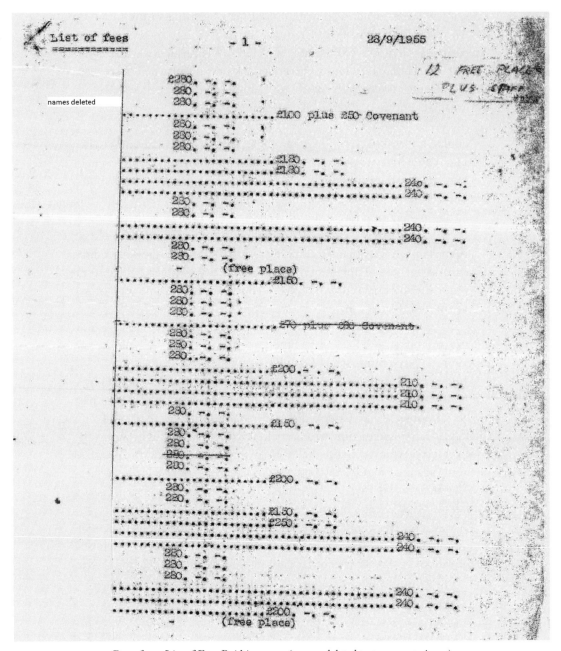

Page from List of Fees Paid in 1955 (names deleted to preserve privacy)

CARMEL COLLEGE

Mongewell Park   Nr. Wallingford   Berks.

Ref.:

Dr. to Carmel College Ltd.   Date: April, 1959

	£	s.	d.
Entrance Fee			
Arrears			
Fees for.................... Summer....Term 1959......, payable in advance	83	6	8
Books and stationery (Detailed account below) 1. 4. 7			
Clothing and Sundries (Detailed account below) 3. 4. 0			
Consultations/special treatment/special medicines -. 2. 0 (Prescrip)			
Extra tuition Oxford & Cambridge Exam. Fee 2. 2. 0			
Music lessons			
Riding lessons			
Railway fares, taxis, travel money, luggage 1. 8.10			
Outings and Films -. 2. 0			
Breakages			
Haircutting			
Pocket Money 2. 5. 0			
Repairs to watch/bicycle/fountain pen			
Tuck shop			
School fees Remission Scheme			
Medical Inspection -.16. 0			
Sports -. 5. 0	11	9	5
11. 9. 5 Total	94	16	1
Special Purposes Fund	-	-	-
Covenant	41	13	4
Less credits:			
Balance due to Carmel College Ltd.	136	9	5

Remarks:

Cheques should be crossed and made payable to Carmel College Ltd.

Books and Stationery Account	£	s.	d.	Clothing and Sundries Account		£	s.	d.
Exercise and note books	-	8	4	Cap	Socks	-	6	11
Special note books				Capel	Socks	-	6	0
Writing paper and envelopes				Blazer				
Geometrical instruments				Tie				
Arts and crafts materials				Scarf				
Pencils, rubbers etc.				Belt				
Miscellaneous				Football jerseys				
				„ shorts				
				„ stockings				
Text Books	-	16	3	Cleaning and repairs		1	18	7
				Pyjama Cords				
				Shoe repairs		-	12	6
				Shoe polish				
Postage Stamps				Shoe laces				
				Soap				
				Tooth paste				
Total	1	4	7	Total		3	4	0

Bill Sent to a Parent in 1959 (name deleted to preserve privacy)

Due to the granting of free places, scholarships, and other reductions in fees, there was a large range in the fees paid and this can be illustrated from a "List of Fees" for all the pupils dated 28 September 1955. At that period, the annual school fees were £280. If there were two brothers at the school at the same time, the fees for each brother were £240, and if there were three brothers, it was £210.[165]

A number of parents paid part of the school fees by covenant. Since this would enable Carmel to recover some money from the income tax authorities, the parents accordingly paid lower fees to Carmel. There is an undated list of all the Carmel pupils which is headed "Covenants." It seems that it was written towards the end of 1956, and comments on the possibility of the parents taking out covenants. In addition to giving the names of those who had already taken out covenants, the various comments in this list include: "cannot now, promised later," "abroad," "not now write," and "No."[166]

There were also a few day boys at Carmel and their annual fees were £75. There were twelve pupils (plus the sons of staff) who had free places. From 1953, Carmel had awarded scholarships of £130, thus making the school fees for such pupils £150.[167] On one occasion, the parent of a scholarship boy found even this amount difficult to pay and following a meeting between the parent and Kopul, the son's fees were reduced to £50 a year.[168]

It was during the latter part of 1955 that the Governors came to the conclusion that the school fees needed to be raised and they accordingly sent an undated letter to the parents, signed by the fourteen Governors:

> This letter is being sent to you from the Governors of Carmel College, and it is our earnest wish that you study it carefully.
>
> The progress made in recent years by Carmel College has given all associated with it cause for great satisfaction. The report of H.M. Inspectors and the full recognition that followed, the remarkably good annual examination results which include a major Open Scholarship to Balliol and two State Scholarships, prove how well the School is fulfilling its original aims and purposes.

---

165. Carmel College, List of Fees, 28 September 1955, (names withheld).
166. List of pupils, headed "Covenants."
167. Carmel College, List of Fees, 28 September 1955, (names withheld).
168. Meeting between KR and parent took place about 1955, (name withheld).

The financial side of the school, however, gives us great concern. The Governors feel that the full facts should be made known to parents:

(1) The school was started without any capital and has been run at a loss during every year of its existence. The money required has been obtained to a small extent from private loans and donations, but mainly by a substantial mortgage from the Bank.

(2) The running of the school – without allowing for capital expenditure is £55,000 p.a. 53% of the cost of running the school goes in salaries. Within the last two years there have been three increases in the Burnham scale; this has meant an additional expense of several thousands of pounds to the school. Furthermore the Governors of Carmel College have followed the policy of paying the members of the teaching staff more than the Burnham scale, because only by doing so have we been able to attract men of the calibre of those of our present teaching staff, who have been so warmly praised in the recent report of H.M. Inspectors. The Governors feel compelled to state that the only exception to this rule of salaries above the recognised scale, is the Principal, Rabbi Rosen, who receives less than would be his salary in a school of corresponding size and status.

(3) The school is compelled by its very nature to have a higher ratio of teachers per boy than other public schools. Whereas other schools might have a master-pupil ratio ranging from 1 – 14 to 1 – 25, Carmel College has a ratio of 1 master for every 9 boys. This is because we must of necessity employ masters who will teach the equivalent number of teaching periods of five full-time teachers to cover the Hebrew throughout the whole of the Prep and Senior schools.

(4) The cost of Kosher catering has risen steadily during the past years; this is equally true of all expenses involved in the running of this establishment. As instances of the increasing financial costs we quote two which have occurred within recent weeks, namely the increased price of solid fuel and laundry charges; this has committed the school to an immediate additional burden of several hundreds of pounds a year.

Parents familiar with schools throughout the country will know that schools have increased their fees very substantially since 1948. A recent article in 'The Times' quotes a number of schools as being '*representative samples*' and shows that the average increase in school fees since 1948 has been approximately £80, a year.

The Governors. therefore, are faced with no alternative but to increase the fees of Carmel College by £15, *per term*; this increase becomes effective from January 1956.[169]

There is a handwritten list of all the pupils with the fees which were due from their parents (for the next academic year) on 1 August 1956. The grand total was £57,552.[170] It would seem from the accounts of Carmel College Limited that approximately this amount was indeed paid.[171]

In December 1956, the Chairman of the Board of Governors brought out a Review of the year 1955/56. After praising the general progress of Carmel, he reviewed the finances, about which he said, "The current financial position still gives cause for great anxiety." Below it can be seen how the Functions Committee of the Development Fund brought out several brochures. However, at this period, the Functions Committee was still a thing of the future, but the idea of a brochure was already being contemplated, as can be seen in this Governors' Review, "The Board of Governors decided to launch a scheme for raising funds by means of a College Brochure." But the timing then was no good. A month or so earlier, Israel had been at war – the Sinai Campaign – and financial appeals had been launched for Israel.

The Review went on to give an "Analysis of Income and Expenditure." On the income side, for every pound Carmel received, 16s 4d came from "Fees and Subscriptions from Parents." On the Expenditure side, for every pound spent, 9s 4d went for "Salaries of Principal, teaching staff, matrons, chef, kitchen, domestic and all other staff"; 4s 0d went to purchase "food, edible milk and general provisions."

Then came a very strong hint that a further rise in school fees was on the horizon, namely, "I am told that the fees of Carmel College are considerably below those of other residential establishments of comparable standards, who moreover have not to incur the extra expenditure of specialised Hebrew teachers."[172]

Indeed, in 1957, there was another increase in fees. This time just over

---

169. Letter from Governors to Parents, undated (latter part of 1955).
170. Fees due 1/8/56.
171. One can only use the word "approximately" since the annual accounts were from 31 August to the next 31 August. Some parents might have paid the first term's fees for the academic year 1956/57 before 31 August 1956, and paid the first term's fees for the academic year 1957/58 before 31 August 1957.
172. Review of the Year 1955/56 by the Chairman of the Board of Governors of Carmel College, 6 December 1956, [henceforth: Review by Governors].

£15 a term and a circular to parents headed "Important" in capital letters stated, "The decision was unavoidable." Teachers salaries had since the last increase in Carmel fees, risen three times.[173] The facts of life are that the more successful the Teachers' Unions are, the more the parents have to pay!

Awarding bursaries from the school's meager funds may improve the quality of the pupils, but will have the opposite effect on the school's finances! Outside sources are thus very desirable in order to finance such bursaries. At a Zionist Conference held in 1954, the then Chairman of the British Zionist Federation, Isaac Solomon Fox, "disclosed that they had just reached an agreement with Carmel College, as a result of which Zionist Federation bursaries would be made tenable at that boarding school, and that similar bursaries would be established in other schools where Hebrew was taught as a spoken language."[174] A few weeks earlier, on 24 March 1954, "some people [had] came down from the Zionist Federation, among them were Levi Gertner, Dr Fox and another gentlemen."[175] This was obviously to see the school firsthand.

Over two years later, a newspaper report of a reception held by the British Zionist Federation presided over by its then Chairman, Abraham Israel Richtiger, states:

> Among the past achievements, Mr. Richtiger mentioned the provision of scholarships and bursaries of the Z.F. [Zionist Federation] for a number of pupils at Carmel College, on whose Board of Directors the Zionist Federation, he said, was represented. It had not been necessary to stipulate that this important boarding school, which catered for 200 pupils and was managed by Rabbi Kopul Rosen, should adopt the educational principles of the Z.F. 'These principles were prevalent at the college even prior to the Federation's association with it,' he stated.[176]

Richtiger did not state who the Zionist Federation's representative was on the Carmel's Board of Governors, but from the lists of Governors, it was almost certainly Isaac Fox. Fox was appointed a Governor on 9

---

173. Undated circular from Carmel College (probably from the Governors in the summer of 1957), the heading: Important. It was probably this letter which KR referred to at a Governors meeting held on 8 October 1957.
174. Jewish Chronicle, 9 April 1954, p.10.
175. Rau letters, 25 March 1954.
176. Jewish Chronicle, 3 August 1956, p.5.

September 1954,[177] just five months after his announcing the agreement for Z.F. bursaries for Carmel, and he remained a Governor throughout the lifetime of Kopul.[178]

Another source of funding for a scholarship to Carmel was the "Charitable Trusts and Educational Committee of the Anglo-Jewish Association." In 1955, they made the award to a boy who had been studying at the Selim School in Aden to enable him to study at Carmel and be trained as a teacher for the Selim School.[179]

At the beginning of 1958, an unsigned "Statement Concerning Scholarships and Bursaries at Carmel College" was written. The statement began, "Each year Carmel College awards a number of free places (described as Scholarships) and places at reduced fees (described as Bursaries) on a competitive basis. The announcement of this Scholarship and Bursary Examination is announced in the Jewish Chronicle in March and the examination takes place in April or early May. The factors that are taken into consideration in granting these awards are: 1. The ability of the boy. 2. The boy's need for Carmel College. 3. The financial means of the parents." The statement went on to state that as at January 1958, there were eighteen boys with free places and a further fifty-two who were paying varying proportions of the fees. It then continued:

> We constantly receive applications from parents who wish to send their boys to Carmel College but cannot pay the full fees. In some cases, after examining the boy, we feel that it is urgent that he should enter Carmel College with the minimum of delay (as, for example, if the boy is living in an area where he has no Jewish environment whatsoever) we admit him and do not ask him to wait until the next year's Scholarship and Bursary Examination. In other cases we ask the boys to wait until the following April when the competitive Examination will take place.[180]

An advertisement in the "Jewish Chronicle" that same year stated that "the Governors of Carmel College are offering a limited number of Scholarships and Bursaries,"[181] which might imply that *only* the Gover-

---

177. CCLtd Notification, registered 24 Nov 1954.
178. CCLtd various Annual Returns.
179. Jewish Chronicle, 29 July 1955, p.26.
180. Statement concerning Scholarships and Bursaries awarded at Carmel College, duplicated unsigned circular, undated (January 1958).
181. Jewish Chronicle, 7 February 1958, p.4.

nors were offering them. However, as time progressed, various people or organisations dedicated bursaries. In an advertisement in the "Jewish Chronicle" in March 1961, it stated, "Scholarships and Bursaries: In addition to those offered by the Governors the following awards will be available. The Michael Bennett Bursary, The Mirel Fabian Bursary, The Irvin Goldstein Bursary, The Hirsch Bursary, The A. Mann Bursary, The St. John's Wood Charity Bursary. The Examination will be held at Carmel College on Sunday April 23, 1961. Application Forms may be obtained from the Vice-Principal . . ."[182] The following year, the same list appeared with the exception of the Mirel Fabian Bursary,[183] indicating that in 1961 five of the bursaries were not allocated. The reason for this non-allocation is not known.

Kopul realised that if a wealthy parent could be persuaded to send his son to Carmel, then having a son at the school, this parent might well be interested in financially supporting the school. Accommodating such pupils could often mean that the already cramped dormitory conditions would become even more cramped! The author recollects:

> The following term [Autumn 1956] found me back on the first floor of the Main Building in dormitory 8. There were three double bunks in it and in one corner a wash basin. When we returned after half-term, we saw that the wash-basin had been removed. One of the boys commented that this removal would give the school the opportunity to squash in a fourth bunk.
>
> Lo and behold when we returned at the beginning of the next term, there was a fourth bunk there. The inhabitants of this bunk were two new boys from very wealthy families! The father of one of these boys later became chairman of the governors. He presented a large silver cup to be presented yearly for something or other – I don't remember what.[184]

By the "law of supply and demand," if one wants first class teachers in a school, one has to pay their salaries accordingly, and also be involved with their accommodation. On this the Inspectors' Report of 1955 writes, "The salary scale for all Masters [at Carmel] is normally 10% above the

---

182. Ibid., 3 March 1961, p.5.
183. Ibid., 23 February 1962, p.38.
184. 7 years, p.99.

appropriate Burnham Scale.[185] In addition, Masters are either provided with free lodging for themselves and their families or with an accommodation allowance of £150 per annum."[186]

On the question of accommodation, Cyril Domb also writes, "Their [Rosen family] home was one large room in the school for thirteen years,[187] first in the main school building in Newbury and later in Wallingford. Building up the school and settling key masters in homes of their own took precedence over personal comforts."[188] Indeed, the school purchased a number of properties for its teachers and the 1960 Auditors' Report includes under the school's assets "cost of three Residential Properties (two occupied by Teaching Staff and one let), £7,801."[189]

Until about 1958, there was no serious building on the Carmel Mongewell estate. That year, two dormitory blocks were built and this was followed by the sanatorium and the Prep School dormitories. Needless to say, this considerably increased the value of the fixed assets of Carmel. Before this building began, these assets (without fixtures and fittings and depreciation) were valued at about £50,000.[190] From then on, this figure increased from year to year. In 1959 it was £101,264,[191] in 1960 it was £155,705,[192] and finally in 1961 it reached £200,902.[193]

THE INSPECTORS ARE COMING!

Buildings are of course very important for any institution, but in order to attract donors, it is strongly advisable for a school to have recognition from the Ministry of Education. Needless to say, before giving such recognition, the Ministry will send in an inspection team and only then issue a report. At the beginning of 1950, the first inspection took place, whilst the school was still at Greenham, and a positive report was received. This was immediately conveyed to the Anglo-Jewish public (including of

---

185. The "Burnham Scale" is the salary scale for teachers in English state schools, and it is revised periodically.
186. Ministry of Education, Report by H.M. Inspectors on Carmel College, issued 8 June 1955, [henceforth: Inspectors' Report], p.3.
187. More accurately about 10 years, but even that is a considerable period!
188. Memories of KR, p.24.
189. CCLtd Auditors Report, 31 August 1960.
190. Ibid., 31 August 1957.
191. Ibid., 31 August 1959.
192. Ibid., 31 August 1960.
193. Ibid., 31 August 1962.

course its millionaires!) by a letter from the Secretary-Bursar of Carmel to the "Jewish Chronicle" which read:

> I have been asked by the Governors to inform you that on June 17, 1950, a communication was received from the Ministry of Education stating that the Minister is prepared to grant to Carmel College provisional recognition for efficiency as a Secondary School.
>
> We feel that this distinction is all the more noteworthy in view of the fact that it was based on an inspection that took place when the school had been in existence only 16 months.[194]

A further Ministry of Education inspection took place between 18 and 21 January 1955. The author recollects:

> They came into the various classes and in one of my classes, the teacher asked certain pupils to hand in their exercise books. These were the best kept books in the class. I am sure that the inspectors realised this!
>
> One of the inspectors was a non-Jewish Professor at a University for Bible studies and he knew Hebrew. I heard that he started teaching a class he entered and he pronounced his Hebrew letter 'vav' as 'wow.' This caused some giggling amongst a couple of boys and as Rabbi Rosen said to the school after the inspection was completely over that this was the only bad incident during the entire visit.[195]

Jeffrey Fisher elaborates on this rather unfortunate encounter between the pupils and this non-Jewish Professor of Bible Studies:

> Since the school was situated very near Oxford, examiners were sent (some, if not all) from Oxford University: among these were non-Jewish experts in Jewish studies. Kopul Rosen brought a group of these experts into our classroom one day for a lesson in Jewish studies: he intended to be our teacher that day and allow them to observe the lesson. Right at the beginning, before the lesson began, he was called away on school business and suggested that in his place, one of the group of observers would teach. I certainly did not know then but it

---

194. Jewish Chronicle, 7 July 1950, p.16.
195. 7 years, p.53.

appears that non-Jewish experts in Jewish studies call the letter Vav (the 6th letter in the Hebrew alphabet) WOW. I don't know if you can imagine the effect on a class of young pupils hearing a teacher say WOW each time instead of Vav. We all very soon had handkerchiefs in our mouths to try and muffle the laughter. Kopul Rosen told us afterwards that our behavior in that lesson had almost sabotaged the entire recognition process. However, the school did achieve recognition at that time, and as far as I remember, none of us were caned by Kopul.[196]

On this inspection, the author also recollects:

> They did not just come into the classrooms. It would seem they went around the dormitories – that was obviously the day when we were told to make them extra spick and span! Their inspection finally finished on a Friday night, when they attended the service and the meal.[197]

Needless to add, the Inspectors also inspected the Prep School. The rumour circulating, that when the Inspectors asked the Prep School pupils, "What is mahogany?" a boy answered "The Scottish New Year Festival," was said to be not true![198]

Following this inspection a boy wrote home that "half-term was extended by two days as Kopul and the masters seem very pleased about the visit of the examiners, although the official result is not yet out."[199]

The Inspectors' report was issued on 8 June 1955 and consisted of twenty pages. It covered almost all the aspects of the school in varying detail. On the Senior School Staff they wrote:

> It is pleasing to record that the teaching skill of the Staff, as a whole, is above average. They bring to their work both in and out of school a sense of responsibility and a generosity of service highly credible to themselves and to their profession. Their relations with the boys appear to be excellent, though at times it seems that more control of

196. Recollections – Jeffrey Fisher.
197. 7 years, p.53.
198. Alpha 1955, p.4.
199. Rau letters, 25 January 1955.

the boys' natural and laudable exuberance and eagerness to answer questions might be exercised to good advantage in the classroom.[200]

There were a couple of pages devoted specifically to the Prep School. On its curriculum, they wrote:

> The timetable shows fifty-four periods in all. These include 'prep' (for all but the bottom form), games, hobbies, and letter-writing, so that by no means all are periods of teaching. All, however, are organised and supervised and there is consequently very little time in the six-day week left free for the boys' own devices. It is understood that more free time is available in summer but it would appear desirable at other times also.[201]

About half the Report was comprised of the Inspectors' specific observations, criticisms, and suggestions on each subject taught in the Senior School, including comments on the various teachers (although not naming them!).[202]

Under the subject of "Hebrew" the Inspectors correctly commented that it "might more accurately be termed Jewish Studies." At that period, there was a serious lack of pedagogic material for Jewish Studies and on this the Inspectors wrote "There is a lack of aids to study; almost the only book available to or possessed by the boys is a Hebrew Bible, and that printed in the Massoretic (i.e. traditional) form: no modern commentary on any book was in use."[203]

The Inspectors were full of praise for the Chemistry Laboratory and wrote that "it would be difficult to find a more efficiently organised, school laboratory, anywhere, and the boys' practical work reflects the very good training they receive in the handling of apparatus and the planning of their practical work."[204]

However, with regards to Geography, the Inspectors were critical. "In the lessons seen the pace was slow, and the teaching itself was too diffuse. In all Forms, the work could be more effectively organised to ensure satisfactory treatment of the topics chosen . . . [The boys'] note-books are

---

200. Inspectors' Report, p.5.
201. Ibid., p.8.
202. Ibid., pp.9–18.
203. Ibid., p.9.
204. Ibid., p.15.

often marred by untidy setting out and needless inaccuracy." However, they added that Geography had been added to the curriculum only one year earlier.[205]

Pupils who had come up from the Carmel Prep School had studied both French and Latin there, but those who had come from outside Primary Schools had not received such instruction. Needless to say, this created teaching problems and on this point the Inspectors commented on numerous occasions.[206]

The Inspectors realised that the topography and facilities of Carmel were a "big plus" for sporting activities, and wrote, "The School is surrounded by woodland and open country and bounded by the River Thames; it has level fields which will, with skilled preparation and maintenance, produce good games pitches. The gymnasium, an attractive, lofty room of good dimensions . . . forms an excellent sports centre that the School may well feel proud and fortunate to possess."[207]

The end of the inspection was on Friday night and on this the report states, "Her Majesty's Inspectors were privileged at the end of the In-spection to be present at the Shabbat (Sabbath Eve) Service, the Group Meetings and the Communal Supper, and they were impressed by the spiritual influences with which the boys are in contact and by the active part taken by the youngest boys in the services and discussions."[208] In their conclusion, the Inspectors wrote:

> Since its foundation six years ago Carmel College has grown in stature and it has already achieved some of its aims in spite of the disturbance caused by its enforced move from Newbury. It appears, however, that the exacting nature of the Hebrew training which all boys re-ceive, fundamental and valuable as it is, threatens to retard progress in several important directions. If this problem can be satisfactorily resolved, there is no reason why Carmel College should not achieve standards in all departments of school life which are in keeping with the tradition of the greatest English schools.[209]

---

205. Ibid., p.12.
206. Ibid., pp.2, 7–8, 12, 13.
207. Ibid., p.17.
208. Ibid., p.18.
209. Ibid., p.19.

The Inspectors, who were all non-Jewish, despite seeing part of a Shabbat at Carmel, it would seem, did not understand the raison d'être of a Jewish school!

Reference to this inspection was found in the columns of the "Jewish Chronicle" under the heading "Carmel College 'Efficient'," and the sub-heading "Ministry of Education's Recognition." The article read:

> The Principal of Carmel College, Rabbi Kopul Rosen, has been informed by the Minister of Education that on the basis of the report by Her Majesty's Inspectors on Carmel College, the school has been granted full recognition by the Ministry as efficient.
>
> A full inspection of Carmel College took place in January of this year. The inspectors subsequently met the governors of the College and gave them a comprehensive and most encouraging verbal report. The printed report will be published shortly. Carmel College, which was established in 1948, received provisional recognition in 1950.[210]

BOOKS COST MONEY!

In mid-1958, Malcolm Shifrin became the first full-time librarian at Carmel. Prior to this, the library had had a budget of at least £150 per annum to purchase books.[211] This was obviously inadequate, and as a result Shifrin wrote in his financial report of the Carmel library:

> In 1958 the school "library" was a common room housing just over 2,000 books which had been gathered together over the years. More than half were out-of-date or in need of urgent repair. The Principal, realizing that books were disappearing almost as rapidly as they arrived, that the collection was completely unbalanced, and that it offered little or no incentive to study, agreed to allow the present writer to develop it, within ten years, into a school library fulfilling a purpose and one which no school need be ashamed to offer its pupils or staff. The librarian was given a free hand organisationally, asked not to spend more than £200 on books before the end of the year, and told to ask for individual items of equipment as required. The ques-

---

210. Jewish Chronicle, 20 May 1955, p.27.
211. Inspectors' Report, p.4.

MINISTRY OF EDUCATION

REPORT BY H.M. INSPECTORS ON

Carmel College, Wallingford, Berkshire

INSPECTED ON 18th, 19th, 20th and 21st JANUARY, 1955.

ISSUED
- 8 JUN 1955

MINISTRY OF EDUCATION, CURZON ST., W.1

IND. 19/55

Cover Page of H. M. Inspectors Report on Carmel College

tion of a budget was to be left until the end of the year. Owing to lack of space, the use of the library was restricted to forms IV, V and VI.[212]

From July to December of that year, Shifrin purchased books to the amount of £184. For the following year (1959), he "was given a book allowance of £250 plus or minus a few pounds." He utilised the "plus" in this allowance and purchased books to the extent of £266. In order that there should also be library facilities for forms II and III, a Junior Library was established, and the book allowance was in 1960, accordingly increased by £150, and that saw an expenditure on books of £470. Due to the change in the history syllabus, it was necessary to purchase a large number of books and since the book allowance for 1961 had already be exhausted, "a special extra grant was allowed for that year only." This resulted in a book bill for that year of £622.[213]

A library does not just involve the purchase of books which may be slung on any shelf. Books have to be catalogued and this requires the purchase of suitable equipment. Furthermore, books which are extensively used, periodically need rebinding. All this costs money and the library budget must, needless to say, be increased. For the second half of 1958, these equipment expenses were £417; for the year 1959, there was an almost identical amount. In 1950 it had shot down to £233, but in the following year had almost doubled to £437.[214]

Shifrin had also made a study of the average price of books. In 1958 it was 19s 8p, and in 1962 had risen to 22s 2d.[215]

He concluded this section of his financial report by stating:

> It can confidently be stated that a) no money allotted to the library is unaccounted for or has been wasted; b) although all books are on "open access" and the library is never closed, during the past twelve terms not more than 20 books have been mislaid – a record envied by any librarian who has heard about it; c) insofar as we have been able to improve our facilities, the boys' work and examination results have improved in direct proportion.[216]

---

212. Carmel College Library, Summary of expenditure since re-organisation in 1958, Memorandum written for the Finance Committee in July 1962, p.1.
213. Ibid., pp.1–2.
214. Ibid., p.1.
215. Ibid., p.2.
216. Ibid.

ADVERTISE!

Although Government recognition and having a first class library are important for the success of a school, on their own they are not sufficient. Just as every product requires repeated advertising in order to keep it in the public's mind, the same thing can be said about a school. Carmel College (as well as other Jewish schools), would therefore regularly display an advertisement in the "Jewish Chronicle." Throughout the "Kopul era," there were several versions of this advertisement, the changes sometimes being quite drastic! However, in most cases the reason for the change in wording is not at all apparent.

During two different periods of the "Kopul era," immediately underneath the Carmel advertisement was one for the Preparatory School. The first was from October 1950[217] and was displayed for just over a year. Towards the beginning of this period, the advertisement stated that the headmaster of the Preparatory School was James Ewart, but when he terminated his office towards the beginning of 1951, his name, needless to say, dropped out.[218] The second of these periods was from July 1956[219] until March 1958, when the separate Prep School advertisement stated that "Carmel College Preparatory School is situated in the same estate but functions as a separate unit. Pupils are admitted from the age of 7."

In some cases the advertisements were wordy and stated "Provides a Public School education together with a comprehensive Jewish training. The entrance age for the Senior School is 12–14 years, and for the Preparatory school from 7 years."[220] However, on other occasions, the advertisements were bland and all they gave was the name of the school, the address, the telephone number, Kopul's name, and "For prospectus apply to the Bursar."[221] In mid-1955, immediately on receiving recognition from the Ministry of Education, in went the words "Fully recognised by the Ministry of Education."[222] In March 1958, this was expanded to read "The only Independent Jewish Residential School recognised by the Ministry of Education."[223]

---

217. Beginning from Jewish Chronicle, 20 October 1950, p.18.
218. Beginning from Jewish Chronicle, 2 March 1951, p.16.
219. Beginning from Jewish Chronicle, 20 July 1956, p.25.
220. Beginning from Jewish Chronicle, 19 June 1953, p.26.
221. Beginning from Jewish Chronicle, 8 January 1954, p.24.
222. Jewish Chronicle, 3 June 1955, p.24.
223. Ibid., 7 March 1958, p.33.

CARMEL COLLEGE,
GREENHAM, NEWBURY,
BERKS.
('Phone: Newbury 1395) –
Principal:
RABBI KOPUL ROSEN, M.A.
PROVIDES A PUBLIC SCHOOL EDUCATION
TOGETHER WITH A COMPREHENSIVE
JEWISH TRAINING
The entrance age for the Senior School is
12-14 years, and for the Preparatory
School from 7 years.
Prospectus and particulars from the
Bursar.

The LAST advertisement with address NEWBURY
Jewish Chronicle 7 August 1953 p.4

CARMEL COLLEGE,
MONGEWELL PARK,
nr. WALLINGFORD, BERKS.
'Phone : Wallingford 3177
Principal :
RABBI KOPUL ROSEN, M.A.
PROVIDES A PUBLIC SCHOOL EDUCATION
TOGETHER WITH A COMPREHENSIVE
JEWISH TRAINING
The entrance age for the Senior School is
12-14 years, and for the Preparatory
School from 7 years.
Prospectus and particulars from the
Bursar.

The FIRST advertisement with address WALLINGFORD
Jewish Chronicle 21 August 1953 p.22

The blandest advertisements were from October 1960,[224] when even the school's telephone number and Kopul's name were omitted.

The name of the officer to whom to apply for a prospectus also changed during the years. At first, it was either the "Secretary-Bursar" or the "Bursar." However the most "dramatic" change was from the end of 1958 when the Bursar was relieved of the task of sending out the school prospectus,

---

224. Ibid., 28 October 1960, p.38.

year after year, to all and sundry, and instead, application to be made to the Vice-Principal.[225]

As can be seen from the advertisements, during the course of the years there was no single term used to describe the person in charge of the secretarial work. Sometimes "Secretary-Bursar" was used; on other occasions "Bursar." When Carmel moved to Mongewell, there was a sign on the school office door which read "Bursar." But in fact this was a misnomer; Mrs. Sophie Walker was not the bursar, but both the school secretary and cashier. Indeed, when a Bursar was later officially appointed, this sign was changed to "School Secretary and Cashier."[226] Norman Cohen describes the situation prior to a Bursar being appointed:

> He [Kopul] was his own Bursar and thus exercised complete control over every aspect of the College. This involved him in more responsibility than he could really cope with and the maintenance of the buildings, with chronic impecuniosity thrown in, left much to be desired. . . . His judgment of persons was oddly faulty at times; more than once he made appointments which he had plenty of leisure to repent. To add one further touch of black to the picture, on at least one occasion he cleared all the outstanding matters on his desk top (it was a very large desk top), into the wastepaper basket, in what he subsequently declared was an excess of efficiency.[227]

THE CAPTAIN IS COMING!

In 1955, the following newspaper advertisement appeared:

> Carmel College invites applications for the post of administrator-bursar. The post calls for initiative and ability and the duties consist of organising, co-ordinating and supervising the household, establishment, and maintenance staff in their daily work routine; similar previous experience would be an advantage but is not an essential qualification; the post offers vast scope for an enterprising person who would like to assist at executive level in the progressive development of an expanding Jewish Public School; commencing salary, including board and residence, would not be less than the equivalent of £1,000 per

---

225. Ibid., 31 October 1958, p.41.
226. 7 years, p.17.
227. Memories of KR, p.113.

annum – Applications giving full particulars which will be treated in strict confidence, should be addressed to Principal, Carmel College, Mongewell Park, Wallingford, Berks.[228]

Come summer 1956 – enter Captain Henry Lunzer, the Bursar! At the time, the "Jewish Chronicle" gave him a write-up and showed his varied history. Born in London, studied in a Frankfurt Yeshiva, went on aliyah, served in British and Indian armies, acted as Field Director for Germany of the Jewish Relief Unit, then to London University, back to Israel to work on Social Welfare, then to United States, and finally to be Bursar at Carmel College.[229]

If one wants to know what work a Bursar at Carmel does, then one can find it in an article the Captain wrote as soon as he joined Carmel:

> 'Please, sir I've been playing cricket behind the classroom block and have broken a window–pane.'
>
> 'The door handle came away in my hand, Sir.'
>
> 'I turned on the shower and was burned by the hot water.' (This must have happened in a dream)
>
> 'Please can I do some painting this afternoon? I've got a 'free pe-riod' ('Now you know there is no such thing')

The Captain then went on to explain the administrative pattern of a large organisation and then showed how it could be applied to Carmel College:

> Carmel College is a fairly large organisation and is fortunate in the fact that its Principal, although by natural inclination and learning mainly concerned with the educational activities of the school, is also keenly interested in the 'tools to do the job'. In these matters he has been most admirably served, since the school was first founded, by Mrs. Rosen, who looked after the domestic side of the college, and by Mrs. Walker who not only ran the office with all its multifarious duties but also kept a good and watchful eye on everything that went on in the college. From time to time an Estate Manager was added to the staff in order to assist the Principal in maintaining the buildings and grounds in a fit and proper condition. All this, however, left the

---

228. News clipping from 1955 – source not traced.
229. Jewish Chronicle, 10 August 1956, p.6.

Rabbi with a host of major and minor problems which no one else had the time, inclination or ability to do. Finance, for instance, both incoming and outgoing, devolved to a large extent on the Principal. Decisions on major policy in this field must, of course, remain in his hands and in those of the Governors, but most of these administrative problems must in due course devolve on the Bursar in order to relieve the Principal and to free him for his major interests. This does not mean that the School Secretary and Cashier (Mrs. Walker) will not be concerned with money matters. Her title indicates the contrary. It is the wider aspects of finance that we are dealing with here. Budgets and budgetary control, fund-raising schemes and projects (although who can compete with Rabbi Rosen in this sphere?), buildings, equipment, and grounds (yes, this includes the broken windows and the door handles), but, perhaps more important than all, co-coordinating the activities of all the departments on the 'tools to do the job' side, the domestic, the office, the grounds and buildings, and the hundred and one large and small things that allow the main work of teaching to continue smoothly. This must, of course, in the final analysis produce an effective knowledge of what can be saved and where, as well as an attempt to increase the source of incoming funds (and there is surely no one connected with Carmel or with many another school who will not recognize this as a most important function). And that in a nutshell is the work of the Bursar and his duties viz-à-viz the Principal and all those who work on the administrative side of the college.[230]

In the Carmel magazine, in the year that Captain Lunzer took up his position, David Saville wrote a poem entitled "Il Bürséro – A Nightmare Macaronic" which was written in a mixed up polygot of languages:

> Il y avait fois un Bursar,
>   Ein mensch sehr gut erat
> Qui était un bon rheetor –
>   Er hat une voix très glatt.
> Hic homo strictus erat
>   Strictissimus indeed.
> Officioque fungebatur
>   Bien qu'é had no need.

---

230. Carmel 1956, pp.15–16.

Agathous edoken nomous
Gravissimos gewiss,
Torat Mosheh gam Hee tovah
Mais nicht so good as his.
Erit ici pour longtemps
Für long que long kann be
So don't worry, mes amis,
We'll love him still, won't we?[231]

However, despite "Erit ici pour longtemps" Captain Lunzer did not remain more than a few years as Carmel's Bursar. Jeremy Rosen writes that Lunzer "found the isolation too much and moved to London after a while."[232]

The Bursar who followed Henry Lunzer was Mercer, and his name was easily remembered by the jingle "Mercer the Bursar!"[233] Michael Bharier recollects that he lived on one of the farms in the area.[234] Mercer was followed by John Squires, who lived in the Lodge at Carmel.[235]

In August 1959, the school put an advertisement in the "Times Educational Supplement" in which they wrote that the school "is seeking a fully experienced Bursar." The advertisement then went on to give the duties of the Carmel Bursar. However, it did not state a salary but asked the applicants to state the "salary required."[236]

Although during the initial years of Carmel, the expenditure was well in excess of the income, in 1956, it was almost equalised out with a deficit of only £390.[237] After that, in the years subsequent to the appointment of a Bursar, the situation radically improved. The year 1957 saw a surplus of £5,415[238] which almost doubled the following year to reach a "record" £10,160.[239] However, in the following years, it dropped to around half of

---

231. Ibid., p.14.
232. Recollections – Jeremy Rosen.
233. Unwritten recollections of author; e-mail from Michael Bharier, 25 August 2013.
234. E-mail from Michael Bharier, 25 August 2013.
235. E-mail from Jeremy Rosen, 11 August 2013.
236. The Times Educational Supplement (London), 7 August 1959. It is possible that this advertisement led to the appointment of Squires, although evidence has not been traced to prove this.
237. CCLtd Auditors' Report, 31 August 1956.
238. Ibid., 31 August 1957.
239. Ibid., 31 August 1958.

this,[240] and by the last complete year of the "Kopul era" there was a small deficit of £694.[241]

To achieve such financial improvement, one of the things that needs to be done is to trim expenditure. One expense in a boarding school is the laundry bills. Not only is there the pupil's personal clothing, there is also laundering of sheets, pillowcases, and towels. On this subject, the author recollects, "At first I don't think there was any limit as to how often one changed one's clothes. When, however, the Bursar [Captain Lunzer] started work, all this changed. For example, only one set of underwear and socks per week, one set of pajamas per fortnight, and only one sheet could only be changed per week. If one exceeded this quota, the extra laundry costs would be put on one's bill."[242] There was indeed an item on the Carmel bills called "Cleaning and repairs."[243]

CARMEL IN THE PRESS

A way to perhaps help pay the enormous laundry bills, and indeed the numerous other bills, was to keep Carmel in the public eye by having supplements or long articles in the press, which would hopefully attract donors. In November 1958, the "Jewish Chronicle" produced an eight-page supplement specifically on Carmel College, although it is true that the equivalent of over half of the area of this supplement was advertisements (one of which occupied an entire page), which, whilst barely mentioning Carmel, were in many cases, for businesses which were run by people with a connection to Carmel. There was a wide variety of articles in this supplement, which included the plans for the next ten years, the financial side of Carmel, conflicts which could arise due to the different standards of religious observance which a pupil might find between the school and his home, the educational standards and achievements of Carmel, and the Old Carmeli Association.[244]

This supplement came out precisely at the period when Carmel was looking for donors to support, in particular, its development costs. Indeed there were several articles with this aim directly in mind. One of them was

---

240. Ibid., 31 August 1959, 31 August 1960.
241. Ibid., 31 August 1962.
242. 7 years, p.18.
243. Carmel College, sample fees bill from 1957 (name withheld). Although this item appeared on the bills from the earliest days of Carmel, charges for laundry which was above the quota, would from the Lunzer era appear on the bills.
244. Jewish Chronicle supplement, 14 November 1958, pp. i-viii.

by Joseph Collier, the Chairman of the Governors, who began, "There are a good many misapprehensions current regarding Carmel College and its finances. People think it is a flourishing concern run for private profit, with only rich man's sons as pupils. If it was as easy as all that I should have a much less anxious time than I do when the Board of Governors discusses financial matters." Collier then went on to refute these misapprehensions, and it can also be seen that he was now accepting Kopul's views that despite the financial problems with the day-to-day running costs, new buildings had to be erected. Collier, the businessman, concluded his article, "As a business it is a pretty poor investment: but as a mitzvah it will go on paying rich dividends."[245]

A year-and-a-half earlier than the above "Jewish Chronicle" supplement, the magazine "The Sphere" had a three-page article on Carmel. However, this article did not mention the financial side of Carmel, but its aim was to show to the non-Jewish world how Carmel "Combines the Traditions of English Education with the Jewish Religion." This theme was illustrated throughout the entire article, which was accompanied by many photographs showing both the Jewish and English aspects of Carmel.[246]

INVITE POTENTIAL DONORS TO EXHIBITION DAYS

An even more effective money raiser than newspaper supplements and articles is to arrange "Exhibition Days" [read: Fund Raising Days] where one can "show off" the school to "carefully selected visitors" [read: potential donors]. On one such occasion at Carmel, held on Sunday 26 May 1957, a whole range of activities were arranged. These comprised demonstrations in all four science laboratories, demonstrations of Physical Education in four different sports, and a performance by the school choir. In the programme, the names of all the pupils taking part in the various demonstrations were listed. There was also an exhibition of Art. Seven members of staff, who included Kopul and David Stamler, showed the invitees around and the programme stated "Visitors are requested to attach themselves to a party being conducted around the school and to remain with their own group and guide." Following the tours, tea was

---

245. Ibid., pp. i, iv.
246. The Sphere, (published by London Illustrated Newspapers, Ltd.), 4 May 1957, pp.191–93.

served in the dining hall.[247] A full report of this Exhibition Day appeared in the Carmel magazine:

> A great Carmel tradition was broken on this occasion for the weather remained ideal for a school function. This special afternoon was to give visitors an opportunity of seeing various activities which are usual to Carmel. On their arrival, parents and guests were given programmes, and members of the staff undertook to conduct organised groups around the school. If ever unemployment should strike the teaching profession, it is certain that posts as tourist guides would not be out of the grasp of our masters!
>
> An art exhibition which contained exhibits ranging from an 'abstract' contributed by a boy in the preparatory school to an Indian painting composed by a senior boy in the sixth form, attracted much attention in the Lecture Hall. The laboratories were the scenes of various scientific displays which were rather perplexing to the layman. Although many of the participating students were 'stumped' by questions such as 'Will this hydrochlorine (sic) acid be good for my figure?', most queries were usually answered promptly. A game of basketball, a physical training display, and cricket practice constituted various other activities.
>
> The highlight among the sporting events was a boat race between two fours made up of senior and junior crews. The more corpulent among the visitors crossed very apprehensively the wooden bridge leading to the boat house island since it threatened to collapse; but all fears proved to be groundless. This event was followed by a return to the school hall in order to hear a concert given by the choir. Their repertoire of Hebrew melodies and negro spirituals was sung extremely well. From here, visitors went into the dining hall to have tea and to hear an address by Rabbi Rosen. Afterwards Exhibition Day came to a close, the visitors departed, and life at Carmel went on as before."[248]

The author also has recollections of an Exhibition Day:

247. Carmel College Exhibition Day, Sunday 26th May 1957, printed programme.
248. Carmel 1957, p.30.

Just before that [Exhibition] day, and with no connection to it, Marks and Spencer had bought new furniture and other materials for their laboratories and they offered their old ones to Carmel College. This 'old' furniture was certainly superior to the furniture in the junior science laboratory. This furniture arrived and the Carmel maintenance men went to work to install it in the laboratory. Also, the roof of the laboratory needed a coat of paint. Rabbi Rosen then told the maintenance staff that the visitors won't notice if there is a bench missing – they will notice an unpainted roof. So get on with the latter.

The potential donors arrived and viewed all the displays put on for their honour. They then went in the dining room for tea and a talk by Rabbi Rosen. At the time, one of the masters then commented, 'People can come to Carmel when there are the most horrible weather conditions, yet Rabbi Rosen will charm them into giving money to the school.'

The cakes which were from Grodzinski's [bakery] were superb. I can say that, because what was left over was given to the boys during their supper that day. They also borrowed from the same place beautiful crockery. It had already been placed on the side when we came into the dining room and being much nicer than the school mugs, some boys started using it – until the kitchen staff put a stop to it.

Whilst they were sipping their tea and munching their cakes, Rabbi Rosen addressed the visitors and they then pledged sums of money. I heard that these proceedings came over the school loud speaker system into the classrooms. I don't know whether this was by design or accident – but I didn't know about this until afterwards; otherwise, I am sure that I would have also listened![249]

It seems that the word had got around that the Exhibition Day Sunday in 1958, was a visiting day for all parents. Kopul therefore sent a firm, but politely worded circular to all the parents to correct this misapprehension:

Please note that June 1st is NOT[250] a visiting day. We are arranging an Exhibition for a number of people in the community who we think will be interested in the work of Carmel College and we respectfully,

---

249. 7 years, pp.130–31.
250. Underlining in original, double underlining under the word NOT.

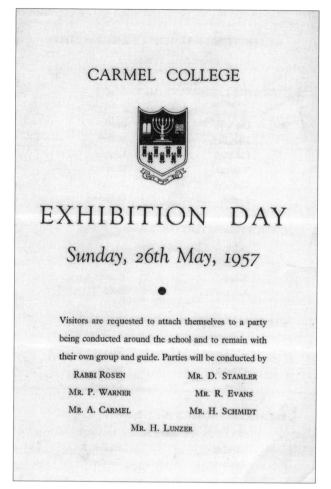

Page from the 1957 Exhibition Day Programme

but firmly, ask parents not to come on that day. Invitations are being issued to a limited number of people who may be particularly interested in assisting the Development Fund in its work.[251]

One could easily imagine that without this circular, there would have been a deluge of parents, almost all of whom did not have the wherewithal or the desire to donate to this Fund, arriving at Carmel. There would then be a mass of humanity, swamping out the invitees, going around the

---

251. Circular from KR to Parents, May 1958, headed: Important notice, please retain.

various stalls in the Exhibition. They would then rush to get a place in the dining hall for tea, grabbing the luscious cakes, and leaving just crumbs for the invitees. Which invitee would want to give money after such a nightmare?!

Unlike the previous year, for this Exhibition Day, the programmes were not printed – they were just duplicated! Also the names of the pupils taking part in the various displays were absent from the programmes. So were the names of the guides – possibly that year they were mere senior boys. The names which did appear were those of the "Masters-in-Charge" of the various displays. The displays took place in the various laboratories, the gymnasium, the sports field, and on the River Thames, and in addition the school choir performed. Following all this, tea was to be served punctually at half past four,[252] and although not stated on the programme, one can be sure that whilst filling their stomachs, the visitors were persuaded to decrease noticeably their bank balances!

CARMEL "FILM-STARS"

There is a saying that "One picture is worth ten thousand words."[253] A film is worth even more than that, and thus in about 1959, a ten minute promotional film entitled "The Road to Fulfilment" was made of Carmel. In describing this film the Carmel magazines writes, "This film covered every aspect of the School life from the sports field to the classroom, and from the laboratory to the Synagogue, In minutes the audience was given an extremely vivid and concise picture of Carmel and Carmel life, and many proud parents amongst the audience fondly toyed with the idea of their sons becoming Hollywood film stars."[254] The author adds some details on the contents and making of this film:

> The producers of this film on the school began by filming Havdalah one Motzoei Shabbat. On the following day they continued with their filming. This included filming in each of the laboratories where a series of experiments had been specially set up for the film. I was in the Physics laboratory doing an experiment on the expansion of solids. The camera crew who had to make a tour of the various laboratories in order to film them, first came into the Physics laboratory and asked

252. Carmel College Exhibition Day, Sunday, June 1st 1958, duplicated programme.
253. It has been suggested that this is a Chinese proverb.
254. Carmel 1959, pp. 6, 36–37.

Mr. Bunney which was the first laboratory to photograph. 'This one,' Mr. Bunney immediately answered. His answer certainly saved a lot of waiting time for us! In addition to the laboratories they also filmed sporting events such as bowling in the cricket nets.

For the evening meal that day, we assembled in the dining hall with Rabbi Rosen and as they filmed, he clapped and said, 'We will now sing Shir Hama'alot, I will give you the note.' We then began singing but he had already told us that it didn't matter how melodiously we sang, since the sound of the singing would come from the school record.[255] Finally, we went out to the playing fields where we were divided into two groups who had to march as the sides of a letter 'V,' who would then meet in a point. This would be superimposed over the model of the master building plan for the school.

From all this filming a very nice black and white film of the school was made with Rabbi Rosen giving the narration.[256]

MONEY RAISERS AND DONORS

Exhibition Days and promotional films are all very well, but a fundamental question was whether they should be utilised in order to raise money to cover Carmel's deficit, or alternatively should the money raised be used to erect new buildings. To which of these two things should one give priority? On this question, Kopul and Joseph Collier (at least at first), did not agree. According to Norman Cohen:

> Collier was cautious and pessimistic, Kopul mercurial and impulsive. . . . Meetings of the Board of Governors were apt, in consequence, to deteriorate into a duologue in which Kopul appealed for new buildings whilst the Chairman [Collier] lamented the increased cost of vegetables. In those years the Board was comparatively small in size and as meetings were held at Collier's office near Olympia at the not very convenient hour of 5.30 p.m., attendances were far from good. There was often no quorum and if, by any mischance, decisions were actually made, they were not necessarily implemented.[257]

---

255. This segment can be seen in the film "Foundation for a Vision" produced by Pearl and Dean in 1965 (at 11 mins 54 secs from the beginning). It was a cut which was taken from the original film "The Road to Fulfilment," produced during the Kopul era; it has not been traced.
256. 7 years, pp.80–81.
257. Memories of KR, p.112.

An example of a quorumless meeting of the Board of Governors is one which took place on 6 November 1957. Only four Governors were present. They included Collier who was in the Chair, Kopul, and Sam Stamler. Eight Governors sent their apologies. In attendance was Norman Cohen the secretary, and David Stamler. The minutes of the meeting began, "There being no quorum present, the Minutes of the previous meeting were not approved and no formal resolutions could be passed."[258]

Despite not being able to muster a quorum at all Governors' meetings, Kopul's plans for new buildings featured prominently in the discussions at these meetings, without his worrying about such things as quorums! At the Governors' meeting held on 8 October 1957, Kopul took along an architect (Rosenberg) and a quantity surveyor (Tillyard) and introduced them to the meeting. At that meeting "Mr. Rosenberg explained to the Meeting that the whole site area of Carmel College had been surveyed and full plans for development had now been approved by the Council. Permission had been obtained for the building of the two-storey dormitory block, but bye-law permission would now have to be sought for the proposed three-storey building."[259]

Even though they were still waiting for planning permission for this three-storey block, the finance had been already settled, as the minutes of this meeting stated, "The Isaac Wolfson Foundation had promised £14,000 for a three-storey dormitory to accommodate sixty boys; the building would be known as the Isaac Wolfson Wing."[260]

There was another problem – sewage! "The present system was not in accordance with statutory requirements." The outlay required for the two dormitory blocks and the sewage plant amounted to £35,000.[261]

The Secretary of the Governors, Norman Cohen wrote up the minutes of the meeting but did not send them straight away to all the Governors, nor even to the Chairman of the Governors. Instead, he first sent them to the school secretary, Mrs. Walker, with a note "I shall be obliged if you will show this to Rabbi Rosen for his approval and then arrange to have it duplicated."[262]

---

258. Carmel College, Minutes of Meeting of the Board of Governors, 6 November 1957, p.1. It is not clear why it stated that there was no quorum; according to paragraph 26 of the Articles of Association, 3 members are quorum and 4 members were present at that meeting!
259. Carmel College, Minutes of Meeting of the Board of Governors, 8 October 1957, p.1.
260. Ibid.
261. Ibid., p.2. The cost of the two-storey dormitory block was £12,000, the three-storey one £15,500, and the sewage plant £7,500.
262. Letter from Norman Cohen to Mrs. S. Walker, 14 October 1957.

"Minutes of meeting of the Board of Governors held at 364/6 Kensington High St, W.14 on 6th November 1957.

Present: Mr. J. Collier (in the chair) Rabbi R. Rosen, Messrs.

A. S. Botman & S. Stanier

In Attendance: Messrs. M. M. Cohen & D. Stanier.

Apologies were received from Sir Maurice Bloch, Alderman Moss & Messrs. Bion, Kleeman, Lyons, Sebag-Montefiore, Sieff, Weber.

There being a quorum present, the minutes of the previous meeting were approved as formal & resolutions could be passed.

Principal's Report

1. Governing Bodies Association
Rabbi Rosen was of the opinion that application ought now to be made for membership. After discussion it was decided the application would stand over until the news & plans for the future were available.

2. A letter had been received from the Middlesex Education Committee containing a very favourable report on the progress made when they had sent to Carmel College for his education.

3. Letters had been sent to various charitable trusts connected with the Marks & Sieff families asking for their support for the College development plans.

Page from Minutes of Governors' Meeting – November 1957
(written in ink on the back of a circular!)

Discussions on the dormitory blocks continued at the next Governors meeting, which was held quorumless on 6 November 1957. The minutes stated that estimates had already been requested for the building of a dormitory building, "Messrs Lovells had submitted an estimate for £17,500 for the three-story dormitory block. The Quantity Surveyor thought this excessive and tenders for the complete project were being sought from other builders, one local and one recommended by Mr. Fierstone."[263]

It was reported at this meeting that "Letters had been sent to various charitable trusts connected with the Marks and Sieff families asking for their support for the College development plans."[264] Why had these letters been sent specifically to them? Nearly a year and a half earlier, at the 1956 Speech Day, when Israel Sieff was the Guest of Honour, Kopul had announced that "a new dormitory for forty boys [is] to be built, financed through a donation received from the Mathilda Marks – Kennedy Fund."[265] It will be seen below, that this Fund had already promised a definite amount, namely £8,000. (Members of the Sieff family were trustees of this fund.) Maybe the reason for these letters could be explained by a statement made in the Chairman of the Governors Review of December 1956,[266] where he reported, "The total estimate for building, furniture and effects and so on [of the dormitory block] will greatly exceed the amount so generously donated by the Mathilda Marks Kennedy Charities, and the additional amount will have to be found by other means." Thus the reason for these letters being sent specifically to the Marks and Sieff families could have been to hint that it was up to them to now make up the difference![267]

As can be seen, despite the precarious financial situation of Carmel, and also despite the Governors' serious reservations, Kopul was actively pushing ahead with his building plans, as Norman Cohen writes, "When his [Kopul's] Board of Governors wanted to consolidate rather than expand he created a Development Fund with the assistance of a number of wealthy parents and other well-wishers from which all the new building work ultimately stemmed."[268]

---

263. Minutes of Meeting of the Board of Governors, 6 November 1957, p.2.
264. Ibid., p.1.
265. Jewish Chronicle, 3 August 1956, p.16.
266. Review by Governors, op. cit., p.3.
267. It was also at this Governors' Meeting of 6 October 1957 that Kopul put forward his opinion that an application ought to be made for membership of the Governing Bodies Association. However following a discussion "it was decided to defer the application until the new dormitory accommodation was available."
268. Memories of KR, p.114.

The first meeting of this Development Fund took place on 30 April 1957. Present at this meeting were Kopul, David Stamler, and seven wealthy parents. Amongst them was Harold Poster who was invited to take the Chair at that meeting. The minutes stated that "those present confirmed that they were prepared to act as a Committee for the purpose of raising funds for building development at Carmel College." At this meeting:

> It was AGREED that the fund be known as the Carmel College Development Fund. Rabbi Rosen was invited and agreed to consult with the College's legal advisers in order to confirm this.
>
> It was discussed and agreed that the initial project should be to build two dormitories and also to improve the amenities of the Sports Block.
>
> The cost of this Rabbi Rosen estimated would be £33,000, and he had been promised a sum of £8,000 from the Matilda Marks Kennedy Fund.
>
> Rabbi Rosen submitted a list of parents invited to the Exhibition Day. Those present were invited to assist where possible in ensuring the attendance of those parents and to give a report of their efforts at the next meeting.
>
> It was suggested that the procedure for Exhibition Day be discussed at the next meeting . . . .[269]

The next meeting was called for 14 May 1957 and the "Procedure to be adopted for Exhibition Day" was indeed on the Agenda. Kopul. David Stamler and seven parents attended.[270]

Harold Poster, who was the Chairman of this Development Fund, was appointed a Governor in March 1958,[271] where he represented the Development Fund.[272] The Development Fund, in turn, set up a Functions Committee under the chairmanship of Gerald Ronson, who was another Governor.

As can be seen in the minutes of a meeting of the Development Fund held on 4 September 1957, the objectives of this Development Fund were

---

269. Minutes of Meeting [to inaugurate a Development Fund], 30 April 1957.
270. Agenda for [Development Fund] Meeting to be held 14 May 1957; the minutes have not been traced.
271. CCLtd Notification, registered 26 March 1958.
272. Carmel College Prospectus, undated, (about 1959).

specifically to raise money for buildings, as distinct from collecting money to cover daily running costs:

> The Committee felt that all donations received by the College, other than those specifically earmarked for educational purposes, should be paid over to the Development Fund. The Secretary [Norman Cohen] explained that the Development Fund was the only fund-raising body now working for the College, so that there was unlikely to be any income from donations that was not the results of their efforts. It could always be arranged for donations to be reported at meetings of the Board of Governors, so that the representative of the Development Fund would be fully aware of all sums received and could thus ensure that no moneys applicable to the Development Fund were retained by the College.[273]

One of the Functions Committee's first fund-raising activities was a Stag Party, which it would seem was held about December 1957. The Development Fund reported at their meeting that "the sum of £1,338 0s 6d had been raised" at this Party. (In the 1950s one could even buy something with a sixpence!) Following the success of this Stag Party, it was suggested that further such parties should be arranged, and the Chairman of the Functions Committee undertook to bring this question up at his next meeting.[274]

However, the major project at that period was a performance of "My Fair Lady" and this became the main item on the agenda at the Function Committee's meeting held in mid-November 1957. The Development Fund had taken over the Theatre Royal Drury Lane for a performance of "My Fair Lady" on 3 June 1958.[275] The first performance at this location was just over a month earlier on 30 April, and thus very few of the potential Carmel audience would have already seen it. Needless to say, to make such a project worthwhile, all the seats must be sold and what is more, for a good price!

At this meeting, it was agreed that the seats in both the Stalls and the Grand Circle, would be sold from 3–10 guineas, depending on their po-

---

273. Carmel College Development Fund, Minutes of Meeting held 4 September 1957.
274. Ibid., 10 December 1957, p.1.
275. Carmel College Development Fund Presents A Special Gala Performance . . . , printed advertisement.

sition, and in the Upper Circle 1–2 guineas.[276] In the Order Form sent round for the purchase of tickets, one could even get a cheaper seat, namely half a guinea, provided one was prepared to sit in the balcony. In order to "panic" people to purchase tickets quickly, accompanying this Order Form was the following statement, "'My Fair Lady' is not only currently the greatest success on Broadway, but one of the most fabulous smash-hits in American musical comedy history. There has already been an overwhelming demand for tickets. Please make your application quickly, remembering that allocations will be made on a 'first-come, first-served' basis." It was realised that some people might not want to go to this performance and they would thus feel that they were exempt from any financial outlay. To cover this eventuality, the Order Form stated "I do not require Tickets and therefore have pleasure in enclosing herewith cheque value £. . . . as a donation."[277]

Members of the Committee made "Promises for Tickets" ranging from £200 – £1,000; presumably this meant that they would make themselves responsible to sell tickets for these amounts, and not that they were going to pay this sum for their own personal seat! It was intended to bus all pupils at Carmel to the theatre and on this the minutes stated "Carmel College Students would occupy guinea seats in the Upper Circle. The expense of their transport would be borne from the proceeds of the Function."[278]

Similarly, at a meeting held nearly a month later, this theatre performance was the only item on the agenda. As with all theatres, there were boxes, and the Chairman took upon himself to deal with the allocation of these boxes.[279] The price for a seat in a box was not recorded in the minutes, but in an order form sent around the price of a seat in a box was from 8 guineas to 50 guineas.[280]

It had previously been decided to bring out a brochure, and at this meeting it was decided that the advertising rate would be 50 guineas for a page and 75 guineas for a double page spread. Some members of the committee made themselves responsible for selling five pages of advertising.[281] "My Fair Lady" was also on the agenda of the Development Fund meeting

---

276. Carmel College Development Fund, Minutes of Meeting held 11 November 1957.
277. Order form for tickets for "My Fair Lady."
278. Carmel College [Development Fund] Functions Committee, Minutes of Meeting held 11 November 1957.
279. Carmel College Development Fund Functions Committee, Minutes of Meeting held 3 December 1957.
280. Order form for tickets for "My Fair Lady."
281. Carmel College Development Fund Functions Committee, Minutes of Meeting held 3 December 1957, pp.1–2.

held on the following week and "it was agreed that the Board of Governors should be asked to help with obtaining brochure advertisements."[282]

Michael Poster (the son of Harold Poster), reported on this visit to Drury Lane in the Carmel magazine:

> For the school it had a more personal significance than for the ordinary theatre-goer but this could only enhance what was a most excellent performance.
>
> The play was outstanding in many respects for its adaptation of G. B. [George Bernard] Shaw's Pygmalion – it kept closely to the original and did not make any concessions other than at the end where like the film, it restored Eliza to Higgins. It treats the original with apparent respect and so retains all of Shaw's wit and humour. . . .
>
> The general décor and dresses were extremely good and the musical score was excellent tending, with such songs as 'With a little bit of luck,' and "Wouldn't it be loverly,' to draw music out of the characters rather than impose it upon them. . . .
>
> No-one I am sure could have left the Theatre without being profoundly aware of having seen a musical comedy with a difference.[283]

Some visitors went home with more than they came with! The author explains, "Certain of the visitors were to be presented with a bouquet of flowers during the interval and certain boys delegated for this task were told where the recipients were seated. One boy jokingly asked why his mother wasn't being presented with a bouquet."[284] Obviously, her bank balance was in overdraft! The bouquets were not limited to visitors. Ian Rabinowitz, who was then the School Captain, presented Julie Andrews, the main female star of the performance, with a bouquet back-stage after the performance.[285]

It was mentioned above that at about this period, a black and white promotional film on Carmel College had been produced. But a promotional film is of not much use, if there is no audience to show it to! An opportunity arose to screen this film for parents and well-wishers in the summer of 1959, when the Functions Committee of the Development Fund of Carmel again took over a place of entertainment, needless to add,

---

282. Carmel College Development Fund, Minutes of Meeting held 10 December 1957.
283. Carmel 1958, pp.32–33.
284. 7 years, p.81.
285. Recollections – Ian Rabinowitz.

Advertisement obtained by:

CARMEL COLLEGE DEVELOPMENT FUND FUNCTIONS COMMITTEE

invite you to assist their efforts to raise funds for
increasing the accommodation and buildings of

CARMEL COLLEGE

by taking space in the Souvenir Brochure of their

SPECIAL GALA PERFORMANCE OF

'The Diary of Anne Frank'

at the CARLTON THEATRE, HAYMARKET, S.W.1

on the evening of

WEDNESDAY, JUNE 10th 1959

To: Messrs. Freedman Publicity Services
   7 Poland Street, London, W.1
Telephone: GERrard 6207

ADVERTISEMENT RATES AND TYPE AREA

Delete space not required
{
Double Page Spread (14″ x 9″)—75 Gns.
Full Page (9″ x 7″)—50 Gns.
Half Page (7″ x 4″)—25 Gns.
Quarter Page (4″ x 3″)—12½ Gns.
}

I/We have pleasure in booking a_____space advertisement in the
Souvenir Programme of the Carmel College Development Fund.

Please delete whichever is inapplicable { Cheque is enclosed
Cheque will be forwarded

Name of Firm_____

Address _____

_____

Date_____

Telephone No._____Signature_____

Please delete whichever is inapplicable {
BLOCK HEREWITH
APPLY FOR NECESSARY BLOCK TO:-
_____

All Copy & Cheques to : FREEDMAN PUBLICITY SERVICES, 7 POLAND STREET, W.1

TEXT OF ADVERTISEMENT

CLOSING DATE FOR COPY 19th MAY 1959

CARMEL COLLEGE DEVELOPMENT FUND FUNCTIONS COMMITTEE	CARMEL COLLEGE DEVELOPMENT FUND FUNCTIONS COMMITTEE
present	*present*
a special Gala Performance of	*a special Gala Performance of*
'THE DIARY OF ANNE FRANK'	**'THE DIARY OF ANNE FRANK'**
at the Carlton Theatre, Haymarket, S.W.1	*at the Carlton Theatre, Haymarket, S.W.1*
on Wednesday, June 10th 1959	*on Wednesday, June 10th 1959*
ROYAL CIRCLE	ROYAL CIRCLE
£10 10. 0. ROW A SEAT 21	£10 10. 0. ROW A SEAT 22

*Order Form and Sample Tickets for Carmel College Special Gala Performance
of "The Diary of Anne Frank"*

for the purpose of fund raising. This was on 10 June 1959 at the Carlton Theatre, Haymarket, and the film was "The Diary of Anne Frank."[286] It was preceded by the showing of the film on Carmel College. The newspaper advertisement for the "Anne Frank" film said that (amongst other dates) 10 June was "sold out."[287] In other words Carmel had bought up the entire cinema for that night. Whether or not Carmel had "sold out" every seat, is not known! The tickets for the performance, printed for the occasion by the Functions Committee, gave the name of the performance, the place, date, seat place, and price of ticket (e.g. 5 guineas, 10 guineas), but for some reason (probably an oversight) the time of the performance was missing![288]

Again that year, a thick brochure was brought out to accompany this activity. As with the previous year's brochure the price for a double page or full page was 75 guineas and 50 guineas respectively. One could also take a half page for 25 guineas and a quarter page for 12 and a half guineas.[289] When produced, the brochure had about ten pages giving "An Introduction to Carmel College" but about ninety per cent of it was advertisements from wellwishers.[290] There were whole-page advertisements from, for example, Bedmax Bros Limited, and Mr. & Mrs. Gabriel Fierstone, and quarter-page advertisements from, for example, S. Eker Ltd, and Shepherd & Woodward Ltd. who supplied sports goods and clothing to Carmel.[291]

A review of the evening appeared in the Carmel magazine:

> The . . . film was one particularly suited to this performance, for it was a film that more intimately concerned us, than do most films. . . . The standard of acting in the film was excellent. . . . Throughout the film one was on tenterhooks; there are numerous scenes when the discovery of their attic hiding-place is averted by a hair's breadth. Too much suspense can lead to a state of apathy in the audience, and if this happens, the whole aim of the film is destroyed. A cut in the length of the

---

286. See: Carmel College Development Fund Functions Committee, sample tickets for a special gala performance of "The Diary of Anne Frank."

287. Jewish Chronicle, 22 May 1959, p.24.

288. Carmel College Development Fund Functions Committee, sample tickets for a special gala performance of "The Diary of Anne Frank."

289. Ibid., circular giving "advertisement rates and type area" for souvenir brochure for the occasion of the special gala performance of "The Diary of Anne Frank."

290. E-mail from George Mandell, 5 March 2013.

291. Introduction to Carmel College, Brochure brought out on occasion of gala performance of "The Diary of Anne Frank."

film would have done much to avoid this danger. Nevertheless, fine acting and clever photography greatly compensated for this weakness. The latter does much to create a claustrophobic atmosphere of the attic, and it is with some measure of relief that we catch brief glimpses of the exterior of the attic, during the film.

'The Diary of Anne Frank' is not only a tribute to a young Jewish girl, but it serves as a reminder to the community as a whole, of the tragedy which so recently enveloped Jewry. The film in itself remains an unforgettable experience, and is most praiseworthy.[292]

A year and a half later, on Sunday, 6 December 1959, the Development Fund arranged a "Gala Evening" at the Dorchester Hotel in London. For those who understand French, here is the complete dinner menu: Le Cocktail à l'Ananas; Le Saumon d'Ecosse Fumé au Citron; L'Oeuf Poché Florentine; Le Delice de Sole Carmel, Les Haricots Verts au Beurre, Les Pommes Delmonico, La Salade de Saison; Le Soufflé Surprise aux Cerises Flambées, Les Friandises; La Corbeille de Fruits; Le Café. For those who didn't study French at Carmel or have since forgotten it, the meal was a fish/milky meal. For the food served later on in the evening, a knowledge of French is not required. At 11.00 p.m. tea was served, and at 12 midnight Kippers, Rolls & Butter, Coffee. The evening was not just food. There were the Loyal and State of Israel Toasts, and a Toast to Carmel College, which was replied to by Kopul. There was also dancing to Van Straten and his Orchestra with his Latin American Group, and there was also a Cabaret.[293]

Due largely to the efforts of the Development Fund, during 1958 both the two-storey dormitory block, which became popularly known as the "M & S Block" and the three-storey Wolfson dormitory block, were erected, as well as the new sewage plant. In 1959, six hard tennis courts were laid but they cost only a 'mere" £3,000. In the following year, a sanatorium was built. It cost £14,000 and was financed by the Wix family.[294] In April of the following year, Michael Wix was appointed a Governor.[295]

The next item to be built was the Preparatory School Dormitories,

292. Carmel 1959, p.37.
293. Carmel College Development Fund, Gala Evening at the Dorchester Hotel on Sunday December 6th 1959, printed programme with Toasts and Menu.
294. Booklet published as a tribute to Kopul Rosen, undated (1962), section headed: Carmel College . . . The Facts.
295. CCLtd Notification, registered 1 May 1961.

whose building was already underway by the summer of 1960. This building was erected by the Development Fund and cost them £25,000.[296] As to be expected, the Development Fund continued in full force with its fund raising. In a letter sent out in July 1960, signed by David Stamler, it stated:

> In order to find the funds for the Prep School and other buildings, the Carmel College Development Fund has been working for some considerable time, and it is hoped to raise the remaining £15,000 required by December, when a Dinner will be held at the Dorchester Hotel, London. The main source of income for this function will be a Brochure and it is in connection with this Brochure that I write to you today for your help.[297]

This letter also stated, "The building of a Synagogue to seat 500 will probably have started by the time you receive this letter."[298] In fact, it was several years later that the Synagogue was built. Again, a year later, in December 1961, the Development Fund held its Annual Dinner and Ball. The Dinner, apart from the food, consisted of speeches and fund raising.[299]

Due to his serious medical state, Kopul could not attend in person. However, he sent a recorded message to be played at this Dinner. The thrust of his message was to compare the British Roman Catholic community with the British Jewish Community, showing how, in proportion to their numbers, the Roman Catholics intended spending far more on the building of new schools in the next three years than the Jewish community would spend. Instead, Kopul stated, the Jewish community would give vast sums of money to national charities, such as hospitals, art galleries, nurses' homes, and the zoological gardens.[300] Whilst on the subject of zoos, Jeremy Rosen reported that Kopul had said in one of his speeches that one Anglo-Jewish millionaire preferred to give money to build a monkey house at London Zoo than to Carmel College![301]

---

296. Booklet published as a tribute to Kopul Rosen, op. cit.
297. Letter David Stamler to Mr. Shifrin, 14 July 1960.
298. Ibid.
299. Letter KR to Malcolm Shifrin, 2 November 1961.
300. Recorded message to guests at dinner organised by the Carmel Development Fund, December 1961.
301. Biography of KR, p.41.

The Boilerman Ted Wetherall (1959)

DON'T FORGET THE BOILERMAN

As we have seen, during the Kopul era there were numerous Governors
of Carmel. However, there was another "governor" (a governor according
to Kopul!), who has not yet been mentioned, but this "governor" did not
appear in the Company Registration Files. He was Ted Wetherall, a man
who had worked on the Mongewell estate since 1910, and who would rise
at 3.30 a.m. to tend to the furnaces and would also tend to the grounds.
However, by the time Carmel took over the estate, he was getting old.
Alex Tobias continues with the events, "Once he maintained a certain
grievance. Younger men were slowly taking over his work. He brought his
complaint into the study of Rabbi Rosen who told him this: 'Ted, you are
not a member of the staff – you are one of the Governors.' Ted went off
enthusiastically to his grass shearer."[302]

Even the pupils gave him "great honour," since in the "General Paper"

302. Reflections – Alexander Tobias.

G.C.E. they would write about Sir Edward Wetherall![303] Maybe the examiners were impressed (or puzzled!) to read the name of a British Knight whom they had never heard of! In an end-of-term assembly held in December 1961, which was just before Kopul died, the "school governor" Ted was presented with a gold watch to mark his 75th birthday, and the school then sang "For he's a jolly good fellow."[304]

ALL'S WELL THAT ENDS WELL

Let us conclude this chapter which deals with the financial side of Carmel with a quotation from the Mechilta which says, "All beginnings are difficult."[305] It is a fact of life that when one starts a new enterprise, however worthy it is, at first it is very difficult to get people to donate. However, when one has already found donors, for example, to build the first few buildings, then further donors are more easily found. This seems to have been the case with Carmel. Already, a few years after building the first two dormitory blocks and the sanatorium, Carmel was able to start building its enormous classroom block. It was in the process of being built when Kopul died, and in the subsequent years numerous buildings were added.

---

303. Unwritten recollections of author (and similar comments by David Shaw) – the idea of using Wetherall's name was taken from the book "The Exam Secret" by Dennis B. Jackson (Wiltshire Book Company, 1970), pp.64–65 in which a non-existent "Lord Pritchard" is "quoted" by a candidate in a G.C.E. history exam in order to impress (or bluff!) the examiner!
304. Recollections – Nigel Simons; Reflections – Alexander Tobias.
305. Mechilta to Shemot 19:5 – the Mechilta is a halachic midrash to the book of Shemot (Exodus).

Chapter 2

Three Carmel Estates

Carmel College was not a transient gypsy encampment but a school which required a permanent locale; during the Kopul era (and indeed during Carmel's entire existence), there were no more than three estates. . . .

AN ESTATE WITH A BOUDOIR AND SMOKING ROOM

By the summer of 1947, well over a year before Carmel College opened, Kopul had already searched and found suitable premises for his planned school, and by about the end of 1947, the property had already been purchased. The property was known as Greenham Lodge, and it was situated near Newbury in Berkshire.

Greenham is an ancient city (not quite as old as Jericho!) with a history as least as far back as William the Conqueror. Indeed it is already mentioned in the Domesday Book, where Greenham was noted as having a total population of thirty-four households which comprised eleven villagers, nineteen smallholders and four slaves. It had land for ten ploughlands, and had two lord's plough teams and seven men's plough teams. Other resources were a meadow of 121 acres, one and a half mills, and a church. The Lord of Greenham in 1066 was Siward Barn. Twenty years later it was Henry of Ferres, who also was the tenant-in-chief.[1]

In 1199, King John (the King of Magna Charta fame, and the one who lost the crown jewels in the Wash) granted Greenham Manor to the Knights Hospitallers, a military order with a monastic life style. (A medieval seal was even found there.) But these Knights did not have it forever,

---

1. Domesday Book: Open Domesday, Berkshire, p.10, Place: Greenham, (Internet).

since in 1540, it was transferred to the Crown. But even the Crown didn't have it forever. In 1746, the ownership of the manor of Greenham passed over to the Croft family.[2] In a book on the history of Newbury written in 1829, by Edward Gray, the author writes. "Mr. Croft built a commodious residence called Greenham Lodge. The whole is now the property of his eldest son, Arthur James Croft, esq."[3]

In 1873, Lloyd Baxendale, a road transport entrepreneur and one of the partners in the Pickford removal company, purchased the Greenham Lodge Estate for £63,000[4] and between 1878 and 1881, a new Greenham Lodge was built, which largely replaced the previous building.[5] The architect for this new building was Richard Norman Shaw and its main façade was modeled on the design of the entrance front of the Elizabethan Shaw House, which is situated on the other side of Newbury.[6]

Soon after, in 1882, Lloyd died, and his son Lloyd Harry succeeded him as lord of the manor of Greenham.[7] Harry died in 1937[8] and in September of the following year, Greenham Lodge was put up to auction as "Lot 20." In the auction catalogue it was described as "The Very Attractive and Renowned Residential Property . . . It is in exemplary condition and erected in the Modern Elizabethan Style of Architecture."[9]

Greenham Lodge was requisitioned by the Air Ministry during the Second World War and served both the RAF and the American Air Force Base station no. 486.[10] It is reported that Eisenhower had lived there and that D-Day had been planned there.[11]

Let us now look at a description of Greenham Lodge. Details of all the rooms in this building, together with their dimensions, are to be found in the Auction Catalogue dated 1938, published just 10 years before Carmel purchased the property. Obviously, the names given to the rooms in this catalogue had little connection with the use to which Carmel put them.

---

2. Greenham and Crookham Common: A Timeline, (Internet).
3. Edward William Gray, *The History and Antiquities of Newbury and its Environs*, (Speenhamland Berkshire: Hall and Marsh:, 1839), pp.196–97.
4. Greenham: a common inheritance, Ten thousand years of History, Victorian Pleasures and Country Life, (Internet).
5. Greenham and Crookham Common: A Timeline, (Internet).
6. *Murray's Berkshire Architectural Guide*, ed. John Betjeman and John Piper, (London: John Murray, 1949), p.105.
7. Greenham: a common inheritance, op. cit.
8. Greenham and Crookham Common: A Timeline, (Internet).
9. Auction catalogue used for the sale of Greenham Lodge on 20 September 1938. Lot 20, (West Berkshire Museum), [henceforth: Auction Greenham], p.19.
10. Greenham and Crookham Common: A Timeline, (Internet).
11. Memories of KR p.24; Recollections – Jeremy Rosen, chap.1.

For example, a "Billiards Room," a "Boudoir," and a "Smoking or Gun Room," were not relevant to Carmel, although some Carmel pupils would surely have liked them to have been!

The building had three floors. On the ground floor, the Entrance Porch had oak-paneled walls and gave access through an arched carved oak screen to the Main Hall, which was also oak paneled and had a large open fireplace with stone surround. Other rooms on this floor included a Billiards Room, a Drawing Room, a Boudoir, a Dining Room, a Morning Room, and a Smoking or Gun Room. They all had open fireplaces and the dining room was paneled in oak.[12] The ground floor also contained the domestic facilities, such as a "large, light and airy kitchen," a scullery with three sinks (useful for meat, milk, and parva) and a "Butler's Pantry."[13]

In order to go up to the first floor there was a Wide Oak Staircase. This first floor included six very large bedrooms, a "Bachelor Suite" (all the Carmel pupils were bachelors!) and a "Nursery Suite" (but the youngest pupils at Carmel were already 7 years old!). The second floor also had a number of bedrooms which were mainly single rooms.[14]

The building even had a basement which contained a wine cellar (where one could store wine for kiddush!), a coal store, and a boiler house. It also boasted mains water supply, gas, and central heating.[15]

In about April 1948, Carmel College put out a Provisional Prospectus. It included a section headed "The College Buildings and Ground" and stated how it intended to use many of the abovementioned rooms:

> The nineteenth century mansion, now the School House, is ideal for its present purpose as it offers the boys a school life in a dignified and cultured atmosphere. The Grand Hall, Gallery and the Dining Hall are panelled in oak; the Library, the Common Rooms, the Play Room and the Study Rooms (classrooms) are all finely proportioned, spacious, well-lighted and ventilated and centrally-heated. The dormitories, bathrooms and resident masters' quarters on the first and second floors all have outside windows. Boys are allocated to dormitories according to their ages, and in the centre of, or close to, each group of dormitories is the room occupied by a member of the staff.[16]

---

12. Auction Greenham, pp.19–20.
13. Ibid., p.21.
14. Ibid., pp.20–21.
15. Ibid., p.21.
16. Carmel College Provisional Prospectus, undated (about April 1948), section: The College Buildings and Grounds.

Sometimes, a prospectus anticipating a future event, says one thing but when it comes to putting it into practice, it is quite different! However, in the case of Carmel, it can be seen from the recollections of David Perl, who was a pupil in the school from its opening day, that the dignified appearance of the various rooms held up to their description in the above Prospectus. Perl writes, "The meals were taken in the baronial-type wood-panelled dining room the ceilings of which, in common with the rest of the ground floor, were magnificently decorated with ornate friezes."[17] Thus the dining room had not changed since at least 1938. With regards to the classrooms Perl writes, "The classrooms were originally lounges and reception rooms whilst the large main entrance hall, overlooked at one end by an elegant minstrel gallery and dominated at the other by a magnificent open fireplace, was used as the general assembly hall. The whole effect was one of extreme elegance."[18] However, those in the second form did not have these luxurious classrooms, but had to make do with a pavilion for their lessons.[19]

With regards to the sleeping accommodation, Perl writes that "there were six dormitories initially, each containing from two to eight pupils,"[20] but he did not state on which floor these rooms were situated. On the dormitories, Jeremy Rosen writes, "Sleeping accommodation was very simple. Large open dormitories with rows of beds and lockers on the second floor accommodated the majority of pupils. Some of the older pupils lived in converted stable lofts down by the greenhouses."[21]

The boys whose dormitories were on the middle floor of the mansion also had an honorable neighbor whose name was Kopul. The Rosen family had an apartment consisting of three rooms plus kitchen and bathroom on the southwest corner of this floor.[22] It is likely that the Rosen apartment was what is described in the Auction Catalogue as the "Nursery Suite" which was comprised of three large rooms plus various washing facilities.[23]

In case one might think that pupils had freedom of movement all over the mansion, Tzvi Hirshfeld points out that this was not the case. "The wooden door to the main entrance was huge (its use was, of course, for-

---

17. The Old Carmeli, no.5, 1968–9, p.27; Reflections – David Perl.
18. Ibid., p.28; Ibid.
19. Reflections – Tzvi Hirshfeld.
20. The Old Carmeli, no.5, 1968–9, p.27; Reflections – David Perl.
21. Recollections – Jeremy Rosen, chap.1.
22. E-mail from Jeremy Rosen, 28 June 2013.
23. Auction Greenham, p.20. Nothing else on this floor seems to fit the description given by Jeremy Rosen.

The Estate at Greenham – Autumn 1948

bidden to pupils). This led to a big wood-panelled hall with its palatial staircase on which the boys could parade their originality on Purim only, but again, out of bounds during the rest of the year."[24]

Away from the mansion there was a glade which had originally been a croquet lawn and a tennis court.[25] David Stamler even found a nocturnal use for The Glade, as recollected by Malcolm Shifrin. He would organise "an all-night nature expedition" when all the boys "camped out in The Glade to watch the rabbits, foxes and the dawn chorus."[26]

There was also a building described in the Auction Catalogue as "The Garage and Stabling Block." The Garage had room for five cars. The Stables consisted of "Six Loose Boxes, together with Harness Room, Boiler Room, Cleaning Room and Store Room and Loft." There was also

---

24. Reflections – Tzvi Hirshfeld.
25. Recollections – Jeremy Rosen, chap.1.
26. E-mail from an early pupil (requested anonymity), 27 September 2013.

a Chauffeur's flat and a Cottage.[27] There was a building which was called the "North Court," which in bygone days had been the servants' quarters and stable block.[28] The Provisional Prospectus stated that this building contained "the Science Laboratories, Study Rooms, Manual Crafts Workshops and married masters' quarters."[29]

The stables on the estate were converted into a Synagogue which was endowed by Henry Freedman of Leeds in memory of his wife. Before being used for prayer, Synagogues have a consecration ceremony. This Consecration took place in Carmel on 15 January 1950 in the presence of the then Chief Rabbi, Israel Brodie. The Consecration service which was conducted by the boys included Reading from the Torah. The leining was done by John Fischer (who was then one month short of his Bar Mitzvah[30]), and the Chief Rabbi was called up to the Torah. Following the service, the audience went to the school hall where two pupils delivered speeches, one in Hebrew and the other in English. The advantage was taken on this occasion to have an "Open Day" and the visitors were conducted around the estate by Kopul and Headmaster Ewart.[31]

David Perl maintained that even after the Consecration one could detect this building's former use, "Looking around during a service one could see the dents that had been produced by the horses' hooves on the wood paneled floors and could actually detect the odour of dried hay laid there as fodder – or was it just our imagination?"[32]

The Greenham estate purchased by Carmel also had extensive grounds – about seventy acres.[33] The Auction Catalogue gives a detailed description of these grounds:

> The Grounds are a very distinctive feature of the Property, and are noted for their magnificent azaleas and rhododendrons of every variety which form the banks of a picturesque small lake and ponds connected by a Stream, giving great scope for making a very attractive Water Garden. The grounds generally are of an informal nature and

27. Auction Greenham, p.21.
28. The Old Carmeli, no.5, 1968–9, p.27; Reflections – David Perl.
29. Carmel College Provisional Prospectus, undated (about April 1948), section: the College Buildings and Grounds.
30. John Fischer commented that "that afternoon served as a useful dress rehearsal for my Barmitzvah one month later in London, (Recollections – John Fischer).
31. Jewish Chronicle, 20 January 1950, p.8.
32. The Old Carmeli, no.5, 1968–9, p.27; Reflections – David Perl.
33. Recollections – Jeremy Rosen, chap.1.

comprise chiefly grass slopes, well timbered with many fine specimen trees and profusely planted with Bulbs and Shrubs. There are also two excellent grass tennis courts and a fine entirely walled kitchen garden entered through wrought iron gates, and containing many es-palier Fruit Trees in full bearing. Herbaceous Borders and productive Vegetable Garden. Orchard. Range of glass houses including Two Vineries, Carnation House and Three Hot Houses. Also a range of good brick-built Potting Sheds and Boiler Houses. Bothy. Timber and thatched garden house.[34]

From the observations of Carmel pupils when they came ten years later, it can be seen that the details given in the catalogue were still operative and that the pupils enjoyed roaming these grounds. One of these pupils was David Perl, who writes:

The grounds were a delight to any boy – the winding and undulating paths, overgrown with rhododendrons, azaleas and other wild plants; the glade, subsequently transformed into the basketball ground; the walled gardens and potting sheds, where many of our vegetables were grown under the careful eye of Old Whitlock, the Head Gardener; the natural lake, behind which was the miniature Grand Canyon type rockery; and the adjoining stream which gave birth to a home-made bridge which was held alternatively by the third and fourth forms depending on who won the battle on that day![35]

Jeremy Rosen also describes these grounds adding details of the fauna and flora of the area:

Life in the countryside was idyllic. The gorgeous grounds were full of secret groves and lakes and pools alive with newts, frogs and water beetles. There were magnificent trees, Cedars, Pines and huge banks of Rhododendron bushes that bloomed each with gaudy blossom and re-ceived visiting hosts of noisy starlings that performed their massing whirls and chattering maneuvers in their season. There were farms to visit and calves to cuddle and have their sand-paper tongues rasp your hands and

---

34. Auction Greenham, op. cit. p.22.
35. The Old Carmeli, no.5, 1968–9, p.27; Reflections – David Perl.

cheeks. Gypsy caravans and fun fairs passed and sometimes stayed on the adjoining Greenham Common.[36]

Almost every new recollection contains material not found in another person's recollections. Several of the observations by Michael Blackstone have such additional material, "The Greenham grounds, outbuildings and orchards, many of which were out of bounds, all had to be explored. There were lakes, waterfalls, many hidden paths through and under the masses of rhododendron bushes, many leading to hidden glades where the boys used to meet for the unofficial dorm fights."[37]

From the recollections of Tzvi Hirshfeld, it can be seen that the scenery and flora were utilised by Carmel for various events throughout the year. He described the lake as "a very effective backdrop to the 'Guy Fawkes' fireworks display always ably put on by Mr. Coles, the chemistry master." and commented that the "abundance of trees and wild flowers were always a source of ample decoration at Shavuot time."[38]

The property also had a Lodge.[39] At that time, Morris Ellman was the Maths teacher and his family lived in this lodge and it has been said that "they were in effective control of comings and goings."[40] To reach the main building from this lodge was "a half-mile long 'drive'." It was not along a smooth road but a "pot-holed track [which] ended by circling around a huge oak in front of the main entrance."[41]

Despite the excellent main building and the magnificent grounds, Carmel College had to do a lot of development and improvement on the estate to make it suitable for the school's needs.[42] Needless to add that this required a lot of money and in those early days of Carmel there were no serious donors, but just a few loaners and many moaners!

At least in the case of the football pitch, they did not have to find money, "Pupils were press ganged into removing stones" and by this means "a rough and meagre football pitch was forced out of the common to the west."[43]

---

36. Biography of KR, p.36.
37. Reflections – Michael Blackstone.
38. Reflections – Tzvi Hirshfeld. (The original says "Shareout time" – this is obviously a printing error for "Shavuot time.")
39. Auction Greenham, p.22.
40. Reflections – Tzvi Hirshfeld.
41. Recollections – Jeremy Rosen. chap.1.
42. Biography of KR, p.33.
43. Recollections – Jeremy Rosen, chap.1.

AN ESTATE WITH A BUTLER'S PANTRY AND KNIFE ROOM

In 1950 Carmel purchased Crookham House, which was situated about 2 miles from Greenham Lodge[44] to serve as the campus for the Carmel Preparatory School.

Crookham, like Greenham, is mentioned in the Domesday Book. It was a much smaller place than Greenham, having only three villagers and one ploughland. The offices of Lord of Crookham in 1066 and in 1086, and also Tenant-in-chief in 1086, were held by the same person – Alwy Chafersbeard.[45]

Well before 1226, the abbots of Reading were the lords of the manor of Crookham,[46] but in 1321 it returned to the Crown.[47] In 1330 it passed into the hands of the Earls of Salisbury, where it remained for 211 years.[48] At a later date, the King would hand it over to various notables.[49] Sometime in the mid-16th century the old manor house at Crookham "ceased to exist" – it had "either been destroyed or allowed to become a ruin."[50]

In 1764, George Amyand, a rich Hamburg merchant, was made a Baronet, and in that year he purchased considerable property in Crookham, and built on part of it the mansion known as Crookham House. About twenty years later in 1790, the Crookham property was sold to Richard Tull.[51]

In 1830, Crookham House "was the site of one of the Captain Swing Riots when agricultural workers, concerned about their standard of living, roamed the countryside breaking the agricultural machinery which they believed was keeping wages down. On the evening of November 30, 1830, a group of men arrived at Crookham House . . . intending to smash machines owned by the lord of the manor, Richard Tull . . . ," but Tull had them arrested.[52]

George Amyand's Crookham House was pulled down by Tull in about 1850, and a new (the present) Crookham House was then built in three

---

44. Google maps, (Internet).
45. Domesday Book: Open Domesday, Berkshire, p.16, Place: Crookham, (Internet).
46. Samuel Barfield, *Thatcham, Berks and its Manors*, vol.1, text, (Oxford: James Parker, 1901), p.247.
47. Ibid., p.256.
48. Ibid., p.259.
49. Ibid., e.g. p.269.
50. Ibid., p.269.
51. Ibid., p.63.
52. Antiques Trade Gazette (London), Issue 2000, 23 July 2011, p.20.

phases between 1850 and 1900.[53] The southern portion of this house contains most of the principal rooms and "some of the walls are about 3 feet in thickness."[54]

In 1939, Crookham House was bought by the Great Western Railway Company, and during the Second World War, their Chief Goods Manager had his offices there.[55]

When, in 1939, Crookham House was put up to auction, the Auction Catalogue gave a detailed description of the building: "Crookham House is solidly built in two main portions, of mellowed Bath stone, surmounted by a stone parapet and slated roofs pierced by attractively designed stone chimney stacks."[56] This building has three floors. On the ground floor, the rooms are designated as The Main Hall, Drawing Room, The Library, The Dining Room, Study, The Billiard Room (a popular sport!), and The Domestic Offices which includes Butler's Pantry, Brushing Room (in a superior building, this is for brushing clothes), Kitchen, Bakehouse, Knife Room (sounds like an Agatha Christie novel! – at a later date in Wallingford, she was indeed one of Carmel's neighbours), and ash dump and Coal House.[57] The first floor had eight large principal bedrooms and nine secondary ones. The top floor was reserved for the servants.[58]

The Drawing Room in particular was exquisite in its décor. "The floor throughout is of oak parquet and the walls are surmounted by moulded and gilt cornices. There is a handsome carved white marble fireplace. . . ."[59] All the rooms had fireplaces. Indeed they were needed since it also states that "Central heating was installed in part of the principal corridors, but is now disused."[60] Outside the main building there were garages for five cars and stabling for twelve horses, and extensive gardens.[61]

Mendel Bloch, who taught at Crookham from September 1952, describes his experiences in this building which show that in addition to being a Prep School it was also a zoo!

---

53. Ten thousand years of history, Country Living, Greenham, a common inheritance, (Internet).
54. Auction catalogue used for the sale of the Crookham House Estate on 22 September 1939, Lot 15, (West Berkshire Museum), [henceforth: Auction Crookham], p.13. This catalogue states that this southern portion was built in 1812, which is not accordance with what is stated above.
55. Ten thousand years of history, Country Living, Greenham, a common inheritance, (Internet).
56. Auction Crookham, p.13.
57. Ibid., pp.13–14.
58. Ibid., p.15.
59. Ibid., p.14.
60. Ibid., p.15.
61. Ibid., p.16.

Crookham House was a large, austere, rustic building which we shared with squirrels, rats, mice and other denizens of Nature with whom we co-existed with much mutual, perhaps unavoidable, tolerance. On one occasion I was ascending the back stairs when a rat slowly ambled downstairs and it seemed to me that he winkled at me as he passed by. Perhaps I was mistaken; at that moment my nerves were not fully under control as I had just left a boisterous class. At Crookham the boys had plenty of room for movement, for tree-climbing and the 'cowboy' games so dear to them, and, in general, they were healthy and high-spirited.[62]

AN ESTATE HAUNTED BY TWO GHOSTS!

Suddenly, a serious problem arose with the location of Carmel College! In 1952, the United States Air Force decided to build a large airfield at Greenham Common and turn it into an airbase for the huge strategic Boeing Jets that were the lynchpin of the nuclear deterrent. The site of this airfield happened to lie between where the Prep School and the Senior School were then situated. The noise of the jet engines would have seriously impaired the tranquility of the school.[63]

The problems that Carmel would have thus faced reached even the national newspaper "The Evening Standard." In an article which appeared in March 1953, under the heading "College Quits as Jets Fly in," it stated:

One casualty caused by the building of a big American airfield at Greenham Common, near Newbury, Berks, is Carmel College – Britain's only Jewish school run on the lines of an English public school. . . . The noise caused by the building of the airfield has been an attraction to air-minded scholars; an irritation to the governors and masters. Now the prospect of competing with the noise of jet-propelled airplanes is too much. The college has decided to move.[64]

Kopul did not wait until the last moment, but already nearly a year earlier he began to look for alternative premises. Information on the progress of finding a new campus filtered through to the pupils and one of them,

---

62. The Old Carmeli, no. 3, 1966–7, p.7.
63. Recollections – Jeremy Rosen; Memories of KR, p.26.
64. Evening Standard (London), 6 March 1953, p.7.

Anthony Rau, reported on this in his letters home. In May 1952 he wrote, "There is a rumour that the school will buy a building that is near Reading and Basingstoke, it has 5,200 *(sic)* acres and a tennis court also, it is enormous."[65] In a subsequent letter he wrote that "there is a rumour that the school might move to the new place (if we buy it) during the winter hols."[66] He did not identify the place but it is likely that it is the place he mentioned in a further letter sent a few days later. "The building the school wants to buy is called Bramshill House and was owned by Lord Brocket; there was an article about it in the Daily Telegraph on Tuesday [8 July] (centre page)."[67] After the Second World War the exiled King Michael and Queen Ana of Romania resided there. Bramshill House was said to be haunted,[68] (but so was the property they finally bought at Mongewell!).

Carmel did not purchase Bramshill House . . . the search continued. In October of that year Carmel was considering another location. Rau writes, "The new place near Salisbury is called 'Norman Court' and it used to belong to the Singers (Sewing Machines) and we will buy it if the Ministry of Town & Country Planning don't object to a school being on that site."[69] One might add that Singers were, in addition to manufacturers of sewing machines, race horse owners and trainers.[70] About this site, Helmut Schmidt writes that it "was somewhere in the middle of the Salisbury Plain, about 20 miles from the nearest railway station," adding that "Doc [Friedmann] was visibly unhappy" about this site.[71] It is not clear whether Doc had gone with Kopul Rosen to see this place or had just heard about it. The above Ministry would, it seems, have given their approval to Carmel, since in the very same year Northaw School purchased the building and accordingly renamed their school "Norman Court School."[72]

Carmel did not purchase Norman Court. . . . the search continued. They came to Mongewell and Kopul took both Doc and Helmut Schmidt to inspect the place. On this visit Schmidt wrote:

---

65. Rau Letters, 26 May 1952.
66. Ibid., (postmarked) 3 July 1952.
67. Ibid., 9 July 1952.
68. Wikipedia – Bramshill House.
69. Rau Letters, 10 October 1952.
70. Norman Court Preparatory School, (Internet).
71. The Old Carmeli Year Book, 1977, p.8; FMF, p.26.
72. Norman Court Preparatory School, (Internet).

I shall never forget that historic drive. We found a clump of RAF huts in the snow around Mongewell Manor House – Agatha Christie's Monkswell Manor Guest House of Mousetrap fame. There was no end to the grandiose vision our flight of fancy took us on that day. We even dreamed of new dormitories, a dining hall, a sixth form campus at Springs, which we also visited, and – typical for Doc and for the Headmaster who both liked doing things in a great style – half in jest and half in earnest a . . . now it can be revealed for the first time . . . Carmel Villa in Florence. The great attraction for Doc, however, was the geographical position of the place between Oxford and London, England's two centres of culinary and cultural excellence.[73]

Jeremy, Kopul's eldest son, also has memories of these searches for new premises for Carmel. "I remember, as a boy of 10, spending the summer holidays of 1952, driving around southern England with my father, looking at decaying stately homes and abandoned estates for a new home. I had a wonderful time exploring cellars and storerooms, with such treasures as suits of armour or piles of deer antlers and climbing up on to dilapidated roofs that housed jackdaws and crows."[74]

On this search for new premises, Michael Ellman adds, "I remember him saying after he had viewed a number that he kept thinking that it would be desirable to have a property which combined the good features of all the various properties he had seen. Fortunately for Carmel, he was looking when the property market was subdued and before the great post-1952 boom in property prices got into its stride."[75]

What was the provenance of the site in Mongewell?

Mongewell in fact has a very long history. It was mentioned nearly a thousand years ago in the Domesday Book:

> Roger de Laci holds Mongewel (*sic*). There are ten hides there. Land to ten ploughs. Of this land there are in the demesne seven hides and therein three ploughs, and five bondmen and six villanes with one knight and eleven bordars have six ploughs. There are two mills of forty-five shillings; and five acres of meadow. Wood one mile and a

---

73. The Old Carmeli Year Book, 1977, p.8, (". . ." is in original); FMF, p.26.
74. Recollections – Jeremy Rosen, chap. 1.
75. Recollections – Michael Ellman.

half in length, and four quarentens broad. It was worth ten pounds; now fourteen pounds.[76]

The Mongewell House (not to be confused with Carmel's "Main Building") was situated where much later both the Rosen and Stamler family houses were built. During the course of building these two houses, an ancient well was discovered on the site.[77] It is likely that this well was the source of water for the old Mongewell House.

This older part of the Mongewell House was built prior to 1649, and at that time it was owned by William Molins. Molins died in 1649, and it was then acquired by Thomas Saunders. At that period it had at least ten rooms, with eight chambers as well as garrets and twelve hearths. It was later inherited by Sir John Guise who had married Saunder's granddaughter Jane. Following that, it was acquired by Shute Barrington in 1770, as a result of his second marriage to John Guise's daughter, who was also called Jane.[78]

Barrington was born in 1734 and following his education at Eton and Oxford University's Merton College, and holding some minor dignities, he was made in 1769 Bishop of Llandaff in Wales, and at a later date he became Bishop of Salisbury, and this in turn was followed by his appointment as Bishop of Durham, a position which he held until he died in 1826.[79] Over the years, Barrington made great improvements to the Mongewell House, probably building the Georgian extension between 1770 and 1773, during the period when he began to stay there regularly. It then had fourteen bedrooms and at least sixteen other rooms. In 1888 Alexander Casper Fraser bought the house from the trustees of Dame Mary Ann Price, the great niece of Shute Barrington.[80]

The Georgian house was replaced in 1890 by a large brick mansion (known in Carmel days as the "Main Building") which had been built for Fraser in a William and Mary style. He lived there until his death, and his

---

76. Domesday Book: Open Domesday, Oxfordshire, p.15, Place: Mongewell, (Internet); Rev. William Bawdwen, *A Translation of the Record called Domesday so far as relates to the counties of Middlesex, Hertford, Buckingham, Oxford and Gloucester*, (Doncaster, 1812), p.62.

77. Carmel 1958, p.5.

78. Berenice and David Pedgley, *Crowmarsh, A history of Crowmarsh Gifford, Newnham Murren, Mongewell and North Stoke*, (Crowmarsh: Crowmarsh History Group, 1990), [henceforth: Pedgley], p.52.

79. Barrington, Shute, *Encyclopedia Britannica*, 11th ed., vol.3, p.437; Wikipedia – Shute Barrington.

80. Pedgley, pp.51–52.

initials and the year 1889 can be seen on the lodge gates to the estate.[81] Fraser was born in Antwerp Belgium in 1835 and later held the office of a Justice of the Peace and Deputy Lieutenant.[82] He died on 30 December 1916, aged 81.[83]

Although Fraser died at the end of 1916, it was two and a quarter years later that a notice appeared in the "London Gazette" that "all creditors and other persons having any claims or demands upon or against the estate of Alexander Casper Fraser of Mongewell Park . . . are required to send in particulars of their claims and demands . . . to the Solicitors for the executors . . ." The two executors were Fraser's two sons John Mathison and Alexander Christian.[84] Meanwhile, the Mansion House had become a hospital for wounded officers from the First World War,[85] a war which ended in November 1918. Hospitals were certainly then in demand since this war had been one of the deadliest conflicts in human history. From just Britain and the Colonies, there were over 1,600,000 wounded.[86]

However, several months before the above announcement for potential creditors and claimants appeared in the "London Gazette," the two executors, on 19 August 1918, sold the estate at Mongewell to an American industrialist and financier, Howard Gould, who had moved to Europe from the United States a year earlier.[87] Howard Gould was born in 1871 and was one of the sons of Jay Gould, an American railroad executive, financier, and speculator.[88]

According to Lucy Ackworth, who was a cleaning lady at Carmel and had worked on the estate since 1918 (except for the period during the Second World War when she was doing war work), Howard Gould was a Jew and had the dome on the Mansion House removed because it made the building look too churchy.[89] However, it seems that this statement is not entirely accurate. Although Howard Gould's second wife, Grete Mosheim, whom he married in 1937, was reported to be of Hungarian Jewish ancestry,[90] there is no evidence that Howard was Jewish. He

81. Ibid., p.50.
82. The Peerage, (Internet), (quoting as its source Burke's Peerages 2003, vol.1, p.1227).
83. London Gazette, 11 March 1917, p.3340; General Register Office index, Births registered in January, February and March 1917, p.57.
84. London Gazette, 11 March 1917, p.3340.
85. Pedgley, p.50.
86. Wikipedia – World War I casualties.
87. Purchase Mongewell, par.8; Conveyance Mongewell. The Fifth Schedule, p.10.
88. Wikipedia – Howard Gould; Gould, Jay, *Encyclopedia Britannica*, 11th ed., vol.12, p.284.
89. 7 years, p.16.
90. Wikipedia – Grete Mosheim.

claimed to be an atheist, and this was to such an extent that he had the path to the church, St. John the Baptist, which was situated on the estate, sunk that he would not see the parishioners attending service![91] It is most likely that for a similar reason, he objected to the "churchy" looking dome and had it removed. From an old photograph of the Mansion House taken at the period when it was owned by Fraser, it can be seen that indeed there was a dome on this building. It was situated approximately over the area of the main hall.[92]

Another idiosyncrasy of Howard Gould's was the relative positioning of the light switches and the actual lights in the main hall. The norm is for a switch to control the nearest lights to it. However, this was far from being the case in this hall. One turned on a switch and the light went on at the other side of the hall! It was said that Gould was frightened that there might be someone at the other end of the hall who was waiting there to harm him.[93]

Gould seemed to have an interest in sports since, soon after he purchased the estate, he built a sports pavilion (in the Carmel era known as the gymnasium) with an outdoor swimming pool adjoining it.[94]

In her autobiography, the daughter of the vicar of Nuffield before the Second World War,[95] writes about a visit she made to Mongewell during the Gould era:

> At a friend's house we met Caroline Wainwright, the Woolworth heiress, who was staying with her uncle, Gould, the American millionaire. She was a charming and attractive girl in her early teens. Her uncle had a huge estate called Mongewell Park, on the opposite side of the Thames from us, with his own golf course. I shall never forget when one evening we took Caroline home after a party. As we approached the drive gates the whole area of the drive and front of the house lit up with brilliant floodlights and the gate opened automatically. Down the steps of the house came her uncle and aunt flanked by two menservants and accompanied by their two dogs, with another servant following behind the group.

---

91. Pedgley, p.50.
92. Photograph of Mansion House (Main Building) Mongewell during the Fraser era (date of photograph stated as unknown), National Trust Collections, National Trust Inventory Number 1251593.
93. 7 years, p.16.
94. Carmel 1957, p.14.
95. Name withheld by request.

The following week Caroline invited me there to see the gardens and the interesting old chapel which was on the edge of the river. I had hoped to see inside the house too but never got any farther than the hall, where I was asked to wait while Caroline went upstairs to fetch her cardigan. While I waited a manservant stood nearby virtually at attention. I thought both the butler and footman looked more like guards and was sure they both had a pistol or two hidden somewhere under their immaculate jackets. Just before the war Gould and his German wife left for Germany;[96] he was, it turned out, a Nazi sympathiser. Caroline went back to America. We did hear from her once or twice after she arrived home.[97]

On 6 August 1940, towards the beginning of the Second World War, Gould sold the estate to the St. Helen's Estate Limited[98] and very likely returned to the United States. Three years later on 10 August 1943, it was sold to John William Henry Charles Hopwood,[99] who owned it until Carmel bought it from him.

However, during the period of ownership of both the St. Helen's Estate and Hopwood, the estate was requisitioned property, the requisitioners being the Air Ministry, and it was occupied by the Royal Air Force until 1945.[100] They erected a number of huts on the site, which later became, together with others, the temporary classrooms, laboratories, and dining hall of Carmel College. In 1942, the estate became the Headquarters of No. 2 Group RAF of Bomber Command led by Air Vice Marshall Basil Embry. The Staff there also included, during the six months before his capture as a POW, World War II night fighter ace, Wing Commander Bob Braham,[101] one of the most highly decorated airman of the RAF in the Second World War.[102] On Mongewell and the Mansion House there,

96. The statement that in 1939 Gould and his wife went to Germany is almost certainly incorrect, since Gould's wife left Germany because of her Jewish origin. Possible evidence that they went to the United States is that in 1947 the Gould's divorced in Nevada (New York Times, 14 January 1947, p.27) and in 1959 Gould died in New York (New York Times, 15 September 1959, p.39).
97. Quoted by Henry Law in an e-mail to author dated 17 July 2014.
98. Conveyance Mongewell, The Fifth Schedule, p.10.
99. Ibid. Hopwood was a Captain, Remount Service, late 9th Lancers, of Attadale Ross-shire, Scotland. His name had not always been Hopwood. A quarter of a century earlier, he had, as a condition of being a beneficiary of the Hopwood family, changed his name by deed poll from Schroder to Hopwood (London Gazette, 26 March 1918, p.3802).
100. Purchase Mongewell, par.7, p.2; Pedgley, p.50.
101. Wikipedia – Mongewell.
102. Wikipedia – Bob Braham.

Braham writes, "I arrived at a Group Staff Officer Night Operation with some trepidation. It was my first staff job. However, I was soon put at ease at Mongewell Park, a beautiful old mansion near Wallingford, Oxford . . . The personnel types were most helpful and a few days after my arrival at Mongewell my two comrades joined me."[103]

Another structure on the Mongewell site was a certain nissen hut. When a teacher at Carmel, Murray Roston, was in a hospital during the 1950s, he met Dr. Mason, a man who had been stationed there during the Second World War. On learning that he was a teacher at Carmel, Dr. Mason asked Roston whether this nissen hut was still standing, which indeed it was. It was in this hut that some important planning for the war took place. Roston invited Dr. Mason to come to Carmel to give a lecture on the history of the Carmel estate, which he did soon after.[104]

It has been claimed that the room which later became Kopul's study was the room in which the final briefing was given to the reconnaissance mission following the "Dam Busters" raid on the dams of the Ruhr valley in May 1943.[105]

At the end of the war, the Mansion House was once again used as a hospital, having been requisitioned by the Ministry of Health.[106] The heated water in the swimming pool had therapeutic value for some of the patients.[107]

When Hopwood purchased the Mongewell estate in 1943, there were some parcels of land on the estate which were owned by other people, but in the early 1950s Hopwood purchased them.[108] There were certain conditions attached to these purchases, and these conditions were sub-

---

103. John Randall Daniel Braham, *Night Fighter*, (New York: Norton, 1962), pp.214–15.
104. 7 years, p.16; Carmel 1956, p.7.
105. Wikipedia – Carmel College (Oxfordshire). The early version of Wikipedia on Carmel College stated that the final briefing before the Operation took place in Kopul's study. However, this was soon refuted. The briefing before the Operation in fact took place in the large meeting room at RAF Scampton's Junior Ranks Mess in Lincolnshire (*Raid Dambusters, Operation Chastise 1943*, by Douglas C. Dildy, Oxford: Osprey Publishing, 2010, p.33). It was from RAF Scampton that the bombers departed. However, the aeroplanes doing the reconnaissance after the Operation left from RAF Benson (RAF Benson website), which is very near Carmel. The later versions of Wikipedia on Carmel College were amended to state that the final briefing before the reconnaissance took place in Kopul's study, but the source quoted for this information, does not mention Kopul's study, nor even the Main Building. However, the book by Stuart Fisher entitled *British River Navigations: Inland Cuts Fens, Dikes, Channels and Non-tidal Rivers* states, "Bomber Command used the [Mongewell] park during the Second World War to study Dambusters raid pictures," (London: Adlard Coles Nautical, 2013), p.215, but this book does not mention Kopul's study.
106. Purchase Mongewell, par.13a, p.3.
107. Carmel 1957, p.14.
108. Conveyance Mongewell, The Fourth Schedule, pp.7–10. One of the sellers was William

sequently inherited by Carmel. The conditions concerned the flora of the area: "For a period of forty years from the date hereof [i.e. date of purchase by Hopwood] not to fell or top any trees on the property hereby conveyed" – (a few listed exceptions are then given).[109]

On 26 January 1953 Carmel College purchased the Mongewell estate from Hopwood,[110] The area of the estate purchased was "Twenty eight acres One rood and Twenty perches or thereabouts."[111] Those who were at school in those days may possibly remember having to memorise in their arithmetic lessons such measurements as "rods, poles and perches"! For those who have forgotten, or never learned this, these three are in fact the same units of length. To mix one up even more, they can also be used as a unit of area. Next maths lesson: Forty square rods or poles or perches, equals one rood, and four roods equals one acre. All this was a nightmare for pupils of bygone days who would have to answer arithmetic exam questions using these units! However, the main question is, what was contained within this area of acres, roods and perches?

The largest area by far, which comprised about twenty-one acres, included (in 1953) the Mansion House, the decorative lawns behind and in front of it, and extended as far as the inner gate of Carmel (next to the Old Mill). It also included the area to just beyond the gymnasium in one direction, and the (Prep School) North Court in the opposite direction.[112] The remaining seven acres included half the width of the Thames extending from the Boat House to the end of the decorative lawns, the main drive up to the Lodge including the Lodge itself, and two close-by cottages, one of them with a garden.[113] When Carmel purchased the estate, these two cottages, as well as the Lodge, had service tenancies. In one of these cottages lived Ted Wetherall, who had worked on the estate since 1910.[114]

However, within this large twenty-one and a half acres was a small area which was not part of Carmel College. It was a church together with a graveyard. The church is St. John the Baptist's Church, Mongewell, and it dates back to the 12th century. Shute Barrington, who during part of his life lived on the estate, had it remodeled in picturesque Gothic style

Henry Madgwick. In the early days at Mongewell, a Mrs. Madgwick worked in the Linen Room. It is possible that she was from the same family.

109. Conveyance Mongewell, The Fourth Schedule, pp.7–8.
110. Purchase Mongewell, par.1, p.1.
111. Ibid.
112. Ibid., First Schedule, part 1, p.4. and plan annexed to contract.
113. Ibid.
114. Ibid., Fourth Schedule, Tenancies to which the Property is subject, p.17.

𝔄𝔫 𝔄𝔤𝔯𝔢𝔢𝔪𝔢𝔫𝔱 made the *Twenty-sixth* day of *January*
One thousand nine hundred and fifty
three B E T W E E N JOHN WILLIAM HENRY CHARLES HOPWOOD of
"Brackenber" Sunningdale in the County of Surrey Esquire (hereinafter called "the Vendor") of the one part and CARMEL COLLEGE
LIMITED whose Registered Office is situate at Greenham Lodge
Newbury in the County of Berks (hereinafter called "the Purchasers")
of the other part W H E R E B Y I T I S A G R E E D between
the parties hereto as follows :-

1.   THE Vendor will sell and the Purchasers will purchase FIRST
for the sum of NINETEEN THOUSAND POUNDS the inheritance in fee
simple in possession subject to the rights and easements and
exceptions and reservations hereinafter mentioned and subject also
to the existing Service Tenancies specified in the Fourth Schedule
hereto but otherwise free from incumbrances of ALL THAT Principal
Mansion House known as Mongewell Park with the outbuildings thereto
and all Landlords' fixtures therein other than the old electric
light engine and plant in the engine house adjoining the garage
premises but including the two timber huts erected on the property
which belong to the Vendor and ALL THOSE pieces or parcels of
land forming part of the Mongewell Park Estate situate in the
parish of Crowmarsh (formerly Mongewell) in the County of Oxford
containing an area of Twenty eight acres One rood and Twenty perches
or thereabouts ALL which said hereditaments are more particularly
described in Part I of the First Schedule hereunder written and are
for the purposes of identification only delineated on the plan
hereto annexed and thereon coloured pink AND TOGETHER ALSO with
the rights and easements referred to in Part II of the said First
Schedule but SUBJECT to the rights reservations stipulations and
provisions specified in the Second Schedule hereunder written
AND SECONDLY for the sum of THREE HUNDRED POUNDS the Tenant's
fixtures and other Chattels in or about the said premises set out
in the Third Schedule hereto which Fixtures and other Chattels will
be paid for on completion by the Purchasers and pass to them by
delivery on such date

2.   THE property will be sold subject to the Conditions known as
the National Conditions of Sale (Fifteenth Edition) so far as they

Page from Contract of Purchase of Mongewell Estate by Carmel College

The First Schedule *above referred to*

Description of the Property hereby conveyed

Number on plan	Parish	Description	Acreage according to Ordnance Survey
7 (part)	Crowmarsh (formerly Mongewell)	Drive verge	.195
9 (part)	ditto	Rough	.112
10 (part)	ditto	Lodge, drive and verge	3.656
13 (part)	ditto	Cottage	.275
15 (part)	ditto	Reservoir	.675
36 (part)	ditto	Cottage garden	.550
38	ditto	Stream	.561
39 (part)	ditto	Mansion and grounds	21.460
43 (part)	ditto	River Thames - half bed	2.050
163 (part)	Crowmarsh (formerly Newnham Murren)	Rough	.034
44	Crowmarsh (formerly Mongewell)	Ditch	.072
45	ditto	Meadow	15.297
46	ditto	Meadow	28.179
47	ditto	Bridle Path	.570
48 (part)	ditto	River	2.175
			76.468

The Second Schedule *above referred to*

Rights and Easements *granted by the Vendor to the Purchasers*

1. The right in fee simple for the purchasers and their assigns the owners or occupiers of the property hereby conveyed at all times hereafter to take and convey water from the reservoir by means of the existing pipes, the approximate position whereof is indicated on the said plan by yellow lines for the use of Mongewell Park aforesaid and all other buildings now or hereafter to be erected on the property hereby conveyed or on some part thereof and the gardens and grounds thereof respectively and to enter upon the adjoining lands under which the pipes are laid and to dig search for and examine the said pipes and to execute effect and do all necessary cleansings and repairs thereto or renewals thereof when and

Page from Document of Conveyance of Mongewell Estate to Carmel College

in the late 18th century. He is buried in the family vault in the church. Periodically some restoration work has been done on the church,[115] which work continued in the 1950s.[116] Included in the deed of sale is a paragraph giving the right of the Parishioners to continue going to and from this church via the Carmel estate.[117]

The area designated in the Contract of Sale and Purchase did not include the playing fields. However in the Deed of Conveyance written about eight months later, the area purchased by Carmel had increased almost threefold to over seventy-four acres.[118] The increase was almost entirely due to the purchase of the playing fields from the same vendor, Hopwood.[119] In the Deed of Conveyance, the playing fields appeared as two adjacent meadows, fifteen and twenty-eight acres respectively.[120] The remainder of the additional area (also purchased from Hopwood) was a bridle path on the eastern side of the playing fields, a ditch, and another stretch of the River Thames.[121] Although the first traced official mention of the purchase of these additional areas was in August 1953, a report of the purchase which appeared in the "Jewish Chronicle" in February 1953 speaks of an "estate of 80 acres."[122] This could indicate that already in the weeks following the signing of the Contract of Sale and Purchase, the two sides had agreed on the purchase of the playing fields.

Cows grazed in the neighbouring fields and, immediately on completion of the purchase, Carmel College was obligated to erect in certain areas a "four strand barbed wire cattle proof fence of a height of five feet" and keep such a fence maintained.[123] Possibly the reason for having to erect such fence was to stop the bovines from entering the Carmel estate.

For any estate, water, drainage, and sewage are crucial elements. For water to reach an estate, the water pipes often have to go via a neighbouring owner's land. Furthermore, the plant receiving one's sewage may well be located outside one's property. In the accompanying map to the "Contract for Sale and Purchase" are shown a number of troughs, a drain, and a "drainage disposal plant," all of them outside the boundar-

---

115. Wikipedia – St John the Baptist's Church.
116. Unwritten recollections of author.
117. Purchase Mongewell, Second Schedule, par.1, p.8.
118. Conveyance Mongewell, p.1, The First Schedule, p.4.
119. Ibid., p.1.
120. The reason for listing these two "meadows" separately, could be because they had different numbers on the Ordnance Survey Plan.
121. Conveyance Mongewell, The First Schedule, p.4.
122. Jewish Chronicle, 27 February 1953, p.9.
123. Purchase Mongewell, par 11, p.3.

ies of Carmel's purchase.[124] Without some form of control and right of access to these facilities, one could have numerous potential problems, should one's neighbours turn out to be uncooperative. It would seem that such an eventuality was foreseen, and in the Carmel Contract for Sale and Purchase most of the First Schedule deals with this subject. Carmel College was granted wide powers which included having the right "to enter upon the adjoining lands under which the pipes are laid and to dig search for and examine the said pipes and to execute effect and do all necessary cleansings and repairs thereto or renewals thereof when and as often as occasion shall require."[125] Needless to say, should Carmel have caused damage when exercising these rights, the school would have had to repair such damage.[126]

Due to the laws of gravity, water only flows downwards. Thus, should one require water at a higher level, it is necessary to incorporate some sort of mechanical device. For this purpose, a hydraulic ram is used. There was such a ram outside the Carmel estate, and the Contract of Sale and Purchase gave Carmel the right to use it.[127]

The sewage plant, which was rather old and built with red bricks, served Carmel until towards the end of the 1950s. At that period, two new dormitory blocks were erected and at the same time a new sewage plant was built adjacent to the old one. This time the brick colour was yellow, to match the new dormitory blocks! The comparison stops there. The sewage plant was not in the name of a person or organisation, nor was there an opening ceremony![128]

The Third Schedule of the Contract for Sale and Purchase gave a meticulously detailed list of "Tenant's Fixtures and Fittings which will pass to the Purchasers by delivery on completion." The rooms then had names which were quite different from the names they had in Carmel's days. There was "The Long Attic," "The Oak Room," "The Green & White Room," "The Drawing Room," "The Bothy," and "The Fernery."[129] There was also "The Butler's Pantry,"[130] but the pupils at Carmel did not merit having their own butler!

---

124. Ibid., plan annexed to contract.
125. Ibid., First Schedule, par.1, p.4; also similar wording in par.5, p.5.
126. Ibid., par.5, p.5.
127. Ibid., par.3, p.5.
128. 7 years, p.101.
129. Purchase Mongewell, Third Schedule, pp.10–16.
130. Ibid., p.14.

The ground floor of the Main Building also had a "Billiards Room"[131] but billiards was not on the pupils' curriculum. In contrast, for a period during the 1950s, when a billiards table was to be found in the Staff Room, it was on the staff's curriculum! However, from Michael Goitein's writings, we can see that the staff's billiard playing did not last forever. Goitein writes:

> Rabbi Rosen decided that this game was undermining the atmosphere of the common room; teachers had become addicted to playing and watching snooker to the exclusion of any substantive conversation. So, not one to idly watch while something he disapproved of was taking place, he decided to get rid of the billiard table during one summer vacation while the staff were away. My mother got wind of this and, typically, offered to take it off his hands. Thus it was that Top Farm [Goitein's house] harbored a world-class billiard table. While this turned me into a semi-respectable snooker player, I am not sure that the transaction endeared me to my teachers.[132]

In a footnote, Goitein adds, "David Stamler recalls being told that the billiard table had been a gift from my mother and that, since it took up so much room, it had simply been returned to her. It sounds as though Rabbi Rosen had woven a tale which shielded him from blame in the matter."[133]

There was a hint at the staff playing billiards in their Staff Room which was then situated next to the Main Hall, in a short verse composed by Philip Refson and Jeffrey Walker, borrowing from the poetry of Charles Wolfe:[134]

> Not a sound was heard not a single note,
> As we walked through that deathly hall,
> Not a junior screamed at the top of his voice,
> Just the click of the billiard ball.[135]

---

131. Ibid.
132. Recollections – Michael Goitein.
133. Ibid., footnote 3.
134. Charles Wolfe (1791–1823) was an Irish poet who wrote, *The Burial of Sir John Moore at Corunna* which begins 'Not a drum was heard, not a funeral note, As his corse to the rampart we hurried; Nor a solider discharged his farewell shot O'er the grave where our hero was buried.'
135. Carmel 1957, p.12.

The list of fixtures and fittings in the Contract for Sale and Purchase almost went as far as to note every nut and bolt to be found on the estate! Here are two examples: "End Room facing River (5): A cornice pole, The metal curtain runners, Two cord electric light pendants and plastic shades, Six hooks in cupboard, The fitment of angle wardrobe cupboard."[136] "The Grey Dressing Room: A plated balance weighted electric light pendant with two frosted glass shades, A rise and fall electric light pendant and plastic shade, A plated electric light bracket, A plated towel roll, A cornice lath fitted brass tramway runners, Four deal batons and eight hooks."[137] The people detailing this Contract for Sale and Purchase certainly had to work hard for their money!

The lake which ran through the estate had swans swimming in it. But if they were unmarked and mute Carmel could lay no claim to them, since they were the property of the Queen of England in partnership, since the late 15th century, with the Vintners' Company and the Dyers' Company.[138] These swans became an integral part of the "initiation ceremony" which took place in 1957 of a then "New Boy," Jacob Fachler, who recollects:

> I was outside the main building when a boy yelled down at me from an upper story, 'Hey, new boy, can you do me a favour?' Once again, delighted to be addressed by anyone, I said, 'Sure.' He continued: 'Can you see down at the bottom of the lawn, just by the lake, my sheet has blown out of the window. Can you bring it back?' 'I thought we weren't allowed to walk on the lawn,' I replied. "That's OK, I'm a prefect, and I allow you.' So off I trundled, happy to be able to be of service to this important person. As I approached the sheet, it turned round and gave an almighty quack. As I ran back to escape the swan, I could hear peals of laughter from the 'prefect' and his mates. Well, I survived my 'tvilla ba-esh' ['being immersed in fire'].[139]

As stated above, the area of purchase of the Mongewell estate by Carmel College included a small strip of half the width of the River Thames. Compared with the total length of the Thames – 215 miles – Carmel's share was miniscule, but even so, they did own a part of this world famous river! However, this miniscule portion does have a certain distinction. It

---

136. Purchase Mongewell, Third Schedule, p.10.
137. Ibid., p.12.
138. Wikipedia – Swan Upping.
139. Recollections – Jacob Fachler.

has the straightest run of the River Thames, and Oxford University made full use of this during their preparation for the annual University Boat Race.[140]

The Thames is a flowing river, but this was not always the case. Between the 17th and 19th centuries, the period of the Little Ice Age, the Thames would freeze over for two months each year and become a skating rink![141] But this is all history! During the years following Carmel's purchase of this part of the River, it would sometimes like to extend its boundaries and "each year flood waters swept through the estate, including the temporary huts, by then used either as classrooms or dormitories. Only permanent buildings on raised grounds escaped the annual floods which came right up to the steps of the Main Building."[142] Neil Acton recollects the "prefab classrooms staying above the annual floods submerging the rest of the grounds."[143] He didn't mention how one got to lessons – swimming or otherwise, or maybe to the delight of the boys the lessons were cancelled!

The Carmel magazine reports on flooding in December 1954, and it was not only in the Carmel area, "Last December floods affected us along with other parts of England. The River came up to the Classroom block, and one wing of the study Block was temporarily evacuated when the floor was covered."[144] On his being rescued on the occasion of this particular flooding, Tzvi Hirshfeld recalls, "One night during the second winter [at Mongewell] I can remember being awakened by one of the housemasters striding into my study making splashing sounds with his wellington boots. He picked me up and carried me over his shoulder to a drier area where the river had not managed to spread its elongated tentacles."[145]

Not only did the flooding obstruct access to the buildings, at the beginning 1955, the football pitch was flooded which naturally caused difficulties in arranging fixtures.[146]

Because of this flooding problem, Carmel's first two new buildings – two dormitory blocks which were built in 1958 – were considerably raised from the ground.

Water wasn't the only hazard at Carmel. The Mongewell estate was

140. Wikipedia – Carmel College (Oxfordshire).
141. Wikipedia – River Thames Frost Fairs; A History of Weather in Epsom and Ewell, (Internet).
142. Recollections – Jeremy Rosen, chap.1.
143. Recollections – Neil Alton.
144. Carmel 1955, p.7.
145. Reflections – Tzvi Hirshfeld.
146. Carmel 1955, p.44.

Stream Running Through the Grounds of Carmel College at Mongewell

haunted by two ghosts! One was the ghost of a 15th-century monk who was murdered and cursed the grounds just before he died.[147] "The Young Carmelonian" has a slight variation on this and writes that this monk "who imitated Cain by slaying his brother, knocks on the windows of certain rooms at a fateful hour."[148] The second ghost was of later origin by about 300 years. This ghost was of the miller of the Old Mill who was found strangled.[149] Maybe this was the reason that the regular reading of ghost stories by candlelight at sessions of the Carmel Union Society was a highly successful activity![150] It was the very same Union Society that held a "highly vociferous debate on the existence of ghosts . . . and after much

---

147. Carmel 1957, p.13.
148. The Young Carmelonian, p.7.
149. Carmel 1957, p.13.
150. Carmel 1956, p.25; Carmel 1957, p.25; 7 years, p.71.

hesitation the floor voted 19 for and 19 against – the first recorded draw in the society's history."[151]

Maybe the ghosts haunting Mongewell were the cause of a boy in the Prep School, David Sheldon, then aged 10, writing this poem:

> The ghost I know is black and white,
> It cannot see, nor can it write,
> It travels through the eerie night
> Rushing forth with all its might.
> Every night I see it pass
> Spacious meadows with green grass.
> But mother told me one bright night
> That my ghost of black and white
> With smoke behind, like horse's mane,
> Was nothing other than a Train.[152]

Let us now leave the world of the super-natural and make a virtual tour of the Main Building, as it was when Carmel took it over. However, first one has to reach the Carmel estate. Henry Law graphically describes the route after arriving at Crowmarsh:

> Carmel was reached by taking the A4074 main road from Crowmarsh to Reading. The road climbed away from the Thames valley onto the chalk of the Chilterns in a beautiful avenue of beech trees whose branches met overhead to form a vault. The main entrance to the Mongewell Park estate and Carmel College was off this avenue on the right. . . . At the entrance, amongst the trees, stood a painted sign with the school shield, with a red brick lodge on the left. A winding pot-holed road led back down towards the river, beside which the school grounds lay.
>
> The road passed through the gates in a wall and to the right was a group of red brick buildings known as North Court, where the preparatory school was situated. It might at one time have been a stable block. A bridge over a stream brought one to the main forecourt of gravel, with a feature of some kind in the centre. To the right of the

---

151. Carmel 1956, p.25.
152. Alpha 1956, p.12.

bridge was a lake. A flight of steps led up to the front door [of the Main Building].[153]

When Carmel arrived in Mongewell in 1953, the walls of this three story Main Building were covered with ivy, but this was soon to be removed, since ivy weakens the walls, although adding to the beauty of a building. Maybe for this reason, a photograph of the main building shown in a prospectus for Carmel brought out in the late 1950s still showed this ivy.[154]

The main entrance to this building was through two enormous copper and glass doors. In the course of the years, the copper on these doors had developed a patina, which beautified them. However, someone gave an order to remove this half-century old patina. Romney Coles, who was a chemistry teacher at Carmel and could thus appreciate what a patina was on copper, was most upset about this.[155]

Pupils were not allowed to enter by this door; they had to use the side door on the eastern end of the building. On going through the main door one came into the big hall. On the western side of this hall was a beautiful wooden staircase up to the first floor. To use it, one had to become a member of the staff or a prefect.[156] One can almost certainly add cleaners, since it is very unlikely that the staff or prefects would have cleaned these stairs! These stairs also proved useful for a Senior School staff photograph taken in the mid-1950s.[157]

There were also a number of very large rooms leading from the big hall. They were panelled in oak and had parquet flooring.[158] One of them became the school library. A big fish that had been caught near the school, was stuffed and put in a glass case, and displayed on the mantelpiece above the fireplace. Before the era of radiators and central heating, people had a coal or wood fire in each room. Even by the 1950s, Carmel had progressed beyond coal or wood fires.[159]

Also leading off the main hall was a loggia, an extension with a glazed wall. It faced south-west and became very hot in the afternoon, which was a good thing in the winter though not so pleasant in the summer. The

153. Recollections – Henry Law, Carmel College days, part 2, p.1.
154. Carmel College Prospectus, undated (about 1959), captioned: Main Building (from the rear).
155. 7 years, p.16.
156. Ibid.
157. Reflections – photograph.
158. Recollections – Henry Law, Carmel College days, part 2, p.1.
159. 7 years, p.16.

Front Entrance to Main Building at Mongewell

loggia was used for teaching small classes, and the newspapers were put out there.[160]

Opposite the library was another large hall, which was the staff room. Pupils were never allowed in this room and could only see what was inside from afar, when a teacher entered. However, there was an occasion when a teacher gave a "Torah lesson" in the staff room. It was probably on a Shabbat. One of the pupils not only took the opportunity to read the staff's private notice board, but he even asked the teacher why a certain notice was not there; the teacher was rather annoyed at this pupil's nosiness! During a parents' visiting day, the then three-year-old younger brother

---

160. Recollections – Henry Law, Carmel College days, part 2, p.1.

of the author, calmly pushed open the staff room door and ran in "where angels fear to tread."[161] The author had to embarrassedly run after him to remove him from this forbidden territory![162]

Another large room leading from the eastern side of the big hall was used as a lecture theatre and at appropriate times it served as a room for public examinations. For the first term at Mongewell, it served as a dormitory. During the latter period of the 1950s, the library considerably expanded and the staff room became the fiction library, whilst the staff then moved (or were moved!) to the lecture theatre.[163]

From the eastern side of the big hall ran a corridor the whole length of the building. The first room in this corridor on the right-hand side was the Principal's study. Jeremy Rosen describes his father's study:

> One of the unforgettable features of Carmel was the headmaster's study. All pupils at some stage stood outside that heavy carved wood door in trepidation, waiting for the lights to flash an instruction to wait or come in or a loud resonating voice calling you in to your fate. The room was large, spacious and wood paneled. Straight ahead lay a huge kidney desk fronted with bookshelves that contained books ranging from Rhadakrishnan to C.P. Snow to the Talmud. On the left was a rococo bookshelf with glass doors covering other volumes. In the eastern corner a door led to a small toilet and then down to what was originally a classroom but later became the headmaster's secretary's office. A small door to the west led out to the back gardens and tennis courts, and also internally to the library.
>
> To the right of the desk was the famous eighteenth century Highwayman's chair with a trapdoor seat. When it was engaged if one sat down on it, it released iron clamps that dropped over ones thighs and prevented escape (until released by someone who knew the mechanism). There was a primitive safety block that prevented the seat from sinking to release the clamps but invariably it was not in place. It was the joke of the school to see which new pupil or visiting dignitary would test the chair and find himself trapped. All the furniture had been bought at local auctions when the school moved in.[164]

---

161. Alexander Pope, *An Essay on Criticism*.
162. 7 years, pp.16–17.
163. Ibid., p.17.
164. Recollections – Jeremy Rosen, chap.1.

According to Henry Law, the arrangement of the furniture in this study was cleverly done. "A visitor would be confronted by the desk, placed diagonally across the corner, with Kopul behind, and behind Kopul to his right was a large window. This meant that Kopul got a better view of the visitor than the visitor got of Kopul, a powerful psychological advantage."[165]

When in the mid 1950s, David Stamler was appointed Vice-Principal, another, but not so elaborate desk was added to this room by the side of the window ledge.[166]

As one continued along this corridor, on the left-hand side was located the school office run by Mrs. Sophie Walker.[167] Beyond the school office was a staircase leading upstairs to the dormitories. This was the only staircase which the pupils were allowed to use.

The next room on the left-hand side was a washroom which was completed soon after the school's arrival in Mongewell. It contained about ten toilets and about twenty washbasins. Why they installed so many washbasins, when the dormitories were upstairs and there were washbasins upstairs as well, was always a mystery. Surely Carmel didn't have a surplus of money at that time! Maybe the school was hoping for super cleanliness! There was also a large cubicle with about eight showers but no partitions between them and next to it a room with four baths. The baths were the "sit-up type" where the back half was about one foot higher than the front half. Maybe the school was frightened that the pupils would drown had they installed normal baths![168] There may have been plenty of washing facilities, but as Tzvi Hirshfeld recalls, "hot water in the bathroom was available by the teaspoon!"[169]

Opposite this washroom was the linen room. There were large laundry baskets where one would put one's dirty clothes. The linen room staff would sort it out, list out what each pupil had put there and send it off to the laundry.[170] Henry Law describes this room and its staff, "[It] had a characteristic fresh smell. Two middle aged ladies seemed to be spending their entire day sorting laundered socks and underpants and putting them in the numbered pigeonholes for each boy."[171]

---

165. Recollections – Henry Law, Carmel College days, part 2, p.2.
166. 7 years, p.17.
167. Ibid.
168. Ibid., p.18.
169. Recollections – Tzvi Hirshfeld.
170. 7 years, p.18.
171. Recollections – Henry Law, Carmel College days, part 2, p.2.

At the end of this corridor there was an annex where some members of the domestic staff lived. Rabbi Rosen once announced that if any pupil were to go into the room of a member of the domestic staff, then that member would be dismissed.[172] The reason is obvious.

In this area there was the only public telephone in the school. Maybe "public" is not the correct term! Pupils were forbidden to use it without permission. This is reminiscent of the Jennings books which are set in a boarding school in the 1950s. When the question of using a telephone arose, Mr. Wilkins, the master, says to Jennings, "You know perfectly well you're not allowed to touch the phone without special permission."[173] However, in Carmel the punishment for this infringement could be much more severe than just a reprimand, as David Mond reported, "My memory of Kopul was soured after he caught me telephoning my parents from the Main Building public telephone box one evening. He banned me from seeing my parents at the showing of the Diary of Anne Frank and the Carmel Film and then 6 of the best on my behind in his study!"[174]

Outside the side door, was a covered area for bicycles – at least at first! But then things changed . . . Henry Law writes, "At first, cycles had been permitted but one day, a boy decided to follow a bird whilst cycling along the towpath. The bird turned and flew across the river. The boy continued to follow. And that was the end of cycling in the school."[175]

On the first floor, most of the rooms were dormitories. The two largest rooms, Dormitory Four and Dormitory Nine held about fifteen to twenty boys sleeping on double bunks. It was almost like the "Black Hole of Calcutta."[176]

There was a boy called Ellis Korn who spoke beautifully and Kopul would use him to show visitors around the school. But he was given instructions not to show them the dormitories! (One can understand why!) He reported that it was the dormitories that the visitors specially wanted to see but he would answer them that he needed special permission to do this.[177]

The last door on this floor led to two rooms and they served as an apartment for the Rosen family. Kopul and his wife lived in one room; on

---

172. 7 years, p.18.
173. Anthony Buckeridge, *Our Friend Jennings*, first edition 1955, (London: Collins, reprinted edition 1973), p.117.
174. Recollections – David Mond.
175. Recollections – Henry Law, Carmel College days, part 2, p.2.
176. 7 years, p.18.
177. Ibid.

one side of this room were their beds and on the other their dining room/ lounge. The second room was a bedroom for their three sons.[178]

Opposite the Rosen's flat was a room which after the move to Mongewell was used as a sanatorium. It had two or three beds in it. A few years later the sanatorium was moved to the annex of the gymnasium. In addition, there was also a dispensary situated near the back entrance of the main building. It was open every morning for pupils who needed medicines or medical treatment for cuts and minor ailments. Pupils would also be weighed and have their heights measured in this dispensary.[179]

During every vacation, the parents received a pink piece of paper to complete and return to the school. This document was headed Carmel College Health Certificate, and this was followed by the solemn declaration (although a Bible was not required!), "I hereby certify that my son . . . . has not been in contact with any infectious disease during the holidays now ending." It had to be signed and dated by the Parent or Guardian.[180] There are no statistics available to ascertain how many parents actually completed and returned this piece of pink paper to the school, but it can be said with certainty that the boys were not checked on their return to school for any germs which might have been lurking around their bodies!

During the course of the Kopul era, there were numerous different matrons at Carmel, some at the Prep School, whilst others were at the Senior School. "The Young Carmelonian" in 1954 described that period "as a great coming and going of matrons," and reported that one current one had "walked the sacred halls of Eton and Sherbourne."[181] One of the first matrons in the Greenham days was Nurse Reppon, a "Spartan German matron who terrified everyone."[182] During Mongewell days, the matrons included Pickard, Garland, Hyland, Spriggs and two Slades.[183] There was one matron who insisted on being called Sister. Miss Watson was designated "Senior Matron" and in addition to her healing powers, she volunteered as gardener and ornithologist.[184] At one end of term assembly, a matron who was leaving was given a presentation. However,

---

178. Ibid.
179. Ibid., pp.19, 129–30; Recollections – Henry Law, Carmel College days, part 2, p.3.
180. Carmel College, Health Certificate.
181. The Young Carmelonian, p.13.
182. Recollections – Jeremy Rosen, chap.1.
183. Various Senior School and Prep School magazines, passim.
184. Carmel 1961, p.5.

Carmel College

HEALTH CERTIFICATE

I hereby certify that my son...

has not been in contact with any infectious disease during the holidays now

ending.

Signed..
Parent or Guardian

Date...

Carmel College Health Certificate

by the following term she was back at Carmel. There is no record of her returning her leaving present![185]

There was one matron who was not frightened by a mump or measle, but instead was terrified of bats! David Shaw relates, "On more than one occasion, Matron, either the skinny one with red hair or 'Battle-axe' came flying in, in a mad panic. Once an inoffensive small Pipistrelle bat was flying around in her bedroom. I had to chase it off but sadly killed it with a racket."[186]

The second floor, which was the top floor of the building could be called the "attic rooms" since they were directly under the sloping roof and had dormer windows and sloping ceilings. The rooms on this floor were smaller than those on the first floor and there were about three to eight pupils in each room.[187]

There were several other brick buildings on the Mongewell estate when Carmel purchased it. One of them was the gymnasium, which was a timber-framed building with a red tiled roof arranged around three sides of a rectangle which enclosed the space where the outdoor swimming pool was.[188] This building consisted of the gymnasium itself which, when Car-

185. Unwritten recollections of author.
186. Recollections – David Shaw.
187. 7 years, p.19; unwritten recollections of author; Recollections – Henry Law, Carmel College days, part 2, p.3.
188. Recollections – Henry Law, Carmel College days, part 2, p.4.

mel first arrived in Mongewell, was poorly equipped with climbing frames. Later, far more gymnasium equipment was added and a basketball pitch was also set up there. There was also a court with wood paneling all over the floor and walls which was built for some American sport, but it was so like an English squash court that it was used accordingly.[189] An annex to the gymnasium was the "long dorm" in which about twenty boys slept and in front of it was the Shul for the Prep School. The upper story of this annex first served as the residence for the Ellman family, Morris Ellman then being the mathematics teacher. After he left in the mid-1950s, this apartment became the sanatorium.[190]

There was another building which Carmel called "North Court," and was originally stables; it was situated, as its name suggests, in the northern part of the estate. This was utilised by the Prep School boys who were aged between 7 and 11. When Carmel arrived at Mongewell, this building was being refurbished and the Prep School was unable to move in for about three months. Until then they were temporarily housed in the top story of the main building.[191] Michael Bharier wrote on this North Court, "We would watch the bats emerge at dusk from under the eaves of that building. One evening we counted over 300 of them before we gave up counting."[192]

At the entrance to the outer gate of Carmel was the Lodge. At first, the Bursar, Captain Lunzer lived there. At a later date David Stamler and his family lived there.[193]

Another building was known as the Old Mill, where the members of staff Dr. Friedmann, Dr. Tobias, and Michael Cox the art teacher lived. This building also had a lower floor with a trap door which could be lifted and gave a view of the trout in the stream which ran below. Of these trout Henry Law wrote, "We tried, never successfully, to catch them with nooses made of electric light flex."[194] He added that "the mill had a spacious loft space. Malcolm Shifrin [Shif], the librarian, set it up as a listening room with the best sound reproduction equipment one could buy at the time: there was a deck with a Garrard 301 turntable and Tan II arm, a Quad 2 preamplifier and amplifier and a Tannoy corner speaker. Stereo was still

189. 7 years, p.19.
190. Ibid.
191. Ibid., p.20.
192. Recollections – Michael Bharier, chap.3, The Environs of Carmel.
193. Unwritten recollections of author.
194. Recollections – Henry Law, Carmel College days, part 2, p.5.

The Classroom Block at Mongewell

in the future."[195] In this area, Michael Bharier writes "I also remember nashing *(sic)* cheese and pasta that Shif had lifted from the kitchen while listening to some of his 20th century music collection."[196]

A school is not only for sleeping and playing sports. Some pupils would like this provided they were adequately fed! However, one needs a place to eat and to learn. During the 1950s all this took place in Second World War huts which had been put up by the RAF whilst they occupied the site. They were built with concrete frames and asbestos cement roofs and wall panels. Henry Law comments on their components, "This material was safe as long as it was left alone. These days the buildings would be condemned, demolished by approved specialists, and the rubble sent for secure disposal. Such buildings were widespread throughout Britain in the 1940s and 1950s. I would be surprised if any of us have had our lives shortened by the experience."[197]

A long hut near the western side of the main building served as the classrooms. The various laboratories were housed in two other huts.[198]

---

195. Ibid.
196. Recollections – Michael Bharier, chap.3, The Environs of Carmel.
197. Recollections – Henry Law, Carmel College days, part 2, p.3.
198. Photographs of these classrooms and laboratories appear in the Carmel Prospectus, undated (about 1959).

Soon after coming to Mongewell, they were named the "Isaac Wolfson Laboratories" and a sign to this effect was erected. However, not long after, this sign came down. Presumably there was a reason for its removal![199]

The dining hall consisted of what seemed to be two huts which had at some period been joined together. At the southern end of this dining hall was the kitchen which was divided into two sections – one for milk and the other for meat. Two hatches joined these kitchens to the dining room. When Carmel came to Mongewell, the entrance to the dining room was in the course of being built and, within a few months, there was a vestibule with a long washing trough for netillat yadayim (washing of the hands) before the meal.[200]

This dining hall had a strange feature. One of the huts had four supporting beams on its ceiling and the other one had five. Soon after coming to Mongewell, Kopul came into the dining hall and said he would give some tuck to the first boy who could answer the following riddle. He explained that he had asked the reason for the different number of beams on the two huts, and had been given the answer, "Because of the echo." The riddle was, what does this answer mean? The solution was, that five in Hebrew is written as "hey" and four is written as "daled." This spells the Hebrew word "hed" which means "echo."[201]

After a few years, the roof of this dining hall developed leaks all over. (The poem by Alfred Lord Tennyson, "Break, break, break, On thy cold grey stones, O Sea!"[202] could easily have been adapted to this situation, "Drip, drip, drip, On my cold baked beans and tea!") Fortunately, within a very short period, the roof was retiled and this water from above ceased.[203]

There were also a few other huts scattered all over the grounds. One of them served as a study block for the upper forms who certainly slept there and, hopefully, also studied there.[204] Henry Law describes this building where he was for a period during his stay at Carmel, "[It was] L-shaped in plan, was divided into rooms for use by the fifth and six formers as individual or shared studies. The study block had the advantage of showers, and an individual room in the study block was much to be coveted, since it was by far the best accommodation in the school."[205]

---

199. 7 years, p.19.
200. Ibid.
201. Ibid., pp.19–20.
202. Alfred Lord Tennyson, *Break, Break, Break*.
203. 7 years, p.20.
204. Ibid.
205. Recollections – Henry Law, Carmel College days, part 2, p.4.

Since it was wartime when the RAF took over the estate, among the buildings they erected was a pillbox near the banks of the Thames, in order to help thwart a possible German invasion.[206] This pillbox was still there when Carmel purchased the estate. The author writes about this pillbox, "When I was in the junior part of the school, I, together with some friends discovered this pillbox. We decided that we would paint it and then maybe it would be our dormitory! One of the maintenance staff gave us some brown paint and together with a broom head (we had no paint brush), we began to paint it. However we soon got tired of this idea!"[207]

Michael Bharier writes on the area behind the Main Building. "Immediately behind the building were some formal gardens with a fish pond, into which we dumped a bunch of goldfish won at a fair in Wallingford, some of which thrived and grew to enormous size."[208] There was an island in the centre of this fish pond and as a "halfway house" there was a large clump of mud which would start to sink if one stood on it for more than about a second. If one was agile one could reach this island by long jumping via this clump of mud without getting one's feet wet![209]

As stated above, in January 1953, the Contract for Sale and Purchase was signed. However at an earlier date the property had been requisitioned by the Ministry of Health, and this requisitioning was still in force. Furthermore, planning permission would have to be obtained for the estate to be used as a school. Therefore, in order not to "buy a pig in a poke," or, as they say in Hebrew "chatul basak" (a cat in a bag), the purchase was made conditional on the derequisition and on planning permission being received.[210] Obviously these conditions were met and the sale went through.

When Carmel purchased the estate in 1953, the playing fields were in a poor state of health! In one area there was a sudden change in levels and this caused the accumulation of a large quantity of rain.[211] Enter the grounds man, Ray Harper, who describes his first day at Carmel:

> The beginning was a meadow, tufts of coarse grass, mole hills and a herd of cows grazing quietly, with a large brown bull casting a wary eye on intruders. I was the intruder!

---

206. Recollections – Jeremy Rosen, chap.1.
207. 7 years, p.20.
208. Recollections – Michael Bharier, chap.3, the environs of Carmel.
209. Unwritten recollections of author.
210. Mongewell Purchase, par.13, p.3.
211. 7 years, p.20.

I had arrived at Carmel College at the request of Rabbi Kopul Rosen to establish a sports field and to restore the estate to its pre-war condition. After two hours of inspection and an attempt to assess the possibilities of beginning work, I received a message from Rabbi Rosen to say that he would come to the sports field at lunchtime to help me drive the cows off to an adjacent field.

While I was waiting for Rabbi Rosen to appear I discovered, under sheets of rusting corrugated iron, a very old tractor, looking most neglected and sad, and under a nearby chestnut tree stood a 1936 ATCO mower, protected from the weather by a dustbin lid. This appeared to be the equipment that I was to use to restore an ailing estate, Despair began to creep in.

Rabbi Rosen arrived at 12.30 and walked out onto the field, elegantly dressed in dark grey suit and very shiny black shoes, in contrast to my corduroy slacks and wellington boots, and I am sure that we made a rather odd picture as we advanced towards the herd which by now was settling down, chewing the cud, looking for all the world like fat old ladies in a tea-shop.

There were a few moments of discussion while we planned our tactics and it was decided to drive the herd to a corner of the field where a gap had been made in the fence for them to pass through. We advanced steadily, the cows coming to their feet and beginning to move. The bull gave Rabbi Rosen a rather long stare and there was a moment's hesitation on the Rabbi's part before he once again moved forward, delicately picking his way between the cow pats until all the cows were through and the fence secured.

We walked back towards the school with a feeling of a job well done and then Rabbi Rosen turned to me and said, 'There you are, Mr. Harper, it's all yours for the next 50 years!'[212]

Why were all the cows allowed to graze on Carmel's fields? The local farmers had grazing rights and Kopul once explained to some pupils that these farmers had to be given a year's notice at Michaelmas (which occurs on 29 September) to terminate these rights.[213] Indeed after several years

---

212. Reflections – Ray Harper.
213. What is the connection between grazing rights and Michaelmas? One can trace this back to the Middle Ages. In order that there should be no overlap between the grazing of sheep and of cattle, the former had grazing rights from Michaelmas to Lady Day (25 March) and the latter up to Michaelmas. (see: Odiham Common – a report on common rights, historic use and encroachments on the Common by Mary Bennett, October 2009, Internet.)

of hard work by the groundsman, the fields were turned into admirable playing fields.[214]

Any building has to be properly maintained and regular repainting is a must, especially in a school. School maintenance must be done during the school holidays but it is not unusual for painters (or indeed any workers) to begin their work well after the agreed date. Carmel's painters were no exception. On returning to the school after one of the holidays, Kopul said to the assembled pupils, "If you tell a Jew that there are fairies, he will believe you. But if you tell him that the paint is wet, he will touch it to make sure." Indeed there was wet paint in the school.[215] This was not the only painting at Carmel, since in the summer of 1956 many of the outside buildings were painted in a variety of exotic colours[216] – maybe this was to frighten off the ghosts who were alleged to haunt the grounds!

As stated above, whilst searching in 1952 for a new site for Carmel College, Kopul together with Doc Friedman and Helmut Schmidt visited "The Springs," and they then had dreams of making it into a sixth form campus. "The Springs" is a Victorian Tudor-Style country house built in 1874 and it overlooks a spring filled lake.[217] It is situated in North Stoke, a village adjacent to Mongewell. Jeremy Rosen wrote that his "father wanted [The Springs] for a Junior [Preparatory] School but he just couldn't raise the cash."[218] A slightly different version is reported by the author, that "whilst we were having a lesson in his study, a person telephoned and Rabbi Rosen said that he couldn't talk too openly since there were people in his study. From what I could understand from this guarded conversation was that the school was interested in buying some property nearby. This seemed to tie up with what his son Mickey had once told me. Apparently, once he had had the option to buy a property near the school for the Prep School but he had turned it down. Later he was sorry about this and was prepared to pay even twice the original price, but the owner was no longer willing to sell. The bottom line was that the school never bought any property for the Prep School."[219] Instead of a Prep School, "The Springs" became a Hotel and a Golf Course – but unfortunately golf was not on the list of Carmel's sporting activities!

---

214. 7 years, p.20.
215. Ibid.
216. Carmel 1956, p.7.
217. The Springs Hotel & Golf Course, (Internet).
218. E-mail from Jeremy Rosen, 3 May 2012.
219. 7 years, p.75; when asked by the author regarding the accuracy of these facts, Jeremy Rosen replied "sounds right," (e-mail from Jeremy Rosen, 3 May 2012).

With all new buildings, there is usually a formal opening ceremony and the Mongewell estate was no exception. Since it was to be held in December, it could not be held in a marquee. Stephen Solomons and Ellis Korn describe the seating arrangement for this ceremony, "The ceremony was held in the Gymnasium and to the great surprise of everybody, except Rabbi Rosen, we managed to seat more than five hundred people in the hall. The boys were seated on a large stand, constructed of tubular steel, which was painted silver for the occasion. Had our visitors seen the unpainted premises a few hours before, they could not have considered such a transformation possible."[220] Before the ceremony, the parents and other guests had been sent invitations which read:

> The Governors, Principal, Staff and Boys invite you to the Opening of the new buildings of Carmel College by His Excellency The Israeli Ambassador Mr. Eliahu Elath and Mme. Elath on Sunday 6th December at 2.30 p.m. . Tea will be served at 4.30 p.m. Carmel College, Mongewell Park, Wallingford, Berks.[221]

At the ceremony the invitees received a programme headed "Carmel College, Opening of the New Premises, 6th December 1953" followed by six numbered items on the agenda of the ceremony.[222] Solomons and Korn describe the proceedings, "The school took up its position five minutes before the ceremony was due to commence, and when Rabbi Rosen led in the impressive procession of masters in their scholastic gowns and hoods, together with the various distinguished visitors, the boys rose from their places. We then greeted our guest of honour, His Excellency The Israeli Ambassador by singing 'The Hatikvah'."[223]

> Ceremonies such as these, customarily begin with a young pupil handing a bouquet of flowers to the wife of the Guest of Honour. However on this occasion there was a glitch! Rouven Dattner, then aged 9, had been delegated for this task and he writes, "I went down to give the flowers to the Ambassador's wife. I went down to the stage, but she was not there. I was told to sit down, so I sat down."[224]

---

220. The Young Carmelonian, p.9.
221. Printed invitation for the "Opening of the new buildings of Carmel College . . . on Sunday 6th December."
222. Duplicated programme for "Opening of New Premises, 6th December 1953."
223. The Young Carmelonian, p.10.
224. Alpha 1954, p.9.

The "Jewish Chronicle" had a long article on the ceremony together with a photograph, and its reporter wrote, "Rabbi Kopul Rosen, the Principal of the College, who presided, said that that day was for them one of deep emotional significance. He referred to the growth of the school from modest beginnings some five years ago at Greenham, Berks. They now had 200 pupils, about a fifth of whom came from overseas countries. This article continues:

> A number of the pupils, introduced by Michael Goitein, welcomed the Ambassador in their native languages. Mr. Elath was greeted first in Hebrew by Benjamin Schalit, of Haifa, then in Finnish, French, Dutch, Spanish, Swahili, 'American,' Flemish, Turkish, Papiamento (a language of the Dutch West Indies). Persian, Swedish, and Arabic. A welcome to the Ambassador, from North Africa, was extended in French.[225]

Solomons and Korn wrote that this was "probably the most stirring of all the great items on the agenda" and commented that "the gathering assumed the appearance of a United Nations Meeting."[226] The "Jewish Chronicle" article wrote:

> Mr. Elath, responding paid a tribute to Mr. Isaac Wolfson for his work for Israel. He went on to stress the importance of building links between Israel and the Diaspora, which would serve to strengthen their common heritage and deepen mutual understanding.
>
> Addressing the boys, the Ambassador said: 'We should be able to see at least some of you in Israel, not because you will be forced to go there but because you will desire to go.
>
> The Principal also added his tribute to Mr. Wolfson who, he said, had been the school's greatest single benefactor. As a token of their esteem for Mr. Wolfson's generosity they were naming and declaring open at the school that day the Isaac Wolfson Laboratories.[227]

---

225. Jewish Chronicle, 11 December 1953, p.12.
226. The Young Carmelonian, p.10.
227. Jewish Chronicle, 11 December 1953, p.12. This was the period when the previous governors all resigned en bloc withdrawing the money they had invested in the school and Isaac Wolfson stepped into the breach and replaced the £14,000 withdrawn by the former governors, (Memories of KR, p.25).

The Governors, Principal, Staff and Boys

invite you to

The Opening of the new buildings

of

Carmel College

by

His Excellency The Israeli Ambassador
Mr. Eliahu Elath and Mme. Elath

on Sunday, 6th December, at 2.30 p.m.

Tea will be served
at 4.30 p.m.

Carmel College,
Mongewell Park,
Wallingford, Berks.

CARMEL   COLLEGE

OPENING OF NEW PREMISES
6th December 1953

PROGRAMME

HATIKVAH

1) Greetings to His Excellency The
   Ambassador of Israel Mr.E.Elath
   and Madam Elath.

   Reply by His Excellency.

2) Opening of school and naming Isaac
   Wolfson laboratories.

   Reply.

3)   v   g of Chanukah lights.

4)   .tions and Declamations from the
      phets.

5) ...nks and Presentation from Pupils.

6) Presentation from Old Carmelis.

School Song
God save the Queen.

Invitation and Programme for Opening of
Mongewell Campus in 1953

"Mr. Wolfson replied in a powerful speech," write Solomons and Korn, "in which he stressed the value of a good name."[228]

It was Chanukah and the next item on the programme was the kindling of the Chanukah lights which was done by Rabbi Rosen.[229]

"Gary Borrow, the youngest remaining member of the original group of boys who were at Carmel College when it opened," write Solomons and Korn, "delivered a speech which was both witty and charming."[230]

This was followed, according to the programme by "Recitations and Declamations from the Prophets."[231] Solomons and Korn in their article give a detailed list: "Henry Schachter recited in a masterly manner from 'King Henry VII', John Fisher followed with a poem by Bialek (sic), and Michael Ostwind recited from the prophet Isaiah, Abraham Levy from Gibraltar gave a convincing performance from Amos, and, finally Avigdor Sperber recited from Jeremiah."[232]

In conclusion, the school presented the Ambassador with the School Crest and the Old Carmeli Association gave him an Old Boys' tie.[233] The ceremony concluded with the singing of the School Song and the National Anthem.[234] Rouven Dattner in his account of this ceremony concludes his report of the ceremony with "Then we went to tea. And that was the end."[235]

About three years later, in 1956, the area of the Mongewell campus was enlarged by 200 acres by the purchase of an estate in the village of Newnham Murren.[236] This village is of ancient origin and is mentioned in the Domesday Book.[237] It is located about a quarter of a mile from Carmel. The estate purchased by Carmel included a large multi-story building which served as the dormitories for a number of senior boys. On one side of this building was a barn or cowshed and on the other side a graveyard and ancient church. In front of the building was a path leading to Wallingford in one direction and in the opposite direction to Carmel. On the

---

228. The Young Carmelonian, p.10.
229. Duplicated programme for Opening of New Premises, op. cit.; The Young Carmelonian, p.10.
230. The Young Carmelonian, p.10.
231. Duplicated programme for Opening of New Premises, op. cit.
232. The Young Carmelonian, p.10.
233. Jewish Chronicle, 11 December 1953, p.12; The Young Carmelonian, p.10.
234. Duplicated programme for Opening of New Premises, op. cit.; The Young Carmelonian, p.10.
235. Alpha 1954, p.9.
236. Memories of KR. p.27.
237. Domesday Book, Open Domesday, Place: Newnham [Murren], (Internet).

other side of this path were two cottages for masters. In one of them lived the family of Yisrael Alexander, who was a teacher at Carmel.[238]

Periodically a "master plan" for buildings of the future were put on the school notice board for the pupils to see and thus realise that one day in the distant, or hopefully, in the not too distant future, they would have more luxurious facilities. In fact the architects seemed to change as the years went by and so did the details of the "master plan."[239]

The Carmel magazine of 1958 gives a diagram of "Future Plans for Carmel College" accompanied by an explanatory article written by the architects, which states that "some of the existing buildings will be re-tained."[240] One of the buildings which it had been planned to retain was the gymnasium. However, soon after, there was talk of a "weak wall" and later it was found to be in a state of collapse, and the whole building had to be demolished.[241]

The architects then went on to explain the many factors that must be considered when planning a new building. These include the topography of the site with its trees and roads, the geological features of the subsoil, local regulations, spacing between buildings, orientation to provide light and air, but concluded that the final deciding factor would be money to finance the building. It is not simple to be an architect for a large estate!

To construct any individual building, one has to go through all sorts of bureaucratic procedures with the local council. Here the local council were not keen to give the necessary permits. Kopul once told some pupils that there was one man on the council who worked hard to get the plans passed and without his help there would have been far more delays.[242]

Even with the necessary permits, one still needed a lot of money to build and "Kopul lost no opportunity in haranguing the Governors and cajoling them into efforts to provide the school with its essential needs. Two important landmarks in this direction were the Wolfson and Matilda Marks-Kennedy dormitory blocks for senior boys which were completed in 1958."[243] These dormitory blocks were of three and two stories high respectively.

They were designed by the well-known architectural firm of Yorke,

238. Telephone conversation between author and David Alexander, 30 July 2013; Carmel 1960, p.4.
239. 7 years, p.21.
240. Carmel 1958, pp.8–9.
241. Unwritten recollections of author.
242. 7 years, p.100.
243. Memories of KR, p.26.

Rosenberg and Mardell (YRM), who were committed Modernists. Amongst the best-known of their buildings is the first phase of Gatwick Airport. One of the architects, Eugene Rosenberg even visited the school one Friday evening.[244]

In order to construct these dormitory blocks, holes were first dug and filled with concrete, steel posts were then erected and joined with horizontal beams, and then this skeleton was filled in.[245] The construction of these buildings was such that the steel posts were outside the building. At one point, the architect came to the school to give a lecture on this building and the first question someone asked him was why these steel posts were outside. He answered "why not?!" He also said that it saved space. The brick walls inside were not plastered but painted with an oil paint. Unlike the baths in the main building which were "sit-up baths," the baths here were normal – one could now luxuriate in the bath, provided of course that no-one else was waiting for his turn! The large room on each floor was divided by partitions of about five feet into small rooms of four beds each. Each boy had his own wardrobe which formed part of these partitions.[246]

Although it might have seemed like paradise after years of sleeping in the crowded Main Building dormitories, Henry Law was very critical about the construction of these new dormitory blocks:

> I was back in the uncomfortable and inadequate new dormitory block. Fortunately, the two other senior boys with me were good company and we joked about the shortcomings of the building. All the way round each dormitory there were large, single glazed windows. Heating was by electric panels on the ceilings. The heating was inadequate, and the loss of heat through the large windows made the buildings icy cold on the clear winter nights. The centre-pivoted windows were liable to stick and then the glass cracked from corner to corner if one tried to open them. It was necessary to be careful when opening the windows if this was to be avoided.
>
> Toilets, washbasins and showers were in an area at the end of each floor, adjacent to the staircase. The toilet cubicles were hilarious. The partitions were clad in mirror finish aluminium which created an infinite regression of reflections. When seated inside, one had the

---

244. Recollections – Henry Law, Carmel College days, part 2, p.4.
245. Ibid.
246. 7 years, p.101.

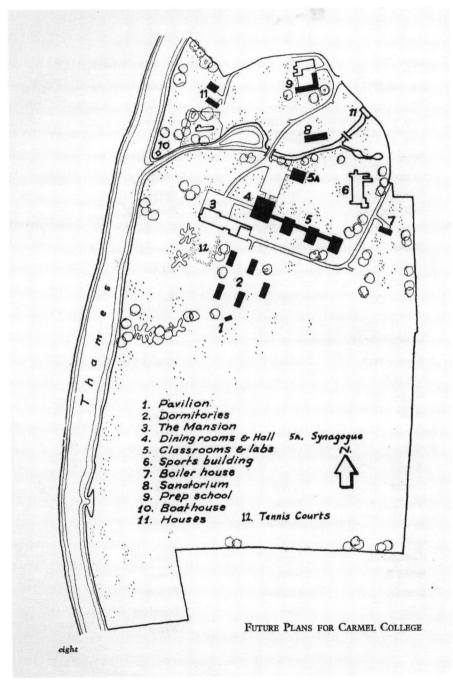

1. Pavilion
2. Dormitories
3. The Mansion
4. Dining rooms & Hall   5A. Synagogue
5. Classrooms & labs
6. Sports building
7. Boiler house
8. Sanatorium
9. Prep school
10. Boathouse
11. Houses   12. Tennis Courts

FUTURE PLANS FOR CARMEL COLLEGE

Building Plans for Carmel College as They Appeared in Carmel
Summer Magazine for 1958

impression of sitting in a hall of bogs. The staircase was noisy. At least the showers worked well and the water was hot, which was some compensation.

It seems strange that such a reputable architectural firm should have got things so wrong, both the big ones and the little ones. There would, for instance, have been no difficulty in providing a few individual study-bedrooms in the building, and this alteration was soon made. And the science of heating buildings was hardly cutting edge.[247]

Possibly this was the reason that in 1959, the Governors decided to change the architects and appointed the firm Erdi & Rabson to "plan the overall future development of the site and the design of individual buildings." Amongst the buildings for which this firm was "responsible for the design and construction" was the sanatorium, the junior [Preparatory] school, the boiler house and both the Rosen and Stamler family residences. They also produced a scale model of the estate.[248]

The Wolfson dormitory block was officially opened by the donors Isaac Wolfson and his wife Edith on Sunday 23 November 1958.[249] Kopul opened the ceremony and then two senior boys spoke. Isaac Wolfson replied, and this was then followed by the opening of the Dormitory and a tour of the school. One must not forget that after all this, tea was served in the Dining Hall.[250] On the day of this opening ceremony, the boys were told to put all their dirty laundry etc. in the store-room downstairs, which would then be locked. Talk of not washing your dirty linen in public![251] It was reported that the donors of the other dormitory block did not want such a ceremony.[252]

In the following year, six hard tennis courts were laid. They replaced the old decrepit tennis courts near the gymnasium and they helped to supply the ever increasing demand for facilities for one of the school's most popular sports.[253]

In 1960, a sanatorium which had been donated by the Wix family was

---

247. Recollections – Henry Law, Carmel College days, part 2, p.29.
248. E-mail from Ronald Rabson to David Shaw, 1 August 2012.
249. The Carmel magazine 1959 p.5, reports that this ceremony took place in February 1959, but this does not accord with the date on the programme.
250. Duplicated Programme on the "Occasion of the Opening of the Wolfson Dormitory on Sunday, 23rd November 1958."
251. 7 years, p.101.
252. Ibid.
253. Carmel 1959, p.5.

built. It was one story high, and it included beds for ill boys, a dispensary, and living quarters for a matron. The opening ceremony was held in the Main Hall of the school in June 1960. In his speech to the assembly, Kopul said:

> When you try to arrange funds for any scheme, almost as important as the amount of money that is given to you is the manner in which it is given. . . . I can truthfully say that never in my experience has a magnificent contribution been given so readily, so generously and with such good spirit as that which has been given by Mr. Wix when I approached him and put before him a scheme for a sanatorium for Carmel College. . . . But this small sanatorium may in your eyes appear to be rather modest, quite humble, when you compare it with the Wix Auditorium in [the Weizmann Institute in] Rehovot, but you know I think that in the course of years the number of human beings who will feel grateful to you for having provided that sanatorium might not be less than the number who will sit in that magnificent building that bears your name in Rehovot. Warmly and sincerely I want to express our deep sense of gratitude to you and ask one of the boys to convey his thanks upon you.[254]

In the course of his speech, this boy said that it would now be a pleasure to be ill![255]

Sometimes a "faux-pas" can lead to wonderful positive results. Such an occurrence occurred at the opening of this sanatorium. David Robbins who was the central figure in this "faux-pas" describes what happened:

> At one point, a new sanatorium was to be formally opened, and Kopul asked me to make a speech thanking the visiting donors and the school matron, Nurse Watson. I had decided to speak without notes, and a few minutes before I was due to begin, I agreed with the Head Boy, Raymond Dwek, that at a pre-arranged point I would stop speaking, and he would start a round of applause. At what I thought was the agreed moment, I stopped speaking, but there was no applause, only complete silence, and the rest of the speech went out of my head. I pretended to be overcome with emotion at the debt which I owed to

---

254. From the recorded speech of Kopul Rosen at the opening ceremony of the Wix Sanatorium.
255. 7 years, p.130.

Opening of the Wix Sanatorium at Carmel College

Matron for her care of me while I was convalescing after an operation to remove an ingrowing toenail. This gave me time to recover my memory and finish the speech. As soon as the proceedings were finished, one of the boys came up to me and said, 'You seemed overcome by emotion, but you can't fool me – you had simply forgotten what you were supposed to say.' Thinking that my cover had been blown, I went later that day to see Kopul in his study in order to apologise. You may remember that in the study was a large Jacobean carved oak chair, and if you sat on it after a catch had been moved, a couple of one-inch thick iron bars would drop down from inside carved side-pieces and pin your thighs to the seat. Well, I apologised to Kopul for my lapse of memory, and he replied 'You have nothing to apologise for. On the contrary. You know that my usual method with prospective donors to Carmel is to imprison them in that chair and then to demand a substantial release fee. But today such a strategy was unnecessary, as many of our guests came to tell me that I had been irresponsible in giving the task of making a speech to such a sensitive boy. You opened their hearts, and they opened their chequebooks'.[256]

After the opening ceremony for the sanatorium, the boys lined the sides of the road from the main building to the sanatorium. The donor, the headmaster and other guests then walked to the sanatorium and as they passed the boys clapped. Two high bushes in flowerpots lined either side of the main entrance to the sanatorium but they did not remain there afterwards.[257]

The year 1960 also saw the start of the building of a Preparatory School Dormitory block, which was financed by the Development Fund. According to David Stamler, the Development Fund originally wanted to erect two dormitory blocks for the Prep School but he persuaded them to erect just one (this must be the first time in history that a recipient persuaded a donor to give less!) arguing that some of the children enrolling in the Prep School were still babies and he thus did not want an increase in numbers of these tender age pupils.[258]

In 1961 the building of the classroom block began. It was completed only after Kopul Rosen had died. A boy reported that when Kopul was already very ill, he saw him walking with a stick to see the progress of the building.[259] It was in the following years that many other buildings were erected on the Carmel estate.

---

256. Recollections – David Robbins. Whether or not Robbins was the pupil who also said that it would be a pleasure to be ill, or it was another pupil, is not recorded.
257. 7 years, p.130.
258. This was heard by the author directly from David Stamler.
259. This was related directly to author by a pupil of the school.

Chapter 3

Guinea Pigs and Their Successors

After visiting a famous British school with magnificent buildings, Kopul remarked that they have the buildings but Carmel has the boys. . . .

ONE TO EIGHT HUNDRED

During the period that Kopul was the Principal of Carmel College, namely, September 1948 to March 1962, about 800 pupils began their studies there.[1] The first intake in September 1948, were the "guinea pigs"; those who came after were their "successors"! Every pupil was allocated a consecutive school number, with the exception of a number 13, since the housemaster was superstitious!

The honour to be pupil number 1 goes to Charles Gale.[2] Another early number is 32, which went to Malcolm Shifrin ("Shif,")[3] who later became the librarian at Carmel. David Shaw clearly remembers his number, 86, since today he signs his Carmel correspondence as "D86."[4] Neil Acton calls himself "Convict number 344"[5] – surely Carmel was not a peniten-tiary but a school, or maybe all the Old Carmelis are today out on parole! The author was 278 and began at Carmel on 5 October 1953, which was the 278th day of that year. His brother Nigel who enrolled eight years

---

1. An almost complete list of (at least) these first 800 pupils was compiled by unknown authors. However, towards the beginning of this list, there are a number of gaps. Since this list was amongst some archival material, which for a period, were stored in Luton, it is popularly known as the "Luton List."
2. Luton List, op. cit.
3. Ibid.
4. E-mails from David Shaw.
5. E-mail from Neil Alton, 4 July 2012.

later was given an anagram of this number, namely 782.[6] However, a study of the alphabetical manner in which the school numbers were given, shows that receiving number 782 was not by design but by chance.[7]

These school numbers, in practice had only minimal use. They appeared on the bills sent to parents for school fees – the "Ref" at the top of the bill was the pupil's name followed by his school number.[8] The clothes lists stated that "Leather Boots and Shoes [are] to be marked with the School number in brass nails on the sole under the instep."[9] These numbers were also utilised in borrowing books from the library and the pupils were instructed "You are expected to know your school number when you come to borrow a book for your tickets are filed numerically when not in use."[10] Michael Goitein, Graham Cohen (and possibly others) certainly never forgot their school numbers; they appeared after their names on their Cash's name tapes which were sewn on all their garments.[11]

AT WHAT AGE WILL CARMEL TAKE ME?

The Provisional Prospectus issued about April 1948, gave the age range for the acceptance of the first pupils, "Candidates for admission in the first school year which commences on 16th September 1948 must be between the ages of 11 and 14½ on that date."[12]

When, in 1949, the Rosen family moved from London to Carmel, their son Jeremy was aged 7, which was well above the legal age for compulsory schooling but too young for Carmel, which created a problem for his family. On this Jeremy Rosen writes:

> There was a brief effort at establishing a small preparatory class for me and some other young children of teachers. Gitta Kohn [Gita Cohen] was in charge of this small preparatory class. But it floundered and for a year I was sent up the road to a small Church of England Village school. That was where I learnt Christmas carols and also got into trouble for making disparaging remarks about Jesus. I must have

6. Luton List, op. cit.
7. Ibid.
8. Carmel College fees bill sent to parents of (name of pupil), August 1957.
9. Carmel College Clothes List issued in 1950s.
10. Carmel College Library, A Brief Guide, second edition, 1962, p.19.
11. Recollections – Michael Goitein; Reflections – Graham Cohen.
12. Carmel College Provisional Prospectus, undated, (about April 1948), section: Admission.

History, Nature and Scope

Carmel College was opened in 1948 at Newbury, Berkshire. The aim of its founder, the present Principal, was to bring into being a boarding school which would provide a general education on a level with that offered by the best Public Schools, together with a comprehensive Jewish training. As a result of its first Inspection in 1950 the School was provisionally recognised as efficent by the Ministry of Education.

In the summer of 1953 the School moved to Mongewell Park, near Wallingford. The Preparatory School, which had formerly occupied a separate building at some distance from the Senior School in Newbury, was accommodated in the same estate and it now shares some of the buildings with the Senior School, but this is regarded only as a temporary arrangement.

The present number of boys in the School is 176, of whom 57 are in the Preparatory School; all are boarders and all are of the Jewish Faith. The majority come from various parts of the British Isles, but 27 of them come from 14 different countries overseas, most of them knowing no English on arrival; and this diversity constitutes a serious problem to which a satisfactory solution has not yet been found. The boys' ages in the Preparatory School range from 7 to 11 years and in the Senior School from 11 to 18 years.

Boys may enter the School at any age up to 14 years after passing a test in English, Arithmetic, and General Intelligence. Some of them come from Preparatory schools where French, Latin, Algebra and Geometry are taught; others come from primary schools where these subjects are not included in the curriculum. This divergence in attainment raises further difficulties which have yet to be surmounted.

Of the 31 boys who left the School in 1954, 22% left at the age of 15+, 23% at 16+ and 55% at 17 or over. Of the 70 leavers in the last two years, 18 have passed on to universities, 11 have gone to other establishments for further education, 21 have entered their parents' businesses and 10 who came from abroad have returned to their homes. About the remaining 10 there is no precise information.

Governing Body

The constitution of the Governing Body is stated in the Memorandum and Articles of Association. There are at present sixteen Governors, but a resolution has been passed raising the number to twenty-five. The Governors meet once a month, and the Principal attends all meetings by right.

Finance

Carmel College is owned by a non-profit-making company known as "Carmel College, Limited". The company has raised its capital by loans; it has no shares and is not subject to income tax. Articles of Association prevent members of the company from receiving financial benefit from the School.

Page from H. M. Inspectors Report on Carmel College from 1955

been responding to jibes about being Jewish but I still wonder how I came to be involved in theological disputes at that early age.[13]

However, by the summer of 1950, the admission age had gone down to 7. David Shaw who began at Carmel that term writes that "at the age of 7 . . . I was packed off [to Carmel]."[14] In a similar vein Julius Nehorai writes, "I was at Carmel about 1951–1958 having joined at Crookham as a snotty nosed 7 year old."[15]

One would expect (and indeed it was so), children of that age to be homesick. On this David Shaw writes, "We were very young and sleeping was difficult because sobbing went on into the night. We were only seven and communication with parents. . . . Well it just did not happen. I remember one really terrifying night when an owl hooted from the window sill."[16] To help pacify the children, one of the Prep School teachers, "Mrs. Glover, used to go round the dorm to kiss us all good night like a surrogate mother."[17] Another surrogate mother "to so many youngsters sent away from home and missing a female touch" was Bella Rosen, Kopul's wife.[18]

Indeed, even older pupils would feel homesick. On this question the author writes:

> On my first morning at Carmel, Rabbi Rosen called all the new boys into his study. He told us that we are going to be homesick at first. He related that the first time he went away from home he was fourteen years old and he cried himself to sleep that night. I was homesick for the first week or so and not only in my first term. For a number of terms when I returned after the vacation, I was homesick at the beginning of the term.[19]

A booklet brought out by Carmel refers to this subject:

> Naturally enough most new boys feel homesick when they come to Carmel. In some schools a new boy seen crying would be ragged cru-

---

13. Recollections – Jeremy Rosen.
14. Recollections – David Shaw.
15. Recollections – Julius Nehorai.
16. Recollections – David Shaw.
17. Ibid. It could not have been Mrs. Glover, since she was not yet a teacher at Carmel; it must have been some other female teacher.
18. Recollections – Jeremy Rosen, p.5.
19. 7 years, p.23.

elly and he would be expected to stand up for himself. We have no faith in that process of toughening. It is quite a common sight at the commencement of a school year to see a senior boy comforting a new boy and assuring him that all have gone through the same emotional process and that he will settle down as the others have done.[20]

However, although almost every pupil mastered the homesickness problem, there were a few who obviously found it too difficult and rather than sweating it out, left permanently after just a few days at the school.[21] In contrast, Graham Cohen wrote home very dramatically about his homesickness, but he sweated it out:

> I hated every minute of it – if it had been possible to cry more I certainly would have done so. I missed home 24 hours each day, and there really didn't seem to be any light at the end of the long dark tunnel. I phoned home (reverse charges) and threatened to run away (no response) to fast (no response), and eventually suicide (no response). I then realised that, like it or not, I was here to stay![22]

In the homesickness of Henry Law, the railway "wizard," there was originality, "I missed my mother. I missed my father. I missed Flip [his dog]. And I missed the constant procession of passing trains at Gospel Oak."[23]

When Kopul Rosen opened the school in 1948, in addition to having to find suitable buildings, considerable finance, and teaching staff of a suitable calibre, he needed pupils. What is the good of buildings, finance, and teachers without pupils?! As Cyril Domb wrote, "And not the least of his [Kopul's] problems was to persuade Jewish parents to allow their children to serve as 'guinea pigs'."[24] From where did these "guinea pigs" come? David Stamler writes:

> The small group of first pupils was a fascinating one. One or two had come because of the closing down of the Jewish House at Perse School,[25] others because their parents felt that in a small group they could make better progress, others because they could not gain entry

---

20. Carmel College 1948–1957, booklet, section: Discipline.
21. E-mail from Michael Bharier, 5 June 2012.
22. Reflections – Graham Cohen. The words in brackets are in the original.
23. Recollections – Henry Law, Carmel College days, part 1, p.3.
24. Memories of KR, p.23.
25. For 44 years, there was a Jewish House called Hillel House at Perse School in Cambridge.

elsewhere, others because their parents wholeheartedly supported the concept of a Jewish School, one or two were simply problem children, and ability ranged from the very able to the backward. However, the smallness of the community, the informal, friendly atmosphere which existed and the enthusiasm which was felt served to weld all together.[26]

Although Kopul needed pupils, when he opened the school it might have seemed that he did not want too many for the first term, since an advertisement in the "Jewish Chronicle" from June 1948 read, "The number of pupils accepted for the first term is strictly limited in order to facilitate the moulding of the school's character and the attainment of a high educational level. Only a few vacancies remain."[27] However, one cannot discount this being a sales gimmick. When people hear that "Only a few vacancies remain," they rush to apply!

The school opened with twenty-two pupils.[28] One might well ask if there were only twenty-two pupils, how it was possible that Gary Borrow and Weinglass, whose school numbers were 33 and 34 respectively, could be amongst this opening number. To this, Gary Borrow answers, "some of the pupils started the following term and some never turned up."[29]

One of these twenty-two boys was David Perl and he described these pupils as "a frightened and straggly looking bunch of lads . . . coming from all parts of the country and from varied backgrounds."[30] Eight of them were still there when the school was about to move to Mongewell in the summer of 1953. However, by that time the numbers at the school had considerably increased, "There were 170 pupils attending Carmel College, and a formidable waiting-list demanded larger accommodation."[31]

At the beginning of 1955, there were a total of 176 pupils, fifty-seven of whom were in the Prep School. The majority of them came from different parts of the British Isles, but there were twenty-seven who came from fourteen different countries overseas, most of them knowing no English

---

In the summer of 1948 this House closed, (Jewish Chronicle, 11 June 1948, p.10 and, 18 June 1948, p.14).

26. Memories of KR, p.103.

27. Jewish Chronicle, 4 June 1948, p.4.

28. Recollections – Jeremy Rosen, chap.1; e-mail from Gary Borrow, 1 July 2013.

29. E-mail from Gary Borrow, 1 July 2013.

30. The Old Carmeli, no.5, 1968–9, p.27; Reflections – David Perl. Perl thinks that the number of pupils was 25 or 27 or even 31. Malcolm Shifrin also quotes the number 31, (Recollections – Malcolm Shifrin). The Gabbai's list of Hebrew names when the school opened in 1948 indicates that there were about 27 pupils.

31. Badad, p.18.

on arrival. The boys' ages in the Prep School ranged from 7 to 11 years and those in the Senior School from 11 to 18 years.[32] By the time the school moved to Mongewell, the school was already "multilingual" and numerous boys were able to greet the Israeli Ambassador, who was the Guest of Honour at the Opening ceremony for the New Buildings, in their own native languages.[33]

Having pupils who came to Carmel from countries where the language was not English, naturally initially caused them difficulties. This can be illustrated by an experience which Moshe Benaim, whose mother tongue was French, had, "I sat through a whole performance of the film Hamlet which was shown in the main Hall of the school that term, not following a word of what Sir Lawrence Olivier or the other actors were saying. When my father later asked me what the film had been about I said that I thought it was about life in a small village! [i.e. a hamlet]."[34] Incidentally, Moshe's acceptance to Carmel was discussed in a pre-arranged meeting between Kopul and Moshe's father "on a train somewhere in England."![35]

Although many pupils from Britain came from cities with established Jewish communities, there were also those from areas with no Jewish communities and to such locations Kopul gave special priority. This point he referred in an "Appraisal of Carmel College" which he wrote in about 1961:

> Clearly if a boy lives in Golders Green or Manchester and he does not measure up to the standard for entry to Carmel we have no hesitation in refusing to accept him, but when boys from Winchester, Ponte-fract, Norwich, the Isle of Man, Jersey, Peterborough, Aberdeen, Kettering, Boston (Lincs), Stoke, for example, apply for admission and their parents plead that we must find a place for their sons who are growing up estranged from all Jewish life, we feel under a moral obligation to take the boy into the school, even if we have to become less exacting in our academic standards.[36]

There were a number of pupils who came from Israel, but they were almost entirely non-observant Jewishly, although they at least passively

---

32. Inspectors' Report, p.2.
33. The Young Carmelonian, p.10.
34. Recollections – Moshe Benaim.
35. Ibid.
36. Kopul Rosen, An Appraisal of Carmel College, 1961.

accepted the school's religious requirements. When considering the matter, it is not really surprising that this was the type of Israeli pupil to come to Carmel. It would generally be non-observant Israeli parents who would want their children to have a British Public School education.

In contrast, there were a number of pupils from Gibraltar, all of whom were Orthodox. One of them Solomon (Momy) Levy was at a later date the First Civil Mayor of Gibraltar.[37] His brother Abraham later became Head of the Spanish and Portuguese Congregation in England.

WHY SPECIFICALLY CARMEL?

For what reason did parents send their sons to Carmel and not elsewhere? One of the early pupils at Carmel was Michael Goitein and he writes:

> My parents sent me to boarding school shortly before my tenth birthday. This was a predictable consequence of their earlier decision to live in the countryside; there simply was not much in the way of excellent schooling available within daily commuting distance . . . But, in any event, in those days it was quite normal for English families of a certain class to send their children away to a boarding school. The job of child-rearing was left to teachers and, far more dangerously, to other children.
>
> From his diaries I learned that my father's first choice had, in fact, been a boy's school in not-too-distant Cheltenham – at which I could possibly have been a day student:
>
> 13 November1945: The Junior school at Cheltenham [probably, Cheltenham College] will not take Michael [Goitein] – they have no prejudice against Jews, but the position might arise when they would not have any vacancies for CofE [Church of England] as it is a CofE foundation! . . . Is a bit of a nuisance, but I suppose allowance must be made for the confusion of the times.
>
> So, Cheltenham was not an option and my parents decided, then, to send me to Carmel College.[38]

In some cases, a younger brother wanted to go to Carmel because his older brother was there. Julius Nehorai writes:

---

37. Postcard "Gibraltar – an example to the World" – showing Solomon Levy with his mayoral robes.
38. Recollections – Michael Goitein.

I pleaded with my parents to send me to Carmel because my older brother Anthony was there which made it seem the most exciting of places. Having joined, perhaps too young, I pleaded with them to let me come home and go to a day school in London which resulted in my leaving at the too young age of 14. Nevertheless I benefited enormously from my time at the school and am sure that most of the worthwhile education I received was gained there.[39]

Likewise the author's younger brother Nigel from the tender age of 3 wanted to go to Carmel.[40]

Some of the children of staff members were pupils there. These included Kopul's three sons Jeremy, Michael and David, Morris Ellman's son Michael, who left when his father left the staff, but returned at a later date, and Yisrael Alexander's son David,[41] and there was also his daughter Leah, who was the first girl pupil at Carmel.[42]

Sometimes, when Kopul knew a parent, he would persuade him to send his son to Carmel. This was the case of Julian Lew. Julian writes:

Rabbi Rosen zt"l was a yeshiva friend of my late father (Rabbi Maurice Lew zt"l). KR spent a Shabbat at our home in South Africa and persuaded my parents to send me to Carmel in the aftermath of the Soweto riots in 1960. From the day I arrived at the school his towering presence and personality was the driving force and a constant inspiration, and his warmth when he saw me made a small help to missing parents, home and the weather in South Africa.[43]

There was a similar situation with Ian Rabinowitz, (and at a later date, his brothers Lionel and Benjamin). Kopul had been a "protégé" of Ian's uncle Rabbi Louis Rabinowitz and had known Ian's father, Rabbi Eliezer Simcha Rabinowitz, in both London and Mir. Ian writes that "in the summer of 1954, Kopul came to Hull to address the local JPA [Joint Palestine Appeal]. When I came home that evening, my father asked me whether I would like to go to Carmel College. Despite never having heard of Carmel, and having no knowledge of its location, I replied that I would."[44]

---

39. Recollections – Julius Nehorai.
40. Unwritten recollections of author.
41. Luton List, op. cit.
42. Carmel 1960, p.4.
43. Recollections – Julian Lew.
44. Recollections – Ian Rabinowitz.

Kopul's remarkable oratory could also attract pupils, as was in the case of Michael Bharier, who writes:

> My grandfather, Benjamin Anderson, a lifelong Yiddishist, socialist and religious skeptic, heard Kopul Rosen speak before his [Benjamin Anderson's] untimely death in 1951. He was tremendously impressed with Kopul's erudition, breadth of knowledge and oratory, and it was his wish and dream that I would go to Carmel. This happened three years later in 1954, when I became pupil No. 331![45]

The parents of Spencer and Anthony Batiste, who were then aged just 8 and 6 respectively, were attracted by Kopul's plans for a Jewish Eton. Spencer wrote that "they believed it [going to Carmel] would be in our best interests. They were immensely impressed by Kopul Rosen's extraordinary personality and his concept of creating an Eton for Anglo-Jewry, where growing up in a Jewish environment and learning about one's roots and heritage went hand in hand with the very best of secular education." Spencer later became Conservative M.P. for Elmet in Yorkshire between the years 1983 to 1997. Anthony died peacefully in his sleep at the sanatorium at Carmel College in October 1962 from a rare virus that had attacked his heart.[46]

Sometimes, family reasons such as illness could result in a boy being sent to Carmel. A case in point was Joe Miller who writes:

> I was nine years old when my mother told me that I was going to change schools. But, this time instead of it being a day school where I came home every afternoon, I was going to a boarding school. Immediately, I started to think about Tom Brown's Schooldays[47] and began to panic, as I had never before left home. The decision had been made due to the fact that my father had suffered a nervous breakdown a couple of years earlier. I did not understand his illness, but for all the right reasons I was about to be protected from the sadness at home.[48]

---

45. Recollections – Michael Bharier.
46. Recollections – Spencer Batiste.
47. *Tom Brown's Schooldays* is a novel by Thomas Hughes on life in Rugby School in the 1830s. There, there were public floggings, bullying and fagging.
48. Recollections – Joe Miller.

Parental illness causing a boy to join Carmel was also the case of David Shaw, who writes, "My father firmly believed in the idea of Carmel and had many a meeting with Kopul about Carmel and much else. My mother became ill, so at the age of 7 so I was packed off."[49] David also writes of the preview he had of Carmel, "I was sent to join a game of football whilst my father and Kopul talked. I did not get near the ball."[50] Another case of family reasons for a boy to go to Carmel was with Jeffrey Gandz, who writes:

> My father died in August 1952, soon after my eighth birthday leaving my mother with two children, my severely handicapped sister and myself, and a newly established retail business to run. Carmel was the answer, and with the financial help of my father's brothers, I found myself in Carmel's Crookham campus in the autumn of 1952. . . . The choice of Carmel was not random. Kopul Rosen had officiated at my parent's wedding . . . in Manchester and my mother had been very impressed with him then. He had also been very responsive to her situation when she called to ask about an immediate enrollment after my father died.[51]

In the case of Henry Law, the breakup of a marriage was the reason, "My mother wanted to secure a Jewish education and was aware that the marriage was on the verge of breaking up."[52]

At least two pupils studied in Aryeh House in Brighton before coming to Carmel. One of them, Neil Alton, found Aryeh House traumatic and was more than delighted at the time to transfer to Carmel. On this Neil writes:

> Like the Jewish joke, I came from somewhere worse. The infamous Aryeh House School (aka Jewish borstal) in Hove. After a Jewish summer camp at the even more infamous Whittingham College in Brighton. I must have upset someone as a kid. Aryeh was up the road from where we'd just moved to, from London. So up the road I duly went, mercifully only as a day boy. I found myself in schoolboy hell. If it were a prison today, they'd close it for excessive abuse. A recent

---

49. Recollections – David Shaw.
50. Ibid.
51. Recollections – Jeffrey Gandz.
52. Recollections – Henry Law, Back to School, p.21.

reunion attended with Jonathan Isserlin, my AHS [Aryeh House School], Carmel and lifetime soul mate, and his dear wife, involved Old Boys cheerfully outdoing each other with their traumas. Being shipped off to open countryside with a gentle name, 'Mongewell Park' as a boarder, while still alive, sounded Heaven. Little did I know.[53]

The other alumnus from Aryeh House was Jonathan Isserlin who, unlike Neil, was a boarder at Aryeh House. He was there from the age of 8, but did not have traumas from it. He writes, "Unlike Neil, and perhaps the majority of the former pupils of Aryeh House, I did not find that it was like Borstal or a prison camp. . . . I am one of the few who really did not feel as if I was in prison. As a result, when I was moved to Carmel in Mongewell Park in 1957, I was already quite an old hand at the boarding school scene, and didn't feel out of my depth at all."[54]

NOT EVERYBODY COULD COME TO CARMEL!

In order to attract pupils to the planned Carmel College, in April 1948 an announcement appeared in the "Jewish Chronicle" which stated, "This school, long-awaited in Anglo-Jewry, will provide a secular education on a par with the best public schools in Great Britain, together with a comprehensive traditional Jewish training." However, from the outset Kopul did not want to accept a boy to the school before seeing his previous school record and interviewing him, and thus the announcement continued, "Admission by examination and personal interview only."[55] The Provisional Prospectus states regarding the first potential pupils:

> The completed form of application should be returned to the Principal not later the 15th May, 1948, together with the original (or a copy) of the boy's most recent school report. An interview will subsequently be arranged during the course of which the candidate will have a short oral examination.[56]

Joe Dwek reports on one of the first interviews that Kopul conducted for a potential pupil. "I attended an interview with Kopul Rosen in 1948

---

53. Recollections – Neil Alton.
54. Recollections – Jonathan Isserlin.
55. Jewish Chronicle, 30 April 1948, p.4.
56. Carmel College Provisional Prospectus, undated, (about April 1948), section: Admission.

when the School was being launched," wrote Joe, "The interview revealed my appalling ignorance on most matters, but I passed the interview and joined the School in September 1949."[57] Another Joe, this time with the surname Miller, also writes about the interview he had with Kopul:

> It was mid December 1954 and the day had arrived when my interview to gain entrance to the boarding school was to take place. I was surprised when my mother told me that a Rabbi was coming to our home for the interview and that my father had known him in Glasgow. . . . The door bell rang and like it was yesterday I remember my mother going to answer the door to our flat that was located above Baker Street Station in Baker Street. I was hiding behind the lounge door, but peering out to view the visitor about to enter. I saw a tall slim man with a full beard, wearing a long coat and dark hat. As he entered the flat his first words were 'what a beautiful aroma' to which my mother responded how nice of you, it's the coffee. Suddenly, my mother realised that we had Christmas decorations up in the hall and trying to make an excuse informed the Rabbi the decorations were for the staff!! The Rabbi smiled and told her that they looked very nice. They both entered the lounge where my father and I were waiting for them. Some talking took place between my parents and the Rabbi. After a while he informed them that he would like to conduct the interview and could they kindly leave the room. As I write these memories it seems as if it was yesterday, being so clear. The Rabbi quickly put me at ease, as he could see that I was very nervous. He told me that he was going to ask me three questions which followed: Captain Cook sailed around the world three times, on which occasion did he die?! Did I like classical music? Did I like football? He then asked me to get my parents back into the room. Without delay he told them I had passed the exam with flying colours, could start the following September and the school uniform could be bought at Harrods. My memory indicates I was both pleased, but worried about leaving my home and family.[58]

For Neil Alton, the interview was not so pleasant. He writes, "My interview aged 8 with Kopul comprised an enormous terrifying man boom-

---

57. Recollections – Joe Dwek.
58. Recollections – Joe Miller.

ing mental arithmetic and general knowledge questions at me from the depths of his beard, in his darkened study. It was something like out of The Rocky Horror Show, though definitely not camp. I hadn't a clue, and got accepted on the spot."[59] Another boy it would seem did not find the interview pleasant, since he described it as a "grilling." He was Michael Bharier, who writes:

> Sometime early in 1954, at the age of 11, I was brought to Carmel College for an interview. I had no idea what to expect but it was made clear that I was very lucky to be considered for this school. I was brought to Kopul's study by a pleasant man with a slight German accent, the teacher Helmut Schmidt. He told me that there would be a lot of people there who would ask a lot of questions but that the questions would not be difficult. (How did he know that?) I don't remember who all those people were but I have a clear recollection of my first view of Kopul sitting behind a large desk in his beautiful wood-panelled study. I remember that the light reflected off his glasses so that I could not see his eyes. I found this slightly intimidating. I was indeed grilled by those present by a barrage of questions. Later we met his wife Bella, who was very warm, as I always found her to be later. She was distantly related to us by marriage.[60]

Harold Berwin who joined the school in 1959 writes on his interview, "My first memory of Carmel was my initial interview by Kopul who asked me about the situation in Tibet. I had read that the Dalai Lama had left his homeland and commented on the position of the Panchen Lama – apparently my knowledge of the religious hierarchy of Tibet passed muster."[61]

Henry Law, who was and is a "wizard" on British transport and can tell anyone which train he travelled on sixty years ago, what its vintage was and what the seats were made of, was excited to be interviewed at Carmel. The reason was not because of the actual interview, which he regarded as "incidental to the whole day out," but because "the prospect of a Sunday morning trip to a place on the Great Western main line was too good to miss." Henry was accepted as a pupil.[62]

Potential pupils who wanted to receive a scholarship, namely reduced

59. Recollections – Neil Alton.
60. Recollections – Michael Bharier, chap.2, Life at Carmel.
61. Recollections – Harold Berwin.
62. Recollections – Henry Law, Back to School, p.21.

CARMEL COLLEGE offers a limited number of free places and scholarships by competitive examination, tenable from September, 1953, to boys aged between 10 and 13½.—For details, write to the Principal, Carmel College, Greenham, Newbury, Berks.

▲ *Jewish Chronicle,*
3 April 1953, p.4.

THE GOVERNORS OF CARMEL COLLEGE

announce that the Annual Examination for the award of

SCHOLARSHIPS & BURSARIES

will be held at

CARMEL COLLEGE, WALLINGFORD

on SUNDAY, APRIL 5 at 10.45 a.m.

For full particulars apply to the Vice-Principal.

THE CLOSING DATE FOR APPLICATIONS IS FEBRUARY 19

▶ *Jewish Chronicle,*
23 January 1959, p.6.

fees, had to endure more than just an interview. There was also a written examination in several subjects. The first scholarship examination was in 1953, and the public at large were informed about it in an announcement in the "Jewish Chronicle." It read:

> Carmel College offers a limited number of free places and scholarships by competitive examination, tenable from September, 1953, to boys aged between 10 and 13½ – For details, write to the Principal, Carmel College, Greenham, Newbury, Berks.[63]

Those asking for details received an application form to complete, which asked for details of medical history, school history and attainments, and Jewish education and attainments. The examination took place on a Sunday a few weeks later.[64] One of the candidates was the author and on this examination writes:

---

63. Jewish Chronicle, 3 April 1953, p.4.
64. 7 years, p.11.

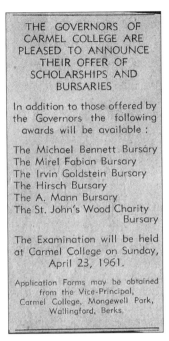

THE GOVERNORS OF
CARMEL COLLEGE ARE
PLEASED TO ANNOUNCE
THEIR OFFER OF
SCHOLARSHIPS AND
BURSARIES

In addition to those offered by
the Governors the following
awards will be available :

The Michael Bennett Bursary
The Mirel Fabian Bursary
The Irvin Goldstein Bursary
The Hirsch Bursary
The A. Mann Bursary
The St. John's Wood Charity
Bursary

The Examination will be held
at Carmel College on Sunday,
April 23, 1961.

Application Forms may be obtained
from the Vice-Principal,
Carmel College, Mongewell Park,
Wallingford, Berks.

Jewish Chronicle, 3 March 1961, p.5.

The candidates were ushered into a classroom and were given a paper in mathematics to answer. Those above the age of eleven and a half were given a more difficult paper. As I remember it, there were ten questions and they got harder as they went along. There was then a paper in English which included a comprehension. In one of my answers to it, I wrote about 'green geraniums'! One also had to write a short essay and one of the subjects was Purim.

The next test was an intelligence test. We were handed out printed booklets and after doing a few sample questions with the teacher in charge, we began the test. One of the questions was to draw a square and inside it write the letter 'B' as seen in a mirror. We had to answer about fifty questions in each section in four minutes, writing in the answers in pencil. The master then said we should turn over and begin the next section. In case one's pencil would break during this test, each candidate was supplied with two pencils. I remember asking the teacher what would happen if we succeeded in breaking both points?! He told me that he had spare pencils.

After this there were the interviews. . . . These were conducted by Rabbi Rosen assisted by several teachers. They asked me a whole variety of questions. I recollect doing a mental arithmetic question on simple interest. The teacher said that my answer was not quite accurate, although when I asked my father who was an accountant, he said that my answer was correct. I also recited part of a poem I had recently learned in school. During the interview I was asked what sporting event would soon be taking place and I answered 'Will the Australians be playing England in cricket?' To this Rabbi Rosen answered, 'Yes they will be.' As I left after the interview, I said 'Shalom' to the teachers.[65]

It was eight years later that the author's brother Nigel took this examination. As before, there was an English and a Maths paper, whose standard depended on the age of the candidates. However the third paper was a General Knowledge paper, amongst whose questions was, 'What do the letters A.M., U.N.E.S.C.O., and N.A.T.O. stand for?' At the interview, Nigel was asked what books he read and told them the "William books" but could not remember the name of the author. A boy who was not accepted for a scholarship "was asked [during the interview] about which TV program which he liked and gave an answer about a Friday night program. His mother thought that was why he was rejected."[66] This is very unlikely, since Kopul made a point of taking boys whose Jewish observance was low in order to instruct them.

Even though boys were tested, at least at an interview, before joining Carmel, it was still necessary when they finally arrived at the school, to determine into which class to put them. Regarding such testing, Jonathan Isserlin, who had been awarded a scholarship to Carmel, writes:

> I had obviously done well in the entrance exam, so I was tested in Maths, Latin and, Hebrew. I had come from an orthodox home and therefore the Hebrew was no problem for me, especially, as . . . Carmel really didn't go in for spoken Ivrit. The other two subjects were taught at Aryeh House by the fearsome principal, Mr. Eliasoff, and so they were my best subjects. Following these really rather rudimentary tests, it was decided that I would be placed in the 5th form, a full 2 years above my age group.

---

65. Ibid.
66. Recollections – Nigel Simons; conversation between author and Nigel Simons on 21 May 2012.

Although this might seem academically sound, it is obviously problematic in other spheres, as Isserlin goes on to explain, "I was small for my age anyway, and it didn't take long for the authorities to work out that I did not belong in the fifth. When they demoted me, however, it was only by one class, so the rest of my time in Carmel was spent a year ahead of my age."[67] A similar situation occurred with Michael Goitein, who was placed in a class where the pupils were two years older than him. On this he writes:

> I was a bright child and already at Glyngarth [his previous school], I was advanced by two classes, so that I was always about two years younger than my peers. As I look back, I see that this was the source of many lifelong problems. Such an advancement can be advantageous from an academic point of view. But it can be – and, I would say, usually is – highly deleterious from the point of view of socialisation. And the problem is exacerbated many-fold in the context of a boarding school in which, instead of a day-school's manageable 6 hour periods for five days a week, mainly occupied with being taught, students are thrust together 24 hours a day, 7 days a week, for months on end – in classes, on the playing fields, during free-time, in shower rooms and dormitories. In addition, being a teacher's pet, as a young bright child eager to please tends to be, does not endear one to one's peers.
>
> If I had to sum up the consequences of being placed two years ahead I would say that they are twofold: On the one hand, one quickly and near-irreversibly learns to adapt to the wishes and whims of others and to fade into the background, becoming as nearly as possible invisible so as to avoid domination, both physical and social, by one's peers. And, on the other hand, one looks for some area in which one can develop self-esteem (in my case, scholastic achievement) and to adopt and pursue it to the exclusion of virtually all other facets of a complete life. This is how one creates a one-sided, socially incompetent, individual.[68]

Henry Law also discusses the problem of having pupils of different ages in the same class, as was the situation in Carmel:

---

67. Recollections – Jonathan Isserlin.
68. Recollections – Michael Goitein.

The school was too small for streaming and the boys were moved around until they were in the class where they could cope with the syllabus. This meant that in each class there was a range of three years between the oldest and the youngest. In some ways it was a good system, but it had the disadvantage that mature, though un-academic boys could be put together with bright though immature ones. This led to tensions. I was initially placed with my own age group, which was the third form, as I had been at William Ellis [his previous school]. But the work was much too easy and after a couple of weeks I was moved up to the fourth form, with mostly older boys, a few of whom resented my presence.[69]

Even though a boy had been accepted to the Prep School, this was not an "insurance policy" that he would later be accepted to the Senior School. The Carmel Prospectus published in about 1951 said, "Although every reasonable allowance will be made for those who are already members of Carmel College, nevertheless, where it is clear that a boy is unfitted for a public school education his parents will be advised to make arrangements better suited to the boy's abilities,"[70] or in less diplomatic language "he will be thrown out!"

RUNNING AWAY FROM CARMEL!

From the Greenham days, running away from Carmel was already on the agenda. On this writes Joe Dwek, "The main preoccupation by some of the pupils was 'running away.' A sort of Colditz mentality. They only got as far as Crewe where they had to change trains for Manchester, were picked up by the police and brought back to Carmel."[71]

During the summer term of 1954, it again became the fashion, on a very limited scale, to

run away from Carmel, or more accurately to run home. One cannot say it was because of homesickness, but it was more of a lark. One boy even ran away twice![72] One of those who ran away was Jeremy Rosen who described this escapade and what followed in some detail:

When I was twelve I ran away from home. Two other boys had decided

---

69. Recollections – Henry Law, Carmel College days, part 1, p.4.
70. Carmel College Prospectus, undated (about 1951), section: Education.
71. Recollections – Joe Dwek.
72. Unwritten recollections of author.

to run away from school so I joined them, on a whim. My excuse was that I was being treated harshly, but in fact no more than everyone else. Besides I could not claim homesickness as the reason. We cycled to Streatley Station and one of them lent me money to take a train to London. At Paddington Station I called my aunt Frances. She was shocked but immediately took charge of the situation and instructed me to take a taxi to her. I poured out my heart to her about how badly I was being treated. She was very supportive and phoned my father to berate him for mishandling me. He had another point of view. He told me I could stay where I was until I apologised. After a few days of idling around, no friends, no football, I was bored. My father came into town for an appointment. He came to my Aunt's house but sat down with a newspaper and just ignored me. I could not stand it. I wanted to go home. I capitulated, apologised. My father relented. I went home, tail between my legs and the matter was never spoken of again.[73]

Another "runawayer" was the author:

If they could, why shouldn't I, thought I. My parents had been at the school a few days earlier on one of these Sunday visiting days and left me some extra pocket money. So I had the fare money.

I chose as my running away partner a boy from my class and after finishing lessons one day at four o'clock, off we fled. We went up the hill to catch the four thirty bus to Reading. We had heard that there was a train strike and therefore might have to get a bus leaving Reading at six o'clock which arrived in London two hours later. This would have made a very tedious journey. However, fortunately there were trains and we got the five fifteen which arrived at Paddington at six o'clock. We took the underground to Baker Street and then I parted from my friend. From there, I took the bus to Edgware and arrived at my house at about seven o'clock.

I must have called out when I knocked at the front door, since my mother thought she heard my voice. I immediately told her that I had 'run away.' My parents wanted me to return that night but I persuaded them to let me spend the night in Edgware. They immediately telephoned the school to tell them what had happened. To inquisitive neighbours, we said that I had a day's holiday.

---

73. Recollections – Jeremy Rosen, p.6.

We were in contact with the other boy's parents and it was arranged that they would take us both back by car on the following night. Towards that evening my mother took me to this boy's apartment . . . and then off we went by car to my alma mater. We reached Carmel just as the other boys were going to bed or had just gone to bed.

The next day, Rabbi Rosen called all the boys who had run away and gave us a talking to. He wasn't 'angry angry,' but this spate of 'running away' stopped.[74]

Later that year, Henry Law immediately after he arrived at the school had similar, but this time unimplemented, ideas. "I think it was mostly lack of courage and the fare money that prevented me from going straight home again."[75]

David Shaw relates a further case of running away, "I seem to remember one runaway to whom Kopul said 'how dare you run off to Oxford' to which the recaptured boy replied 'Reading sir.' Kopul responded 'Reading . . . Oxford . . . what's the difference?' 'About twelve miles sir' 'mmmmm'."[76]

REVEILLE TO PREP AND BED

Although for a period at Greenham, the day began with a cross country run in all weathers followed by a cold shower,[77] the boys were denied this "pleasure" in Mongewell! There, the daily programme from year to year was similar, and one's life was ruled by bells.

The history of the "Bells of Mongewell" at least during the Kopul era, has been written about by the author, (but here there are no "Oranges and Lemons" as with the "Bells of St. Clements!):

> The first bell when we came to Mongewell was a century old bell which was hung (or maybe it was already in position before we came) over the well in the quadrangle in front of the Main Building. After a term or so of pounding, it developed a crack and from then on, it was only fit for decorative purposes.

---

74. 7 years, pp.24–25.
75. Recollections – Henry Law, Carmel College days, part 1, p.3.
76. E-mail from David Shaw, 23 September 2012.
77. Recollections – Jeremy Rosen, chap.1.

In its place, some rusty drainpipes were suspended in some nearby bushes and they were banged on with some other metal implement. It was not very musical. This was our 'bell' for a year or so.

Bell number three became a permanent feature in Carmel life and it was an electronic system whose peals could be heard in every corner of the school. When we returned to the school in January 1955, it was already installed. It comprised a pendulum clock connected to a glass fronted box containing a whole collection of cogs and wheels. It was pre-set to ring bells at various times throughout the day, to signify such things as the start and end of lessons, and meal times. Before Shabbat it was switched off.[78]

Here now, as an example, is the weekday programme for the Senior School in October 1957: "Rise and Shine" was at 7 o'clock with a warning bell five minutes prior to that. Since Shacharit was longer, on Mondays and Thursdays, "rising out of bed" was ten minutes earlier on those two days. One then had 20 minutes to get to Shul. Then came breakfast at 8 o'clock. After filling one's stomach with school food, it was back to the dormitories for inspection. On the sound of the next warning bell, one had to rush to the classrooms for lessons (preceded by a school assembly on Mondays). Then there were five lessons of 40 minutes each, with a break after the third lesson. Then more food, known as lunch, at quarter past one. Then Minchah followed by four more lessons (with the exception of Sundays and Fridays) in the afternoon with a break for tea (with a slice of cake thrown in) in the middle. On a rotating basis, on one day a week, there were games instead of two lessons, or maybe games should also be called lessons, as the saying goes "All work and no play makes Jack a dull boy." Then Ma'ariv, which was followed by supper. The poor boys were still not free, since after supper there were one and a half hours of Prep. Finally, after all the hours of slavery, there was Bedtime and Lights out which ranged from 9 o'clock to 10 o'clock, depending on one's age.[79]

Now for the yearly programme. As was customary in almost all schools, the year at Carmel consisted of three terms. Details of term and holiday dates for the academic year 1958–59 were published in the "Roll and Calendar" for that year – for some reason just a one-time publication. Each term day – but not holiday days – was given about half an inch space in

---

78. 7 years, pp.52–53.
79. Carmel College, Daily Time-table, Duplicated sheet, October 1957.

```
CARMEL COLLEGE, MONGEWELL PARK, WALLINGFORD, BERKS.

                 DAILY TIME-TABLE.              October, 1957.

Warning      Bells
Bells
Every day.
6.55                           Warning bell for rising (Mon.and Thurs.
                                                            6.45)
             7.00             Rise          (Mon. and Thurs. 6.50)
7.15                          Warning bell for Service (Mon.and Thurs.
                                                            7.05)
             7.20             Service       (Mon.and Thurs. 7.10)
7.55         8.00             BREAKFAST
             8.30             Inspection of Dormitories and tidying
                                      of rooms.
Monday only.
8.50                          Warning bell (2 x 5 secs.) for Assembly
                                      in Hall.
             8.55             Assembly of whole School in Hall.
Sunday, Tuesday, Wednesday, Thursday, Friday.
8.55                          Warning bell for Assembly of Forms in
                                      Form rooms.
             9.0/9.05         Assembly of Forms in Form rooms.
             9.05             Dismiss Forms to Period 1.
Every day.
9.05         9.10/9.50        Period 1
             9.55/10.35       Period 2
             10.40/11.20      Period 3
             11.20/11.40      BREAK.
             11.40/12.20      Period 4.
             12.25/1.05       Period 5
1.10         1.15            LUNCH
             1.45 approx.     Service
Sunday only.
             2.10/3.55        GAMES as rota below.
                              No lessons p.m.
3.55         4.00             TEA
Monday, Tuesday, Wednesday.
             2.10/3.55        GAMES, as per rota below.
2.10         2.15/2.55        Period 6
             3.00/3.40        Period 7
3.55         4.00             TEA
4.25         4.30/5.10        Period 8
             5.15/5.55        Period 9
Thursday
                              no games p.m.
2.10         2.15/2.55        Period 6
             3.00/3.40        Period 7.
3.55         4.00             TEA
4.25         4.30/5.10        Period 8
             5.15/5.55        Period 9
Friday
                              No games p.m.
                              No lessons p.m. (unless indicated for
Sunday,Monday,Tuesday,Wednesday,Thursday.        certain groups.)
6.25         6.30             Service
6.40         6.45             SUPPER
7.25         7.30/8.00        Prep. 1
             8.00/8.30        Prep.2
             8.30/9.00        Prep.3
Friday
Every night  8.30            Arrangements for changing as   posted each
             9.00            Bed 1       Lights out 9.00           week.
             9.30            Bed 2       Lights out 9.30
                            Bed 3       Lights out 10.00
GAMES ROTA      Monday    III M.  III A
                Tuesday   IV    +  IVA
                Wednesday Shell VA/B LVI LVI/SVI
                Thurs.    IIA
Signals:        Fire:     Several 1-sec.rings separated by 1 sec.or
                Assembly: 2 x 5-second rings            (whistles.
                All other signals above:  1 single 7-second ring.
OCTOBER 1957.                                R. COLES.
```

Carmel College Senior School Daily Time-table as of October 1957

this calendar, possibly for pupils to doodle in or, alternatively, for pupils who were followers of Samuel Pepys[80] to write in their diary entries!; each week occupied one page.[81] Usually, but not always, the autumn term began before Rosh Hashanah.[82] However, for the academic year 1958/59, there was an unusual occurrence, and the term began during Chol Hamoed Sukkot.[83] Two years earlier, it had originally been planned to begin the term during Chol Hamoed Sukkot,[84] but it was later decided that it was not appropriate to begin during Chol Hamoed and the start of term was accordingly postponed.[85] In the style of the Pesach Mah Nishtanah one could well ask, "Why is academic year 1958/59 different from all other years?" However, unlike the Pesach Mah Nishtanah, no answer has been traced for this difference! This term continued until Thursday 18 December, although the pupils did have a respite from their noses to the grindstone with a half term weekend at home from Thursday 13 November to Monday 17 November.[86] The spring term lasted from Tuesday 13 January until Thursday 2 April, again with a half term at home from Thursday 19 February to Monday 23 February.[87] The summer term extended from Tuesday 5 May until "Speech and Prize Day" on Sunday 26 July, but the long suffering boys were not given a half-term holiday.[88]

SCHOOL CAPTAINS AND OTHER OFFICES

As with other schools, Carmel had its School Captain. The first one, appointed after the school moved to Mongewell, was Maurice Lipsedge,[89] who later went to Lincoln College in Oxford to read English.[90] Those who held the position of School Captain permanently had their framed photograph in Kopul's Study.[91] If you want to be school captain, make sure you are photogenic! There were also a number of prefects and

---

80. A famous diarist who lived in the 17th century (Wikipedia – Samuel Pepys).
81. Carmel College, Roll and Calendar 1958–59.
82. Carmel College, sample school reports, (name withheld). The reports gave the dates of the following term.
83. Roll and Calendar, op. cit., p.8.
84. Carmel College, sample school report, summer 1956, (name withheld).
85. Unwritten recollections of author.
86. Roll and Calendar, op. cit., pp.14, 15, 19.
87. Ibid., pp.20, 25, 26, 31.
88. Ibid., pp.32, 44.
89. Carmel 1954, p.10.
90. Ibid., p.9.
91. Unwritten recollections of author.

sub-prefects, all chosen by Kopul. The Prep School had its own prefects, whose names appear in the various Prep School magazines.

The following year, the office of Vice Captain was added, the first position being held by George Mandel.[92] George won a State Scholarship and later an Open Scholarship at Balliol College, Oxford. The pupils were particularly excited about this award, since they, as a result, got a school holiday![93] Three years later he received a first class honours degree in Physics[94] and during the following year he used to come to Carmel once a week to teach that subject "thereby helping to remove the teaching congestion on the science side."[95]

Towards the end of 1956, a Sixth Form Council was established, whose membership consisted "of those sixth form boys who have not had the onerous task of prefectship imposed upon them."[96] This body met once a week and assisted in certain aspects of the school's organisation.[97] At a later date, this Council involved itself in the question of lost property.[98]

Michael Goitein, unlike his predecessors, was just a two-term school captain – autumn 1956 and spring 1957[99] since he had been awarded an Open Scholarship at Balliol College, Oxford[100] and thus departed from the school at the end of the spring term.[101] He was popularly known as "Hippy." Michael explains how he got this name:

> The story of how I got my nickname exemplifies a youngster's need to establish an area of acknowledged personal achievement. It was during the course of evening dinner, soon after I had come to Carmel. Meals were noisy affairs with many dozens of children, seated several to a table, chatting away at full volume. The staff sat at a head table and, when some announcement needed to be made, the senior master present would clap for silence. Rabbi Rosen had done so, but I, no doubt caught up in whatever conversation I was having, kept on talking. 'Goitein,' he boomed out, 'come here at once' – and up to the head table I went. 'Goitein,' he asked me, simulating amazement

92. Carmel 1955, p.4.
93. Ibid., p.6.
94. Carmel 1958, p,5.
95. Carmel 1959, p.5.
96. Carmel 1957, p.6.
97. Ibid., p.28.
98. Carmel 1959, p.32.
99. Carmel 1957, p.4.
100. Ibid., p.5.
101. Ibid., p.8.

Kopul Rosen in his Study with the Prefects

at my lack of compliance, 'I just called for silence and you kept on talking. Are you stupid?' 'No Sir,' I spontaneously replied. 'I am a highly intelligent person.' At that, Rabbi Rosen roared with laughter and said that from then on he would address me by the initials 'H.I.P.' – and, so, 'Hippy' I became from then on.[102]

The 1957/58 school year had Ian Rabinowitz as School Captain.[103] Regarding his appointment, Ian writes:

The results [of my A-level examinations] would have allowed me to take up my offered place at Manchester University in the autumn. However, Kopul phoned my father and asked him to allow me to stay on for the 3rd Year [in the] 6th [form] to be School Captain. After

---

102. Recollections – Michael Goitein.
103. Carmel 1958, p.4.

discussion, it was agreed. I took A Levels for the 2nd time in Summer 1958. I thank Kopul once again, for giving me what was a formative experience which included presenting Julie Andrews with a bouquet back-stage after a performance of 'My Fair Lady' in aid of Carmel.[104]

Ian further explained that being School Captain was not a bed of roses:

I had to work very hard as School Captain. It may have been 'chicken and egg' but somehow the staff seemed to leave everything to me, particularly at weekends. And I, out of necessity, became quite a tartar. For meals, the School Captain sat with any staff at the top table. If there were no staff present, and I was in charge, then I was not pleased if, when I stood up to make the announcements, there was not absolute silence within 3 seconds. Well, one Sunday the noise continued for 5 seconds. I told the boys (and, of course, it was only boys in those days) that, because of this lack of discipline, after the meal they should all go to the Main Building hall where they would stand in silence for 10 minutes. I am sure that pupils in modern times would not have complied, but, on this occasion, *all* the boys (I went through the school roll to check) went to the hall.

As the boys were standing there in complete silence, with me in the front facing the staircase at the back, Kopul started to descend the stairs from his flat on the first floor. He really was a majestic figure, tall and handsome and impeccably dressed. He slowly made his way to me at the front and asked 'Ian, what is going on here?' I told him that the school had misbehaved and that they were standing for 10 minutes in silence as punishment. 'Don't you think that you should have told me?' he asked. 'Well,' I answered, 'I am the School Captain.' He nodded and, without saying anything else, proceeded to his study.

The next day, to my utter consternation, I saw a notice on the board announcing the appointment of two new prefects. I ran to Kopul's study, pounded on the door, burst into the study, and demanded of Kopul 'how could you appoint two prefects without a discussion with the School Captain'. Kopul spread his hands and said 'Well,' he answered, 'I am the Principal.' My final thank you to Kopul is for teaching me a lesson in humility.[105]

104. Recollections – Ian Rabinowitz.
105. Ibid.

In the academic year 1959/60, Raymond Dwek was School Captain.[106] On his period of office, Raymond wrote, "I tried to put into operation many of the ideals which had kept me going over the years. Thus I tried to persuade the teachers not to give punishments to any of the boys without first giving me an opportunity to speak to them to see if there was another way. Surprisingly, the school ran for a year without a single punishment being given. It was, I think, a happy school."[107]

When Raymond left the school in the summer of 1960, he was awarded the Jerrold Roston Cup and Kopul spoke at some length about Raymond:

> There is one boy in the school today who is leaving; he is Captain of the school, has been in the school eleven years . . . I don't think the boys themselves are aware what a remarkable liaison officer Raymond Dwek has been between you and the staff. On many occasions during the course of the term he has come to my study and has told me in very polite but firm words that he thought my judgment or my attitude to a boy or a group of boys had been somewhat harsh or that he had to give me more information which he thought I had not had when I came to a certain decision. We have had captains in the school every year. I will not praise him too highly when I say that we have never had a better Captain and I shall be more than satisfied if those who follow him will be as good.[108]

Towards the end of that Speech Day ceremony, Raymond spoke on behalf of the pupils who were leaving. Regarding his school captainship he said, "I would like to say how deeply grateful I am for having had the opportunity of being School Captain. It has been a fruitful and challenging year and I want to express my deepest thanks to you my fellow Carmelonians for the wonderful loyalty and co-operation which you have shown."[109]

The next School Captain was Jeremy Rosen, Kopul's son.[110] In order to anticipate the immediate cry that it was "nepotism," Jeremy explains, "I was elected Head Boy in a secret ballot of all the pupils. Normally the Headmaster would have made the appointment but as I was his son, my

---

106. Carmel 1960, p.4.
107. Recollections – Raymond Dwek.
108. Recording of 1960 Carmel Speech Day, at 39 minutes 10 seconds from beginning.
109. Ibid., at 1 hour 2 minutes 50 seconds from beginning.
110. Carmel 1961, p.4.

father had decided to open it up to a referendum. I really was surprised by the result."[111]

SCHOOL MASTERS OR FRIENDS

How in Carmel did the masters relate to the pupils? This subject was summarised in a booklet brought out by the School in 1957:

> Authoritative persons have remarked that the relationship of the staff with the boys is excellent. Jewish boys are more demanding and demonstrative than others and it is difficult and indeed undesirable that a rigid informal relationship should exist between master and pupil. A respectful distance however must be maintained and we feel that in Carmel we have achieved a balance between formality and personal friendship. The generosity of service given by the staff can be seen by the amount of time they spend with their pupils outside the classroom. Sitting in a master's room drinking coffee, listening to records, or walking in the grounds discussing matters not directly connected with his syllabus, the boy receives as much and more educational influence from his teacher than he does in the classroom. Because this aspect of education is so important in a residential school we appoint men to our staff not only on the basis of their qualifications and experience but on the strength of their personalities and ability to give of themselves.[112]

Already, whilst the school was still in Greenham, pupils were invited to the teachers' rooms. George Mandell recollects:

> On Friday evenings Friedmann held open house and fifth and sixth-formers would fill his rooms, sitting on the bed and the floor when there were no chairs free, looking through his art books, talking about literature, art, or politics, drinking tea, coming and going as they pleased. It was a kind of salon . . . Simply to know Friedmann in such circumstances was a liberal education.[113]

---

111. Recollections – Jeremy Rosen, p.10.
112. Carmel College 1948–1957, booklet, section: Staff.
113. FMF, p.22.

When the school moved to Mongewell, Dr. Friedmann took up residence in the Old Mill, and his hospitality was unchanged. Geoffrey Paradise is sure that many pupils remembered "being entertained by Yoshke Friedmann . . . . in the mill house with jam sandwiches on a Sunday afternoon."[114]

Abraham Carmel, the Housemaster of the first floor of the Main Building, had his room on that floor, where he would extend hospitality to boys. As Moshe Benaim recollects, "Often on Friday evenings, some of us would be invited to Mr. Carmel's room where we would have nibbles and talk about philosophical matters."[115]

On a floor above, although at a slightly later period, Rabbi Moshe Young had a one-room "bachelor flat." He writes that to this room "would come four students where we would talk and learn Torah and talk again. There was food too. I think it consisted of Maneschewitz fishlets and Tam Tams, if I'm not mistaken."[116]

Visits to teachers' rooms were not always limited to food and talk. Michael Cox, the Art teacher also lived in the Old Mill, and Michael Bharier, who had a particular interest in music, writes that he remembers in this building "following Stravinsky's full score of his Symphony of Psalms with Mr. Cox."[117]

On occasion, a whole class received an invitation to a teacher's residence. This occurred when on one Simchat Torah, David Stamler was one of the Chatanim. He did not limit his activities to being called up to the Torah as Chatan, but invited an entire class to his house which was then situated in the school's Lodge building.[118]

Contact between the staff was not limited to the period during which they were still at Carmel. After both pupils and teachers had left, it was not unusual for alumni to visit staff, usually in their houses. The locations of these visits included Tel-Aviv,[119] New York,[120] Majorca,[121] London,[122] and Shillingford.[123]

---

114. Recollections – Geoffrey Paradise.
115. Recollections – Moshe Benaim.
116. E-mail from Rabbi Moshe Young, 17 December 2012.
117. Recollections – Michael Bharier, chap. 3, The Environs of Carmel.
118. 7 years, p.38.
119. E-mails from Jeremy Rosen 13 March 2013, David Shaw 11 March 2013, and Emmanuel Grodzinski 11 March 2013.
120. Reflections – Alexander Tobias.
121. Recollections – David Shaw.
122. E-mail from Gabriel Chanan, 4 April 2013.
123. E-mail from Neil Myeroff, 8 August 2013.

CORPORAL PUNISHMENT, VARIOUS TORTURES
AND OTHER SANCTIONS

Despite the less formal relationship between teachers and pupils than found in other schools, the boys often needed disciplining and a method used all over England and elsewhere during the Kopul era was corporal punishment. At Carmel this took many forms and was administered by a number of the teachers, both officially and unofficially. Joe Dwek recollects that "the slipper and the cane were frequently used."[124]

In addition to the teachers giving corporal punishment, Jeremy Rosen writes, "Initially prefects were allowed to use corporal punishment too, but over the years the frequency of caning declined."[125] However, a pupil relates that "Prefects would also administer the slipper, a la English public school, until Kopul found out. He then visited the prefects' dorm and made it quite clear that there would be no corporal punishment by prefects ever again at Carmel 'and that is that with a capital T,' a saying that became a prefects' catchphrase for some time after."[126] However, at a later date, prefects again resorted to corporal punishment. Two prefects from the Senior School upper sixth form were assigned to the Prep School and they slept there. Their job was to maintain discipline and slippers were the tools of their trade (at least with some of these prefects). On this Franklin Koppel, who was a pupil in the Prep School from 1959 to 1961 writes, "One of the two prefects was [name of prefect] who was a known sadist. Prefects were allowed to give corporal punishment, he gave someone the slipper every night."[127]

Carmel was nicknamed the "Jewish Eton" but its corporal punishment was "mild" compared with Eton. In Eton until 1964, pupils could be birched on their bare buttocks in a semi-public ceremony.[128] In Carmel it was "just" the cane on trouser covered buttocks in a "private ceremony."

Kopul would use the cane for a variety of offences ranging from using the telephone without permission[129] to not doing the leining allocated by him.[130] A major recipient of corporal punishment was Kopul's son Jeremy

---

124. Recollections – Joe Dwek.
125. Recollections – Jeremy Rosen, chap.1.
126. E-mail from an early pupil (requested anonymity), 27 September 2013.
127. E-mail from Franklin Koppel (Dov), 16 April 2014. The author also witnessed such slippering when he visited the school as an Old Boy in the summer of 1961.
128. Wikipedia – Eton.
129. Recollections – David Mond.
130. 7 years, p.31.

who writes, "As a troublesome and rebellious pupil I was slippered and caned regularly, even by my father. It made little difference at all other than to persuade me that corporal punishment was not very effective."[131]

When a boy was to be punished by Kopul, was there room for negotiation? David Uri answers this question in the negative! "It was sheer terror to stand outside his study at 8.50 in the morning waiting to be caned: then incur his wrath by trying to negotiate a compromise sentence."[132]

Caning was not always limited to the backside – sometimes the hand was the target. David Shaw writes, "I once giggled nervously during the Shema at bed time. You know sometimes the harder you try to stifle a giggle the more difficult it is to do so. That was the only serious caning I ever had, and it was on the hand. I will never forget it . . . or the teacher . . . Mr. Bloch."[133]

Instead of a cane, William Phelps, who taught French and Latin for just one year at the school, used a ruler on the hand. Put out your hand . . . swish . . . Ow! that hurts![134] A slight variation on the ruler punishment was administered by Arthur Hoffman, who held a position in the Prep School for part of the time whilst it was at Crookham. Emmanuel Grodzinski reports that "he used a ruler for chastisement. The ruler had a metal strip inset into one side, to protect from wear, and he would rap you across the knuckles metal side down. And he didn't even bother to say 'this hurts me more than it hurts you'."[135]

Abraham Carmel, who wrote in his autobiography, "Indeed, during my early days [at Carmel] many a spoiled mother's darling made an intimate acquaintance with my slipper."[136] As housemaster, he also had a cane which was in fairly regular use.[137]

Charles Marshall, the P.E. teacher, used the tools of his trade, namely a gym shoe, to administer punishment. David Sheldon describes it as "slip-

---

131. Recollections – Jeremy Rosen, chap.1. On his recollections of his period as Headmaster, he wrote on the use of corporal punishment. "When I [Jeremy] entered the headmaster's study for the first time as Headmaster, I found the bamboo canes that had been used to beat me often enough, still there in the same bookcase behind the Headmaster's desk. I got rid of them." (Recollections – Jeremy Rosen, chap.4).
132. Reflections – David Uri.
133. Recollections – David Shaw.
134. Unwritten recollections of author.
135. Recollections – Emmanuel Grodzinski.
136. Abraham Carmel, *So Strange my Path*, p.145.
137. Unwritten recollections of author.

pering which turned out to be a good kick up the behind instead."[138] The author recollects:

> To misbehave in front of him would be immediately dealt with and the punishment would really be felt. He regarded with great severity boys taking other boys' gym kit. As a result of this 'borrowing' and not returning, after a time a lot of boys were missing their gym kit and Mr. Marshall decided to act. He assembled the whole school (except the upper forms) during break in the quadrangle in front of the main building and everyone had to stand in rows in absolute silence. Any boy guilty of the slightest infraction would be liable to immediately receive Mr. Marshall's standard punishment. The boys who had gym kit missing stood in the front row. This was repeated day after day.
>
> Meanwhile, some public spirited boys went through the unclaimed gym kit and gave it to the boys whose kit was missing. As a result the front row got shorter each day and when it had gone to zero, these 'assemblies' ended.[139]

David Uri describes a different form of physical punishment from Marshall, "Some hapless, unsuspecting soul [might] incur Mr. Marshall's wrath by being so 'very very' late on the sports field and be chased from one end of the playing field to the other, only to be finally shaken till his teeth rattled."[140]

A strong advocate of corporal punishment was Joshua Gabay, who taught French. Harold Berwin writes, "Josh Gabay soon made his presence felt and would dispense swift justice using a variety of implements to inflict sometimes cruel and unusual punishments." However, Berwin then adds, "Notwithstanding this, I found him to be a caring and very human man and was delighted some years later to invite him to the inauguration of the Gibraltar Chapter of the Junior Chambers of Commerce, which my Chapter in Leeds had helped to found."[141] After all these years, David Marks still remembers "the famous Gabay slipper."[142]

Another instrument used for punishment was the blackboard cleaner which consisted of a small implement about five inches long, one side

---

138. Recollections – David Sheldon.
139. 7 years, p.52.
140. Reflections – David Uri.
141. Recollections – Harold Berwin.
142. Recollections – David Marks.

wood, and the other side cloth. This was used on the hands of naughty boys by Alex Tobias – but maybe, as can be seen from the words of Joe Miller, he intended missing the target! "We had to hold a hand out three times for Dr Tobias to hit us with the wooden side of the brush. If you could pull your hand away quick enough, he missed and you continued for the three times. I am not sure if he missed intentionally each time, as I cannot recall him ever hitting anyone."[143] If Miller was correct, then Tobias was unique in this respect amongst the Carmel teachers!

Meir Gertner, the Hebrew teacher who came from Israel, was famous for slapping boys around the face. The author was amongst his candidates for this punishment. "On one occasion he [Gertner] asked us what the root of the word 'shifcha' was. I answered, without trying to be funny, that it was related to 'shiksa'. For that I received his standard punishment and then he added that in a minute I would get a like punishment for the plural of shiksa. Fortunately, I didn't!"[144]

Even the School Captain was not exempt from a face slapping in public, although this was not by Gertner! The author elaborates:

> On one occasion, when a certain teacher who was on duty [in the dining hall] was in a querulous mood, he publicly rebuked the School Captain and said he should be showing an example. The School Captain went over to this teacher and asked whether he would like to do his job. At this, the teacher gave the School Captain a slap around the face. I was told that the School Captain and the prefects then went to this teacher and said they were not prepared to act when he was on duty. At this the teacher apologised to the School Captain, saying his hand slipped![145]

Howel Pugh Roberts, a teacher who was at the school whilst it was at Greenham, used his foot instead of his hand, as explained by John Fischer, who was one of his pupils. If a boy was not paying attention in his class, he would receive a kick under the table.[146]

The choir master Dudley Cohen also resorted to corporal punishing using a board duster. Julius Nehorai writes:

---

143. Recollections – Joe Miller.
144. 7 years, p.48.
145. Ibid., p.94.
146. E-mail from John Fischer, 11 October 2012.

Once, in his class I'd misbehaved in some way and in a fit of temper he flung the blackboard duster, with its heavy wooden handle, right at me. I didn't see it coming and it hit me square on the forehead where an ugly purple bump soon appeared. These days I'm sure he'd be suspended and all sorts of enquiries and worse would ensue but as I think about it, with half a century's hindsight mind you, I was in the wrong. He probably didn't mean to hit me, I was too slow in ducking so, I learnt a lesson.[147]

The French teacher, Mrs. Whitfield, one of the only women teachers in the school, had another "diploma," namely, her "incredible accuracy with a blackboard duster thrown across the room at a sleepy child."[148] Whether or not the recipient received "an ugly purple bump" is not recorded!

A more unusual punishment, or probably, in this case, torture, was administered by the teacher who made a pupil put his finger in a desk and then slammed the desk lid on it. This same teacher also made a boy put his head in the class rubbish bin   less painful physically, but the unpleasantness was proportional to what was already in the bin![149]

A non-corporal punishment (although one could not always be sure) was to be told to wait outside Kopul's study. On this Geoffrey Paradise writes:

> There have been many mentions of Rabbi Rosen's (it still seems disrespectful to me to call him Kopul) punishments; the worst one for me – which I endured on many, many occasions, was being told to wait outside his study. The non-Jewish masters used to refer to him as 'The Rabbi' as in 'Wait outside the Rabbi's study.' The wait was in a dark little annex to the main corridor and seemed interminable, with a fearful prospect at the end of it when 'The Rabbi' finally turned up to enquire what I was doing there. Usually it just ended in a telling off though – or perhaps being told to learn a passage of Tanach by heart.[150]

Julius Nehorai describes this wait outside Kopul's study in more dramatic terms,

---

147. Recollections – Julius Nehorai.
148. Recollections – Jeffrey Gandz.
149. Unwritten recollections of author.
150. Recollections – Geoffrey Paradise.

'*Outside my studaay*' boomed the rich baritone voice of which, one was in absolute awe if not fear. So, off one went petrified while thinking about what was in store. Was it the Chinese drip torture waiting for hours not knowing if he was ever coming to administer who knows what punishment or the quick immediate response of the ruler on the open hand or, for really serious offences the cane on the rear-end? There were occasions when I'd stood there for what seemed like hours and assumed I was forgotten so I slunk off wondering if that was the punishment; the anguish of not knowing one's fate and worrying, would I be missed if I dare leave? Or, maybe, he had a sneaking admiration for those that did not hang about indefinitely and took destiny back into their own hands.[151]

The trauma of being summoned to Kopul's study was referred to humorously by Phillip Clein in giving the vote of thanks to the Guest of Honour, at the 1960 Speech Day. "I was told that Rabbi Rosen wanted to see me in the Study. I should explain that the Study is a place to which prefects go reluctantly, senior boys in fear, junior boys in a trance and the Prep School [boys] have to be carried in screaming in tears."[152]

Sometimes Kopul had the ideal punishment to fit the crime – "Measure for Measure!" Jack Coleman writes:

> One morning I decided to give shul a miss. Wouldn't you know it, that was the morning Kopul decided to visit the sleeping quarters. 'What's your problem this morning Coleman.' 'Don't feel very well Sir.' So off to the sanatorium to see nurse. Of course she couldn't find anything wrong and I returned to the daily routine. That afternoon there was a school cricket match and being in the team I turned up. Low and behold Kopul was there. 'What are you doing here Coleman, you can't play in the match today, you are sick.' Needless to say I attended shul each morning and that I am happy to say is the case today.[153]

David Shaw was once punished because his activities led to his ripping his trousers. He writes: "There was a fir tree [at Crookham] with close set branches where you could safely climb to the top and jump. You then

---

151. Recollections – Julius Nehorai.
152. Recording of 1960 Carmel Speech Day, at 1 hour 6 minutes 43 seconds from beginning.
153. Recollections – Jack Coleman.

flowed from one layer of fir to another until . . . one fine day my trousers caught and ripped. The result was that I was barred from climbing trees ever again. Indeed I was not allowed in my favourite parts of the grounds. Disaster."[154]

Writing of "lines" is another traditional school punishment and on its use (or should one say uselessness!) in Carmel, Jeremy Rosen writes:

> Many teachers and prefects simply handed out 'lines.' One had to write out some banal sentence in English or Latin to the effect that 'I must not misbehave in school,' anything up to a thousand times. Whenever I watch the Monty Python film 'The Life of Brian,' the scene where John Cleese gets Brian, the Judean rebel, to paint the lines 'Romans Go Home' in correct Latin, it always reminds me of my youth.[155]

But it is much more educational, if pupils can benefit from their punishment. On this David Shaw writes, "Kopul was very sensible about doling out punishment. No, I do not mean his making you wait outside his study in terror. Instead of mindless lines he used to make you learn a sentence from Perek or something in Hebrew. I still remember some of it. On occasion I have impressed by quoting it. Of course they do not know how I came to learn it."[156]

Just as prisoners are confined to their cells or the military to their barracks, Carmel pupils would be confined to their classroom after hours, commonly known as "detention." On this, a naughty boy named Jeremy Rosen writes, "I confess that in 1955 I held the school record for twenty hours of detention in one week."[157] On a more serious note, Jeremy continues:

> One of the great benefits of the school was the large number of after school activities, ranging from extra sport, to chess, debating, model making, art, music, rambling, debating and many more. Being in detention meant one had to forgo those far more attractive options. But the worst detention was on an afternoon when one was allowed to

154. Recollections – David Shaw.
155. Recollections – Jeremy Rosen, chap. 1.
156. Recollections – David Shaw.
157. Recollections – Jeremy Rosen, chap. 1.

Raphael Loewe Throwing a Confiscated Ball into the River Thames

go into town. On various afternoons different sections of the school could walk the two miles across the fields into Wallingford.[158]

Kopul was strongly against what he called "the mob taking over," even if it was in the framework of Purim fun. Alan Gold reports, "I can recall one Purim when the fourth form became prefects and we went for a revenge mission on the study block. Kopul decided that this was the mob taking over and we were barred from breakfast and told to pick up paper. Or when he didn't like the way I was talking and made me put some kind of wedge in my mouth and recite poetry."[159]

Raphael Loewe once gave an unusual punishment. It "followed a classroom ball throwing incident" and David Shaw elaborates, "He took us down to the river where the ball was ceremoniously discharged [i.e. thrown into the River]. I have the photographic sequence. It was like Tashlich."[160]

Romney Coles, who taught Chemistry, did not often hand out punishments, but Anthony Rau wrote of a case which occurred in July 1951:

---

158. Ibid.
159. Recollections – Alan Gold.
160. Recollections – David Shaw; there is also a photograph of this incident.

On Sunday night there was no prep because a dozen boys made a terrific noise during supper, even when told not to speak. And after supper there was a free fight among the same boys and another dozen, they made such a noise that Mr. Coles heard them in his cottage and he came to see what the noise was, he called an assembly immediately after shool [shul] for the whole school. The punishment was to assemble in the dining room for 10 mins. [minutes] in complete silence then to go down to the shool also in complete silence and wait there for 10 more mins. and then to return to the dining room. This was repeated 6 (SIX) times by everyone. We started at 8.15pm and finished at 10.30pm. We walked altogether 1752 yards!! I worked this out by pacing the distance to shool and multiplying by 12, once there and once back. I had nothing to do with any of the disturbance at all.[161]

Although not exactly in the area of punishment, a pupil could feel very uncomfortable when Kopul was not pleased with him. Michael Bharier writes, "Kopul himself could be very moody. He didn't suffer fools gladly and he could be rough with timid or retiring pupils. I personally was a victim of his ire several times." However, Michael continues, "He could also be, and was, a warm father figure to countless numbers of us. I was a recipient of this too."[162]

David Stamler writes about Kopul, "His ability to demolish an argument was shattering. Yet he did so in such a way that often the parties felt crushed as persons, whilst feeling that their arguments remained valid."[163] The author had an experience of this:

On one occasion, he asked the class which berachah can only be said on a Wednesday or Thursday? He then told us that the answer was the berachah for Eiruv Tavshillin. I then commented that since the same berachah was said for Eiruv Chatzarot and Eiruv Techumim and in these cases were not limited to Wednesday and Thursday, the question should be phrased as 'Which *Mitzvah* can only be performed on Wednesday or Thursday?' Although my comment was perfectly valid, Rabbi Rosen replied that my chutzpah was inversely proportional to my size, [I was rather on the short side][164]

---

161. Rau Letters, 10 July 1951.
162. Recollections – Michael Bharier, chap.5, Carmel memories.
163. Memories of KR, p.102.
164. 7 years, p.75.

CARMEL BOY USUALLY DOES NOT FIGHT BOY

The concern that Carmel pupils had for their fellow pupils was almost always praiseworthy. This can be illustrated by David Robbins' experience:

> I came to Mongewell Park in 1956, after two years at an old-established English public school where there was a strict informal rule that no boy could speak to a boy who was his senior unless he had been spoken to first. Third formers couldn't speak first to fourth formers, fourth formers couldn't speak first to fifth formers, and so on. And if two boys began to fight in the playground, the proper etiquette was to surround them in order to prevent the fight being interrupted, and then to bet (for cash only) on which boy would win. A few months after arriving at Carmel, I was astonished to see a junior boy go up to two boys who were clearly older than he was, and who were fighting, and say to them 'Come on, stop this nonsense.' Obviously Carmel was a very different type of public school, and I am very glad to say, it remained so even after it had been admitted to the Headmasters Conference. Kopul taught us that we were indeed our brothers keepers.[165]

However, it would not be true to say that there were no exceptions. Neil Alton describes: "Certain 'senior' i.e., bigger boys, who specialised in Chinese burns, knuckle-punches, and name-calling. I could name some names myself now. But they're probably human rights campaigners for all I know. Carmel moves in mysterious ways. At the time I thought 'You wait'."[166]

Kopul did not allow bullies to get away with their activities scot-free. Jacob Fachler reports, "Kopul was particularly sensitive to cases of bullying. I remember once that he chastised a group of boys for bullying (I don't remember who the victim was) by richly insulting every one of them to see how they liked it."[167]

There was also an "original" form of what might be called bullying, and most terrifying to those who were claustrophobic, on which David Shaw reports:

---

165. Recollection – David Robbins.
166. Recollections – Neil Alton.
167. Recollections – Jacob Fachler.

Talking of being smart for Friday nights you had to be ready and down by a certain time, Teachers in front, School in rows facing. Discipline strict. Well we had a way to disrupt proceedings. In each dorm was a wicker linen basket. Somehow we managed to 'persuade' a luckless individual in to it. When we closed the lid and slid it under a bed he was trapped. You imagine the rest.[168]

Although not strictly bullying, new pupils are sometimes terrified when "old timers" tell them what to expect from the school. Michael Bharier reminisces. "I remember that Roger Rudd and Julian Black were in my compartment [on the train to Carmel] and, since they were 'old timers,' they started telling the 'new boy' what to expect at the school, some of it scary."[169] Obviously Carmel's "new boy" treatment was not unique, In common with Jennings and Darbishire, the pupils at most boarding schools receive the same treatment on their first day at boarding school![170]

NO SHORTAGE OF SUBJECTS TO STUDY!

Numerous subjects were taught at Carmel both in the Prep School and the Senior School.[171] The Jewish subjects were the various branches of Jewish Religious Knowledge and Modern Hebrew. On the secular side, there was English Language, Mathematics, the various Humanities, both ancient and modern languages, and the various Sciences. The non-academic subjects included Arts and Crafts, and there was also Physical Education. Music was not on the timetable, but was taught as an extra for which parents had to pay.

In the Prep School, Mathematics was limited to Arithmetic, Algebra, and Geometry. French and Latin were on the curriculum; this proved to be a problem for boys who joined the Senior School from state primary schools where French and Latin were not taught. In Crookham, the pupils also learned General Science, Hygiene, and Elocution.[172]

In the Senior School, Mathematics included Trigonometry, and in the higher classes Calculus, Analytical Geometry, and Mechanics. The Sci-

168. Recollections – David Shaw.
169. Recollections – Michael Bharier, chap.2, Life at Carmel.
170. Anthony Buckeridge, *Jennings Goes to School*, (London: Collins, 1953), pp.27–31.
171. Inspectors' Report, passim.
172. Inspectors' Report, passim; Various Carmel College Preparatory School sample school reports.

EDUCATION

CARMEL College consists of a preparatory school for boys from 7 to 12, and a senior school for boys from 12 to 18. The two are conducted independently of one another. The senior school is at Greenham, Newbury, and the junior is at Crookham, three miles away. The latter, also serves as the main building for married masters' quarters.

The preparatory school has three classes and form I. Pupils passing through the school at an even pace should be ready for the senior school at the age of 12 to 13.

The curriculum includes English language, Literature, History, Geography, Mathematics, Elementary Science, Art and Crafts, Latin, French, Music, Physical Training and Current Affairs.

Carmel College Preparatory School follows the curriculum for the Common Entrance Examination but does not coach pupils for special entrance examinations to other schools.

Admission into the Preparatory School does not carry with it any assurance that the boy will be admitted into the Senior School. Although every reasonable allowance will be made for those who are already members of Carmel College, nevertheless, where it is clear that a boy is unfitted

Page from Carmel College Prospectus – about 1951

ences were divided into Chemistry, Physics, and Biology, each having its own laboratory, with a general science laboratory for the lower classes. Additional languages which sometimes appeared on the curriculum were German and Spanish.[173] However, exotic languages from the Far East, such as Kuki-Chin (which is spoken by the Bnei Menasheh from India who have converted to Judaism), did not appear on the curriculum, nor was Yiddish, Kopul's "mameloshen" (mother-tongue).

Below the fifth form of the Senior School, the pupils studied both Arts and Science subjects. When they reached the fifth form, pupils had to choose between Arts or Science. Even within this division, there were further sub-divisions, for example Maths or Biology. There was friendly rivalry between those opting for arts and those opting for science, and a humorous article appeared in the Carmel magazine on how each group viewed the alternative group. The Arts boys wrote:

Already the Science Sixth are getting out of hand. Even the dreamy silence of an English lesson conducted by the side of the lake is occa-

---

173. Inspectors' Report, passim; Various Carmel College Senior School sample school reports.

sionally disturbed by a series of bangs and groans accompanied by a yellow mushroom cloud of evil smelling gas drifting in our direction from the Chemistry Lab. where scientists are indulging in a riotous orgy. Whereas the absence of those dear animals (Matron's last four dogs!) has been due to the fact that there is a line of captured canine carcasses hanging up in the window of the Biology laboratory, waiting to be dissected; even Tinker, Matron's poodle, is not allowed out after dark.[174]

And now what the Science boys wrote:

The scientist would say, 'I ascended the hill.' The arts student would express this, 'The sun was blazing down' (which is an untrue statement because blazing implies oxidation or burning, and everyone knows that the sun's heat is derived from a thermonuclear fusion reaction) 'and the birds were chanting melodiously' (which they do all the year) 'as I ambled over the gently undulating' (a stupid phrase; it is not an accurate description and it would be better to say: gradient 1 in 5) 'countryside.'[175]

Having such a variety of subjects involved finding and employing qualified staff to teach these subjects. Some were at Carmel for very short periods, even less than one year, whilst others were on the staff for decades.[176] Some could teach, others could not, some would scream and some would swish.

In addition to their formal class teaching periods, the teachers had other duties. Almost all of them were involved in the school's extra-curric- ular activities, such as sports and societies.[177] There was no "homework" at Carmel – no! The boys did not get a bonus of free-time; instead of "homework" they were burdened with what is called "prep" for an hour and a half each night. Just as there was a lesson timetable, there was a prep timetable. The teachers would set assignments for this prep and afterwards mark it.

---

174. Carmel 1958, p.17.
175. Ibid., p.19.
176. See Section 2 of this book.
177. See Various Carmel magazines.

Chemistry Laboratory at Mongewell

OY VEY! EXAMINATIONS

Competition at Carmel was not limited to sporting activities or debating societies. There were also learning competitions – or in less pleasant language for the pupils – examinations! On these examinations in the Senior School the author reminisces:

> One's school life seems to be full of examinations. If it's not external examinations, then it's internal examinations and if it's not internal examinations then it's tests and more tests and . . . . even more tests.
>
> Every teacher kept or should have kept a mark book. In it were entered the marks a pupil obtained for his homework, for his tests and whatever else the teacher decided. In a term where there were end of term examinations, these marks counted as much as the examinations for one's form position that term. In a term when there were no examinations, the form positions were based entirely on these marks.
>
> There are two ways to calculate such a form position. One is to add up the percentage mark a pupil has gained in each subject and then find the average, arrange them in descending order and you then have

the form positions. The second method is to add up the positions in class that a pupil obtained for each subject and arrange them in ascending order to determine the class position. . . . Carmel College used this method to calculate the form positions. . . .

It is usual to calculate form positions only on the basis of academic subjects. A subject such as Art, in which generally one can do well, or alternatively, not do well however much one tried, would not be taken into account when working out form positions. For some reason, Carmel College was different in this respect, and Art was counted in the same way as English or Geography.

As a rule, the end of term examinations were held twice a year – in December and July. The question papers were as a rule duplicated, with most teachers having their papers typed on a stencil and then run off, although there were a few teachers who would write them in their own handwriting on to the stencil. . . . Before each session of examinations, we would be given a timetable for them. Should a paper have been of short length, for the remainder of the time, we had to remain in our classroom and revise for our exams still to come. . . .

The paper on which we answered the questions was file paper which had been specially marked by Mr. Coles. He would take reams upon reams of this paper and with a brush go from top to bottom over the top edge of this paper with a bluish copper sulphate solution. This left an easily identifiable mark several millimetres deep on the top edge of each sheet of paper. Only such paper could be used in these exams.[178]

However, Romney Coles did not give out starter's guns and stop-watches to the teachers for the exams! Maybe this was an oversight!

Strict security is required before an exam to ensure that pupils do not get prior access to exam papers. But sometimes there are slip-ups. The author recollects one such incident which occurred with one of Helmut Schmidt's end of term examinations, "Some boys got hold of the questions in Mr. Schmidt's Geography paper. But it didn't help them. Without saying anything, Mr. Schmidt just changed in ink on every question paper details of the questions. For example, when the question asked to write about a particular country or city, he changed the name to a different country or city!"[179]

178. 7 years, pp.108–09.
179. Ibid., p.110.

Needless to say, there were also external examinations and for these exams the school utilised the Oxford and Cambridge Schools Examination Board. These examinations were designated by different letters – O, A and S, namely Ordinary, Advanced and Scholarship levels. There was also something known as Alternative Ordinary level, although it is not clear why the term "Alternative" was used. The author also has recollections on these examinations:

> The examinations in foreign languages routinely set by this Board were limited and included French, German, Italian, Spanish, Welsh and Irish. If one wanted some other language or subject, one had to apply to the Board for the papers to be specially set. It wasn't free – the school had to pay for it. Carmel wanted each year O-levels in Classical Hebrew and also a Hebrew alternative to one of the regular Scripture Knowledge papers. In some years, there was also A-level Classical Hebrew.
>
> It also came to my knowledge that at least on one occasion there was O-level Modern Hebrew. I managed to get hold of a past set of papers, and I observed that they were very easy indeed. I accordingly spoke to a number of boys and found a great interest in wanting to take this subject. I then spoke to the school about having a paper set that next year. Mr. Stamler then told a boy that on one occasion when they had set it, it was so difficult that even the teacher was looking up words. It was as a result of these complaints that they had on the next occasion set the very easy paper which I had obtained from the Board. In the end nothing came of my initiative to have it set that year. . . .
>
> All the administrative work concerning these examinations was done by Mr. Coles. The various subject teachers would decide whom they wanted to enter for their own subject and pass on their list to Mr. Coles. The names were then entered up on a large broadsheet with details of the names of the pupils, their birthdates and the subjects they were being entered for. Under the regulations, pupils who were under 16 could only take these examinations with the consent of their headmaster. This seemed to be more of a formality, since all this involved was the Headmaster signing just once for all such pupils in his school, at the bottom of this broadsheet.
>
> Once the broadsheet was ready to be sent up to the Secretary of the Board, Mr. Coles would go through the list, boy by boy, checking his personal details and the subjects he was entered for. Amongst the

Subjects		Classification	Remarks	Master
Hebrew	Language Torah	(c)	Promises to do very well, needs to be livelier however.	H.G.
English	... ...	c. B.	Satisfactory He has worked well, and made progress.	KR AC
History	... ...	(a)	A very good beginning	AH.
Geography	...	80%	Made very good progress	WS
Latin	... ...	B	Satisfactory.	AC.
Greek	... ...			
French	... ...	(a)	A sound term's work	AH.
German	... ...			

(a) = 65% and above (b) = 55% - 65% (c) = 45% - 55%
(d) = 35% - 45% (e) = 35% and below

Page from Senior School End of Term Report (name deleted to preserve privacy)

personal details of the boys, were their full names and this, sometimes included names which their friends did not know they had, and perhaps more to the point, the boy would prefer them not to know! I recollect that one boy had the middle name 'Jack' and when this was read out, his classmates thought this was very funny!

A problem which arose was that this Board also set papers on Saturdays. Carmel College was allowed to take these papers on Sunday. On the weekends when this was implemented, no boy was allowed to enter the school from the time the paper was taken on Saturday by the non-Jewish schools and the time it was taken on Sunday by Carmel College. It was also forbidden to use the telephone during this period. The school was effectively in quarantine.

In connection with this, there were some interesting situations. There were some non-Jewish day boys studying in Carmel who lived in Wallingford. When one of them was entered for a Saturday paper, which Carmel was taking on Sunday, this non-Jewish boy had to come to the school on Saturday morning before the exam was taken in other schools and sleep over in Carmel that Saturday night.

These non-Jewish boys had classes in Christian Scripture and there was an occasion when this paper was set on a Saturday. There was no reason for them not to take this paper on Saturday and a classroom and non-Jewish teacher was set aside for them to do so. Exams were thus being taken in Carmel all seven days of the week!

Sometimes due to internal timetabling arrangements, a paper programmed by the Board to take place in the morning, took place in Carmel in the afternoon and vice versa. During such days, these 'quarantine' arrangements were in force in Carmel.

Mr. Coles informed the school that should a boy need to make a telephone call, for example, in connection with his travel arrangements, he would have to make it in the office, in the presence of the school secretary. Similarly, if a boy had a dental appointment in Wallingford, he would have to go down accompanied by the Matron.

The Board built its timetable on the basis that a pupil would not take a 'peculiar' combination of subjects. But some boys in Carmel did have such combinations. One boy had for his A-levels a combination of Arts and Science subjects – I believe it was Maths, Physics, and History. There was a day when each of these subjects had a paper and as a consequence those taking History had to take their paper from five o'clock until eight o'clock at night. . . .

After a particular exam was finished, the scripts would be handed to Mr. Coles for arranging in alphabetical order and dispatch to the examiners. Before dispatch, the subject teacher would often look over them to see how his pupils had fared in the exam and sometimes would even estimate what mark they would obtain. If a pupil's effort was catastrophic, he might withdraw the script and the pupil would be listed as being absent from the examination.[180]

The Scripts were then put into a large envelope and dispatched with a "proof of postage."

More complicated was the dispatch of the dissection specimens of the candidates following an A-level Biology exam. They had to be packed well – perhaps in a biscuit tin. The post office authorities would not have been amused if the juices from a dissected dogfish or catfish had oozed out in transit all over the other items of post, and moreover the recipients would not have liked the fishy smell of their post on its arrival!

The results of the summer exams were sent to the school during the summer holidays. Fortunately, the boys did not have to sweat it out until they returned to school at the end of the holidays. The secretarial staff prepared a list of all those who had passed their G.C.E. [matriculation] exams and dispatched it to them by post.[181] For the December exams, pupils did not have this luxury. However, the consolation was that they did not have to sweat for a long time, since the results only came out a few days before the end of the holidays.

One's results quite often differ from one's first impressions after an exam; the pupils, would often come out of an exam room happy or sad, and likewise there were these reactions when they received the results. David Shaw reports on a happy boy who "came out of an O-level English exam beaming from ear to ear. One essay question was 'Birthday Presents.' He related a wonderfully witty and sarcastic essay on the merits of receiving a toothbrush."[182] It is not reported whether or not this boy was happy when the results of his essay writing were published.

There was a certain period of time that was the norm to prepare for an external examination. Sometimes, however, a "crash course" became a necessity. Henry Law reports on one such case in which he was personally involved:

---

180. Ibid., pp.112–15.
181. Carmel College Sample lists of G.C.E. results, Advanced level 1958, Ordinary level 1960.
182. Recollections – David Shaw.

We then got a new syllabus. For the first time ever, I had a teacher, Murray Roston, the English and Latin teacher, who was able to teach Hebrew in a systematic way. Some kind of deal was made between Murray and the class that we would have a go at getting O-level Classical Hebrew that summer. We had just two terms. Less, actually. And we all passed. Murray obtained a decent text book. We learned the grammar systematically. I discovered that behind the strange characters lies a language artificial in its simplicity. An eight year old could have learnt it if anyone had had the wit to try and teach it properly. But I was fourteen before I came across someone who would.[183]

Henry Law had a similar experience with his A-level Physics:

Chemistry continued to go smoothly, under the superb guidance of Romney Coles. Physics was another matter as we had learnt next to nothing during the Lower Sixth year and had to do the entire A-level syllabus in, effectively, two terms. Julyan Bunney obtained the best text books of the time, including some by Nelkon who had been the Physics teacher at my old school, William Ellis. With his inspiration, and the camaraderie of what had become a group of friends, we passed and mostly with flying colours.[184]

There was an occasion when a non-Carmel pupil (with a hyphenated surname) sat his A-levels at Carmel College. The author reports on this:

It was that year [1959] that an external pupil . . . came to take his Science and Maths A-levels at Carmel. . . . Mr. Bunney commented that as a consequence of his taking the exams at Carmel, the school had to buy an extra set of equipment for the Physics practical. He then added that Carmel sometimes sent its pupils to other schools for language oral examinations. It would seem that he had complained about having to buy this additional equipment and this was the reply he had received. However, this does not seem a parallel to me, since taking an oral exam at a school does not involve extra expenditure, except maybe a cup of tea![185]

183. Recollections – Henry Law, Carmel College days, part 2, p.12.
184. Ibid. p.20.
185. 7 years, p.121.

Needless to say, in external examinations, the school wanted its pupils to get one hundred per cent! Michael Goitein recollects:

> Close to the time when I left Carmel, I was at home on holidays and Rabbi Rosen called up to let me and my family know the results of a national exam I had taken at the end of term. 'I was very disappointed in the results of your Math exam,' he said to me sternly. My heart sank. 'You got three questions wrong. How can it be that someone who can answer ninety-seven questions correctly can't get all one hundred right?' How, indeed? Of course, he meant his comment as a joking compliment. But, it cannot have been all that funny given that I still remember the conversation – and, indeed, the exact spot where I stood during that phone call – over 50 years later.[186]

One would have expected that should a Carmel boy be taking external examinations, he would not be burdened at the same period with taking school internal examinations. But that was not so, as the author reports from personal experience:

> At first, we understood that this would be the situation [i.e. no internal examinations]. But we were soon disabused of this. Mr. Bunney, the Physics teacher, came into our class and said quite clearly that neither Mrs. Whitfield, the French teacher, nor himself were prepared to forgo their end of term examinations. In the middle of our O-level, there was a day without exams and these two utilised it to its fullest extent – and I literally mean 'its fullest extent.' Not only did Mrs. Whitfield gives us two papers in French; in the break between two papers, she, in addition, managed to squeeze in a French dictation. Mr. Coles, who I think would not have insisted on a Chemistry examination, also gave us one, but on a different day. Dr. Friedmann then said he would give us a History exam, but in the end he didn't.[187]

SPEECH DAY – READ: A BORING AFTERNOON!

At the end of every academic year, on a Sunday afternoon,[188] there was the ceremony known as Speech Day, when the all the pupils (and the staff

---

186. Recollections – Michael Goitein.
187. 7 years, pp.110–11.
188. In 1958, the Sunday which normally would have been Speech Day, namely 27 July, was the

wearing their academic robes – gowns, hoods, and mortar boards) had to sit through, for at least two hours, speeches without end. The compensation was that after this ceremony, the pupils would have a two months holiday. Parents were also invited[189] and "were allowed to arrive on the morning of speech day at about eleven o'clock in the morning and take their boys out but they had to arrive back by the start of the ceremony, which was about two o' clock."[190]

The programme was similar from year to year. It would begin with Kopul's report, which would be followed by an address by the Guest of Honour. The prizes would then be presented by the wife of the Guest of Honour. Recitations and declamations by various pupils came next, although sometimes these came before the presentations of prizes. Finally there was a vote of thanks to the Guest of Honour and the ceremony ended by the singing of the school song, and also the Hatikvah and the National Anthem.[191]

Governors and potential donors would also be present at these ceremonies and Kopul would make extensive preparations to ensure that the ceremony passed off without a hitch. The author recollects these preparations:

A few days before each Speech Day, a marquee was erected, usually on the lawn behind the classroom block but on occasion on the lawn in front of the gymnasium. Even though Speech Day was held in the month of July, the weather could well be rainy and wintry. Indeed on a number of Speech Days, it poured with rain. On one occasion the weather was so nice, that the erected marquee was not used and the ceremony was held outdoors.[192]

In contrast, one year there was a fierce gale raging on that Sunday afternoon. The marquee, which had been erected near the gymnasium, was full of people and at the same time to prevent it blowing over, senior boys were holding on to guy ropes to try and steady the

fast of Tisha b'Av. Obviously the ceremony could not be held on that day, [circular to parents from KR, dated May 1958, headed Important notice, please retain] and it was postponed to the middle of the following academic year. Since it was in mid-winter, it was not practical to hold it in a marquee and instead it was held in the Main Hall. Since the seating capacity was far less than in a marquee, only the parents of prize winners were invited (7 years, p.129).

189. Carmel College Speech Day invitations for Sunday 25 July 1954 (including Sports Day which was cancelled because of rain), and Sunday 24 July 1955.

190. 7 years, p.127.

191. Carmel College Speech Day programmes for 1955 and 1960.

192. 7 years, p.126.

Carmel College Speech Day at Greenham

marquee. It could have been dangerous to have held the ceremony in the marquee under such conditions. Therefore Rabbi Rosen came in and told every person there to take his folding chair into the nearby gymnasium where the ceremony would be held. The pupils were told to stand in the gangway by the wall and the prizewinners in a nearby room adjacent to the dais. Rabbi Rosen was an expert at dealing with emergency situations . . .[193]

The seating in the marquee was in three blocks. In the centre block sat the pupils and on the side two blocks the parents. After the marquee had been erected, Rabbi Rosen would assemble all the pupils there and decide on which seat each pupil would sit. The more presentable pupils would sit near the front and the less presentable ones further back. On one occasion, a boy said that his school blazer was dirty and torn, to which Rabbi Rosen replied that he would seat him in a place

---

193. Ibid.; This emergency change of venue was also reported in the Jewish Chronicle, 3 August 1956, p.16.

where the dirt and tears wouldn't show. . . . The prize winners would be seated at the end of the rows to enable them to go out quickly when their names were called. He would also do a practice with a number of prize winners, by calling out their names and they would go out to him as if to receive their prize . . .

Another tradition in these prize days was for a senior boy to give a vote of thanks to the guest of honour and he would end by saying, 'And now Carmelis, let us give our guest of honour the traditional school cry 'Carmel College – ko lechai'.' The pupils would then call out in a loud voice 'ko lechai.'[194]

Jeremy Rosen supplies further details of Speech Days:

> Speech Days became showcases for the school when parents and visitors would drive down to the estate. Kopul orchestrated the proceedings. He got pupils to declaim speeches or extracts from literature and classical texts, both secular and Jewish. He was anxious to grandstand them to show off the cultural mixture that Carmel wanted its pupils to aspire to. Pupils were drilled to walk in and out in a disciplined way and to sing the school song both in Hebrew and in English.

On "ko lechai," Jeremy notes, "Kopul always insisted it be a united roar of enthusiasm. Something not all pupils were capable of. It was often forced. But Kopul's own voice was so powerful that he made sure there was enough volume in the reply."[195]

One of the declaimers of secular texts was Michael Goitein who writes, "Being a 'good boy' I was impressed into reciting by heart poems and suchlike at the end-of-year prize days. I recall memorizing and reciting a small part of Milton's 'On his Blindness' and still remember the opening lines. And, for a later event I recited John Donne's memorable sermon 'For Whom the Bell Tolls.' Such exercises, which seem burdensome at the time can have a lasting benefit."[196] As for Jewish texts, which were declaimed in Hebrew, on one occasion Mordell Klein recited the "Song of Devorah," and Jeremy Rosen, "The Valley of Dry Bones" from the book of Ezekiel.[197]

---

194. 7 years, pp.126–27.
195. Recollections – Jeremy Rosen, chap.1.
196. Recollections – Michael Goitein.
197. 7 years, p.128.

Despite all the extensive preparations by Kopul, Romney Coles, and possibly others for the Speech Day, in 1957 there was a serious mishap with the prizes, as explained by the author:

> I was awarded a prize for Chemistry and after I received the book, I saw that it was a book from the school library complete with the library stamp and catalogue marks. I wondered what had happened and how would I be able to erase these marks! After the ceremony had finished, it was announced that the prize winners should remain behind. Mr. Coles then told us that not enough prizes had been bought and so he had quickly gone into the school library and taken books which looked newish, in order to give the impression that they were prizes. We therefore had to return the library books to him and he added that during the following term, they would purchase books for us.[198]

At these Speech Days, even parents had to be on their best behavior, otherwise they would get a reprimand from Kopul! Alan Gold elaborates, "[I remember] on Speech Days [Kopul] caustically telling parents, some of whom have never recovered from the shock, that perhaps one day all the parents would have the courtesy to arrive on time and then perhaps the proceedings wouldn't be continually interrupted while they sat down."[199] The Carmel boys displayed courtesy towards these late comers, but Kopul intervened as described by the author, "On one occasion, parents who had arrived late came into the centre block and pupils with good manners had offered them their seats. However Rabbi Rosen announced that these parents should remove to the side blocks set aside for parents."[200]

Speech Days (and other visiting days) were utilised by some parents, as an opportunity to show off their wealth, or sometimes fictitious wealth. Jeremy Rosen elaborates, "It was interesting and often surprising to see what a pupil's parents were like. Wealthy parents came in their Rolls Royces, fathers smoking cigars and mothers decked in furs. It was said that some parents hired luxury cars for the day just to impress. Lesser cars brought more modest parents and families. And other parents had to make use of public transport."[201] On this subject, (although, apparently, not on Speech Day), Neil Alton writes of, "One dad driving his family

198. Ibid.
199. Memories of KR, p.128.
200. 7 years, p.127.
201. Recollections – Jeremy Rosen, chap.1.

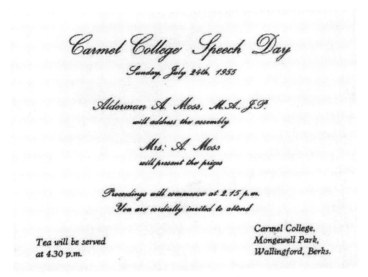

Carmel College Speech Day
Sunday, July 24th, 1955

Alderman A. Moss, M.A., J.P.
will address the assembly

Mrs. A. Moss
will present the prizes

Proceedings will commence at 2.15 p.m.
You are cordially invited to attend

Tea will be served
at 4.30 p.m.

Carmel College,
Mongewell Park,
Wallingford, Berks.

Invitation to Speech Day of 1955

down in a Rolls to be shown round, getting his son accepted, and driving them home – to replace the Roller back in his 2nd-hand car showroom."[202]

On the 1961 Speech Day, which was to be Kopul's last one, the author recollects, "Rabbi Rosen ended the proceedings by telling the audience only to watch worthwhile television programmes during the holidays. He got a laugh for that because on that evening he was due to speak on television about the Eichmann trial."[203]

Immediately following Speech Day, the pupils would leave Carmel as quickly as possible for their long awaited "freedom" and in many cases Continental travel. However, the staff had a further activity, a very pleasant one, as Charles Marshall describes:

> It had become a tradition that the last day of each academic year was also the occasion of Carmel's annual Speech Day, attended by large numbers of parents. On the same evening after parents and pupils had left the school for the summer vacation, Kopul always hosted a formal dinner for all members of staff and their spouses. On one such

202. Recollections – Neil Alton.
203. 7 years, p.140.

memorable Sunday, Kopul had accepted an invitation from the BBC to appear on a prime time Sunday evening live discussion about the Eichmann Trial which was due to take place in Israel. After a typically charismatic performance for Speech Day he drove to London and made a very impressive contribution to the TV discussion, along with a leading historian and two other authorities from different disciplines. Following the TV appearance he drove back to Mongewell and became the perfect host for our staff dinner.[204]

MORE INCOME TO BRITISH RAILWAYS!

At the beginning of each term and also at the end of every half-term, the boys would travel in a specially chartered train from Paddington Station to Wallingford Station, and from 1959 when Wallingford Station was closed for passenger travel,[205] (this was even prior to the "Beeching Axe" of Dr. Beeching, the Chairman of the British Railways who closed numerous train lines.) the journey terminated at Cholsey Station. The train left Paddington Station at 3.33 p.m. (an easy time to remember!). There were a number of teachers to supervise the boys on the train.[206] Joe Miller reports that on one occasion "Rabbi Rosen was waiting for us on the platform [at Paddington] to greet us, but did not join us on the train, instead driving ahead to meet us at the school."[207] In view of the "speed!" in which this Carmel train travelled, this was not a difficult assignment! Henry Law gives a graphic description of this journey:

> Carmel began at Paddington. Term began the moment our tickets were clipped by the blue-serge uniformed inspector as we passed through the barrier . . .
>
> Simmering at the end of the line [at Paddington Station] was a large black shunting engine of rugged outline, and next to it, the 'school train' three coaches attached to the back of an ordinary express. The school train must have been made up of any spare carriages which happened to be lying about; very often they were Edwardian timber-bodied, and elaborately paneled on the outside. At other times,

---

204. E-mail from Charles Marshall, 17 March 2013.
205. Goods traffic only ceased from Wallingford Station in 1965, (Wikipedia – Cholsey and Wallingford Railway).
206. Unwritten recollections of author.
207. Recollections – Joe Miller.

we enjoyed the very comfortable coaches of the 1930s, with individual pull-down armrests and reading lamps and, at least once, we were treated to a train of brand-new stock . . .

We settled down, a few leapt on at the last minute, and then we were on our way, at a spanking pace, it seemed, bringing us to Reading about 40 minutes later. . . . There our coaches were detached, the express train went on its way, and now, with our own engine we continued down the main line, eventually leaving it for the Wallingford branch which curved sharply away to the right at Cholsey.

Standing in the forecourt at Wallingford station, two or three black and orange coaches waited to take us on the final stage of our journey. Tappin's Coaches were an integral part of the school scene, being the usual means of conveyance for school outings. They were typical vehicles of the time, lavishly upholstered, always well kept.[208]

Henry Law also writes on the closing of Wallingford station:

The Wallingford branch was what was officially known as 'unrenumerative' – funny how words come and go. It went out with a bang. One warm Shabbat evening in July 1959, we were sitting outdoors in a group with Kopul Rosen when the peace was disturbed by a series of detonations. Kopul enquired what was happening, and when someone explained, he pondered for a moment. 'They've shot it,' he declared.[209]

At the end of term or the beginning of half-term, the journey (to the delight of the pupils!) was reversed. On rare occasions, instead of the train, the pupils travelled all the way by coach. It should be added, however, that going home for half-term was an innovation from Mongewell days; before then, it was limited to a visit by parents once a term for just a few hours on a Sunday,[210] even though some parents had put in a request in November 1951, for pupils to be allowed home in the future for half-term.[211] Despite this "no homes" policy, there were in fact two pre-Mongewell occasions when the boys went home for half-term. One of them was in

---

208. Reflections – Henry Law.
209. Ibid.
210. Recollections – John Fischer.
211. Rau Letters, 9 November 1951.

the summer of 1952, when they had a five-day-long weekend at home, the reason being that the school could not get any domestic staff for the Whitsun weekend,[212] and the second was in June 1953, on the occasion of the Coronation when the pupils were given a few days at home to enjoy the event with their families,[213] (with acknowledgements to the Ministry of Education who granted all schools a three-day-holiday from their studies.[214])

For the return to "home sweet home," the school had to organise the purchase of tickets and the dispatch of pupils' luggage. The author describes this:

> Before each return home for a holiday or half term, the school had to make extensive travelling arrangements. A circular was sent to all the parents telling them that there would be a special school train to Paddington. There then followed a long list of trains to the various provincial cities where the various pupils lived and the parents were informed that pupils will be escorted across London to the various terminals from where these trains departed.
>
> A few weeks before the vacation, following supper, the master in charge of travelling arrangements would go through the pupils one by one asking for details of their travelling. For the end of term, this included the luggage they intended sending in advance.
>
> All this was very tedious and when Mr. Epstein took over this task, he would hand out forms which pupils would fill up with the details. Once, when he had collected them in, he commented that 'trunk' was not spelled 'trunck'!
>
> All the tickets were then purchased and on the night before the half term or the end of term, they were given out.[215]

Other than the fairly rare visiting days, parents were not allowed to visit their sons, nor were the boys able to spend a weekend, or even a day at home.[216] There was no physical contact between the boys and their

---

212. Ibid., 11 May 1952.
213. Recollections – John Fischer. When a year and a half earlier, the King had died, a special assembly had been called "where the news was announced in solemn tones" (Recollections – Michael Ellman), and there was a further assembly which was called a few days later to hear the Proclamation of the new Queen (Rau Letters, 8 February 1952).
214. Badad, p.2.
215. 7 years, p.25.
216. Carmel College, duplicated circular from KR to parents, 7 April 1954.

families; more than that, even audio contact was forbidden, namely no telephone calls! The only contact was the impersonal contact of letters between the boys and their parents.

The light at the end of the tunnel was that after many months at the grindstone, there would be "Home Sweet Home!"

Chapter 4

Bed, Bread, and Blazers

Bedside lockers, jumbo sized saucepans, and wellington boots were no less a part of Carmel life than were the blackboards and chalk. . . .

HARD MATTRESSES AND PILLOWS

Carmel was not the Hilton! Even though it was called the "Jewish Eton," the pupils at Carmel did not have their own individual bedrooms, as was the case in Eton.[1] Instead, numerous bunk beds two-tiers high were stuffed into the rooms which were called dormitories. Some dormitories were large, others smaller, but whatever the size, almost all of them had double bunks. Next to his bed, each pupil received an itsy-bitsy size "wardrobe," to store his soap bag, towel, and other little memorabilia. For his clothes he was allocated a small cubicle in the ground floor linen room at Mongewell. The Prep School boys had their own dormitories in the building known as North Court and some members of the Sixth form had a bedroom-cum-study, with two pupils in each room, in one of the former RAF huts. When the first two new dormitory blocks were built, there were beds and not bunks for those fortunate enough to sleep there. Every boy there also had a smallish wardrobe next to his bed to store his clothes.[2]

A bed requires a mattress – unless one is in the Far East where one sleeps on a mat on the floor! Henry Law writes on Carmel mattresses,

---

1. Eton College official website – School Life – Boarding, (Internet).
2. Unwritten recollections of author.

"The mattresses were hard, though there were a few foam rubber ones to be had, if one was sharp at the beginning of term. I managed somehow to get hold of one and keep it."[3]

Unfortunately, Carmel did not have maids who went round the dormitories to make the pupils' beds every morning – this was a job for the pupils themselves. Harold Berwin comments how as a new pupil he was "initiated into the regime of making my bed with hospital corners."[4]

Pupils were allocated to dormitories according to age. This was logical, since in general the younger the pupil, the more sleep he required and hence "lights out" would be earlier. Although this was then the time for sleep, it could also be the time to clandestinely listen to radio programmes, which could be a risky enterprise! David Shaw writes:

> On my set I mainly tuned in to the ever fading Radio Luxemburg '208 Meters Medium Wave' and concerts on the Third programme. One night, Kopul entered the dorm when I was listening under the covers. If you held the speaker to your ears the volume could be very low. I did not have time to turn the set off. Had I tried it may have made a tell-tale whine or, knowing me, I would have turned the volume the wrong way and . . . confiscation . . . Or the Bastinado! As radios were disturbing after lights out, we blocked the signal by tuning in to a certain frequency. . . . Then, silence.[5]

Talking after "lights out" could lead to painful consequences. Jeffrey Gandz writes in his reminiscences of the physically "cold" dormitories at Crookham, and "Being slippered for talking after lights out – not so bad back then but today would be considered barbaric."[6] The author also received a caning for this misdemeanor, as he recalls:

> I remember at least one occasion, when together with some boys, I received this punishment [caning]. We then returned to bed and a few minutes later Mr. Carmel [the Housemaster] heard talking again. He came in and asked whether I had been talking. I honestly could not say yes or no and I did not want to lie and so I answered that I could

3. Recollections – Henry Law, Carmel College days, part 2, p.3.
4. Recollections – Harold Berwin.
5. Recollections – David Shaw.
6. Recollections – Jeffrey Gandz.

not remember. Mr. Carmel was not satisfied with that answer but another boy came to my rescue and said that I had not. Incident closed.[7]

After a tiring day, one might finally try to get into one's bed but find one it "mission impossible" – someone has made you an "apple-pie bed"! On this Michael Goitein writes:

> One of my vivid memories is of the dormitory in which I was placed when I first entered Carmel College. Perhaps eight or so iron beds, covered by dull grey blankets, situated side by side with neither privacy nor protection. I was intimidated by most of my dormitory-mates who would secretly turn back the over-sheet of my bed making it impossible to get wholly into bed, which often happened embarrassingly under the eyes of a supervising master.[8]

"Apple-pie beds" were not the only hazards in the dormitories. Sometimes one had to share them with non-humans! It is reported that:

> Momi Levy [a pupil at Carmel] felt a creeping sensation up and down his back during dovening one morning and, having scratched, and scratched, and all in vain, ran off to a room where he stripped, and still all in vain, until, pressing the sleeve of his coat, a squeak was heard. This indicated the presence of a timid mouse seeking refuge from the giants of the study block. After some encouragement, the poor 'wee timorous beastie' emerged and bolted to the fireplace."[9]

Pillows are not just for laying one's head on to sleep. They are universally also used as weapons in pillow fights. Carmel was no exception. Ian Rabinowitz writes "A pillow fight broke out in my dormitory on my first Friday night, and the formidable Kopul appeared on the scene. Although I was not involved, he sent me to stand outside his study where he left me for two hours, being very apologetic when he finally turned up."[10]

Another escapade was the hiding of slippers (and a "good hiding" with "slippers" which it led to!). Jacob Fachler relates, "Who will ever forget the slippers escapade (Stuart Cohen and two other criminals) – they took

---

7. 7 years, p.97.
8. Recollections – Michael Goitein.
9. The Young Carmelonian, p.13.
10. Recollections – Ian Rabinowitz.

one slipper from every boy in the Wolfson [dormitory] Block and hid them in a bath. The next morning, we all rushed to the window to see the boys hopping around. Despite Josh's [Gabay] promise of leniency, he slippered all 3."[11]

PRIVATE ENTERPRISE

Dormitories were allocated by the staff, and to change rooms, one needed permission. However, on two occasions during his school career, the author more or less took the law into his own hands, using dubious "permission," to make more than just small changes in the dormitory accommodation! Regarding the first of these two occasions, the author writes:

> At the beginning of my third year at the school (autumn 1955), my friends found themselves in different rooms. By that time we were more experienced in school life and routine and we decided to act and bring ourselves together into Dorm 7, which had about eight beds.
>
> We came to the necessary agreement with the boys who were then in Dorm 7 to move to other dormitories and went to speak to our housemaster who was still Mr. Carmel. He answered us, 'No changes today.' We very liberally interpreted this as 'but yes changes tomorrow!'
>
> The following day, taking advantage of the fact that he was not in the school, we implemented these changes. When he returned, he was not very pleased, to put it mildly, and I heard it reported that he said 'Who does Simons think he is making all these changes?' That evening he stood up in the dining hall and announced that anyone who had changed dormitories without permission must change back, especially those involving Dormitory 6. *I* had moved from Dormitory 6. Since we had moved 'tomorrow' and not 'today,' we 'conveniently' decided that the announcement did not refer to us! Fortunately, he never followed up the matter and we remained in Dormitory 7.[12]

The second occasion was over three years later:

---

11. Recollections – Jacob Fachler.
12. 7 years, p.97; similar version appears in "Reflections."

By the time I reached the lower sixth, these newly built dormitory blocks began to be in use and I slept in the M & S block. At this period, some of the lower sixth were given studies in the rooms on the top floor of the main building. The remainder of these small rooms were occupied by junior boys. I did not understand at the time – (I still don't understand!) – the reason why these junior boys were not put in the new dormitory blocks and the sixth form given these rooms. However, I decided that this had to be remedied. I chose a room which would make a good study for myself with two other lower sixth formers. These were Moshe Leibovich and Reuben Sawdaye. The latter had come from Iraq, where his family still lived and he had a 'guardian' in England who looked after him. I did not tell the junior boys in this room of my plans. They would have obviously done the maximum to thwart them. I couldn't just swap them over with us, since they would then have been in a room with boys of a completely different age. I had to do far more complicated changes to avoid this problem. But I soon found other boys who were glad to have an opportunity to move into the M & S block.

Since I was not the 'supreme authority' in Carmel College, I had to get some sort of permission to implement such changes. [At that period, there was a day when Kopul was in] an exceptionally wonderful mood. . . . I immediately went with Moshe Leibovich with the list of my proposed changes and asked [Kopul] whether we could implement them. He answered in the affirmative. [He did not even study the proposed list of changes!] We thus had our license. Half term was about a week away and we decided to stay behind after the school [had left] . . . and hey presto, do all the moving. . . . [This we did] . . . After several hours work in moving beds, bunks, mattresses and blankets we finished the removal work.[13]

Even prior to the above incident, when studies were limited to the "Study Block," there were complaints regarding the allocation of studies which resulted in a Letter to the Editor of the "Carmel Clarion" signed by "Disgruntled." He wrote:

---

13. 7 years, p.102. It should be mentioned here that Kopul had different "moods." On this Norman Cohen, the then Company Secretary of Carmel College Ltd. wrote, "There were days . . . when staff and boys queued up to see him, because he would refuse nothing, and there were other days when all who could, kept well away, for he would then agree to nothing." (Memories of KR p.112).

The Two Dormitory Blocks Built in 1958

I should like to protest over the unfair allocation of studies in the school. Admittedly, there is no distinction between the Shell and the Fifth form, but there are certain boys in the latter form who work hard and who require and deserve these rooms. There was a spare study in the Study Block recently, but this was given to two members of the Shell, and although I do not wish to offend these boys, and if I do so I apologise, it is obvious that they deserve this room far less than certain boys who are at present in the dormitories.

On what basis, then, are studies given? It is definitely not on merit, certainly not on hard work, nor on maturity. Perhaps an explanation will be forthcoming in the next issue of the 'Clarion.'[14]

Abraham Carmel was the Housemaster for the lower classes of the High School and his room was "Number 10" (not Downing Street!). For him, being Housemaster was not limited to supervision of the boys during their hours of sleep. He would regularly make house parties for the members of the dormitories under his care. Apart from the food, pupils as well as members of staff would put on different sorts of acts.[15]

These parties were compèred first by Brian Seaberg and later by Jeremy

---

14. Carmel Clarion, vol. 1, no.1, (p.3, pages unnumbered).
15. 7 years, p.98.

Rosen. During their compèring they would play a gramophone record of some man playing the piano and singing at the same time. Meanwhile, they would be sitting in front of a piano pretending to play and moving their lips as if singing![16]

Of the first such party, which was held in 1954, the Carmel magazine writes, "Mr. Carmel scored a spectacular success with his Junior House Party. The outstanding features were Mr. Roston's unsuccessful attempts to blow out a candle, George Mandel being eaten by a lion, and a musical dramatisation of Peter and the Wolf."[17]

One of these parties was held on Chanukah, where Mordell Klein, acting as a grandmother, and the author, acting as her grandson, put on a skit with Chanukah connections.

Here is a very, very brief extract:

Grandma: We must get the tree ready.
Grandson: It's not Christmas.
Grandma (knocking on her head): Come in, come in. Ah it's Purim.
Grandson: No grandma, it's Chanukah.
Grandma: Chanukah, Purim, what's the difference?!

Later during the course of the skit, a very long thick branch of a tree dragged onto the acting area, was thought by the "grandmother" to be "Mother Hubbard's clothes prop," but her "grandson" corrected her and said that it was "Goliath's toothpick."[18]

Abraham Carmel's Junior House Party no 6, took place in November 1956 as a "Welcome Home Rabbi and Mrs. Rosen!!"[19] Fourteen different acts were performed during this house party. They included, "Don't be late for class," "Never kick a radio," "Buns for Prefects," "Verses from the Rookery," and "We want Dave."[20]

---

16. Ibid.
17. Carmel 1954, p.10.
18. 7 years, p.98.
19. In the autumn of 1956, Kopul had gone on a fund raising tour in Australia, not for Carmel, but for Mount Scopus College (Memories of KR, p.95); even though Carmel was in a serious financial situation, Kopul would help other institutions raise money (Memories of KR, p.31). Later, Bella Rosen joined him in Australia (Carmel 1957, p.4).
20. Mr. Carmel's Junior House Party no.6, 26 November 1956, duplicated programme.

GRUB UP BOYS!!

How could one describe Carmel food – ugh or yummy?[21] Jeremy Rosen, when talking about Carmel food, comments, "School food was a constant irritant. It could never compete with home cooking of course. But over the years cooks and caterers came and went, some more successful than others. . . . Often pupils demonstrated their dissatisfaction and whenever attempts were made to establish a School or Students council or complaints committee, food always topped the list of student complaints."[22] Back in November 1951, a boy wrote in his letter home, "The food here is deteriorating,"[23] and in a later letter "We do not get enough FRESH fruit and vegetables, could you [his parents] complain to Kop [Kopul] next Sunday (half term)?"[24] On the Shavuot fare he wrote, "The cheese cake we had was simply awful, it had no flavor whatsoever."[25]

However, there was one potential pupil who had a different view of Carmel food! This occurred on a day when boys turned up at Carmel College to take the annual scholarship examination, and during the course of the day the candidates were given dinner which included kneidelach in soup – maybe it was to surreptitiously inspect their table manners! One candidate remarked that it was the best meal he had had in his life![26] The school probably thought that if he could say this about Carmel food, he would be a wonderful advertisement for Carmel College! An alternative explanation could be, that one might reasonably ask, Oy vey! What sort of food does he have at home? We had better, therefore, give him a scholarship!!

During the Kopul era, there were numerous cooks, chefs, workers, or whatever you want to call them, who worked in the kitchen. The food served, both qualitatively and quantitatively (although the latter might have been controlled by budgets), would depend on who was in charge of the kitchen. A pupil wrote on the catering during the last term at Greenham, "The food is better this term and there is still the quantity. The chef left and Miss Halberstadt is in charge of the kitchen."[27] One later chef was called Jim, but he was relegated to menial cleaning jobs, because he

---

21. Ugh and yummy are words which appear in the Merriam-Webster's dictionary.
22. Recollections – Jeremy Rosen, chap.1.
23. Rau Letters, 21 November 1951.
24. Ibid., 25 October 1952.
25. Ibid., 22 May 1953.
26. Recollections – Nigel Simons.
27. Rau Letters, 8 May 1953.

was rude to Bella Rosen.[28] Most of the kitchen staff have been forgotten, but one who will never be forgotten is Mr. Bitner! The author reminisces about him:

> I remember him screaming at someone towards the end of one breakfast, 'Breakfast is finished,' and this could be heard all over the dining hall. . . . I don't think I will forget the 'Bitner Marmite meal.' The first course was soup flavoured with Marmite. The gravy in the next course was flavoured with . . . yes, with Marmite. The last course was ice-cream – he didn't actually add Marmite to it, but by that time, I am sure that all one could taste was Marmite![29]

Stephen Morris also remembers Bitner's food, and mentions "Mr. Bitner in the kitchen and cold spaghetti sandwiches on a day out to watch the rowing on the Thames."[30]

THE DAILY STOMACH FILLER

The pupils at Carmel did not starve, unless of course they did not want to eat the food! Every weekday they were served with three meals. First was breakfast at eight o'clock. Henry Law describes this meal:

> Breakfast consisted of a dry cereal and milk. A couple of days a week it was porridge. There was no main course. On the table was sliced wholemeal bread, specially baked for the school, and that was excellent. To spread on the bread were butter, which had to be divided into seven pieces, and something sweet, usually jam or marmalade, or that old British staple, Marmite. If there was only a sweet spread I would eat plain bread and butter. Sometimes there would be very overcooked hard-boiled eggs which I found inedible. The best things were cottage cheese or thinly sliced Dutch cheese, ordinary cheddar not being kosher. As the cheeses were unpopular, when they were served I could usually get what was meant for the entire table.[31]

The recollections of the author on this meal add some further details:

---

28. 7 years, p.94.
29. Ibid.
30. Recollections – Stephen Morris.
31. Recollections – Henry Law, Carmel College days, part 1, p.12.

For breakfast every morning there was bread – as much as one could eat, butter, jam, tea, a cereal and something else. About half a packet of butter was put on each table. When I first joined the school, it was already cut into seven portions – this was the number of boys on each table. Later however, the whole chunk was put on each table – there wasn't a 'smash and grab' raid for it – someone on the table would divide it up. The cereal on some days was corn flakes, on others Weetabix, on others Sugar Puffs, on others porridge and so on. The 'something else' could be a whole variety of things, such as grapefruit, prunes, sweet corn, eggs, and so on.[32]

Julius Nehorai was not very happy with the Carmel breakfast, "Then there was breakfast with the interminably fried eggs wallowing in oil. There were over 200 boys, did they have a gigantic frying pan to cook them all in? The eggs were only slightly more desirable than the glue-like porridge."[33]

In all fairness, one could not completely describe the breakfast menu as "take it or leave it" – there was an appearance of democracy, at least in theory, on what was served. The author explains:

> The boys were sometimes given an opportunity to state their food preferences. On one occasion we had a written questionnaire. I think there were five questions on it. Amongst them was, 'What do you prefer, Cornflakes or Weetabix?' . . . On another occasion they asked the pupils to answer by a show of hands whether they would prefer hot or cold milk for breakfast. They explained that hot milk would not only be for the cereal but also for the tea. Two thirds of the school voted to keep the milk cold.[34]

Dinner was served for the Senior School at one fifteen in the afternoon; for the Prep School it was earlier. Almost every day of the week there would be a meat meal. It might be sliced beef or chopped meat or sausages or viennas, but not chicken. It would be accompanied with potatoes and various vegetables. The desert might be a tart or fresh fruit. The drink would be just a jug of water on each table – no fancy drink![35] Henry Law

32. 7 years, p.92.
33. Recollections – Julius Nehorai.
34. 7 years, p.95.
35. Ibid., p.92.

adds that the menu on Friday was "fish and chips" and that "portions were generous."[36]

In this connection, one might well ask, whether there were "seconds" of food or "just firsts and that was it!"? On this the author writes, "Sometimes there was sufficient for some boys to have seconds. For example, they might have served eights slices of meat for the seven boys on the table or there may have been a surplus in the kitchen waiting for takers."[37] Some "heads of table exercised dictatorial powers and could . . . deprive them [members of his table] of food or dispense 'seconds' to his favourites"[38] or, they might first of all take for themselves. However, other heads of tables "would be more 'democratic' and there would be a rota around the table for the allocation of these seconds."[39]

These "dictatorial powers" of the head of table often resulted in their taking the food first as soon as it reached the table. However, David Stamler intervened and said they had to take last, arguing that if there was not enough food on the table and as a result, the head of table did not receive any, he would jolly well make sure that more food arrived from the kitchen! Research was never undertaken to see if Stamler's ruling was just a "dead letter."[40]

There was an occasion when Kopul announced to the school that they should let him know if there was not enough food, adding that he couldn't promise all the food that everybody liked. Obviously there are foods where pupils would like seconds, thirds and even fourths and fifths but there is a limit, even at home![41]

Despite this, Spencer Batiste's parents could never be persuaded that the pupils "were not always on the verge of starvation." Therefore on sports days they would make a large picnic to which his friends were also invited.[42]

Supper was at quarter to seven for the Senior School and earlier for the Prep School. The menu is described by Henry Law. "The evening meal was usually a light supper of things like cheese, tinned fish, salad, potato salad, and plenty of the wholemeal bread. Sometimes there would

---

36. Recollections – Henry Law, Carmel College days, part 1, p.12.
37. 7 years, p.93.
38. Recollections – Jeremy Rosen, chap.1.
39. 7 years, p.93.
40. Ibid.
41. Ibid., p.95.
42. Recollections – Spencer Batiste, p.4.

be chips. These were by far the most popular dish."[43] In the words of Jeremy Rosen, "The pupils just wanted 'Chips with everything.'"[44]

It is not surprising that chips were the boys' favourite dish. But one cannot fry chips for two hundred people using a frying pan over the gas. Kopul realised this and soon after arriving at Mongewell, the school bought a "chip machine." He would keep the pupils updated regarding its installation with such comments as "we are waiting for a plug for it." Finally the great day came and, hurray, chips were added to the Carmel menu.[45]

Although usually the supper was milky, there were occasions when there was a second meat meal of the day. To the list of foods given by Henry Law for the supper, the author adds that sometimes there was also a soup and sometimes baked beans.[46]

The menus were not just drawn out of a hat like a conjurer's rabbit. The meals were planned since the "school wanted to offer a balanced and healthy diet."[47] Bread served at the meals was sometimes white and sometimes wholemeal. On one occasion there was a lecture in the school on nutrition and the outside speaker came out in favour of wholemeal bread. In the question time after the lecture, Bella Rosen, who used to plan out the menus for the school, told the speaker that as a result of this lecture, she would increase the percentage of wholemeal bread served at the school.[48]

In addition to the three daily Carmel meals, there was a drink served at the morning mid-day break for anyone who wanted it. "A large pan of milky cocoa would be left outside the dining room [in the vestibule] with a ladle and supply of mugs."[49] Julius Nehorai describes this drink with a certain amount of sarcasm:

> I must tell you about the cocoa. Carmel was in a culinary class of its own when it came to the beverage at morning break or 'elevenses' as the Mums of the day would call it. We'd walk to the foyer of the dining hall, . . . and finally you were rewarded with this lavender coloured drink; sugar with a bit of cocoa and surely oodles of mauve dye, served

---

43. Recollections – Henry Law, Carmel College days, part 1, p.12.
44. Recollections – Jeremy Rosen, chap.1.
45. 7 years, p.95.
46. Ibid., p.92.
47. Recollections – Jeremy Rosen, chap.1.
48. 7 years, p.92.
49. Recollections – Henry Law, Carmel College days, part 1, p.12.

from a giant pan with a ladle. The winters were so cold that you'd have drank it if it were arsenic for the warmth it provided.[50]

But beggars can't be choosers and Neil Alton describes this cocoa as "undrinkable but desperately welcome."[51]

In the afternoon, tea and sponge cake were left on a trolley in this vestibule.[52] At least the pupils at Carmel could be reasonably sure to have tea served to them each day. But not so the visitors who came to the Speech Day of 1960. At the end of the ceremony Kopul explained:

> In previous years we have tried to provide tea for all our visitors. It has proved an impossible task. We haven't a hall that can accommodate approximately 700 people and the last year we found the experiment to provide tea was a complete failure. Very few people could fight their way into the small dining hall and those who did found that more tea was spilt on their clothes and their suits than they were able to drink. If we do not provide tea today please don't regard it as any lack of hospitality on our part. I want to assure you that as soon as we have the facilities to be able to invite you to stay after Speech Day you will not find us lacking in warm hospitality.[53]

Eliot Katz poetically warns of the potential risk of even the boys not receiving their afternoon daily cake:

> He drops his book and grabs his scarf
>   And dashes for the door,
> Down the hill, across the lawn
>   And over the muddy floor;
> And as he nears the line of boys
>   He hears a person shout,
> "Too late, my boy, you've missed your chance,
>   The cake's been given out!"[54]

---

50. Recollections – Julius Nehorai.
51. Recollections – Neil Alton.
52. Recollections – Henry Law, Carmel College days, part 1, p.12.
53. Recording of Carmel College Speech Day 1960, at 1 hour 10 minutes 53 seconds from beginning.
54. Carmel Clarion. vol.1, no.1, (p.20, pages unnumbered).

Dinner at the Prep School at Crookham and the risk of not receiving one's due share is dramatically described by Julius Nehorai:

> . . . in the bleakness of faraway Crookham, Berkshire with its cold corridors and freezing dormitories and still colder food? Mashed potatoes with lumps and strangely tasting Kosher bangers, which must have been a Jewish concoction because they were shorter but fatter and the colour of no other meat I've ever seen since. That was if you were lucky enough to get one with Dr. Tobias, Toby behind his back, as head of table complaining how the boys 'steal the very food from my mouth.' But at least here you were out of range of his pinching your cheek till it bruised and affectionately exclaiming 'Mushkalano,' does anyone know what it means?[55]

In addition to their regular meals, the Prep School children whilst at Crookham had an extra "treat!" Julius Nehorai explains:

> Every night before bedtime we were given a spoonful of Malt. Radio Malt[56] it was called although I'll never know why, did it broadcast good health? There we were, all the boys in a line with the housemaster, or was it the matron, spoon in one hand and jar of malt in the other doling it out mouthful by mouthful. Was the spoon changed can anyone remember or, was that in the days when we were less fussy about such things? Gooey and sweet it was but then disaster; a new matron came on the scene and replaced it with Cod Liver Oil.[57] Ugh, ugh, ugh . . .[58]

However this "treat" did not end with Crookham. It even reached Mongewell and Joe Miller seems to have actually enjoyed it. He reports, "Going back to my first term at Carmel in September 1955, I can clearly remember all the pupils in the Prep School having to attend the Sanatorium for regular spoonfuls of Radium (*sic*) Malt. It was sweet and was supposed to help prevent us getting colds during the winter months. I

---

55. Recollections – Julius Nehorai.
56. Radio Malt was an early to mid-20th century brand of malt extract which contained vitamin A and whose contents were sickly sweet. It was supposed to ward off winter illnesses and colds and build up children's bodies.
57. Cod liver oil is a nutritional supplement which is derived from the liver of cod fish. It has high levels of omega-3 and also contains vitamins A and D.
58. Recollections – Julius Nehorai.

actually think it worked for me."[59] Jeffrey Gandz sums it up in a few words "Radio Malt – good. Cod liver oil, the liquid stuff – bad."[60]

Now to the dining room facilities during the Kopul era. When the school arrived in Mongewell, the entrance to the RAF hut dining hall was in the course of being built, but within a few months, there was a vestibule. The purpose of this vestibule was not just to protect the "poor delicate boys" from getting wet whilst waiting impatiently for the doors to open for "grub up." It was also to hold a long washing trough for netillat yadayim (washing of the hands) before the meal.[61] The numerous taps were of the push-button type, the water was cold and the towels, however often changed, never stayed clean and dry for long.[62] At a later date, paper towels were introduced. When this occurred, David Stamler told the school that he was sure that for the first few days, pupils would keep going in and out to wash their hands in order to use these paper towels, but after the novelty had worn off they should be used sparingly.[63]

Henry Law describes the dining hall furniture at Mongewell, "The tables were, I think plastic laminate with steel legs. The chairs were of a type known as Rebel Stackabye. They had tubular steel frames and the back and seat was formed of a single curved metal sheet. They were cold and uncomfortable. Apparently they are now regarded as a vintage collectable."[64] However, the boys did not have to suffer eternally with these chairs, since later in the 1950s, they were replaced by folding wooden chairs.[65]

In the dining hall there were three rows of tables along the whole length of the hall. On each table sat seven boys: three on either side, and at the end a prefect or sixth former. However, at the beginning of the Mongewell era, a teacher would sit at the head of some of the tables. At a later period, the dining room had a stage constructed along the right hand

---

59. Recollections – Joe Miller.
60. Recollections – Jeffrey Gandz.
61. 7 years, p.19.
62. Recollections – Henry Law, Carmel College days, part 1, p.11.
63. 7 years, pp.27–28.
64. Recollections – Henry Law, Carmel College days, part 1, p.12; photograph of dining hall appears in "Reflections."
65. This can be seen in the Carmel College film "Foundations for a Vision" at 11 minutes 40 seconds from beginning.

Dining Hall at Mongewell

side with a long table where all the teachers sat facing the boys.[66] This special table did not grant the teachers special food. There were no secret extras on their menu![67]

However, did the staff have better food on one Purim? Kopul said yes, but it was to laugh off a certain situation which arose! What happened was that the Governors came to the school for the Purim meal. There was no room to put all of them on the staff table and so they had to sit on tables amongst the boys. In order to avoid any possible offence, Kopul jokingly said, "We have put you on tables with the boys so that you can eat *their* food and not *our* food."[68]

After every meal, pupils, working on a rota, had to pile up the dirty plates and cutlery and carry them to the counter next to the kitchen. The head of the table invariably did not participate in these "menial" tasks. He was served but didn't serve![69] There the used utensils were washed – not by the boys – there were kitchen staff employed to do that. The pupils

66. 7 years pp.92–93; Recollections – Henry Law, Carmel College days, part 1, p.11.
67. 7 years, p.93.
68. Ibid., p.41.
69. Ibid., p.93.

were once asked in a food questionnaire whether the plates were clean. It is reported that ninety-five per cent of the school replied in the negative.[70]

LINE UP FOR EATING

What was the procedure for assembling the pupils in the dining hall for meals? This is described by Jeremy Rosen:

> In preparation for meals pupils had to assemble outside according to class in a vestibule in front of the Dining Hall with long metal troughs to wash hands. Officially everyone had to wash ritually before the meal. In practice most pupils tried to avoid it on the principle that any compulsion was to be avoided if possible. Prefects lined them up and ensured that no one moved in until instructed. Marshalling the restive students was no easy matter and it became a test of effectiveness that all new prefects had to go through. Everyone eventually filed in. Meal times in the early days were dominated by the teachers sitting up on the High Table. A different master would be on duty during the week. A small hand bell was at his disposal to get the pupils' attention.
>
> Some teachers commanded respect and could project their authority. Others struggled and a favourite pastime was to see how many pings of the bell it took to get the school to be quiet. Taking a meal was a sort of ritual blooding of new teachers who usually showed their inexperience right away. The student body was adept at testing and probing and seeing how far they could push a newcomer. One could tell whether the teacher in charge was respected or feared or not. Often the Prefects, zealous to protect authority, subtly kept control from the body of the students when teachers failed to do the necessary.[71]

Having reached their places in the dining hall, the pupils were supposed to stand by their chairs in silence. The author explains what then followed, "The master on duty would then ring the bell on the top table or would say 'Baruch' – sometimes even a non-Jewish master would say 'Baruch' – and the pupils would then say the blessing over the bread. At the end of the blessing, the master would again ring the bell, the pupils would take a piece of bread and sit down and eat it."[72]

---

70. Ibid., p.95.
71. Recollections – Jeremy Rosen, chap.1.
72. 7 years, p.28.

By the time the pupils entered the dining room, the plates and cutlery had been laid for each pupil, just like in a five-star hotel! However, the quality of the crockery did not match that of such a hotel! For milk meals, in place of a quality hotel's bone china cups, there were thick mugs – never cups! The school probably bought up surplus unused supplies from somewhere, since the cups had all sorts of names of institutions on them. For meat meals, it was more in the style of a hotel – a glass was placed on the table for each pupil.[73]

The waiters who brought the food from the kitchen were the pupils themselves.[74] The "waiters" were even in uniform – their school uniform! Pupils can sometimes, if not often, be noisy and as a result, on occasions they had to eat their meals in silence.[75] Did one have to gobble down one's food or could one eat leisurely? Henry Law writes:

> Meals always seemed to be rushed. It would take a while for all the tables to get served, and then the teacher would ping the bell to end the meal whilst I was in the middle of a mouthful, with half the meal still uneaten. . . . Later on in my time at Carmel I was able to grab more to eat after the meal had officially ended. If I was lucky I could get a full tub of cottage cheese and a couple more slices of bread.[76]

Different masters were on duty at the various meals during the week. Amongst them was Helmut Schmidt who was on duty at suppertime on one day of the week. In order to bring supper to an end so as to get the pupils into the classrooms for prep he would say "The exams have never been so close."[77] Rabbi Young would also speed up the meal but for a different reason. He writes, "One thing I recall, and that was about the length of time week-day lunch took when I was on duty. I always made a point that it should not take longer than necessary. The boys loved it. Before you looked around, I would press the bell, the boys would bentch (Grace after Meals), and their break before lessons would thereby be extended."[78]

A meal finishes with Birchat Hamazon (Grace after Meals). The author explains the procedure in Carmel for an ordinary weekday:

---

73. Ibid., p.93.
74. Ibid.
75. Ibid.
76. Recollections – Henry Law, Carmel College days, part 1, p.13.
77. Recollections – Michael Bharier, chap 4, Helmut Dan Schmidt.
78. Recollections – Rabbi Moshe Young.

During the course of the meal, a senior boy would go around the dining hall and would choose a boy to lead Birchat Hamazon. He would
write his name on a slip of paper which he would hand to the master
on duty. When the end of the meal arrived, the master would either
say 'Birchat Hamazon' or would read the name from the slip of paper.
Mr. Coles who was on duty every dinner-time, would do the latter.

The boy leading grace would then say the 'zimun,' with the other
boys answering him. The grace which was recited on ordinary weekdays was the 'Shorter Form of Grace.' The boys would recite together
until 'hazon et hakol' and then the boy leading Grace would repeat
'Baruch ata HaShem, hazan et hakol.' The boys would say 'amen' and
then continue 'nodeh lecha' until the end of that berachah and the
boy leading grace would say 'Baruch ata HaShem al ha'aretz v'al hamazon.' Then the boys would say 'amen' and continue with 'rachem'
until the end of the grace.

When I joined the school, I (as well as some other boys who had
joined at the same time) were used to the full grace and this shortened
version muddled us up. We were sitting near Dr. Tobias on one of
our first meals and he tried to point out the words in the shortened
version which didn't appear in the full version. Rabbi Rosen was also
present at a meal at this period. When he saw that some boys were
puzzled by this short version, he explained that on weekdays they said
this version.[79]

Following Birchat Hamazon was announcement time. At the dinner meal,
all the pupils would stand, but not necessarily "stand to attention," the
teachers would leave, and Romney Coles would make the announcements.[80]

THE CARMEL KOSHER KITCHEN

Needless to say, the kitchens at Carmel were kosher. Basically this meant
two things. Firstly, all the food coming into the kitchen had to be kosher
and, secondly, there had to be a strict separation between meat and milk.
To have kosher products is not so easy when one is living a long way from
an established Jewish community. Neither Newbury nor Wallingford had

---

79. 7 years, p.28. The shortened form of Grace after Meals is not some "modern composition,"
   but it appears in the writing of the Rabbis from many hundred years ago (Introduction of
   Magen Avraham on Shulchan Aruch, Orach Chaim, chap.192).
80. 7 years, p.93.

such communities. The problems of obtaining kosher food are illustrated by what David Perl wrote about the first term after Carmel was established:

> We were given meat on two occasions only and there was not a day that passed without us eating fish of some kind whether it was kippers, smoked haddock, boiled fish, fried fish or indeed any other fish that you can think of. As you can imagine we became a little upset with this monotonous routine and were seriously wondering whether some dietician had persuaded the school authorities that this was the best way of feeding us, or whether some Rabbi had decreed that this was now in strict accordance with current Jewish dietary laws! It was some months later that we learnt that neither was the case. In fact certain arrangements with the nearest Kosher butcher, who was in Reading, had not yet been completed.[81]

Fishy complaints were not limited to Carmel's first term. Joe Miller writes about the latter part of the 1950s, "For several months and it seemed like an eternity, we had pilchards every Saturday and forever after, including now I cannot look at a tin of pilchards." Joe put it down to the school buying "job lots of food" for financial reasons."[82] According to Neil Alton this resulted in the "Great Pilchards Revolt" but the kitchen staff had the last laugh by "dishing up extra cholent." According to Neil, the moral is "Be careful what you wish for."[83] Another Old Carmeli to report on "pilchards" was Harold Berwin, who recollects "Food – a topic never far from a Jewish teenager's thoughts – was better than I expected, apart from the pilchard issue. It appeared that Mr. Bitner had secured a job lot of tinned pilchards, the thought of which still turns my stomach."[84] David Shaw has a slightly different version – it was Kopul who bought this "job-lot,"[85] or, maybe Shaw was referring to a different occasion.

When the school was in Mongewell there was an attempt on one occasion to put duck on the menu, but it failed! Jeremy Rosen relates:

> I remember one incident in which several dozen ducks were bought at the local market and released onto the lake with the expectation

---

81. The Old Carmeli no.5, 1968–9, pp.27–28; Reflections – David Perl.
82. Recollections – Joe Miller.
83. Recollections – Neil Alton.
84. Recollections – Harold Berwin.
85. Recollections – David Shaw.

that they would be served up as a Shabbat meal. But the school had become so fond of them, they would feed them scraps and fend off marauding foxes, that when a shochet was brought down to kill them, no one was prepared to eat them.[86]

It was only towards the end of the 1950s that chicken would appear on the menu, and then only very occasionally. The reason was technical. It is much harder to prepare chicken than beef when dealing with hundreds of portions.[87]

Another basic commodity is bread and there was no Jewish baker in the area. The school, therefore, had their bread specially baked at a local bakery; Bella Rosen would go to the bakery to check that it was being baked according to our kashrut requirements.[88]

Another popular food, especially amongst school boys, is ice cream. In the mid-1950s, Carmel began to serve Snowcrest ice cream as the dessert on Friday night, in place of the fruit salad which they had served previously. On the first occasion when it was served, Kopul explained to the school that ice creams such as Walls or Lyons were not kosher and the school was thus buying Snowcrest.[89] A few years later, pupils could themselves buy Snowcrest ice cream at the school.[90]

Needless to say, one could not purchase Snowcrest ice cream in Wallingford. It had to come from London. Ice cream melts quickly and so it was packed in dry ice – "cardice" (solid carbon dioxide), which is much, much, colder than ordinary ice, before being sent to Carmel.[91]

After the ice cream arrived at Carmel, the dry ice was discarded in a rubbish bin just outside the entrance to the Main Building. This was rather an irresponsible thing to do, since some of the pupils would then "rescue" this dry ice and use it for their experiments which were somewhat dangerous. Julius Nehorai explains:

> Dry ice was a schoolboy's irresistible temptation and bound to lead to trouble. You couldn't touch it or it would burn your skin. Pour ink on it and it would colour beautifully, but that was one of its more peaceful

86. Recollections – Jeremy Rosen, p.5.
87. Recollections – David Shaw; 7 years, p.32.
88. Recollections – Jeremy Rosen, p.1.
89. 7 years, pp.27, 32.
90. Ibid., p.96.
91. At atmospheric pressure carbon dioxide changes from a gas to a solid (dry ice) at a temperature of $-78.5°C$, compared with ice which turns to water at $0°C$.

applications. Put it in a sealed bottle with some water and you have a Molotov cocktail but no one told us that. We found out for ourselves when we threw such a bottle into the Thames and a few moments later, in an explosion of water and broken glass one boy got a deep cut in his leg and had to be rushed off to the hospital for stitches.[92]

Spencer Batiste was also once involved in a dry ice explosion. This time a boy was not injured – it was Kopul's car which received the brunt of the explosion! Spencer reports:

> I remember, after a chemistry lesson with Romney Coles about dry ice, a group of us decided to explore those properties further. In all innocence we made a dry ice bomb which we located in what we thought was a safe position and retreated to watch the results. Unfortunately, Kopul chose that moment to park nearby. The explosion was much greater than we had expected and Kopul did not take kindly to the shrapnel damage to his car. I resolved there and then not to make my career in the arms trade.[93]

It is not recorded what punishment the perpetrators received – physically painful or otherwise.

There was yet another group of pupils, namely David Shaw & Co, who wanted to increase their scientific understanding of dry ice. David Shaw explains, "One game was to find a bottle with a good stopper and put some ink in it. We then put dry ice in and sealed it. We used to go to the shallow part of the river by the Boat House and throw the bottle in. After a while it exploded with force sending a plume of blue down-stream. Our ordnance experiments on dry land were, I admit very dangerous."[94]

Many pupils came from homes where kashrut was not observed and as Jeremy Rosen writes, "Finding ways to import non-kosher food into the school became something of a game of cat-and-mouse."[95]

It was impossible to stop pupils bringing food from home at, for example, the beginning of term, some of which might well have been non-kosher. The non-kosher status of these foods could have been inadvertent, since, especially at that period, many Jews, who would never dream of

92. Recollections – Julius Nehorai.
93. Recollections – Spencer Batiste, p.3.
94. Recollections – David Shaw.
95. Recollections – Jeremy Rosen, chap.1.

going to a non-kosher butcher, did not realise that such things as cakes or
biscuits, might well contain non-kosher ingredients.

During term time, parents would find ways to pass on to their sons at
Carmel, foodstuffs which might not be kosher. Michael Goitein relates
how he received contraband cakes during term time:

> I was very fond of a particular really delicious coffee cake made at a
> small tea shop, the Bindery, in Broadway. Knowing this, my mother
> on one occasion smuggled in one of these cakes to me. Both the
> cake and the visit from my mother were highly illegal; boys were not
> supposed to hoard food, and parents were not supposed to visit their
> sons except on the very infrequent designated parents' visiting days.
> However, my mother was not one to be stopped by such trifling reg-
> ulations. I stashed the cake in the back of my bedside cabinet – and
> never touched it! At the end of term it was discovered: uneaten, hard
> as a rock, and covered with a green mold. Since I really liked this kind
> of cake and would normally have devoured it at one sitting, this was
> all very odd, and it must have had some strong significance, but to this
> day I do not understand what that might have been.[96]

Maybe the answer is Heavenly intervention! There was another incident
of a cake that did not go moldy – it had no opportunity to do so since it
was eaten post-haste, but not by its intended recipient pupils. It was David
Shaw's birthday cake and he relates:

> I am minded of a time when my mother baked me a birthday cake and
> sent it to the school for me. We had a kosher home but I was not al-
> lowed to take it 'in case' it was not kosher enough for the school. The
> next thing I knew the staff were eating it. I threw a tantrum. What I
> did not know was that the staff had made me another one. By the time
> they told me it was too late. . . . No cake . . . sob sob.[97]

Pupils were allowed after receiving an exeat [written permission to leave
school grounds] to go down to Wallingford. It is not at all surprising that
some used the opportunity to patronise the local restaurants there. David

---

96. Recollections – Michael Goitein.
97. Recollections – David Shaw.

Frome writes, "who can forget the cream teas at the Fleur de Lys in Wallingford – heaven."[98]

In addition to going to restaurants whilst in Wallingford, some pupils would order food from that town and have it delivered secretly. Stephen Morris writes, "The taxi coming down the back drive, lights off, at night with the fish and chips from Wallingford. What was the name of that firm?"[99] Joe Miller elaborates:

> There were many school societies that placed notices on the notice board outside the dining room. I formed a society that requested you to put your name on the list below if you wished to attend. But it was in fact a decoy for those wishing to order fish and chips. We ordered them and met Jims Taxi at the bottom of the back drive. On one occasion we had to hide in the ditch enabling Mr. Schmidt to pass in his bubble car without seeing us![100]

TUCK SHOP – READ: THE CARMEL MONOPOLY

As in many other schools, Carmel had a tuck shop, but as Anthony Rau commented in October 1950, "The Tuck Shop is quite good but quite expensive."[101] The tuck shop was originally run by Miss Valerie Arons. Julius Nehorai writes about one of Miss Arons' food specialties, "[She] "introduced me to homemade cream cheese. The preparation required two muslin bags of cream-cheese to be hung on a clothes line outside the kitchen to let the moisture drip out which were forever known as Mrs. Aarons *(sic)* knickers!"[102] Moshe Benaim has a particular memory of this tuck shop, "I remember the tuck-shop with the lady in charge [Miss Arons] asking us if we decided to purchase a packet of crisps as to whether 'Mit or Mittout' (salt)."[103]

Valerie Arons would take payment in the tuck shop in any form, even if it was a crossed postal order with a pupil's name on it.[104] The tuck shop, which was housed in a shed near the dining room, was the place most pupils made a bee line for the moment the bell went for mid-morning or

---

98. Recollections – David Frome.
99. Recollections – Stephen Morris.
100. Recollections – Joe Miller.
101. Rau letters, 5 October 1950.
102. Recollections – Julius Nehorai.
103. Recollections – Moshe Benaim.
104. 7 years, p.95.

mid-afternoon break. The main items were of course chocolates, sweets, crisps, and soft drinks.[105] After Valerie Arons left,[106] various senior prefects took over the tuck shop with varying degrees of success until Raymond Dwek in 1959 became the supremo. For the first time, commercial expertise and a surprising degree of professionalism were brought into running the tuck shop, expanding the stock, increasing efficiency, and providing a really expert service.[107]

One might think that on a visiting day one could get a large sum of money from one's family, and with it buy tuck galore! At least on one occasion such dreams of eating mounds and mounds of tuck came to naught! Anthony Rau explains, "On Monday morning, Kop[ul] came round all the classes and collected all the money that parents (& rich uncles) had given these boys on Sunday. He collected the money because he made a rule that no money other than pocket money was to be received by boys during the term."[108] This gathering in of the money was surely to the financial detriment of the tuck shop!

Various opinions were expressed on the quality of the stock-in-trade of the tuck shop. Julius Nehorai had some mixed comments about the potato chips sold at the tuck shop:

> You could buy a packet of Smiths Crisps for thruppence. Inside a little bag of salt was neatly tied in blue greaseproof paper. I'm not sure why because it was usually too soggy to use anyway. Boy they tasted good but was it because I was forever hungry or because, to me, they were the top of the line and like today's Kettle crisps which fetch premium prices?[109]

The tuck shop had a monopoly, at least officially, in Carmel. The author explains:

> You couldn't even go into competition with the tuck shop, by your Yiddishe Mamma sending you tuck parcels. This was forbidden and to

---

105. Ibid.; Recollections – Jeremy Rosen, chap.1.
106. She then found a job in the kitchens of Jews' College. When the author had occasion to visit that place in the early 1960s, she said, "I recognize you!" It seems that she lived on the premises of Jews' College, since there is a Jewish New Year Card from her with her address given as that of Jews' College, (National Trust Collection, Inventory Number 92082).
107. Recollections – Jeremy Rosen, chap.1.
108. Rau Letters, 9 November 1951.
109. Recollections – Julius Nehorai.

*Miss Valerie Arons running the Carmel College Tuck
Shop*

make sure you kept the rules, all packages received by the boys went
through the 'censoring department.' They were opened and any tuck
inside them would be retained and only be handed over to you at the
end of each term. It was unfortunate for you if it were perishable.[110]

110. 7 years, p.96.

A few months after moving to Mongewell, Kopul sent a circular to parents which included this subject:

> The school tuck shop has an abundant supply of fruit, biscuits, choc-
> olates and sweets of every variety . . . In view of the existing tuck
> shop, no food parcels are necessary and *parents are hereby informed*
> *that parcels of food or confectionary must not be sent to the school. We shall*
> *enforce this rule strictly, and any parcels which are sent will be readdressed*
> *to the sender.*[111]

The consolation is that by returning them to the sender, the perishables would not have perished, but according to the recollections and personal experience of the author, this was not the case – they were retained at the school and handed over at the end of term![112] This was an example of the maxim "Publish or Perish!" Kopul published one thing, but in the end the tuck often perished!

Needless to say, pupils tried to get around this monopoly. One of them was Stephen Gold who writes:

> Those of us who survived the terrible food and the expeditions to
> the tuck-shop where Ms. Arons[113] ruled supreme, may sympathise
> with [the] following story. My late Father ran a Kosher restaurant and
> because his darlings shouldn't go hungry, shipped food parcels care
> of Wallingford post office, (poste restant), where I was delegated to
> shlap down to the village and rescue said food! Koppel *(sic)* got to hear
> of this wheeze and captured me one winter's evening and confiscated
> said food parcel!! Oh the shame oh the hunger! and soon after my
> leaving school, Koppel *(sic)* often ate in the restaurant and on one
> happy occasion I confiscated his lokshen soup! He of course saw the
> joke!![114]

Another example of bringing in tuck, but this time on a "commercial scale" following the half-term home visit during the spring term of 1954, was reported in "The Young Carmelonian." "On their return [from half-

---

111. Circular to Parents from KR dated 7 April 1954, section: Pocket Money and Tuck Shop, underlining in original.
112. Unwritten recollections of author.
113. There is a photograph of Miss Arons in the tuck shop in "Reflections."
114. Recollections – Stephen Gold.

term], many boys were found to be in possession of sufficient tuck to open a large departmental store. The House masters had a very busy time removing large quantities of food from the dormitories."[115]

In the late 1950s, the school acquired a coca cola machine and various chocolate machines. Carmel magazine added humorously that "the rumour that the school is to purchase cigarette machines and pin-tables is entirely unfounded."[116]

However, maybe there were some pupils who considered that tuck included cigarettes, but for some reason, perhaps because of an "oversight!" they were not sold in the school tuck shop. It is possible, that they were reserved for staff since the Carmel magazine writes on this that "Rabbi Leperer . . . has quickly established himself as the Tuck Shop's leading customer for tobacco."[117] Pupils, however, had to obtain nicotine products either by buying them elsewhere, or, perhaps in a less honest manner. Julius Nehorai makes a confession:

> Not many of my contemporaries may know this but the Principal [Kopul] kept a small stash in one of his desk drawers. I confess a guilty secret when I tell you that I, and a compatriot who shall remain nameless because I can't remember who he is, but would be very happy to hear from him if he is familiar with this tale, crept down to his study and became thieves in the night by helping ourselves to a supply from his hoarde. There, I've lived with it all of these years, catharsis, the guilt is expunged.[118]

The first Carmel sports pavilion burnt down, at the beginning of January 1958.[119] According to Neil Alton, pupils' cigarettes caused this conflagration. He writes, "Those heroes who smoked theirs behind the cricket pavilion and burned it down."[120] Jeremy Rosen comments, "Nineteen fifty-eight had started off ominously with a fire that destroyed the cricket pavilion during vacation time, a surprise in itself given the amount of smoking that went on around it during term time."[121]

However, the "Jewish Chronicle had a news item which more than

---

115. The Young Carmelonian, p.27.
116. Carmel 1958, p.6.
117. Carmel 1961, p.4.
118. Recollections – Julius Nehorai.
119. Jewish Chronicle, 10 January 1958, p.28.
120. Recollections – Neil Alton.
121. Recollections – Jeremy Rosen, chap.1.

hinted at the culprits for this conflagration. It was headed "Fire at Carmel College" with the sub-heading "Cricket Pavilion Destroyed." The article continued:

> The timbered cricket pavilion donated by Sir Lewis Sterling to Carmel College in 1954 was completely destroyed by fire last week.
>
> The fire, which is thought to have been started by a cigarette, blazed the more easily as pots of paint had been stored in the building, and the fire brigade was unable to save any of the sports equipment kept in the pavilion.
>
> Rabbi Kopul Rosen, the Principal of Carmel College, estimated the cost of the damage at £1,200.
>
> The fire occurred while the college was on holiday, but the school buildings were being used by participants in the Jewish Agency's Hebrew Seminar.[122]

The Carmel boys thus had an alibi which was "beyond all reasonable doubt!"

NO TOP HATS!

Even though Carmel was called the "Jewish Eton," unlike in Eton, the boys did not wear top-hats. The clothes were more conventional and had similarities to other schools. Like other boarding schools, Carmel brought out a series of clothes lists.

The first of such lists appeared in the "Provisional Prospectus" issued in the spring of 1948. The section dealing with clothing was headed "Uniform and Outfit" and began:

> For daily informal use all boys will wear the school uniform of a grey flannel shirt with a collar attached, grey shorts, grey stockings and black shoes or boots, with the addition in cold weather of a grey long-sleeved pull-over and the college navy-blue blazer. This uniform is smart, practical and healthy.
>
> For formal or best wear: dark grey flannel suits (long trousers), white shirts and collars, the school tie, grey socks and black shoes.

---

122. Jewish Chronicle, 11 January 1958, p.28.

*The Original
Carmel College Cap*

The College cap will be worn when head wear is necessary. (Straw hats will not be worn by the boys.)[123]

This introduction to the clothes list speaks of a "college navy-blue blazer," "school tie," and "school cap." One can immediately see from the colour of the blazer, namely "navy-blue," that it was not the well known purple Carmel blazer. Indeed, the original uniform was quite different from that of the latter days. Jeremy Rosen elaborates, "Originally the school uniform was simple and non-descript. Two silver letters C faced each other on the front of a blue cap and on the pocket of a blue blazer. The uniform was available at a department store called Daniel Neale that used to be situated just off Oxford Street."[124]

The prospectus then went on to give a detailed list of clothing and the quantity of each item. In addition to the items mentioned above, it included: two sets of underwear, six handkerchiefs with the additional note "khaki or some other dark neutral colour is recommended," an overcoat and macintosh, a warm dressing gown, one pair of strong leather slippers, and the various items of clothing for football and gym. The list ended,

---

123. Carmel College Provisional Prospectus, undated (about April 1948), section: Uniform and Outfit.
124. Recollections – Jeremy Rosen, chap.1; the school cap with the "two C's" can be seen in a photograph of a pupil taken at that period.

"one toilet bag containing brush and comb, tooth brush and paste, soap box and soap, flannel or sponge." The list also included two medium or large towels.[125] Strangely enough, pyjamas were not included on the list.

The school bills of that period had an item "toothpaste" and since on the school bill for Charles Gale, dated August 1949, there is an extra of 10 pennies for toothpaste, it would seem that the school kept a supply of this commodity.[126]

During the first years of the school, ties only had to be worn with formal dress. From photographs of the pupils taken during this period, it can be seen that there are some pupils with ties, whilst others are tieless with open neck shirts.[127] Any laxity in school dress was not allowed to continue indefinitely and in January 1951, a pupil, Anthony Rau, wrote home in a postscript to a letter, "Clothing rules will be very strict. You might have to buy me another grey suit.[128] A few days later he wrote, "Only black shoes & grey suits may be worn. So I cannot wear my brown shoes,"[129] and a few weeks later, "The school pullovers (official, made by Harrods) have arrived; they cost 35s 6d, and it is COMPULSORY to have one."[130]

But despite this tightening up of school dress, did the pupils then have to wear a tie all the time? An undated Prospectus brought out in about 1951,[131] refers to both "informal" and "formal" wear, only the latter requiring a tie. Only in "informal" wear was the School blazer, the Harrods purple one, included, and the shirt that one had to wear was as before, "grey flannel with collar attached." The formal wear did not include the school's purple coloured uniform, with the exception of the tie, and the pullover which was referred to as an optional extra. In "formal" wear, in place of the school blazers, grey suits were to be worn, and the shirts were to be white, "preferably with a loose collar."[132] The school had presumably come to the conclusion that the boys would make their white shirt collars dirty faster than the rest of their white shirts, and so they recommended detachable ones!

---

125. Carmel College Provisional Prospectus, undated (about April 1948), section: Uniform and Outfit.
126. Carmel College school bill for Charles Gale, dated 18 August 1949; (since this bill was reproduced in "Reflections," the name has not been withheld here).
127. There are photographs of groups of Carmel boys from the Greenham era, with some wearing ties, whilst others had open necked shirts.
128. Rau Letters, 12 January 1951.
129. Ibid., 16 January 1951.
130. Ibid., 31 January 1951.
131. The clothes in this Prospectus accord with what Rau wrote.
132. Carmel College Prospectus, undated (about 1951), section: Uniform and Outfit.

The school's purple coloured uniform must have seemed strange to the locals in Newbury as Tzvi Hirshfeld writes, "Our outings to Newbury always aroused curiosity with the local townsfolk, especially with our peaked, purple caps and purple blazers with their odd looking badge!"[133]

Meanwhile, a new clothes list had been brought out by the school. It was more comprehensive than the original list[134] and it probably came out when in about 1950 the school uniform was drastically changed to the famous Carmel purple coloured uniform, obtainable from Harrods.

The headings on this clothes list give: the numbers of each item that the parent had actually sent to the school; the minimum number of an item required; the name of the item; the number received at the beginning of the term, and the number returned at the end of the term.[135]

The first item on this list was a trunk to transport the boy's clothing and effects backwards and forwards at the beginning and end of each term. Trunks were made of different materials and were of different vintages. Henry Law writes about his trunk and its dispatch, "A 1930s cabin trunk was obtained second hand from somewhere. . . . All the things were packed into the trunk and collected by a British Railways van for delivery to the school. That was a service costing five shillings . . . which made it excellent value for money."[136] An alternative way of sending the trunk was by Carter Paterson (later known as British Road Service) but it took longer.[137]

During term time, these trunks had to be stored somewhere, and in Mongewell there was a red-brick outhouse about fifty yards behind the Main Building and in this building the trunks were piled sky high. Towards the end of each term, these trunks were brought into the corridor of the Main Building and this was the sign that the holidays (read: freedom!) were near![138]

The next item on this clothes list was a "Playbox." This was a medium sized wooden box with a lock, not usually for toys but for storing tuck – thus a "tuck box" would be a more appropriate name.[139] This indeed was the receptacle in which pupils could store the tuck they brought from home at the beginning of term, or they purchased from the tuck shop, or

133. Recollections – Tzvi Hirshfeld.
134. Carmel College Clothes List, issued about beginning of 1950s.
135. Carmel College Clothes List, issued during the 1950s.
136. Recollections – Henry Law, Carmel College days, part 1, p.1.
137. 7 years, p.13.
138. Ibid., p.24.
139. This was the period when the Jennings books by Anthony Buckeridge were written and in a picture in the frontispiece of Anthony Buckeridge's *Jenning's Diary* (London: Collins, 1953), one can see part of such a playbox. Jennings' school also had a tuckbox room (ibid., p.25).

CARMEL COLLEGE

Clothes List from about 1950

CLOTHES LIST

Name..   School No..............   Term................

Filled in by Parent Number Sent	MINIMUM Number Required		Filled in by Matron	
			Number Received	Number Returned
		ALL TERMS		
	1	Trunk		
	1	Playbox		
	1	Handbag or Case		
	1	Travelling Rug		
	1	Raincoat		
	2	Grey Flannel Suits, long trousers		
	*1	Blazer		
	1	Flannel or Grey Tweed Jacket, for rough wear		
	2 prs.	Grey Flannel Trousers		
	1 pr.	Grey Flannel Trousers, for rough wear, etc.		
	*1	Grey Pullover, for best wear, sleeveless if preferred		
	*1	Grey Pullover, strong, with sleeves, for everyday wear		
	6 prs.	Grey Socks		
	3	Grey Flannel Shirts, collar attached, for everyday ("Viyella" or "Clydella" are recommended)		
	3	White Shirts, collar attached, for best wear		
	3	Vests or Singlets		
	3 prs.	Pants or Under-shorts		
	1 pr.	Dungaree Overalls		
	1	Warm Dressing Gown		
	3 prs.	Pyjamas		
	3	Bath Towels		
	3	Smaller Towels		
	4	Sheets		
	3	Pillow Cases		
	10	Handkerchiefs		
	*1	Cap		
	*2	Ties—School ties ONLY may be worn		
	*1	Belt		
	*1	Scarf		
	1 pr.	Cotton Shorts for P.T. and Games		
	1	Cotton Singlet for P.T. and Games		
	2 prs.	Strong Leather Shoes (at least one pair must be black)		
	1 pr.	House Shoes		
	1 pr.	Bedroom Slippers		
	1 pr.	White Canvas Gym. Shoes		
	1 pr.	Wellingtons		
	4	Double Coat-hangers		
	2 ozs.	Grey Mending Wool		
		Supply of Name Tapes for School use		
	2	Brushes and Blacking for Shoes		
	1	Shoe-bag, 18-in. x 2-ft.		
		Braces and Garters		
		Hairbrush and Comb		
		Sponge Bag, Flannel, Soap-box, Nail-brush, Tooth-brush and Paste, Nail File and Scissors		
		SCIENCE BOYS ONLY		
	1	White full-length coat, detachable buttons		
		WINTER AND SPRING TERMS		
	1	Overcoat, Grey Tweed is recommended		
	1 pr.	Warm Gloves		
	*2	Football Jerseys		
	2 prs.	Football Shorts, 1 white, 1 blue		
	*2 prs.	Football Stockings		
	1 pr.	Football Boots (at least one size SMALLER than size of shoes)		
		SUMMER TERM		
	§1	White Sweater		
	1 pr.	Bathing Trunks		
	1 pr.	Cricket Boots or Shoes		
	1 pr.	Strong Sandals		
	1 pr.	White Flannel Trousers		
	2	Extra White Shirts for Cricket		

THIS LIST SHOULD BE FILLED IN CAREFULLY AND RETURNED IN TRUNK

All articles marked :— * To be obtained from the official outfitters, HARRODS Ltd Knightsbridge
London SW 1

§ Are not essential.

Flannel Suits for best wear and Flannels for everyday wear should be MEDIUM GREY in colour. Navy and Brown Suits may not be worn.

Grey or Azure Aertex Shirts may be worn instead of Flannel Shirts during the Summer Term.

Toys and Books to be listed and packed in the Playbox.

The Handbag should contain:—Health Certificate, Ration Book, Keys to Trunk and Playbox, Towel, Brush and Comb and all Toilet necessities, Two Handkerchiefs, Pyjamas, House Shoes.

It is requested that boys return to School in their everyday clothes.

All Clothes and other articles to be marked clearly with the owner's name with Cash's name tapes. (Indian ink marking is not sufficient). An additional supply of name tapes for School use to be sent. Leather Boots and Shoes to be marked with the School number in brass nails on the sole under the instep. Key rings to have a brass or other metal name-plate. At least 2 keys must be sent; one key will be retained in linen room.

The Carmel College Clothes List from about 1950

they surreptitiously smuggled into the school! The school had to find a place where pupils could store their tuck boxes, and also where they could have reasonable access to them. Carmel's first location was Greenham, and David Perl writes, "There was a basement [at Greenham Lodge] in which was housed the boiler room and the tuck room – the words "tuck shop" were not known to us. The tuck room housed our tuck boxes each containing our most precious belongings and edibles behind carefully and securely locked lids."[140] In Crookham, the gymnasium had a concrete floor and the walls were lined with the tuck boxes.[141]

In Mongewell, there was what seemed to be a wartime damp brick air-raid shelter, very close to the Main Building, which was used to house the tuck boxes. Jeffery Gandz' memories of this room are not pleasant ones, "I can smell the dank, sour odour of the tuckbox room at Mongewell Park."[142] It is always tempting to eat one's tuck "today" and not think of "tomorrow." Julius Nehorai writes, "No matter how you stuffed them [tuck boxes] you'd run out of tuck by the first week or ten days of term with nothing much left for the remainder."[143]

In 1958, there was a change in the tuck box room arrangements which led to a anonymous letter in the "Carmel Clarion" (although it is not clear why the writer did not want to sign his name!):

> I would like to bring to your readers' attention the congested and untidy state the Senior School tuck-box room is in, since the recent change. This gives about *30* boxes belonging to Prep. School boys more than ample room, whilst at least *150* boxes are crammed into the other room; it is a lucky boy who can get to his box without climbing over mountains of tuck-boxes and heaving three others off it before he eventually gets to his own.
>
> On account of the congested condition it is impossible to clean the room, and there is no lighting other than a fairly small window which lets in very little light anyway. This could lead to a dangerous fall.
>
> If a return to the old system is not practicable, I only hope that some way will be found to solve this problem.[144]

---

140. The Old Carmeli no.5, 1968–9, p.28; Reflections – David Perl.
141. Recollections – David Shaw.
142. Recollections – Jeffrey Gandz.
143. Recollections – Julius Nehorai.
144. Carmel Clarion, vol.1, no.1, (p.15, pages unnumbered).

Let us also now return to clothes lists. Although the revised clothes list included the items which were on the original list from 1948, there were now additions in both the various items and in the quantities. For example, instead of two sets of underwear there were three; instead of six handkerchiefs there were now twelve. This time pyjamas appeared on the list (and by at least 1957, "pyjama cords" appeared as an extra on the Carmel bills[145])! Under the item "Gray Flannel Shirts, collar attached, for everyday" was a bracketed comment "'Viyella' or 'Clydella' are recommended."[146] It was not reported whether "Viyella" and "Clydella" were the names of those who donated to Carmel, or whether it was just a free advertisement for shirts!

Also new on this list were dungaree overalls, to be worn during art lessons, and for "science boys only" there was a white full-length coat with detachable buttons. The list also had the sports clothes for the summer term (in addition to the sports clothing for the winter and spring terms). Sheets and pillow cases also appeared on this list, as did a travelling rug. The pupils did not use this rug to cover their knees when travelling to and from Carmel. It ended up as a blanket on their beds, and this possibly enabled Carmel to purchase fewer blankets![147]

Joe Miller recalls another item of clothing which was then on the clothes list, namely "some very strange black house shoes with elastic across the front instead of shoe laces that were to be worn when we returned to the dormitory in the evening."[148] Although this item, called "House Shoes," appeared on the clothes list,[149] the author cannot recollect anyone, even if they had bought such shoes, bothering to change into them when entering the dormitory!

Many of the items of clothing, such as the blazer, cap, tie, scarf, pullover, socks, and some of the football items were specifically Carmel uniform (which from about 1950 was the purple uniform and remained throughout Carmel's history), and had "to be obtained from the official outfitters, Harrods Ltd."[150] Jeremy Rosen elaborates on this:

---

145. Carmel College, sample school bill, April 1957, (name withheld).
146. Carmel College Clothes List, issued about beginning of 1950s.
147. Carmel College Clothes List, issued about beginning of 1950s; unwritten recollections of author.
148. Recollections – Joe Miller.
149. Carmel College Clothes List, issued about beginning of 1950s.
150. Carmel College Clothes Lists, issued in the 1950s.

The school designed a completely new outfit based on a purple blazer which was now available at Harrods. Purple was dominant, together with red, blue, silver, and gold. These were the primary colours of the Biblical Tabernacle. The central motif of the school crest was the Seven Branch Candelabrum of the Tabernacle and Temple, which initially was also the official symbol of the State of Israel. Two smaller icons on either side of candelabrum represented the Ten Commandments symbolizing the Written Law and a book representing the Talmudic tradition. Below were seven Torah scrolls, the 'Seven Pillars of Wisdom' as referred to in the Book of Proverbs. The school motto, 'Know Him (G-d) in All Thy Ways,' also came from Proverbs (3:6) and was taken to mean that one should follow the values and ideals as laid down in the Bible in whatever one did in life. The acrostic of the three Hebrew words, Bechol Derachecha Daeyhu , also stood for the term that Balaam used to describe the Israelites in Numbers 23: 'A people that dwells alone (BaDaD).'

The school tie was purple with silver, gold and blue stripes. Sub-prefects had ties of blue with one silver stripe and prefects had ties of silver with two blue stripes. . . . Not only was all this expensive but the supplier, Harrods, was not a cheap store.[151]

The Carmel cap had a certain peculiarity as the author relates, "[The] Carmel cap had a very long peak and I recollect a boy in Edgware calling after me 'violet long peak'."[152]

Another item of school uniform, although it did not appear on the school clothes list was the school cuppel which was, like the uniform, purple. Jeremy Rosen reports, "[a] purple cuppel, [was] required for religious services, meals and Jewish Studies but not obligatory at other times. Most pupils chose not to."[153] John Fischer, who was one of the first pupils at the school, says that not only was it "not obligatory" but that "it is worth recalling that with the exception of learning Hebrew, praying and eating, boys were actually discouraged from wearing a kippah, as it was considered unnecessary; only if our parents requested it could we do so – unimaginable these days!"[154] However, one might add that at about

151. Recollections – Jeremy Rosen, chap.1.
152. 7 years, p.13.
153. Recollections – Jeremy Rosen, chap.1.
154. Recollections – John Fischer; similar comments from Abraham Levy.

that period the Hasmonean Boys School had the same principle, as related by an Old Boy of that school, "Hasmonean was started by Yekkes. In the German Jewish tradition, the 'capple' was used *exclusively* in religious contexts, e.g., praying. In the early years of Hasmo, the school rules required pupils to wear it during religious studies lessons, and *forbade* wearing it in secular contexts. Only pupils (typically of eastern European extraction) who brought a note from home saying it was their custom could wear one all the time."[155]

One did not always have to traipse around the shops to buy clothes! Shepherd and Woodward, a clothing shop from Oxford, would periodically come to Carmel to sell their wares[156] – only when the parents got the next school bill did they learn what their offspring had bought![157]

How could the clothes of one pupil be identified from those of another pupil? Underlined instructions appeared towards the bottom of the Clothes List, "All Clothes and other articles to be marked clearly with the owner's name with Cash's name tapes." This was followed by "Indian ink marking is not sufficient." To cover the eventuality that a name tape might become detached or that, during term-time, a pupil might buy an item of clothing from, for example, Shepherd and Woodward, there was a further instruction, "An additional supply of name tapes for School use to be sent." But what about shoes where it would be very problematic to sew on a Cash's name tape? For this the instruction was "Leather Boots and Shoes to be marked with the School number in brass nails on the sole under the instep." Pupils had to bring a key ring to school holding the keys of the trunk and tuckbox. Generally speaking the key rings of different pupils are of similar design and so the instruction was "Key rings to have a brass or other metal name-plate." To cover the eventuality that a pupil might lose his key ring and thus cause a problem at the end of the term when the time came to pack his trunk, the instruction continued, "At least 2 keys must be sent; one will be retained in linen room."[158]

Towards the end of the 1950s, a slightly amended clothes list came out. A few items, namely, the travelling rug, the scarf and belt and a white sweater for the summer term were deemed "not essential." Dungarees had disappeared from the list. Suits had also disappeared from the list, the

---

155. Hasmo Legends XV!, Itzy Sabo, (Internet).
156. Two receipts from Shepherd and Woodward, Oxford, for two pair of socks, (price 6s 0d and 6s 11d) dated 22 January [1959] (name withheld).
157. Carmel College school fees bill dated April 1959, (name withheld).
158. Carmel College Clothes Lists from the 1950s.

reason being that at that period the school had instituted the wearing of a school "tunic."[159] On the breast pocket of this tunic was emblazed the school crest. These tunics became the weekday uniform for classes below the sixth form.[160] Unlike other school uniform items which were obtained from Harrods, the clothes list stated that "School tunics can be obtained at the College."[161] Prior to their being issued, someone went around the classes to measure each pupil to know the size tunic he required. Not only were the sixth form allowed to wear suits instead of the school tunics, they were also allowed to wear a trilby instead of the school cap.[162]

Clothes lists can only itemise which clothes are required, but whether a boy wears such clothes in a smart manner or in a slovenly one, depends to a large extent on the pupil. Kopul would have been happy if every boy would have been as particular in his dress as he personally was, but with a school of hundreds of pupils, this was just a pipe dream!

159. Carmel College Clothes List from end of 1950s.
160. Unwritten recollections of author.
161. Carmel College Clothes List from end of 1950s.
162. Unwritten recollections of author.

Chapter 5

The Most Memorable Days

One could not booze, at least officially, at Carmel, but the select few could at least have the taste of Kiddush wine. . . .

THE UNIQUE DAY OF THE WEEK

One of the most memorable facets of Carmel life, which was remembered by the alumni, even long after they left the school, was Shabbat at Carmel. In an article which appeared in the Carmel magazine for 1954, one of the pupils writing under the pen-name "A Nistar" (which can be loosely translated as "anonymous") wrote an article summarising and commenting on a Carmel Shabbat:

> Whenever I think of Shabbat in Carmel one thought seems uppermost in my mind – Shabbat is the most memorable day of the week. There is little organised activity and yet much seems to take place. I would like to record some impressions but there are so many and they are all so vivid that whatever I write will be only a very pale image of the real experience.
>
> The services are unlike those we know elsewhere; they are jollier and we take part in them with the 'Sheliach Tzibbur.' I do not think that the pleasant atmosphere is due only to the fact that the boys conduct the services and the reading of the law; everyone seems less formal and freer to pray and sing, and the final handshake with the masters puts a stamp of friendliness on the occasion.
>
> The Zemiroth at the table are a unique feature. We have grown so accustomed to the singing that we cannot judge what an impression

the Zemiroth make on visitors who spend Shabbat at Carmel for the first time. What a glorious untrained rapturous noise we make when we are caught up by the rhythm and melody of a popular 'niggun,' and how the school responds quickly when hearing a melody for the first time.

The Shiurim when masters give informal lessons teaching many subjects that are not covered in the normal time-table. When one of the masters, whose name I shall not mention, is in good form, the Shabbat lesson becomes one long session of laughter and we leave with enough jokes to fill a booklet.

Much more, so much more that cannot be described, at least not by me; I cannot, however, fail to mention the Havdalah, this lovely ceremony with which the Shabbat concludes. As we sing 'Hamavdil' and 'Eliyahu Hanavi' we feel that a memorable experience has ended and we are passing gradually into the mundane world of daily routine.

I recall a story that Rabbi Rosen tells. A new boy joined Carmel and after Havdalah on his first Shabbat he came running to Rabbi Rosen, shook hands with him, wished him 'Shavua Tov' and said 'Sir, will we have Shabbat again next week?'

In a year or so, I shall leave the school. The childish question of this young prep-school boy will have a deeper significance for me; on my last Shabbat I shall ask myself, 'Will I have a Carmel Shabbat again next week?'[1]

The above article is needless to say just a summary of Shabbat at Carmel. The author elaborates on the Shabbat services at Carmel:

At the start of Shabbat, we would go to the Synagogue for davening [praying]. . . . During almost all the time I was in Carmel, the Synagogue was in the main hall. The boys' seats were in a large block extending from the front to the back of the hall and a smaller block in the alcove in the southern side of the hall. The masters sat in a row at the front facing the pupils. Those who regularly attended the services on Shabbat were Rabbi Rosen, Mr. Stamler, Dr. Friedmann, Mr. Carmel and Mr. Epstein. In my last year at the school [1959–1960] there was Rabbi Young and Mr. Alexander . . . On Shabbat, the Ark, which during the week was kept in an alcove of the hall, was moved to

---

1. Carmel 1954, p.30.

the centre of the hall at the front. As at that period, in many Shuls in England, the leining was done (and also the Chazan took the service) from the front of the Shul. This was also followed in Carmel. On the two sides of the fireplace at the front of the hall were two faces which had been carved into the stone. To accord with the Jewish law regarding idols, their noses had been chipped off and also during the services they were covered up with a small flag shaped cloth.

Before each service, Rabbi Rosen would ask if any boy would like to be the Chazan. I sometimes volunteered for this. Although at that period, it was rare to find a Shul in England who used the modern Hebrew pronunciation for davening, Rabbi Rosen had instituted this at Carmel.

In the Kabbalat Shabbat service, the entire congregation sung the whole of 'Lecha Dodi' together. In my first year, after the Friday night service, the school would sing 'Shalom Aleichem' although only twice (instead of the usual thrice) for each verse. When the days became longer that summer, this was stopped and it was never restarted.[2]

As with the evening service, the morning service was also conducted by the boys. This was followed by the Reading of the Torah. Since the people reading from the Torah need to do an extensive preparation for the reading, before the end of each Shabbat, Kopul would give out the leining for the following Shabbat. The author elaborates:

> I think he wanted every boy in the school to be able to lein, although I don't think this objective was every reached. When there was a short portion in the leining – say, about 5 verses – he would usually give it to a person who had never leined before. I was one of the more regular leiners amongst the boys. One year, Rabbi Rosen was giving out leining for the double Sidrot Matot-Masei, when he reached the fourth portion and offered it to me. I asked him how long it was and he thereupon turned over page after page after page in his Chumash and then answered 72 verses – (this is the longest portion in the Torah). I politely declined his offer! I think I did instead the fifth portion which is much shorter. At my last Shabbat at the school, we also read Matot-Masei and I asked to be able to lein this fourth portion, which I did.

---

2. 7 years, pp.31–32.

There were occasions when a boy failed to do the leining he was given. This did not just pass off without comment or should I say action. He was likely to receive a summary punishment from Rabbi Rosen. The leining in such cases would be done by Rabbi Rosen or one of the masters, such as Mr. Epstein, and without any preparation or warning.[3]

Because of these "sanctions" administered by Kopul, a number of Old Carmelis clearly recollect how they tried to avoid being chosen to lein. Harold Berwin remembers, "Shuffling out of sight line of Kopul behind the clock in the hall of the main building when leining was given out."[4] However, as Martin Slater reports trying to hide did not always work, "His eyesight was amazing. On three occasions he picked me out in semi-darkness on motzie Shabbat cowering behind big boys for leining."[5] On this subject, Jonathan Isserlin writes in retrospect, "I regret ducking down and avoiding being caught for layenning by him because I never learned how to learn to layen quickly and easily. I do it, but it is a real chore. Had I sat up straight and been seen by him on Shabbat evening more often, I am sure I would be better at it."[6] Michael Bharier summarises the situation in general terms, "While a small number of students were very keen to do this, many of us would try to hide or remain otherwise inconspicuous, so that he [Kopul] would not pick on us to do it."[7]

The Prep School had its own services (with some Senior School boys davening there to make up the minyan), and there the leining was done by Dr. Tobias, who was an expert leiner.[8]

David Shaw recollects the Shabbat morning services in Greenham and wrote that, "If you were late, you stood outside in the porch for the duration." He continued by relating how when he was once late, although receiving this punishment, he received a "treat" which those inside the shul missed! "I was late and was parked outside in the porch. After a few minutes there was a low throbbing sound that increased in intensity. It was a squadron of spitfires, followed by Lancasters, Wellingtons, Mosquitos, then the jets, yes jets, in 1950 and planes of all sorts, Meteors, Vampires, Hunters. . hundreds of them . . . thousands of them. Them inside could

3. Ibid., p.31.
4. Recollections – Harold Berwin.
5. Recollections – Martin Slater.
6. Recollections – Jonathan Isserlin.
7. Recollections – Michael Bharier, chap.2, Life at Carmel.
8. 7 years, p.31.

Consecration of Carmel College Synagogue in Greenham in 1950

only hear the tantalising noise. I could see the flypast that went on and on, right overhead. Oh joy!!"[9]

Needless to say, when it came for the Barmitzvah of a boy, he would go home to his local Synagogue for the occasion. The author recollects a few exceptions to this:

> I remember two occasions when there was a Barmitzvah during the service. One was Rabbi Rosen's son Mickey (his eldest son, Jeremy's Barmitzvah was during the summer holidays). The other case was of a boy who did not have a father. His mother came down to the school for that Shabbat and both the boy and his mother sat on the masters' table. Rabbi Rosen gave an address during the service on having one's Barmitzvah at the school.[10]

Soon after the reading of the haftarah, there is the Prayer for the Queen. Unlike in many Anglo-Jewish synagogues where it is recited in English, in Carmel it was recited in Hebrew. Furthermore Carmel had something

9. Recollections – David Shaw.
10. 7 years, p.34.

unique in this prayer – the Queen was given the Hebrew name Elisheva!![11] Did not Queen Victoria order that all her descendants be circumcised[12] and is not circumcision linked with giving a Hebrew name?![13]

Needless to say, services in Carmel were not limited to Shabbat. Every weekday there were three services – Shacharit, Minchah, and Ma'ariv. At first they were all compulsory for the entire school. In addition, at Shacharit, all boys over the age of Barmitzvah were required to put on Tephillin, which they all did. At a later date, Kopul made Minchah voluntary, and on this the author recollects, "About 20 boys attended. At the time, Rabbi Rosen commented that the pupils may think I have made it easier for them now that Minchah is voluntary. In fact it is harder for them. Now they have to decide themselves whether or not to attend."[14]

Some pupils enjoyed the services, but not everybody! Henry Law wrote "The long Shabbat morning services were a misery, especially when it was a sunny day and I would want to be outside after a week spent cooped-up in a classroom." To pass the time during the service, Henry Law would imagine he was on a train and, being an expert on trains, would periodically calculate at which station he was then passing. He would also sit by the school clock which was located in the main hall and commented, "The boredom could be alleviated by watching the swinging of the pendulum, the turning of the toothed escape wheel and the drop of the gravity impulse arm every thirty seconds."[15]

Whether or not pupils enjoyed the services, the Shabbat meals, however, with their accompanying zemirot, are events which remain in the memories of many Old Carmelis. Of these meals, Jeremy Rosen comments:

> The communal meals on Shabbat were of a very different character to those of weekdays. Led invariably by Kopul, his charisma, his great singing voice, his passion for a Jewish life, his way of presenting Judaism as both traditional and modern, impacted on the school. He managed to blend authority with sympathy and concern and found a

11. Ibid; written evidence for this can be seen in the "Prayer for the Royal Family" recited during the "Order of Service at the Consecration of the Joseph Collier Synagogue" at Carmel College, on 26 July 1964, p.6.

12. Royalty and Circumcision (Internet).

13. Siddur – Service at a Circumcision.

14. 7 years, p.28.

15. Recollections – Henry Law, Carmel College days, part 1, pp.9–10.

R. Nagley	אַהֲרֹן בֶּן אַרְיֵה זְאֵב
R. Newella	שִׂמְחָה אַהֲרֹן בֶּן אֶשֶׁר
Mr. Stanle	מָרְדְּכַי דּוּד בֶּן נַפְתָּלִי צְבִי
P. Cohen	פִּנְחָס בֶּרְל בֶּן שַׁבְּתַי 8
Chajes	בָּרוּךְ בֶּן חַיִּים זְאֵב
Gale	יְחֶזְקֵאל בֶּן רְאוּבֵן 1
Pex	דָּוִד בֶּן יִצְחָק
Sherman	אַבְרָהָם מָרְדְּכַי בֶּן אֶשֶׁר
Tober	דָּוִד אֶשֶׁר בֶּן מֹשֶׁה דֹּב 10
	אַחְרִים בֶּן אַבְרָהָם
Kaufman	אָבִים בֶּן יִשְׂרָאֵל חַיִּים
Shifrin	... 23
Speter	מֹשֶׁה ... דֹּב ... יִשְׂרָאֵל
Cohen S.	יְעוּתִיאֵל ... בֶּן אַבְרָהָם דָּוִד
Wolf	יוֹסֵף מֹשֶׁה בֶּן אַבְגְּדוֹר
Black	מְנַשֶּׁה בֶּן יַעֲקֹב
Gold	כָּלֵב בֶּן חַיִּים 18
Bear	
Goldfar	... אַהֲרֹן בֶּן דָּוִד 5
Rose	שְׂמוּאֵל בֶּן אַרְיֵה 20

Page from Carmel College Synagogue's Gabbai's List of Hebrew Names from 1948

way to make the Shabbat meals and services both intensely traditional and yet enjoyable, even on occasion light-hearted. But he turned them into learning experiences and was very conscious of the need to teach everything. The students were expected to learn and join in with traditional songs and take verses. Sometimes this was voluntary and impromptu; on other occasions victims were given a week's notice to learn a verse.

Control was exercised by Kopul clapping his hands for attention. Finding a balance was hard. The relaxed atmosphere often misled pupils into thinking they could overstep the mark. If talking rose to

Carmel College Preparatory School Synagogue at Mongewell

too high a pitch, Kopul would clap and insist on silence for a few minutes.[16]

The author describes the technical arrangements for the Friday night meal:

> The boys would do netillat yadayim, enter the dining hall, and stand in silence by their places. Rabbi Rosen would make Kiddush and after drinking some wine himself, would call out the names of a few boys to come out and drink the wine. (I recollect that on one occasion during my first year at the school, Mr. Carmel made the kiddush, even though Rabbi Rosen was present.) Rabbi Rosen would then go into the kitchen. He once told us that a boy asked him why he goes into the kitchen after making Kiddush each week. The reason of course was to do netillat yadayim.

---

16. Recollections – Jeremy Rosen, chap.1.

Meanwhile Dr. Friedmann would make Hamotzi on the two chal-
lot on the top table. On the boys' table was only sliced challah. On the
top table were seated the staff together with their wives. Sometimes
there were also some non-Jewish staff at the table. . . .

There was no fish course (oy vei! Shabbat without gefillte fish!),
and the meal would begin with lockshen and soup. In the early days at
Mongewell, a member of the kitchen staff would come round with the
soup saucepan on a trolley and would dish out plate by plate. However, this method was soon changed and each table was given a soup
tureen – this was certainly much quicker. The next course was meat,
roast potatoes, and gravy. It was much simpler to prepare meat than
chicken when catering for hundreds of people. However, in my last
years at Carmel, chicken started to occasionally appear on the menu.

The dessert course in my first years at the school was fruit salad.
Afterwards the school began to buy Snowcrest ice cream. At first we
got a cup each but afterwards they would put a block of ice cream,
already cut up according to the number of boys on the table. On one
occasion, when I was head of a table, there were two slices missing.
The kitchen staff refused to remedy this. Maybe they thought we had
secretly gobbled it up. I thus went up to Rabbi Rosen and he gave me
two slices from the head table's plate.

There was also a jug of water on the table. For some reason which I
don't know, Rabbi Rosen refused to let the boys go into the vestibule
to refill it."[17] This reminds one of what Samuel Taylor Coleridge
wrote in his 'The Rime of the Ancient Mariner,' 'Water, water, everywhere, Not any drop to drink.'[18]

The Shabbat lunch menu included cold potato salad and cold meat, with
vegetable salad, and at a later date chulent was served.[19]

Zemirot played a memorable and important part of the Shabbat meals.
The boys did not know the words of the zemirot by heart and it was thus
highly desirable for them to have a zemirot book in front of them. The
Carmel teacher, Alex Tobias, filled this need by bringing out in October
1955 the Carmel zemirot book containing sixty-eight pages and entitled
"Beshir Vekol Todah," and it was classed as "Carmel College Publications,
No. 1." Kopul wrote the "Forward" to this book:

---

17. 7 years, p.32.
18. Samuel Taylor Coleridge, "The Rime of the Ancient Mariner," part 2, lines 39–40.
19. Recollections – Henry Law, Carmel College days, part 1, pp.12–13.

We have been aware for some time that it will be necessary for Carmel College to produce books of its own to cover certain requirements of school life which are singularly Carmeli. One of the most outstanding features of life at Carmel College is the Shabbat; those who have been present at the 'Friday-Evening-Table' when a new Nigun has been taught and the first wave of enthusiasm is spreading through the dining hall, will readily agree that such an experience is not easily forgotten. Our choice of Nigunim and Zemirot is wide, and this has compelled us to produce a book of Zemirot containing more than the two or three well known table hymns which are printed in the ordinary prayer book.

We are indeed fortunate in having a scholar of the calibre of Dr. A. Tobias on the teaching staff of Carmel College, and it is to him that the full praise for this production must be given. Although this book is intended primarily for Carmel College and its purposes, we believe that it might have a wider appeal and will be regarded as useful by individuals and groups to whom the singing of Shabbat Zemiroth is a precious and inspiring feature of their religious life.[20]

In the "Preface" to this zemirot book, Alex Tobias wrote:

This book is designed to give us a collection of Zemirot, our table songs for Sabbath and Festivals. We have here those songs best known to us. . . .

Our 'Zemirot,' or 'songs' combine the words of Torah and devotion with the fervour that comes from singing. . . .

In some cases we know who the author was, in others we venture a guess. Some Zemirot are very plain in their meaning, and others, especially of the French and German schools, are so laden with Talmudic allusions of an intricate nature as to make any attempt at translation formidable. . . .

No reference has been made in the introduction to the songs to the metrical rules observed by the composers, nor is it intended to give any enlightenment on medieval Hebrew verse in general, but the Zemirot do possess a definite rhythm. It would be a thrilling experience if we were to discover the tunes to which these Zemirot were originally set, although we should find their singing very strange,

---

20. *Beshir Vekol Todah*, Carmel College Publications, no.1, first edition, 1955, p.3.

since, in those days, composers used modes unknown to us. Perhaps some of the authors were themselves 'Minnesingers' or 'Troubadours' and there were such artists among the Jews of Germany and France of the Middle Ages. . . .

Much of our own singing at school consists of Biblical passages – verses from the Prophets and Psalms.[21]

This book contains no fewer than sixteen Zemirot which are to be found in larger siddurim. For each of them, Alex Tobias writes when known, the name of the author, and brief biographical details. Often, the name of the author is obtained by means of an acrostic found in the text of the zemirah. Some of the authors were from Eretz Yisrael, and others from Germany, Spain, and North Africa.[22] Tobias also included some interesting snippets, for example: 'Yom ze l'Yisrael,' has in fact eleven verses, and not just five as is found in many Zemirot books;[23] 'D'ror Yikra,' can be sung to any tune which is used for Adon Olam, since both have the same meter;[24] Avraham ibn Ezra, the author of the zemirah 'ki Eshmera Shabbat' visited London on a foggy day and compared it with the Biblical plague of darkness that was in Egypt.[25]

In a few cases, the Zemirot book contains translations which were reproduced with permission from other sources. In addition, it contains the text of kiddush, havdalah, birchat hamazon, and material for Chanukah and Purim. The last two pages are headed "miscellaneous" and contain eighteen songs, almost all from verses from the Tanach.[26]

Almost, but not all, of the Zemirot and the "miscellaneous" items in this book would be sung at the Carmel Shabbat table. The author describes the procedure for the singing, "Not anybody could start a zemirah. It was rigorously controlled by Rabbi Rosen. He would clap to silence the school, begin to sing a zemirah, stop, say achat, shtayim, shalosh [one, two, three] and everyone would start singing together. He once related to us that one of the non-Jewish teachers had asked him why all our songs begin with 'shlosh'!"[27] Jeremy Rosen adds further details, "[Kopul] con-

21. Ibid., pp.5–6.
22. Ibid., passim.
23. Ibid., p.22.
24. Ibid., p.33; (It could also be noted that "Eli Tzion" which is one of the last kinot recited on Tisha b'Av has the same meter.)
25. Ibid., p.37.
26. Ibid., passim.
27. 7 years, p.32.

7   PREFACE

Jews who, because of the late composition of some of the Zemirot and the uncertainty of their authorship prefer to sing only Biblical verses and certain passages based on the Zohar, the most famous of Kabbalistic works.

Our own school repertoire is large and includes in addition to the traditional items a number of songs of recent origin.

Thanks are due to the "Singers' Prayer Book Publication Committee" for permission to use the English texts of the Authorised Prayer Book for the translation of יום זה (p. 23), יה רבון (p. 25), צור משלי (p. 27), אתה אחד (p. 43), המבדיל (p. 51), the text of the Shorter Grace (p. 60) and the excerpts and translations for Chanucah and Purim, and to Mrs. I. Abrahams for permission to use the translation of כי אשמרה (p. 39) which appears in the Companion to the Daily Prayer Book (by the late Dr. Israel Abrahams). Acknowledgment must be made to the work "Medieval Hebrew Minstrelsy" by the late Herbert Loewe, for the valuable information which it contains.

A. TOBIAS

Carmel College
Cheshvan, 5716
October, 1955

PREFACE   6

music to its zenith was moved to add the human voice to his orchestra when he wished to convey his religious theme of confidence and triumph.

The introductions that head the songs show not only the vast period they cover in the annals of our people's history, but also the wide area over which the scattered communities of Israel found refuge. The Land of Israel, Spain, France and the Rhineland and North Africa with its ancient community of Fez are represented in our collection.

In some cases we know who the author was, in others we venture a guess. Some Zemirot are very plain in their meaning, and others, especially of the French and German schools, are so laden with Talmudic allusions of an intricate nature as to make any attempt at translation formidable. Neither would the result, if such attempt were made, do justice to the talent of the author.

No reference has been made in the introductions to the songs to the metrical rules observed by the composers, nor is it intended to give any enlightenment on medieval Hebrew verse in general, but the Zemirot do possess a definite rhythm. It would be a thrilling experience if we were to discover the tunes to which these Zemirot were originally set, although we should find their singing very strange, since, in those days, composers used modes unknown to us. Perhaps some of the authors were themselves "Minnesingers" or "Troubadours" and there were such artists among the Jews of Germany and France of the Middle Ages. The traditional melodies which have come down to us from those bygone days and which we still employ on Sabbath and Festivals (especially on Rosh Hashanah and Yom Kippur) have so altered with the passage of time as to conceal their original forms.

Much of our own singing at school consists of Biblical passages—verses from the Prophets and Psalms. There are many devout

Two Pages from the Carmel College Zemirot Book

ducted the school and made sure they followed his rhythm. Otherwise, if he was dissatisfied either with the participation or the rhythm he would clap his hands loudly and start again. Indeed, his loud clapping was always how he got attention. Sometimes he would rub his palms together slowly and ostentatiously to give notice that he was about to call for attention."[28]

There was an exception to the "formal" way that Kopul would start the Zemirot. Jacob Fachler explains, "Who remembers that on Shabbat afternoon, at the seuda shlishit meal, Kopul would start singing Mizmor Ledavid[29] quietly while we were in the middle of eating. Usually he would clap, and we would start singing something. But that one time in the week, he started singing without clapping, and gradually we heard it and joined

---

28. Recollections – Jeremy Rosen, chap. 1.
29. At seuda shlishit, it is customary to sing "Mizmor leDavid" – Psalm 23; some sing it three times.

in."[30] An unsigned article in the Carmel magazine describes the singing of this Psalm as "restrained. No boisterous singing as we enjoy for 'Tzur Mishelo', no rhythmic lilt or exultant tone, but a melodious murmur – slow, meditative."[31] Jonathan Isserlin found this tune "melancholy" and "wonderful" and writes that it is "full of poignant memories."[32]

"On some occasions," the author recollects, "he [Kopul] would ask the boys for suggestions of what zemirah to sing but the decision whether to accept the suggestion was his alone."[33] Phillip Nagley (the son of the teacher Harold Nagley), when he was a very small boy would eat at the Carmel Shabbat table, and he relates the following incident:

> On one occasion (I am not sure if it was during my father's tenure at Carmel or on a subsequent visit), Kopul Rosen turned to me on Friday night, between the end of one zemirah and the start of the next, and asked me if I would like to choose the next one. As a small boy then (and even now, as I write this), I can feel all the eyes upon me, teachers and pupils alike, while they wait for my reply. 'Shevach notnim lo . . .' I venture. Suddenly, I realise it may not have been be a suitable choice for Friday evening, as the pasuk comes from the Shabbat Shacharit prayers. What a great relief it is to me when the whole room bursts into song: 'Shevach notnim lo, kol tzvah marom, tiferet ugdulah, serafim ve'ofanim vechayot hakodesh!' To this day, I cannot pass through the K'l Adon prayer without this memory flashing into my head![34]

Kopul liked Yiddish and amongst the repertoire of songs for the Carmel Shabbat table was one in Yiddish. Robert Cannon reports:

> I remember with great delight the singing at Shabbat meals – the Zemirot. I found the names all very hard: I liked the tunes so much but could never, with any confidence call out the songs' titles when it came to requests. Except for one: the Yiddish 'So shal sein die Gullah.' I couldn't pronounce that either but I tried once – Heaven only knows what I made of it. But Kopul understood and, without correcting me

30. Recollections – Jacob Fachler.
31. Carmel 1954, p.31.
32. Recollections – Jonathan Isserlin.
33. 7 years, p.32.
34. E-mail from Phillip Nagley, 25 July 2012.

began 'Achat, Shtei'm, Shalosh . . .' and whenever I put my hand up for a request there was never any question: he simply nodded and began that song.[35]

Kopul liked to pick boys to sing verses from the Zemirot and then the whole school would join in for the chorus. Examples of this included verses from "Yom ze l'Yisrael" and "Tzur Mishelo." For one tune of "D'ror Yikra," boys in the Prep School would sing, "lei lelei lelei" after each phrase. Some pupils were reluctant to sing these verses alone and tried to avoid Kopul's gaze, while others eagerly wanted the chance to sing solo.[36] David Saville asked in his quiz on Carmel, "Who was the greatest on Friday nights singing the last verse of Tsur Mishelo," and he gave as the answer – "Jacky Coleman."[37]

"When I first came to Carmel," writes the author, "on the last Shabbat of the term we would sing amongst the Zemirot, the song 'hayamim holchim.' After a time this was stopped. The reason for this being that one of the words was 'hamanginah' and some boys changed this word to 'ha-monkey nuts'!"[38]

Strangely enough, Alex Tobias did not like the singing of the Zemirot at Carmel and on this he writes:

> The highlight of the week was the Friday evening (Shabbat) meal. Strange as it may sound, although I compiled the Zemirot Book, I have never liked Zemirot. Sometimes this meal would develop into High Mass. I always felt that Rabbi Rosen's singing was a quarter of a tone flat and that he was sorely slow in tempo. The latter feeling may have been due to my being very fast. I would never dare to be sacrilegious and discuss this with anyone (I mean the flatness). He did like the minor scale whereas my singing was given more to the triumphant. I disliked dining in public. . . . This became an inhibition of the most serious type and contributed not a little to my leaving [Carmel].[39]

---

35. Reflections – Robert Cannon.
36. Recollections – Jeremy Rosen, chap. 1; unwritten recollections of author; 7 years, pp. 32–33.
37. Recollections – David Saville.
38. 7 years, p. 33.
39. Reflections – Dr. Alexander Tobias.

However, this was not the view of many of the pupils. Neil Alton comments, "As everyone remembers, singing our hearts out during Shabbat."[40] Michael Bharier elaborates on this:

> Without question, the events that affected me the most, starting from my very first days at Carmel, and continuing to affect me to this day, were those of Shabbat and the Jewish holidays. There was a *ruach*, a spirit, on those days that transformed the whole school into a warm family, especially at meals. Kopul had a strong, pleasant baritone voice and would lead us in singing *Kiddush*, the *Z'mirot* and *birchat hamazon*. We all rapidly became familiar with the tunes, including alternative versions of many of the *z'mirot*, and Kopul would often ask us which melody we would like to use. For *Y-ah Ribon* he seemed to favor the 'Italian' tune, a melody that sounded quite Neapolitan. We might ask for the Yemenite tune, an oriental-sounding tune with vocal appoggiaturas that would set us off in giggles.[41]

In contrast, Henry Law did not enjoy the Zemirot. On this he wrote, "We kept breaking off to sing Zemirot (religious songs) while the food got cold on our plates. I was not interested in singing songs. I wanted to get on with the meal."[42]

A tradition in the school was for boys who were leaving that term to make a leaving speech in the dining hall during the meals of the last Shabbat of the term.[43] The speeches were of about five minutes in length, but there was a notable exception as was reported in the Carmel magazine:

> Many School records and achievements have been recorded this year [1958–1959] from the sphere of sport to achievements in new buildings. But, perhaps no-one was unimpressed this February when R[affy] Ettisch broke all existing records when he delivered his 44-minute record farewell speech. Assisted by a break for Grace after Meals in the middle of his sermon, Ettisch skillfully went on touching all points concerned and unconcerned with school life. His marathon

---

40. Recollections – Neil Alton.
41. Recollections – Michael Bharier, chap.2, Life at Carmel.
42. Recollections – Henry Law, part 1, Carmel College days, p.13.
43. 7 years, p.138.

of oratory ended, the thundering applause clearly expressed the audience's pleasure.[44]

The author recalls a leaving speech "which had the school in fits of laughter and enthusiastic clapping." It was delivered "by a boy who had a reputation of going out with girls. . . . He said, 'Now there are three [name of family] in Carmel College. Soon there will be four.'"[45] Geoffrey Paradise recalls how Kopul saved him from embarrassment in his farewell speech, "I told a good joke quite badly and nobody laughed. So I muttered that it sounded better in Yiddish – and KR [Kopul] cracked up with his booming laugh of enjoyment."[46] David Saville remembers the farewell speech of Michael Pildus, who was one of the original pupils in 1948. "You are the only father I knew, and I also recall Sir Robert Menzies the former Prime Minister of Australia, speaking of Churchill after his funeral – We who have lived in his times have been touched with his greatness – how much more so the students of Kopul Rosen at Carmel."[47] The author began his farewell speech by saying "This Shabbat we read the Sidra of Masei, which deals with the journeys of the Children of Israel in the wilderness. Being in Carmel is a stage in the journey of life."[48]

David Shaw left Carmel "almost on the spur of the moment" and gave a farewell speech. Afterwards, Kopul wrote to his father, "I was rather surprised to hear David's farewell speech."[49]

Jeremy Rosen in summing up the farewell speeches writes, "they were often humorous, complimentary, thanking teachers who had helped them. Occasionally they were critical or acerbic. There was always a frisson as rebellious seniors rose to speak and the junior pupils wondered how far they dared go in revealing their real feelings."[50]

Every meal ends with Birchat Hamazon. The author describes the procedure on Shabbat:

> After singing Shir Hama'alot, Rabbi Rosen would call out the name of a boy to lead the grace. Since often, the names of two boys sounded similar, there were occasions, where a boy, not intended by Rabbi

---

44. Carmel, 1959, p.7.
45. 7 years, p.138.
46. Recollections – Geoffrey Paradise.
47. Recollections – David Saville.
48. 7 years, p.138.
49. Recollections – David Shaw.
50. Recollections – Jeremy Rosen, chap.1.

Rosen, led the grace. The boy leading would say the grace out loud and in numerous places, the school would join in singing. Towards the end of my stay at Carmel, I had learned a tune for 'bamarom'[51] and when I led the grace I incorporated it. Afterwards Rabbi Rosen made some humorous remark about it.[52]

On Shabbat afternoons, there were organised programmes. John Fischer recollects:

In the afternoon, especially during the summer term, on the school lawn weather permitting, Rabbi Kopul Rosen would give a shiur on Pirkei Avot or on Tanach to boys in an advanced stream for Hebrew studies. The challenge was to learn by heart for the next shiur whichever verse or section we were asked to memorise; although this was a chore at the time, in later life I personally found it invaluable![53]

On these shiurim, Henry Law also comments positively:

We studied and discussed verses from the Ethics of the Fathers (Pirke Avot) and the conversations encompassed a wide range of important ethical issues. That has stuck for life. It is a pity what was said was never written down. Kopul was forwarding a form of wholly orthodox Judaism that was in tune with, and answered the needs of, the contemporary world.[54]

In the autumn term 1961, there were on Shabbat afternoon three Gemara shiurim, an elementary one given by Kopul, an intermediate one by Rabbi Sydney Leperer, and an advanced one by Jacob Epstein.[55]

The author reports on another Shabbat afternoon activity:

At one period, Rabbi Rosen instituted a 'sha'a limud.' This was for an hour on Shabbat afternoon, when the boys were supposed to learn a Torah subject of their own choice by themselves. I heard it called by one boy 'Charlie Mood.' He would have a Torah book open and

---

51. A passage which occurs towards the end of Birchat Hamazon.
52. 7 years, p.33.
53. Recollections – John Fischer.
54. Recollections – Henry Law, Carmel College days, part 1, p.11.
55. Recollections – Nigel Simons.

some novel. As long as there was no-one to check up, the novel was open – when a teacher appeared, the novel miraculously disappeared! On one occasion, Rabbi Rosen asked boys what they had learned. One boy answered that he had read a book on the Holocaust but Rabbi Rosen did not feel that that was the intention of this hour.[56]

What else did the boys do on Shabbat afternoon, especially in the long summer days when Shabbat ended about 10.30 at night? Could they play with a ball on the playing fields? On this Michael Blackstone writes, "On Shabbat, no objection was made to us playing cricket or football provided a) we did not change our clothes including shoes b) no stumps or goal posts were used. Consequently in cricket, mainly French cricket was played, and of course c) playing did not clash with any official school activity – services, shiurim, meals, rest periods, etc."[57] However, in contrast, Melvyn Ackerman recollects that, "[Kopul] caned me for playing with a football on Shabbat afternoon."[58] Other pupils would occupy themselves with less problematic activities, as John Fischer reports, "Leisure activities on Shabbat would include reading, playing chess, etc."[59] In a similar vein Jeffrey Gandz recollects, "The lazy Shabbat afternoons sitting in the Ha-Ha or tucked away in the library just reading or dreaming."[60]

Helmut Schmidt asks, "What did Carmel boys and their headmaster do on a Cup Final or a Boat Race Saturday? Only the Lord knows and is discreet."[61] Jeremy Rosen, less discreet, discloses, "Some found willing non-Jews nearby who would allow them to come in and watch Television."[62] Ted Wetherall lived in a cottage on the Carmel estate and Jeremy writes, "that's where I used to go on Cup Final days to watch TV!!!"[63]

Many boys came from homes where Shabbat was not observed and at their homes lights would be freely turned on and off on Shabbat. One could say with certainty that they were not aware of the details of the laws of Shabbat. The author reports on an incident which occurred on Shabbat:

---

56. 7 years, p.35.
57. Recollections – Michael Blackstone.
58. Recollections – Melvyn Ackerman.
59. Recollections – John Fischer.
60. Recollections – Jeffrey Gandz.
61. Reflections – Helmut Schmidt.
62. Recollections – Jeremy Rosen, chap.1.
63. E-mail from Jeremy Rosen, 3 May 2012.

On one occasion during the meal on Friday night there was a power
cut and we were in complete darkness. The non-Jewish kitchen staff
started bringing in lighted candles to put on each table. Some boys
then went into the kitchen to help them. When Rabbi Rosen saw
what was happening, he clapped his hands to silence the school and
said, 'What sort of Jewish homes do you come from? Don't you know
that you mustn't carry lighted candles on Shabbat?'[64]

All good things come to an end, and one of them is Shabbat each week.
The school would assemble for Ma'ariv, Kopul would allocate the following week's leining, and would then make havdalah. The author recalls,
"One boy was called on to hold the candle and another boy the spice box.
The lights were then turned off. The only light one could see was that
from the Havdalah candle. After Havdalah, the boys would sing 'Hamavdil bein Kodesh Lechol' and 'Eliyahu Hanavi.' Sometimes we would also
sing another tune for 'Hamavdil' which went 'tumbuy, tumbuy, tumbuy,
hamavdil bein kodcsh lcchol. . . .'"[65] Joe Miller adds, "Everyone will remember the sight of our Rabbi Rosen lighting the Havdallah candle as
Shabbat came to a close with his shadow rather spookily moving on the
wall behind him."[66] Anton Dell also recalls these moments, "We were all
sitting in the hall in Mongewell Park. As darkness came he [Kopul] lit the
Havdalah candle and his huge shadowy flickering image was reflected on
three walls combined with the smell of the incense."[67]
    Recalling the termination of Shabbat at Carmel, Henry Law reminisces:

At the end of Shabbat there would be more prayers and a period of
meditation whilst waiting for the end of it. This was an altogether
more positive experience. At dusk, it could be a time of intense and
sometimes numinous quiet. Kopul Rosen cultivated this time and the
spirituality got through to me. It might have got through to everyone.
It was precisely here that Kopul achieved his aim.[68]

Comments of a similar nature were made by Jeffrey Gandz:

---

64. 7 years, p.33.
65. Ibid., p.35.
66. Recollections – Joe Miller.
67. Recollections – Anton Dell.
68. Recollections – Henry Law, Carmel College days, part 1, p.11.

I remember the spirituality of Carmel . . . To this day, I treasure the memory of the Havdalah ceremony as we stood in the main hall at Mongewell and watched the light disappear behind the high-set window, the smell of the burning, tapered candle, the voices raised in unison. Never a choir – that would have been too orchestrated. More the spontaneous, unified commitment of many to one act of observance.[69]

A pupil composed a poem entitled "The Motze-Shabbat Sky" which appeared in the Carmel magazine, and shows the spirituality of a Carmel Shabbat:

> For nearly thirteen years now I have trained my naked eye
> To recognize the beauty of the Motze-Shabbat sky.
> From Sunday night to Friday the Heavens look so good
> And radiate such beauty as only Heavens could,
> But on a Shabbat evening, when darkness walks the land,
> It's only then that beauty can disclose her glorious hand,
> And then it is when reddened skies can penetrate one's thought,
> After forgetful moments when real purity is caught.
> And every Shabbat evening I come to think this way,
> It is a fitting ending to a really thoughtful day,
> For once a week, to just forget is proper relaxation,
> A type of haze which, for a week should give one stimulation,
> And later on when things go wrong, as things do, by and by,
> I think of heaven's beauty, and the Motze-Shabbat sky.[70]

Michael Blackstone summed up Shabbat at Carmel in a few chosen words, "Shabbat, [was] always a highlight, even if some of us weren't very religious. It was a different day, essential to our life."[71]

CYCLE OF THE JEWISH YEAR

The author has extensive recollections of the Festivals at Carmel:

> With the exception of Pesach, we were in school for all the Festivals, at least some years. This was very good, since had they been at

69. Recollections – Jeffrey Gandz.
70. Carmel 1955, p.21.
71. Reflections – Michael Blackstone.

home, many of the boys would not have celebrated the Festivals in the traditional manner. Certain events concerning these Festivals still remain in my mind, although I cannot always remember to which year they appertain. On at least one Lag B'Omer, we made a bonfire and I remember the school giving to each of the boys an orange as an extra dessert on Tu BiShvat. I shall now go through the Festivals one at a time.

Yamim Noraim

When Rosh Hashanah occurred at the end of September or the beginning of October, we were often in school. . . . Rabbi Rosen took most of the services and also blew the shofar superbly. Many of the piutim recited in many Shuls during the service were omitted.

Before my first Yom Kippur at the school, Rabbi Rosen called together all the boys in the senior school who were not yet Barmitzvah and said he thought that they should fast the whole day. However, some of them went into the dining hall to eat with the prep school.

Since many of the piutim were omitted, each year there was a break of several hours between Mussaf and Minchah. One year, I asked Rabbi Rosen to give a shiur during part of this break to the few boys who wished to attend. The subject was on the laws and customs concerning Minchah and Neilah on Yom Kippur. . . .

During the summer holidays before my last year at the school, Rabbi Rosen slipped whilst jumping from a boat on to the landing stage and broke his leg, his arm and some of his ribs. That Rosh Hashanah he was confined to his house. Before the service on Yom Kippur, a big armchair and a small chair were set up in front of the Chazan's desk. Just before Kol Nidrei, Rabbi Rosen arrived in a wheel chair, used his crutches to reach the armchair, sat on it and put his broken leg up on the other chair. He then conducted Kol Nidrei, although his voice was weaker than usual. He came again for Neilah, which he conducted from the armchair. When he reached 'Shema Yisrael' at the end of the service, he asked for his crutches, and stood up to recite it.

There were still some moments until the end of Yom Kippur and he utilised them to relate a story regarding Rabbi Israel Salanter. At the end of one Yom Kippur, he told one of his students in his Yeshivah to take all the bread and not give it to the other students. They were all eager to eat after the fast and they started squabbling. Rabbi Salanter entered the

Yeshivah dining room and reprimanded them saying that though Yom Kippur had just ended they were already arguing with each other! Rabbi Rosen then said to us that Yom Kippur for fasting was ending, but Yom Kippur for repentance goes on the whole year.

Sukkot

My first Sukkot in Carmel was in 1954. That year the Sukkah was built on the western side of the dining hall and was rather primitive. Part of it was problematic since there was an overhanging tree. (When building a Sukkah, trees always seem to be in the most inconvenient places!) On the whole, all the boys who wanted to eat in the Sukkah could do so. Rabbi Rosen brought the entire school into the Sukkah for Kiddush and then those who wanted to eat in the dining hall went there for their meal. On Yom Tov it was full and the numbers thinned out during Chol Hamoed.....

The following year the Sukkah was built far more professionally and was at the eastern side of the dining room. Again the numbers of those eating in the Sukkah decreased as Chol Hamoed progressed. Since a number of the boys eating there were younger and thus smaller (perhaps more accurately in this context 'thinner'!), four of these boys sat on each side of the table instead of the usual three.

Food had to be brought from the kitchens into the Sukkah and after the meals, the dirty crockery dishes had to be returned to the kitchen. Who would be the 'waiters' for these jobs? Rabbi Rosen had the original idea of making the 'Ushpizin' for that particular day do these tasks. [Ushpizin are the various Biblical personalities who traditionally visit our Sukkot on each day of the Festival.] For example on the First Day of Sukkot it is Avraham. Therefore all boys whose Hebrew name was Avraham found themselves as waiters that day and if there were not enough boys with that name, they would be supplemented with boys whose English name began with the letter "A," such as Anthony or Andrew. . . .

I should mention that after a few years on the eastern side of the dining hall, the Sukkah returned to the western side, and it was built at a site where there was no overhanging tree. . . .

Every year Rabbi Rosen would buy two sets of Arba'at Haminim for the school. . . . Before Hallel on the days of Yom Tov, Rabbi Rosen would stop the service and all the boys would line up to fulfill the Mitzvah on the Arba'at Haminim. This took a long time to complete, but the entire school observed this Mitzvah.

Carmel College was next to the Thames and on its banks were many willow trees. On a number of occasions on the day before Hoshanna Rabba, I went with a number of other boys to pick willows for the following day's service. As far as possible we tried to tie them into small bundles for each boy. Towards the end of the service on the following morning, the boys would give the willows a good bashing.

Simchat Torah

On Simchat Torah one dances and sings with the Sifrei Torah both in the evening and in the morning. In Carmel they had a custom I have never seen anywhere else. There was a candelabrum, which had seven branches, and I understood it was found when they took over the premises at Mongewell. Seven lighted candles were put in it and a person would hold it walking backwards in front of the Sifrei Torah during each hakafah.

Before each hakafah, Rabbi Rosen would announce who would hold the Sifrei Torah and who would go with the lights. For each hakafah there would be singing and dancing and each hakafah would end when Rabbi Rosen called out 'tzon kedoshim.'

Simchat Torah is the day when everybody is called up to the Torah – even boys who are not yet Barmitzvah. To call up each boy individually in Carmel was well nigh impossible. The service wouldn't then finish until about three o'clock and the pangs of hunger would be ghastly. To avoid this, Rabbi Rosen organised the boys into groups and then all those in a particular group were called up together. . . .

As I have already mentioned, just before my last year at the school, Rabbi Rosen as a result of his accident was in a wheel chair. That Simchat Torah, he could not get to the service, although his wheelchair did. Mr. Stamler jokingly announced that there was an old custom to wheel a wheel chair in front of the Sifrei Torah before each hakafah and he each time he called out a boy to do so. I think that some of the boys even swallowed what Mr. Stamler was saying!

Chanukah

Every evening during Chanukah, the whole school would assemble in the Main Hall for the lighting of Chanukah candles. At least on the first year when I was in Carmel, the school used the seven branched candelabrum which they had found at Mongewell. At one end was placed the shamash and from the other end the Chanukah candles. I don't remember what they did on the last two nights.

There were a number of boys who had brought their own chanukiot to school and after the school lighting, they would light them on a table near the window. Some used candles and others oil. Some boys made their own chanukiot by simple improvisation, in one case with eight drawing pins on the lid of a metal geometry box. One friend of mine went to Wallingford, where he bought some small candle holders which he attached to a piece of coloured cardboard I had given him, and on it he wrote 'l'hadlik ner shel Chanukah.' At that period they were selling coloured Christmas candles, which were about the same size as Chanukah candles and he bought a sufficient supply. Later he discovered that he could have bought a box of Chanukah candles at a far cheaper price.

One year Rabbi Rosen managed to obtain, I believe free of charge, a large supply of miniature plastic chanukiot. He had wanted to be able to give them out to each pupil free of charge but the British customs had demanded customs duty on them, even though he tried to tell them that they were religious appurtenances. He therefore had to make a small charge for boys who wanted one. Some however had arrived broken and Rabbi Rosen said that pupils could have these for nothing and maybe they could repair them by heating the plastic. The candles were like birthday candles and did not last half an hour and the boys were therefore told not to make the Berachah when lighting these candles. Several tables were set aside in the hall for these miniature chanukiot. . . .

Purim

Most of the years I was in Carmel, the Megillah was read by Dr. Tobias. The banging at Haman's name was very strictly controlled by Rabbi Rosen. Before each reading, he said that banging could only take place when one read 'Haman ben Hamdata.' On one occasion, the boys started banging at a different Haman. This didn't just pass over. (I can't complete this sentence with the customary words 'in silence,' since I was never taught how to bang 'in silence'!) Rabbi Rosen immediately stood up and reminded the school when they were allowed to bang . . .

One year, on Purim night, a group from Israel who were in England at the time – I think that they were a Yemenite group – came to the school and gave a very enjoyable performance. They succeeded in getting the whole school to join with them in singing. Unfortunately, the performance had to be cut short, since they had to be rushed back to Reading station to catch a return train to London . . .

Each Purim the school had an excellent programme. It began with a fancy dress competition and was followed by what they called a 'social' in which both teachers and pupils could put on acts. This was followed by the Purim meal.

The fancy dress parade would take place in the hall and Rabbi Rosen would call out the title of each contestant or contestants and they would then walk down the wooden staircase in view of the judges and the school. Rabbi Rosen would choose the judges. One year at least they were composed of teachers and teachers' wives.

The winners that year [1954] were three boys from Gibraltar, who had hired three fancy dresses of monkeys and they called themselves, I believe, the 'Saviours of Gibraltar.' (It has been said that as long as monkeys are found in Gibraltar, the colony will remain British.) One of these 'monkeys' even slid down the banister. They easily won the first prize. . . .

In my last year at the school, a number of us in the sixth form did as this fancy dress parade a short skit. There were other skits by sixth formers and the judges decided that the size of the applause would determine the winner. The winners, which were not my group, received applause well in excess of the other groups.

Generally the winners in such a competition are not judged on the magnificence of their fancy dress but on how it is put over. One year the winner was a boy holding a guitar and as he came down the stairs, he said the following ditty:

> My name is [the name of a then current pop singer],
> I am just an ordinary kid
> But wouldn't you all be
> For fifty thousand quid. . . .

In my last year at the school, a number of the boys in the sixth form, including myself, did a presentation of the Book of Esther with the characters modelled on the masters at the school. Mr. Rafael Loewe was designated as Rafael Haman and he was going to be hanged but at the last moment reprieved. Rabbi Rosen said he wanted to see our play before we did it in front of the school. When he saw that Mr. Loewe was going to be hanged, he told us that we couldn't hang a master, even if the sentence is not carried out. We therefore realised that some change had to be made, but hadn't time to plan out this change.

When it came time to punish Rafael Haman (and this was where Rabbi Rosen had demanded a change), Rafael Haman ran off the stage saying 'it's not my fault, it's my dog Sharia's.' This change was made on the spur of the moment by the boy acting Rafael Haman. I don't remember any further details of the play. I do know that the audience, including Mr. Loewe, were in fits of laughter, and it was very successful.

Shavuot

Shavuot occurs after counting 49 *complete* days of the Omer. This means that one cannot bring in Shavuot before nightfall. Therefore on the night of Shavuot we davened late and then went into the dining room for kiddush and cake and to do some learning. Rabbi Rosen said that boys could deliver 'divrei Torah' at this gathering. . . .

One year, during this gathering, Rabbi Rosen said that any boys who wanted to go to bed could do so. Quite a number left and after they had gone Rabbi Rosen said that he had let them go, since he wanted to give out a packet of crisps to each boy but he did not have enough packets!

It is customary to decorate the Shul with flowers for Shavuot. On one occasion, I, together with some other boys, collected together flower petals of various different colours, and with them we made a number of different pictures on the floor at the front of the Shul. One of them was the school crest.[72]

Anthony Rau also wrote in his letters home in 1952 brief comments on the Festivals at Carmel whilst in Greenham. Regarding the Tishri Festivals he wrote:

[Mr. Stamler] and Robin Gilbert and David Perl (and his sister) came down for Yom Kippur. On Kol Nidre we began at 7.15pm and finished at 8.45pm. On Yom Kippur we had the morning Service from 10–12.30 and Mussaf from 2–3.45pm and Mincha, Nila and Maariv from 5pm to the end of the fast. The meal they gave wasn't bad. First we had a snack of cakes and then a half-hour later we had a proper meal of meat and sausage.[73] . . . The whole school ate in the Succah

---

72. 7 years, pp.35–42.
73. Rau Letters, 1 October 1952.

for the first three days, but it grew so cold and windy, that Kop[ul] told everyone to eat inside. There are also a lot of wasps which are a nuisance.[74] . . . On Simchas Torah, we were given some beer, it was absolutely foul, even the masters who are drinkers thought it was shocking.[75]

Anthony Rau also wrote on the fancy dress held the previous Purim, in which boys dressed up as "King Farouk," who was then the King of Egypt, a "chain-gang," and "the girls King Achashvarosh rejected."[76]

More has been written on Purim at Carmel than on any other festival in the year. It was one of the jolliest (or even the jolliest) day in the Carmel calendar. In addition to the annual fancy dress parade and the "social," a number of years the school captain and the prefects were demoted and boys in lower classes were appointed in their place![77] One year there was "impromptu mud-slinging (in verse) between Rabbi Rosen and George Mandel."[78] Jeremy Rosen also has Purim recollections:

In many ways Purim was the highlight of the year when dignitaries and favoured parents were invited down to the school to witness or judge a fancy dress competition and then a revue which always included teachers making fun of pupils and vice versa. Not even Kopul was immune. Nevertheless he always invited Governors and potential donors down for Purim celebrations even if he knew full well that he would be the butt of jokes. He gave as good as he got and was very good at composing rhymes that made fun of people impromptu, a skill he picked up from the Yiddish Yeshivah tradition of 'gramen.[79]

Joe Miller writes on his Purim recollections:

Purim was a time for fancy dress and it became harder each year for us to try and come up with an idea for fancy dress. I recall one year about ten of us not having any ideas, went as the Shoe Shiners of Shushan, with just shoes being cleaned by us as we walked through the staged

74. Ibid., 10 October 1952.
75. Ibid., 16 October 1952.
76. Ibid., 15 March 1952.
77. Carmel: 1958, p.6, 1959, p.6, 1960, p.5.
78. Carmel 1955, p.4.
79. Biography of KR, p.46.

Lighting of Chanukah Candles in the Hall of the Main Building at Mongewell

area. At least we created a smile on our teachers faces that of course included Kopul Rosen![80]

On Purim 1960, a "Revue" consisting of a collection of a total of 16 songs and sketches, written by the teacher, Hyam Maccoby, was performed twice at the school. The songs in this Revue included items headed "Flowers for Ophelia," "The Outsider," "The Telephone Directory," and "The Abominable Snowman." The sketches included "Top Ten Secret," "Six-Gun Goldberg," "Master Move," and "Boots."[81] On the preparations for this revue, Michael Bharier writes:

---

80. Recollections – Joe Miller.
81. Youth, A Revue, Purim 1960, Carmel College, Programme (designed and printed by the Carmel College Press).

He [Maccoby] asked me to write music for several of the numbers and he contributed melodies too. There was one specific number about which he was very particular. He brought me to his home in Marlow with the words and I spent an afternoon with him and his wife brainstorming about the melody. My first efforts were totally unacceptable to them. It took a while to hammer the piece into shape. What emerged was 'The Abominable Snowman,' which I sang in the revue accompanying myself on the piano while Michael Brown and Norman Gerecht pranced about in snowman costumes on stage. I have written a large amount of music since, much of it far more complicated and demanding, but this notorious ditty has pursued me all over the world, wherever Old Carmelis of that era see me. Oy! Thank you Mr. Maccoby.[82]

The Carmel magazine reported on the actual performance and wrote:

However, like all good productions, the success obviously does not hinge on the writer's ability alone. A revue has to be well cast, and in this respect the roles could hardly have been more suited to the actors.

Gold, who had by far the most parts to play, proved himself to be an excellent comic, with near professional ability. Kaufman's interpretation of a teen-age idol was almost too realistic. Shenderey came to force in 'Boots,' a witty sketch in which he portrayed a not-so-beautiful female intent on getting the masculine attentions of Kaufman, a small but elegant policeman. Lament proved his worth in such sketches as 'Six-Gun Goldberg,' 'The Shorts and the Proberts,' and 'Master Move,' where he showed his capabilities both as an actor and as an impersonator.

"Gerecht and Fisher J., proved to be masters of the guitar as well as convincing actors, and Dell added zest on the bongos. Bharier deserves praise for his lively performance in "The Abominable Snowman,' and also for his services as musical director.

The Revue enabled those boys who took part to show their talents in public for the first time. It is hoped that this experiment will be continued with equal success in future years.[83]

---

82. Recollections – Michael Bharier, chap. 2, Life at Carmel.
83. Carmel 1960, p.29.

Chapter 6

Not Everything Is Lessons

The Carmel day consisted of lessons and then more lessons, and after all that, prep and then more prep. But despite this, there was still time for a large variety of extra-curricular activities. . . .

SING A SONG

Music played an important part in life at Carmel. Of Kopul Rosen and music, Cyril Domb writes:

> There was a tradition of chazzanut in the family, and Kopul's father was a capable Baal Tefilah with a pleasant voice. Kopul inherited these talents. Interest in music and chassidism remained with him for the whole of his life. He was fond of stressing the chassidic dictum that whatever the origin of a song there was no Tum'ah (impurity) associated with the melody, and it could be used for any sacred purpose.[1]

When Kopul was just 17, he spent a Shabbat with Rabbi Louis Rabinowitz. On this Shabbat, the latter wrote, "The tuneful manner in which he sang the Zemirot made that Sabbath eve a memorable Sabbath of delight."[2]

Several decades after the event, Kopul's singing whilst he was at Mir Yeshivah was still remembered by another student, Theodore Lewis, who

---

1. Memories of KR, p.13.
2. Ibid., p.85.

was there at the same time, "On these occasions [such as Purim and Simchat Torah] we did a lot of singing, Kopul, the leader in everything that
he did, was the life and soul of these parties. He would initiate a niggun
and with some of us who could sing fairly well, he would harmonise to the
delight of all present."[3]

Thus, not unsurprisingly, the provisional Prospectus for Carmel College, written in 1948, almost certainly by Kopul, had a section on music,

> The normal curriculum will include classes in vocal and instrumental
> music and every effort will be made to foster in the boys a love and
> appreciation of music. A Choir and an Orchestra will be formed;
> well-known musicians and singers will be invited to visit the College
> and the boys will be allowed to attend any outstanding concerts and
> recitals which take place in the neighbourhood. Private lessons in
> instrumental music (Piano, Violin, 'Cello, and all wind instruments)
> will be arranged.[4]

All this was not just wishful thinking on Kopul's part. During the course
of his lifetime, most of these items became part of the school life.

With regard to Carmel having its own choir, in 1956 Kopul arranged
that Rev. Leo Bryll, who was lecturer of chazzanut at Jews' College, come
to the school to train such a choir. On this subject, the "Carmel Fanfare"
wrote, "He [Bryll] came down to Mongewell, once in the Autumn [1955]
and is now [May 1956] coming every week. Rabbi Rosen said that he
hoped the Choir would develop into a Hebraic culture of Carmel College."[5] The Carmel magazine reported favourably on the choir's progress
saying that "it has developed beyond recognition and should very soon be
good enough to perform publicly."[6]

A once a week visit to Carmel was insufficient to make a first class
choir, and therefore in January 1957, Dudley Cohen, the choir master
of the Zemel Choir,[7] joined the full-time staff of Carmel College as its
first Director of Music and established what was known as the "Carmel
Boys' Choir." In a report which appeared in that year's Carmel magazine,
Dudley Cohen wrote:

---

3. Ibid., p.59.
4. Carmel College Provisional Prospectus, undated, (about April 1948), section: Music.
5. Carmel Fanfare, p.3.
6. Carmel 1956, p.7.
7. The Zemel choir was a mixed-voice Jewish choir established in 1955 by Dudley Cohen.

The School Choir was formed in January of this year [1957] and consists of approximately 65 boys who come from all parts of the school.

As with most boys' choirs, our greatest difficulty has been in finding altos and tenors, but we now have a good alto section though the tenors are a little weak. In May the addition to the Choir of seven very enthusiastic boys from Prep. School strengthened and improved the treble section considerably. We are, I feel, fortunate in having a very powerful and reliable bass section which adds body and depth to the general tone of the choir.

While the choir still has very much to learn about tone production, voice control and choral singing in general, the boys are capable of producing pleasant and joyful harmonious sounds and are now able to learn new songs very quickly. I feel sure that the Choir can improve to a really high standard since it already shows great promise.[8]

On this choir, Michael Bharier writes:

He [Dudley Cohen] did a remarkable job. He took a bunch of enthusiastic but unruly youngsters, mostly people who could not read music, and produced a choir of some quality. After a couple of years of singing we were brought to London and made a record, a 10 inch LP, which I still have. The music was mostly popular Israeli songs of the day but we also sang Dudley's own arrangement of Yossele Rosenblatt's melody for Shir Hama'alot, Malcolm Sargent's arrangement of Little David Play on Yo' Harp, and a Hebrew version (with different words) of En Natus Emmanuel by Michael Praetorius. Kopul came and joined the choir for that session and his voice can be heard clearly at some points.[9]

Regarding Kopul's contribution to this record, Martin Slater recollects "when we made the Carmel Boys' Choir Record, his [Kopul's] 'Bim bong, bim bong, bim, bim' etc. was the loudest."[10] This "bim bong" was on the last of the ten songs on the record and was in the song in Hebrew entitled "The Orchestra." The author (who being tone-deaf was not a member of this choir – they only wanted boys who could sing in tune!) also has some recollections of this recording:

---

8. Carmel 1957, p.28.
9. Recollections – Michael Bharier, chap. 3.5, Music at Carmel, a personal recollection.
10. Recollections – Martin Slater.

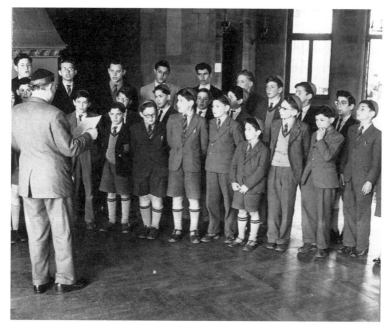

Choir Practice at Mongewell with the Choirmaster Dudley Cohen

As the end of the school year drew near, Dudley Cohen made an appointment with a recording studio in London. A few days before the scheduled recording, he said he was thinking of cancelling it – he felt the choir wasn't ready. However, after some more rehearsals and I would think, some 'prodding' from above, there was no cancellation. Off went the choir to the recording studio. I understand they had some trouble with one of the songs, but Rabbi Rosen then turned up at the studio and together with his singing, this song was recorded.[11]

This was still the era of gramophones (if you today want to know what one looks like, pay a visit to a pre-historic museum!) and a gramophone record of the "Carmel Boys' Choir," recorded at the E.M.I. Recording studio in London,[12] came onto the market. On the dust jacket was a drawing of rows and rows and rows of boys. They can be seen wearing an outer

11. 7 years, pp.72–73.
12. Carmel 1957, p.28.

garment of purple colour, the colour of the Carmel blazer. However, the Carmel tie seems to have changed colour in this drawing![13]

Even before making this record, the Carmel Boys' Choir gave public performances. The Carmel magazine reports that "Its first public recital with quite good success" was on Purim of that year.[14] A few months later on Lag B'omer, a concert was held at Carmel at which both the Carmel Boys' Choir and the Zemel Choir performed. A report appeared in the Carmel magazine:

> On May 19th, Lag B'omer, the Zemel Choir came down to sing to us for the second year running. The first half of the concert was given before supper, and then the School Choir sang two songs. During supper, the Zemel Choir had a comprehensive tour of the grounds, with Mr. [Dudley] Cohen and a few senior boys acting as guides. The second part of the Zemel Concert was made noteworthy by the solos sung by David Scheiner in "Swing Low Sweet Chariot," and Greta Brenner in "Hariu." The whole concert was very entertaining, and no boy went away dissatisfied. There was only one complaint and that is it did not last long enough.[15]

Carmel had Monday morning assemblies which began with a piece of music. Michael Bharier writes on an embarrassing situation which once occurred:

> Kopul himself was very interested and always played recorded music at the Monday morning school assemblies as well as at other times. For a while he let me pick the pieces. One Monday I picked a piece by Bach that I especially loved. I didn't pay attention to the name of the piece, Jesu Joy of Man's Desiring. As Kopul marched in, he heard what was playing then told me to take it off immediately, giving me a wink![16]

Kopul would try to interest the Carmel pupils in classical music. Solomon (Momy) Levy, from Gibraltar, was already a pupil in Carmel when it was at Greenham. Of Kopul and music he writes, "My love of classical music is

---

13. Cover of gramophone record of Carmel Boys' Choir.
14. Carmel 1957, p.28.
15. Ibid., p.29.
16. Recollections – Michael Bharier, chap. 3.5, Music at Carmel, a personal recollection.

due to him. When I first arrived at Carmel College, I knew nothing what-soever about classical music and, during the week after lunch, he would take a group of us to his study and play small excerpts of music especially Swan Lake which really gave us an insight and a love for classical music.'[17]

When Carmel moved to Mongewell, Kopul reintroduced these "after lunch" record recitals. In the first academic year, the music played was from a whole variety of classical composers. These included Johann Se-bastian Bach's Brandenburg Concertos, some of Ludwig van Beethoven's Symphonies, pieces by Wolfgang Mozart and Franz Schubert, overtures by Gioachino Rossini, and selections from ballets.[18]

Periodically, Kopul would want to test the general knowledge of the boys at Carmel and would hand out pages of questions to be answered under exam conditions. These would invariably include a whole list of classical music compositions and the boys would have to write who the authors were.[19]

One of them would be "The Unfinished Symphony" by Schubert. There was a boy at Carmel who had a rhyme which was sung in Hebrew to the tune of one of the movements in this Symphony:

> Zeh hamanginah
> Asher Shubert lo gomar
> (this is the tune which Schubert did not finish)[20]

There were occasions when "appropriate music" was played in front of the school. The Carmel magazine explains, "Instead of confiding their academic failures (or successes) to their parents alone, boys have now to face the music publicly at the end of term assemblies. Form Masters re-port (usually somewhat humorously) on their forms' progress during the term, and appropriate music for each form is played."[21] Unfortunately, no examples of this "appropriate music" were given in this article!

Although it is very nice and convenient to hear music coming out of a machine, usually from (at that period) a gramophone, it is far more natural to hear music live and see the musicians playing. This is what Carmel periodically did, and musicians, some of them very well known,

---

17. Recollections – Solomon Levy.
18. Carmel 1954, p.43.
19. 7 years, p.112.
20. Unwritten recollections of author.
21. Carmel 1959, p.5.

came to Carmel, from the Greenham days onwards, and gave recitals.

One of these recitals was by the Newbury String Players, conducted by Gerald Finzi. It took place in March 1951 and included compositions by Mozart, Bartok, and Bach.[22] The then Carmel music teacher Houghton-Dodd was involved with the composer Gerald Finzi, and it was he who brought them to Carmel for this concert. Malcolm Shifrin (better known as Shif), an Old Carmeli, writes on this concert that it "was a remarkable feat due to the combined charm of (yes, we did call him Hottentot [Houghton-Dodd], I fear) and Kopul."[23] In July of that year the boys at Carmel heard a different musical instrument played by a non-member of the school. It was a Piano Recital by Ruth Oldman, which included compositions by Mozart, Brahms, and Chopin.[24]

These musical recitals continued in Mongewell. One of them was by Lady Barbirolli, an oboist, who was a neighbour of Carmel, since she lived in Wallingford. She came with members of the Camden Trio. Not only did they play their instruments, they even explained to the pupils, with humour and charm, the capabilities of their instruments, thus making the occasion most memorable.[25]

Needless to say that over the course of centuries, some of the instruments used in an orchestra do change. (The piano was only invented about 300 years ago![26]) In 1957, a concert was given at Carmel using various types of medieval instruments.[27]

The alumnus Malcolm Shifrin, returned to Carmel to reorganise the library, but he at the same time established a group called "Musica Viva." This began towards the end of 1958, and David Saville wrote a report on it in the Carmel magazine:

> During the winter and spring term [1958/59], a small, though select, group of senior boys met weekly to listen to, and discuss, the music of the modern world. Mr. Shifrin, the organiser of the group, first introduced us to Nielsen, and his Symphony No. 5 was soon appreciated by all. We then progressed (or degenerated) to Orff, and before long, various members of the Sixth Form could be heard chanting bawdy

---

22. Orchestral Concert at Carmel College Greenham on 17 March 1951, programme.
23. Recollections – Malcolm Shifrin.
24. Piano Recital at Carmel by Miss Ruth Oldman on 15 July 1951, programme.
25. Carmel 1956, p.6.
26. Wikipedia – Piano.
27. Carmel 1957, p.6.

CARMEL COLLEGE   GREENHAM, NEWBURY.

ORCHESTRAL CONCERT
===========================

7.15 p.m.   Saturday
                                       17th March 1951

NEWBURY STRING PLAYERS

Leader May Hope

Conducted

by

Gerald Finzi

Symphony   No. 4   Boyce
   Allegro Vivace-   Gavott-Allegro

"Eine kleine Nachtmusik"   Mozart
   Allegro-Andante - Menuetto & Trio Rondo(Allegro)

Three movements from
"The Holberg-Suite"   Grieg

   Prelude -Sarabande - Rigaudon.

Rumanian Dances   Bartok

Flute Concerto   Quantz

Allegro Arioso   Allegro Vivace

Giant Fugue   Bach

Programme of Orchestral Concert Held at Carmel College in 1951

Latin songs all over the place. By the end of the winter term, our ears were attuned to Barber, Milhaud, Copland, Janacek, and many others.

Our success of the spring term was Walton's 'Belshazzar's Feast', which was a favourite with everyone, as was the 'Alexander Nevsky Cantata," by Prokofieff, and by the end of the term, we had met Dohnanyi and Bruckner. During the term, some of us went to the Festival Hall, where many of us could feel at home with 'Rio Grande' and the 'Glagolithic Mass.'

Finally, I would like to extend our sincere thanks to Mr. Shifrin for innovating Musica Viva, and for spending much of his time in discussing the music; indeed, he must be regarded as a sine qua non. We look forward to next year, when we can further convince ourselves that good music is still being written in the twentieth century.[28]

In addition to just playing the music of the composers, Shifrin, in November 1958, prepared a duplicated chart for the Musica Viva Group headed "Modern music in perspective" and explained that "this rough chart aims to place modern composers in chronological perspective against the earlier Masters. Dates are shown as accurately as possible and no attempt has been made to include every modern composer of merit; rather to place a few useful landmarks. The chart also shows varying shifts of the musical centres in Europe." As an example, under "Scandinavia, East Europe and Russia," Chopin appeared as a purely 19th-century composer, Nielson spanned both 19th and 20th centuries, whilst Shostokovich was entirely a 20th-century composer. It also showed that from the beginning of the 19th century there were numerous composers in Germany and Austria, such as Beethoven, Schubert, and Mendelssohn. However, until the latter part of the 19th century, there were almost none in Great Britain, and the United States; in contrast, in the 20th century these countries could boast of many composers.[29]

The boys' interest in music was not always limited to just listening to music. There were two pupils, Alexis Grower and Richard Lament, who wrote what could be called an obituary to the American Jazz saxophonist, Sidney Bechet, affectionately known as "Pops" Bechet, when he died in the summer of 1959 aged 69. Extracts from this obituary read:

---

28. Carmel 1959, p.31.
29. Carmel College, Musica Viva group, Modern music in perspective, duplicated chart, November 1958.

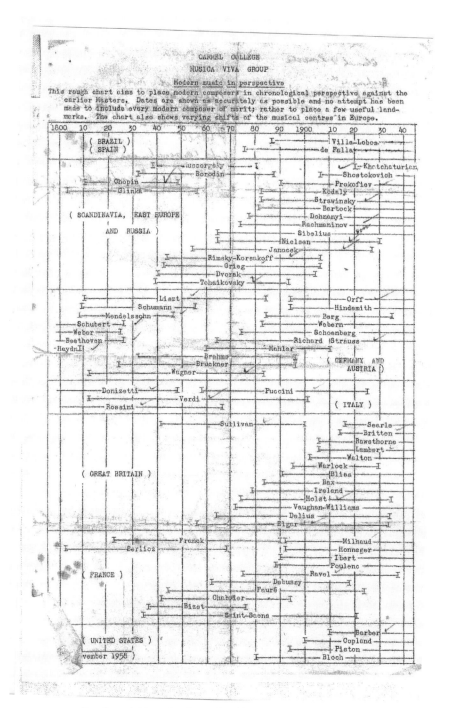

Duplicated Chart for Carmel College Musica Viva Group

His friendship with Louis Armstrong[30] was as firm as the way they played. Although this sounds quite natural, it was nearer a miracle than anything else, for, in New Orleans there was bitter hatred between the Credos (those, like Bechet, of Spanish descent) and the Negroes. . . . But even at the height of his New Orleans career he still had some doubts about the security of a musician's life, and he opened a tailor's shop in Harlem. This was not at all successful, perhaps because instead of trying to promote sales he spent the time in practicing the soprano sax. However, the call of Jazz proved too much for him and he re-entered the world of jazz, playing with the spark of genius and the fire for which he was renowned. . . . When he died all France mourned her adopted son.[31]

Some months later, towards the end of 1958, Grower and Lament wrote an article in the "Carmel Clarion" entitled "A Short History of Jazz" in which they offered a defense of jazz:

> Contrary to public opinion, Jazz is not just a cacophony of sound, and it certainly is not the same kind of music as Rock 'n Roll. It is very old and is founded on very sound principles of music. Right back in the early nineteenth [century], in New Orleans, negroes lived in certain communities. They were very high-spirited and they were liable to play their own brand of music whether they were authorised or not. In fact, they often played their 'hottest' numbers at a funeral. However, the white people soon began to enjoy their music and they used to look forward to these street recitals. . . .

They then went on to describe some leading jazz players, how jazz slowly became commercialised, and the change in musical instruments being used in jazz. In conclusion, after having made their case for jazz, they wrote "We hope that we have clarified the picture as far as jazz is concerned, and that the next jazz record that you come across you will listen to in a different frame of mind."[32]

Enter Mr. George – enter Gilbert and Sullivan. The Carmel magazine wrote, "Mr. George has come to teach Physics, but in addition to his sub-

---

30. Louis Armstrong was an American jazz trumpeter and singer, (Wikipedia – Louis Armstrong).
31. Carmel 1959, pp.12–13.
32. Carmel Clarion, vol.1, no.3, December 1958, (pp.4–5, pages unnumbered).

ject has also introduced Gilbert and Sullivan into the school."[33] Michael Bharier recollects, "Mr. George was a big fan of Gilbert and Sullivan and he got a group of us going on excerpts from their light operas. There is an image still in my mind of him sitting straight as a rod at the piano bringing out the triplet accompaniment to 'When the foeman bears his steel taranta ra taranta ra'."[34]

In 1955, there was a singing group at Carmel called the "Gil and Glee Club." In order to join, one had to go to an audition where one had to sing, "I want to join the gil and glee. Please let me join the gil and glee."[35] This Club was run by Kopul and had a membership of thirty to thirty-five older boys. The members would sing "unison songs, some of them of unusual interest, with fairly well-controlled tone and much enthusiasm."[36]

Not all the singing in Carmel was in English or Hebrew. The year 1956 saw the establishment of a French club, which met weekly, whose programme included "more or less harmonious renderings of traditional songs." The Carmel magazine wrote that "no session was considered complete without the singing of our famous chant adapted from 'Lycée Papillon':

> On n'est pas des imbéciles
> On a même de l'instruction,
> Au collèg' Carmel (bis)
> Au Collège Carmel."[37]

During the following year, another French song, home-produced, came onto the agenda. The Carmel magazine reports that "During the last meetings of this term [Summer 1957] the 'clou'[38] of the evening was a whimsical song composed by M. Gluck, the Chairman, and T. Lutvak, the Secretary of the Club. The song describes goings on at Carmel College and is based on the melodies of well known opera and Folk tunes. Its very popular chorus is:

> Cinq minutes de plaisir avec nous.
> Ce soir nous allons chanter pour vous.
> Seulement, seulement pour vous."[39]

---

33. Carmel 1956, p.4.
34. Recollections – Michael Bharier, chap.3.5, Music at Carmel, a personal recollection.
35. 7 years, p.72.
36. Inspectors' Report, p.17.
37. Carmel 1956, p.28.
38. "Clou" is the French word for highlight.
39. Carmel 1957, pp.27–28.

In September 1959, Yisrael Alexander came over from Israel for three years, and joined the staff at Carmel. He immediately organised a singing group to teach Hebrew songs, and as he taught the various songs, he would bring out duplicated sheets with their words. On the first sheet he brought out, he wrote that "if you hang on to this sheet and those to follow you will have your Hebrew song book by the end of this school year."[40] The author who was a member of this group recollects, "He began by teaching us "Rananu tzadikim" which is from the Psalms.[41] This was his favourite tune, and we would begin each lesson with it. . . . Towards the end of the school year, he recorded us singing all the songs he had taught us on his tape recorder."[42]

One could receive instrumental tuition at Carmel, but unlike other subjects, such lessons were not part of the curriculum. Pupils opting for these lessons would be called out of their normal lessons for them. In addition, parents had to pay extra for these lessons and there was an item on the school bills entitled "Music lessons."[43] Piano lessons were given by Charles Colquhoun and violin lessons by Lilian Edwards.[44]

Music was not confined to the four walls of Carmel. There were also outings to hear musical performances. The Carmel magazine describes one such outing:

> Perhaps one of the most delightful of Gilbert and Sullivan's opera is the 'Mikado', which was seen by a number of boys from various forms of the senior school. It was presented by the D'Oyley Carte Opera Company at the New Theatre, Oxford. The music, which was conducted by Isadore Godfrey, impressed the audience and the spirit of the cast produced a wave of infectious enthusiasm. Ko Ko, the Lord High Executioner, portrayed by Peter Pratt, was exceptionally good. The scenery, and the Japanese dress, were first class. Gilbert's words to the opera were highly amusing and Sullivan's music made it a great comic opera. The boys felt that it was an experience they will always remember.[45]

---

40. Notes on Song-Sheet No. 1/2, September 1959.
41. Psalm 33, verses 1–2.
42. 7 years, p.76.
43. Carmel College school fees bills, e.g. bill shown in "Reflections."
44. The Young Carmelonian, p.17.
45. Carmel 1956, p.29.

David Shaw writes on an outing to London to hear an opera, "Can you imagine a school outing to Covent Garden today! Well we went on one to see Joan Sutherland no less, playing Gilda in Rigoletto. The date was 28th February 1958. I have the programme. In the coach on the way back a group of Latin scholars were singing Postea te vidibo 'I'll see you afterwards' to the tune of 'La Donna e Mobile'."[46]

Michael Bharier likewise writes on an outing to a concert, but this time to hear some famous musicians:

> We heard Sviatoslav Richter playing both Lizst piano concerti with the London Symphony Orchestra under Kyril Kondrashin at the Royal Albert Hall. For an encore he played Lizst's Hungarian Fantasy with the orchestra. We heard I. Musici playing Vivaldi. Kopul and I differed on our tastes in Vivaldi – we exchanged words about it once! He loved Vivaldi. I was more interested in the observation, from high up in the gods, that all of those musicians from Italy appeared to be bald.[47]

Some pupils became so attached to classical music that they wanted to attend concerts outside the framework of official school outings. David Shaw reports on one such incident:

> Samuel Sheldon said that he knew famous pianists including Shura Cherkasky. He was desperate to go to a LPO [London Philharmonic Orchestra] concert at the Festival Hall. We asked the Head, possibly Mr. Sewell if we could go. He replied that we could if we did not miss any lessons. . . which of course meant No!!! . . . It was a problem, but solved it was! We contacted our families for transport (a night at home and some decent food). We were ready, and directly after the bell ending the last period of the day we dashed to the station, met our parents at Paddington and were taken to the concert which luckily did not start till 8.00 p.m. . . . At the interval we went behind the scenes and told the Conductor [Sir Adrian Boult], what we had done. He was most amused and signed our programmes price one shilling plus a third one for the Headmaster for the following morning . . . just to

---

46. Recollections – David Shaw.
47. Recollections – Michael Bharier, chap.3, The environs of Carmel.

rub it in. We were back just before class. The concert included Jeux by Debussy, The Planets and Prakofiev's First Piano Concerto.[48]

David Shaw adds, "When Samuel could not get to a piano he ran his fingers over anything he could find, mantle pieces, desks, whatever.[49]

There was a school outing which could be considered to be on the borderline between a musical activity and a dramatic activity. The author elaborates. It was called "'Let's make an Opera.' From the price of the tickets, someone commented that it was more like 'Let's buy an Opera.' This performance consisted of three parts. The first was of pupils planning to make an opera. In the second part the compère taught the audience how to sing the various songs which they, the audience, would sing during the opera. The final part was the performance of the opera itself."[50]

LET US NOW ACT!

Dramatic performances were already put on by the boys whilst the school was in Greenham, the location being the large wooden paneled hall. Michael Goitein describes his acting in two of these performances, the first of which was a French play which was given before an invited audience of parents:

> As it was a boys' school with no girls to take the female parts, the boys had to do so, and so it was that I got to play a French housewife out on a shopping expedition. I have never been sure whether the laughter that greeted my first appearance on stage was due to the very gay scarf that I had to wear tied around my head, or to the heavily-framed glasses that I wore which quite removed any hint of femininity. Then there was the play 'Hassan,' written by James Elroy Flecker no doubt for somewhat more sophisticated audiences than we could provide. This time I had a lead role – that of Yasmin, a sultry widow, who was loved by the confectioner Hassan, but only became interested in him when he was able to save the Caliph's life and was made rich. She then bribes a servant to let her into Hassan's bedroom. Finding her, Hassan enquired what she was doing there. I then had the hapless duty of replying rhetorically 'Why does a woman lie in the bed of a man?'

---

48. Recollections – David Shaw.
49. Ibid.
50. 7 years, p.81.

This was an incredibly exciting question to young boys. The line was taken up and memorised by the entire school and subsequently not a day passed when it was not mouthed in my presence, accompanied by taunting giggles.[51]

The first dramatic performance put on by the boys at Mongewell was in the summer of 1955. Originally this performance was planned "weather permitting" to be in an outside location on Sports Day after the sports competition.[52] However, the rain decided otherwise and the performance had to be postponed. But this was England, and who was to say that it would not rain on the new proposed date?! The author elaborates, "The school decided then to buy lighting equipment, so that if, on the date to which it had been postponed it again rained, it could be held inside the gymnasium. To cover the cost of this equipment, tickets were sold for the performance. In fact the weather was glorious that day and it took place outside."[53] Two performances were held towards the beginning of July. The location was the terrace in front of the swimming pool, where the producer made use of the pillars and the natural amenities of the setting. The audience sat on the lawn.[54]

The first item on the acting agenda[55] was scenes of the Interlude from "A Midsummer Night's Dream." In an account of the acting, the reviewer wrote:

> Wootliff, as Bottom with a ripe Lancashire accent, extracted every particle of humour. At times, he over-acted and relapsed into buffoonery unrelieved by pathos: he should remember that all great clowning is on the verge of tears. Schachter, as Thisbe, had the same faults and the same virtues but not the same accent. Golker was a quieter but none the less effective Quince. Seruya, as the Duke, looked majestic and carried himself regally. His court were all very competent and his Philostrate had a good delivery. The minor parts (which included in R. Rudd a minute and charming lion) were all well done. The costumes were a miracle of skilled improvisation by Mr. Cox and his helpers

---

51. Recollections – Michael Goitein.
52. Carmel College Athletic Sports Day, 1955, programme, p.7.
53. 7 years, p.82.
54. Carmel 1955, p.10.
55. Scenes from "A Midsummer Night's Dream" and from "Job," duplicated programme.

and a word of praise should go to the efficient backstage activities of Victor Keller and his confrères.[56]

The item on the programme which followed was described by the reviewer as "the most complete contrast imaginable – perhaps too complete." It was the Biblical book of Job (Iyov). The programme described it as "a dramatisation of the book of Job translated from Hebrew into modern English prose. Apart from selection, no alteration has been made to the original text."[57]Apart from the actors on stage, the voices of G-d and of Satan were spoken offstage via a "mechanical amplification" which the reviewer described as "not all it might have been, which was a pity, for both [speakers – Henry Schachter and Ivor Wolfson, respectively] enunciated clearly and feelingly." The difficulty in this production was that there was "almost no action" and there were "long speeches" during which it was "hard to keep the thread." The part of Job was played by Michael Ostwind, and he "accomplished the difficult task of delivering them [his speeches] from a variety of uncomfortable positions with real dramatic force. His performance – much the most difficult of the day – was something of a *tour de force*." In summing up this production of Job, the reviewer wrote:

> Job was a moving and a remarkable experience. It was not wholly successful; at times it rose to a climax only to lapse into anti-climax. The producer might perhaps reconsider some of his groupings, and the author shorten some of his longer speeches to give them more dramatic intensity. But to both we extend our sincere and humble congratulations, and our astonishment that they have so successfully united in one man [namely, Murray Roston, who taught English].[58]

In 1959, just after he joined the staff of the school as head of English, Frederick Nelson reintroduced dramatic activities to the school curriculum. The Carmel magazine in its "School Chronicle" writes on this, "Mr. Nelson turned a blind eye to the lack of dramatic facilities in the School and proceeded to revive successfully the Dramatic Society. In the course of the year a considerable number of plays have been produced, and many

---

56. Carmel 1955, p.10.
57. Scenes from "A Midsummer Night's Dream" and from "Job," duplicated programme.
58. Carmel 1955, pp.10–11.

of them attained an excellent standard. A consequence of this achievement is that the School development plan now includes a stage."[59]

Later in this magazine appears a full-length article on the activities of "The Dramatic Society":

In the first full year [1958–1959] the Dramatic Society has been one of the liveliest of School activities. A production has been staged in each of the three terms, and, all told, some sixty boys have appeared on the stage; many others have given valuable help in preparing stage properties and behind the stage. . . . No full-length play has yet been attempted, as the aim of the newly-formed Society was to offer as many acting opportunities as possible without making the demands on the boys' time which could not have been avoided had inexperienced actors been asked to learn large parts and rehearse them to a high standard.[60]

During the first term of that academic year, two one-act plays were performed on 16 December 1958. The first of them, "The Bishop's Candlesticks," was based on an episode in Victor Hugo's novel "Les Miserables," and it contained several moral and ethical lessons. In contrast, the second, "The Rehearsal," was a comedy whose contents were summarised in the duplicated programme for the performance, "We present a rehearsal of 'Macbeth' by Mr. Shakespeare and the company of the 'Globe' Theatre." Amongst those supplying the properties and costumes were the Carmel Kitchen Staff (please take note that they did more than just stuff the boys with both edible and inedible food!) and the Oxford Playhouse.[61] On the contrast between the two plays, an article in the Carmel magazine comments:

One valuable lesson was learnt from these two plays: that while a mixed programme of serious drama and comedy makes the best evening's entertainment, it is better to be ambitious in choosing the serious play than to perform, as on this occasion, a 'simple' but slow and

59. Carmel 1959, p.5.
60. Ibid., p.29.
61. The Carmel College Dramatic Society presents Two One-Act Plays . . . Tuesday, December 16th, 1958, duplicated programme.

undramatic story. For this reason the two plays performed together in the Spring term[62] were chosen with an eye to dramatic effect.[63]

The plays were A. A. Milne's "The Man in the Bowler Hat," and "Happiness my Goal," the first of which was produced by a student from Pembroke College Oxford, who at the time was doing his teaching practice at Carmel.[64]

In the summer term, a Junior School Festival was held in which each of the lower five forms performed a short play. One of them was "The Crimson Cocoanut" which was "a comedy of bombs and anarchists," and another was "The Letters of Fate" which was "a farcical melodrama of smuggling and spying for Napoleon." What was remarkable about the play "Doctor Till," which was produced by the third form, was that the cast contained every pupil in that form.[65]

A dramatic performance does not just require actors. There also have to be sound and light effects. At first, some primitive lighting equipment was used which comprised a few rheostats screwed on a board, which in one of the performances fused all the lights! For the performance put on in 1960 (and described below), far superior equipment was constructed at the school. The author explains:

> This time, the librarian Shifrin made himself responsible for the lighting and sound effects. He had a long meeting with Mr. Coles to discuss the construction of a frame to hold the lighting equipment and another one to hold the sound equipment. The materials for these frames came from old iron beds. For the lighting, the rheostats were taken from the original boards and attached to these frames.[66]

The first time that the school put on a full-length play was in the spring term of 1960. It consisted of four acts, and was produced by Frederick Nelson. It was a slightly adapted version of S. Ansky's[67] Yiddish classic,

---

62. On 30 and 31 March 1959 in the School Hall.
63. Carmel 1959, p.29.
64. Carmel College Dramatic Society, "The Man in the Bowler Hat" . . . "Happiness my Goal," duplicated programme; Carmel 1959, p.4.
65. Carmel 1959, p.30.
66. 7 years, p.82.
67. Shloyme Zanvl Rappoport (1863–1920) known by his pseudonym S. Ansky (without specifying what the "S" stood for!) was a Russian Jewish author, playwright, and researcher of Jewish folklore (Wikipedia – S. Ansky).

"The Dybbuk." A four page duplicated programme was brought out which listed a cast of twenty-four, although in some cases the same person played two or even three different parts. In addition there was a technical staff of about twenty, whose functions included lights, sound, wardrobe, and make-up.[68] Another first was that "the actors had the benefit of curtains and no longer had to walk off in Shakespearean style."[69]

The author adds further details of this production:

> The English text for the performance had been translated from the Hebrew – in fact it had been over-translated! Even expressions such as 'David Melech Yisrael . . .' which should have left in the original Hebrew had been translated. Rabbi Young was therefore asked to go through the script and decide which phrases should be left in the original.
>
> During this play, shofars are sounded. The blowing of the shofar was not done live on the stage (very wise, since shofars don't always blow when you want them to!) but had been pre-recorded and the actors put models of shofars to their lips.
>
> A problem in the production was that the script spoke of taking seven Sifrei Torah out of the Ark. The script was first changed to 'the Sifrei Torah' without specifying a number, but even this was not so simple since one could not use real Sifrei Torah in a theatrical performance. To solve this problem, some dummy ones were constructed with the aid of the rods used to hold the daily newspapers. The performance which I saw went very nicely and was most enjoyable.
>
> A story I once heard regarding productions of 'The Dybbuk' was that the author died on the day of the first production. Since then, an extra candle has been lit in the scene where the actors carry candles. Accurate or not – I really don't know.[70]

Again in the summer term of that year, the Juniors took over, and what is more they did not act in the English language, nor in just one foreign language, nor in just two, but they became tri-lingual, namely they produced plays in three languages, "Miles et Senex" in Latin, "Chalif Storch" in German, and "Nous les Gosses" in French. The Carmel magazine com-

68. Carmel College Dramatic Society presents The Dybbuk by S.Ansky, duplicated programme.
69. Carmel 1960, p.28.
70. 7 years, pp.82–83.

"The Dybbuk" takes place in White Russia about
1800. The characters are members of the Chassidic
sect, in whose beliefs there was (and is) a strong
mystical element, seen here in the emphasis on
Channon's presumption in "meddling with the Kabala."
The play concerns the casting out of a Dybbuk - the
spirit of a dead person which has taken possession of
a living body - a ceremony of which there are many
records in the lives of the great Rabbis of this
period.

ACT ONE

Evening. In the synagogue of Brainitz, a small town
near Miropol.

Interval

ACT TWO

Two weeks later. In the square of Brainitz, in front
of Sender's house. On the left is the synagogue.

Interval

ACT THREE

Shabbat evening, some time later. Rabbi Azrael's
house in Miropol.

Interval

ACT FOUR

The next day. Rabbi Azrael's house.

Page from the Programme of the "Dybbuk" Acted by the Pupils of Carmel College

ments, "The outstanding characteristic of the performances was the high
standard of pronunciation and the authenticity of the national atmosphere
produced."[71]

As with music, acting was not limited to the four walls of Carmel Col-

---

71. Carmel 1960, p.29.

lege; there were also actors beyond the walls and the boys were often taken to see them.

Let us start with Stratford-on-Avon and the reason is simple! A Shakespearean play was a compulsory paper on the English Literature O-level examination. (In Carmel one could never get away from exams!) What could be better than seeing such a play acted, and what place could be better than Stratford-on-Avon. Indeed the Carmel boys would often visit the place. In May 1951, whilst the school was still at Greenham, a group of boys went to the Shakespeare Memorial Theatre in Stratford to see Richard II,[72] in October of the following year, there was a visit there to see Macbeth,[73] and in May 1953 to see "Antony and Cleopatra."[74] On this last visit, there was a report in the Carmel magazine "Badad," which concluded with the critical comment, "We all deplored the fact that such a delightful little English town [Stratford-on-Avon] should be exploited for the sake of the ever-powerful dollar."[75] The Carmel magazine for 1957 describes a further such visit:

> In June, the Union Society paid its annual visit to Stratford-on-Avon, this time to see 'As You Like It.' This quaint Warwickshire town has much to offer visitors other than the Memorial Theatre and our boys occupied themselves before the performance in visiting the birthplace of Shakespeare, the parish church to see his bust and the entries in the registers, and also, perhaps, in a glance at the Shakespeare Art gallery at the rear of the Theatre.
>
> 'As You Like It' is one of the less often produced plays, and most of those present were seeing it for the first time. The play is in complete contrast with Shakespearean tragedy, but the Memorial Theatre Company made it a welcome contrast. It is one of the comparatively few plays which contain songs, and they were well sung though not, perhaps, sufficiently emphasised in this production. It was pleasant to see Miss Peggy Ashcroft as Rosalind, for one cannot help admiring the talent of such a gifted actress.
>
> The annual Stratford outing is always an enjoyable affair, and this year was no exception.[76]

---

72. Rau Letters, 22 May 1951.
73. Ibid., 16 October 1952.
74. Ibid., 26 May 1953.
75. Badad, p.5.
76. Carmel 1957, p.30.

However, this mention of "annual visits" to Stratford is not supported by the various Carmel magazines. The theatre to which there were a number of visits by Carmel boys to see Shakespearean performances, was the Old Vic Theatre in London. There, what the Carmel boys saw, included, "Julius Caesar,"[77] Michael Bentham's production of "King Lear,"[78] and "Richard II."[79] The various performances of the Shakespearean plays seen by the Carmel pupils were not limited to period costumed productions. There was a visit to Oxford to see Macbeth acted in modern costume[80] – an anachronism of many hundreds of years!

One does not have to see acting live at a theatre – there is also the option of viewing films. Indeed Carmel boys both at the Prep School and the Senior School had regular film shows at their respective schools, and there were also occasions when they went to the cinema.

The numerous films shown to the Prep School included the American science fiction film "The Day the Earth Stood Still";[81] "The Count of Monte Cristo" which is based on an adventure novel written in the 19th century by the French author Alexander Dumas, and today regarded as a literary classic;[82] the comedy film "The Belles of St. Trinians" whose location was a girls' high school;[83] and Agatha Christie's crime story "Witness for the Prosecution."[84]

For the entire Senior School, between 1954 and 1957, Romney Coles would project a number of films each term. The author elaborates:

> This was done in the Main Hall, with the film projector being placed by the eastern wall and the screen by the western wall. (No religious significance for these placings – just the topography of the hall!) Mr. Coles once told us that when he borrowed a film to show at the school, he had to fill up a lot of forms certifying that it was only a private performance and was not open to the general public; pupils, teachers and even parents of pupils were part of the school. He added that if anyone else 'happened to be present' he 'didn't know about it'! After a time I learned that instead of sitting in the hall, I could get a

---

77. Carmel 1956, p.29.
78. Carmel 1958, p.32.
79. Carmel 1960, p.32.
80. Carmel 1958, p.32.
81. Alpha 1955, p.4.
82. Alpha 1956, p.3.
83. Preparatory School Magazine 1958, p.11.
84. Preparatory School Magazine 1959, p.6.

better view by sitting on my bedside locker by the edge of the railing to the staircase on the first floor – a grandstand view. I don't think this was officially allowed but I was never caught when doing this.[85]

The films were on a whole variety of subjects. There were some films of Shakespeare's plays – "Hamlet" and "Romeo and Juliet"; biographies of Marie Antoinette and of the German Field Marshal Erwin Rommel in the latter stages of the Second World War; Jane Austen's novel "Pride and Prejudice" which dealt with issues of manners, upbringing, morality, education, and marriage in the society of the landed gentry of early 19th-century England; Victor Hugo's book "Les Miserables" which focused on the struggles of an ex-convict and his experience of redemption; the war film "Stalag 17" which tells the story of a group of American airmen held in a Second World War German prisoner of war camp, who come to suspect that one of their number is an informant; "State Secret" where a famous American surgeon is decoyed to a middle European country where he discovers that he is to operate on a dictator; the adventure film "Golden Salamander" which is about an archeologist in North Africa who runs afoul of a crime syndicate; the American western film "Winchester '73"; the two comedy films "Doctor in the House" which follows a group of students through medical school; and "Genevieve" where two couples are comedically involved in a veteran automobile rally.[86]

In those days, films were graded by the British Board of Film Classification into "U," "A" and "X" films. Children under 16 were not admitted to "X" films.[87] Since the showings at Carmel were private, these restrictions did not apply. One of the films shown at Carmel was H. G. Wells "The War of the Worlds" and it was classified as an X film. This was not surprising since there were some very scary scenes. The creatures from Mars flew overhead spraying the earth's inhabitants with deadly material. Even a clergyman who tried to approach them to talk peace suffered the same fate.[88]

Indeed, over the years, the pupils at both the Prep and Senior School were treated to a whole variety of films, without having to travel to a cinema.

---

85. 7 years, p.80.
86. Carmel: 1954. p.10; 1955, p.7; 1956, p.6; 1957, p.6; explanatory information on the various films is from the appropriate articles in Wikipedia.
87. Wikipedia – History of British film industry.
88. 7 years, p.80.

LEAVING THE CONFINES OF CARMEL

In addition to concerts, theatres, and cinemas, there were outings to a large variety of places, often in co-ordination with various subject teachers.

In October 1957, "Inbal" the National Ballet and Dance Theatre of Israel, performed at the Theatre Royal Drury Lane for three weeks,[89] and a group of boys went to see the performance.[90] The author elaborates:

> The Inbal Dance Troupe from Israel was in London putting on a performance which included the 'Song of Devorah' from the book of Judges. Rabbi Rosen wanted to take a group of pupils to see this performance and on a Friday night after the meal, a group of pupils, including myself, assembled in his study to study this passage from the Tanach. During this meeting, one of the boys said that that Motzoei Shabbat was the last performance. We therefore decided that we would go that following evening, which we did.[91]

That same term there was a visit to the Royal Albert Hall for an international folk-dancing festival.[92] The author elaborates, "We went to the Royal Albert Hall, to see troupes of dancers from numerous different countries in the world. Included was Israel and the troupe began with a person singing from the Song of Solomon 'El ginat egoz.' The evening ended with all the dancers from the different countries dancing, to the tune 'Ushavtem mayim b'sason'."[93]

The author also relates that on one of these trips which took place in the summer of 1958, there were no London buses – they were on strike![94] On another occasion,

> when I was in the upper fifth, there was an exhibition in the British Museum on the excavations in Hazor in northern Israel. Mr. Loewe arranged a trip to London for us to see this exhibition. In one corner of this exhibition there was some crib with the remains of some baby. A week or so later, Mr. Schmidt took his Economics class on a field trip to London. Before our first stop which was near to the British

---

89. Jewish Chronicle, 11 October 1957, p.23.
90. Carmel 1958, p.32.
91. 7 years, p.81.
92. Carmel 1958, p.33.
93. 7 years, p.81.
94. Carmel 1958, p.32.

Museum, we had a short time to spare and so we went in to see the Hazor exhibition, since many of those participating in the Economics trip had not gone to London in the previous week. In fact we saw almost as much of this exhibition on that day as we [had] seen in the previous week, when we had travelled especially to London for it. Our first official stop was at the Trade Union house where we were given a lecture on trade unions. I remember it was an exquisite lecture hall, beautifully furnished. O to be a trade union leader!"[95] [The Carmel magazine adds that "We were overawed by the architecture [of this building] and by Epstein's overpowering statue. This visit made Trade Union history, for we were the first public school ever to have visited the headquarters."[96]]

Our second destination was the department store Harrods in Knightsbridge. Here in a less exquisite lecture hall, we were told all about the running of Harrods. The lecturer told us that it was almost the biggest department store in Europe. He showed us their method of sending information from the various departments to the office via pipes with high pressure air which would speedily transfer the orders, which were placed in metal containers before being inserted into these pipes. In the vote of thanks to Harrods given to the lecturer by one of the boys, he said jokingly that one of our smaller boys nearly got lost in one of these pipes! We were finally taken down to the staff canteen where we were given cakes and other confectionary for tea. One of the boys asked Mr. Schmidt whether the food was kosher and he replied 'Eat as much as your conscience permits you.'[97]

In the same term "visits were made to Reading Museum to see an exhibition of Roman remains and to the Royal Apartments at Hampton Court, followed by a trip down the river. A large party made a journey to The Cheddar Gorge and they saw the remarkable stalagmite formations in The Cheddar Caves."[98]

During the "Kopul era," if one wanted to see what was going on in the British Parliament, one had to go there in person. Television was rigorously excluded from the Parliament, even still photography was not allowed and had to be done clandestinely. There were at least two out-

95. 7 years, p.83.
96. Carmel 1958, p.32.
97. 7 years, p.83.
98. Carmel 1958, p.33.

ings to the Houses of Parliament. The first one was in the spring term of 1958 when "the English and Economic sets of the Sixth Form went to the Strangers' Gallery of the House of Commons where rather desultory debating and speaking was heard."[99] It is a matter of luck what one hears; sometimes it can be more interesting as was the case of a visit to both the House of Commons and the House of Lords two years later. When on their visit "they were privileged to witness part of an instructive debate on betting licences."[100] Did any Old Carmelis after that become bookies, or in more refined language, "Turf Accountants"?

LET'S ESTABLISH ANOTHER SOCIETY!

In Carmel there were numerous societies[101] – almost as many societies as pupils! However, unquestionably the main society was the Union Society. Everyone there became a "Mr."

The most common item in meetings of the Union Society was debating. In such debates there would be two speakers proposing the motion and two opposing it. The debate would then be thrown open to the floor. Both sides would then sum up and the floor would vote on the motion. The boys were told that they had to vote on the arguments of the speakers and not come in with pre-conceived ideas.[102]

The debates involved not only boys versus boys. In the early days of Carmel in 1950, there was a debate on whether blood sports should be abolished, and the speakers were Kopul versus two fourth form boys.[103]

Although the younger boys at Carmel never actually paraded with posters with the slogan "Down with the Prefects," there was indeed in February 1954, a debate in which members of the 4th and 5th forms deplored the "prefectorial system." The Carmel magazine reports that "the speeches from the floor were unusually numerous and of a high standard, G[eorge] Mandel [then a sub-prefect] making a particularly treacherous attack upon the prefects. The motion was surprisingly defeated, despite the fact that three prefects present voted in favour of it."[104] In summing up that year's debates, the Carmel magazine reports:

---

99. Ibid., p.32.
100. Carmel 1960, p.32.
101. Various Carmel magazines, section on Societies.
102. Unwritten recollections of author.
103. Rau letters, 6 June 1950.
104. Carmel 1954, p.40.

The most encouraging feature of these two terms has been the promise shown by members of the Fifth Form as speakers; this means that
we should not be left in a year or two, when the present sixth-formers
leave, with no-one in the school experienced enough to speak, as we
were at the beginning of this year. The floor speeches have, however,
been generally disappointing throughout the year, more so in quantity than in quality. For a debate to be successful, the house should
be made to feel strongly enough on the motion to wish to discuss
it themselves afterwards; and I hope that this will be rectified in the
future.[105]

The Carmel daily menu included both cake and bread, but not everyone
in the world is so fortunate. It was during the following year that there was
a debate on the motion 'That no man should have cake until all men have
bread'. The Carmel magazine reports on this debate, "Mr. M. Ostwind
and Mr. E. Schwartz [note the "Mr." when referring to the boys!] both declaimed vehemently on behalf of egotism and both were strongly attacked
for their apparent selfishness. It is interesting to note that this motion was
defeated, an apparent instance of evil triumphing over good."[106] So "Let
them eat cake!" Did not a famous head-chopped-off French Queen say
this?!

Even film stars and cricket batters entered the Union Society debates
(as least by name, if not in person). This was in the year 1956 and as the
Carmel magazine relates:

> [There was] an interesting debate on the advantages of sport over
> culture. The house finally decided that it would rather be Sir Lau-
> rence Olivier than Dennis Compton, Esq. The wittiest speaker of the
> evening was not on the proposition or opposition, but on the floor.
> An unpleasant feature of the meeting was the success of the disruptive
> elements at work who proposed abstention and in fact who gained
> more supporters than either side.[107]

It is the unusual which attracts attention and this was indeed so even in
the Carmel Union Society. During the academic year 1958/59, there were
a number of somewhat unusually worded motions which included "The

---

105. Ibid., p.41.
106. Carmel 1955, p.12.
107. Carmel 1956, p.25.

UNION SOCIETY

THE ACTIVITIES OF the Union Society during the last year have been both numerous and diverse, and although a general decline in the number of orators was noticed, the debates were lively in the extreme.

The Autumn term opened with an enjoyable, if slightly hilarious, meeting where a session of 20 questions was held. The panel was immensely successful. At the following meeting, on the 3rd October, a heated debate took place. The motion was that "this house proposes that the English language be reformed". All the speakers, members of the teaching staff, spoke well and the motion was finally carried.

Following meetings were: —a discussion group on "Imperialism in this modern world" and an original panel game in which Mr. Schwartz won a speaking prize.

A highly vociferous debate on the existence of ghosts was held and after much hesitation the floor voted 19 for and 19 against—the first recorded draw in the society's history.

On Monday, the 21st of November, Dr. Friedmann gave a lecture on Goethe, rather poorly attended, one thought, for so brilliant a speaker who is an authority on the subject.

The last meeting of the Autumn term was a highly successful ghost-story-reading session. This particular type of evening has now become a permanent feature on the society's agenda and not without good cause.

The Spring term opened with a resounding success where 9 persons tried their hands, or rather their tongues, at speaking for the first time in public. All the speakers were good, some particularly so and it augurs well for the future oratorical prowess of the Union Society. Mr. Korn, though not the most powerful speaker—Mr. Moshi must claim that honour—won the Society's speaking award with his speech on 'Spirtualism'.

"Etymology" was the subject of an intriguing talk by the Society's vice-president, Mr. Warner, and provoked much thought-searching study.

The debate of the meeting of Tuesday, the 7th of February, was agreed by all to be the most serious debate the society has held for a long time. The motion was the time-worn, but nonetheless still topical debate—"that this house *deplores* capital punishment." Mr. Keller and Mr. Winkleman proposed; Mr. Goitein and Mr. Hirschfeld opposed. It was a fiery debate by any standards—there was perhaps too much heckling from the floor—and the standard of speaking was generally high. Moral issues were thrashed out over and over again and the final voting carried the motion fairly conclusively by 19 votes to 12.

The following three meetings were of cultural interest. One was a literary evening interspersed with gramophone records; the second an informal debate on "the British Press" and the third an illuminating lecture on Mozart given by Mr. Cox with the aid of long-playing records.

The next meeting was an interesting debate on the advantages of sport over culture. The house finally decided that it would rather be Sir Laurence Olivier than Denis Compton, Esq. The wittiest speaker of the evening was not on the proposition or opposition, but on the floor. An unpleasant feature of the meeting was the success of the disruptive elements at work who proposed abstention and in fact who gained more supporters than either side.

The last meeting of the year was a Symposium. The pieces submitted were of a very high standard and after a re-vote between the secretary's "Sioux

twenty-five

*Report on Carmel College Union Society Activities
in Carmel Summer Magazine of 1956*

house deplores the sending of rockets to the moon" which was defeated, "All men are neurotic, but some are more neurotic than others," which was carried, and "This house believes that culture is bunk," which was defeated. "Highlights of the debates included five pound notes being waved about by E[llis] Korn, piles of authoritative books in front of M[ichael] Ellman, and D[avid] Lewis trying to persuade the Society that the moon was made of green cheese."[108]

Let us be like Parliament and have filibustering in Union Society debates, decided pupil Mr. Segal, aided and abetted by fellow pupils Messrs. Robson and Schreiber! They thus set up in 1960 a "Filibusters Club." The Carmel magazine reports on this that Segal "was so imbued with reforming zeal, that, practically single-handed, he managed to see to it that the procedure of the Society adhered as strictly as possible to that of the Oxford Union. We are as yet naturally unable to appreciate the full magnitude of the service which he has rendered us."[109]

The lessons of a debate did not always end at the end of a meeting. Jeffrey Gandz elaborates:

> The joy of discussion and debate. I loved the cut and thrust of debating, of learning how to defend a position even if you didn't believe in it and of finding the holes in others' arguments. Both the appreciation of this and some of the modest skills I developed at Carmel gave me a foundation for later years as an academician, an educator and consultant to businesses and governments for which it is critical to be able to understand others' perspectives and points of view and to frame cogent arguments.[110]

There were also activities of the Union Society, other than debates. In October 1951, whilst the school was still in Greenham, a meeting was devoted to hearing a collection of records called "The Sounds of Time," accompanied by a running commentary by the teacher Gilbert Warner.[111] These records gave extracts of numerous memorable speeches and sounds between the years 1934 to 1949. The vast majority were connected with the Second World War; one of the more unusual being a cab driver reporting how all that a woman standing in the middle of bombed ruins

---

108. Carmel 1959, pp.26–27.
109. Carmel 1960, p.26.
110. Recollections – Jeffrey Gandz.
111. Rau Letters, 29 October 1951.

could say was "you ain't seen my bleeding milkman round, have you?" However there were other sounds which included the voice of the reporter witnessing the giant airship Hindenburg bursting into flames, King George VI speaking of his anxiety about Britain's economic plight, and Chaim Weizmann speaking with pride of the new State of Israel.[112] In 1955, the Union Society gave a repeat performance, again conducted by Warner, enabling a new generation of pupils to hear these records.[113]

In a symposium held by the Union Society, a paper entitled a "Memoir of a Foreigner," received more votes than a paper entitled a "Sioux Indian's visit to a dentist," but maybe it was a consolation to the "Sioux Indian" that this was only after a revote. Competition was obviously stiff since "the pieces submitted were of a very high standard."[114]

Over the course of the years, the agenda included lectures, on a whole variety of subjects, which were given either by an outsider or by a member of the Carmel staff. The subjects included the German writer Johann Wolfgang von Goethe,[115] The Meaning of History,[116] Heraldry, the Compatibility of Science and Religion, and Tibet (which was illustrated by Tibetan coins, scarves, and knives).[117]

The upper forms did not have a monopoly in Union Society activities since the lower forms in the Senior School, had their own society called the Junior Union Society. Its agenda included debates, brains-trusts, hat-debates, and lectures. Even though the members were younger than those of the Union Society, they were still addressed as Mr.[118]

The magazine "The Young Carmelonian" reported on a debate held during the academic year 1953/54:

> It was most successful, and the standard of speaking was very high. The motion was 'The pen and the tongue are mightier than the sword.' Mr. A. Levy assisted by Mr. Moshe, spoke for the motion, and Mr. H. Benjamin, seconded by Mr. E. Fine, opposed. The debate revealed talent of a most promising nature, and the Society justly feels a sense of pride in its work of training debaters for the Senior Union

---

112. The Sounds of Time 1934–1949, (Internet).
113. Carmel 1955, p.12.
114. Carmel 1956, pp.25–26.
115. Ibid., p.25.
116. Carmel 1958, p.27.
117. Carmel 1959, p.28.
118. Carmel 1956, p.28.

[Society]. Our President, Rabbi Rosen, graced the assembly and made a most eloquent defence of the pen and the tongue.[119]

A couple of years later a debate "That this House considers that the ancient Britons were happier than Modern Man" was held. Maybe in those days they used their pens, tongues, and swords differently than today, and the Carmel magazine comments that "Our members evidently would prefer to live in the Neolithic era, for the motion was passed." In a further debate on the abolishment of capital punishment, the same magazine notes "Carmel is compassionate and once more the motion was passed."[120]

The following year, the Junior Union "went political!" and set up a "Junior Parliament" – why should such an organisation be limited to Westminster?! The Carmel magazine elaborates:

> Another aspect of the Society has been the Junior Parliament, modeled on Westminster, which has brought to the Junior School an interest in world affairs. There has been considerable rivalry between the Conservatives who formed the Government, the Labour opposition and the Liberals and Independents. It has been interesting to note that although the Government have had a majority, they have not had any victories because the Independent parties have sided with the Opposition. What will happen when the House reassembles next year is yet to be seen.[121]

However, this Parliament seems to have had a very long recess during the following year and the politicians only returned in the 1958/59 academic year, when "Roland Joffe was returned as Prime Minister and David Linton as leader of the Opposition." Another activity that year was a mock trial for murder. Following a moving plea for the defence, the accused was found "Not Guilty" by a jury of twelve.[122]

Whilst on the question of political parties, in 1960 the author co-established a political "Liberal Society." The author elaborates;

> A society established in the school by Barrie Schreiber and myself, when we were in the upper sixth form, was a political "Liberal Soci-

119. The Young Carmelonian, p.6.
120. Carmel 1956, p.28.
121. Carmel 1957, p.26.
122. Carmel 1959, pp.28–29.

ety." On one occasion, we brought a speaker and had a joint meeting with the Union Society. This meeting took place in Rabbi Rosen's study.

However the main activity of this Liberal Society was the bringing out of a newspaper. We had planned to bring out six editions and people paid in advance the sum of 12 pennies, namely 2 pennies per edition. In the end we brought out 5 editions, with the last edition being of extra large size priced at 4 pennies.

This was prior to the days of home computers. We therefore had to type the text on to a Gestetner stencil, and correct any mistakes with red correcting fluid. To make a paper look attractive, it is nice to finish every line at the same point. In those days it was not so simple as it is today with computer programs. The librarian Shifrin told us of a method on how to do this, although it would involve typing the item twice. Since this method was tedious, I believe we limited it to just the first page of the paper.

We ran off the newspaper in the school office and immediately paid Mrs. Walker for the outlay. On one occasion when we told her that we had run off *about* 500 pages, she informed us the cost would be fifteen shillings *and one penny*. One cannot say that Mrs. Walker wasn't precise!

Included in this newspaper was a guest article, a cartoon, and a quiz. We also left a column blank until just before running off copies of the paper on the office duplicator. This was a "stop press" column and we would get the latest news from the radio which we then put in this column. . . .

One of the cartoons was called "The Battle of Trafalgar." At a demonstration which had then just taken place at Trafalgar Square, there were fights between the Fascists and some other groups and in this cartoon one saw the Fascists waving Nazi flags and the opposing side different flags. Another cartoon showed a man watching television and in his window was a notice "indoor aerial." The point was that people not seeing a television aerial on his roof would think that he could not afford a television. Amongst the quizzes was one asking for the names of the Prime Ministers of a long list of countries and in another quiz the capital cities of countries.

At that period, there was a motion before the governing body of Oxford and/or Cambridge Universities to drop the entrance requirement for Latin for science students. In our newspaper, we wrote that those science students who were already burning their Latin books should stop. This motion still had to go through one further stage until it was passed, although it was likely that it would get through.[123]

In a report in the Carmel magazine, Barrie Schreiber adds some further details and comments:

> When it [Liberal Society] was started . . . all ideas of a modest nature had to be abandoned as sixty would-be members attended the first meeting. Throughout, we had to remember that this was a school, and so our policy was to educate in politics rather than to shout slogans. Now we can justifiably claim that the boys of the school woke up to the fact that important and vital events happen every day in the world . . . The discussions [in the meetings] ranged far and wide over many important topics: Defence, Apartheid, the Ombudsman, Proportional Representation, Cyprus.[124]

In the spring of 1958, the Prep School pupils suddenly saw on their timetable a period called "The Prep School Union." Some pupils wrote that, "We wondered what it was at first, but on the following Sunday, we found out it was a club, in which we had debates and quizzes, etc.," which had been set up by Abraham Carmel.[125] One of its first debates was on the motion "This House considers that Atomic Energy is a Curse to this World," a motion which was carried.[126] It also held a number of "Hat Debates" about which "The Prep School Magazine" was very enthusiastic saying that these debates "first prepared boys to speak, and a number who, prior to this year had never spoken in public, have become capable little orators."[127]

Carmel also had a science society which was called the "Haber Society" after the German Jewish scientist Fritz Haber.[128] Over the years there were numerous papers delivered by boys of Carmel at this Society's meetings. These included "Coffee in Kenya" which was delivered by Henry Hirshfield who came from Kenya; "Crystallography" by Leon Norell,

123. 7 years, pp.71–72.
124. Carmel 1960, p.31.
125. Preparatory School Magazine 1958, p.6.
126. Ibid.
127. Preparatory School Magazine 1959, p.6.
128. In 1918 Haber was awarded the Nobel Prize in Chemistry for the synthesis of ammonia from its elements, (Wikipedia – Fritz Haber).

who at the same time "showed some of the magnificent crystals which he had prepared"; Jack Coleman who spoke on "Perfumes" whilst passing samples around the audience; a talk on "Railways" by Henry Law, who could be called an authority on this subject, and he illustrated his talk with his own diagrams and drawings; and "Defects of the Eye and Modern Methods of Correction" delivered by Michael Blackstone.[129]

There were also many outings. One of the early visits was to the Reading and District Gas Undertaking. On this visit the Carmel magazine says that "this was one of the most interesting visits so far arranged; the senior members found the visit particularly interesting, because of the chemistry involved in the Gas Works, which is on their syllabus for the G.C.E. We saw the extraction of some of the constituents of coal-gas. And also saw producer-gas being prepared on a large industrial scale."[130] During the following year, the outings "included a visit to the Southampton Corporation Water Works . . . where we saw water from both wells and rivers being softened and purified for domestic use. Our visit to Morris Motors, Oxford, was of interest to our engineering enthusiasts, who saw, besides the ordinary mass production, the assembly of a prototype model and the testing of a similar type."[131] The "boozers" obviously enjoyed an outing during the next year which the Carmel magazine describes as being to a site "enthralling as the name suggests" – the name was Simonds' Brewery and it was situated in Reading which was relatively close to Carmel.[132]

Regular films were shown to members of the Haber Society by Romney Coles, who was the Master-in-Charge of the Society (unlike the other school societies, he did not want to be called the President!). These included the Chilean nitrate industry; the extraction and uses of aluminium which was preceded by a talk on the subject; colloids and emulsions; and on a variety of topics ranging from the industrial preparation of chemicals to modern aircraft.[133]

Following 1956, there was a sudden lack of interest in this society and it went into "cold storage" for two years. "[Then] it was impressed upon the members that the society could only continue to function, provided that it had the support it deserved, and it is pleasing to record that the response was very impressive."[134] Following this "resuscitation" a number of talks

---

129. Carmel: 1954, p.41; 1955, p.13; 1956, p.26.
130. Carmel 1954, p.41.
131. Carmel 1955, p.13.
132. Carmel 1956, p.26.
133. Carmel: 1954, p.41; 1955, p.13; 1956, p.26.
134. Carmel 1960, p.30.

were given by boys during the subsequent years on subjects which in-cluded "Modern Processes in Dyeing," "Radio," "Animal Behavior," and "Bacteria," and a visit was made to the National Smelting Corporation near Bristol where a lot was learned about the metallurgy of zinc and the general operation of heavy industry.[135]

Even though Biology is a science and things connected with it could come under the auspices of the Haber Society, there was in fact a sepa-rate Biology Society, which was established in the winter term of 1953. Its activities consisted of lectures by pupils, teachers, and also by visiting lecturers. In addition there were outings. The lectures given by the boys included "Life on Other Planets" and "Birds Past and Present."[136]

Not only was there human singing at Carmel, there was also bird song. This occurred when at a meeting of the Biology Society, the Bi-ology teacher, William Warren, "delivered a short talk on Ornithology interspersed with, and helped by, gramophone records of bird songs. The recordings were made into something of a quiz and Mr. Nickson [even in this Society, the boys were "Mr."] showed his ornithological ability by guessing most of the recordings."[137]

The boys at Carmel liked to go on "expeditions" [read: holidays] to the sunny South of France, but there are people who prefer to go instead to the frozen North, and afterwards come to Carmel College and describe to the Biology Society their "holidays" in these places, These included Hans Sellman who spoke on "My expedition and exploration into Spitz-bergen"[138] and Mr. Gwynne on his visit to Lapland, when he spoke on many of the habits of the Lapps.[139]

In the autumn term 1955 a "Junior Biology Society" was founded "for the more junior boys who were interested in Biology and were too young for the Senior Biology Society . . . the agenda being lectures by members of the Society, hat-debates, biological parlour games, brains trusts and country hikes. . . . Lectures have also been given by visiting lecturers." During the first year there was a lecture on "Tracking and Making Plaster Casts of Tracks"[140] and in the following year one of the many lectures was one "given by the Curator of the Reading Museum and illustrated with

135. Carmel: 1958, p.31, 1961, p.28.
136. Carmel 1954, p.42.
137. Carmel 1956, p.27.
138. Carmel 1955, p.13.
139. Carmel 1956, p.27; there are no further mentions of the Biology Society in the Carmel magazines.
140. Carmel 1956, p.28.

lantern slides. Afterwards he kindly presented us with a stuffed kestrel, found in the grounds, which will go into our biological museum."[141]

In January 1958, the Junior Biology Society published its own magazine.[142] In its Editorial, it states, "We have tried to include topics which are of interest to everyone."[143] Indeed the magazine included a large variety of material, and plenty of advertisements which obviously defrayed the cost of publication!

There are short articles with interesting information on a variety of fauna. One of them is an article written by Ian Gerecht on "The St. Bernard Dog":

> The St. Bernard is a massive dog, one of the largest in existence. It is bred by the monks of the Hospice of St. Bernard, and has a remarkable standard of intelligence. . . . [It] is trained for rescuing people who have been lost in the snow, or trapped by snowfalls or avalanches. . . . Unfortunately sometimes when these dogs are saving people in the dark, they are mistaken for wolves, and are killed by the persons they are trying to rescue. A notable example of this misfortune occurred last year when a St. Bernard dog named 'Barry' was shot by a soldier he was attempting to save.[144]

Another article, written anonymously, headed "Insects," with a sub-heading "Sight" stated that "Insects have two kinds of eyes; firstly the simple type . . . and secondly the compound eyes . . . The latter . . . consist of thousands of tiny eyes. You would suppose that thousands of similar images would be seen. This is not so. Each separate eye can only see what is immediately in front of it. The impression that the insect gets therefore, is that of a mosaic pattern."[145]

One page of the magazine was headed "Miscellaneous paragraphs from our Members." One of these "miscellaneous paragraphs" was by Martin Alpren on "Looking after pets – the rabbit." Alpren began, "First, you must have a very deep dry hutch. Deep, because the rabbit is inclined to

---

141. Carmel 1957, p.27.
142. Junior Biology Society Magazine, January 1958, Only one issue has been traced; it is not known whether there were further issues.
143. Ibid., (p.2, pages unnumbered).
144. Ibid., (p.3, pages unnumbered).
145. Ibid.

stand up on its hind legs, and if you have a shallow hatch, when the rabbit stands up it will disfigure its ears. . . ."[146]

It also had some "Health Tips," one of them being "Be true to your teeth or they will be false to you."[147]

Jokes also found their place in this magazine:

Junior Biologist: Please sir, I have brought this plant for your Mathematics Exhibition.
Maths. Master: Indeed. What connection has it with Mathematics?
Junior Biologist: Sir, it has square roots.[148]

Towards the end of the magazine was a quiz entitled "What do you know about food?" and one had to identify a list of various foods. Unfortunately for many pupils, these foods never appeared on the Carmel menu. The list included Irish Peach, Bombay Duck, Truffle, Risotto, and Minestrone.[149] The magazine gave the answers on the following page. For those wanting to try these dishes here are the answers: Irish Peach is not a peach but a very rare variety of apple said to have originated from Ireland; Bombay Duck is not a duck but a kosher fish found in the Far East; Truffle is the fruiting body of a subterranean mushroom; Risotto is a type of Italian rice dish cooked in broth to a creamy consistency; Minestrone is a thick soup of Italian origin made with vegetables, often with the addition of pasta or rice. Enjoy them, or as they say in Israel, "b'tayavon"![150]

There was at one period, a further "Science Society," historically probably Carmel's first scientific society, and it was particularly active whilst Carmel was at Greenham. Towards the end of 1950, the Society tried to arrange a number of educational outings, but without success. A film studio answered in the negative.[151] The Royal Mint suggested a date[152] but the society was tardy in confirming it and they received a telegram from them "Regret visit to Royal Mint cancelled letter follows."[153] A car

---

146. Ibid., (p.7, pages unnumbered).
147. Ibid., (p.6, pages unnumbered).
148. Ibid., (p.4, pages unnumbered).
149. Ibid., (p.9, pages unnumbered).
150. This is an expanded version of the answers given in the Junior Biology Society Magazine, (p.10, pages unnumbered). The information comes mainly from various Wikipedia articles.
151. Letter to Carmel College from Twentieth Century Fox Productions, 13 November 1950.
152. Letter to Carmel College from Royal Mint, 8 December 1950.
153. Telegram from Royal Mint (undated); Letter to Carmel College from Royal Mint, 20 December 1950.

factory could only give a mutually convenient date several months later, which was in February of the following year,[154] and the boys visited the factory on that date.[155]

During the following years, the Society had greater success with their requests and received positive replies which included Gestetner Duplicators,[156] the Royal Aircraft Establishment,[157] Esso Petroleum,[158] and Kodak Films.[159] Whether they actually visited these places is not known.

What is known, however, is that a proposed visit to the textile factory of Courtlands in Coventry had to be cancelled at the last moment due to an outbreak of mumps at Carmel.[160] Anthony Rau counted the number of "mumpy" boys by dates: 12 November, just 1; by 17 November it had jumped to 15 and on the following day, he was included in the number making the comment, "I am now in the sick bay . . . so I have got the mumps after all. Too bad . . . At any rate we get better food here and I will have to miss the exams, but I don't want to." By 6 December the number had escalated to 32, but Rau added "nobody's quite sure [of the number] because if you start counting by the time you've finished another boy has reported ill." He also commented that the cook Miss Arons had come to visit the sick.[161]

Towards the end of 1951, the Society decided that they wanted to go towards the core of planet Earth, namely a visit to a coal mine. The parents of the boys were required to give the school their consent in writing, and ten parents did so accordingly. The letters all took the format "I have no objection." One parent added, "I think he will find it very interesting and instructive."[162] There is no report of whether they actually went down this coal mine. If they did, it can be said for certain that they also came up!

However, outings of this Society which are known to have taken place during 1951 were to Riley and M.G. Car Works at Abingdon,[163] Reading Power Station, Osram Bulbs (where the boys received samples),[164] and

---

154. Letter to Carmel College from The Car Company Abingdon, 1 December 1950.
155. Rau letters, 8 February 1951.
156. Letter to Carmel College from Gestetner Duplicators, 19 March 1951.
157. Letter to Carmel College from Ministry of Supply Royal Aircraft Establishment, 24 October 1951.
158. Letter to Carmel College from Esso Petroleum, 23 January 1952.
159. Letter to Carmel College from Kodak, 16 November 1953.
160. Letter from Carmel College to Courtaulds, 30 November 1951.
161. Rau letters 12, 17, 18 November, 6 December 1951.
162. Ten letters from parents to Romney Coles, November 1951.
163. Rau letters, 8 February 1951.
164. Ibid., 30 May 1951.

$CM|P|2$

FROM DR. LEO RAU

25, HIGHPOINT,
NORTH HILL,
HIGHGATE, N.6.
MOUNTVIEW 3307. London.

Nov.11th.1951.

Dear Mr. Coles,

This is just to confirm
that, as I told you, Anthony has my
full permission to visit the coal
mine with the school party. I think
that he will find it very interesting
and instructive.

Yours sincerely,

*Letter from a Parent Giving Permission
for his Son to Go Down a Coal Mine*

British Railways Maintenance Department (still the days of Steam Engines).[165]

In 1954, the members of this Society received a lecture on "Alchemy" – which is, amongst other things, trying to change lead into gold! (a pity that no-one thought of this to raise money to cover Carmel's enormous deficit!) Another paper read to this society was by Malcolm Shifrin, entitled "Growth and Form." In it, Shifrin spoke "on the statistical facts of growth, illustrating his points with several diagrams which included numerous graphs. He then showed the Society some amusing mathematical

165. Ibid., 26 June 1951.

facts dealing with the similarity between various animals, ending up by comparing the human being to a monkey."[166]

The Society's programme at that period also included some outings. One was to the "Kodak Films' Factory on 10 December 1953, where they saw "the manufacturing process for all photographic materials, including roll films and cameras."[167] (Today, one has to visit a museum to see roll films – everything is now digital!) The Factory had informed the school that they offered tea to their visitors,[168] but to this Carmel replied, obviously for kashrut reasons, "I notice that you mention that you provide tea. I would like to thank you very much for this, but we would not require cakes or any other solid refreshment."[169]

Almost every Londoner travels on the Red London buses, but some, including Carmel boys, are also curious to know how the buses are put together and their curiosity was hopefully satisfied by a visit to the "Associated Engineering Companies" [A.E.C.] on 15 March 1954.[170] Prior to this visit, Carmel was informed that they had to adhere to "conditions under which visits are permitted."[171] A request to visit the studios of "Viking Films"[172] was answered in the negative since at that period there were no films in production.[173]

It is stated in the Talmud that the world never has less than thirty-six righteous men.[174] Based on this, in 1961, a new society called "The Thirty-Six Club" was established at Carmel. Its membership was limited to a maximum of thirty-six.[175] Who were the privileged thirty-six in Carmel? According to Spencer Batiste, "It was very democratic – he [Kopul] appointed all thirty-six members."[176] (However, by the following year the number of members had increased to forty-one,[177] which according to any maths teacher is more than thirty-six!!). The policy of this Club was "to invite distinguished guests to address it on subjects of their own choice." That year, the speakers included Professor Hugh Trevor-Roper on "Phi-

166. Carmel 1954, p.42.
167. Ibid., p.41; Letter to Carmel College from Kodak, 16 November 1953.
168. Letter to Carmel College from Kodak, 9 November 1953.
169. Letter from Carmel College to Kodak, 11 November 1953.
170. Carmel 1954, p.41.
171. Letter from A.E.C. to Carmel College, 22 February 1954; the page setting out these conditions was not traced.
172. Letter from Carmel College to Viking Films, 14 January 1954.
173. Letter to Carmel College from Viking Films, 9 February 1954.
174. Babylonian Talmud: Sukkah 45b, Sanhedrin 97b.
175. Carmel 1961, p.27.
176. Recollections – Spencer Batiste, p.2.
177. Carmel 1962, p.9.

lo-semitism in the 17th century England"; Huw Weldon on "Television," and Glyn Daniel on "Pre-historic Cave Paintings."[178]

However, as with all organisations, sometimes at the last moment the speaker does not arrive, and one has to improvise. Spenser Batiste reminisces on one such occasion:

> What I most remember was an occasion when a speaker let us down at the last moment and Kopul decided we should have a debate ourselves. This was during the US election campaign between Jack Kennedy and Richard Nixon in which Kennedy's Catholicism was an important issue as there had never been a Catholic president before. So our debate was to be about whether it was appropriate. He first asked for someone to argue that it was wrong. We were all opposed to religious discrimination and so there were no takers. So he took up the task and gave a really convincing tour de force. So much so that, when he finished, no-one would volunteer to put the opposite point of view. So he then proceeded to put the other side of the argument with equally persuasive force. There were a lot of lessons to be learned from that. Obviously he demonstrated the importance of learning to speak in public. But more important was his demonstration by example that there were two sides to every argument and most issues are in shades of grey rather than black and white. We had lots of opportunities to try this out for ourselves and with gusto in the Union Society. I remember with relish those debates.[179]

In Greenham there had been a photographic society but when the school moved to Mongewell, it was unable to continue because of the lack of a fully equipped dark room.[180] It was only in 1960, that a report of its activities appeared in the Carmel magazine stating that this society had "sprouted forth into active existence." A dark room had been acquired which was used for developing and printing. The members also received a "most illuminating (or exposing) lecture on 'Colour and Composition'."[181]

Needless to say, the Prep School also had its own societies. One of them was the "Debating and Dramatic Society" which was established in the

178. Carmel 1961, p.27.
179. Recollections – Spencer Batiste, p.2; there is a similar account by Spencer Batiste in "Reflections."
180. Carmel 1954, p.42.
181. Carmel 1960, p.32.

spring term of 1954. Its first debate was chaired by Mendel Bloch and the subject was "This House considers that all Jews should live in Israel." The voting was a tie – six in favour and six against. Usually in such a case the Chairman gives the casting vote, but in this case he declined to do so.[182] During the following year there were numerous debates. These included "That reading comics is a waste of time" – it was carried. It is not reported whether the pupils then stopped reading comics! Another debate that year was "That Guy Fawkes Day should not be celebrated" and it was defeated.[183] Obviously the pupils liked fireworks and burning a guy! During the following year, again there were many debates, one of them being "That it was a pity Television was invented," but it was defeated.[184] It was not reported whether every dormitory in the Prep School (or better still every boy) then received a television!

CARMEL IS ALSO ABLE TO PUBLISH!

During the "Kopul era," a number of different magazines catering to different ages and tastes were published at Carmel. The main magazine (or one might even use the term "official" magazine) of Carmel College was the annual magazine called "Carmel" which was published every summer from 1954 onwards, namely from the time that Carmel moved to Mongewell. In general, each year this magazine began with the "School Chronicle" whose contents were the news headings for that year. Then followed sections on Literary Output, Societies, School Outings, Sports (including House reports), and sometimes reports on the Old Carmeli Association. For most years there were also several pages with photographs and drawings of various sorts.[185]

From 1955 onwards, there was a page listing the names of boys who had joined or left Carmel that year. At first they were headed "Salvete" and "Valete."[186] These words are not the names of ointments but are the Latin for "Hello" and "Good-bye"! In 1958, Latin was replaced by Hebrew and the words "Shalom" and "Le-hitra-ot" were used.[187] However in 1961 it was "valete" to Hebrew and "salvete" to Shakespeare,[188] and those leaving

---

182. Alpha 1954, pp.5–6.
183. Alpha, 1955, p.5.
184. Alpha, 1956, p.5.
185. Carmel magazines from the various years.
186. Carmel 1955, p.8.
187. Carmel 1958, p.7.
188. William Shakespeare, "As You Like It," act 2, scene 7.

were headed by "They have their exits" and those joining the school by "and their entrances."[189]

The 1961 magazine spoke of doing "hagbag" with the school's Sefer Torah![190] What on earth is "hagbag," and how does one do it with a Sefer Torah? The mystery was solved in the following year's magazine. It was a printer's error and the word should have been "hagbah"![191]

Whilst still in Greenham, the magazine "Badad" was published. According to the Editorial, "We should like this magazine to become an annual publication."[192] But in Shakespearean language, this was "not to be"[193] and the only issue to come out was this one in July 1953. In mitigation, one could argue that it was superseded by the annual Carmel summer magazine, since the subject headings in the two magazines were similar. The Editors also commented on the name "Badad" for the magazine, to which they gave a lot of thought, stating that it is the initial letters of the School Motto, "Bechol Derochecha Da-aihu."[194]

A magazine written by the Junior part of the Senior School was brought out in 1954 by Abraham Carmel. It was entitled "The Young Carmelonian" and, as in the case of "Badad," although it was called "volume 1," no "volume 2" ever came out! It was obviously, at least largely, financed by the advertisers, since there are no fewer than 13 full pages of advertisements, plus acknowledgements to various donors and, in addition, to obtain a copy one had to give, not a payment, but a "subscription – two shillings and sixpence." Its contents were news and a "gossip page" on Carmel, prose and poems written by junior pupils, a brief description of the then teaching staff, jokes, a quiz and photographs.[195]

For an even younger age, there was the annual magazine named "Alpha" brought out by the Prep School. Its first edition came out in 1954 and the Editorial Board hoped "that Alpha will become what it is intended to be: an historical record and a field for literary effort." The Editorial had begun, "A village cricketer who bowled too many no-balls, when asked why he did so, scratched his head and replied: 'Dunno, just a 'abit. I reckon.' Editorials are, we imagine, just a habit too, for there seems to be no really adequate reason for them; yet they appear to be as inseparable

189. Carmel 1961, p.7.
190. Ibid., p.5.
191. Carmel 1962, p.9.
192. Badad, p.1.
193. William Shakespeare, "Hamlet," act 3, scene 1.
194. Badad, p.1.
195. The Young Carmelonian, passim.

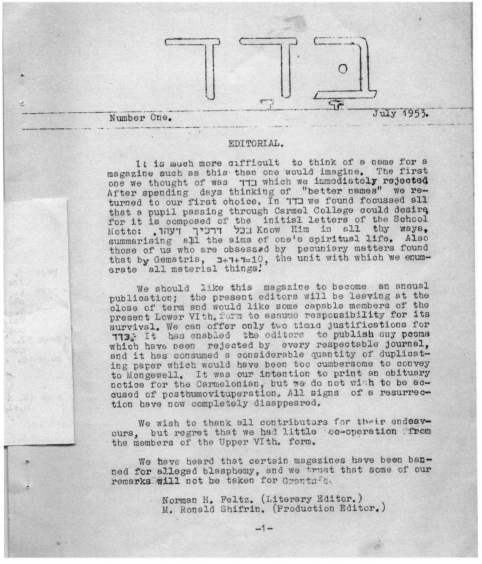

Number One. July 1953.

EDITORIAL.

It is much more difficult to think of a name for a magazine such as this than one would imagine. The first one we thought of was בדד which we immediately rejected After spending days thinking of "better names" we returned to our first choice. In בדד we found focussed all that a pupil passing through Carmel College could desire for it is composed of the initial letters of the School Motto: בכל דרכיך דעהו, Know Him in all thy ways, summarising all the aims of one's spiritual life. Also those of us who are obsessed by pecuniary matters found that by Gematria, ד+ד+ב=10, the unit with which we enumerate all material things!

We should like this magazine to become an annual publication; the present editors will be leaving at the close of term and would like some capable members of the present Lower VIth. form to assume responsibility for its survival. We can offer only two timid justifications for בדד. It has enabled the editors to publish any poems which have been rejected by every respectable journal, and it has consumed a considerable quantity of duplicating paper which would have been too cumbersome to convey to Mongewell. It was our intention to print an obituary notice for the Carmelonian, but we do not wish to be accused of posthumovituperation. All signs of a resurrection have now completely disappeared.

We wish to thank all contributors for their endeavours, but regret that we had little co-operation from the members of the Upper VIth. form.

We have heard that certain magazines have been banned for alleged blasphemy, and we trust that some of our remarks will not be taken for Granta's.

Norman H. Feltz. (Literary Editor.)
M. Ronald Shifrin. (Production Editor.)

-1-

Page from "Badad" – The First Duplicated Carmel College Magazine

from School Magazines as is duck from green peas." The Editorial writer however, then had second thoughts, since he concluded, "If Editorials are just a habit, perhaps they are not so bad a habit as the village cricketer's no-balls."[196]

---

196. Alpha, 1954, p.3.

"Alpha," however only came out in 1954, 1955, and 1956. In 1957 there was no Prep School magazine. For the following two years Abraham Carmel was editor of the Prep School magazine. It was no longer published under the name "Alpha," but "Carmel College Preparatory School Magazine." In his Editorial, Abraham Carmel wrote:

> It is to the youngest pupils of the School, that we must look to fulfil the best hopes for the future. That is why it is so important to encourage them at an early age, to give expression to the 'Carmel' spirit. When we consider the ages of our contributors, we feel confident that the present edition maintains the high standards demanded of Carmel publications. It is a cause of much gratification, that the pupils of the Prep. School should have displayed such enthusiasm in submitting articles. So great was the number of satisfactory articles sent in, that we have experienced considerable difficulty in selecting the best.[197]

The following year's editorial stated that "We received five times as many contributions as we were able to use," and to the unsuccessful contributors it went on to say, "[You] will be lucky next time, so keep on trying![198]

Another magazine, was the "Carmel Fanfare," but it was limited to news items on Carmel and a very brief lost property section entitled "Has anyone found." It was published in May 1956 and labeled "Vol. 1 No.1" but there was never a No. 2![199] "On this, one of the Editors wrote in answer to a question, "No it was the one and only – best forgotten!!!" When asked why "best forgotten" the Editor wrote, "Long story KR [Kopul Rosen] got us into it at the age of 10 and then forgot all about us."[200]

Another magazine, which in the "best Carmel tradition" was a onetime production, was called "The Phoenix." However, it differed in two ways from other Carmel magazines. The first, as the Editorial stated:

> This singular magazine does not cover any field that is specifically applicable to Carmel College. We aim to present to you the talent of the school without any relation to the school itself. This should be sufficient excuse for such a publication. . . . We have divided the magazine into two sections, literary and critical. We fear that this may

---

197. Preparatory School Magazine, 1958, p.3.
198. Preparatory School Magazine, 1959, p.3.
199. Carmel Fanfare, 20 May 1956.
200. Two e-mails from Alan Gold, 5 June 2012.

restrict its popularity since neither sensationalism nor sport are within these spheres.[201]

The second difference was that this magazine is undated![202] Kopul wrote "An Explanatory Note" in which he said:

> "The Phoenix" is the private venture of a few individual pupils who have both the confidence and impatience of happy youth; confident that they have talents which should be more widely acclaimed (masters alas fail to appreciate their obvious genius) and impatient to appear in print so that the world can recognize and applaud their literary gifts. Now, though I write this introductory note in a somewhat facetious manner, I am pleased that a number of boys have displayed the initiative, talent and administrative ability which made this publication possible. They deserve encouragement and congratulations.[203]

A magazine which had far more than one issue was the "Carmel Clarion," which brought out its first issue in the first term of the 1957/58 academic year.[204] Originally the Editors had grandiose plans to bring out two editions every term, but due to practical realities this was considerably toned down![205] Still, when during the next term the second edition came out, (statistically unusual for a Carmel magazine!) the Editors wrote, "We are immodest enough to announce a resounding victory over the cynics of Carmel in that we have succeeded in producing a second issue of the 'Clarion'."[206] To defray the publication costs, these magazines contained a number of pages of advertising material from businesses situated in Wallingford.

In the last edition of this magazine during the Kopul era, one can see in the Editorial, the results of a Carmel education in Shakespearian English literature! "At the beginning of the term we thought the Clarion was Much Ado About Nothing, and that we could take it As We Liked It, but by the Twelfth Night of the term we were in a Tempest and our

---

201. The Phoenix, p.1.
202. By virtue of the date that the Editors of "The Phoenix" left Carmel, this magazine could not have come out later than 1957.
203. The Phoenix, p.2.
204. Carmel Clarion, vol.1 no.1 (undated). This issue gives the names and forms of the contributors and from the form lists, one can deduce that this issue was published in the autumn term of 1957.
205. Carmel Clarion, vol.1, no 1, (p.2, pages unnumbered); vol.1, no 2, (p.2, pages unnumbered).
206. Carmel Clarion, vol.1, no.2, (p.2, pages unnumbered).

Midsummer Night's Dream turned and Leared at us" . . . and so on . . .
The Editorial finishes "If you do not think this Editorial is a Hit, don't
give the rest of the magazine a Miss."[207]

There was also an occasion when a pupil tried to publish a magazine by
"private enterprise." However, David Stamler did not look on this with
favour and wrote a memorandum:

> The magazine was produced in Jan 1958 with neither the knowledge
> nor the consent of any school official. Advertisements were solicited
> (and payment obtained) from local tradespeople by [name of pupil] –
> the self-appointed editor. While his zeal is commendable, his actions
> are not. He was mildly reprimanded, encouraged to continue his work
> under official supervision and the advertisement revenue was returned
> to the donors.[208]

CARMEL BOYS COULD ALSO WRITE!

Carmel had a large literary output, much of the material appearing in the
various Carmel magazines. As to be expected, the major magazine "Carmel" had a "Literary Section." Included in this section were historical and
fictional articles, including some humorous ones. Although the vast majority of the articles were in English, there were also a number in Hebrew
written both by Israelis and non-Israelis. Poetry formed an important part
of this section and there were a number of poems in various languages,
in general written by boys in their mother tongues. Although not strictly
literature, this "Literary Section" included drawings and scraperboards.[209]

One of these articles was about a family with three boys who succeeded
in fleeing at night from Eastern Europe towards the end of the Second
World War[210] and, some years later, were enrolled at Carmel. A vivid
description of this flight appeared in the Carmel magazine:

> The moon lit the dark streets of the big town. Here during the night
> it was terribly cold. Walking in file near the dark walls was a family
> wearied and depressed, with all the signs of utter despair. The feeble
> little boy said to his father: 'Daddy, I feel hungry'. The father, with

---

207. Carmel Clarion, autumn 1961, (p.2, pages unnumbered).
208. Memorandum from David Stamler, January 1958.
209. Carmel magazines from various years.
210. Recollections – Henry Law, Carmel College days, part 1, p.20.

tears in his eyes, looked up to the moon with a sorrowful heart. He did not answer, except, after a pause, indirectly; 'In two weeks' time you will be, my son, in the biggest city of the world, in New York,' . . .

Because of his exhaustion, the child's eyes were beginning to close. However, they continued walking. The old man's wife, a haggard but once lovely woman, held a small baby in her arms, and was finding the pace difficult. They went on, crossing many unknown streets, where darkness and the silence gave the town an air of tranquility. . . .

In the darkness, the shape of a ship was reflected on the water of the port. It was full of colour, and it was as if they had witnessed a miracle. Here was freedom at last. . . .[211]

Another topic of interest in the magazine was Wallingford Castle, located in the ancient city of Wallingford, adjacent to Carmel College. In this city, till this day, one can still see the ruins of Wallingford Castle which is a "Grade I listed building." This Castle was built soon after William the Conqueror became King of England in the mid-11th century. During the course of its history, the Castle survived multiple sieges, one of which was in the mid-12th century by King Stephen of England.[212]

The writer of a paper in the Carmel magazine gives a "first-person" account of one of those in this Castle under siege, followed by how the siege was broken:

The army encircled us on three sides; on the other, the mile-wide marsh with a river in the middle stopped all who would bring us food. Like a tightening snake, the army lay around, throttling the very life out of us. Day by day the supplies of salted meat and corn grew less. In the bailey store-hut you had to go right to the back to see the pitifully small and rapidly dwindling bags of oats. All the animals had long since been killed; all the animals, that is, except the rats – and those we endeavored to kill for extra food. We could not afford to be choosers. . . .

Then they came. With an unintelligible shouting that rent the winter's air, with a wheeling of horses and an array of colours darkened in the dim light of the early morning, a line of horseman fell on the encircling snake. The snake had been sleeping and was taken by

---

211. Carmel 1956, p.21.
212. Wikipedia – Wallingford Castle.

MODERN HEBREW LITERATURE

MODERN HEBREW literature is a child of the secularising tendencies of the 19th century, a product of the rebellion against the ghetto, a combination of secular and Jewish national cross-currents. It was often taken as a sign of heresy if the yeshiva bachur of a generation ago perused the first periodicals of essays, poems and stories, and left for a moment his sacred Talmudic Texts. Yet today we find in Israel a vast fast-growing literature of a young nation. How did this come about?

The Talmud and the Jewish scholars of the middle ages belong to the history of the spirit of Israel rather than to its literature. While it is clear that it is almost impossible to assign an exact date to the beginning of a literary movement, some consider Moshe Hayim Luzzatto, who lived in Italy from 1707 to 1747, to be the founder of Modern Hebrew literature. He was among the first to indulge in secular writing; he wrote plays such as "Migdal Oz" and "Layesharim Tehilla" on the subject of the good and bad in the life of man. But Italy was not the ideal setting for the development of Hebrew literature, and the scene moves to Germany where Moses Mendlesohn was the first Jew to mix secular learning with Jewish teachings. His greatest work was the translation of the Bible into German with a new commentary. Though Mendlesohn was the father of the Haskala movement, it was Wessely (Weisel) who was the first German Hebrew writer, writing in a figurative pseudo-Biblical Hebrew on secular, yet still Biblical, subjects. At that time the first Jewish periodical started in Berlin called "Ha'measef".

Towards the end of the 18th century the scene shifts again, this time to Lithuania and Russia where writers such as Adam Hacohen turn up.

The Romantic period began with Joseph Levensohn, and Abraham Maper who wrote novels again in the Biblical style, with highly complicated plots similar to those of the early renaissance, but this time with the specific aim of attacking corruption within the Jewish community, and particularly those of certain Chassidic groups.

Next comes the realistic period which was started by Y. L. Gordon. His greatness was not so much in writing as in the fact that he attempted to write in a style and upon subjects which more closely followed the non-Jewish writers of the day. His contemporary was Mendelei Mocher Sepharim, who wrote novels and satires which are read with much pleasure to this very day. His most famous satire is "The Journeys of Benjamin III", in which he attacks the poverty of spirit of the ghetto Jew, his attitude of nonchalance to the world around him, and suspicion of secular learning.

The period of the beginning of Zionism helped and filled with zest the new literature. We see Y. L. Peretz, Ahad H'am, writing novels, N. H. Imber composing "Hatikvah" in the 1890's and then H. N. Bialik and Tchernichovsky who brought to its peak modern Hebrew poetry, combining the Hebrew of the Cheder with the newly coined words of the recently set up V'ad Ha'lashon. At the same time people such as A. D. Gordon preaching Zionism in their poems and lyrics. In the same category are Agnon, Shimeoni Rachel and many others writing in the time when the basis of the state of Israel was being built, writing on everyday subjects, bringing up the problems of the time or simply singing a song of praise to the idealists.

With the setting up of the state of Israel the number of Hebrew writers and poets rose rapidly. In recent years the number of books written has been very

eighteen

A Sample Page from the Literary Section of the Carmel Summer Magazine of 1957

surprise. . . . Within half an hour, after all the singing of arrows and sighing of swords had done, we trooped out of the castle . . .[213]

The siege had finally been broken by the forces of the future King Henry II of England. Now to move on several hundred years. In the Carmel magazine, there was a scholarly article on Shylock in Shakespeare's "Merchant of Venice." The writer put forward a theory as to where Shakespeare got the plot for this play, but he then discounted it:

> How did Shakespeare arrive at his plot? He is not a story teller but a dramatist. His stories are borrowed. It is related in the biography of Pope Sixtus V (published in Venice in 1587) that one day news reached Rome that Drake had conquered San Domingo. A Jewish merchant, Simson Ceneda, refused to believe this news, which he had heard from the Christian merchant Paolo Secchi. The Jew undertook a wager that he would give a pound of his flesh that the report was false. Secchi staked a huge sum of money against him. Secchi was right and demanded his flesh. The case was eventually submitted to the Pope. Some held they were both imprisoned – others that they were condemned to death – others say that they were sent to the galleys. We ought perhaps to mention that the whole thing is a legend. It is significant that the roles played by the Christian and the Jew are reversed. It is peculiar that Italy, which was full of Jews, is, in this case, gentle to the Jew, whereas Shakespeare, who knew no Jews, should have been so unkind to them."[214]

Let us now go from the Arts to the Sciences. An article headed "The Priobolic Theory of Light" appeared in the Carmel magazine. A non-scientist who reads it might reasonably assume that this is a serious scientific paper. However there are statements which might make even him suspicious! "Diffraction cannot be explained on this theory and therefore does not exist. It is merely an optical illusion." If this does not make one think something is strange about this paper, then the instructions for the practical examination which regularly accompanies a written paper should make one ask what is going on here?! "Wash your hands CAREFULLY and apply the given bandages to them." But if one is still credulous, the

---

213. Carmel 1957, pp. 11–12.
214. Carmel 1961, p. 18.

book reference "Auf Trasch fun der Rubisch" (unless one's knowledge of German is zero), would give the game away. The paper is in fact scientific "trash and rubbish" written for a laugh or for science fiction purposes![215]

Science fiction articles were indeed included in the literary section of the Carmel magazine, and one boy went nearly fifty years into the future, to the year 2000, to describe a holiday to a faraway planet:

> The best holiday that I have ever had was when my father took me and my sister Mari to Planet 35. The Planet was newly discovered and we were wildly excited when at 5 o'clock we were woken up by the pressure clock. My mother with her usual foresight had switched on the automatic bed turn-over, so that if I had any ideas of staying in bed a minute too long they were frustrated by this stupid modern invention. Of all the modern age's curses this is certainly the worst. I looked out of the invisible window and saw the hoverplane anchored to the ground as usual. My father was busy loading it with air-compressed clothes. I quickly got Charlie, the automatic servant, to dress me, and luckily the effects of last year's superwash hadn't worn off yet. . . .
>
> When we arrived at the airport, we had to pass through the Interplanetary Customs, and then we entered the rocket ship 'Lunar II'. . . . After an hour of pleasant cruising we drew in to Planet 35, only suffering a few minor bumps from flying meteors. . . . We soon arrived at our hotel, and my father chose the rooms in the fifth dimension as he liked the spectrum.
>
> We spent two weeks very pleasantly swimming in water gas and sun-bathing from Planet 35's two suns . . . My polythene bed was very comfortable and I only had to wash it once . . . . . Alas, all good things must come to an end and the day came for the departure. Like a flash we were back in London; but I shall always remember this as my best holiday.[216]

One can see today that the writer in the 1950s was too optimistic as to the progress that man would make!! Let us now for a change go back in time! Had Carmel College been established 600 years earlier, it would not have been possible to hand out textbooks left, right, and centre. In those days, there was no such thing as printing! All books had to be tediously hand

215. Carmel 1960, pp.23–24.
216. Carmel 1959, pp.23–24.

copied. An article on printing of books appeared in the Carmel magazine. On the inadequacy of textbooks, this article states:

> The lack of literary material led to great hardships in the schools. Some students had to retire to bed at an early hour while their friends used the few available books. The former would have to rise at a very early hour in order to read the folios which had been left for their use by those students who had spent the night in study. These difficulties often encouraged diligent folk who could afford the necessary writing materials to copy the works which they needed most. Even renowned Rabbis used to apply to wealthy friends and relatives for the use of private copies. One of them mournfully writes: 'My weapons are not with me at present for all the books of my brother-in-law are at Graz (Austria) and my own books do not satisfy half my requirements.' Even the copying of books was hindered by the difficulty of obtaining materials. Old manuscripts from which the original text had almost disappeared had to be used for writing. The reign of miracles began when the printing press made its appearance in Europe.[217]

Even though textbooks are today freely (or more accurately for a cost – just look at a bill from Carmel!) distributed to schoolboys, there are some boys who are not happy with their school, and Carmel was no exception. A fictional account of such a boy, albeit at a day school, appeared in the Carmel magazine:

> Derek, in his small room upstairs, would often lie awake and listen to the distant rumble of the trams. He would lie awake, often because he was unhappy; because of some injustice committed against him at the small school with the din-infested playground he attended so wearily all day, the injustice aggravated by the indifference, or even antipathy of the masters, whose desire for a quiet life led them to regard any complaint and its maker as an insignificant nuisance – an attitude which usually made the enemy's triumph even more complete and humiliating. Or, occasionally some incident at home.
>
> On that particular day, both had occurred. Firstly, he had been late for school, where he was sentenced to an hour's detention after lessons, and secondly an incident had occurred during break. He had just

---

217. Carmel 1958, p.12.

come out of a Mathematics lesson, and maths was his worst subject. That lesson, however, he had distinguished himself, and had known the tremendous pleasure of suddenly understanding and mastering a subject which had long been incomprehensible to him. He felt strangely exhilarated, and was still thinking about it in the corridor, when the headmaster came out of a door almost opposite and saw him.

The Headmaster was held in awe by everyone, particularly first-formers like Derek. Derek was privately not very fond of him, as representing the forces of law and order, with which Derek was not usually associated; but just then he felt strangely drawn to him in his new-found achievement. He vaguely hoped he would notice him, and tried to smile weakly as he passed.

'Boy!' The tone was sharp and curt. 'You look absolutely like a scarecrow! Go and wash immediately, and don't walk about like that again.' Derek stood still for a moment, white-faced, and then slowly walked on. He knew it was true that he was untidy; but to him this was unimportant. He had been living in a new-found respectability, and he knew that the Head had classed him mentally on sight as one of the school 'urchins'.[218]

"Derek" was obviously born in the country where he was schooled. However, this was not so with many Carmel pupils. The customs and the way of life in England are often different from those in Israel. A pupil from Israel describes this:

> The murmur of the plane's engine was just dying behind me, as I strode quickly towards the reception desk. Arriving there, I found a queue formed, and since I am used to this sort of chastisement from Israel, I decided to push forward. To my amazement no sound of protest was heard from the crowd and when I accidently stuck my elbow into a large soft body, I only heard: 'Sorry, my fault.' I gulped, gasped and then decided that my victim was mentally deranged.
>
> By Jove! The shock I got when I left the airport in a bus which was rolling on the left-hand side! Why did it have to be upside down? But before long I had to get use to everything being just the opposite of what I expected. . . .

---

218. Carmel 1955, p.22.

The shrill noise of bell [of the bus] and then a sound like 'Kew, Kew' and that was my first meeting with the conductor. 'Tuppeny, please!' I looked up, I knew there were pennies, shillings, pounds, but what fatuous creatures of the treasury were tuppenies? Using his two fingers he managed to clarify his desires. I gave him a shilling and received the ten pennies change. But surely, ten minus two equals eight, so I have received two pennies too much. . . .

When I eventually boarded one [a taxi] I could not even enjoy the scenery, since my eyes were glued to the meter which kept going up in geometrical progressions with a self-satisfied click. You judge me: the meter shows a fabulous amount of money, I gave it, and what then? Well, I learned some new words in the English language which won't be found in any self-respecting dictionary. And all that because I did not know that you are supposed to give even more than the meter says. How could I have guessed? 'Am I a prophet or a son of a prophet?'[219]

The Literary Section of the Carmel magazine also contained a number of items of poetry. One such item was a poem on some mysterious creature called a "Whippersnapperelahawk" (there are still a few longer words in the English language![220]):

> fish, a bird, a man or a beast
> It doesn't resemble this in the least
> A whippersnapperelahawk
> A funny name of which to talk . . .
> Its body is like a hard-boiled egg
> And its nose is like a cloakroom peg
> A whippersnapperelahawk
> Each finger and toe like a wine bottle cork . . .
> Its eyes pop out a yard or two
> A thing like this you never knew
> This whippersnapperelahawk
> After three years it grows a stalk . . .[221]

Another poem which was entitled "Progress" had ecology in mind: . . .

---

219. Carmel 1954, p.24.
220. Examples of such words are: floccinaucinihilipilification and antidisestablishmentarianism.
221. Carmel 1954, p.18.

> The dust, the dirt, the crowds, the fumes,
> Din of steady streams of traffic,
> Monotonous as spinning looms
> Past shop windows' luring magic.
> Advance and progress, see the effects;
> Unblinded by dazzle one detects
> Under neon-filth and lice
> Painted evil, drugs and vice.[222]

Carmel poetry was not limited to the English language. The pupil body in Carmel was multi-lingual and in the 1961 Carmel magazine, appear poems in three non-English languages: German, Hungarian, and Afrikaans.

The German poem was written by E. Gartner and is entitled "So ist die Liebe":

> Es war in Toledo
> Da traf Don Alfredo
> Die schwarze Olalita Kantarcs;
> Sie war die schönste des Tages . . .[223]

Janos Hadju wrote his poem "Tavaszi Mese" in a language from behind the then "Iron Curtain" – Hungarian:

> Fólyomentén öreg tölgyfa
> Nyári zöldös kabát hordja,
> Fal nélküli kárja helyett:
> Télen hideg: meleg szerett . . .[224]

For the last of these three poems, the authors come from the southern extremity of the continent of Africa. The poem entitled "Die Aang is Hier" was written by Gerald Simon and Harris Sidelsky in the Afrikaans language:

> Die skape luister,
> Bome fluister,
> En kriekies sing hul lied.
> 'n Uil kom loer . . .[225]

---

222. Carmel 1958, p.16.
223. Carmel 1961, p.24.
224. Ibid.
225. Ibid., p.25.

Another item of poetry which appeared in the Carmel magazines was a translation into poetic English of poems of medieval and modern Jewish poets. One of them was a translation of the famous "My Heart in the East" by Yehuda Halevi who lived between 1075 and 1141. Throughout the generations, Jews in the Diaspora yearned for Eretz Yisrael, and this sometimes, found expression in their compositions:

> My heart is in the East, my body far in the West,
> How can I taste my food, and how can it give zest?
> How can I keep my vows and promises when
> Zion is in Edom's grip, I in an Arab chain?
> I could with ease leave all my fortunes here in Spain
> More precious to me are the Temple's ashes and dust to gain.[226]

Carmel pupils did not magically become literary geniuses on the move to Mongewell. Those who were in Greenham could also write! Thus the magazine "Badad" also had a literary section of prose and poetry. One such article was titled "Classification in Science":

> An illustration of this passion for classification was the Theory of Aristotle. He considered that there were four fundamental types of matter: solids, liquids, gases and fire. An object could possess any two of four fundamental properties. Thus a liquid was cold and wet, and fire was hot and dry . . .
> By this theory, a liquid, which is cold and wet, on heating becomes hot and wet, i.e. a gas. This can be shown to be correct; on heating water, it boils, turning into steam. Similarly a solid (dry and cold) on heating burns or forms fire, which is dry and hot. If a solid is wetted, it dissolves to become a liquid, etc. This theory, although, of course, discredited now, is interesting, and well worth studying.[227]

In "The Young Carmelonian" an article appears on the death of a mother. It was written by Morad Zahabian, who came from Persia (Iran), and was then aged 14. The editor writes that he had "refrained from changing the poetic phrases of our gifted author from the East":

---

226. Carmel 1955, p.31.
227. Badad, pp.10–11.

My beloved one is taken away, the one who undertook the pain of my birth; the one who, when I was born, kept me by her bosom and taught me how to walk and talk. She who in the cold, cold winter nights kept awake to guard me, she who moved my girdle by day and night to give me comfort. The companion of my childhood, the one who, when my father died, devotedly worked all hours of the day to provide breath for me, and fulfil her duty, sending me to school, because she knew well that I had to be nourished with knowledge and understanding. She was the one who gave all, that I might live.

O, my mother, I can hear that sweet voice of yours no longer; Mother, my heart grieves for you; now that you enter the resting place with hundreds of others resting beside thee. I find nothing by your grave, except the lonely, weeping grass, moistened by the dew and rain.[228]

The Prep School magazines also had literary items, both prose and poetry. Some of this material was contributed by staff members. One of the articles, written by a boy aged nine, was entitled "The Lost Penny" where the penny itself described its wanderings all over the world: "I am a penny, and I was born in 1952. My adventure started like this. A lady owned me, and one day she took me to the Midland Bank. The cashier put me into a metal safe for a time, and there I met ten pounds. They were very boastful. One of them said: 'Look who's here, a little penny. Not able to buy a thing with that,' and the others said: 'We are worth much more than you,' . . ." The article continues how this penny made a world tour going to Canada, India, Tibet and finally back to London, where on Coronation Day it fell "in the road just outside Westminster Abbey. After a few minutes the Queen came out of the Abbey and picked me up and took me to her palace . . ." After further adventures, the penny arrived back to the original owner.[229]

A few years later, a Prep School boy wrote on an unpleasant encounter at the dentist:

After some minutes, the 'Executioner' strode into the room. He spoke to my mother and then came over and said, 'Now young man I am going to pull out your tooth, and no nonsense do you hear?' Before I could answer, he thrust me back into the chair, and reached for

228. The Young Carmelonian, pp.13–14.
229. Alpha 1954, pp.11–12.

some big steel pincers. He put them firmly on a tooth and pulled. 'Ow! Ouch! Oof!' I screamed jumping from the chair and doing some 'Rock 'n' Roll!' round the room, 'Give him a banana, then show him out' said the dentist to his assistant.

The story ends with the banana peel thrown on the floor, the dentist sliding on it and the dentist himself then screaming![230]

Maybe because Dr. Sewell had given David Sheldon the nickname "monkey," as he "was a rather cheeky chap as an eight-year-old and loved to climb ropes"[231] that Sheldon was prompted to write the following poem entitled "The Monkey in the Zoo," in the Prep School magazine "Alpha":

> I am a little monkey in the Zoo,
>   As everyone can see;
> If humans were here with me too,
>   I'm sure they would not flee.
> They all throw nuts and laugh at me;
>   If only they could see
> What monkeys see, they'd change their minds –
>   They'd see what fools they'd be!
> I know I play some nasty tricks,
>   I pull off hats and bite;
> I only do it to annoy,
>   Not really out of spite.[232]

The content of the "Carmel Clarion" was largely literary, and on occasion the articles were topical. The first edition of this magazine came out soon after the Soviets had launched their Sputnik. The pupils of Carmel did likewise and launched their "Carmelnik"!! After the article had described the launching, it continued, "The members of the staff were interviewed by a reporter from a certain glossy magazine. Each was asked what he thought of the Carmelnik:

Rabbi K.R. 'This project exists only in the minds of its promoter. It is a purely psychological phenomenon best explained by the theory of Freud.'

---

230. Preparatory School Magazine 1958, p.14.
231. E-mail from David Sheldon, 5 July 2012.
232. Alpha 1955, p.14.

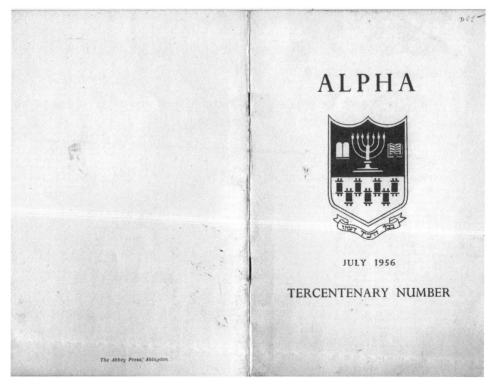

Cover of Carmel College Preparatory School Magazine Alpha

Mr. D.S. [Stamler] 'This project may well shed more light on the intergalactic relationship between the Dead Sea Scrolls, and the Indo-European and Semitic linguistic groups.'

Mr. R.C. [Coles] 'I am looking forward to a genuine sample of space to add to my collection.'

Mr. J.B. [Bunney] 'Despite all the Jiggery-Pokery, make no mistake about it, this is of vital importance in A-level.'

Dr. F.F.F.F. [Friedmann] 'I do not know what the consequences of this will be, because the Manchester Guardian has not yet arrived, but with the definite bent towards the science side which there is in the school, I have no doubt that it is of importance.'

Mr. F.N. [Nelson] 'I think Carmelnik is good stuff, but I cannot stop to talk just now as I must make a phone call to Oxford [to my fiancée].'[233]

---

233. Carmel Clarion, vol.1, no.1, 1958, (p.6, pages unnumbered).

Another topical item was a poem in the Autumn 1961 issue which read:

> Sitting down in Trafalgar Square
> The Police gave them a bit of a scare,
> Get into a Black Maria van
> And try and get out as quick as you can.
> Earl Russell has gone more grey
> Because he caught a cold today.
> Tristan da Cunha refugees
> Have just seen their first T.V.'s . . .
> Kennedy and Kruschav started to digress,
> And once again the world's in a mess . . .[234]

This magazine also included "Letters to the Editor." Each edition had a number of such letters on a variety of subjects such as Community Service Badges,[235] the Carmel Cadet Corps,[236] and Stag Hunting.[237] But perhaps the most original letter was in the Autumn 1961 issue, "Dear Sir, I can think of nothing to write for the Carmel Clarion. Yours sincerely."[238]

Each earlier issue had a crossword puzzle with a ten shilling prize for the winner.[239] The third issue quoted the prize as twenty sixpences. This is the same as ten shillings, but the magazine explained why the change in wording, "useful for Sixth Form Council fines."[240]

The author recollects an exhibition of various Carmel magazines which included two written during the first years of the school:

> Only one copy was made of each and they were handwritten and hung on the school notice board at Greenham. One of the articles dealt with a Carmel boy who was very ill and therefore asked his mother to hold his Siddur (instead of writing it with an 'S', they spelled Siddur with a 'C') whilst he davened. However 'Siddur' was spelled, it was wonderful to see how a Carmel boy when very ill, was concerned not to miss out on davening.[241]

---

234. Ibid., Autumn 1961, (p.10, pages unnumbered).
235. Ibid., vol.1, no.1, 1958, (p.7, pages unnumbered).
236. Ibid., vol.1, no.2, 1958, (p.14, pages unnumbered).
237. Ibid., vol.1, no.3, 1958, (p.5, pages unnumbered).
238. Ibid., Autumn 1961, (p.9, pages unnumbered).
239. Ibid.: vol.1, no.1, 1958, (p.19, pages unnumbered); vol.1, no.2, 1958, (p.14, pages unnumbered).
240. Ibid., vol.1, no.3, 1958, (p.23, pages unnumbered).
241. 7 years, p.88.

The poetry output of Carmel was not limited to school magazines. On one occasion, a poem was engraved on a marble slab. The author elaborates:

> Due to the regular use of Siddurim, Chumashim and other religious books, they will eventually reach a state where they can no longer be used. Unlike secular books, they cannot be thrown in the dustbin – they have to be buried. These holy pages which are being buried are known as 'Shemos' – from the plural of the word Shem (name) – since they contain many times the Divine Name. On at least one occasion, I, together with some friends attended to this burial. We dug a 'grave' near the wall by the outhouse where the trunks were kept and buried them. We then found a marble type stone in the school and we scratched on it a suitable poem we composed, and then filled in the scratches with ink. I still remember our poem:
>
> > The Shemos which we bury here,
> > Were to us precious and dear.
> > Outwardly they may wither and die,
> > But up to Heaven they will fly.

To ensure that the non-Jewish ground staff, not knowing what "Shemos" were, might remove the stone or worse still, plough up the area, we added at the top of the stone 'HOLY.'[242]

READ, READ MORE AND EVEN MORE !

Every organisation worth its salt has a library and Carmel College came under this category of being worth its salt! At first, various teachers would take on the task of organising the library. The 1954 Carmel magazine reported on the state of the library after Carmel had been at Mongewell for nearly a year, "The Library, under the supervision of Mr. Roston, has expanded considerably since we came to Mongewell Park. Rabbi Rosen has presented many books, and a large number of books have been added to various sections, particularly the Jewish Section, English Literature, and Classical Translations. In addition, Biology, Geography, and Economics sections have been started recently."[243]

---

242. Ibid., p.30.
243. Carmel 1954, p.9.

At the beginning of 1955, there were about 2,500 books in the library. There was then an allowance of at least £150 a year [in those days a large sum] to purchase books and Heads of the various Departments would submit suggestions for new books to the Master responsible for the library, who would then decide whether to buy them.[244] At that stage the Judaica books did not include a set of the Talmud nor the Soncino English translation.[245]

After Murray Roston left Carmel, the author recollects:

> Mr. Schmidt was in charge of the library, and books were catalogued into subjects by having different coloured stars stuck on their spines.
>
> There was no set of the 'Jewish Encyclopaedia' in the library, (the Encyclopedia Judaica was still decades away!) and I once asked Mr. Schmidt when he was getting a set. He thought I had asked about an up-to-date set of the Britannica and he said it would soon be arriving. In fact the library did soon after also get a set of the 'Jewish Encyclopaedia.' Rabbi Rosen had a set in his study and boys were often referring to it and so he decided to put it in the school library.
>
> The up-to-date edition of the Britannica also soon arrived at the library. Whilst on the subject of the Encyclopaedia Britannica, one of the boys in the school wrote up to them for a catalogue. He also got a bonus – a personal visit by their salesman who came specially all the way to Carmel College. What did this salesman think – he was going to sell an expensive set of Encyclopaedia to a school-boy? Needless to say he made no sale in Mongewell that day. Rabbi Rosen was not very happy with this unexpected visit to the school and he clearly informed the pupils, that if you want a catalogue, use your home address.[246]

In May 1958, Malcolm Shifrin, and in the initial stages together with Dr. Tobias, began a complete reorganisation of the library which included cataloguing the books using the Dewey system.[247] That month, Shifrin wrote a memorandum for Kopul setting out his plans for the School Library:

> IMMEDIATE TASK: Calling in of all books for complete rearrangement of shelves.

---

244. Inspectors' Report, p.4.
245. 7 years, p.84.
246. Ibid.
247. Carmel 1958, p.4.

CLASSIFICATION: The "Dewey" system which is now adopted in all Public Libraries should be used in the School Library. Although the Library will, for some years, remain a "small" library, the system (obviously intended for large collections) will be useful as a training for boys who should be able to use the classification method and make *full* use of the facilities now offered by the Public Libraries of Great Britain. In such classification HEBRAICA and JUDAICA will be kept apart and all Jewish subjects be under these headings, e.g., 'HISTORY OF THE JEWS IN SPAIN' will not be classified under History but in the historical section of JUDAICA; 'HISTORY OF JEWISH PHILOSOPHY' under the philosophical section of JUDAICA.

DISTRIBUTION: Each volume must be labeled on the inside of the front cover with the name of the College and space for stamping date of RETURN. A pocket must be stuck on the corner of the same inside cover to contain the borrower's card which may be withdrawn for any reason such as malicious damage or continued failure to return books at the proper time. An index system will be arranged for such cards as is the practice in the Lending Libraries. Should any assistance be enlisted from the Prefects in the work of distribution, such assistants must first be conversant with the system. A loose leaf filing index will be kept of all volumes in the Library with the description of the book – Name of Author – date of publication and name of publisher.

AUGMENTATION: A 'suggestion book' will be kept in which 'boys' may insert the title of any book which they believe will be a useful addition to the Library. Each month the book will be handed to the Principal who will decide on the material to be chosen as additions to the Library.

SECTIONS: The Lending and Reference sections will be classified separately. Any volume belonging to the Reference Section will have the letter 'R' on the spine. No Reference book must *ever* leave the Library.

JEWISH SECTION: Owing to the Hebrew and Religious bias of our School special attention will be paid to this department which should contain attractive literature. As the foundation of such a section, there must be an attractively bound set of SHASS, a Jewish Encyclopedia, etc. The Modern Hebrew section should be attended to and the works of BIALIK, etc. must be given a place of honour. Shakespeare should appear in Hebrew if only in two or three plays.

BINDING: From time to time books will be rebound. The present lack of binding arrangements leads to the loss of valuable and interesting books.

FURNITURE: Apart from the need for erecting new shelves from time to time as the number of volumes increases, there should be a 'distinct' type of chair for use in the Library. Such a chair will be recognised as a 'Library Chair' should it be removed from the Library.

OUTSIDE HELP: The College Library should be affiliated to the 'School Library Association' (fee: one guinea p.a.).

CONCLUSIONS: There is no valid reason why, within a period of say five to ten years, Carmel College should not possess one of the finest School Libraries in the country.[248]

At that period, Shifrin and Tobias put out a notice to the pupils outlining their aims and pointing out that their work "would cause some inconvenience to the boys and 'to sweeten the pill' they would explain what they intended doing."[249]

During the following year, Shifrin explained in some detail in an article in the Carmel magazine what he had done to the library:

The past year has seen a 'bloodless revolution' – though not all would accept the adjective – in the College Library. It was decided that this should be enlarged and completely reorganised. The first step was to expand spatially and the old Staff Room was converted into a Fiction Library and Reading Room; the Loggia into a Newspaper and Magazine Room.

Many additional bookcases were acquired, the Library closed for two weeks and the task of sorting, classification and cataloguing began. Of an initial stock of 2,800 volumes, 200 were rejected and disposed of, and the remainder divided into those of Jewish, and those of secular, interest. All the books in the latter category were classified according to the Dewey Decimal Classification . . . and then boys volunteered, were begged, were cajoled, were press-ganged into sticking in numerous seemingly useless labels.

At this stage the Library was re-opened, and the remainder of the work was carried out while the books were in use. . . . A trolley was

---

248. Memorandum, The School Library, written by Malcolm Shifrin, May 1958.
249. 7 years, p.84.

obtained and, following standard library practice, no reader was allowed to replace books on the shelves. Initially, this procedure was found irksome and many boys had to be discouraged from 'helping the librarian' by replacing the books. This has now been accepted as normal . . . The looseleaf book catalogue was decided upon as it was felt that these can be used, in the manner of a normal book, much more easily than a card index file.[250]

In the summer term of 1959, Shifrin brought out a five-page memorandum which elaborated on points made in his Carmel magazine article and also included additional points. He wrote that the recent additions to the library included 400 books, over half of which were either gifts or were bought second hand. The new library equipment "included fourteen three-foot bays of shelving, cataloguing and marking equipment, plastic jackets for all new books and a trolley."

On the cataloguing he wrote that "Each fiction book has two entries in the catalogue and non-Fiction books have from two to six, the average being two and three-quarters entries per book. This compares exceptionally well with the catalogues of the Public Libraries in Reading and Oxford and is probably much better than the majority of School Libraries." To anticipate anyone who may have thought that Shifrin had wasted school money and manpower in producing this catalogue, he immediately added that "it cannot be too highly stressed that properly used . . . the catalogue increases the use of the books beyond imagination." The books on a subject which appeared in a dozen different locations in the library, could thus be found at a glance using this catalogue.

Shifrin had made a breakdown of books which had been borrowed from the Library: "Fiction, Biography, Travel, and Economics were the most popular sections but it must be stressed that poetry reading was almost nil."

In any library, there are books which need to be thrown out. The Carmel Library was no exception and on this Shifrin wrote, "A large proportion of the books at present in the Fiction section have no real value and it is proposed to remove most of them during the next year as books are added."[251]

Nearly three pages of this memorandum were devoted to the "Future

250. Carmel 1969, pp.33–34.
251. Carmel College Library, Memorandum, Summer term 1959, pp.1–2.

Plans" for this library. One of them was to build up "a library of the spoken word on records. This should lead to greater use of the Poetry and Drama books." Shifrin reported that during the previous term, the room for the Fiction Library "was chaotic at all times" and that this was due to it's invariably being used for "other purposes." He also stated that although the Prep School had its own library, the Junior part of the Senior School did not. This was being remedied and a "preliminary list of three hundred books" to be purchased for such a Junior Library had already been compiled, but the actual purchase would be dependent on the necessary finance being available.[252]

Memoranda and articles are all very nice, but one also needs contact between the librarian and the pupils themselves. The author recollects such a meeting between Shifrin and the pupils:

> When the reorganisation of the library was complete, Shifrin called each class of the school in turn to the library and explained how the new system worked and potential problems we might find in using the catalogue. He also said that we would probably see how this loose leaf catalogue could be opened and that expulsion would not be sufficient for a boy trying to open it. It, for example, had taken them three hours just to arrange the entries beginning with the letter 'e' in alphabetical order.[253]

Even the largest library in the world cannot have every book which has been published, and this is all the more so for a relatively small library such as at Carmel. As a result, enthusiasts of various disciplines were disappointed. One of the disappointed was Henry Law who commented, "Disappointingly for me, however, there was nothing on the shelves where the 625 range [in the Dewey system] should have been. There were no books published by Ian Allen,"[254] who is one of the world's most established independent publishers for Aviation, Rail, Modelling and Road Transport enthusiasts . . .[255]

Shiftin brought out two "Brief Guides" for the library, the first a duplicated one in 1960 and the second a printed one, two years later. Although the table of contents of both were very similar, the second one was lon-

252. Ibid., pp.3–5.
253. 7 years, p.85.
254. Recollections – Henry Law, Carmel College days, part 2, p.1.
255. Ian Allen Publishing, (Internet).

ger, especially in the section describing the cataloguing of the books.[256] Between the writing of these two guides, the library had expanded the area it occupied, the number of books had increased from about 4,500 to 6,000 books[257] and so had the library rules – they had doubled from three to six![258]

The Dewey system, although suitable for secular books, lacks the necessary comprehensiveness for Jewish books. Shifrin therefore prepared his own "Carmel Classification" for the Jewish books. As with the Dewey system, the "Carmel Classification" is divided into ten main classes: 000 General works (includes encyclopaedias, etc.); 100 Bible; 200 Mishna; 300 Babylonian Talmud; 400 Palestinian Talmud; 500 Midrash; 600 Medieval literature; 700 Modern Literature; 800 Jewish life; 900 Jewish history and environment. These classes were then further subdivided.[259] The author adds "He [Shifrin] bound his typed out copy of this system as a small book which was then put in the library. At a later date, a second enlarged version was brought out." For some period during this work, one could not refer to books in the Judaica section of the library.[260]

An integral part of a library is a room for newspapers and periodicals. The "Carmel Library Guide" elaborates. "The newsroom [loggia] . . . houses a representative selection of British and foreign daily and weekly newspapers, newsmagazines and weekend reviews. Newspapers, being particularly fragile, should be treated with care and replaced on the paper rack as soon as you have finished with them. Each periodical is kept in a transparent-fronted cloth-bound case."[261]

The school subscribed to periodicals such as the Jewish Chronicle, Punch, and the Listener, and also received several serious daily newspapers such as the Times (which still had its front page filled with advertisements), the Daily Telegraph, and the Manchester Guardian.[262] On this latter newspaper, Henry Law comments:

---

256. Carmel College Library, A Brief Guide, 1960, passim; Carmel College Library, A Brief Guide, 1962, passim.
257. Ibid., p.1; Ibid., p.5.
258. Ibid., p.2; Ibid., pp.5–6.
259. Carmel College Library, A Brief Guide 1962, p.10; The "Carmel Classification" in the Carmel College Library, A Brief Guide 1960, p.5, is slightly different.
260. 7 years, pp.84–85.
261. Carmel College Library, A Brief Guide, 1962, p.7; similar wording in Carmel College Library, A Brief Guide, 1960, p.1.
262. 7 years. p.85.

- 5 -

'FOL'   -   This is an abbreviation for Folio Book - one
that is larger than average. These are shelved
on their own in a larger bookcase. Most of
them are also Reference Books and are shown by
the symbol 'R.FOL.'

'q'   -   Quarto books - not as large as Folios and usually
not Reference. These are shelved either on the
bottom shelf of the bookcase they would be in if
they were normal size books, or else on the top
right shelf of the Folios bookcase.

'B'   -   Biography and autobiography. These are shelved
in their own bookcase. Biography books have no
number, but the letter 'B' is followed by the
first three letters of the surname of the person
the book is about, e.g., the call number of 'Trial
and Error' by Chaim Weizmann is B.WEI. That for
'The small woman' by Alan Burgess is B.AYL because
the book is about Gladys Aylward.

'S'   -   Indicates a book from the Special (Jewish) Library.
(See below).

Fiction books shelved in the Fiction Library have no numbers. Their
call numbers consist only of the first three letters of the author's
surname, e.g., 'Nothing so strange' by James Hilton is HIL.

THE CARMEL CLASSIFICATION   Our own classification for Jewish
books is also a decimal classific-
ation and works in the same way as the Dewey Classification. All
these call numbers are preceded by the letter 'S'.

The table below gives the ten main classes into which Jewish
books have been divided. The full schedule of tables is in the library (R. 025. 49 CAR)

000	General works (includes encyclopaedias, Jewish Theology, Festivals, etc.)
100	Bible
200	Mishna
300	Talmud (Gemara)
400	Midrash
500	Liturgy
600	Medieval literature
700	Modern Hebrew and general Jewish literature
800	Language
900	Jewish History

Page from Carmel College Library Guide of 1960

The Manchester Guardian was still printed in Manchester then and did not arrive until the middle of the afternoon. Dr. Friedman would be waiting for it and ask in his heavy German accent 'Yah, where is the Manchester Guardian,' and grab it when it eventually arrived. This made the Manchester Guardian desirable reading amongst the boys as the idea was to be reading it so that he would have to ask for it.[263]

Pupils were also given the opportunity to suggest which books the library should purchase. For this purpose, in 1958, "Suggestion Slips" were duplicated and made available for pupils. One fifth former suggested the "Careers Encyclopædia" published by the Oxford Press, whilst another fifth former suggested the "Focal Encyclopædia of Photography" published by the Focal Press.[264] It is not known whether or not these books were purchased.

As with almost all libraries, the pupils could borrow books by going through a certain procedure.[265] For the teachers, the borrowing was much simpler. All they had to do was remove the bookcard from the inside back cover of the book and leave it on the lending desk in the catalogue room together with a slip of paper on which was written their name. Teachers could also borrow books for the holidays by completing a certain form.[266]

In 1959 Carmel entered the "printing industry" when a printing press, an 1886 Chandler & Price treadle platen machine was donated to the school, and the library incorporated it as its "newest division." This aroused "great interest" in the school and the Carmel magazine writes, "a printing society has been formed, and already a high standard of work has been achieved."[267] That year there was a printer's strike, and as a result the Carmel "Printing Society" got to work and printed that year's Preparatory School magazine.[268]

To add to all the numerous Carmel rules and regulations, as stated above there were also library rules. If you want to eat, go in the Fiction Library. If you want to write, fill up your pen before entering the library. With regards to talking, there were different degrees of decibels of sound that could be emitted from one's lips. The strictest was in the Reference Library where even moving one's lips was forbidden, and woe betide a

263. Recollections – Henry Law, Carmel College days, part 2. p.2.
264. Carmel College Library, sample completed Suggestion Slips, dated October 1958.
265. Carmel 1959, p.34.
266. Notes on lending procedure for Members of Staff.
267. Carmel 1959, pp.5, 35.
268. Preparatory School Magazine, 1959, p.3.

Carmel College Senior School Library at Mongewell

boy who transgressed this![269] The "Carmel Clarion" summed it up, "If there are more than two boys in the library, no two may talk to each other; if there are only two, they may not talk to each other; if there is only one, and he talks, the bogey-man will come and take him to the Fiction Library."[270]

CARMELISMUS

The term "Carmelismus" seems to have first appeared in the "Jewish Observer and Middle East Review." There it was the heading of a report of the 1954 Speech Day at Carmel.[271] At a later date, this word was taken over to describe the Carmel College Archives. There is an undated mem-

---

269. Carmel College Library, A Brief Guide, 1962, pp.6–7.
270. Carmel Clarion, vol.1, no.3, 1958, (p.10, pages unnumbered).
271. Jewish Observer and Middle East Review (London), 30 July 1954, p.9.

orandum (very likely written about the end of the 1950s) by Malcolm Shifrin on "Carmelismus." He began referring to the universal problem of storage space and the inevitable solution:

> In common with the remainder of the school, both the administration department of the Library and my own room, are hopelessly inadequate in storage facilities. I am, therefore, in the process of a ruthless clearing out operation, burning all old letters and destroying all other pamphlets and literature which is not 100% necessary to my existence.[272]

He continued that Carmelismus items were overflowing everywhere, adding that there was an unnecessary waste of space, since entire issues of newspapers were being stored just because there was one article on Carmel College in that newspaper. He commented that the availability of scrapbooks would help but not entirely since many items such as school magazines and prospectuses could not be stuck in a scrapbook. Furthermore, it would be unsatisfactory to stick photographs in a scrapbook since they might be required at a later date to be reproduced in a brochure or magazine.[273] To solve the problem, Shifrin suggested:

> All news cuttings, photographs, pictures, etc. should be individually mounted on cards (or thick sheets of paper) 8 inches by 10 inches or 8 inches by 13 inches and filed chronologically. This ensures that items can be temporarily removed for any necessary purpose with ease. Interspersed with these cards – and in the same chronological sequence – should be filed all magazines, brochures, etc. A card index 5 inches by 3 inches might be kept giving dates of items to which reference might need to be made. This is standard Library practice.[274]

In the course of this memorandum Shifrin had commented:

> I assume that it can be taken for granted that Carmelismus *does* fulfil a need and must be continued in its present comprehensiveness. It will, presumably, be essential material in the compilation, at any future date, of a history of the College.[275]

272. Memorandum re Carmelismus, undated, p.1, par.1.
273. Ibid., p.1, par.2–4.
274. Ibid., pp.2–3, par.7.
275. Ibid., p.2, par.5.

Chapter 7

Play the Game!

During the exams at Carmel, the boys had to manage on their own resources; during the sports at Carmel, they were members of their House or School. . . .

BACK TO GREENHAM AND CROOKHAM DAYS

From the school's inception, sports were an integral part of the daily life of Carmel. The Provisional Prospectus published in about April 1948 has a whole section headed "Games" which states:

> Football and Cricket will be played as the official organised team games, but boys who do not show any particular aptitude for these will be able to find some game or form of exercise, both suitable and enjoyable, from among the variety of voluntary games and sports which will be available. These will include lawn-tennis, basketball, athletics, boxing and playground games.[1]

The same Prospectus had a clothing list which included a games kit, namely, two football shirts, one pair football shorts, one pair football stockings, one pair football boots and one pair gym shoes.[2] But there was no mention of a cricket kit in this list; surely they were not expected to play cricket wearing football boots! Maybe, the reason was that it would be a half year before the following summer.

---

1. Carmel College Provisional Prospectus, undated (about April 1948), section: Games.
2. Ibid., section: Uniform and Outfit.

Right from the opening of Carmel, early morning running was instituted by the Headmaster James Ewart. David Perl, who was at Carmel
from its inception writes:

> We were awakened each day, apart from Shabbat, at 6.40 a.m. by a
> loud clanging bell. . . . Every boy (other than those who had managed
> to coax matron to provide them with an excuse) assembled in a dazed
> and untidy looking mass by the back door dressed only in a pair of
> plimsolls and running shorts. Whether it was warm and dry, wet and
> cold, icy or foggy, we then proceeded to run round the overgrown
> grounds covering a pre-determined course of something like a mile,
> Obviously the purpose of this was to tone us up for the day ahead and
> also as will be clearly seen by anyone meeting one of us first-termers,
> to make real men of us! Having returned, albeit scratched by over-
> hanging branches and stung by stinging nettles, to the building we
> hurriedly washed and dressed.[3]

In answer to the question as to why Carmel began every day with such
"Spartan demands," Jeremy Rosen explained that, "During those early
years, Carmel tried very hard to emulate aspects of the English public
school system."[4]

There was, however, one pupil in particular who did not like these "aspects." Jeremy Rosen elaborates:

> Kopul loved to tell the story of Dov Weinberger. Dov was the brilliant
> son of two cultured German refugees who had settled in Jerusalem.
> His father was a successful lawyer. His mother Gustle was well known
> on the international Inter-Faith circuit. Dov was a passionate student
> but athletically uninterested and uncoordinated. He argued strongly
> against the obligatory morning run and protested this waste of time
> and glorification of pagan Greek ideals with all the means at his dis-
> posal. In the end the crude force of school discipline won and he went
> on his first run. To everyone's surprise he came back in exceptional
> time, amongst the leaders. When Kopul was next at the school he
> went up to Dov to congratulate him. Dov looked at him with blazing

---

3. The Old Carmeli, no. 5, 1968–9, p.28; Reflections – David Perl.
4. Recollections – Jeremy Rosen, chap.1.

eyes and said 'I only did it to get back to my studies as quickly as possible.'[5]

The Prospectus spoke about football and cricket. For these sports, playing fields are required. David Perl elaborates:

> On one, and sometimes two afternoons a week, a period was devoted to games. Now at that time there were no playing fields available so we played, rugger in the winter and cricket in the summer, on the back lawns. Even though we wore plimsolls for both games I feel sure that the previous owner would have been horrified at the sight of 10 or 15 hefty lads running amok on those erstwhile well maintained ornamental lawns. The playing field eventually came into existence some 12 to 15 months later after much sweat and toil by both the workmen from the building contractors and the pupils. The area set aside for this was found to be extraordinarily densely covered with stones and no sooner were they cleared than another layer seemed to rise to the surface. This presented the hard hearted and callous prefects with a ready-made punishment 'Ableson for talking in line you will spend one hour of your free time clearing stones'! Eventually the task was complete and the playing fields were laid and ready for use.[6]

David Shaw also recollects that there was such a punishment, "I am reminded that a punishment was to be sent with a bucket to pick stones from that [sports] field for a period."[7] Michael Blacktone described this as the "main punishment" at Greenham and it could well be that the boys had to fill a certain number of buckets![8]

The Provisional Prospectus also stated that swimming would be on the curriculum, and said, "Every boy will be taught to swim during his first summer in the College."[9] One such boy was David Shaw who wrote on "the trip to Newbury Baths. They were outside, unheated and cold, very cold. The first trips must have started early on because I still have the hand written certificate (somewhere) saying that I swam one width. wow! Because of the cold the body reacted and on the coach trip back

5. Biography of KR, p.35.
6. The Old Carmeli, no. 5, 1968–9, p.28; Reflections – David Perl.
7. Recollections – David Shaw.
8. Recollections – Michael Blackstone.
9. Carmel College Provisional Prospectus, undated (about April 1948), section: Games.

GAMES

FOOTBALL and Cricket will be played as the official organised team games, but boys who do not show any particular aptitude for these will be able to find some game or form of exercise, both suitable and enjoyable, from among the variety of voluntary games and sports which will be available. These will include lawn-tennis, basket-ball, athletics, boxing and playground games.

Every boy will be taught to swim during his first summer in the College. Classes in life-saving will also be held.

Exercises in the open air will not be confined to organised and voluntary games; boys will be encouraged to make the fullest use of the College estate and of the magnificent open country which surrounds it.

MUSIC

THE normal curriculum will include classes in vocal and instrumental music and every effort will be made to foster in the boys a love and appreciation of music. A Choir and an Orchestra will be formed; well-known musicians and singers will be invited to visit the College and the boys will be allowed to attend any outstanding concerts and recitals which take place in the neighbourhood.

Private lessons in instrumental music (Piano, Violin, 'Cello and all wind instruments) will be arranged.

HOBBIES—SCHOOL SOCIETIES

THE boys will be given facilities, encouragement and assistance to make the fullest and most profitable use of their leisure time according to their individual abilities and inclinations. It is proposed to organise Music, Debating, Natural History and Art Societies early in the first school term; others will follow when a sufficient number of boys show a genuinely keen interest in any particular activity such as Stamp Collecting, Model Engineering, Chess or Gardening.

The College has an excellent Reading Library.

Page from Carmel College Provisional Prospectus from 1948

somehow your frame bristled with an inner warmth."[10] David Shaw then managed to find this certificate. It was issued by "Carmel College Preparatory School" and states, "This is to certify that D. G. Shaw swam one length, July 1953" and it is signed by J. S. N. Sewell, who was then the Master-in-Charge of the Preparatory School.[11] David Shaw, however, had a confession to make, "[It was] actually at the shallow end and my feet touched the ground once."[12]

Games were not limited to official school games. Jeffrey Gandz writes about a game he played with his friends whilst he was in the Prep School at Crookham. "I remember playing the game," he writes, "Kingy I think it was called – where a crowd of boys used a ball to hit other boys who

---

10. Recollections – David Shaw.
11. Carmel College Preparatory School, Swimming certificate issued to D. G. Shaw, July 1953.
12. Recollections – David Shaw.

then had to drop out of the game. The last one standing was the king. I was never the king."[13]

There was another sport at Crookham but it was not played by the pupils – it was fox hunting by outsiders whom the pupils actively opposed. "Fox Hunts came through the grounds," wrote David Shaw, "and I delighted in sending them the wrong way. I remember farmers shooting rooks right near the school. I gathered some friends and we pelted them with stones from the drive from slings made from our handkerchiefs. They were not happy."[14]

Needless to say, in the various sports there were competitions between opposing teams. Some of these competitions were internal school house matches whilst others were against other schools, both local and not so local, and organisations, such as Oxford University Jewish Society, R.A.F. Benson and Henley Police.[15]

From its second year, Carmel would regularly play soccer[16] against outside teams and a handwritten record was kept of the matches played during the academic years 1949/50, 1950/51, and 1951/2. These records show the date of the match, the team played against, whether it was a home or away match, the players in the Carmel team and the field positions they each played in, and the result of the match. It was also recorded which players scored the Carmel goals. For the first two of these years the records were written by Martin Law, with the first recorded game being a home match against Thatcham County. The Carmel team consisted of Sperber, Oberman, Law, Wolfson, Rottstein, Sarsby, Kreps, Boxer, Buckman, Jackson, and Bornstein J. That match was lost by four goals to nil. Other teams played against during that year included Thatcham Church, Hermitage, Lambourn, and Avigdor (the London Jewish school). During that season Carmel lost six matches, won three matches and there were no draws. During the following season, again six matches were lost, but this time Carmel only won one match and two were drawn. The following year saw the introduction of a second eleven.[17]

From 1951 onwards, one of the schools which Carmel regularly met in sports competitions was Mary Hare School – four times during the

---

13. Recollections – Jeffrey Gandz.
14. Recollections – David Shaw.
15. Various Carmel College magazines.
16. During its first year, the school played rugger rather than soccer, (e-mail from an early pupil who requested anonymity, 27 September 2013.). There is a photograph of the pupils playing rugger.
17. Detailed handwritten record of football matches played between 1949–1952.

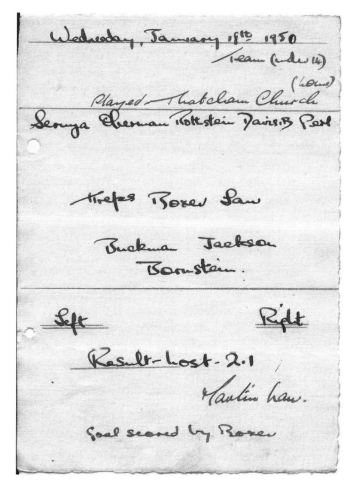

Details of Carmel College Football Match from 1950

1957/58 football season, with Carmel winning three of these matches.[18] This is a school for pupils who are, unfortunately, deaf. It is of interest to note that the Mary Hare Primary School is located in Greenham Lodge, where Carmel was located when it was founded.[19]

About half of the football matches against outside teams were "away" matches, which involved travelling to the various venues. Phillip Nagley,

---

18. Carmel 1958, p.34.
19. Mary Hare Primary School for deaf children in Thatcham, (Internet).

the son of the teacher Harold Nagley, who was then a pre-school aged boy, still recollects these journeys:

> Another memory of singing, this time secular [songs], is the school sports song that the boys would sing on the bus going to the football matches with rival schools. The rhythm 'dunderumm, dunderumm, . . .' or something like that is part of that memory. My father told me there were one or two variants of the football song, and there were also many other favourites sung on the bus. Maybe 'Green grow the rushes, O', was one of them.[20]

An Editorial in the Carmel magazine writes of "riotous sing-songs in a coach on the way back from a football match" in 1950.[21]

THERE WERE ALSO HOUSES FOR SPORTS

Initially the school had two houses – Gilbert and Alexander. What was the origin of these names? They were named after two of the original governors of Carmel – Joe Gilbert and Alexander Margulies.[22] At a later date, as the school grew, a third house was added, called Montefiore, although it is not clear which Montefiore it was named after. When Montefiore was established, there was also some reshuffling of houses. Some boys who were in Gilbert, found themselves in Alexander and also the reverse, and a number of boys from both Gilbert and Alexander then found themselves in Montefiore. The author reports, "I saw the dissatisfied expression of one boy who originally was in Alexander, now finding himself in Gilbert."[23] Each house had its distinctive colour, which corresponded to the colour of the sport's shirt worn by the boys. For Gilbert it was blue, for Alexander it was red, and for Montefiore it was yellow.[24]

The reorganisation of the Houses was an ideal opportunity to dispense with the names Gilbert and Alexander and choose new names, especially because of the serious rift between Kopul and the Governors, which had resulted in Joe Gilbert and Alexander Margulies, together with all the other founder governors, resigning and withdrawing their loans to the

20. E-mail from Phillip Nagley, 25 July 2012.
21. Carmel 1955, p.3.
22. Recollections – Jeremy Rosen, chap.1.
23. 7 years, pp.76–77.
24. Recollections – Jeremy Rosen, chap.1.

school. But Kopul did not dispense with these names, thus giving support to Jeremy Rosen's statement that "after his victory [in his fight with the governors] he magnanimously made it up with his opponents and I for one never heard him recriminate or even pass a critical remark."[25]

The author explains the competition which went on each year between the houses:

> Every year there was an inter-house sports competition, with the winning house receiving the house-cup on Speech Day. The sports included for this competition were football, basketball, cricket, tennis, squash, athletics, cross country running and chess. For these sports the school was divided into two sections, a senior and a junior. For athletics, it was divided into three sections.
>
> For football, basketball and cricket, the top house obtained twelve points, the next house eight points and the last house four points. For the remaining sports, the points were eight, five, and two. The reason for this difference was that these first three sports involved teamwork. A football game requires a referee and a cricket match an umpire. Even in sports, anarchy is not recommended! It was decided that the house master of the neutral house would take on the function of referee for the senior teams and a senior boy from the neutral house for the junior teams.[26]

When having three houses competing, one can sometimes have a strange situation whereby losing a particular game, you can gain the house cup![27] The author reports that "this indeed occurred one year and members of one house were talking about deliberately playing badly to lose. The head of another house heard about this and warned that should this happen, he would immediately call a meeting of all the houses, in order to have the house deliberately losing, disqualified from receiving the cup."[28]

---

25. Biography of KR, p.41.
26. 7 years, p.77.
27. Consider the following theoretical scenario: Gilbert and Montefiore are running neck and neck for the inter-house cup. The last sport to be played is tennis. However, Gilbert are so far behind in tennis that whatever happens they will come last in it. The last game of the season in tennis is between Gilbert and Alexander. If Gilbert wins, then Alexander will come second in tennis and Montefiore first. Should however Gilbert lose, then Alexander will come first in tennis and Montefiore will only come second, and this will enable Gilbert to win the house cup!
28. 7 years, p.78.

KOPUL'S LOUD VOICE AT SPORTS MATCHES!

Any home match was not limited to the Carmel players. The non-playing pupils were expected, or even required, to come out and give encouragement to the Carmel team.[29] Kopul himself would come out. Jeremy Rosen explains, "Many pupils just loved his performance as a spectator. He shouted phrases of abuse picked up on the terraces of Tottenham Hotspur during his youth. He encouraged school teams but criticised players, demolished them, making fun and exposing their shortcomings to ridicule."[30] This is well illustrated in a Carmel promotional film, in which Kopul goes to watch a Carmel football match. One first sees him cheering on the pupils. Then, when someone does something he doesn't like, he waves his hand in disgust. Later, when something really displeases him, he puts his hand in front of his eyes, turns around and walks away.[31] Michael Blackstone's described Kopul's loud comments at football matches as a "booming voice from the touch line."[32]

Kopul would also be a spectator at Carmel cricket matches and shout out comments. Martin Slater writes "I can still hear him when standing on the boundary at a first team cricket match howling at our bowler 'bowl a length boy'."[33]

Kopul's bellowing was not limited to when he was a spectator, as is related by Michael Blackstone. "Kopul always like to be Captain in whatever football or cricket team he played, and with his deep loud voice he bellowed at his team throughout the match."[34]

There was a pupil whose surname was Isserlin, but Kopul "delighted in referring" to him as "Misserlin," because he would miss opportunities in sporting events![35] Jonathan Isserlin reports on one of these "missing" occasions:

> When Colan Linton called me out of the blue from his home in Fredrickton, New Brunswick several years ago . . . he began by asking if I remembered him. How could I not, I replied, when I had dropped him when he had scored just seventeen runs in a House [cricket]

---

29. Ibid.
30. Biography of KR, pp.45–46.
31. The film "Foundations for a Vision" at 10 minutes 15 seconds from the beginning.
32. Recollections – Michael Blackstone.
33. Recollections – Martin Slater.
34. Recollections – Michael Blackstone.
35. Recollections – Jonathan Isserlin.

match and he went on to score 117, the only time I could remember anyone ever scoring a century in a house match (or any match for that matter) at Carmel.[36]

SOME LOVE SPORTS WHILST OTHERS HATE THEM!

Sports were not limited to competitions between houses or schools. It was also part of the school timetable. Jeremy Rosen writes, "The twice weekly 'Games Afternoons' were looked forward to as a chance for letting off steam. Most of the teaching staff were involved in sports afternoons, either coaching a sport or supervising games outside. Pupils could only get off games with an 'Off Games Slip' from the school nurse at the Sanatorium."[37] David Uri writes of "the thrill of getting an 'Off Games' slip from Matron and not having to go cross country running on a bitterly cold day."[38] At one period, there was a boy who forged such slips! The author explains:

> There were pupils who didn't like sport and if one could get a slip from the matron that one was 'not fit' that day for sport, one would be exempt. The blanks of these slips had been typed and then run off on a Gestetner duplicating machine. The matron then wrote in the details of the boy and date. At one time there was even a boy who forged these slips and he really made a good job of it. I once asked him if he utilised a typewriter to make them. He answered in the negative and said that he wrote out each letter by hand with black ink. All the more praise to him – maybe I shouldn't praise a 'forger'! I think the word must have got out what was happening, since it was announced that there were forged slips going around.[39]

There were pupils who loved sports and would take part in a large variety of them. For others this was not the case, one of them being Anton Dell who wrote that "watching a wet dirty hard football flying towards me was almost as terrifying as a red hard cricket ball – so sport was not my thing."[40]

---

36. Ibid.
37. Recollections – Jeremy Rosen, chap.1.
38. Reflections – David Uri.
39. 7 years, p.49.
40. Recollections – Anton Dell.

It happened that when there were two brothers in Carmel, one of them might love sports, whilst his brother had the opposite inclination. This was the case with the Nehorai brothers, Anthony and Julius. "Anthony was a great sportsman," wrote Julius, and then continued:

> Personally, sports were never of any great interest to me, he [Anthony] must have inherited all the family sports genes. I've thought of consulting a psychiatrist about it because I seem to be missing so much when I see the pleasure my friends get from following their team or actually playing themselves. Every so often I force myself to a football stadium but it's no good, more often than not I nod off. Strange really because my son is a great sportsman and played college football in the United States and enjoys spectating as well as playing amateur basketball.[41]

On cricket, Michael Ellman writes, "I did not like cricket because most of the time one just stands around, and when one is a batsman one is at the receiving end of a fast hard ball."[42]

Even the various Prospectuses for Carmel recognised the fact that not every pupil has an affinity for sports and stated "Where a boy shows marked disinclination to take part in games, other forms of outdoor activity are arranged during the games period."[43] However, the author cannot recollect other forms of activities actually being arranged.[44]

However, even a pupil who is hopeless at sports could play his part in the administrative work of sporting activities at Carmel. Michael Bharier who described himself as "awful at sports" writes:

> Imagine my surprise, then, when I was approached by Charlie Marshall and Josh Gabbay and asked to become the school sports secretary. They told me that they felt it was important for me to become involved in the school's sports programme and this is where they felt I could contribute. My job was to contact other schools and set up a schedule of games with Carmel. I enjoyed doing it. Some were schools we had played before but others were schools with which we

41. Recollections – Julius Nehorai.
42. Recollections – Michael Ellman.
43. Carmel College Prospectus, undated (about 1959), section: Games and Sports; similar wording is found in all the other prospectuses.
44. Unwritten recollections of author.

had not had contact. It worked out quite well and I am grateful for their insight and wisdom in getting me involved.[45]

Likewise, the author was hopeless at sports (although on one occasion the author was a player in a junior house football match),[46] but helped on the administrative side:

> For a period, I was the official scorer for Carmel in these cricket matches. I would sit in the veranda of the pavilion next to the official scorer of the opposing team. On one occasion, even though one of the teams had officially won the game, I continued to keep the score but in a different colour ink, pointing out the reason for the different colours. This difference was not just academic but was needed when working out the batting and bowling averages of the various players."[47]

Whilst on the subject of batting averages, despite the hopelessness of the author in sports, the author had the highest batting average in the school in one particular year!! How did this come about?! "*played* – 1; *runs* – 1; *not out* – 1; *average* – infinity."[48] One can say with certainty that "The Guinness Book of Records" would not accept this as a record!

Pupils at Carmel came from different countries, and thus had different sporting traditions. Basketball originated in the United States towards the end of the 19th century and it was they who later introduced it to other countries.[49] Thus the Americans might consider themselves the experts in this game! Elliot Katz wrote that he was "perhaps the first Yankee to attend Carmel" and how he "tried to teach the Brits how to play at basketball, alas to no avail."[50] In contrast to basketball, cricket originated in England and although some cricket has been played in the United States for some centuries, the United States Cricket Association was only founded in 1961.[51] Despite this Elliot Katz writes, "However my natural athletic skills allowed me to become Carmel's first Yank wicket keeper."[52]

---

45. Recollections – Michael Bharier, chap.2, Carmel Memories.
46. 7 years, p.77.
47. Ibid., p.78.
48. Ibid., p.79.
49. Wikipedia – History of basketball.
50. Recollections – Elliot Katz.
51. Cricket in the USA, (Internet).
52. Recollections – Elliot Katz.

Each year the Carmel Magazine would include "Pen Portraits" of the members of Carmel's first team in various sports. In one of the "Football Pen Portraits," Charles Marshall describes Katz' abilities in football, with allusions to his basketball skills, "Katz: Played in goal, with very little experience of football, as only a basketball enthusiast would. He made some good saves and some which were spectacular. Frequently a source of amusement for the spectators. He has qualities of anticipation, speed and good ball handling which could help to make a good goal-keeper."[53]

GETTING WET DURING SPORTS

Carmel had its own small swimming pool at Mongewell in front of the Gymnasium. but it had been badly neglected. The filtration and chlorination system had long been defunct. However, Carmel managed to use it by filling it up and dosing it with buckets of bleach, which would work for a few days but then the water would start to go green and thus had to be changed.[54]

The Prospectuses brought out in the 1950s stated that "Boys are taught to swim in the school's swimming bath, attached to the gymnasium."[55] However, from the words of Henry Law, this was not the case. "There were no formal lessons," Henry wrote, "but we had free access. By getting in the water often enough and long enough, I finally succeeded in swimming a tentative breast stroke, first half a width, then a width. I was not very good – barely seaworthy, but I was no longer a non-swimmer."[56] It is often stated that the quickest way to teach a person to swim is to throw him into the deep end. This is indeed how Neil Alton learned to swim as he reports that "[He learned] to swim by – being chucked in!"[57]

The River Thames was also adjacent to the school – or to be more precise half the width in the Carmel area, according to the "Document of Sale and Purchase" and the "Deed of Conveyance" belonged to Carmel.[58] There was no authorised swimming in the Thames for the pupils although

---

53. Carmel 1957, p.33.
54. Recollections – Henry Law, Carmel College days, part 1, p.14.
55. Carmel College Prospectuses: undated (about 1956), undated (about 1959), section: Games and Sports.
56. Recollections – Henry Law, Carmel College days, part 1, p.14.
57. Recollections – Neil Alton.
58. Purchase Mongewell, First Schedule, part 1; Conveyance Mongewell, The First Schedule, p.4.

The Carmel College Swimming Pool at Mongewell

Michael Ellman writes "Amongst things I remember . . . swimming across the river."[59]

Another member of Carmel using the Thames as a swimming pool was Kopul, but he didn't need anyone's permission! Ian Rabinowitz writes:

[Rabbi] Louis [Rabinowitz – Ian's uncle] visited Carmel, and I had an order to meet him on the steps outside the Main Building. When I arrived, he and Kopul were standing there in bathing robes and with towels over their shoulders, having been swimming in the Thames (which at Mongewell had a very powerful current). After a chat, Louis presented me with a £5 note. . . . I thank Kopul once again because I

59. Recollections – Michael Ellman.

am sure that, if he had not been present, then Louis would not have given me such a large sum.[60]

In addition to intentional swimming in the Thames, some ended up in this River under rather different circumstances! A contributor to the magazine "The Young Carmelonian," pen-named "Keyhole," reports in the "Gossip Page," "I learn that David Perl, an Old Boy, staying for the week-end, fell into the Thames in a vain attempt to rescue a lifebelt which had fallen from the boathouse into the water."[61]

FOOTBALL AND SMUGGLING!

Despite all the financial and other limitations he was working under, Kopul did the maximum to put together the best staff and instructors that were on the market, not only for academic subjects but also for sports. Helmut Schmidt relates one such instance:

> One outstanding master in his field, however, was smuggled into the school unannounced. How Kopul loved an occasional leg-pull! How he anticipated with glee the long faces of the surprised boys watching the dramatic rout of their football eleven!
>
> It was only on the day of the annual staff match against the boys that the arrival was announced of a new gardener who would be playing in Rabbi Rosen's staff team. The November wind was driving the last leaves across the playing field when the referee's whistle blew for the kick-off. Several members of the staff, like their captain, were in their late forties and were no match against the boundless energy of Carmel's young manhood. The new gardener playing with the staff also appeared past his prime and lost the ball on the few occasions when he could have scored. The superiority of the boys was obvious from the start. The junior boys cheered mightily every time the ball landed in the staff goal. The boys' goal-keeper, on the other hand, had little to do except suppress a yawn or two. Once or twice a mocking young voice rang out 'come on, sirs, get your socks up!' which encouragement was echoed by a general merriment from the sidelines. The masters were well and truly clobbered and their dear pupils took

---

60. Recollections – Ian Rabinowitz.
61. The Young Carmelonian, p.12.

a great delight in their defeat. Poor old fogeys, they soon looked exhausted, probably thinking about a hot shower back home with just enough strength left to listen to the news about the Eichmann trial, President Kennedy's space program or about the rebellious French army in Algeria. Half-time drew near. They could take it easy in the second half and merely defend their decisive advantage. Yet the bearded captain looked anything but dismayed and even managed a wistful smile.

The whistle went for the second half and the staff team seemed a little more lively. Before anybody knew what was happening, the new gardener had sent the ball from the half-way line as if it was a guided missile straight into the top left of the goal. Players and spectators were stunned. A lucky shot, no doubt, as rare as eight draws on the pools. Why should fortune deny her favour to a gardener once in a while? Even a blind hen finds a grain. But the gardener was no blind hen. The boys had hardly recovered from the unexpected blow when from a distance of 20 yards another rocket hit their goal. The boys rightly decided to pay more attention to that inside forward and keep him covered. They tried to tackle him when he advanced with the ball. He just danced and rotated around them in a spectacular show of football ballet. No, there could be no question any longer of chance or luck. Here was a virtuoso who fired his shots with the calculated, deliberate precision of a champion of first-class football.

The football fans of the Vth Form who had watched with utter surprise the dramatic turn of events racked their football brains. They knew the style and looks of all the top footballers in the land and no longer had any doubt about the true identity of the 'new gardener' they had been privileged to watch so closely and free of charge. They were in the presence of none other than Jackie Milburn, the great Jackie Milburn. Good Heavens, the goalscoring legend of Tyneside who had helped Newcastle United win the FA Cup twice in succession. The school could now be told by the headmaster at the end of the thrilling match that Mr. Milburn had agreed to coach Carmel's young footballers for two terms.[62]

Neil Myeroff also describes the above event which included a number of points not found in Helmut Schmidt's account:

---

62. Reflections – Helmut Schmidt.

As we were going in for lunch Melvyn Green approached me and said 'I am sure I just saw the ex-Newcastle United and England centre forward Jackie Milburn get out of a car.' I said to him jokingly, 'well the staff and teachers are playing the first XI this afternoon and you know how seriously Kopul takes these matches. May be he has pulled in an ex-pro.' After lunch I went out on to the playing field to watch the game and both sides were warming up. A few hundred yards away walking past the cricket pavilion Kopul was walking on to the playing fields and next to him was another tall gentleman with the same kit on as the staff and teachers. There was one particular moment in the game when from at least 35 yards (or was it 40!) this player shot at goal with the ball smashing against the crossbar. I can remember the school goalkeeper Roger Fierstone saying after the game that it was the hardest shot he had ever faced but somehow the crossbar survived. After the game Kopul spoke to all those who were present at the time and announced that the school had managed to get the services of the great Jackie Milburn and for approximately one year we had the pleasure of his coaching. Carmel's very indirect connection with England winning the world cup in 1966 was that Jackie left the school to take up the job as Ipswich Town manager when Alf Ramsey was made manager of the England team.[63]

To this, David Robson adds that Kopul even "offered him a permanent job and free education for his son."[64]

A "goalscoring" player is not limited to FA Cup Finals. It also occurred in a Carmel inter-house football match which was played at the beginning of 1954. "Spectator" reports on what transpired:

There was chattering in the School Hall on the morning of 3rd February. Most of the boys were round the notice board. One was asking another, 'Will there be a House match?' They asked that question because there was snow on the ground, and a bit of ice. Well, that afternoon the question was answered. There would be a Junior House match: Gilbert v. Alexander.

At half-past two, both teams were out on the field, and Alexander took the centre. After four minutes of play Gilbert were on top of

---

63. e-mail from Neil Myeroff, 24 July 2012.
64. e-mail from David Robson, 15 September 2013.

Alexander's goal. All the boys were cheering their respective Houses. The noise was intense, and the last two minutes before the first goal was scored were very exciting. Then the goal was scored: one up to Gilbert. Isi Weinberger, who was playing for Gilbert, kicked the ball over to Reynolds, the Gilbert right wing, who kicked it in. Alexander then took the centre again. They got the ball to Gilbert's goal, but a back passed it to the rear. Quite a while passed till the next goal was scored. Reynolds again smashed the ball in.

Alexander took the centre and got the ball down to Gilbert's goal. They scored. The victor was John Loftus. Then there was a long interval. Both sides going up the field, complaining about the cold. Then the third and last goal was scored for Gilbert. Yes, it was the same player; Reynolds completed his hat-trick. And so victory for Gilbert, 3 – 1.[65]

USE ONLY YOUR FEET!

Football has eleven players in each team. However Carmel was probably unique with a number almost ten times as large. David Frome relates, "I remember the 100-a-side football matches on the long summer evenings led enthusiastically by Rookie Rosen – who knew he was really called Jeremy?!"[66]

In a football match, if one wants to help the other side, one kicks the ball into one's own goal; it is then a goal for one's opponents! Michael Blackstone describes an incident that happened in a school match, "One player, Jackson, managed, in a school football match against one of the local rivals, to score for both teams."[67] Well, at least Jackson managed "to atone for his sins!"

Football matches demand a referee. Needless to say, he needs to be an expert on the rules and have expertise in the practical side of the game. However, on one occasion in Carmel, these criterions were not adhered to and the results were thus disastrous. Michael Bharier, who was on this occasion the referee explains, "The biggest disaster was when I was asked to referee a football match between the staff (including Kopul) and the boys. I don't know how or why I agreed to do it. What happened was casually

---

65. The Young Carmelonian, pp.26–27.
66. Recollections – David Frome.
67. Recollections – Michael Blackstone.

summed up later by Mr. Bunney, 'You were asked to do the impossible so naturally you couldn't do it'."[68]

There are two kinds of football played in England today, Association football and Rugby football, the latter being named after Rugby school where it is traditionally said to have begun.[69] The teacher Joshua Gabay was an excellent player of Association football and Neil Alton would tease him saying that Rugby football was superior. Neil writes on this:

> A special word on Josh [Gabay] and football. He was mesmerising on the field. Constantly scanning the pitch and instructing, while executing his own brand of ball control wizardry. My home football team was 3rd Division Brighton & Hove Albion. I felt Josh could out-dribble any of them. He obviously loved the sport. So I loved 'playing up' rugby to him as a superior game, which I relished on holidays tv [television]. The Northern lads could talk League v. Union rugby. As a Southerner, I only had broad comparisons for the Josh Exchange. We'd banter over ball-handling, rugger catching and passing, positioning, athleticism, upper body strength, all rugby's distinct hallmarks. Nothing phased, Josh would counter with equivalent footie skills. To great effect, as he had them in abundance. I treasured those moments. When Josh was receptive to my cautious teasing, he was kind, smiling, interested, understanding, and another encouraging influence. The opposite to his public face of strict disciplinarian.[70]

Melvyn Ackerman in his own words was a "fanatical Spurs supporter" and in an encounter with Kopul, he succeeded in persuading Kopul to let him out of school to watch Spurs play. Melvyn recollects:

> One Shabbat in the winter of 1961/62 I was strolling the grounds when Kopul who obviously knew he was seriously ill at the time, came up to me and said 'Hi Young Ackie' (My older brother Laurence was at the school at the time), and then said, 'If I were to make you principal of Carmel for a day what changes would you make?' It was a no-brainer. Spurs were playing in the European cup and a few sixth-formers were going on an excursion to London for the next Spurs game against I think Dukla Prague. So I responded, 'Well sir, I think

68. Recollections – Michael Bharier, chap.2, Carmel Memories.
69. Wikipedia – Rugby football.
70. Recollections – Neil Alton.

all Spurs supporters should be allowed to go to London on the coach to see Spurs play their European cup game.' He laughed and said, 'I can't let the whole school go but you can.' For a week or two I was the talk of the school and did get to go to the match.[71]

However, the bottom line is that for the boys of Carmel, football was just a spare time hobby, their having no intention of taking it up professionally. However, professional coaches sometimes have other dreams for their top-rate students. This can be illustrated by the Carmel pupil Ady Kaplan and the coach Jackie Milburn. Spencer Batiste relates, "I remember him [Milburn] once saying to Ady Kaplan (then the school soccer captain and talented sportsman) that he could get him a contract to play for Newcastle, and being rather stunned when Ady thanked him but said he wanted to be a lawyer."[72]

EVEN HOCKEY AT CARMEL

For a short period in the late 1950s, hockey became a sport at Carmel, under the leadership of Ronald Evans. However, it only lasted for a limited period and it never became one of the sports in the inter-house competition.[73] Michael Ellman writes that the reason that it was "abandoned quite soon" was that "it was too dangerous – the boys used their sticks to hit other boys' ankles."[74]

Strangely, the official annual Carmel magazines make no mention of hockey at Carmel. The only mention is in the first issue of the "Carmel Clarion" published during the autumn term of 1957. In it, Geoffrey Levy in his "Sports Report" is not happy about hockey since he writes "Next term is devoted to Hockey, and football is not played at all. It would be interesting to see what the opinion of the boys is in this matter. Is Soccer or Hockey preferred in the school? It is hoped to organise a 'Clarion' ballot whereby boys will be able to show their preference."[75]

---

71. Recollections – Melvyn Ackerman.
72. Recollections – Spencer Batiste, p.4.
73. Unwritten recollections of author.
74. Recollections – Michael Ellman, Senior School par. 5.
75. Carmel Clarion, vol.1, no.1, 1958, (p.20, pages unnumbered).

Cricket XI at Mongewell

Carmel College Cricket XI at Mongewell

HOWZAT!!

The winter is for football and the summer for cricket. Indeed, the "Carmel Clothes List" had a section headed "Summer Term" and it included Cricket Boots or Shoes, White Flannel Trousers and Extra White Shirts for Cricket.[76]

Cricket is not just randomly throwing and hitting a ball! There is a lot of technique in the game which accordingly requires expert guidance. In addition to the teachers at Carmel, there were some sports coaches. One of them was Don Banton who played cricket for Oxfordshire and at Carmel coached the first XI in the nets once or twice a week. Jonathan Isserlin has recollections of him, "He was an excellent coach who bowled legbreaks for Oxfordshire but was able to teach all sorts of styles. I particularly remember him having special composition balls that he coated one side with some sort of substance that made them swing beautifully."[77]

As with other sports, cricket was played against numerous outside teams

76. Carmel College Clothes Lists from 1950s.
77. Recollections – Jonathan Isserlin.

at both at home and away venues, and it also featured in the inter-house sports competition.[78]

In addition, there were both pupils and staff who wanted to play cricket at least once a week and during the first season at Mongewell (1954) the school was divided into seven teams who formed a league. The names of the teams were all water birds, maybe because Carmel was on the banks of the Thames. The names of these swimming fauna were Coots, Geese, Herns, Swans, Snipes, Drakes, and Ducks. The teams were captained by masters and two members of the first eleven, and play took place on three days each week. The games produced new talent particularly among the younger boys.[79] On these matches Jeremy Rosen comments, "It was one of the bonuses of being in a small school, playing together with staff, both proficient and clumsy ones. When the weather was good it was delightful."[80]

On a more formal level, there was the "Carmel College Cricket Club," that would bring out a card with the cricket fixtures for that year. It had four columns: date of fixture, name of the opponents, whether a home or away venue, and the result of the match. The last column was naturally left empty (one would need prophetic vision to know the result in advance!) and was to be filled in by the pupils after the match. The opponents for the 1958 fixtures included Rabbi Rosen's XI, Oxfordshire Constabulary, Wallingford Grammar School, Reading School 3rd XI, and the Staff of "Jewish Chronicle."[81]

The first match each year was the pupils versus Rabbi Rosen's XI "and is more in the nature of a trial match than a competitive game." In 1957, Rabbi Rosen's team was well and truly beaten. The pupils made 115, which included Colan Linton making the first half century of the season, while Rabbi Rosen's team made a mere forty-one runs.[82]

A cricket match, whilst the school was still at Greenham, merited an article under "Incidentally" in the "Jewish Chronicle." It was written by "Chronicler" and was headed "Rabbi at the Wicket":

After bidding farewell on Sunday to his distinguished guests, Mr. Justice and Lady Karminski, Rabbi Kopul Rosen, the Principal of

---

78. Various Carmel school magazines.
79. Carmel 1954, p.47.
80. Recollections – Jeremy Rosen, chap.1.
81. Carmel College Cricket Club, season 1958, Fixtures 1958.
82. Carmel 1957, p.34.

Cricket Practice at Carmel College in 1959

Carmel College, changed into flannels, donned his pads and went in to bat in the mixed masters' and boys' [versus the parents] cricket match on the school playing-field. The tall, bearded rabbi made an impressive figure as he took guard and faced the bowling. Equally impressive was his first stroke, a stylish cut to the on for two. His next was a lucky snick through the slips for four. Most striking was his fast running between the wickets. His short but merry innings enabled him to reach double figures. His batting partner, a boy, made a nice scoring shot which drew the comment from one lad in typical public-school drawl: 'He ought to say a beracha, that's his first this season!' There was some gentle leg-pulling at dinner in the masters' common-room after the match. Rabbi Sperber, who was visiting his son, complained that he had not been invited to play in the parents v. boys match. 'Ah,' retorted Rabbi Rosen, 'that was because we wanted the school to win, and you would not only have used a bat and ball but tehillim [recited Psalms] as well.'[83]

As with other sports, cricket at Carmel had its exciting and interesting occurrences. The author recalls one such event, "In one senior cricket

---

83. Jewish Chronicle, 4 July 1952, p.6.

match, the last over had been reached. Number ten of the opposing side was batting. On the fifth ball he was bowled out. The last batsman went in. If he could survive the last ball of the match, the game would be a draw. If he was out, Gilbert would win. The bowler bowled and the batsman was bowled out, thus giving Gilbert a win."[84]

Winning on the last ball of the match also occurred in a match held at the end of the Newbury era in the summer of 1953, between the staff and the pupils which, unusual for a school match, was of two innings. The magazine "Badad" reports:

> The Staff Match was generally considered most enjoyable. Mr. War-ner, who was Captain, provided a team of formidable stature which included the School Coach, Mr. Slatter. He bowled eight consecutive maiden overs and took three wickets. However, in spite of this fine bowling analysis the Masters only secured 37 runs. We [the pupils] scored 43 for 4 declared, and decided that it would be pleasant to watch the Masters perspire at the wicket once more. They obtained 52 runs for the loss of one wicket and left us to make 47 in order to win in only 15 minutes. To the great delight of the boys the winning stroke came from the last ball of the day.[85]

There was even a more exciting finish to a junior house cricket match between Gilbert and Montefiore. Montefiore were all out for 14. In their innings which followed, Gilbert had apparently made 15 runs for the fall of just three wickets, but the umpire had declared that one of them was a "short run." So one more run was still needed to win. Geoff Levy, who was the house captain of Gilbert, turned to Danny Bernstein and said "I am not moving from this spot until the winning run is scored."[86] But it never came. All the Gilbert batsmen from then onwards were bowled out for ducks. So the game ended in a tie. Geoff then said that this "short run" would cause Gilbert to lose the house cup that year. However, due to good tennis playing, which followed a few weeks later, Gilbert finally gained the house cup.[87]

A "carbon copy" of the above cricket match occurred in 1956 in the Prep School in a match between Gilbert and Alexander – (there was no

---

84. 7 years, p.77.
85. Badad, p.8.
86. E-mail from Daniel (Danny) Bernstein via Neil Myeroff, 24 July 2012.
87. 7 years, p.77.

Montefiore in the Prep School). The Prep School magazine "Alpha" reports on this match:

> This year's match worked itself up to a climax which caused the spectators to forget the 'breathless hush' associated with the more tense moments of the game and to voice their excitement in frenzied shouts which startled the dignified Seniors playing a School match on an adjacent pitch. Alexander batted first and made 43. Gilbert had almost overhauled this score with several wickets in hand when over-eagerness caused a number of batsmen to be run out. Their final score was 43 and the result of the match was a tie. An attempt was made by some (misguided) persons to cast doubt upon the arithmetical capacity of the scorers and an appeal was made to the senior Umpire who confirmed that the match was a tie.[88]

David Shaw remembers a case of "blind" cricket. The match was against Rutlish School. The batsman was Robert Seruya whose specialty was "goalkeeper" in football but he also "doubled as wicket keeper." David Shaw reports that "their front line bowler ran up delivered. Our 'goalkeeper' danced up the pitch, closed his eyes and swung, and swung again, and to the bewilderment of the bowler yet again, projectiles disappearing high into the trees. The umpire later said 'this is the first time I've witnessed a batsman hitting a ball without even looking'."[89]

Michael Blackstone recalls a cricket match, when (at least in the early stages) no batsman in the team, including himself, "ran." He recollects, "Playing cricket against another public school (I think it was Leighton College in Reading) when we were 0 runs for four wickets, I had taken about twenty-five minutes to make my 0."[90]

The year 1959 saw the breaking of a cricket record. For the first time in Carmel history, a team, in a senior inter-house match, made over 200 runs in an inning, the majority of them being made by one batsman, Colan Linton, who scored 121 not out.[91] As spectacular as it was for Carmel, it did not reach the pages of Wisden![92]

---

88. Alpha 1956, p.9.
89. Recollections – David Shaw.
90. Recollections – Michael Blackstone.
91. Carmel 1959, p.7. Another report states that Linton made 117 runs in a house match (Recollections – Jonathan Isserlin); whether or not the reports of 117 runs and 121 runs, refer to the same game and there is a faulty recollection of the exact number of runs, is not known.
92. Wisden Cricketers' Almanack is a cricket reference book published annually in the United

OFFICERS 1958

CAPTAIN:

G. N. LEVY

SECRETARY:

C. LINTON

FIXTURES 1958

Date	Opponents	Venue	Result
May 4	Rabbi Rosen's XI - - -	Home	....
„ 7	St. Catherine's, Oxford, 2nd XI	Home	....
„ 11	St. Bart's G.S., Newbury, Bdrs.	Away	....
„ 14	Oxfordshire Constabulary -	Away	....
„ 21	Leighton Park School 2nd XI -	Away	....
June 4	Lord William's School, Thame	Away	....
„ 11	Wallingford Grammar School -	Away	....
„ 18	Reading School 3rd XI - -	Home	....
„ 22	SPORTS DAY		
„ 25	Rutlish School 'A' XI - -	Away	....
„ 26	Culham College 2nd XI - -	Away	....
„ 29	Staff of "Jewish Chronicle" -	Home	....
July 20	Staff - - - - -	Home	....
	UNDER 14 FIXTURES		
June 4	Lord William's School, Thame -	Home	....
„ 11	Wallingford Grammar School -	Home	....
„ 12	Reading School - - -	Away	....
„ 25	Rutlish School - - -	Away	....

Carmel College Cricket Fixtures in 1958

There were occasions when, because of a shortage of players, pupils with injuries had to play in cricket matches. Jonathan Isserlin refers to one such match, "I batted in a house match with the cast on [because of a broken leg] because we were short of batsmen."[93]

A player doing well in a game can also lead to some personal embarrassment, as Michael Blackstone explains, "There was one well-built lad, a very nice person, . . . the memory stays with me of him catching the ball in a cricket match and as he stooped down, his trousers split along their seam."[94]

Every year a cricket match took place at Carmel against the "Jewish

---

Kingdom. It is considered the world's most famous sports reference book. From 1993 for a non-continuous period of 10 years, Matthew Engel, an Old Carmeli, was the editor of Wisden, (Wikipedia – Wisden Cricketers' Almanack).

93. Recollections – Jonathan Isserlin.

94. Recollections – Michael Blackstone.

Chronicle." In fact it was more than just a cricket much – it was a whole day's outing for the staff of the "Jewish Chronicle" together with their spouses and offspring. The first visit was in 1955. Kopul "welcomed the visitors and said that the 'J.C' was regarded as an institution in Anglo-Jewry, which the College also hoped to become."[95] Needless to say, the "Jewish Chronicle" reported on this occasion in full together with a photograph, with the sub-heading "Rabbi Kopul Rosen's Fine Batting and Bowling." Although Kopul made 28 not out, and took three wickets for 14 runs, it was the "Jewish Chronicle" that won by 38 runs.[96] In the same edition, the "Jewish Chronicle" commented that the number of runs they had made was 114, which was precisely the age of the newspaper.[97] Carmel, however, did not disgrace themselves, since they made far more than 7 runs, which was the then age of Carmel! The following year it was Carmel's turn to win and indeed they did with a heading in the "Jewish Chronicle," "Carmel College Beats 'J.C.' by 8 Wickets."[98] In 1958 the J.C. "battled unsuccessfully in the last few seconds of the game to gain the two vital runs needed to win" and so the game ended in a draw.[99] The "Jewish Chronicle" heading for the 1959 match was "Exciting Finish to Cricket Match" and indeed it was an exciting finish! It was four byes which won the match for Carmel College. Carmel was three runs behind the J.C, and "the four byes came when a fast ball . . . sped past the batsman and wicket keeper to the boundary."[100]

These "Jewish Chronicle" visits began with dinner and the author relates what happened one year:

> On that day there would be two sittings for that meal – one for the 'Jewish Chronicle' contingent and the other for the boys of the school. After this had been done successfully for several years, Mr. Bitner became in charge of the kitchen. Rabbi Rosen related to us that when Mr. Bitner heard about having to have two sittings for dinner that day, he ran to him saying that it was impossible to do this. Rabbi Rosen informed him that it been done for several years and he told us that he had given Mr. Bitner the day off![101]

---

95. Jewish Chronicle, 15 July 1955, p.19.
96. Ibid.
97. Ibid., 15 July 1955, p.6.
98. Ibid., 13 July 1956, p.27.
99. Ibid., 4 July 1958, p.19.
100. Ibid., 3 July 1959, p.17.
101. 7 years, p.78.

Carmel played many "away" cricket matches. On one of the away pitches, at Leighton Park School, (a school in Reading opened in 1890 by the Quakers[102]), Jonathan Isserlin writes about its idiosyncrasy, namely that there was "an Oak tree encroaching onto the pitch at mid-wicket (or extra cover depending on which side was batting) and which caused the boundary to be so short that they gave you 2 runs instead of 4 if you hit it!"[103]

Certain fauna had no respect for the Carmel cricket pitch and would barrow in it leaving mounds of earth all over the place. These were the moles that habited Carmel College. In 1969, the school purchased a jeep to chase these moles away. At the same period, to make it easier to get to "away" venues, the school bought a 12-seater van.[104]

SEE THE COUNTRYSIDE BY RUNNING

Being situated in the countryside, Carmel could easily make a route for a cross country run, which it indeed did. The author elaborates:

> [In Mongewell], there were two courses for this cross country run – one for the juniors and a longer one for the seniors. The juniors ran along the far edge of the sports field until the end of it, turned left and continued until the main road; left again and along the main road until they came to the hill leading to the back gate of the school; down the steep hill and this was the finish.
>
> The senior boys however didn't have this 'luxury!' They had to start by running up this hill – one was exhausted before one really got started! Then right turn and run along the road until the village of North Stoke. Turn right again and continue along the road till one reaches the fields. Again right and run on and on and on until one gets to the back road of the school. You have now finally finished and so you can take a long, long rest and have a nice drink!"[105]

The Carmel magazine reported that Carmel boys wearing running clothes became quite a familiar sight to the residents of North Stoke.[106]

Cross country running was one of the sports included in the inter-house

---

102. Wikipedia – Leighton Park School.
103. Recollections – Jonathan Isserlin.
104. Carmel 1959, p.5.
105. 7 years, pp.48–49.
106. Carmel 1955, pp.51–52.

competition. Not running the entire course would disqualify that pupil, irrespective of which position he came in the running. The author explains how this occurred in a certain year and how it made a difference as to which house gained maximum house points:

> One year, it was initially found that Gilbert was just lagging behind another house on this run. One of Gilbert's cross country runners, who was one of the best in the school, developed a 'stitch' and returned to base, thus apparently causing Gilbert to lose the winning points. I said 'apparently' because it then came to light that one of the runners from the house which had apparently won, had started his race from the study block, which was a very short distance after the starting line. He therefore had not run the entire course and had to be disqualified, thus giving the winning points to Gilbert.[107]

A boy could be, in the words of Henry Law describing himself, "useless at the usual team games of football, rugby and cricket" so much so that "nobody wanted me in their team," which turned out to be "a deficiency which earned me no social kudos," yet at the same time could state that "I could indulge my talent at cross country running instead." Henry had his own technique to succeed in the Carmel cross country run route. "I was a lightweight," he wrote "and could keep up a decent pace indefinitely. It got me out of the school grounds. I did well in the annual competitions. My strategy was to charge up the hill out of the valley at the start of the course. This would bring me amongst the front runners. I would then ease off for the downhill stretches and maintain speed up the hills, which gradually brought me forward."[108]

Not all pupils carried out this cross country run as prescribed by the school regulations. Neil Alton elaborates with two alternatives. The first was "short-cutting the cross country and acting a finish 'out of breath'"; the second involved the full route but doing one's shopping on the way "going the distance with the help of extra glucose, sweets from the shop in North Stoke en-route."[109]

Another pupil who took a "short cut," but of a different sort, on a cross country run was Joe Miller. "Running gave me the stitch" he writes, "and when it came to the cross country run that went through North Stoke, I was lucky to be able to jump into the back of that funny little van that Mr.

---

107. 7 years, p.78.
108. Recollections – Henry Law, Carmel College days, part 1, p.13.
109. Recollections – Neil Alton.

Bumpus [a member of the maintenance staff] drove and he brought me back to the school!"[110]

Michael Blackstone describes a slightly different method to make the cross country run easier! "Cross country running at Mongewell Park – we were allowed to run clockwise or anti-clockwise round the cross country course which I think included North Stoke. Consequently some of us ran clockwise for 100 yards then hid behind a hedge for 25 to 30 minutes then returned running anti-clockwise not feeling too tired from our run."[111]

The Biblical Book Bamidbar (Numbers) states "Be sure your sins will find you out."[112] This indeed happened to boys from Gilbert house who took short cuts, and their House Captain wrote of them in the Carmel magazine, "Boys proved themselves to be most ingenious in discovering short cuts during practice runs. However, this policy brought dire effects when the actual race was run, and we finished last."[113]

The Carmel cross country running even appeared in the Carmel literary output. It was David Saville who wrote a long "Ode on a School Cross Country Race":

> My eyes are in front
> Full ready to go
> All set for the good pace
> "By Monty!" , I know
> Who'll win this great race!
> Not I . . .
> I'm now twenty-ninth
> From thirty in all.
> I past the last fellow
> Since I made him fall
> Who leads there in yellow?
> Not I . . .
> I come next to last,
> Not in the first ten
> And if you ask me,
> "Will you run again?"
> My answer will be,
> Not I

---

110. Recollections – Joe Miller.
111. Recollections – Michael Blackstone.
112. Numbers chap.32 verse 23.
113. Carmel 1958, p.40.

Sports Day at Carmel College in 1957

EPILOGUE
To those boys who like
Cross country running,
A message for you:
In your ears it will ring,
But still it is true:–
You're crazy[114]

RUN, JUMP, AND THROW

Every year during the summer term, Carmel had a day known as "Sports Day," to which parents were invited. More accurately, this day should have been called "Athletics Day" since it was the day of inter-house *athletics* competition.

Even though it took place in the height of the summer, being England one could not foresee what the weather would be like and, indeed, at Mongewell there were days planned as "Sports Days" which turned out to be "Washout Days." In fact the first time in 6 years that there was no rain

---

114. Carmel 1957, p.9.

on Sports Day was in 1956.[115] As an "insurance policy," Sports Day was fixed about a month before the end of the summer term, since this gave leeway in the event of bad weather. This lesson was learned from the first planned Sports Day in Mongewell in 1954. It had been scheduled to have taken place on the last day of term immediately before the Speech Day, but the weather eliminated the sports part of the programme, and also possibly changed the winner of that year's inter-house cup.[116]

The following Sports Day "was marred a little by a continuous drizzle of rain," the Carmel Magazine reported. "But thanks to the hard work put in by the Officials and House Athletic Captains everything ran very smoothly, and the quite large number of spectators who defied the rain witnessed a keen competition."[117] The longest distance run at the Carmel Sports Day was a mile. That year the mile-long race was won by Ian Caller of Gilbert House.[118] Caller was the House Captain of Gilbert and on this achievement of Caller's, Gilbert Warner who was the Housemaster of Gilbert (there is no evidence that "Gilbert" being both his name and his House was by design!) wrote, "As his own victory in the Mile in the Athletics proved, he has distinguished himself at all he has undertaken and shown a magnificent example."[119]

There was rain again on the day designated as Sports Day in 1958.[120] Kopul then sent out a circular to the parents":

> Due to the unfavourable weather on Sunday, 22nd June, our Sports Day had to be cancelled; we are unable to organise another Sports Day on a Sunday this term, as unalterable fixtures have been made.
>
> If the weather is favourable, however, we shall have the School Sports on Thursday, 3rd July, at 2 p.m.
>
> I want to make it perfectly clear that Thursday, 3rd July, is not a *normal visiting day* but parents may come to the School after lunch, at 2 p.m. to witness the sporting events. If the weather on Thursday, 3rd July, is unfavourable, normal lessons will take place.[121]

---

115. Carmel 1956, p.31.
116. 7 years, p.131; unwritten recollections of author.
117. Carmel 1955, pp.50–51.
118. Ibid., p.51, photograph.
119. Ibid., p.40.
120. Carmel 1958, p.5.
121. Duplicated circular to parents from KR, 24 June 1958, underlining in original.

The author adds that "I remember hearing comments at the time that even if there is rain in Mongewell, who said it won't be fine in, for example, London. How are parents supposed to know. Long distance telephone calls were not like those of today! The bottom line was that the athletics were able to take place on that day."[122]

Every year, a duplicated programme of events on Sports Day was prepared and distributed. The cover page was a sketch of some form of athletics. For example, in 1956, it was of the "throwing" events, and in 1957 it was "running" events. The programme also it made it clear that parents could not utilise the afternoon as an opportunity to take their offspring on a half-day outing. There were definite limitations, as it clearly stated at the end of the programme. "Please note: "All boys must be present during the events and distribution of prizes. Parents and guardians may take the boys out after the end of sports, but must bring them back to school by 6.30 p.m. (Prep School) or 8 p.m. (Senior School)."[123] In 1955 it was planned to follow the Sports Day by a dramatic production. The Sports programme for that year accordingly stated, "At 5.00 p.m. (weather permitting) the school will present two short plays, using as its stage the open-air theater in front of the swimming pool. We sincerely hope that parents will stay for these and thus encourage this new venture . . ."[124] But weather did not permit and "rain stopped plays"![125]

After the events come the mathematics! Accordingly, the 1960 Sports Programme gave explanations on "Scoring." "For each win, second place, and third place, three points, two points and one point respectively are awarded. In the event of a tie, the points for those places are divided equally between the contestants concerned. (e.g. two boys tie first – two and a half each). In each age group, the boy who earns the most individual points is awarded the Victor Ludorum for that group."[126] "Victor Ludorum" was not the name of the donor of this cup but is the Latin for "winner of the games"![127]

The Sports Day programmes began by listing events which had already been decided prior to Sports Day, and this was followed by "Programme

122. 7 years, p.132.
123. Carmel College, Athletics Sports, 1956, programme, p.10, Carmel College, Athletics Sports, 1957, programme, p.10.
124. Carmel College, Athletics Sports, 1955, programme, p.7.
125. Carmel 1955, p.10.
126. Carmel College, Athletics Sports, 1960, programme, p.7.
127. It was traditional at some British Public School sports days to present this cup to the athlete who had won the most events or who had accumulated the most points through competing in many events (Wikipedia – Victor Ludorum).

<u>SENIOR SCHOOL</u>

<u>220 Yards</u>   1st - Fine   )   (A)
                 1st - Wootliff   )   (G)
                 3rd - Dee   (A)

Winning Time 25.4 seconds
(Record 25.6 secons Fine (A) - 1956)

<u>Javelin</u>   1st - Wootliff   (G)
                 2nd - Fine   (A)
                 3rd - Blackstone   (M)

Winning Throw 107 ft. 0 in.
(Record 89 ft. 8 ins. Burton (G) - 1956)

<u>880 Yards</u>   1st - Wootliff   (G)
<u>Senior</u>   2nd - Linton   (M)
                 3rd - Fine   (A)

Winning Time 2 mins. 15.5 secs.
(Record 2 mins. 29.4 secs. - Fine (A) - 1956)

<u>Discus</u>   1st - Burton   (G)
                 2nd - Staal   (A)
                 3rd - Refson   (G)

Winning Throw 111 ft. 9 ins.
(Record 109 ft 0 ins. Burton (G) -1956)

<u>High Jump</u>   1st - Wootliff   (G)
                 2nd - Dee   (A)
                 3rd - Linton   (M)

Winning Jump - 4 ft 10½ ins
(Record 4 ft 10 ins. Burton (G) -1956)

Page from Carmel College Sports Day Programme of 1957

of Events for Today." It was sports day for both the Prep School and the
Senior School, although naturally, due to the differences in ages, the
nature of the events were not identical. The Prep School races were of
shorter length (80 yards to 220 yards) and included "three-legged races"

and throwing was limited to the cricket ball. The Senior School races went up to a distance of one mile and included throwing the javelin and the discus and putting the shot.[128] Items found in other athletics meetings such as pole vaulting and hurdles did not form part of the Carmel Sports Day, although from the cover of the 1958 Sports Day Programme, one may well think that they did![129]

The programmes listed the name of the contestants for each event and the Carmel record (in the case of the Senior School) for that particular event. As an example, it stated for the Senior Mile "Record 5 mins. 14.9 secs. Linton – 1957."[130]

Sports Day of 1959 saw many school records broken. Amongst them, Colan Linton beat his previous record and this time broke the five-minute mile,[131] by a fraction of one second,[132] and Michael Selby[133] in the high jump, reached a fraction of an inch less than five feet.[134] Although one might expect that each year there would be some new record, in 1960, in the events which took place before Sports Day, not even one Carmel record had been broken.[135]

At the end of the Sports Day events, there was the presentation of prizes, namely, a miniature cup to the winner of each event. At this ceremony, which took place on the athletics field, (at least in one year) stood Kopul, on his left Charles Marshall, and on Kopul's right Bella Rosen, who handed out the prizes.[136]

There was even an unlisted contestant in the races, who wasn't even old enough to be in the Prep School. His name was David and he was of Kopul and Bella's offspring. He didn't come first but he received a consolation prize presented to him publicly on the athletics field by his mother.[137]

Heblish is a mixture of Hebrew and English. Alan Gold and Jonathan Isserlin decided to describe a Carmel Sports Day, not in Heblish but in Latlish – a mixture of Latin and English (but with the latter greatly pre-

---

128. Various programmes for Carmel College Athletic Sports.
129. Carmel College, Athletics Sports, 1958, cover of programme.
130. Ibid., p.8.
131. Carmel 1959, p.46.
132. Unwritten recollections of author.
133. In the Maccabi Championship that same year, Selby cleared 5 feet 4 inches. (Carmel 1959, p.43).
134. Carmel 1959, p.46.
135. Carmel College, Athletics Sports, 1960, programme, pp.1–5.
136. Memories of KR, photograph between pp.40–41.
137. Memories of KR, photograph between pp.40–41; Batiste cine film of Sports Day 1955.

Sports Day at Carmel College in 1957

dominating!) under the heading "Dies Ludorum – ab Auro et Igne." They wrote:

> The day appointed having arrived and the sun having been made to shine, the hordes of parenti in their chariots did descend at the meridian upon Carmel. As it came to pass that rain-clouds were put to flight, it became necessary that the sports should by some other means be delayed in their starting.
>
> The praetor who had taken command of the van on which the loudspeaker had been positioned said himself to be unable to make the loudspeaker that it might work. After the passing of half an hour the praetor said himself to have discovered the cause of the loudspeaker's reluctance to make itself heard and it was made able for the sports to commence. Thereupon H.S. put himself in command of the usage (+ ablative) of the loudspeaker warning those who spectated by the side of the track of the sports concerning the "Ides of June" sun lest their heads might be burned unless (+ present indicative) there was a covering of their above mentioned. J.B. having possessed himself with an ultra-modern weapon made himself present at all the runnings

(gerund) that he might start them. The events of the track having been run, and the spears and discoi having been thrown, the prizes were awarded according to the timings of R.C.'s hourglass. The cups having been presented (the majority, by many, to a certain Diskinius) and all the runnings having been raced, the hordes returned, leaving behind many great fragments of spoil for those who reside at Carmel (locative) that they might collect them.[138]

House points for athletics were not always limited to Sports Day. In 1955, half of the points came from what was known as "standards." For each different athletic event, a "standard" was established, namely run a certain length within a certain time, jump a certain height or length, throw something a certain distance. If one succeeded in doing this, it would be recorded and the house whose members achieved the highest number of standards would be awarded the highest number of house points and so on. This system was instituted to encourage boys who might not have won any events on Sports Day to go out and train and reach a certain standard.[139]

Boys would go out and train for the various athletic events, sometimes with unexpected results. Michael Davis reports on what happened in 1961:

> I was 15 and on the sports field practicing javelin-throwing when an abrupt voice yelled 'D-A-V-I-S! I hear you can throw that thing!' (You guessed it, Charlie Marshall) 'Ye-Ye-Yes Sir' I replied. 'Well let's see what you are made of, throw it over there towards that pylon.' 'But Sir, it looks quite near to me,' I said. 'Look lad you throw it and I'll take the responsibility, OK?'
>
> With that, I thought to myself, if ever in my life I had a chance to make a name for myself it was now. Please G-d, I pleaded, give me strength.
>
> I slowly walked back 20 paces (how many times I had practiced this technique), three deep breaths and then 'Zulus' eat your heart out, here I come. I had never put so much power into my javelin. It took off at a perfect angle, reached its maximum height and leveled off. Then it touched the first main cable of the pylon and bounced onto the second cable. There was a bright flash, then a bang followed by another flash. Sparks flew and then my charred javelin fell to the

---

138. Carmel 1959, p.12.
139. Carmel 1955, pp.39, 50; also referred to in Carmel 1957, p.36.

Throwing the Discus at Carmel College

ground. I have never seen Charlie Marshall open mouthed, just stand-ing there, silent and dumbfounded,

The result was a cold dinner for the whole school. I had made my mark.[140]

Michael Davis later related that "the teacher who taught carpentry, Mr. Taylor, took the javelin and embedded it in concrete and has it to this day."[141]

Carmel did not limit its athletic activities to internal events. The boys also entered external competitions and on occasion excelled. In 1956, A. Burton became the Oxfordshire county youth champion in throwing a discus and, moreover, his throw was only a few feet behind the county record.[142] The following year there was a near miss in discus throwing in this competition. Yomtov Sabah missed the county championship by just two inches.[143]

140. Reflections – Michael Davis.
141. E-mail from Michael Davis, 30 July 2012.
142. Carmel 1956, pp.6, 31.
143. Carmel 1957, p.7.

CARMEL ALSO HAD OTHER SPORTS

Another sport which in 1954 found its way into the school's sports curriculum was boxing. The coach was David Stamler, who had "undertaken to teach the noble art of self-defence to the boys each Sunday," wrote "The Young Carmelonian" which then went on to warn, "In future, anti-Semites will not find life so easy."[144] (Advice to pupils who were due to receive corporal punishment from David Stamler – Beware!!) On this subject, the Carmel Magazine wrote, "His [Stamler's] skill and patience have already produced results. Enthusiasts have improved, not only in boxing, but also in their general physical fitness."[145] Boxing however did not become a sport in the inter-house championship.

The Mongewell estate had tennis courts, but they had lain unattended for some seasons before Carmel purchased the property and were thus in a decrepit state. To rectify such a situation, one could rely on Ted Wetherall, who at that period had already worked on the estate for over forty years, and was thus certainly not a youngster. The Carmel magazine writes on his work on these tennis courts, "[Wetherall] applied himself to the task of renewing them. The result of this was that, although no tennis was expected last term [Spring 1954], there were in fact three full week's play." This magazine then goes on to report on the immediate mass popularity of tennis at Carmel. "This term [Summer 1954] saw the formation of a Tennis Club with a membership of over seventy boys."[146] By the following year, the numbers had increased, and eighty boys had entered for the school tournaments. Even the Prep School had formed their own tennis club which already had thirty pupils, and had the younger members not been excluded, there would have been many more! Tennis courts require constant maintenance and on this the Carmel magazine continues, "A special tribute should be paid to Mr. Wetherall . . . He has lived up to his name ["Weather–all"], and in all weathers he can be seen carefully tending the courts which he has looked after for the last half-century."[147] These refurbished courts were only a pro-tem solution and towards the end of the 1950s, six brand new hard tennis courts were built at the school.[148] Izzy Gletzer, Captain of Tennis commented on this "small!" number of

144. The Young Carmelonian, p.6.
145. Carmel 1954, p.48.
146. Ibid.
147. Carmel 1955, pp.48–49.
148. Carmel 1959, p.5.

Old tennis court at Mongewell. Gymnasium in background,
October 1956.

new tennis courts, "This number [six new courts] might, at first, seem large (it is in fact, possible to allocate thirty-six courts a day), but so great is the clamour for courts that they are often hard to come by."[149]

As can be seen, in Mongewell the actual playing of tennis was extremely popular. However, in Newbury, instead of the physical exertion required to actually play tennis, there were other preferences! The magazine "Badad" explains, "In spite of a reproving letter sent to the All England Club Secretary last year, the Wimbledon Tennis Championships again clashed with our tennis tournament. As a result, our competition has been scratched, for it seemed that our players much preferred the close atmosphere of the television room, to indulging in the game itself."[150]

Ping Pong, not here the name of a Chinaman, but tennis played on a table, began in Britain in the 1880s where it was played among the upper-class as an after-dinner parlour game.[151] This sport, needless to say, also reached Carmel College. It gained popularity in Carmel in 1955, after the table tennis table had been moved to a better and more suitable room. That was also the year when this sport became re-included in the inter-house sports competition.[152]

Not only did Carmel play the usual sports found in other schools, it also had at least one "unusual" sport. This was volleyball which was introduced

149. Ibid., pp.4, 45.
150. Badad, p.8.
151. Wikipedia – Table Tennis.
152. Carmel 1955, p.50.

to Carmel in 1958. On this, the Carmel magazine wrote that "it seems to be one of the favourite pastimes of the Principal. Indeed volley-ball is the foreign boy's substitute for cricket, and the grass tennis court has been transformed into a volley-ball court."[153]

Already, at Greenham, basketball had been one of the sports. The school converted the glade in the extensive grounds into a basketball pitch.[154] The "Badad" magazine in 1953 wrote that "Basketball has also had an excellent complement of supporters, a few of whom were enthusiastic to the extent of having an illicit game at midnight."[155] In Mongewell, the basketball pitch was set up in the gymnasium,[156] but it was not always in that location. In the summer of 1957, the basketball nets were taken outside the gymnasium and set up there. The first game to be played outside was towards the end of May, on Exhibition Day,[157] the day when Kopul announced Carmel's new building project.[158] .

Basketball is one of the sports where supporters giving verbal and other encouragement to the players can be of advantage. This message was brought home by Ellis Korn, the Gilbert House Captain:

> My criticism lies not with those who participated in the [basketball] game, but with those who should have been watching. I shall never forget the occasion of the Montefiore v. Gilbert senior basketball match when the spectators' gallery was packed with Montefiore supporters shouting jingoistic slogans, and waving yellow house shirts. Unfortunately not one Gilbert supporter turned out to watch the game and this contributed a great deal to our resounding defeat.[159]

For the opposing team, Colan Linton, the House Captain of Montefiore wrote "It was during the Basketball matches that the spirit of the non-playing members of the House really made itself apparent."[160]

The gymnasium building also had a court with wood paneling all over the walls and floor, which had been built for the American version of squash. (Squash is not only a soft drink, or the effect of the high density

---

153. Carmel 1958, p.5.
154. The Old Carmeli, no.5, 1968–9, p.27; Reflections – David Perl.
155. Badad, p.9.
156. Carmel College 1948–1957, photograph on p.10; Carmel 1957, p.34.
157. Carmel 1957, p.34.
158. Ibid., p.6.
159. Carmel 1959, p.48.
160. Ibid., p.50.

The Squash Court at Mongewell

of passengers on the London Underground during the rush hour; it is also the name of a sport!) This American style court had been constructed during the period when the building had been commandeered by the United States Army during the Second World War.[161] The Carmel magazine commented that this deviation from a conventional squash court "prevents us from playing as many matches as we might wish. This tends to be rather galling, as squash has undoubtedly become one of our best sports, and one in which we could hold our own against most schools."[162] Despite this, there were outside teams who came to Carmel for squash matches. Needless to say, they were at a disadvantage. One such team who came was the Oxford Jewish Society. However, being "unaccustomed to our [Carmel's] faster American-type squash court, the [Oxford Jewish] Society was decisively beaten, but they put up a much harder fight than the score of 7–0 suggests."[163] In 1959, the walls of the squash court were painted white. This did not make it more conventional but at least it made

161. Recollections – Jonathan Isserlin.
162. Carmel 1955, p.49.
163. Carmel 1954, p.49.

the "most of the inefficient lighting system."[164] That year the squash secretariat passed into other hands, and Izzy Gletzer commented ironically, "I feel sure that he [the new squash secretariat] will not give way under the barrage of letters that will be expected"![165] By 1961, the gymnasium had come to the end of its life and was in danger of collapse. With that, squash as well as basketball "vanished from Carmel life."[166]

Near to the Greenham Lodge is the Newbury District Golf Club. The 1938 Auction Catalogue states that the property of Greenham Lodge is to be sold with vacant possession "save a strip 15 feet wide by the Drive, let on lease to Newbury District Golf Club at an apportioned Rental of 1/- [one shilling] per annum."[167] According to the magazine "Badad," "the golf course, or at least the nineteenth hole, afforded some pleasure to the more discerning sportsmen."[168] The "nineteenth hole" is a slang term used in golf, generally referring to a pub, bar, or restaurant on or near the golf course, and it can thus be seen what the priorities of the 1953 Carmel pupils were! In 1958 golf was introduced for the first time, at least officially, into the school. Lessons were given by a visiting professional from a nearby golf course. About fifteen boys participated and there was considerable enthusiasm.[169] The Carmel magazine adds that golf is "for the extreme individualists or more usually for the prematurely middle-aged!"[170] Where the "nineteenth hole" was is not stated, but it might well have been the Carmel tuck shop!

Horses also entered the Carmel sports programme in the 1953/54 academic year. The Carmel magazine describes this riding activity:

> On many days of the week, after lunch, a group of boys may be seen setting off down the bridle path in the direction of the stables, dressed in an assortment of clothes which can rarely be encountered elsewhere.
>
> Because of the increase in custom, the stable-mistress has bought several horses of slightly greater stature than usual, to fit our more sizeable pupils from Turkey, and even from the sandy wastes of Morocco. The Berkshire Downs have been well covered in our excur-

164. Carmel 1959, p.44.
165. Ibid.
166. Carmel 1961, p.5.
167. Auction Greenham, p.22.
168. Badad, p.9.
169. Carmel 1958, p.35.
170. Ibid., p.5.

sions, and some excellent scenery has been revealed to us. The sport is a healthy one, entailing strenuous exercise of a novel type. And above all, a great deal of time is spent in the open air.[171]

ROOKS, KNIGHTS, AND BISHOPS

For those pupils who preferred to use their brains and not their muscles, there was chess in the sports programme. As with the other sports, there were inter-house chess matches and also many fixtures against other schools and adult teams. Furthermore, Carmel entered into a number of organised county and national chess championships.

In 1956, Carmel first entered the Berks and Bucks Chess Tournament, and succeeded in reaching the finals where they were defeated by Eton by a score of five and a half against a half.[172] The Carmel Magazine wrote that "Eton has in past years dominated the tournament and must start favourites if only by virtue of their superior numbers."[173] In fact Eton had over 1,300 pupils as against Carmel's 200. The following year, Carmel again reached the finals, but this time the result was less lopsided and Carmel were only narrowly defeated three and a half against two and a half. "That night, Mr. Bunney announced the result in the dining hall saying that the Carmel team did very well and were narrowly beaten."[174] A report of the match was published in the Londoner's diary in the Evening Standard on 12 June and in many local papers.[175] It was in the following year, 1958, that Eton were beaten by Carmel in the Zonal Finals of the Sunday Times tournament.[176] If one had thought that one would have the opportunity to see the distinctive Eton uniform – black tailcoat, waistcoat, false-collar and pinstriped trousers[177] – when the team came to Carmel, one would have been disappointed, since the boys came wearing normal clothes![178]

The winning side in a chess competition was not always the side which won the most games. Sometimes the age of the players could determine who had won. One such incident is related by Ian Panto:

---

171. Carmel 1954, p.48.
172. 7 years, p.79.
173. Carmel 1956, p.33.
174. 7 years, p.79.
175. Carmel 1957, p.6.
176. Carmel 1958, pp.6, 28; that year Carmel won the Berks and Bucks Chess Tournament, but Eton did not enter it that year.
177. Wikipedia – Eton College.
178. Carmel College 1948–1957, p.22, photograph.

Chess Tournament Held at Carmel College

The story I wish to tell is regarding chess. I was a good chess player, having represented my County (Sussex) when I was just 10 years of age! So it came to pass that I was Captain of the chess team whilst I was in the fourth form. It was my duty to formulate the team and pick players for each match. In each year that I was captain, we always reached the finals of the Sunday Times Boys Chess Competition and inevitably we played Eton. This competition allowed age to be taken into account — so if you had a low aggregate age you could win by taking only 2 out of the 6 games!!! In 1961 this is exactly what happened — I picked a prep school boy to play the number 6 slot. His name was Cohen and he was about 8 or 9 nine years old. We won by drawing 3 3, as a result of our age. Kopul Rosen heard about the result and called me to his office. I thought he was going to congratulate me, but I knew things were not quite right when the first thing he said, at the top of his voice, was 'PANTO what do you think you are doing

putting an 8 year old into the Chess team? THAT IS GAMESMAN-
SHIP NOT SPORTSMANSHIP.' I, of course, replied that the prep
school boy had obtained a half and indeed merited his place!!! Anyway
I was read the riot act for at least five minutes and just as I was walking
away I noticed a twinkle in Rabbi Kopul Rosen's eye! I am sure he was
really proud of us!![179]

The Prep School indeed had its own Chess Club, whose activities included an inter-pupil competition with a chess "ladder." In addition to
chess being one of the sports in the inter-house competition, there would
be inter-form competitions and also matches with the lower part of the
Senior School.[180]

   The norm is for chess to be played one to one. However, often chess
masters will play a large number of contestants simultaneously. This occurred in Carmel when Raphael Joseph Arie Persitz, the ex-Israeli boy
champion, then aged 20, played fifteen Carmel players at the same time,
winning on every board.[181]

ROWING ON THE WAVES

Since Carmel was not only situated by the side of the River Thames, but
in fact owned part of the river (admittedly only a miniscule amount!), it is
natural that rowing became a major sport at the school. There was even
an old boat house on the Carmel estate.

   At the 1960 Speech Day, Kopul explained the advantage of rowing as a
team sport:

> There is perhaps no sphere of athletics which takes longer in which to
> achieve success than that of rowing. In cricket, one or two outstanding
> boys can carry a team, an outstanding batsman, an outstanding bowler
> can achieve victory for a mediocre side. This cannot be achieved in
> rowing, the stroke can't row faster than everybody else. It's a team and
> it takes years before one sees some success.[182]

179. Recollections – Ian Panto, capitals in original.
180. Alpha: 1954, p.5; 1955, p.6; 1956, p.6.
181. Carmel 1954, p.49.
182. Recording of Carmel College Speech Day 1960, at 28 minutes 1 second from the beginning.

The Carmel College Boathouse at Mongewell

Carmel instituted rowing as an official sport just one term after moving to Mongewell. But soon after, rowing stopped – not because of lack of enthusiasm, but because the Thames froze over! Fortunately two weeks later, it thawed and rowing was resumed.[183] On Speech Day that year, although the athletics programme had to be cancelled due to heavy rain, a boat race between two teams went on as planned.[184]

At first, the boats had to be borrowed[185] but in 1957, two clinker four boats were donated to the school by Jack Saville. These two boats were

183. Carmel 1954, p.48.
184. Carmel 1955, p.6.
185. Ibid., p.43.

named "Jacob" and "Esther," presumably after the donor and his wife.[186] It is not recorded whether a bottle of kosher champagne was smashed against the sides of these boats on naming them!

Rowing even entered the field of Carmel poetry, as can be seen in P. Adler's poem:

> "Turn towards the river, bow!"
>   Says cox'n to the crew;
> "Stroke side under when I say now!"
>   Says cox'n to the few.
> "Now the boat is in for sure,"
>   Says cox'n to the crew;
> "Everyone in and fix his oar!"
>   Says cox'n to the few.
> "At the start we all get ready,"
>   Says cox'n to the crew;
> "Come forward all, and get her steady!"
>   Says cox'n to the few.
> "Pull more water as we go,"
>   Says cox'n to the crew;
> "We've passed the post – and what a show!"
>   Said the cox'n to the few.[187]

As the rowing teams progressed, Carmel started to enter regattas. Over the years these included Pangbourne, Reading, and Hereford.[188] However, many regattas were held on Shabbat and so Carmel could not participate in them. At the Carmel Speech Day in 1960, Kopul spoke of the "unique feature" of the Carmel College Rowing Club:

> Almost every rowing school in the country that has competed against Carmel, and this includes some of the most prominent rowing schools, knows full well that Carmel will not row on Shabbat, and where there is a regatta on Saturday, our crew does not put in an appearance. Now the reaction to this on the part of Headmasters and rowing masters of schools throughout the country is quite remarkable, and I wish some prominent persons of Anglo-Jewry could have said to them what has

186. Carmel 1957, p.31.
187. Carmel 1961, p.35.
188. Ibid., p.37.

been said to me by Headmasters of well-known schools concerning this attitude of the boys, that even if they were to enter for an event in which they would reach the final, if that final were rowed on Shabbat, they would scratch and not row. One Headmaster of a prominent school, King's School Chester, said to me 'I wish we had some such moral principle to make boys realise that there are more important things than athletic prowess,' and our rowing master, Mr. Marshall, will tell you that at all regattas this has been a talking point amongst the Christian schools that have been there, that there is a Jewish school that rows, that can give you a good fight even if they lose but row with a sense of sportsmanship, but will not desecrate their Sabbath. And of course I am biased, I admit my prejudices, but I believe that this does more to create a sense of goodwill based on mutual respect than all the lectures and propagandist pamphlets which the community might publish. (applause) I am hopeful that within a few years we will put a crew in for the Henley regatta. I dare not hope that they will reach the final and thus have to scratch because the final is raced on the Saturday. But if my hopes did carry me so far, I would go one stage further and say, as I have expressed on some previous occasion, that one day, who knows, both the Oxford and the Cambridge crews might be composed of Old Carmelonians and the boat race will have to be raced on a Monday. (applause)[189]

The problem of regattas being held on Shabbat was already mentioned by Kopul on the first Speech Day at Mongewell and he related how one day the rowing instructor came excitedly to him and told him there was a regatta on Whit Monday, but Kopul had to inform him that Whit Monday that year coincided with Shavuot![190]

The rowers had special "privileges" in connection with their eating and sleeping conditions. In this connection the author recollects:

As the years went on, rowing as a sport was intensified in Carmel. The players did weight-lifting exercises to strengthen their bodies. The rowing teams were allocated to a dormitory of their own and

---

189. Recording of Carmel College Speech Day 1960, at 34 minutes 28 seconds from the beginning; This last remark of Kopul's regarding the university boat race being held on a Monday, was again related by Abraham Levy, an Old Carmeli of the Kopul era, in a film on Israeli Television in 1985 on Carmel College, entitled "English Gentlemen."
190. 7 years, p.127.

tables of their own in the dining room. The reason for this was that with their training exercises, they might well be eating and sleeping at different hours from the other boys and having separate facilities would minimise any mutual disturbances.[191]

On the subject of the rowers' "luxury" food, Joe Miller commented that there were those who got "extra food" – the rowers – and he noted that this was "another good reason for being a rower!" adding that "being growing lads was always on my mind."[192]

One of the rowing boys, Michael Goitein, described the unconventional style of instruction of one of the rowing coaches, "Our coach, Mr. Hooper, would ride precariously along the towpath on his ancient bicycle, risking life and limb as he looked sideways at us rather than ahead to where he was heading, all the while shouting instructions through his hand-held megaphone."[193]

Hooper was not the only person to endanger himself for the sake of rowing, as the Carmel magazine relates, "At one time Mr. Marshall, in the capacity of rowing coach, had to sprint along the bank when training his crews – a courageous undertaking at the best of times. All that has changed however, and now, thanks to the generosity of Mr. Cope, he corrects and criticises imperviously from the bows of the new school motor-launch 'Evadne'."[194]

In 1960, the Carmel magazine described a mysterious happening at the Carmel boathouse. "The area down by the boathouse, where the school fours are kept and launched, was recently cordoned off, and within hours the inevitable rumours were circulating. All curiosity was satisfied however, when a fresh-laid concrete landing stage gradually emerged from the confusion."[195]

People have been putting ships in bottles for well over 200 years.[196] However, the new art teacher, Dennis Mills, amazed everyone at Carmel by putting the Carmel boats into a polythene bag![197]

According to Henry Law, the Carmel boats were not only used for racing – sometimes they were used for a Sunday pleasure sail. He writes:

---

191. Ibid., p.79.
192. Recollections – Joe Miller.
193. Recollections – Michael Goitein.
194. Carmel 1960, pp.5–6.
195. Ibid., p.5.
196. The Modern Method of Building Ships in Bottles, (Internet).
197. Carmel 1961, p.5.

A group of us – not the heavyweights who were in the school rowing team – learned how to handle the boat, to get in and out safely and use the oars, and we would take a boat out on a Sunday morning for a couple of hours. One fine summer morning we rowed, at a comfortable pace, all the way up to Benson lock, back past the school, down to the railway bridge at Cholsey and then back to school. We were pleasantly and satisfyingly tired after a couple of hours in the fresh air, and came back with hearty appetites.[198]

PHYSICAL JERKS

In addition to Carmel's sports programme, there was also in the lessons timetable Physical Education instruction, which consisted of physical jerks of all kinds and the climbing of frames and ropes and all manner of other equipment.[199] Jeremy Rosen elaborates:

There was a distinction between the afternoons of compulsory sport which were designed to engender team spirit and competitiveness and on the other hand the weekly Physical Education period, a requirement of the educational curriculum. The latter as an agony suffered at the hands of often ex-military men determined to force young muscles to do things they were not designed for. For pupils who were good at sport their position in the school pecking order or popularity stakes was guaranteed. Hero worshipping was inevitable. But for those who were neither athletic nor strong the ways to excel were more limited. Chess, music, drama and of course academic success were alternatives and indeed some fortunate pupils were good at everything.[200]

In the Prep School magazine "Alpha," one of the pupils, D. Samuels, devoted the first verse of his poem to his Physical Education lessons:

First we have P.T.,
Much beloved by me;
We swing upon the ropes
And exchange little jokes.[201]

---

198. Recollections – Henry Law, Carmel College days, part 1, p.14.
199. Carmel College 1948–57, p.10 photograph; Reflections – photograph.
200. Recollections – Jeremy Rosen, chap.1.
201. Alpha, 1956, p.14.

Although not strictly fitting under the heading of sports, yet an activity that requires physical coordination, is being a member of a group such as a Cadet Corps. However, it would seem that it was not the original intention of Kopul when founding Carmel to have a Cadet Corps since he wrote in the Provisional Prospectus:

> Instead of J.T.C., A.T.C. [Air Training Corps], Sea Cadet Corps or Boy Scouts, the College will have a voluntary organisation – the To-ranim – which will aim at providing practical training in citizenship (communal tasks in the Carmel estate, assistance in time of emergency to farmers or other neighbours, visits to factories, farms and other centres of industrial and agricultural activity, exchange visits with schools abroad, etc.); and at developing initiative, resource, endurance and spirit of self-reliance (camping, first-aid and life-saving, map reading, cross-country excursions, etc.).[202]

However, later Kopul had a change of mind and in January 1957, he established a Cadet Corps in Carmel. This was at a period when Britain had compulsory military service, which required every able-bodied man to serve two years in the armed services,. Furthermore, all British Public Schools had cadet forces which were trained by different branches of the military, and in many schools the Cadet Corps was the most elite and sought after of all the school activities. At first there was great enthusiasm for the cadets. Being a cadet could result in a person having a higher rank when conscripted, which would carry with it privileges and status.[203]

Amongst the kit which was distributed to the cadets were rifles. For a cadet who was of short stature there was a problem, as related by David Waldman, who identified himself as the "titch" in a photograph of the Carmel cadets.[204] Waldman explained that because of his size he couldn't hold his rifle properly![205] Neil Alton also remembered the big rifle, "Along came the Cadets, with big rifles, crawling along the Ha-Ha[206] in

---

202. Carmel College Provisional Prospectus, undated (about April 1948), section: Toranuth.
203. Carmel 1957, p.29; Recollections – Jeremy Rosen, chap.1.
204. E-mail and photograph from David Waldman, 10 November 2011; e-mail from David Waldman, 11 November 2011. David Waldman used the term "titch" in his e-mail to describe himself.
205. E-mail from David Waldman, 6 May 2012.
206. "Ha-ha" is a term in garden design that refers to a trench one side of which is concealed

uniform, which I joined and had some fun at last."[207] Neil later elaborated:

> We were issued with uniforms of a kind, rifles, and our marching orders. Literally. So we drilled. Giggling to start with. Then more seriously. An esprit de corps developed. Not exactly to war film levels. Rather, fun mixed with togetherness. On to activities, missions, praise, gentle criticism plus positive suggestions to improve – my first experience of enjoyable group activity. What a change from being school underdogs, 'schnips'. For short sessions, we were 'it' instead. I put my later rowing abilities down to the Cadet Corps. Neither side knew it at the time. But it may have been the start of a new Alton.[208]

"Titch" Waldman was once photographed on parade to the right of Jeremy Rosen who was also one of the Carmel cadets.[209] Of this Carmel Cadet Corps, Jeremy writes:

> Pupils were taught to polish their boots till they could see their faces in them, to spend hours greasing and priming their kit with blanco. They were commanded to stand to attention, chin in, chest out. They were drilled, to square bash and march up and down the main school square. Old army Enfield rifles were handed out to take apart and learn to fire and trips to the Benson shooting ranges were the highlights. The Carmel soldiers in the making competed against each other for the title of expert marksman.[210]

Another Carmel cadet, Michael Goitein adds his recollections:

> A bunch of us were conscripted, given uniforms complete with shiny army boots, and taught to march in formation. My friend, John Goldsmith, whose uniform was always impeccable, was immediately identified as officer material and made squadron leader – but he suffered from not being able to march in step so his left foot would move forward in near-perfect synchrony with the two dozen right feet which followed him. I recall one exciting exercise in which we were shown

from view.

207. Recollections – Neil Alton.
208. E-mail from Neil Alton, 8 August 2012.
209. E-mail from David Waldman, 11 November 2011.
210. Recollections – Jeremy Rosen, chap.1.

how to launch grenades, and another in which was demonstrated how to camouflage oneself so as to be undetectable in the undergrowth. Alas, our competence and attitude did not match the army's expectations.[211]

However soon after its formation, "the early interest waned – perhaps the proposed ending of National Service contributed – and mass resignations took place." But there were those who continued. Every Thursday and Friday parades were held in Carmel when members of the Cowley Barracks provided instruction of a very high quality,[212] and following an exam, a few of the cadets were promoted to N.C.O.s.[213] However, the Carmel Corps came to an end in 1958.[214] Julius Nehorai attributed its demise to the "hopeless[ness of] attempts to train pampered Jewish boys for becoming soldiers."[215]

One of the leading Carmel cadets was Anthony Mothew, who following the exam became a Lance/Cpl.[216] Just before its demise, Mothew wrote a "Letter to the Editor" of the "Carmel Clarion" strongly criticising the waning of interest in the cadet corps, a letter which reinforced both Alton's and Nehorai's comments:

A few terms ago a new feature was introduced into the school. A feature that is encouraged in the finest of British Public Schools; namely a School Cadet Corps.

At first, a great many boys showed an interest in this project. Unfortunately, this interest has somewhat waned.

I have reason to believe that the majority of boys in this school are either physically too weak, are unaware of the many benefits and fun they are missing or are simply bone lazy, when they claim not to have enough time for the Carmel College Cadet Corps.

They do not realise that by devoting an hour to the Cadet Corps each week improves their character. It teaches its members to show self discipline, leadership, courage, initiative and many other qualities of the gentleman.

---

211. Recollections – Michael Goitein.
212. Carmel 1957, p.29.
213. Carmel 1958, p.31.
214. Carmel 1959, p.33.
215. Recollections – Julius Nehorai.
216. Carmel 1958, p.31.

Carmel College Cadet Corps

It is true that some boys are unwilling to spend five minutes cleaning their kit. This is sheer laziness. The qualities are not taught brutally, but in a fashion that can be enjoyed by any one. The army cadet syllabus is specially designed to send a boy out into the world with invaluable knowledge that will show him benefit throughout his lifetime.

Boys of this school should take advantage of the instruction and free use of equipment given to them by the government, if only to improve their character, to get some free pleasure or to support the school's morale. (A cadet corps is a feature in all public schools), they should join the cadet corps as soon as possible."[217]

A vacuum was not left in Carmel. The Carmel Cadet Corps was replaced by the Jewish Lads' Brigade. The Carmel magazine writes of them:

The Carmel Platoon of the Jewish Lads' Brigade has a full complement of 26 Cadets. It has regular weekly meetings, where its activities include drills, map reading, field craft and first aid. After only four weeks' training the Carmel contingent took part in the London Regimental Review. Although it was the largest company present it was

217. Carmel Clarion. vol.1, no. 2, 1958, (p.14, pages unnumbered).

the only unit where there were no fainting casualties (in spite of the excessive heat), and was commended by the commanding officer.[218]

A report of this event appeared in the "Jewish Chronicle" under the heading of "J.L.B. Contingents on Parade." Carmel was specifically mentioned in this report, "Among the 14 companies represented on parade was "that newly formed at Carmel College."[219] The following year, the lads were given a further treat – attending a J.L.B. week end camp.[220]

---

218. Carmel 1959, p.33.
219. Jewish Chronicle, 10 July 1959, p.8.
220. Carmel 1960, p.27.

Chapter 8

The Eternal Link

Two of the appellations given to boys at a school are "New Boy" and "Old Boy." A "New Boy" is one who has just enrolled in a school; an "Old Boy" is not one who is drawing his old age pension, but is one who receives this title the day he leaves his school, irrespective of his age. Many schools have a guild to link their Old Boys together. Carmel College was no exception....

SETTING IT UP

By just over four years after Carmel College's establishment, there were already a small number of Old Boys; an Association for these Old Boys was therefore planned and was soon after established.

It all began in October 1952, when an Old Boy, David Perl, wrote to his friends, the "Friends" being former Carmel pupils:

> For some time now, a number of us who were at Carmel College have been discussing the formation of an Old Boys' Association. Although we realise how few are the numbers who have passed through the school, we feel that the time has come when a start should and can be made.
>
> We are therefore calling a meeting at 8.30 p.m. on Saturday, November 1st, at 8, Raleigh Close, Hendon, when it is hoped to formulate and ratify a constitution for the association and elect officers and a committee.
>
> We do hope you will make every effort to attend and help us in this project and we look forward to seeing you there.[1]

---

1. Duplicated letter from David Perl to Friend (i.e. former Carmel pupil), October 1952.

In his letter, Perl referred to "ratify[ing] a constitution." Indeed, an organisation without a Constitution is like turkey without plum-pudding (or in Jewish circles, the Rosh Hashanah apple without honey). Thus prior to sending out his letter, an unidentified Old Boy had been asked to draft out such a document. (There is still extant part of a typed draft of such a Constitution, dated 17 September 1952.)

The meeting[2] duly took place on the arranged date.[3] The number of Old Boys who attended (according to the best recollections of David Perl) were five, and "a committee was formed consisting, naturally enough, of the five of us present."[4] Another Old Boy, Malcolm Shifrin reports that at this meeting, Kopul was made the President and the Vice-Presidency was "offered to Mr. J. C. Gilbert," who at the time was a Governor.[5]

Perl also wrote of this meeting, "Rabbi Rosen kindly attended. At this meeting a constitution was formulated and ratified."[6] It is very likely that at this meeting, those present went through the draft constitution, word by word. As can be seen from the original draft, numerous handwritten changes were made on it, some of them barely legible.

Let us now look at some of the typed clauses of this draft constitution and the subsequent handwritten changes:

Paragraph 1 stated: "The Association should be called the "Old Kopulians Association." In the handwritten amendment this was changed to "Old Carmeli Association."

Paragraph 2 was titled "Objects" and read:

(a) To keep Old Boys in contact with Carmel College, in particular by encouraging personal visits to the School.

(b) To maintain and foster intercourse between Old Kopulians and to furnish information concerning Old Kopulians and new activities. The word "Kopulians" was of course crossed out, and replaced by "Carmelis."

(c) To organise such dinners, sports functions and other gatherings, as shall, from time to time, be determined upon. In the handwritten amendments, the words "by the committee" were added.

---

2. A brief report of this meeting appeared in the Jewish Chronicle, 6 February 1953, p.6.
3. Badad, p.6.
4. Jewish Chronicle supplement, 14 November 1958, p. vii.
5. Badad, p.6.
6. Carmel 1954, p.35.

Draft Constitution of OCA with handwritten amendments (last page missing) 17.9.52.

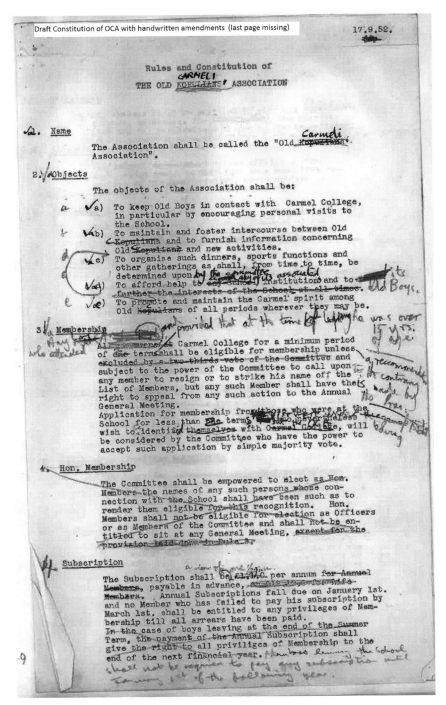

Rules and Constitution of
THE OLD ~~KOPULIANS'~~ *CARMELI* ASSOCIATION

1. Name

The Association shall be called the "Old ~~Kopulians'~~ *Carmeli* Association".

2. Objects

The objects of the Association shall be:

a) To keep Old Boys in contact with Carmel College, in particular by encouraging personal visits to the School.

b) To maintain and foster intercourse between Old ~~Kopulians~~ and to furnish information concerning Old ~~Kopulians~~ and new activities.

c) To organise such dinners, sports functions and other gatherings as shall, from time to time, be determined upon *by the committee associated*.

d) To afford help to ~~and School of~~ *institution* and to ~~further the interests of the School at all times.~~ *Old Boys.*

e) To ~~promote~~ and maintain the Carmel' spirit among Old ~~Kopulians~~ of all periods wherever they may be.

3. Membership

All ~~who were at~~ Carmel College for a minimum period of ~~one term~~ shall be eligible for membership unless ~~excluded by a two-thirds vote of the Committee~~ and subject to the power of the Committee to call upon any member to resign or to strike his name off the List of Members, but any such Member shall have the right to appeal from any such action to the Annual General Meeting.

Application for membership from ~~those who were at the~~ School for less than ~~six terms~~ ~~who nevertheless~~ wish to identify ~~themselves with Carmel College~~, will be considered by the Committee who have the power to accept such application by simple majority vote.

4. Hon. Membership

The Committee shall be empowered to elect as Hon. Members the names of any such persons whose connection with the School shall have been such as to render them eligible for ~~this recognition~~. Hon. Members shall ~~not be eligible for election~~ as Officers or as Members of the Committee and shall ~~not be entitled to sit at any General Meeting, except for the provision laid down in Rule 3.~~

5. Subscription

The Subscription shall be £1.1.0 per annum for ~~Annual Members~~, payable in advance, ~~on his £3.3.0 for life Members~~. Annual Subscriptions fall due on January 1st. and no Member who has failed to pay his subscription by March 1st. shall be entitled to any privileges of Membership till all arrears have been paid.

In the case of boys leaving at the end of the Summer Term, the payment of the Annual Subscription shall give the right to all privileges of Membership to the end of the next financial year.

Page from Draft Constitution of Old Carmeli Association – September 1952

(d) To afford help to any School institution and to further the in-
     terests of the school at all times. The handwritten amendments
     show that changes were made so that it read, "To afford help to
     Carmel, any of its associated institutions and to its Old Boys."
     (Also this clause (d) was moved to stand before clause (c).)
(e) To propose and maintain the Carmel spirit among Old Kopu-
     lians of all periods wherever they may be. Once again, the word
     "Kopulians" was crossed out.

Paragraph 3 dealt with the qualifications for membership. The typed draft
suggested one term at Carmel, but the written amendment spoke of 2
terms and added the words "provided that at the time of leaving he was
over 15 years of age."

Paragraph 4 which was titled "Hon. Membership" was crossed out.

Paragraph 5 was titled "Subscription" and the typed draft stated one
guinea per annum, but the handwritten change made it a (minimum (?) –
change not clear) of one half guinea.

Paragraph 6 was titled "Privileges" and read "All members shall be entitled to wear Old Kopulian (changed in written amendment to Carmeli)
colours, to receive the Carmelonian (changed in written amendment to
School Mag), the Address List and all publications issued by the Association. Then followed a handwritten addition, "Members serving compulsory national service are exempt from paying subscriptions during their
service."

The subsequent paragraphs dealt with technical and procedural details,
which included: the Committee, the President, Vice-President, Election
of Officers, Meetings of Committee and Duties of Officers. A number of
these paragraphs had a lot of handwritten amendments. (The third page
of the draft is missing.)[7]

A duplicated three-page "Rules and Constitution of the Old Carmeli Association" was prepared in 1953. It had fifteen paragraphs and it followed
to the letter, the draft constitution with its handwritten amendments.
The paragraphs which were on the missing page of the draft, dealt with
"Special General Meeting," which required fourteen days notice; "Notice
of Motion," which required at least fourteen days notice; "Alterations of

---

7. Rules and Constitution of The Old Kopulians' (amended to Carmeli) Association, dated 17
September 1952, first two pages (third page missing) of Draft Constitution for The Old Carmeli Association (OCA), with handwritten amendments.

Constitution," which required a two-thirds majority; and the right for any member to inspect the constitution.[8]

In an article in the Carmel magazine "Badad" published in July 1953, Malcolm Shifrin reported on three motions which were passed at the meeting of 1 November 1952:

(a) A person wishing to join the Association must have been a member of Carmel College for at least one year.

(b) The annual subscription shall be one half-guinea.

(c) The Committee's term of office shall be one year.[9]

However, there is a slight difference between the first above quoted motion and the final constitution. The motion speaks of being a member of Carmel "for at least one year," whereas the constitution speaks of two terms, "provided that at the time of leaving he was over fifteen years of age." The second and third motions, however, are in agreement with the constitution.

In 1954, David Perl wrote an article in that year's Carmel magazine explaining the raison d'être for such an organisation of Old Boys:

One of the traditions linked with the public schools of Great Britain is, that they have attached to them an Old Boys' Association.

Why are these Associations formed? Surely because it gives those pupils who have left school not only an opportunity to keep in constant touch with friends they have made at school, but also to retain an active interest in the progress and welfare of the school in which they have spent most of their life. Indeed that is why in the summer of 1952 a few of us who had had the opportunity of being educated at Carmel College decided that an Old Boys' Association affiliated to the school was essential.[10]

GREAT PLANS AND EARLY ACTIVITIES

Having set up this Association, there was much work and planning to do, and on this David Perl wrote in his 1954 article that "we soon found

---

8. Rules and Constitution of The Old Carmeli Association, three-page duplicated document, 1953.
9. Badad, p.6.
10. Carmel 1954, p.35.

ourselves settling down (with the help of Rabbi Rosen and Mr. David Stamler) to the important tasks of submitting designs, to a well-known London store, for the manufacture of an official uniform, seeking advice for the design of letter-headings, arranging future events, and numerous other jobs essential in all associations."[11]

Regarding the uniform, Shifrin wrote in mid-1953, "A uniform has been designed and, at the time of going to press, members are able to obtain wired blazer badges and Old Boys' ties. These ties are of silk in navy blue with a silver Menorah as the motif. If one is to judge from the ties, it augurs well for the Association."[12]

The Old Carmeli notepaper was headed OLD CARMELI ASSOCI-ATION and on the right hand side was the school crest, with the letters O.C. in Gothic type below it. The left hand side had the name of the current officers of the Association.[13]

As with many new organisations, the organisers had grandiose plans, but they were soon toned down. The Old Carmeli Association (OCA) was no exception, as Perl writes:

Naturally being eager and inexperienced in these matters, we soon found our ideas were getting rather too big for such a small association. However, after our initial eagerness, it did not take long before we calmed down and had things running smoothly. Our first large social function took place in June 1953, in the form of a Coronation Dinner-Dance[14] which was held at Selby's restaurant. I am sure that even if the Association had been established seven years instead of seven months the function could not have been more of a success.[15]

Shifrin also agreed with this assessment, "Although sparsely attended (for obvious reasons), the affair was an undoubted success and we look forward with eagerness to next year's Dinner and hope that all our new Old Boys will attend."[16]

Shifrin then concluded, "Some of the greatest work of Carmel College will be done by its Old Boys' Association and for that reason we hope that a lively interest will be taken in it, especially by our boys from overseas."[17]

The next activity was a reunion of Old Carmelis for Shemini Atzeret and

11. Carmel 1954, p.35.
12. Badad, 1953, p.6.
13. Sample note paper of Old Carmeli Association.
14. The coronation of Queen Elizabeth II had been at the beginning of that June.
15. Carmel 1954, p.35.
16. Badad, 1953, p.6.
17. Ibid.

Simchat Torah 1953 at the new premises at Mongewell. Incidentally that year the term began on 5 October, which was several days later, and so the Old Boys saw the new premises before the pupils! On this reunion Perl writes, "The fact that fifteen members attended this reunion was in itself something for us, the committee, to be proud of. But what really made us swell with pride was that half of these boys came not from London but from the provinces, some having been compelled to travel overnight in order to arrive before Yom-Tov."[18]

A few months later, in February 1954, the OCA sent a letter to their members informing them of the next activity:

> On the Sunday following Purim, i.e., March 21st, we are arranging a day's outing to the School's new premises. Full details will be sent in a further circular, but the following arrangements have been provisionally made.
>
> A football match against the School in the afternoon, followed by a Buffet-Dance in the evening.
>
> The journey to the School will be made by coach, which will leave central London during Sunday morning.[19]

The planned football match took place with the final score being Carmel College 4, Old Boys 1. On commenting on this match, the Carmel magazine wrote, "It is hoped that this match, in all respects a complete success, will now become an annual fixture. The muddy state of the pitch was obviously a great handicap to both teams, but the School won in a far more convincing manner than the score of 4–1 suggests."[20]

In his beautiful handwriting, Shifrin wrote out an invitation to David Stamler, who was still a bachelor, "The Old Carmeli Association requests the pleasure of the company of Mr. D. Stamler and friends at their Second Annual Dance to be held at Carmel College on Sunday 21st March 7.30 p.m. Informal Dress."[21] Reporting on this Dance, the Carmel magazine wrote that "The School Hall shed its customary air of academic dignity for one of elegant frivolity on the occasion of the Old Boys' Purim Ball on Sunday, 21st March."[22]

---

18. Carmel 1954, p.35.
19. Letter from Old Carmeli Association to (left blank to write individual names, it would seem, to Old Carmelis), February 1954.
20. Carmel 1954, p.45.
21. Handwritten invitation to Mr. D. Stamler and friends to attend Second Annual Dance at Carmel College on 21 March (1954).
22. Carmel 1954, p.9.

A few weeks later on Sunday, 4 April 1954, the OCA held its first annual meeting at the Primrose Jewish Youth Club in Finchley Road, London. The agenda included the election of the honorary officers.[23]

It was probably in 1954 that the Old Carmeli Association began to bring out a duplicated Bulletin, with Number 2 being dated 7 July 1954.[24] The Bulletin included a Report of a meeting which had taken place at Carmel between several members of the OCA and a team of speakers from the Association for Jewish Youth (AJY). At this meeting "each of them [AJY] told us something about his particular work in the Youth Clubs[25] which comprise the AJY and about some of the many difficulties which they have to face today. After a discussion between the Team, the tea *(sic)*, our Members and several Sixth-Formers, Mr. Drage [from the AJY] summed up and told us of some practical steps which we might take immediately to help them. It was decided that both Carmel College and the OCA should closely associate themselves with these clubs, particularly those which are doing such fine work in the East End of London." The Bulletin added that the OCA had received an invitation to visit these clubs to see how they could help with the work.[26]

One of the activities of the OCA was the "Monte Carmel Car Rally" (a play on the words "Monte Carlo Car Rally"). In this annual OCA event, which that year took place on 18 July, the cars began from Mill Hill in North West London.[27] That year, the OCA had received a silver challenge cup to be awarded annually to the winner of this Rally.[28] The next Bulletin reports that that year it was awarded "in the Association's Room at Carmel at the end of the Summer Annual Sports and Speech Day. Over six pounds was raised for the Association's funds. We are told that it was enjoyed by all who took part. (It was also enjoyed by the Organisers!)"[29] That year the "Jewish Chronicle" also gave a report of it, "The Carmelites *(sic)* Association (Old Boys of Carmel College) held their annual car rally

23. Jewish Chronicle, 9 April 1954, p.14.
24. Old Carmeli Association Bulletin number 1 has not been traced.
25. The massive inflow of Jews fleeing from Eastern Europe in the period following 1880, had made their homes in the East End of London. However, as time passed the more affluent Jews moved out of that area and so by the middle of the 20th century, the Jews remaining there were the poorer, disadvantaged Jews and thus the help provided to their youth by the AJY was invaluable.
26. Old Carmeli Association Bulletin, no.2, 7 July 1954, pp.2–3.
27. Ibid., p.3.
28. Ibid., p.2.
29. Old Carmeli Association Bulletin, no.3, 5 October 1954, p.3, bracketed words in original.

OLD CARMEL ASSOCIATION

BULLETIN

Number Four	15th. Oct. 1956

Comment.   After a short but beneficial rest the "Bulletin" reappears with its fourth issue and renewed energy.

It is a custom in certain Orthodox families that if a son marries 'out of the Faith' then they sit Shiva for him as though he had died. Rabbi Rosen tells the story of a family who was sitting Shiva for its 'dead' son when on the fourth day the son came in to comfort the mourners! Having read our Obituary in the last issue of "Carmel", we feel in a similar position.

We now have a Membership of 75, and less than half these Members reside in London. The majority live in the provinces or abroad. A year or so ago the percentage of London Members was even lower. We tried to arrange Socials, Dances and serious meetings and when we found there was only a very limited response we wrongly became discouraged and decided to wait till the Association was a little larger. But we also omitted to keep Members in touch with the School and with each other. We believe that if we face the fact that we erred rather than gloss over it then we can profit by our experience and rectify matters.

At this stage it might be worth mentioning that in the same way that views expressed in "Bulletins" are those of the contributors rather than of the Editor; so those expressed in 'Comment' are those of the Editorial Board rather than of the whole Committee. Neither should this necessarily be taken to mean that there are Committee Members who do disagree.

Carmel is going from strength to strength. We intend that the O.C.A. should do likewise.

School Appointments.   We should like to congratulate Mr. David Stamler upon his appointment as Vice-Principal of Carmel College. The Association is still young enough for it to be unnecessary for us to tell any Member who Mr. Stamler is. We wish him luck for the future in his new position.

We should also like to welcome Captain H. Lunzer who has been appointed College Bursar.

Page from Bulletin of Old Carmel Association from 1956

last week. Starting from Mill Hill, the route was over a 50 miles' course finishing at London Airport."[30]

The activities of the OCA were not limited to fun and games! There

---

30. Jewish Chronicle, 30 July 1954, p.19.

were also educational activities. The last weekend of the summer term was a "Discussion Group Weekend," to which members of the OCA were invited. On the agenda were several talks on the theme of "The New Israel and the Rise of the Nationalistic Movement in Asia." The speakers included Kopul, Meir Gertner, and Dr. Friedmann.[31]

In 1954, the OCA staked a claim to a portion of the Carmel real estate, "The rooms above the boathouse have been finally taken over by the Old Carmeli Association. The validity of their claim over that of the Prefects has been reinforced by appearance of a notice on the balustrade."[32]

The third OCA Bulletin came out before Rosh Hashanah of that year and began with a seasonal message from Kopul:

> To all Members of the Association, I send warm greetings and wishes for a year of fruitful achievement.
>
> This period is one of supreme 'Cheshbon Hanefesh', (Self-examination). During these days every Jew must analyse and examine his behaviour and recognise frankly, without self-deception, how far he has succeeded, or failed, in Life's purpose.
>
> You, who bear the name of Carmelis, admit by that term, that you wish to be openly associated with what Carmel stands for. It is appropriate, therefore, that during this period of 'Cheshbon Hanefesh,' you should show yourselves to what extent your lives have accorded with the pattern of Carmel. The true Carmeli is not merely one who pays his subscription regularly (though I am told by the Treasurer that this is not unimportant), but one who moulds his life to the pattern of Carmel ideals.
>
> After self-examination must come resolve for the future, and I can only hope fervently that there will be a firm resolve on the part of all of you to live a life during the coming year that will make your Membership of the Old Carmeli Association, not a matter of formal registration, but a living reality.[33]

This Bulletin reported that "at a Committee Meeting of the Association held recently it was decided that invitations should be sent to certain past

---

31. Old Carmeli Association Bulletin, no.2, 7 July 1954, p.3.
32. Carmel 1954, p.9.
33. Old Carmeli Association Bulletin, no.3, 5 October 1954, p.1.

Carmel College Masters asking whether they would like to become Associate Members of the Old Carmeli Association."[34]

The excitement of football for many Carmel pupils obviously continued into their alumni days since the Bulletin announced, "We have obtained a block of good seats for the floodlit match between Arsenal and the Maccabi-Tel Aviv Team . . . on Tuesday 26th October . . . Please guarantee your seats by applying IMMEDIATELY."[35]

OBITUARY FOLLOWED BY REINCARNATION

The successful start of the OCA did not last long. But in all fairness, at that period there were not many Old Boys. They "rarely mustered more than a dozen boys" at their activities and as Perl wrote, "I believe we all felt that we should sit back for a while until the number of boys who were eligible for membership had grown, and consequently the Old Carmeli Association was dormant for quite a while."[36]

This dormancy resulted in a "bombshell!" In 1956 there appeared an "Obituary" in the Carmel magazine which read "We regret to announce the quiet passing away of the Old Carmeli Association plus funds. The association, which was founded in 1952, had a very spasmodic existence and now appears to have given up the ghost. We can but hope for a reincarnation."[37]

In response to this "Obituary" notice, the next Bulletin, which came out a full two years after the previous one (thus giving credence to the obituary!) began:

> It is a custom in certain Orthodox families that if a son marries 'out of the Faith' they then sit Shiva for him as though he had died. Rabbi Rosen tells the story of a family who was sitting Shiva for its 'dead' son when on the fourth day the son came in to comfort the mourners! Having read our Obituary in the last issue of 'Carmel [magazine]', we feel in a similar position.[38]

Fortunately, there was a reincarnation and the following year, the follow-

34. Ibid., p.2.
35. Ibid., p.3.
36. Jewish Chronicle supplement, 14 November 1958, p. vii.
37. Carmel 1956, p.44.
38. Old Carmeli Association Bulletin, no.4, 15 October 1956, p.1.

ing notice appeared, "We are pleased to announce that the obituary notice in the last issue of Carmel [magazine] has had its desired effect and we can now report that the Old Carmeli Association has been resurrected."[39] A further Bulletin had come out in May 1957 which updated Old Carmelis to what was new in the school, such as the choir and the Cadet Corps.[40] The Hon. Treasurer also "requested that the 'Bulletin' remind some procrastinating Members that Subscriptions are overdue!"[41]

The financial bankruptcy of the OCA – "funds of OCA negative" – featured in an early paragraph in the minutes of a sub-committee meeting of the OCA held at Carmel College on 2 June 1957. Three members attended whilst two were absent. Despite the OCA's unfortunate financial situation, no fewer than seven suggestions were put forward for future activities of the OCA. These included the "Car Rally with supper dance at school," "Get a block in theatre for show/concert – (idea is to keep Old Boys united as far as possible)," "Very informal social evening – dancing, talking, raffle, etc." and "Have a small coach to C.C. [Carmel College] and charge a couple of bob extra for D. Toben's treasury."[42] There is no record whether any of them actually materialised.

In June 1958, the Chairman of the OCA sent out a letter to the members informing them of the Annual cricket match which would take place on 20 July. The letter continued:

> As you will probably recall from previous years, this fixture always proves to be lots of fun for both spectators and players and everyone gets his full share of laughter and excitement – especially when the 'old-uns' (the O.C.A., of course,) start performing.
>
> Please do try and prove the old saying "the more the merrier" correct, by coming along and joining in the fun. If you don't feel energetic on that day, there's no reason you shouldn't just laze around and get that lovely Carmel tan!
>
> Incidentally, the fun is due to start at 2.00 p.m. G.M.T,[43] not J.M.T. [Jewish Mean Time] Be seeing you.[44]

39. Carmel 1957, p.41.
40. Old Carmeli Association Bulletin, no.5, 13 May 1957, p.2.
41. Ibid., p.1.
42. Old Carmeli Association Sub-Committee Meeting at Carmel College, 2 June 1957, minutes of meeting.
43. Since at that period of the year there was Summer Time in Britain, surely the fun started at 2.00 p.m. B.S.T.
44. Letter from David Perl, Old Carmeli Association to Members of OCA, 13 June 1958. The problem is that by "tradition," it usually rains on Carmel activity days!

Other *reported* activities of the OCA during that period were almost zero, and this was despite a "resurrection!" They were limited to a football match with Carmel in 1958, where the School won by a score of five goals to two,[45] and another football game in 1959, when Carmel won by the same score.[46]

There was some action in 1962 as stated in the Carmel magazine, "As a result of the labours of the Old Carmeli Association, an appeal was launched on J.N.F. lines, but with much greater success, for bricks (5/- [five shillings], apply to . . .) which when finally assembled will provide a boathouse. The noble effort was not purely altruistic in nature, as it will provide a physical rallying point for the Old Boys."[47]

After leaving Carmel, the Old Carmelis would, hopefully, get married, and Kopul realised that it was important that they find acceptable partners, and that the OCA would be a good forum [read: Shadchan!] to accomplish this. Jeremy Rosen writes:

> Kopul invested a great deal in the Old Carmeli Association. He wanted the alumni to stay in touch with him and the school. He was worried that graduates of Carmel might not be able to find partners with the same Jewish experiences that they had. To Kopul, Carmel's Judaism meant a commitment to living a Jewish life but at the same time openness to secular culture, a committed yet open minded Judaism. He used to arrange dances[48] for Old Boys and tried to match them with suitable young ladies. Not too successfully it must be said.[49]

It was a policy of Carmel to welcome Old Boys to visit the School, especially for a Shabbat. On this, in 1954 "The Young Carmelonian" writes, "The Old Boys continue to show a very welcome interest in their Alma Mater. From time to time they arrive for the week-end and confiscate all spare beds, and linen. 'Shif' is said to have a private line from Hampstead to Wallingford; we utterly reject the suggestion that he is a Governor without portfolio. More power to their elbows!"[50]

---

45. Carmel Clarion vol.1, no.3, 1958, (p.22, pages unnumbered).
46. Carmel 1959, p.40.
47. Carmel 1962, p.8.
48. Although mixed dancing is not in accordance with the halachah, it is a fact that in the 1950s (and before) mixed dancing regularly took place even amongst Modern Orthodox Jews.
49. Biography of KR, p.49.
50. The Young Carmelonian, p.7.

LIVES OF THE OLD BOYS

In the Carmel magazines for 1955, 1956 and 1957, there is a page or so on "Old Boys' Activities" which covered a whole range of activities.

There were those who were continuing their Religious studies in Yeshivot: "Both Maurice Levine (1951–54) and John Fischer (1948–54) have settled down very well to their work at Jews' College. They have been preparing to take exams this summer, and despite their modest comments to the contrary they will do very well. Besides his own studying, Maurice has also been teaching in the local Hebrew classes, where he is highly respected."[51] "Abraham Levy is now studying at Jews' College, London, and we are told makes a most impressive figure in his bowler hat."[52] "Ivor Wolfson is now studying in Yeshiva at Montreux. He has just come over to England for a week or so."[53]

A number of Old Boys were studying at institutes of higher education: "Jeffrey Leifer (1952–54) has been studying at the Regent Street Polytechnic. He is taking his work very seriously and intends to carry on to take up chartered accountancy."[54] "Our heartiest congratulations go to Dov Weinberger who is our first old boy to get a degree. He was awarded a B.A. in Classics at the Hebrew University."[55] "Maurice Lipsedge has not yet been sent down from Lincoln College, Oxford, where he is studying P.P.E."[56]

A few old boys were combining religious and secular studies, something which Kopul encouraged: "Victor Sperber (1948–53) is going up to St. John's College, Cambridge this autumn. During the past eighteen months he has been learning at a Yeshiva, and also studying a good deal of Greek, as he intends to do Classics at University."[57] "Robert Seruya has been studying French in Switzerland and has had Hebrew coaching from Ivor Wolfson who is still at Montreux Yeshiva."[58]

There were those old boys who were doing their National Service in various countries of the world: "Alex Mizrahi (1949–52) has been called up to H.M. Forces for his National Service. He seems to have settled

---

51. Carmel 1955, p.56.
52. Carmel 1956, p.43.
53. Ibid.
54. Carmel 1955, p.56.
55. Carmel 1956, p.43.
56. Ibid.
57. Carmel 1955, p.56.
58. Carmel 1957, p.40.

down very well, and as far as I can gather he is as cheerful as usual."[59] "Also serving in Her Majesty's armed forces is Solomon Levy doing his six months National Service in Gibraltar."[60] "Malcolm Black has completed his national service in Israel and hopes to come and visit the school this summer when he is coming to England for a holiday."[61]

Finally, there were old boys who went into business: "Henry Bentwood (1952–54), also in business, is also progressing well. He hopes that his monthly pay packet will soon be increased."[62] "Michael Green is the prosperous owner of an Espresso coffee bar in London and we hear rumours that he is buying another."[63] "Martin Law is with a big gown firm in Manchester."[64]

TOWARDS THE END OF THE KOPUL ERA

In December 1961, the Development Fund held its Annual Dinner and Ball. A month prior to this Kopul wrote to Malcolm Shifrin, as a representative of the Old Boys:

> The members of the Development Fund, the Governors and I would very much like to see a large number of Old Boys present, but we realise that the cost of the ticket for the Dinner and Ball is rather substantial, especially since we hope those who come will bring their wives, fiancés, girl friends (strike out which does not apply) with them. We have agreed, therefore, to extend an invitation to Old Boys and tell them that if they wish to forego the Dinner (which in any case will be largely a matter of speeches and fund raising) and come after dinner for the dance, that is, round about ten o'clock, we shall be delighted to welcome them as our guests and, of course, there will be *no charge whatsoever*.[65]

Kopul would correspond with Old Carmelis, right up to the time of his death. One of these letters, written just some months before he died, was to Gary Borrow, who was from the original Carmel intake of September

---

59. Carmel 1955, p.56.
60. Carmel 1956, p.43.
61. Carmel 1957, p.40.
62. Carmel 1955, p.56.
63. Carmel 1956, p.44.
64. Carmel 1957, p.41.
65. Letter from KR to Malcolm Shifrin "Shif," 2 November 1961, underlining in original.

1948, and was then doing his National Service in "Advance Base British Forces" in Belgium. Kopul wrote:

> My dear Gary,
> I was delighted to receive your letter. You sound as charming and as breezy as ever.
> As soon as the Queen is able to dispense with your services come down to Carmel and let me have the pleasure of seeing you again.
> With affectionate regards.
>
> Yours sincerely,
Kopul Rosen."[66]

A couple of months before he died, Kopul made a tape recording in which he described what he saw to be the functions of the OCA:

> A few weeks ago, one of the Old Carmelis came to see me at my home and he said to me that he didn't know what the Old Carmeli Association was supposed to do, and I said to him it isn't supposed to do anything in the sense in which you are using the word "do." It isn't meant to build, it isn't meant to raise money; at least that's not its primary purpose. If it does raise money for certain activities in the school or elsewhere, splendid. But that's not the raison d'être of the Old Carmeli Association. The Association is, primarily, to establish an association of young men who later will become, I hope, leaders and factors for good in the community, young men who have one thing in common at the moment, which is, that they spent several years, their most impressionable years perhaps, in Carmel College. Now you must believe me and I am sure you will, that I am not in a state of mind to tell lies or even mild exaggerations, which I believe in moments of enthusiasm, I used to be very much capable of doing. I am not exaggerating when I say that as a result of my viewing of world Jewry and more especially Anglo-Jewry with a certain air of detachment, I say that Carmel College in the next twenty-five years or beyond that can be the greatest source of light. I use that word deliberately, the greatest source of light in Anglo-Jewry. This doesn't mean to say that I am pleased with everything that Carmel has done

---

66. Letter from KR to Gary Borrow, 20 November 1961. Photostat of letter is reproduced in The Old Carmeli, no.2, 1965–6, p.8.

or that I think our standards in any department where the secular or religious are such that we ought to sit back smugly and be pleased with ourselves. This is not so. We are only at the commencement, barely at the commencement, of what Carmel will become with the help of G-d and of course, the help of G-d, through our own efforts. But I see, clearly, how in every sphere of Jewish life, synagogal, charitable, educational, whether amongst students, or whether later amongst adults, the young men who have been through Carmel will gradually, or perhaps not so gradually, begin to exert a greater influence and an impact for good, because seriously, when you live in Carmel College itself which is a very closed community, or even when you go out into the world and live within little pockets of closed communities, you lose the sense of an overall picture of what is happening in An-glo-Jewry. The truth of the matter is, boys, and I suppose I should call you young men, but the truth of the matter is, that outside isolated pockets of religious and educational activity, there is almost a state that I would best describe as a desert, a sheer wilderness, and I think that only young men like you who have a reasonably good general education, who will have learned how to deal with people as a result of having lived in a community and been thrown together with fellow human beings and who have at least a minimum knowledge of what religious life is, that you young men will exert an enormous influence far greater than you imagine, because potentially you are all greater, we are all greater, than we realise, but you must do this deliberately, you mustn't wait for opportunities for service, you must go out and seek these opportunities and this is what the Old Carmeli Associa-tion primarily is, an association of people who have a good common denominator and who seek to perpetuate and spread the ideals and the light, according to how far we have been able to absorb light and how far we have been able to give it in Carmel College. Of course this means meeting at functions, having of socials, having some other denominator of activity but never losing sight of what the Carmeli Association is supposed to be. Finally, I understand as well as anyone, the number of distractions that will cut across your interests in the Old Carmeli Association. When you are 20, 22, 23, there are so many things that do distract you. But don't lose the vision of Carmel. Come down frequently when you marry and you have children. You are then as much members of Carmel, and in one respect perhaps even more members of Carmel, than when you were actually in the school, because when you were in the school you were taking root, but now when you have left the school and when you marry, when you have children, when you establish homes of your own, that is the time when you will produce the fruit when we will really know whether your root and your planting in the Carmel soil was a healthy one. Now this will sound very much like one of those Shabbat afternoon talks that I used to give in my study and I suppose the atmosphere and the general milieu is wrong for this kind of talk now, but I have said I think what is in my heart and I want you, and I am not in a position to say "stand outside my study" if you don't do it, but I really want you to make the Northern branch of the Old Carmeli Association a strong one and bear in mind what I have said again that the Old Carmeli Association which is just another branch or another phase of activity of Carmel can be, and you must make it a great source of light for Anglo-Jewry and even for world Jewry. Well G-d bless you all.[67]

---

67. Tape Recording made by KR, early 1962. (For beginning of text of recording, see chapter on "End of the Kopul Era.")

Chapter 9

End of the Kopul Era

Came the autumn of 1961. Buildings had already started to sprout in Carmel. Two dormitory blocks, a sanatorium, and Prep School dormitories, had already been built and now a classroom block was in the course of construction. Also the academic and sporting achievements were increasing in leaps and bounds. At last Kopul was able to see the fruits of 15 years of hard labour. But then tragedy suddenly struck . . . Helmut Schmidt describes it as "being struck by lightning on a cloudless day."[1]

Charles Marshall reports how the teaching staff at Carmel College heard about Kopul's illness:

> I first heard about the diagnosis of Rabbi Rosen's fatal illness at a staff meeting convened by David Stamler whilst Rabbi Rosen was receiving treatment at a nursing home in Oxford. The news came as a shock for which none of us had been prepared. Following the meeting we all felt stunned and somehow three of us gravitated together. Jack Epstein, Josh Gabay, and myself had very different roles at Carmel but had become good friends. We felt a compulsion to visit Kopul that evening and arranged to drive together to visit him at the nursing home. On the drive we all felt some apprehension about how our visit might be received. However, immediately after we were shown into Kopul's room our nervousness was completely dispelled. He welcomed us very warmly and with smiles he waved us towards chairs.

---

1. Reflections – Helmut Schmidt.

Conversation flowed easily and included some details of discussions with his doctors about his illness.[2]

What occurred at the following Carmel staff meeting, is also described by Charles Marshall:

> Again, there had been a general atmosphere of apprehension before the meeting which Kopul somehow dispelled immediately. He began by recognising that we were all aware of his condition and told us that he had been advised by his doctors to continue working normally and he asked that we should all continue with our work and our dealings with him in the same way as before.
>
> He wanted us all to know that he considered Carmel's financial future to be very secure and he could see no reason why those of us who wished to continue with our career at Carmel should not do so. (I formed the impression that news of Kopul Rosen's condition had stimulated a surge of financial backing from people within the Jewish community who wanted to help him see more realisation of his vision for the future of Carmel.) Kopul even joked that he wondered whether, if he recovered from his illness, some of the donors would want their money back![3]

The sequence of events at that period is related by Cyril Domb. "In November 1961 he [Kopul] went down with a bad cold which was particularly difficult to shake off. Blood tests taken in December showed an abnormally low count and further tests indicated that he was suffering from lukaemia."[4] When such a situation arises many Jews go and consult with great Rabbis. Kopul went to New York where he spent several hours with the Lubavitcher Rebbe. Domb continued, "The Rebbe proceeded to consider in detail the educational programme at Carmel and made a number of suggestions for its improvement. He liked to regard Carmel as a 'breakthrough' for Anglo-Jewry and he hoped that a generation of Rabbis would emerge who would take Kopul as their model. Kopul should intensify his efforts particularly in personal religious practice, and should symbolically let his beard grow longer."[5] On that period the author recollects:

---

2. E-mail from Charles Marshall, 17 March 2013.
3. Ibid.
4. Memories of KR, p.28.
5. Ibid., p.29.

The Old Carmelis received a letter saying that as a result of Rabbi Rosen's serious illness, a meeting would take place at Hillel House. A large number of Old Boys turned up and Mr. Stamler briefed us on the situation. He said that Rabbi Rosen would like to meet all the Old Boys and we should visit Carmel for this purpose. Mr. Stamler also suggested that the Old Boys raise money for a building in the school and various suggestions were put forward as to which building to raise funds for. It was also agreed that a board be put up in the school and for a minimum of three guineas, the name of the Old Carmeli would be inscribed on it. This last suggestion was implemented.[6]

Following this meeting, Malcolm Shifrin ("Shif") suggested that Kopul make a tape-recording for the benefit of the Old Boys who could not attend the meeting which had been called at Hillel House. On the sleeve of the gramophone record of Kopul's speeches, including this speech, it states regarding it, "Those who knew him [Kopul] will find it difficult to believe that he did not know why he was being asked to make the recording, yet it is typical of the man, of his faith, and of the manner in which he continued his life during the last months, that he sat down in front of the microphone immediately, paused for a few seconds, and spoke."[7] The content of the tape recording began by Kopul briefly talking about his illness. The main part of the recording was on the functions of the Old Carmeli Association. The recording begins:

> Good Evening Old Carmelis. This record on the tape recorder that I am making now was Shif's idea. I think it is an excellent one and I am very glad to be able to make this tape recording and send this message to you to your meeting. I don't want to talk too much about myself because I suspect that there is far too much talking going on about me behind my back, and that people are discussing what doctors have said. Well I know what they said and I don't take too much notice about this. Generally speaking you shouldn't take too much notice of what doctors say. You can judge this fact from your own observation. I mean, look at the boys in Carmel who want to become doctors. Only the bad types, the really good fellows go into business! But to be serious for a moment, those who have visited me in Carmel and those

---

6. 7 years, pp.140–41.
7. Sleeve of gramophone record of selected speeches of KR.

who are living with me will tell you that I am not in the least disturbed by what the doctors have said, or are saying, or for that matter will say. I always taught, and this conviction has now become an unshakable certainty in me, that there is only one source of life and it's in this source which I think one ought to name and say it, Almighty G-d. This one source gives life and can take life and if one has trust in Him it is very much like being in the arms of one's father and one knows with absolutely inflexible certainty that whatever happens it is not for one's harm. Having said this and perhaps having left you in a state of doubt, let me assure you that I still intend continuing my function for another thirty years or so and hope to welcome you frequently when you come with your children and grandchildren to visit Carmel College. Now that wasn't said just as a pious hope nor was it an expression of wishful thinking, though I suppose that some element of wishful thinking is inevitable in this kind of situation. But it does lead on to what I want to say to you about the Old Carmeli Association. . . .[8]

Despite his illness, Kopul would keep up correspondence with, amongst others, Old Carmelis. A letter written on 11 January 1962 said:

Dear Martin,
The Old Carmeli bulletin is splendid, short, pithy and readable. I was very pleased to read it. Hope to see you soon.

Yours,
Kopul.

P.S. Doctors are an ignorant and arrogant bunch of people, aren't they. You have to compel them to admit the truth; and by the bones of Bohunkus, I will.

K.[9]

After his illness had been diagnosed, Kopul invited all the Old Boys who were either doctors or medical students to visit him. Jonathan Isserlin reports on this meeting, "I remember being in his office . . . He was convinced he was going to survive his illness (which he probably would

---

8. Tape Recording made by KR, early 1962. (For continuation of text of recording, see chapter "The Eternal Link.")
9. Letter from KR to Old Carmeli Martin, 11 January 1962. Photocopy of letter is reproduced in: The Old Carmeli, no.1, 1964–5, p.3, and in Memories of KR, opposite p.192.

have, had he had it now instead of then), and wanted to know if we would publish an article about him in the BMJ or Lancet to say that as a deeply committed Jewish Rabbi he had believed all along that he would recover. Sadly we were not able to do that."[10]

Many other people also came to visit Kopul in the period after his illness was diagnosed and they wrote their impressions. Ivor Wolfson, an Old Carmeli and a past School Captain, who went to study full time in Yeshiva after leaving Carmel, wrote to Jeremy Rosen, "I have never in my life seen a person arrive at such a high Madrega (spiritual level), even visibly so, as your father when I saw him then just a month before his passing."[11]

Another person to visit Kopul just before he died was Lord Sieff of Brimpton, who wrote, "The last time I saw Kopul Rosen in life was three weeks before he passed away. He was completely aware of the fate that would soon overtake him. Yet the serenity of his demeanour, his conversation, his hopefulness of the Jewish survival and his faith, filled me with wonder. But above all was his serenity."[12]

Jeremy Rosen writes of Kopul's last weeks, "It was increasingly hard for him to engage or even talk. Finally he died on the 9th of Adar Sheni 5722, March 15th 1962."[13]

The Carmel magazine of 1962 wrote:

> To the end, Rabbi Rosen displayed an unswerving interest in Carmel. On the eve of his death he expressed the hope that Carmel would do well the following day in the Head of the River regatta. Carmel did, although he did not live long enough to know it, but it expressed very aptly that determination that carried the school through its early difficult days and that optimism which triumphed in the face of all opposition.[14]

Neil Alton elaborates:

> Therefore a bit of a shocker, when the 1st Eight departed to compete in the Head of the River Race in London, after I got the mother and father of pep talks from Himself ill in bed. During the race we expe-

---

10. Recollections – Jonathan Isserlin.
11. Memories of KR, p.188.
12. Ibid., p.7.
13. Biography of KR, p.60.
14. Carmel 1962, p.3.

One of the Last Letters Written by Kopul Rosen

rienced an out-of-body calmness, throughout a mad threshing row. We finished incredibly well, 24th I think out of hundreds, after 67th the previous year. I was deputed to phone him with the brilliant news. Only to be told he'd passed away in the middle of it! Hardened seniors that we thought we were, we felt he'd been with us all the way, and that he already knew.[15]

Charles Marshall also has recollections of that day in connection with the regatta:

On the day of Rabbi Rosen's death our rowing crews had been entered for the Schools Head of the River Races on the Thames between Hammersmith and Putney. Before our coach left school for the journey to Hammersmith I received a message from David Stamler saying that Rabbi Rosen had asked that I should convey his good wishes to

---

15. Recollections – Neil Alton.

the crews and tell them that he hoped that they would 'have a good row.' The rowers and I heard that Rabbi Rosen had died that morning only after the races had finished. We had been invited to the home of Jeffrey Coorsh, a member of the crew, and heard the shocking news from his mother at their home. I learned later, that news of Rabbi Rosen's death had reached the school before our departure but had been withheld by Romney Coles until after our coach had left. Some of the rowers were among the prefects who carried the coffin at Rabbi Rosen's funeral on the following day.[16]

Even though he had died on a Thursday morning, it was possible to insert a short news item on the front page of that week's "Jewish Chronicle." Headed "Death of Rabbi Kopul Rosen," it continued, "Rabbi Dr. Kopul Rosen, the founder and Principal of Carmel College, died at the College yesterday (Thursday) at the age of 48. He had been ill for several months. The funeral is today."[17]

Before he died, Kopul asked to be buried on the grounds of Carmel. But it wasn't so simple as just digging a grave. One needed the agreement of both the civil and the religious authorities for such a burial. It was not easy and it required a lot of negotiation with these authorities and this was done by Kopul's father-in-law.[18] There was also opposition from one of the dayanim of the London Beth Din, who wanted Kopul to be buried in London.[19]

The author describes the funeral:

> There was a large turnout of Old Carmelis and numerous other Rabbis and other friends. The non-Jewish masters were in their caps and gowns standing by the side. Since there was no cemetery there, the ground had first to be consecrated and we walked around the area designated to be the grave, seven times reciting a Psalm. The service was conducted by Dr. Tobias and he first announced that the burial was conditional. If for some reason the school was sold or for any other reason, the body could be moved elsewhere. This condition was with the agreement of the widow, the sons, and the brother. The only person to speak at the funeral was Mr. Stamler. Following the

---

16. E-mail from Charles Marshall, 17 March 2013.
17. Jewish Chronicle, 16 March 1962, p.1.
18. Recollections – Jeremy Rosen, chap.1.
19. Related to the author by someone who had heard this directly from Henry Shaw.

funeral, we went to the Rosen house to comfort the mourners and then we hurried back to London, since it was a Friday in the month of March.[20]

And so the "Kopul era" of Carmel College came to a sudden tragic end. . . .

20. 7 years, p.141.

List of Carmel College Archival Material and Recollections

The vast majority of the source material quoted in the footnotes to Section 1 of the book has been copied on to a DVD. It is divided into 7 headings and is limited to the Kopul era.

01: CARMEL COLLEGE ARCHIVAL MATERIAL

A detailed index to these archives is to be found at the beginning of these archives.

02: RAU LETTERS

Extracts of letters written home from Carmel College by the pupil Anthony Rau between the years 1950 and 1955.

03: RECOLLECTIONS OF OLD CARMELIS FROM THE KOPUL ERA

About fifty Old Carmelis from the Kopul era have written down their recollections. They are of varying length, and in a few cases they are part of the autobiographies of these Old Carmelis. They appear in alphabetical order.

04: REFLECTIONS

In 1988, the Old Carmeli Association brought out a book in which members of staff and alumni of Carmel wrote their recollections of the school, many of them appertaining to the Kopul era.

05: 7 YEARS AT CARMEL COLLEGE

The detailed recollections of an Old Carmeli, who was a pupil at the school between 1953 and 1960.

06: MEMORIES OF KOPUL ROSEN

In 1970, a book entitled "Memories of Kopul Rosen" was published, parts of which deal directly with Carmel College.

07: HISTORY OF GREENHAM, CROOKHAM AND MONGEWELL

A selection of documents illustrating the history of these three locations, and especially of the Carmel estates at these locations.

Index to Carmel College Archival Material

1947–1962: The Era Of Rabbi Kopul Rosen

NOTE: The originals of many of the documents in these archives were pale, with some being almost illegible. This was the result of age, the use of worn carbon paper or inadequate ink being used in the duplicating or printing process. Also, some of the newspapers had yellowed over the period of time. Using a computer program, an attempt was made to make the words on these documents darker, which sometimes resulted in the background taking on a yellow-brown tinge. Should the words on any documents still be difficult to read, it is suggested that one enlarges the words on the screen of the computer.

HEADINGS OF ARCHIVAL MATERIAL

01 Kopul Rosen Correspondence
02 Carmel College Limited
03 Governors' Activites
04 Purchase of Mongewell Estate
05 Fees and Covenants
06 School Fees Bills
07 Invoices and Orders
08 Prospectuses, Etc.
09 Ceremonies
10 Lists of Pupils
11 School Reports
12 Gce Results
13 Magazines
14 Science Society

15 Music and Singing
16 Dramatic Activities
17 Sports
18 Library
19 Clothes Lists, Etc.
20 Books and Booklets
21 Memoranda by Kopul Rosen
22 Miscellaneous
23 Old Carmeli Association
24 Photographs
25 News Cuttings
26 Audio Recordings
27 Film Clips

DETAILS OF ARCHIVAL MATERIAL

01 KOPUL ROSEN CORRESPONDENCE

01 *Pre-opening of Carmel*

001–193: Correspondence of Kopul Rosen (almost 200 letters) between June 1947 and May 1948, namely prior to the opening of the school. Almost all of it deals with the subject of loans in order to purchase the Greenham Estate and for the initial running costs of Carmel College.

02 *January 1949*

01–04: A handful of letters dated January 1949 on the same subject.

02 CARMEL COLLEGE LIMITED

01 *Incorporation*

01–03: Incorporation document and certificate of Incorporation of Carmel College Limited.

02 *Memorandum*

01–08: Memorandum of Association of Carmel College Limited.

03 *Articles of Association*

01–16: Articles of Association of Carmel College Limited.

04 *Annual Accounts*

001–091. Annual Accounts for the period between 11 December 1947 and 31 August 1962 of Carmel College Limited submitted to the Companies Registration Office.

05 *Annual Returns*

001–096: Annual Returns for the years 1949 to 1962 of Carmel College Limited submitted to the Companies Registration Office. These returns list the names and particulars of the Governors and the Secretaries.

06 *Notifications*

001–106: Notifications between 1948 and 1961 to Companies Registration Office of Changes in Governors, Secretaries, Registered Offices etc.

07 *Draft Minutes*

01: Draft Minutes of first meeting of Carmel College Limited held on 17 December 1947.

03 GOVERNORS' ACTIVITES

01 *Minutes of Governors' Meetings*

01–06: The minutes of two meetings. (These are the only ones which have been traced.)

02 *Minutes of Development Fund*

01–11: The minutes of four meetings. (These are the only ones which have been traced.)

03 *Kopul Rosen versus the Governors 1953*

01–03: Two letters sent to parents by Governors and one sent to parents by Kopul Rosen.

04 *Governors' Review 1955–56*

01–03: Review of the year 1955–56 by the Chairman of the Governors.

05 *Life Associate Scheme*

01: Circular giving details of the Life Associate Scheme – about 1953.

06 *Fund Raising Activities*

01–13: Taking over theatres for "My Fair Lady," "The Diary of Anne Frank" (including sample pages of a brochure) and the menu of a dinner at the Dorchester Hotel.

07 *Exhibition Days*

01–08: Detailed programmes for Exhibition Days held in 1957 and 1958.

08 *Increases in School Fees*

01–03: Two letters sent to parents announcing the increase in school fees.

09 *Scholarships and Bursaries*

01: Statement on the awarding of scholarships and bursaries.

10 *Covenants*

01–02: Two sample covenants in favour of Carmel College.

11 *Miscellaneous*

01–06: Miscellaneous material including some letters and a list of Governors.

04　PURCHASE OF MONGEWELL ESTATE

01　*Contract for Sale and Purchase*

01–19: Contract for sale and purchase of the Freehold Mansion House and premises known as Mongewell Park dated 26 January 1953.

02　*Conveyance of Property*

01–15: Deed of Conveyance of Mongewell estate (written in copperplate writing) dated 7 August 1953.

05　FEES AND COVENANTS

01　*Fees*

01–09: Two lists of fees paid for each pupil (names have been deleted).

02　*Requests for Covenants*

01–07: List of parents with the possibilities of them taking out a covenant to pay school fees (names have been deleted).

06　SCHOOL FEES BILLS

01–11: Sample school fees bills and receipts which were sent to parents. (names have been deleted).

07　INVOICES AND ORDERS

01–14: A number of miscellaneous invoices and orders.

08　PROSPECTUSES ETC

01　*Provisional Prospectus 1948*

01–08: An 8 page prospectus with 3 photographs brought out in about April 1948, namely before the school opened.

02　*Prospectus 1951*

01–18: An 18 page prospectus, 7 of the pages being photographs, brought out in 1951.

03　*Prospectus c.1956*

01–18: An 18 page prospectus, 11 of the pages being photographs, brought out about 1956. (It is possible there were some further pages which are now missing.)

04　*Prospectus c.1959*

01–20: A 20 page prospectus, 11 of the pages being photographs, brought out in about 1959.

05 *Carmel College 1948–1957*

01–30: A 30 page booklet with numerous photographs brought out to mark the 10th anniversary of the founding of Carmel College.

06 *Carmel Tribute to Kopul Rosen*

01–10: A booklet brought out in memory of Kopul Rosen.

09 CEREMONIES

01 *Visit of Viscount Samuel*

01: Invitation to meet Viscount Samuel on his visit to Carmel College in May 1951.

02 *Opening of Mongewell campus*

01: Invitation and programme for the opening of Carmel Mongewell campus in December 1953.

03 *Opening of Wolfson dormitory.*

01: Programme for official opening of Wolfson dormitory in November 1958.

04 *Speech Days*

01–07: Speech Day invitations for 1954, 1955, and programmes for 1955 and 1960.

10 LISTS OF PUPILS

01 *Luton List*

01–11: The names of the about 800 pupils who joined the school during the Kopul era. There are some gaps towards the beginning of this list. (This list was prepared by some unidentified authors and because for a period it was stored in a warehouse in Luton, it became popularly known as the "Luton List.")

02 *Roll 1957*

01–06: Three lists of all the Senior School pupils with their forms, one of them is for the summer term 1957 and two for the autumn term 1957.

03 *Roll and Calendar 1958–59*

01–24: A booklet with the staff list, lists of pupils in Senior School, and diary for all the days in the academic year 1958/59.

04 *Roll 1958*

01–02: List of all the Senior School pupils with their forms for the summer term 1958.

11 SCHOOL REPORTS

During the Kopul era, there were various formats of school reports for the pupils of both the Preparatory School and the Senior School.

01 *Preparatory School*

01–16: Sample Preparatory School reports during the Kopul era (names have been deleted).

02 *Senior School*

01–17: Sample Senior School reports during the Kopul era (names have been deleted).

12 GCE RESULTS

01–04: Sample pages of pupils' successes in both O-level and A-level examinations sent out by the Carmel College office during the summer vacation.

13 MAGAZINES

01 *Carmel*

Every summer from 1954 the official Carmel College magazine entitled "Carmel" was published.

01 Carmel 1954

01–49: vol.1 no.1. 49 pages of printed matter and drawings.

02 Carmel 1955

01–57: vol.1 no.2. 57 pages of printed matter, photographs and drawings.

03 Carmel 1956.

01–45: vol.1 no.3. 45 pages of printed matter, photographs and drawings.

04 Carmel 1957

01–47: vol.1 no.4. 47 pages of printed matter and photographs.

05 Carmel 1958

01–48: vol.1 no.5. 48 pages of printed matter, photographs, and an architect's drawing for Carmel College of the future.

06 Carmel 1959

01–57: vol.1 no.6. 57 pages of printed matter, photographs, and drawings.

07 Carmel 1960

01–53: vol.1 no.7. 53 pages of printed matter, photographs, and some thumb-nail sketches.

08 Carmel 1961

01–51: vol.1 no.8. 51 pages of printed matter, photographs, and some thumb-nail sketches.

09 Carmel 1962

01–51: vol.1 no.9. 51 pages of printed matter and photographs, and a tribute to Kopul Rosen who had died during that academic year.

02 *Badad*

01–20: A magazine with 20 duplicated pages which came out in July 1953 and had just one issue.

03 *The Young Carmelonian*

01–43: A magazine for the Junior part of the Senior School which came out in March 1954 and had just one issue. Of the 43 pages, there are a number containing advertisements.

04 *Carmel Fanfare*

01–06: A 6 page duplicated magazine which came out just once in May 1956.

05 *The Phoenix*

01–19: A duplicated undated (about 1957) magazine with 19 pages which only had one issue.

06 *Carmel Clarion*

A duplicated magazine with advertisements; the cover and some of the advertisements are in colour. A number of issues came out.

01 Carmel Clarion no.1

01–21: vol.1 no.1. 21 pages. It came out towards the end of 1957.

02 Carmel Clarion no.2

01–19: vol.1. no.2 19 pages and is entitled "Purim edition," spring term 1958.

03 Carmel Clarion no.3

01–24: vol.1 no.3. 24 pages. It came out in December 1958.

04 (2 pages from) Carmel Clarion 1960

01–02: Only two pages from the entire magazine have been traced.

05 Carmel Clarion 1961

01–24: 24 pages. It came out in the autumn of 1961.

(The 1959 issue and the remainder of the 1960 issues are missing.)

07 *Junior Biology Magazine*

01–11: The Junior Biology Society brought out its own magazine with 11 pages in January 1958.

08 *Preparatory School magazines*

The Preparatory School brought out its own magazines.

01 Alpha 1954

01–12: vol.1 no.1. 20 pages of printed matter with no photographs or drawings. It came out in July 1954.

02 Alpha 1955

01–12: vol.1. no.2. 20 pages of printed matter with one photograph. It came out in July 1955.

03 Alpha 1956

01–11: vol.1 no.3. 19 pages of printed matter which includes several photographs.

It came out in July 1956 and is labeled "Tercentenary Number" (1956 marked 300 years since the Jews had been readmitted to Britain).

04 Preparatory School Magazine 1958

01–12: 20 printed pages and a photograph of the Main Building on its cover. It came out in July 1958.

05 Preparatory School Magazine 1959

01–12: 20 printed pages and a photograph of the lake in the Carmel grounds on its cover. It came out in July 1959.

(There was no magazine for 1957 and no magazine has been traced from 1960 onwards.)

09 *Correspondence*

01–03: Miscellaneous correspondence in connection with Carmel magazines.

14 SCIENCE SOCIETY

The only Carmel society whose records have been traced is the Science Society between the years 1950 and 1955.

01–77: The records are almost entirely correspondence between the Science Society and numerous organisations asking that the members of the society be able to visit the organisations.

15 MUSIC AND SINGING

01 *Concerts*

01–03: Programmes of three concerts held at Carmel College whilst it was at Greenham.

02 *Musica Viva*

01: Sheet on composers of modern music written by Malcolm Shifrin for his "Musica Viva" Group, dated November 1958.

03 *Hebrew Song Sheets*

01–10: Hebrew song sheets; on some of them the Hebrew words have also been transliterated into English letters.

16 DRAMATIC ACTIVITIES

  01 *Acting*
    01–13: Programmes of several dramatic activities put on by the Carmel Dramatic Society, and of a Purim Revue on Purim 1960.
  02 *House Parties*
    01–03: A programme and invitations to House Parties.
  03 *Juke Box Joe Show*
    01–02: Programme for a variety show put on by some pupils in 1958.

17 SPORTS

  01 *Football Matches 1949–1952*
    01–33: Very detailed handwritten accounts of the Football matches played by Carmel College against outside teams.
  02 *Cricket Matches 1958*
    01–02: A card issued by the Carmel College Cricket Club giving all the fixtures for the 1958 season.
  03 *Sports Day Programmes*
    Every year on Sports Day a duplicated programme was distributed giving the results of events already decided and of the events to take place on the actual Sports Day.
    01 Sports Day 1955
      01–07: A 7 page programme.
    02 Sports Day 1956
      01–11: An 11 page programme.
    03 Sports Day 1957
      01–11: An 11 page programme.
    04 Sports Day 1958
      01–10: A 10 page programme.
    05 Sports Day 1960,
      01–14: A 14 page programme.
    06 Miscellaneous
      01–02: An invitation to a Sports Day, and a circular regarding a postponed Sports Day.
  04 *Swimming*
    01: Swimming certificate awarded by the Preparatory School.

18 LIBRARY

01 *Library Memoranda*

01–13: Several memoranda written by the librarian Malcolm Shifrin.

02 *Carmel Library Guide 1960*

01–09: A 9 page duplicated guide on how to use the Carmel Library.

03 *Carmel Library Guide 1962*

01–16: A 21 page printed guide on how to use the Carmel Library.

04 *Suggestion Slips*

01–02: Two sample completed suggestion slips for purchase of books for the Carmel Library.

05 *Carmelismus*

01–03: A 3 page memorandum on the situation of the Carmel archives "Carmelismus" in the late 1950s.

19 CLOTHES LISTS ETC

01–04: Three different Clothes Lists issued in: 1948, about 1950, and late 1950s, and a Health Certificate.

20 BOOKS AND BOOKLETS

01 *Carmel College Zemirot Book*

01–36: The first edition of the Zemirot book "Beshir vekol Todah" brought out in October 1955 by Dr. Alexander Tobias for use at the Shabbat meals at Carmel.

02 *Education Inspectors' Report*

01-20: A 20 page Report by H.M Inspectors following a full inspection of Carmel College made in 1955.

21 MEMORANDA BY KOPUL ROSEN

01 *Appraisal – typewritten copy*

01–18: An 18 page undated typewritten copy of "An Appraisal of Carmel College" written by Kopul Rosen.

02 *Appraisal – printed copy*

01–09: A 9 page undated (about 1960) printed copy of "An Appraisal of Carmel College" written by Kopul Rosen.

03 *Carmel College in Israel*

01–07: A 6 page typewritten memorandum by Kopul Rosen on his plans to set up a Carmel College in Israel.

22 MISCELLANEOUS

   01 *Shul Gabbai's list of Hebrew names 1948*
      01–02: The list of Hebrew names of teachers and pupils who were at Carmel when it opened in 1948 for use of the Shul gabbais when they called up a person for the Reading of the Torah.

   02 *Book Reading List*
      01–02: A suggested list of books that the pupils should read which was brought out in the early days of Carmel College.

   03 *Circulars and Letters from Kopul Rosen*
      01–05: Two circulars sent out to parents, and two letters written to individual Old Boys by Kopul Rosen in the months before he died.

   04 *Letter from Abraham Carmel*
      01: Letter written by Abraham Carmel to Malcolm Shifrin in July 1957.

   05 *Timetable 1957*
      01: The daily timetable of the Senior School brought out in October 1957.

23 OLD CARMELI ASSOCIATION

   01 *Constitution*
      01–05: Draft Constitution of OCA together with handwritten amendments (last page missing), and Constitution from 1953.

   02 *Letters*
      01–05: Various letters in connection with the OCA.

   03 *Bulletins*
      01–12: Periodic Bulletins brought out by OCA between 1954 and 1957 (number 1 is missing).

   04 *Miscellaneous*
      01–02: Sample OCA notepaper, and an invitation.

24 PHOTOGRAPHS

   01 *Greenham Estate*
      01–11: Inside and outside Greenham Lodge and the surrounding Estate.

   02 *Synagogue at Greenham*
      01–15: Consecration of Synagogue by Chief Rabbi Israel Brodie in 1950.

   03 *Speech Day at Greenham*
      01–05: Scenes during the Annual Speech Day.

   04 *Science Laboratories at Greenham*
      01–05: The laboratories and science lessons.

05 *Staff at Greenham*

01–07: A staff photograph and individual members of staff.

06 *Pupils at Greenham*

01–13: Groups of pupils in some cases together with a teacher.

07 *Miscellaneous at Greenham*

01–08: Various groups which include parents, teachers, and pupils.

08 *Crookham Estate*

01–02: Includes photographs of the Estate in 1939.

09 *Mongewell Estate*

01–28: Different areas of the Estate including the outside of the Main Building, the dining hall, the swimming pool, and the boathouse. There is also a very old photograph of the Main Building with a dome over the area of the main hall.

10 *Science Laboratories at Mongewell*

01–06: Pupils working in the various science laboratories, in some cases with the teachers.

11 *Lessons at Mongewell*

01–08: Different lessons in progress, some in the classrooms whilst others outside, and also the choir rehearsing.

12 *Library at Mongewell*

01–05: Pupils looking for books, reading and working in the library.

13 *Chanukah at Mongewell*

01–03: The lighting of Chanukah candles in the Main Hall.

14 *Staff at Mongewell*

01–10: A group picture and individual members of staff, and the elderly groundsman Ted Wetherall.

15 *Pupils at Mongewell*

01–07: Groups and individual pupils.

16 *Miscellaneous at Mongewell*

01–08: Various groups of pupils, and Miss Arons serving in the tuck shop.

17 *Opening of the Wix Sanatorium 1960*

01–03: The ceremony and the donors touring the sanatorium.

18 *Various Sports*

01–52: Includes rugger, cricket, athletics, tug-of-war, squash, tennis, gymnasium scenes, rowing, and chess.

19 *Miscellaneous*

01–18: Includes pupils involved in various activities, and scenes in the kitchen.

20 *School Photographs*

Every other year from 1953 onwards a photograph was taken of the entire school.

01   Prep School 1953

   01–03: scanned in 3 overlapping sections.

02   Senior School summer 1953

   01–03: scanned in 3 overlapping sections.

03   Prep and Senior Schools 1953

   01–06: scanned in 6 overlapping sections.

04   Prep and Senior Schools 1955

   01–05: scanned in 5 overlapping sections.

05   Prep School c.1956–1957

   01: scanned in entirety with 1 scan.

06   Prep and Senior Schools 1957

   01–08: scanned in 8 overlapping sections.

07   Prep and Senior Schools 1959

   01: scanned in entirety with 1 scan (it can be enlarged on the screen).

08   Prep and Senior Schools 1961

   01–08: scanned in 8 overlapping sections.

A large number of photographs are also to be found under different sections of these archives.

25   NEWS CUTTINGS

01   *Press Advertisements*

   01–12: Selection of regular advertisements for Carmel College in the "Jewish Chronicle."

02   *Advertisements for Teachers*

   01–06: Selection of advertisements for teachers in the Jewish and national press.

03   *Scholarships*

   01–06: Advertisements in the "Jewish Chronicle" announcing scholarship examinations

04   *Governors*

   01–05: News cuttings concerning the Governors of Carmel College.

05   *Bursar*

   01–04: Advertisements for a bursar and news cuttings on the bursar Captain Lunzer.

06   *Speech Days etc.*

   01–14: News cuttings on the annual Speech Days, consecration of Greenham Synagogue, and visitations of prominent Anglo-Jews.

07 *Sports reports*

   01–09: News cuttings on cricket, chess, and rowing.

08 *Jewish Chronicle at Carmel*

   01–07: Report on the annual visit of the Jewish Chronicle staff and families to Carmel with particular reference to the cricket match played during that visit.

09 *Old Carmeli Association*

   01–05: News cuttings on the formation and activities of the OCA.

10 *Miscellaneous*

   01–10: News cuttings on a variety of matters connected with Carmel College.

11 *Jewish Chronicle supplement*

   01–08: An 8 page supplement of the "Jewish Chronicle" on Carmel College dated November 1958.

12 *The Sphere article*

   01–03: A 3 page article on Carmel College which appeared in "The Sphere" in May 1957.

13 *Jewish Observer article*

   01–04: A 3 page article plus cover page on Carmel College which appeared in the "Jewish Observer and Middle East Review" in February 1962.

26 AUDIO RECORDINGS

01 *Carmel College Choir*

   01.mp3–10mp3: Recordings of ten songs sung by the Carmel Boys' Choir, conductor Dudley Cohen, in about 1958.

02 *Carmel College Speech Day 1960*

   01 Track 1.wma: A recording of the entire ceremony (with the exception of the distribution of the prizes).

03 *Speeches of Kopul Rosen*

   Speeches which are connected with Carmel College.

      01.wma: Speech delivered by Kopul Rosen at the opening ceremony of the Wix Sanatorium at Carmel College in the summer of 1960.

      02.wma: Speech recorded by Kopul Rosen for a fund raising dinner in aid of buildings at Carmel College, towards the end of 1961. Due to Kopul's state of health he could not be present in person, but sent a recording of his speech.

      03.wma: Recording made by Kopul Rosen for the Old Boys. It was made just a couple of months before died.

27 FILM CLIPS

01 *Sports Days*

01: Colour cine clip from Sports Day 1955. Includes "little" David Rosen competing against the "big" Senior Boys!

02: Colour cine clip from Sports Day 1956.

03: Colour cine clip from Sports Day 1959.

04: Colour cine clip from Sports Day 1961.

02 *Cricket*

01: Colour cine clip of a cricket match played in 1955.

03 *Kopul Rosen*

About 1958, a black and white film of Carmel College was produced. Although this film has not been traced, clips from it were used in a film made in the 1960s.

01: Kopul Rosen watching a Carmel football match.

02: Kopul Rosen in the dining hall.

TEACHERS AT CARMEL –
THIS IS YOUR LIFE!

"What you will be, you are now becoming."

—Proverb of Kopul Rosen

Introduction

When I came to write this book, I found that Old Carmelis of the Kopul era knew nothing, or almost nothing, about their teachers at Carmel, in many cases not even what their first names were! I therefore decided that it would be beneficial and interesting to write up brief biographical details of the Carmel teachers. This is especially so, since a number of teachers became world authorities in their fields. Kopul certainly knew how to choose teachers!

To obtain such biographical details of teachers, with many of whom contact was lost half a century ago, was not an easy thing to accomplish. However, as the result of sending out many hundreds of e-mails, making numerous telephone calls to all over the world, searching on the internet, looking for newspaper obituaries, and utilising many other methods, it was possible to build up, at least partial biographical details of a large majority of the teachers. In many cases the biographical sketches cover their whole lives, in other cases there are gaps, and in a relatively small-ish number, especially teachers in pre-Mongewell days who only taught at Carmel for a short period, no details have been found. (Biographical details of teachers who joined the staff during the academic year 1961/62, the year Kopul died, have not been included in this volume; they are more appropriate for Volume 2 on the History of Carmel College.) Many of the activities of the teaching staff whilst at Carmel are to be found in the first section of this book. However, in order not to make the teachers' activities at Carmel seem bland, some of their activities at Carmel during the Kopul era, have been "reserved" for this section.

Numerous individuals and organisations supplied, and even researched for me, biographical information on the former Carmel teachers. Their names or organisations appear in the footnotes, and to all of them go my sincere gratitude and thanks.

I must begin by adding a word of caution. In research of this type, one cannot 100 per cent exclude the possibility that as a result of coincidence of names, an item of information attributed to a Carmel teacher is in fact that of an entirely different person with the same name!

The various methods which I used for building up the teachers' biographies will now be explained for some of the teachers.

I should start by stating that it is unfortunate that although the annual Carmel magazine for the Senior School went into great detail on the social and sportive activities of the School, and gave a list of pupils who joined and left the school during that particular year, it did not give a staff list. The closest it got to that, was that the section headed "School Chronicle" usually, but not always, gave the names of the teachers who joined or left the school during that academic year. The Preparatory School magazine, however, almost always gave a Prep School staff list. The school Prospectuses which were brought out periodically did give such a staff list, but by only coming out periodically, some teachers, who were only at Carmel for a short period "fell through the gaps."

From the various Carmel magazines and from recollections of Old Carmelis of the Kopul era, I was able to obtain many details of the activities of the various members of staff whilst they were at Carmel.

School reports are also a valuable tool in this matter, since they give who taught what and when, and also give the initials of a teacher, which in some cases were not known. However, I only have in my possession a miniscule proportion of the boys' school reports, and they therefore cannot be regarded as a representative sample. As a result, they cannot give a complete picture of a teacher's timetable in a particular year, and certainly not of his timetable throughout his tenure at Carmel. Needless to add, the footnotes giving "sample school reports" are only examples of lessons given by a particular teacher and often do not represent the entire period the teacher was at Carmel.

A few of the teachers from the Kopul era were still alive when writing this book. In such cases, if they could be tracked down, they themselves would give their biographical information. If however, they were no longer alive, but one could locate a close relative, one might also be able to obtain such information, but this would be second-hand material which could well be less reliable. One should also bear in mind that whether the information was first-hand or second-hand, these are recollections, given only after half a century or more of the events. It thus follows that the most reliable information is documentary material written at the time of the actual event itself. For this reason, even when I received information from the teachers themselves, I would try to corroborate it from documentary evidence, such as from the university or the school that the teacher studied at or taught at.

In some of the cases where the teachers are still alive, such as David Stamler, Julyan Bunney, Charles Marshall, Murray Roston, Rabbi Moshe Young, and Mary Evans, their contact details were on the Old Carmeli lists, and I either contacted these teachers by telephone or by e-mail to get the necessary information about them. In addition, an Old Carmeli gave me the contact details of John Toalster, who I duly contacted. In his article in "Reflections," Dr. Alexander Tobias gives an autobiographical account from the time he joined Carmel.

In a number of cases, I managed in various ways to trace a relative of a deceased teacher. As I pointed out in my letters to the Old Carmelis of the Kopul era, one small fact can lead to a mass of material. A case in point is that of Dr. Purley. At first, all that some Old Carmelis knew about him was that in the 1960s they had visited him in Frishman Street in Tel-Aviv, but even these Old Carmelis did not know his first name! The breakthrough came when one Old Carmeli remembered that his only son was killed in the Yom Kippur War. Following up on that lead, I traced his grandson and from him, Dr. Purley's daughter. I telephoned her and she gave me a biographical sketch, which in turn led to my obtaining further details, including finding his German doctorate thesis in the Jewish National Library in Jerusalem. I was also able to obtain recollections of him from a former pupil who remembered him as a teacher at Aryeh House School in Brighton, and in addition from a person who remembered him as a Madrich in the Sunshine Hostel for Children. Before I had located his family, I came across on the internet a photograph of a Martin Purley in a British army uniform. I sent it to several Old Carmelis who had been taught by him, and asked whether it was our Dr. Purley. They were reasonably certain that it was.

Rev. Bernard Ward was a Latin teacher from 1957. In order to try and get biographical details about him, I sent a message via the website of the village of Brightwell-cum-Sotwell, where he was a pastor whilst at Carmel, and a representative of the village replied that my request would be put in their newsletter. A few weeks later, I received an e-mail from Rev. Ward's daughter. She gave me biographical details and recollections of her father and also sent me a news clipping from the local paper where he had been a Minister, headed "Minister is Part-time Postman."

Although St. John's College Oxford, where Frederick Nelson had studied, was not prepared to give me any information about him, they were prepared to forward to him my request for information, and as a result his son Paul made contact with me and gave me biographical details. (At the time Frederick was very ill, and died soon after.) Above, I wrote that documentary evidence is invariably more reliable that recollections, but here there was an exception. A school at which he had taught, had written to me that Frederick was a teacher there until 1973, on which Paul commented, "That's funny (and a little upsetting of the school to not know). He taught me and I left 1979. He was there a number of years after."

Charles Marshall gave me the address in Canada of Gerald Thomas. Since I did not have his e-mail address, I sent him a letter by "snail-mail" asking for his biographical details. Very soon after that Gerald died. I therefore asked some Old Carmelis living in Canada whether they had any contact with the Thomas family. Their answer was in the negative, but they gave me some internet links to some obituaries which had been written about him by some swimming organisations with which he had been very active. A few weeks later I received in answer to my letter, a curriculum vitae of Gerald which his family had compiled.

With regards to Harold Nagley, a teacher from Greenham days, I started off with an advantage. My paternal grandmother was a Nagli (that was the original spelling!), although I have never managed to trace my family link up with Harold. Because we are relatives (albeit the link untraced) I had been in contact with his son Phillip (who lives in Australia) several years earlier. He now supplied me with a mass of information on Harold. He also put me in touch with Mendel Bloch's daughter-in-law who also lives in Australia, and also with Hermann Ehrmann's sister-in-law, and he also sent me some printed material on Esra Shereshevsky.

Another teacher whose relatives I traced, were those of Jack Epstein. I made contact with his widow who lives in London and his sister who lives in Jerusalem and they supplied me with biographical information. In addition, they sent me a number of documents, which included a curriculum vitae which Jack himself had prepared during his lifetime. Prior to Jack going to Carmel, there were a number of short items about him in the "Jewish Chronicle" which I located, and these included his receiving his university degrees and becoming a Reverend.

From an Old Carmeli who lives in Gibraltar, I was able to obtain the telephone number in Gibraltar of Joshua Gabay's widow. Following a telephone conversation with her, she sent me a curriculum vitae for Joshua. In the 1980s he had returned to Gibraltar and was involved in a number of public activities, including being elected to the Gibraltar Parliament. As a result, there was material on him in publications from Gibraltar, which were on the internet, and I found these very useful.

Much of the biographical material on the teachers was obtained from university and school records and the magazines of various schools. Of the universities, the records of Oxford and Cambridge were the most comprehensive. Their records often contained date and place of birth, schooling, university studies with details of degrees awarded and, in the cases where the records had been updated for their alumni, their places of subsequent employment. Most Colleges (but not all) were prepared to share this information with me without question (and a few of them asked me to let them have the information that I found to complete their own records, which I happily obliged).

However, with London University it was a different question. They wanted evidence that the teacher had died (although the individual Colleges of the University were prepared to give information without such death evidence). I provided them with such evidence for Jack Epstein, Bernard Steinberg, and Rabbi Sydney Leperer.

However, for one teacher, the maths teacher Harry George, I did not have evidence of death. However, since he was born in 1895, he would have been 118 years old. I pointed out this fact to them, but the answer was "no" until I provided evidence of death! I argued that if he were still alive it would be a world record and that his name would be in all the newspapers, adding that even the British census which is a strictly confidential document puts all its information in the public domain after 100 years. I thus suggested that they consult with their legal adviser in this matter. They obviously did do, since after about a week they replied with the information I had requested with "apologies for the confusion."

There is on the internet a list of London University graduates who graduated up to 1930. Should the University know that the graduates are deceased then their names are removed from this published list. I searched this list and found Romney Coles' name – they obviously had not received information that he was dead. However, prior to my even requesting information on Harry George, I had made a search on this list for his name, but without success. I thus concluded that either he had received his London degree after 1930, which is quite possible since it was the second degree he had been awarded (an earlier degree was from Oxford in 1921). Alternatively they had received information that he was deceased; in such a case there was no reason to withhold information!

I also contacted the various schools that teachers had studied at, or had taught at. Some of them kept excellent archival records and they supplied me with much needed information. This, on occasion, even included the pupil's record card, and I could see what his marks were and his form position! One school sent me the teacher's completed application form for the position of a teacher at that school together with his testimonials. Others had more skimpy records which just gave the years they joined and left the school, whilst others had no extant records or did not answer my enquiry, even after a reminder.

There were some teachers who, before or after (or, as in the case of Morris Ellman, both before and after) teaching at Carmel, were on the staff of the Hasmonean Grammar School for Boys in London. One of them was Mendel Bloch and one of the teachers who was there at that period had memories of him. Furthermore, on the internet there are "Hasmo Legends," namely recollections of Hasmonean alumni of their school, and one of them, who is also an Old Carmeli, wrote of his recollections of Bernard Steinberg at the Hasmonean.

In a few cases, biographies of teachers had been published. One of them was an anthology giving a selection of the writings of Meir Gertner, and the book began with a fairly detailed biography of him. Another case was that of Dr. Friedmann, where after his death a booklet, "In Memory of F. M. Friedmann" was published, in which a whole collection of individuals (including several Old Carmelis) wrote on different phases of his life. In fact, I learned about this booklet before I began writing this book on the history of Carmel. I was reading Martin Gilbert's book "The Boys," when I came across a "Dr. 'Ginger' Friedmann" (he was not yet known as Yoshke!). Immediately, the Carmel Dr. Friedmann came to my mind and a few pages on, I saw that it was indeed the same person. These two books (on Gertner and Friedmann) gave me plenty of the information that I required. Likewise, much of the biographical information on Kopul I found in the book "Memories of Kopul Rosen" and also in Jeremy Rosen's biography of his father.

There was a teacher who wrote his own autobiography which I found very useful. It was Abraham Carmel and his book was entitled "So Strange my Path." Not only did Abraham Carmel write about his own life, he also described encounters with some of the staff at Carmel College who were there when he arrived in 1951. In the first edition of the book, he wrote the actual names of the Carmel staff, but in a later edition the names were distorted. Hoffman became Toffman, Dr. Purley became Dr. Rurely, and Dr. Alexander Tobias became Dr. Antonius London; however Roberts and Warner did not have changes made in their names!

One can usually get a lot of biographical information from obituaries and indeed several of the Jewish staff had obituaries in the "Jewish Chronicle." Raphael Loewe and Hyam Maccoby even had obituaries in the British National press, which I found very helpful. If a person is prominent enough, he will even merit a mention in "Who's Who," and indeed one of Carmel's former teachers reached this book. He was Robert Gavron who became Lord Gavron, and he had a detailed biography in the "Who's Who." Within the "Jewish Year Book,' which is published annually, some Carmel teachers appeared and I managed to glean a few facts here and there on the biographical details of these teachers.

Some of the teachers at Carmel were authors, before and/or during and/or after their tenure at Carmel. Lists of their publications were found in the various national library catalogues, e.g. "Malmad" for Israeli Libraries and "Copac" for British Libraries. A number of teachers had been awarded masters or doctorate degrees from various Universities, especially London, and on the internet one could find from the University library catalogues details of these theses.

Many of the staff were in the armed forces during the First World War, or especially the Second World War, with the younger ones doing their national service at an even later date, and a few members of staff served in the armies of other countries. A promotion in rank in the British armed forces is often publicised in the "London Gazette." All the past editions of this paper are to be found on the Internet and it is very easy to search these issues by just typing in, for example, the name of a person. I did this and obtained information, such as their promotion in the armed forces, for these members of staff. According to items of information I had received, two members of the Carmel staff had worked at the Decoding Centre at Bletchley Park during this war. Bletchley Park also has a website which contains the names of the countless thousands of people who worked there, called the "Roll of Honour." I found just one of these two staff members on this list. However this list states that it is incomplete.

At least six of the teachers at Carmel acquired British naturalisation. From the website of the "National Archives," one can find the file number of a person's certificate of naturalisation. From the certificate one can find some biographical information of the person. Photocopies of these certificates can easily be ordered. The cost of the photocopying is nominal, but the cost of the packing and postage is far, far greater than the actual photocopying! I ordered photocopies of these certificates for these six teachers. A person acquiring naturalisation also gets a mention in the "London Gazette," but the biographical information there is less than on the certificates.

When teachers (or their relatives) had unusual names such as John Swindale Nanson Sewell, or Arveschoug, or Romney Coles (or his son Revel), I sometimes found the search engine "Google" to be a useful tool in obtaining further information about such teachers, but with common names such as Evans or Rose, as to be expected, it was useless!

During the first years of Carmel College, there was a Headmaster called James Ewart. The only biographical information I had of him came from Carmel printed material from that period, namely that his name was followed by "M.A. (Cantab)" – nothing else! Thus knowing which University he had studied at, I contacted Cambridge. His College, Jesus College, had a number of biographical items about him. From these I could see that he was a world traveler – he had been in education in Barbados and the Far East. I also searched the Carmel advertisements in the "Jewish Chronicle" which came out with regularity. These advertisements would include his name as the Headmaster: first as Headmaster of Carmel College, then later as Headmaster of the Prep School, and towards the beginning of 1951 his name completely disappeared from these advertisements, thus indicating that at that stage he left Carmel. The Jesus College records also stated that he then became Headmaster of Coombe House School (and that he died in 1987). Searches on the internet showed that this school closed in 1964, possibly because it had got burnt down. There were also some recollections of him on "Friends Reunited" by some former staff at that school. But what did he do after Coombe House School closed, until his death? I decided to ask a question on this on the Wikipedia Reference Desk. I indeed received an answer. He became headmaster of the Princess Mary's Village Homes located in Surrey. This institution had also since closed and so I contacted the Surrey County Council and they were able to give me a few smatterings of information about him there. I also found on "Facebook" the recollections of the institution itself by someone who had learned there during part of Ewart's tenure (but she did not mention Ewart). I succeeded in contacting this person and I received some of her recollections of Ewart.

Simcha Neuschloss was on the staff of Carmel, it would seem, just for the first term (or just half of the first term) of the school's existence. He was a refugee from Germany who came at first to Manchester. From the internet, I found under "Jewish Telegraph Roots Directory" someone who was looking for old friends and amongst the names she mentioned was Simcha Neuschloss. I contacted her and she sent me very positive recollections of him, he being her Cheder teacher in Manchester. Helmut Schmidt was also a refugee from Germany, but he first went to Eretz Yisrael. There he studied at the Hebrew University. On searching their records for that period, they found a Helbut Schmidt, saying that "Helbut" rather than "Helmut" was likely a writing error, and they then supplied me with details of the subject of his degree and the year it was awarded.

H. P. Roberts was on the Carmel staff at Greenham. However, his pupils could give me no biographical information about him. They did not even know what the H. P. stood for. Two small bits of information which I managed to glean from various sources was that he came from Wales, and that when he taught at Carmel he had a house in Greenham. From this, I was able to find out what the letters H. P. stood for – Howel Pugh. Following this, I was able to find on the internet a brief biography of his wife who was an artist, and this biography also contained some information on Howel. This led me to discover that for over thirty years he had been a teacher at Stationers' Company School in London. Their alumni gave me guest access to the School's past magazines which were on the internet (viewing was normally limited to alumni) and which were published three times each year. Going through nearly 100 magazines, I gleaned material on the numerous extra-curricular activities in which Roberts participated at that school. (They later asked me to write a biography of him for their magazine "The Old Stationer," which I did, and it was published in their 2014 edition.)

There was a Biology teacher at Carmel called Rose, who joined the staff when the school moved to Mongewell, but at first I did not know even the initials of his first name. I then discovered an invoice which the school received on his ordering of some equipment. It was to G. A. Rose, and on it one could see that originally it was a "J" which had been altered to a "G." At the same period, I saw in the Government Inspectors' Report for Carmel, that the Biology teacher was a student from Oxford who was at the same time studying for his doctorate. On enquiring at Oxford University, I was given information on Geoffrey Arthur Rose. One can understand why the "J" had been changed to a "G' – the clerk writing the receipt first thought that it was spelled Jeffrey! My continued research showed that he later became a very well known Professor and when he died, several obituaries were written about him, one of them appearing in the British Medical Journal.

A teacher who was at Carmel just for one term was Dr. Dirk Bijl. On the internet, I found the memoirs of his wife describing life in Holland during the German occupation. She wrote how in the building where her family lived, a young Jewish child was hidden, and when the Nazis made a surprise search of that building, Dirk smuggled him out in his rucksack and took him to a safe house. It is possible that this was the reason that Dr. Bijl came to spend a term in a Jewish school.

For just one year, there was a Physics teacher called Tonks. A school report showed that his initials were L. H., but at the time, that was the sum total of my biographical knowledge about him. A study of library catalogues showed that some geology books had been written by a Laurence Henry Tonks, but my question was whether or not it was the same Tonks? Further research showed that prior to coming to Carmel, the geologist Tonks had been a Maths teacher at a grammar school. Since he also taught Maths at Carmel, this increased the probability that it was the Carmel Tonks. I had from a Carmel school report a sample handwriting of the Carmel Tonks, and for comparison purposes I tried to obtain a handwriting sample from his previous school, but without success. However the clincher came when I saw in the Government Inspectors' Report on Carmel that one of the Science teachers then at Carmel was a geologist.

Due to a change in surname when a woman gets married, unless one knows her maiden name, a problem will arise when trying to obtain her biographical details. One case in point was Mrs. M. F. Whitfield. Not only was her maiden name not known, even what her initials M. F. stood for were also not known. I asked Julyan Bunney, but even he didn't know. He explained that in those days, the teachers would address each other as Mr. or Mrs. – (unthinkable today!). A breakthrough came when Mary Evans told me that Mrs. Whitfield's husband had been the Director of Education of Berkshire. An enquiry to the Berkshire Record Office gave me his name, which fortunately was a very unusual one – Trevor Drought Warburton Whitfield. With this information I looked up on the internet on "Free BMD" records his marriage and from this I got Mrs. Whitfield's first name and her maiden name. From a Carmel prospectus, I learned that she had graduated at Trinity College Dublin. I contacted this College and got documentary evidence of her two degrees which were awarded to her there. (I could not do this earlier, since I then did not know her maiden name.) Quite independently of this, I managed to get the e-mail of her daughter and she sent me quite a lot of information about her mother.

Another woman teacher at Carmel was Mrs. Evans. Since she was still alive, I telephoned her to get her biographical details. However, due to her state of health, I could only receive limited information from her. One of the details she gave me was her date and place of birth (and from this I was able from "Free BMD" to find her maiden name), and that she had received her diploma from the Chelsea College of Physical Education, an establishment which was no longer in existence. However, I discovered from the internet that Dr. Ida Webb had received her doctorate on researching the history of this College. I made contact with her – it had to be by telephone and regular letters, since she did not have a computer or e-mail! She was extremely helpful and carefully went through all the past magazines of the alumni of this College extracting all the numerous bits of information on Kathleen Mary Bown (the future Mrs. Evans).

There was also a problem which arose with teachers who did not have a University degree – there was no University to write to for biographical information! This was generally the case with teachers for non-academic subjects. One of them was Michael Cox, the Art teacher. One Carmel publication stated that he had received an Art diploma in London – that was it! The problem is that there are numerous schools of Art in London. I therefore had to send an e-mail to a large number of them, and finally I had success. He had received his diploma from the Slade School of Fine Art and they were able to supply me with some information about him. My next question about him was where did he go after he left Carmel? A couple of Old Carmelis told me that in the 1960s they had visited him at the Quintin Kynaston School in St. John's Wood London, where he was head of Art. On "Friends Reunited," I found some very complimentary comments about him at that school from his former pupils, and I tried to make contact with them and other potential former pupils of his to obtain further information but was not successful. I telephoned the school, but they informed me that they did not keep records for more than seven years. At a later date, one Old Carmeli suddenly recollected that Cox had been involved with the "Little Missenden Festival." Using the internet I was able to locate the Chairman of this Festival and on contacting him, he was able to supply me with various items of printed material on Michael Cox, and also put me in contact with a relative of his and also a lifelong friend. The latter (then aged 88) was able to supply me with much biographical information which filled in the various gaps in my information about him.

The Art teacher who followed Michael Cox was Dennis Mills, who also did not have a University degree. The only scrap of information I had to make contact with him (if he were still alive) or with his family, was from an Old Carmeli who said that in the early 1990s he would see Dennis in Brighton and that he had a son called Tarquin. Fortunately "Tarquin" is an uncommon name and I managed to locate a Tarquin Mills – unfortunately it was not the right one! I also managed to find on the internet a Tarquin M. Mills, and that one could send a message to him via "Facebook" which I did. Meanwhile I found a T. M. Mills living in Brighton. I was sure that I had found the right person, but I was too hasty, since when telephoning this person, it was someone else! However, some time later I received a reply from Tarquin (this time the correct one!). He had only just seen my message. He put me in contact with his mother and she was able to supply me with information on Dennis' wartime activities.

I had heard that Yehuda Ofir had returned to Israel and had since died. I know that the Israel National Insurance Institute keeps excellent records and I contacted them. They indeed had records of him and contact details for his widow. They contacted her and she was happy to speak to me and she gave me biographical details of Yehuda. She even gave me a copy of his death certificate and with this I was able to get further details from Gray's Inn in London where he had taken his Bar finals and also from Leeds University from where he had graduated. Without documentary proof of death, they were forbidden by the Data Protection Act from giving me any information.

Although Mrs. Glover had been a teacher at the Prep School for many years, no-one I asked could give me any biographical details of her. The only thing I could find was her address in the "Old Carmeli Association Occupational Directory 1991." I wrote a letter to this address which was in Reading, addressing it to "The Occupants." I soon received a reply from "The Occupant," who, amazingly, was an Old Carmeli (who was at the school at its inception)! He had had no idea that Mrs. Glover had once lived there and he described it as "creepy." At my request, he asked his neighbours about the Glovers, but no-one could help. I then wrote a "Letter to the Editor" of the various Reading local newspapers asking to hear from a Glover family member or a friend who had known her. I received one reply and this was from Sidney Gold, a local resident who is interested in family history. He did some research for me and obtained her maiden name (Elizabeth Joyce Rawlings), and the years and place of her birth, marriage, and death. I contacted the Archives of the Local Council where she was born and they found in their archives that an Elizabeth Rawlings had been admitted to one of their schools. However, before I could get further details, a fungus infestation was discovered in the room where their archives are kept, and the room was immediately closed off and it remains so.

Although I had biographical details about Gilbert Warner until he went to Ethiopia, after that period it was a blank. An Old Carmeli then told me that he had retired to the Irish Republic, was no longer alive, and that his son Dick was an important person in Irish Television. It was then not difficult to obtain his son's telephone number and thus make contact with him, and he gave me his father's post-Ethiopia history. Thus knowing the various places he had worked, I was able to obtain further details, including an almost unobtainable article (located in Folkestone library) he had written whilst he was the first warden of Eversley College.

When building these biographies, I was able to refute some common misconceptions about certain teachers. Mrs. Whitfield was not a French Canadian and neither was she a motor racing enthusiast, and that Healey had never been a county cricket player (although he possibly played in a 2nd XI county team). A mystery I never conclusively solved is why people called Healey "Tim" when his name was Arthur Joseph!

But even after all the research, I am still left with unanswered questions: for example where did William Phelps, Ernest Gray, Dennis Mills, and Martin Coombe go after they left Carmel?

In conclusion, I will mention that during the course of my research, I found some interesting snippets of information regarding the top echelon of staff. Kopul, at one period of his life, had the nickname "Bunny" (even his son Jeremy did not know this), and I learned also of the "post box escapade" of the undergraduate David Stamler, and Romney Coles' "heating trays"!

For further details – read on!!

From Cradle to Old Age or Grave

The biographies are in the approximate chronological order in which the teachers joined the staff at Carmel College.

RABBI KOPUL ROSEN

Kopul Rosen, the founder and Principal of Carmel College was born on 4 November 1913, in Notting Hill in London,[1] to Shlomo and Feige (née Bialystock) Rosen (Rosrazowski), the name having being changed from Rosrazowski to Rosen when they arrived in Britain in 1910.[2] Although, his name was registered as Kopul,[3] this was only discovered many, many years later![4] As a boy, in school at least, he was called Cyril.[5] Kopul's Hebrew name was Ya'akov[6] and on his tombstone in both Carmel College and later on the Mount of Olives, his name is given as Yisrael Ya'akov Kopul.[7]

He was a "born orator." Towards the end of the First World War when bombs were falling, Kopul then aged about four, called out in Yiddish

---

1. Biography of KR, p.2.
2. Ibid., p.3. This is confirmed from Kopul's birth registration which has the name Rosen, showing that the name Rosen was already used by the time Kopul was born, (General Register Office index, Births registered in October, November and December 1913, p.R-367).
3. General Register Office index, Births registered in October, November and December 1913, p.R-367.
4. Memories of KR, p.50.
5. Ibid.; Biography of KR, p.4.
6. Biography of KR, p.4. Kopul is a Yiddish diminutive of Ya'akov.
7. Memories of KR, photograph opposite p.177 of his grave at Carmel College; Mount of Olives cemetery website (Internet). When a person is seriously ill, some have the custom of giving the person an additional name. After Kopul's final illness was diagnosed, he visited the Lubavitcher Rebbe, and about a month before Kopul died, the Lubavitcher Rebbe gave him the additional name of Yisrael (e-mail from Jeremy Rosen, 8 December 2013).

"people should not throw bombs, we should all be friends." About four years later, he wrote a strongly worded essay, in which he criticised his teacher's view on the Creation of the world, restating it as given at the beginning of the book of Bereshit. At the age of eleven, he spoke at an outside "soap-box" meeting for the local Labour party, beginning "Comrades and friends" and went on to deliver a diatribe against wealth and privilege, but not for two minutes as requested but for ten minutes – that was until the police had to move the crowds who filled the whole area and impeded the traffic flow.[8]

Kopul spent a number of his teenage years and his early twenties, studying at the Etz Chaim Yeshiva, in the East End of London.[9] Anthony Rau writes that Kopul once told him that whilst he was at Yeshiva, his fellow students gave him the nickname "Bunny."[10] It was during this period, when he was just seventeen years old, that he gave a sermon in a London Synagogue, the subject being the "High Priest's Trousers."[11] He studied at the Etz Chaim Yeshiva until Dayan Yechezkel Abramsky told Kopul's parents that he was wasting his time and talents in London and he must therefore go to Mir Yeshiva in Poland.[12]

So in the autumn of 1935, off Kopul went to Mir. Mir was a very small hamlet which did not even appear on the map. The Polish Consul in London had never heard of Mir! The Yeshiva had neither dormitories nor dining hall. The students boarded out with local Jewish families. A peasant woman would collect laundry each week and return it a few days later clean and pressed. There was no water in these houses – it had to be drawn from a well. Toilets were outhouses. The only place in Mir to have running water, bathrooms, and toilets was Mir Yeshiva.[13]

Cyril Domb wrote how the mashgiach of Mir Yeshiva, Rabbi Yeruchom Levovitz (or Reb Yeruchom as he was universally known) had a greater influence on Kopul than any other single person.[14] This is even more noteworthy since Reb Yeruchom became very ill about six months after Kopul arrived at Mir and died soon after in the summer of 1936,[15] and so

---

8. Memories of KR, pp.43, 44, 46; Biography of KR, p.4.
9. Memories of KR, pp.13–14.
10. Reflections – Anthony Rau.
11. Memories of KR, pp.85–86.
12. Ibid., p.50.
13. Theodore Lewis, *Remembrances of Mir Yeshiva* (Internet); Letter from Mir 1932 by Rabbi Judah L. Gordon (Internet).
14. Memories of KR, p.15.
15. Theodore Lewis, op. cit.

their period of association was short. A framed picture of Reb Yeruchom hung in Kopul's study at Carmel.[16]

Kopul's "Rebbe" at Mir was R' Simcha Sheps, who was one of the most brilliant students at that Yeshiva.[17] R' Sheps succeeded during the Second World War in escaping from Europe via Siberia and Japan and then reached New York. There he was on the staff of Torah Vodaas Yeshiva until he died in 1998 aged 90, and he is buried on the Mount of Olives cemetery in Jerusalem,[18] the cemetery in which Kopul is now buried.

There is a list of students who were at Mir Yeshiva in 1937–1938. A study of this list shows that the name "Kopul Rosen" appears twice, one of them as originating from Dublin (where Kopul came from) and the other one as originating from Bialystok[19] in Poland, a city where in the 1930s over half the city were Jews. It could have been by coincidence that there were two Kopul Rosens in Mir Yeshiva at the same time. Alternatively, it is plausible that since Bialystok, apart from being the name of a city, was also the maiden name of Kopul's mother,[20] it was this fact that caused confusion when compiling the student lists.

Before leaving Mir, Kopul received semichah (or as they say in the vernacular "was ordained as a Rabbi"). This was a great help in his future University studies, since Manchester University accepted this "ordination" as equivalent to a B.A. and he was thus able to go straight to an M.A.[21] which he was awarded in 1943 for his writing a thesis entitled "A Study of the Musar Movement."[22] Two years later, his book "Rabbi Israel Salanter and the Musar Movement" was published by the Narod Press in London.[23] Towards the end of his life Kopul obtained a Ph.D. from London University for his thesis, "The Concept of Mitzvah in Rabbinic Literature."[24]

In the summer of 1940 Kopul married Bella Cohen in the Salford

16. Unwritten recollections of author.
17. Memories of KR, p.57.
18. Who was R' Simcha Avrohom Hakohen Sheps? (torah.org) (Internet); Rav Simcha Avrohom Hakohen Sheps zt"l on his Yahrzeit today (Internet).
19. Avraham Bernstein, *Yeshivat Mir – Hazericha b'paatei kedem* (Bnei Brak, 1999–2001), vol.3, pp.1014, 1016.
20. General Register Office index, Births registered in October, November and December 1913, p.R-367.
21. Biography of KR, p.16.
22. "Copac" library catalogue.
23. Ibid.
24. Senate House Libraries, University of London, Catalogue of Theses.

area.[25] Even though his father-in-law's name was Cohen, he was not a Kohen – he was a Levi! Jeremy Rosen explains how this anomaly arose:

> My grandfather's family were called Shumacher in the town of Kribitz in the Ukraine. When they migrated in the early twentieth century to Tredegar in Wales, the resident Jewish godfather was called Cohen, possibly a distant relative, and for various reasons still disputed (convenience, preference, obligation, etc.) they agreed to change their name to Cohen even though they were Leviim.[26]

After returning from Mir, Kopul held different Rabbinical positions, one after another, all within the course of just one decade. The first was Rabbi of a Manchester Synagogue and he also then served on the Manchester Beth Din. This was followed by being Communal Rabbi of Glasgow,[27] which was soon followed by his appointment as Principal Rabbi of the Federation of Synagogues. Then came the major achievement in his life – Carmel College.[28]

Kopul was very meticulous in the way he dressed.[29] Rabbi Louis Rabinowitz comments that Kopul, then aged 17, visited him one Shabbat, and he was "impeccably and elegantly attired."[30] On this subject, David Stamler also wrote, "The great attention he paid to his dress, rarely spending less than £50 on a suit even in the early 1950s." Kopul was even concerned that his beard should be perfect, and he once advertised in "The Times" for "a barber who could trim his beard as he liked it."[31]

Kopul was very strong in his principles, even to the extent of taking the law into his own hands, as Jeremy Rosen writes:

> On one occasion [when he was Communal Rabbi of Glasgow] he personally battered down the door of a kosher butcher to find, as he thought he would, non-kosher meat products that the owner had brought in to pass off as kosher. This actually led to court proceedings

---

25. General Register Office index, Marriages registered in July, August and September 1940, pp.C-313, R-173; Memories of KR., p.15.

26. E-mail from Jeremy Rosen, 26 August 2013.

27. Whilst in Glasgow, he would write thin booklets entitled "Views Letter" which would be printed and distributed to the Jewish community of Glasgow.

28. Memories of KR, passim.

29. An Old Carmeli of the Kopul era, Solomon (Momy) Levy writes "the way I dress, I owe it to him," (Recollections – Solomon Levy).

30. Memories of KR, p.85.

31. Ibid., p.103.

in which Kopul was admonished for breaking in illegally, but praised for his zeal in upholding religious standards.[32]

At Carmel, Kopul was an expert at answering "awkward" parents. Abraham Carmel in his book reports of one such case:

> A mother of a pupil was arguing with Abraham Carmel that she wanted to be able to send her son chicken twice a week and for him to have a rubber-foam mattress. At the right moment Kopul turns up and answered, "Yes, yes . . . you want [boy's name] to have chicken twice a week, and three rubber mattresses a month! When he gets home in December he'll need them all, I'm sure, but meantime the bell is just about to ring, and I shouldn't like you to be swept away by a hundred young savages charging downstairs!" . . . At that, Mrs. . . . , discomfited, routed, bereft of words possibly for the first time in her loquacious life, and also a little fearful, too, of the threatened avalanche down the stairs, retreated . . .[33]

Kopul's retorts were not limited to his tongue. When necessary he would use his pen. On several occasions he wrote reprimanding letters to the "Jewish Chronicle."

He did not like a "Silhouette" written by that newspaper on the occasion of Rabbi Dr. Schonfeld's 50th birthday.[34] He wrote that "It is possible to present a selected number of facts, each one which is not inaccurate, and yet produce a total impression which is a grotesque distortion of the truth." After mentioning several activities in Dr. Schonfeld's life, Kopul continued, "Of, course, he does not always 'hit it off' with people. My relationship with him has not always been smooth (on the occasions when we differed he was in the wrong, *of course*) but one can hardly expect a colourful and headstrong personality to be widely popular in a community that *esteems mediocrity*. You have not produced a silhouette of Dr. Schonfeld but a daub."[35]

Another letter written to the "Jewish Chronicle" by Kopul during the last half year of his life followed a lecture given by Robert Graves to the

---

32. Biography of KR, p.25.
33. Abraham Carmel, *So Strange My Path*, pp.146–47; whether or not this is an accurate report of what occurred, it does show Kopul's expertise in answering such people.
34. Jewish Chronicle, 5 December 1958, p.11.
35. Ibid., 12 December 1958, p.20; Memories of KR, p.32.

Hillel Foundation on a subject connected with "Higher Criticism." In his letter, Kopul described Graves' lecture as "a monumental example of superficial pseudo-scholarship. . . . What Robert Graves delivered was not a scholarly lecture but an exhibition of skill in the intellectual game known as 'higher hooey'."[36]

Kopul pronouncements were not limited to retorts. He also had his own collection of "Proverbs":

"What you will be, you are now becoming."[37]

"There are two opinions you can have on this subject, boys, the wrong one and mine."[38]

"If it goes without saying, it goes better with saying."[39]

"If Freud could do it so can I."[40]

"Don't let the mob take over."[41]

"By the bones of Bohunkus."[42]

"You need more oomph."[43]

"It sounds better in Yiddish."[44]

"[The columns of the magazine are open] not to those who want to say something, but to those who have something to say."[45]

Kopul would do a little class teaching, and he liked to teach English. He would sometimes have to fill in for gaps for different subjects.[46] On one occasion he taught the second form Modern Hebrew and Mathematics (the latter of which Jeremy Rosen writes was "not his strong point"[47]). The author who was in that class reports, "Modern Hebrew was the last period each day and we were taught it by Rabbi Rosen. He also taught us Mathematics and he introduced us to algebra. He began by asking what is 'a' plus 'a'? We probably answered 'b' since one automatically thinks of the alphabet!"[48] Emmanuel Grodzinski writes on one of Kopul's maths lessons:

---

36. Ibid., 3 Nov 1961, p.26; Ibid., pp.35–36.
37. Recollections – David Saville.
38. Ibid.
39. Recollections – Michael Bharier.
40. Ibid.
41. Ibid.
42. Ibid.
43. Ibid.
44. Ibid.
45. Memories of KR, p.15.
46. Carmel College Prep School and Senior School, sample school reports: autumn 1952, Prep form 3; autumn 1950, Senior form 3; spring – autumn 1953, Senior forms 2 and 3; autumn 1954, Senior form 2. (names withheld).
47. Biography of KR, p.44.
48. 7 years, p.46.

My Maths reports for Spring and Summer 1953 were written by Kopul. I do not remember him teaching us regularly, but I do remember him filling in one day when the regular teacher was absent. The subject was geometry; Kopul wanted to describe a circle on the blackboard and the divider was missing. So he extracted a large white handkerchief from his pocket, placed one corner in the centre of the board, held the chalk with the opposite corner and drew the most perfect circle.[49]

In Kopul's lessons, syllabuses were often "irrelevant." On this David Stamler writes:

> A lesson with him [Kopul], ostensibly on one of the Prophets, could range easily to Yeats via Tagore. A period marked as 'Sidra' on the timetable could deal with his future plans or with a pithy analysis of the Anglo-Jewish Establishment. A pre-arranged syllabus was never completed, but a class of boys would be wiser human beings as a result of their term's work. His absences frequently took him away from the school and as a result his class would be unattended. There could be few teachers whose absence from a lesson would be so genuinely missed by the boys.[50]

There was an occasion when Kopul taught a boy how to swim, albeit in an unconventional manner. David Sheldon was the boy and he recollects, "Rabbi Rosen taught me to swim in the old swimming pool by swimming on his back holding me in his arms, when I was 8 years old, then letting go of me in the deep end with the words 'You should be alright now!'"[51]

He would also give voluntary extra-curricular lessons in his study, which included Gemara. The author recollects:

> One of these lessons was Gemara. Throughout the school, this did not appear in the curriculum. The first Gemara that we learned was the perek 'Eilu Metziot' from Masechet Bava Metzia. This perek is traditionally taught to children beginning Gemara. A reason I have heard is that children often find things belonging to others and they

---

49. E-mail from Emanuel Grodzinski, 11 March 2013.
50. Memories of KR, pp.107–08.
51. E-mail from David Sheldon, 24 June 2014.

thus learn that there is not 'findings keepings.' After learning that lost objects are returned on the basis of identifying marks, Rabbi Rosen asked me if I lost my watch, how would I identify it. I answered that one of the numbers was partly eradicated and he replied that this was a very good identifying mark.

On one occasion, there was a lady visitor in his study during the Gemara lesson and in order to test whether one of the boys understood the Gemara, he asked him to explain it so that the woman would understand it. After the boy had gone through the explanation, he asked the woman whether she had understood it and she answered that she didn't but that was due to her ignorance. 'No,' said Rabbi Rosen, 'He didn't explain it well.'[52]

Once a boy did not give the right answer in his Gemara lesson, and Kopul is reported to have said to him, "Out, out, and I don't want to see you again."[53]

One of the O-level subjects taken at Carmel was Scripture Knowledge. This consisted of two papers, one from the Tanach, which the non-Jews call the "Old Testament," and one from what they call the "New Testament." There was a possibility, for pupils whose parents objected on religious reasons to take a "New Testament" paper, to do two "Old Testament" papers. However, instead Carmel opted to have a special paper on the Hebrew text of a book of the Torah. For this paper, the boys had to study on their own.[54] To instruct the boys for the other paper, Kopul would give a compulsory lesson on Shabbat afternoon. The author reports on this:

> We all went to his study carrying our Bibles and we would read through the set-books. Rabbi Rosen would ask us questions which showed whether we *understood* the text. One such question was whether the seer (Samuel) wore distinctive clothing. The text as such doesn't specify this point. However, the fact that Saul approached Samuel and asked him where the seer's house was, to which Samuel replied that he was the seer, indicates that he wasn't wearing distinctive clothing.[55]

---

52. 7 years, pp.73–74.
53. Recollections – David Saville.
54. Unwritten recollections of author.
55. 7 years, p.74.

Kopul realised that after leaving the school, the boys would have missionaries trying to draw them away from Judaism. The author explains how Kopul instructed the pupils on countering their arguments:

> Rabbi Rosen told us how to answer alleged Christological references in the Tanach. He spoke about 'Kiss the Son' – the Son referring to Jesus – which some Christian 'scholars' gave as the translation of the last verse of Psalm 2, by translating the word 'bar' which is the *Aramaic* for son. He explained that it is illogical for a Psalm written entirely in Hebrew, to have just one word in Aramaic. The word 'bar' in Hebrew means purity and the correct translation is 'Kiss purity'.' Another example was *their* translation towards the beginning of Isaiah 'And a virgin shall conceive' – which according to these 'scholars' referred to Jesus' mother. Rabbi Rosen then explained that the translation of the Hebrew word 'alma' is not virgin, but 'young woman.' I personally found this lesson most useful when I went to University and had to contend with such claims.[56]

Gilbert Warner's son Dick has a recollection of Kopul, whilst the school was still at Greenham. He writes, "The first television programme I ever saw, [was] when I was invited into Rabbi Rosen's study to watch the coronation of Queen Elizabeth II [in June 1953] . . . I was fond of Rabbi Rosen because he had a habit of giving small boys very large tips (half a crown!)"[57]

Sadly, at the period when one could see that the fruits of his fifteen years of infinite efforts were beginning to show visible results, Kopul was stricken with his fatal illness and died on 15 March 1962, at the early age of 48, and was buried on the grounds of Carmel College.[58] After Carmel College closed and the estate was sold to property developers, his grave was transferred to the Mount of Olives Cemetery in Jerusalem.[59]

---

56. Ibid.
57. E-mail from Dick Warner, 17 December 2013. On the occasion of the Coronation, the pupils were given a few days holiday at home.
58. Memories of KR, p.30.
59. Jerusalem Post, 23 July 1999.

DAVID MARCUS STAMLER

Stamler was born[60] in London on 4 November 1928 to Herman and Brucha (née Roshandler) Stamler,[61] his father being a Fur and Skin Merchant.[62] His bar mitzvah was held at the Chesham Synagogue where he read Maftir and Haftarah.[63]

He was educated at Battersea Grammar School, and in 1941 continued at Berkhamsted School[64] (which was founded in 1541 by John Incent, the Dean of St. Paul's Cathedral[65]). The pupils were assigned to one of the Houses, which had such names as Adders, Bees, and Swifts;[66] David Stamler was in Hawks House. In December 1944, he passed his School Certificate, and in 1946 the Higher School Certificate in Zoology, French, English, Botany, and Scripture Knowledge. He told the School that his intended profession was to be a Doctor. At the School he was a House Prefect and was on the Committees of both the Sixth Form Discussion Group and the History and Debating Society. He studied at that school until July 1946.[67]

Of his relationship with Kopul, Stamler writes:

My own first meeting with Kopul Rosen was on April 2nd 1947. At the time I was National Chairman of the Jewish Youth Study Groups and it was our practice to invite an outside speaker to address the annual conference of Group Chairmen. Kopul Rosen's name was proposed but, never having heard him speak and knowing nothing of his reputation, I felt reluctant to accept the suggestion. I was never to regret allowing myself to be persuaded and he spoke on 'The duties and functions of the Rabbi in the community.' From the first moment of our meeting we 'clicked' and before the afternoon was over he suggested that once he came to live in London – as he planned

60. He was registered at birth as Marcus David Stamler (General Register Office index, Births registered in January, February and March 1929, p.S-188), and when he began at Carmel in 1948, he was called up to the Torah as Mordechai David (Carmel College Gabbai's Shul list of Hebrew names from 1948).
61. General Register Office index, Marriages registered in January, February and March 1925, pp. R-163, S-208.
62. Application form of David Stamler to Berkhamsted School, dated 27 November 1940.
63. Jewish Chronicle, 7 November 1941, p.3.
64. Record card of David Stamler at Berkhamsted School.
65. Wikipedia – Berkhamsted School.
66. Ibid.
67. Record card of David Stamler at Berkhamsted School.

to do shortly – I should come and learn with him. I rapidly came to see what a fascinating teacher he was. Never before had I so looked forward to a 'shiur.' I had never been enamoured of Gemara, but in Kopul Rosen's hands, even the driest of subjects became vividly alive. 'Nach' we both loved and Rabbi Rosen rightly felt that all we studied should be learned by heart. A year or so later when he was speaking in Lauderdale Road, we walked from his house to the Synagogue, a thirty-minute trip, reciting alternate verses of Proverbs by heart. Occasionally, captivated by a particular phrase, he would declaim it loudly to the mild astonishment of the Saturday morning shoppers in Kilburn High Road. Even his lack of punctuality and reliability only served to make my trips from Chesham (where I was then living) more unpredictable and unusual. No teacher I had ever had before had been late for a lesson (or even failed to turn up at all) because he had completely forgotten about it or had gone swimming![68]

These Shiurim continued regularly until September 1948 when Carmel opened and Stamler joined the staff at Newbury.[69]

From 1950 to 1952 he was a House Master at Carmel.[70] For one term in 1950 he was a Form Master.[71] In 1950 and 1951 he was teaching Biology to the lower Forms,[72] and in 1952, Jewish Studies.[73]

He then went to St. Catherine's College in Oxford University where he studied Oriental Studies (Hebrew and Arabic). He finished his studies for a B.A. in 1955 with a Second Class Degree (which became an M.A. in 1960).[74]

At University, as with many other undergraduates, he got up to pranks. David Saville elaborates:

He once told us when he was studying at Oxford he went to a post box with a few friends and spoke inside as if there was someone there and said 'Don't worry George, we'll get you out, the fire brigade is

---

68. Memories of KR, pp.99–100.
69. Ibid., p.97.
70. Carmel College Senior School, sample school reports: summer 1950 – summer 1951, forms 2 – 3; spring 1952 – summer 1952, form 4 (name withheld).
71. Ibid., autumn 1950, form 3 (name withheld).
72. Ibid., summer 1950 – summer 1951, forms 2 – 3 (name withheld). There are also some photographs of him teaching biology at that period.
73. Ibid., spring and summer 1952, form 2 (name withheld).
74. e-mail from St Catherine's College Oxford, 25 October 2012.

on the way, there is nothing to worry about, etc., etc.' and after a few minutes when a considerable crowd had come, he and his friends simply slipped away.[75]

In addition to his pranks, at his University Stamler was a boxer, but because all the University matches were on Friday nights, he could not take part in them.[76] During 1954 he would come down to Carmel from the University every Sunday "to teach the noble art of self-defence."[77] He also played cricket for his Oxford College.[78]

In 1955, the year he graduated, he was awarded an English Speaking Union and Fulbright Fellowship to do research during the following year in Semitic languages at Brandeis University and Harvard University.[79] He lectured extensively on the Dead Sea Scrolls.[80]

At that period, he co-authored the book "Backdrop to Tragedy: the Struggle for Palestine." The three authors of this book were: an American scholar; David Stamler the Zionist; and an Arab, who each undertook to present from their respective points of view the background to the Arab-Israeli issue.[81]

After completing that year in America, Stamler returned to Carmel and was appointed Vice-Principal.[82] At the same time, he taught Tanach at Carmel and his University studies were evident from the contents of his lessons.[83] Michael Ellman recollects something else that Stamler taught him. "He introduced us to Tom Lehrer,"[84] an American singer-songwriter, satirist, pianist, and mathematician.[85]

On one occasion, he gave his class a holiday task – to research and write an essay on a subject of their choice on Modern Zionism.[86] On another occasion, he wanted to test the Jewish general knowledge of the pupils and for this purpose he set the pupils an examination consisting of questions requiring one-word answers. This included identifying people in Jewish

75. Recollections – David Saville.
76. e-mail from David Stamler to Jeremy Rosen, 27 October 2013.
77. The Young Carmelonian, p.17.
78. Jewish Chronicle, 17 August 1956, p.7.
79. Carmel 1955, p.5; Jewish Chronicle, 17 August 1958, p.7.
80. Jewish Chronicle, 17 August 1956, p.7.
81. Foreign Affairs (New York: Council on Foreign Relations), January 1958, Review by Henry L. Roberts, p.360.
82. Carmel 1957, p.4; Jewish Chronicle, 17 August 1956, p.7.
83. Unwritten recollections of author.
84. Recollections – Michael Ellman.
85. Wikipedia – Tom Lehrer.
86. 7 years, p.54.

David Stamler (in the white coat) Giving a Biology Lesson at Greenham.

history from Biblical to modern times. However, some of them were non-existent people, one of them being "Hotzmach"![87]

When he was Vice-Principal, Stamler built up a card index of the boys in the school in which he wrote the various good and bad deeds done by the pupils, and this was kept on the window ledge by his desk in the study he shared with Kopul. One pupil, whose name was right at the beginning of the alphabet, succeeded, when he was in this room, in opening by the tiniest amount the drawer of this card index and was able to read his card![88] On one occasion he wrote on the school report of a boy, who had come 19th out of the 20 pupils in his class, "If you had tried harder you could have come bottom of the class."[89]

---

87. Ibid., p.112.
88. Ibid., p.17.
89. Recollections – Michael Goitein; this is also found with similar wording in Recollections – David Saville.

In September 1957 he married Micheline Lindenbaum.[90] Whilst building a bungalow for the Stamlers on the Carmel campus in 1958. . . . The Carmel magazine continues, "On the site where Mr. Stamler's house is being built, an event no less important than the discovery of the Dead Sea Scrolls took place; a well thought to be Anglo-Saxon was unearthed."[91]

When Kopul died in 1962, David Stamler was appointed as Headmaster[92] (from then on, the term "Headmaster" was used instead of "Principal"). In 1969, he was elected to the Headmasters Conference. On this Jeremy Rosen wrote, "This was the ultimate accolade for Carmel to be recognised as a 'proper' public school."[93] However, in the autumn of the following year, he had a stroke and as a result resigned as Headmaster of Carmel.[94]

After leaving Carmel, he went to Israel and there ran the Rad (Rural Arts Development) Family Foundation until 1977. He then moved to Geneva where he worked with the World ORT Union. A couple of years later, when ORT left Geneva, he moved to the United States.[95]

As of 2013, David Stamler lived in New York.

JAMES ARCHIBALD EWART

He was born on 22 May 1907 in Suez, Egypt.[96] By 1911, he was living in Langport in Somersetshire.[97]

Ewart's schooling between the years 1917 and 1926 was at Taunton School in Somerset, where he reached the position of Head School Prefect. At that school, he excelled in its sporting activities. He became the School Captain for Rugby football in 1925–1926 and a year earlier, 1924–1925, had been awarded School Colours for this sport. He was also House Captain for Rugby and received House Colours for it. Furthermore, he represented Scottish Public Schoolboys against English Public Schoolboys in Junior International Rugby. He was also School Captain for Water Polo, and received House Colours for Cricket and sports. In

90. Carmel 1957, p.4.
91. Carmel 1958, p.5; (also see chapter "Three Carmel Estates").
92. Carmel 1962, p.3; Recollections – Jeremy Rosen, chap.2.
93. Recollections – Jeremy Rosen, chap.2.
94. E-mail from David Stamler, 10 February 2013.
95. E-mail from David Stamler, 11 February 2013.
96. E-mail from Jesus College Cambridge, 9 January 2013.
97. British 1911 census.

Swimming he was the winner of two lengths and the clothes race in 1924-1925-1926, and received House Colours for this sport.[98]

He was admitted on 22 October 1926 to Jesus College Cambridge University. He first studied History for the Historical Tripos. In the examinations for Part 1 of this Tripos in 1928, he was awarded a lower second class pass. He then switched to studying English for the English Tripos. In the examinations for Part 1 of this Tripos in 1929, he was awarded a third class pass. He graduated with a joint honours degree of B.A. in History and English, on 18 June 1929 (and this became an M.A. on 17 May 1935).[99] He also played rugby for the College.[100]

Ewart then taught in Barbados,[101] and in 1935 became a member of the Royal Society of Teachers.[102] Accordingly, on the Carmel notepaper of 1948, the letters M.R.S.T. appeared after his name and degree.[103] His teaching in Barbados was followed by his being appointed in 1939 as headmaster of the Shan Chiefs' School in Taunggyi,[104] the capital of the Shan state in Myanmar (Burma). This was a school founded by the British administration to train the sons of the ruling families.[105]

Between 1939 and 1945, the years of the Second World War, Ewart served in the intelligence corps in W. [West ?] country, India and Shan state,[106] with him being promoted to the rank of 2nd Lieutenant on 4 December 1942.[107]

At the beginning of 1948, he was appointed as the first Headmaster of Carmel College. In the Provisional Prospectus published about April 1948, Kopul writes:

> We have been extremely fortunate in obtaining the services of Mr. J. Ewart, M.A. (Cantab.) who will be the headmaster responsible for the administration and secular education of the school. His personality, ability, qualifications and wide educational experience encourage us

---

98. Two e-mails from Taunton School, 10 January 2013.
99. E-mails from Cambridge University Archives, 8 January 2013, and Jesus College, op. cit.
100. E-mail from Jesus College, op. cit.
101. Ibid.
102. Teachers Registration Council Registers 1902–1948 (Findmypast.co.uk), (Internet).
103. Sample of Carmel College notepaper from 1948.
104. E-mail from Jesus College, op. cit.
105. Wikipedia – Sao Saimong; Wikipedia – Taunggyi.
106. E-mail from Jesus College, op. cit.
107. Supplement to the London Gazette, 29 January 1943, p.535.

The Headmaster James Ewart and his Wife

to believe that we shall reach that high target which we have set our-selves.[108]

It is desirable that in a boarding school, the headmaster should live on the campus and indeed Ewart lived in a small cottage in the grounds of Carmel.[109] David Shaw has some memories of him, "I was proud of my telescope and remember seeing the Headmaster, Mr. Ewart, in his two-seater, coming and going, for miles from my roost [the giant redwoods which he climbed]."[110]

In all the "Jewish Chronicle" advertisements of Carmel, his name ap-peared with the title Headmaster of Carmel College.[111] However, from October 1950, it appeared as Headmaster of the Preparatory School.[112]

---

108. Provisional Prospectus, undated (about April 1948), section: The Intention of Carmel College.
109. Recollections – Joe Dwek.
110. Recollections – David Shaw.
111. e.g., Jewish Chronicle, 6 August 1948, p.3.
112. Jewish Chronicle, 6 October 1950, p.19.

That was until the beginning of 1951, when his name disappeared from the Carmel advertisements, indicating that he no longer worked at Carmel.[113]

Ewart then became Headmaster of Coombe House School in New Malden and remained there until it closed in about 1963, and the buildings and land sold to property developers.[114] A former teacher at that school, Michael Webb, who was appointed in September 1961, writes:

> My 'interview' was a brief bluff chat with Mr. Ewart, a breezy ex-army officer type (don't know if he was) who more or less said 'You'll take the job then? Splendid – staff meeting day before start of term.' . . . During the so-called staff meeting on that first day, Mr. Ewart turned to [the teacher] Jim Gallaher and said 'We'd better have a caning on the first day, Mr. Gallaher,' as if it was a matter of choosing rugby practice times . . .[115]

Indeed, that very day, in accordance with Ewart's orders, Gallaher "flogged" a pupil, chosen at random, "in front of his awed classmates."[116]

From 26 April 1971 to 31 March 1976, he was the Headmaster at the Princess Mary's Village Homes in Addelstone, Weybridge, Surrey.[117] These homes had been founded to care for girls in need of care and protection because their parents had been committed to prison; the homes became an approved school for girls in 1927. In an article in the local paper dated 2 June 1972, it stated:

> The aim of the headmaster, Mr. James Ewart, and his staff is to plant seeds of integrity, discipline and high domestic standards, so that their pupils will be able to maintain good homes of their own. Training received by the girls is in one sense punitive – rather it concentrates on character-building and formation of a well-balanced outlook of present problems.[118]

---

113. Beginning from Jewish Chronicle, 2 March 1951, p.16.
114. Coombe House School, Friends Reunited, recollections from alumni Roger Lewis and Bob Evans (Internet).
115. Ibid., recollections from Michael Webb.
116. Ibid.
117. E-mail from Surrey gov uk, 1 February 2013.
118. E-mail from Runnymede gov uk, 6 February 2013.

Irini Baawuah was a pupil at this Village Home from 1974 to 1980 (the first part of which Ewart was its Headmaster), and has recollections of him there:

> I was at Princess Mary's Village Homes when Mr. Ewart was a head-master, it was a care home for girls from an age range of 8–16 with problem backgrounds. It had a school on the premises and he was the overall headmaster. He was strict and would not tolerate bully-ing, rudeness to staff and smoking. I remember he would make the houseparents search our rooms whilst we were at school and destroy any cigarettes that were found but no one was punished for it. We later found out that he had a close relative pass away from a smoking related illness. But we still found it unfair as other care homes allowed smoking (and as a mother and grandmother I can now understand why he was like that). We used to go home for the weekends and one of the punishments was grounding for the weekend (but the house-parents made it a pleasant weekend for the grounded girls and I'm sure it was with his knowledge and blessing). I cannot fault him, he did a good job of the running of the place. There was a huge oval lawn on the premises that we were not allowed to step on but even the staff would run across it if they thought he wasn't around and I'm sure he was aware of it and turned a blind eye. He also had a sense of humour. He once signed my passport picture, I was 12 at the time and I had long hair, a casual t-shirt, and a serious look on my face. I looked like a proper hippy. He duly endorsed the picture, put it in an envelope, and wrote on it To Irini 'dumb dumb face.' When he left the school, the first thing they done (*sic*) was they allowed us to smoke but when he came back for his leaving-do we were asked not to smoke and not one of us did, so there was respect for him because as wayward teenagers I'm sure we would have retaliated. He was also a tennis fan because come the tennis season he would not bat an eyelid when a teacher would bring a portable tv [television] in the staff room and they would go off and watch it.[119]

Ewart died on 29 April 1987 after a stroke,[120] at the age of almost 80.

---

119. E-mail from Irini Baawuah, 28 February 2013.
120. E-mail from Jesus College, op. cit.

ANDREJ (ANDREW) SIMCHA NEUSCHLOSS

He was born on 30 April 1920 in Bratislava, Czechoslovakia to Andor and Gisella Neuschloss, both of them Czechoslovakian citizens.[121]

Neuschloss arrived in England from Czechoslovakia and went to live in the Manchester area. At that period there were numerous refugees from Czechoslovakia who had arrived in Britain and, in a list brought out by a British Committee for these refugees, 13,398 names are listed, one of them being Andreas Neuschloss.[122]

In 1944, he was awarded the degree of B.A. with First Class Honours in Semitic Studies by Manchester University, and two years later in 1946 he received a Teacher's Diploma (Second Class) following a course of initial training in teaching by the same University.[123] He also studied at the Manchester Talmudical College (Yeshiva).[124]

He was the Headmaster of the Higher Crumpsall Hebrew Classes from 1944 to 1946.[125] On her recollections of him at these Hebrew Classes, Glo McNeill writes:

> He taught [at the] Cheder at Higher Crumpsall during the war years, from I believe 1940 – 1944. He was our leader in Bnei Akiva and formed a girls' group called Bnot Torah, and led children's minyans during those years.
>
> Some of the many things he taught us were wonderful nigunim [tunes] and introduced some beautiful melodies to biblical passages and prayers. . . . Nobody I have met has known these particular songs. . . . He brought unity and comfort to a group of young people in a very dark and uncertain time during World War II.[126]

In a further e-mail, Glo adds, "He was a staunch early Zionist and was always singing the praises of life on the kibbutz. I believe he spent some

---

121. British Certificate of Naturalisation dated 27 February 1948.
122. Czech and Slovak Things, British Committee for Refugees from Czechoslovakia . . . , Names of Registered Individuals and Associated Persons, Part 4 of List, (Internet). In documents his name would sometimes be spelled as slight variations of Andrej.
123. E-mails from Manchester University, 21 January 2013.
124. The Dropsie College for Hebrew and Cognate Learning, Register 1949–1950, p.49; Jewish Chronicle, 26 November 1948, p.14.
125. Jewish Chronicle, 26 November 1948, p.14.
126. E-mail from Glo McNeill, 23 July 2012; her recollection of the actual years he taught there are inaccurate, but this is understandable after such a long period of time.

time in the 30s on a kibbutz also. I know many of the songs he taught us youngsters were from those early days."[127]

From 1946 to 1948, Neuschloss was Senior Master at the Manchester and Salford Jewish Day School.[128] In March 1948 he received a British certificate of naturalisation.[129]

When Carmel opened in 1948, he took charge of the Jewish Studies and religious activities.[130] However, he was only at Carmel for just one term,[131] or even less.[132] A pupil of his commented on his very short stay at Carmel, "Great pity. A wonderful, kind man, especially to those of us who knew little about Judaism. Made me feel at home and started to teach me my bar mitzvah (held late). David Stamler arrived as he left, and took over from him."[133]

It was towards the end of 1948 that he was awarded a Research Fellowship in Jewish History at the Dropsie College in Philadelphia,[134] and he then became a student (probably a post-graduate student) there.[135] In 1956 he submitted a dissertation in partial fulfillment of the requirements for the degree of Ph.D. It was entitled "Rabbi Akiba Eger: his life and times."[136]

By the end of 1962, he was already on the staff of Yeshiva University in New York giving lectures in Jewish History to the "Jewish Studies Program"[137] for the second to the fourth years.[138] For several decades he gave

---

127. Further e-mail from Glo McNeill, 23 July 2012.

128. Jewish Chronicle, 26 November 1948, p.14.

129. British Certificate of Naturalisation dated 27 February 1948; London Gazette, 13 April 1948, p.2354.

130. Memories of KR, p.103.

131. Neuschloss' name appears in the list of students in several annual Registers up to 1955 of The Dropsie College for Hebrew and Cognate Learning. Since it is stated in the Register that he began as a student in the second term of the 1948/49 academic year (Register 1949–1950 p.49), he was thus no longer at Carmel at that period.

132. E-mail from an early pupil (requested anonymity), 27 September 2013 who states just half a term.

133. Ibid.

134. Jewish Chronicle, 26 November 1948, p.14.

135. The Dropsie College for Hebrew and Cognate Learning, Register 1949–1950, Students 1948–1949, p.49.

136. E-mail from Pennsylvania University, 22 January 2013; ResearchGate, publication 34316527.

137. This was a 4-year programme in Jewish Studies, given by the "Jewish Studies School" of Yeshiva University for students who wanted to pursue Jewish Studies whilst taking a regular secular college programme. In 1965 this School was renamed the "James Striar School," (Wikipedia – James Striar School of General Jewish Studies).

138. Lecture from Rabbi Morris Besdin to Dr. Samuel Belkin, dated 14 November 1962.

these lectures (and on occasion also lectures in Rabbinics and in Jewish Liturgy),[139] and was still on the staff in 1984.[140]

Neuschloss was also on the staff of Touro College and in May 1977, at a conference sponsored by the Medieval Institute of Western Michigan University, he delivered a lecture entitled "The Responsa of Yishaq al-Fasi as a Source for Jewish-Moslem Relations in Twelfth Century Spain."[141] According to a note written by Neuschloss, this was the first time that this Institute had sponsored a specifically Jewish panel.[142]

He died on 4 August 1994, probably in New Jersey,[143] at the age of 74.

OSCAR DAHL

In May 1948, Dahl was living in Wolverhampton, and was on a short list of candidates to be interviewed for the teaching staff for Carmel College for that September. The interview was arranged by the Headmaster James Ewart and took place in London on 23 May 1948. Dahl's travelling expenses for the interview amounted to £2 0s 0d.[144] He was appointed as the Housemaster,[145] and because of him, there was no pupil with the school number "unlucky" 13.[146]

A pupil who was at Carmel from the inception has recollections of Dahl, "[He was] into corporal punishment and torture with a shelf of books on the subject on the top shelf of his bookcase. Each of his canes was named after a Roman emperor known for his cruelty. [He] instituted the original prefect system. His aim to get every boy caned at least once during the first term."[147] He was only at Carmel for a very short period.[148]

139. Yeshiva University, New York, James Striar School, Schedule of Courses: e.g. Fall 1968, Fall 1969, Spring 1970, Fall 1970, Spring 1973, Fall 1977.
140. Yeshiva University, New York, "Masmid" 1984, p.34.
141. Twelfth Conference on Medieval Studies, May 5–8, 1977, Western Michigan University, programme, p.6.
142. Note by Andre Neuschloss to the Editor of "Inside Yeshiva University," September 1977.
143. Persons born 30 April 1920 in the Social Security Death Master File (Internet).
144. Carmel College, Appointment of teaching staff, expenses of visits to London for interviews on 23 May 1948.
145. Memories of KR, p.103.
146. E-mail from an early pupil (requested anonymity), 27 September 2013.
147. Ibid.
148. The pupil (requested anonymity) in his e-mail writes one term; however there is a photograph of him (together with a group of pupils) at Carmel with the inscription "Spring 1949."

HAROLD AARON NAGLEY

Nagley was born on 30 November 1913 in Leeds, his parents, Lewis and Tilly, having arrived in that city from Eastern Europe in about 1870. After the First World War his father built a pier on the sea front in Tel Aviv, which they named Nagliah. Harold attended the City of Leeds Central High School from 1925 to 1931, where in addition to his academic ability, he was an able sportsman participating in a number of sports.[149]

Nagley then attended Leeds University, where he graduated with Second Class honours in both French and Latin;[150] his studies included four months at the Sorbonne in Paris.[151] The following year he was awarded a Diploma in Education from Leeds University.[152] Between 1935 and 1940, he taught various subjects, and specialised in P.E. at Castleton County School in Armley Leeds. In 1940, he volunteered to the army where he served as Sergeant Instructor in the Army Physical Education Corps, and was later promoted to Lieutenant. For many years during this war, he served in the Middle East.[153]

After being demobilised in 1946, Nagley taught French, Latin, and P.E. at Bedlington Grammar School in Whitley Bay, Northumberland. In an account of his life he writes:

> I was the only member on the staff at Bedlington who was Jewish. One colleague who knew of my fond feelings for Palestine, and realised that I might be happier in a Jewish school, sent me an advertisement that he had seen in the paper. The advertisement was for a new Jewish boarding school, Carmel College. . . .
>
> I took his advice, and this became the turning point of my career. 'Everything in life is pre-destined, but we have the power to choose our own path.' I had the free will and I could have ignored the advertisement, but with circumstances being as they were, I applied for the job.

149. "My Name is Aaron," (compiled by Nagley's student Nerada Stern, 1983), pp.1–2; Suzanne D. Rutland, *If you will it, it is no dream – The Moriah Story 1943–2003*, (Caringbah, N.S.W: Playright Pub., 2003), p.85; letter from Harold Nagley to Liverpool Hebrew School, 23 March 1951.

150. Certificate from University of Leeds for Degree of Bachelor of Arts, 2 July 1934.

151. Rutland, op. cit., p.85; Letter from Nagley, op. cit.

152. Certificate from University of Leeds for Diploma in Education, 26 June 1935.

153. Rutland., op. cit., p.86; Letter from Nagley , op. cit.

I was interviewed in London[154] in early 1948 for a teaching position at the new boarding school, by two gentlemen: the headmaster elect [James Ewart], and the Principal, the late Rabbi Koppel (*sic*) Rosen who was to become the person who had the most influence on me throughout my life. . . .

At the interview, Rabbi Rosen asked me about my Hebrew knowledge and whether I could speak Hebrew. I said that I did not speak Hebrew, but I had wanted to acquire the subject. He answered on the spot 'You will.' This became an inspiration to me. I was appointed to teach French, Latin, and Physical Education, but before long, I was also put in charge of the bar mitzvah boys. . . .

The experience of teaching and pioneering in an educational experiment was most enriching for me. Mainly because I had come into close contact with a most impressive personality, as well as other members of the Jewish teaching staff. The distance from my family's quarters to the room which was used as a synagogue was only a matter of a flight of stairs, and services were held there daily on Shabbat and festivals. Meals in the dining room were in themselves an experience. Not only on Shabbat and festivals, but every single day! One of the advantages was that my son Phillip, who was then two years old, could be sent home if he lost interest in the services. . . . .

Being close to London was also a great advantage, as we could maintain contact with cultural activities in the capital, both Jewish and general. Also well known personalities would be brought to the College as visitors, both to inspire the students and staff, as well as an excuse to show off this new Jewish public school.[155]

Nagley began at Carmel from its inception in 1948, and in addition to teaching French, Latin and P.E., he would also teach Hebrew.[156] At Carmel, he also organised basketball, stationery and pocket money.[157] A pupil recollects, "[He was] the first inhabitant with his wife, and later two children, of a flat in North Court. Owned the first TV set I ever saw. Think he may have been form master of the Remove. Either the first or second

---

154. There is receipt for £4 4s. 0d to cover his travelling expenses for this interview in London.
155. "My Name is Aaron," op. cit., pp.5–6.
156. Carmel College Senior School, sample school reports, summer 1950 – summer 1951, forms 2 – 3, (name withheld); Letter from Nagley, op. cit.
157. Old Carmeli Association, Bulletin no.3, 5 October 1954, p.2.

Harold Nagley with a Group of Carmel College Pupils
Teacher: *Harold Nagley.* Back row L to R: *Freedland, Feltz, Boxer,*
Mizrahi, Caller? Middle row L to R: *Oberman?, Colin Gold, —, —,*
Fischer, Law, Ziff. Front row L to R: *Wolfson, Sperber, Davis*

summer holiday, he took a group of students to France on the first school
trip. It was great success."[158]

In the course of his career, Nagley received a number of certificates and
medallions from the "Royal Life Saving Society."[159] This indeed became
useful in Carmel as it is reported that "his [Nagley's] main claim to fame
in student folklore was rescuing one of the pupils, 'Scotty Freeman,' who
got into difficulties on a school trip to the municipal swimming pool in

---

158. E-mail from an early pupil (requested anonymity), 27 September 2013.
159. Letter from Nagley, op. cit.

Newbury."[160] Alan (Scotty) Freeman confirms the accuracy of this piece of "student folklore."[161]

In 1951, he applied to be Headmaster of the Liverpool Hebrew Day School. In his letter of recommendation, Kopul wrote of him:

> His work in the School can be described as educational pioneering. He is one of the most stable, reliable and conscientious persons I have met.
>
> In everything that he has undertaken, whether in teaching, school administration, physical training, games or other out of school activities, he has shown exceptional organising and administrative ability and efficiency of rare quality.
>
> He is a natural teacher and a natural disciplinarian. He has been extremely popular with both pupils and staff. I cannot speak too highly of his work or over-estimate what an important asset he has been to Carmel College.
>
> On the Hebrew side of the School he has been responsible for training boys for Bar mitzvah and has in many cases achieved remarkable success. He has been of service to us in the Hebrew curriculum although he was not originally engaged for that purpose. As one who has advocated Hebrew schools for many years and has been engaged in their establishment, I am able to say that Mr. Nagley possesses that combination of modern culture and traditional outlook which enables him to plan and direct a Hebrew school along the desirable course.
>
> I have always felt that one day he would seek a Headmastership, for which he is so well suited, and whilst being happy for his sake that this opportunity has arisen, I regret that this will mean his departure from Carmel College.[162]

He left Carmel in the summer of 1950, and at a later date after the Old Carmeli Association was established he became the first Associate Member[163] and later one of its Vice Presidents.[164]

Nagley was appointed to the position of Headmaster of the Liverpool Hebrew Day School which he took up in 1951. In 1957 when the King

---

160. Recollections of Jeremy Rosen, chap.1.
161. E-mail from Alan Freeman, 15 July 2014.
162. Testimonial for Harold Nagley from KR, 19 March 1951.
163. Old Carmeli Association, Bulletin no. 3, 5 October 1954, p.2.
164. The Old Carmeli Year Book 1977, p.2.

David School was opened in the Childwall district of Liverpool, to his "amazement" he was not appointed as Headmaster. He remained at the Liverpool Hebrew Day School until 1961, meanwhile applying for other positions and received the position of Vice-Principal of the Mount Scopus College in Melbourne. This meant moving to the other side of the world and it took his wife eighteen months to decide! Just three years later, the position of Principal at Moriah College in Sydney was advertised. Nagley applied and was accepted.[165] He remained there until he retired, aged 65 in 1978.[166]

Nagley died on 6 November 1989,[167] at the age of 76.

DR. FRIDOLIN MORITZ MAX FRIEDMANN

Friedmann was born on 2 June 1897 in Burgkunstadt Barvaria in Germany to Louis and Rosa Friedmann.[168] When he was a child, he moved to Munich[169] and went to the State Secondary School Munich Abiturium.[170] During the First World War he fought in the trenches where he was slightly wounded[171] and was awarded the Iron Cross. On this, Spencer Batiste writes that "I recall Dr. Friedmann illuminating a lesson on 20th century history by producing the Iron Cross which he had been awarded in the German trenches of the First World War. It didn't protect him from the Nazis. Suddenly history came alive."[172]

Friedmann then studied at the German Universities of Munich, Heidelberg, Erlangen and Cologne, and in 1925 received a doctorate from the University of Erlangen on a topic connected with Moses Mendelssohn.[173] He passed the First State Exam, which is a science examination for teachers for Higher Schools, in Cologne in July 1928, and a Second State Exam, which is a pedagogical examination, in Berlin in September 1929, and in the following month received a teacher's certificate for High

---

165. "My Name is Aaron," op. cit., pp.7–8.
166. Ibid., p.12.
167. E-mail from Phillip Nagley, 26 June 2013.
168. British Certificate of Naturalisation dated 6 October 1947.
169. *In memory of F.M. Friedmann*, (Oxford, 1978), [henceforth FMF], p. v.
170. E-mail from Warwick School, 25 January 2013.
171. FMF, p. v.
172. Recollections – Spencer Batiste, p.3.
173. FMF, p. v.

Schools.[174] He also did scholarly research in Königswusterhausen near Berlin.[175]

In November 1925 Friedmann received his first teaching appointment, at the Odenwaldschule,[176] a progressive boarding school in Heppenheim,[177] founded in 1910. Although he was only there for one year, he is listed in a Wikipedia article[178] on the school, as one of three notable staff members. This was followed by his teaching at a grammar school in Königswusterhausen near Berlin,[179] and then at the Samson School which was a Jewish boarding school at Wolfenbüttel near Brunswick[180] which had been established in 1807.

In April 1932, he joined the staff of the Jüdisches Landschulheim Caputh, a Jewish co-educational boarding school near Potsdam, which he developed in 1933 when Jewish children were forced to leave the German state schools. There he taught German and History, and he eventually became its headmaster.[181] A month after joining this school, Friedmann was granted a teaching certificate from the Potsdam school administration.[182] He remained in this school until April 1937.[183]

He then moved to the Oberschule der Jüdischen Gemeinde zu Berlin, which was a secondary school in the Wuilsnackerstrasse newly founded by the Jewish community, where he taught until May 1939.[184]

In 1938–1939, Friedmann led some kindertransports to England. He managed to get out of Germany in the summer of 1939, and he immigrated to England. After arriving in England, he learned English at the Regent Street Polytechnic and then worked with Youth Aliyah, at first in Ashford Kent, and when this became a proscribed area, the Youth Aliyah group moved to Bydown near Swimbridge in Devonshire. During this period he was briefly interned as an enemy alien, and he was upset that his release "came a few days too early as it interfered with a play he was producing in the internment camp."[185]

174. E-mail from Warwick School, op. cit.; Wikipedia – Fridolin Friedmann.
175. Wikipedia – Fridolin Friedmann.
176. E-mail from Warwick School, op. cit.
177. FMF, p. v.
178. Wikipedia – Odenwaldschule.
179. FMF, p. v.
180. Wikipedia – Fridolin Friedmann.
181. FMF, p. v.
182. Wikipedia – Fridolin Friedmann.
183. E-mail from Warwick School, op. cit.
184. FMF, p. v; e-mail from Warwick School, op. cit.
185. FMF, pp. v, 12, 34.

He then taught (his appointment being classed as "temporary") mainly German, but also History and the History of Arts, in Warwick School (which is one of the oldest boys' school in England with a history dating back nearly 1,100 years[186]), from September 1941 to October 1945,[187] (which was when the former teacher of German returned from the Armed Forces). In addition, Friedmann would produce the annual Shakespeare play at the school.[188] Even many decades later, he was still spoken about in Warwick School, as Marta Dannheisser relates:

> On hearing that I had a friend [Friedmann] who, about 30 years ago, had been a master at Warwick School, my grandson, who is a pupil there, enquired about his name. I did not imagine that it would mean anything to him. However, when he heard the name, he said 'Friedmann, Oh, they still talk about him at the school, he was so good at drama and getting up plays.'[189]

Not unexpectedly, his involvement in drama was remembered more than his teaching of German! However, sporting activities were not his specialty, as recorded by his nephew Walter Black, "His spell on games duties as referee led to the most appalling breaches of the rules of cricket and soccer."[190]

The British Government had given a permit for 1,000 children, who were survivors of concentration camps, and Friedmann took charge of some of them in Wintershill Hall, Southampton, and at a later date in Northern Island.[191] At the latter place, he wrote and produced a play about Pharaoh and Joseph which was acted by the boys and was put on for the Jewish community.[192] At that period he received the nickname "Ginger Friedmann,"[193] no doubt because of his ginger colouring. From August 1946 to July 1948 he taught at Bunce Count, a boarding school which had moved in 1933 from Southern Germany to Kent, and whose pupils were refugee children from Germany;[194] at least part of this time, he was its headmaster, but the interference by the "boss" made his position there

---

186. Wikipedia – Warwick School.
187. E-mail from Warwick School, op. cit.; FMF, p.13.
188. FMF, p.13.
189. Ibid., p.29.
190. Ibid., p.34.
191. Ibid., pp. v-vi
192. Martin Gilbert, *The Boys* (London: Phoenix, 1997), p.328.
193. Ibid., e.g., pp. 315, 328, 366.
194. Ibid., p. vi.

ultimately untenable.[195] In October 1947, he became a naturalised British citizen.[196]

He joined Carmel in 1949,[197] where he taught history throughout the Senior School,[198] and (at least) in 1950 even in the Prep School.[199] Jeremy Rosen writes of Friedmann's teaching, "At Carmel he taught histrionically, acting parts and peppering his Germanic English with malapropisms."[200] On one occasion he related to the class how a bunch of crooks had nearly smothered him to death in a Paris hotel by lowering the roof of a canopy bed whilst he lay in it. Friedmann did it with such expression that the class believed that this was an occurrence that had actually happened to him. The only thing was that it was in fact a story by William Wilkie Collins![201]

When he began at Carmel, he was known as Doc Friedmann. However, this was only until one day when he gave a talk about Jesus and as a result, from then on, he was given the nickname "Yoshke."[202] Henry Law gives a different explanation for this nickname, namely, "because of his habit of opening his arms wide."[203] Friedmann did not only teach History, but he also taught English to the lower classes in 1950,[204] even though English was not his native tongue. In fact, Mollie Panter-Downes who interviewed him at Wintershill Hall at the beginning of 1946 wrote, "He speaks excellent, lively English, and his pronunciation is perfect except for an occasional confusion of the letters 'v' and 'w'."[205]

Friedmann was also involved with the cultural activities of Carmel. In November 1953, he delivered a paper to the Union Society which dealt with the life and philosophy of Socrates, and its impact on Greek civilisation,"[206] and two years later he gave a lecture to the same society on

195. AJR (Association of Jewish Refugees) journal, vol.11, no.6, June 2011, p.6.
196. British Certificate of Naturalisation dated 6 October 1947; London Gazette, 21 November 1947, p.5504.
197. Martin Gilbert, *The Boys*, p.315.
198. Carmel College Senior School, sample school reports, between summer 1950 and summer 1958, classes from form 2 upwards, (names withheld).
199. Carmel College Prep School, sample school report, summer 1950, form 1, (name withheld).
200. Recollections – Jeremy Rosen, chap.1.
201. Unwritten recollections of author. The story by Collins (1824–1889) was entitled "A Terribly Strange Bed" and it can be found in "Masterpiece Library of Short Stories" vol.8, pp.424–37.
202. Recollections – Jeremy Rosen, chap. 1. "Yoshke" is the Yiddish for Jesus.
203. Recollections – Henry Law, Carmel College days, part 1, p.4.
204. Carmel College Senior School, sample school reports, summer and autumn 1950, forms 2 – 3 (name withheld).
205. Mollie Panter-Downes, "A Reporter at Large – A Quite life in Hampshire," The New Yorker, 2 March 1946, p.52.
206. Carmel 1954, p.40.

Goethe.[207] He was also a great fan of the daily newspaper then called the "Manchester Guardian,"[208] but coming from the North of England, he had to wait till the afternoon for it to arrive.[209]

Although he was far from being strict in his ritual observance of Judaism, Friedmann did give it a lot of respect; he would always attend the Synagogue services on Shabbat and it was he who made the "hamotzi" aloud at the Shabbat meals.[210] George Mandel writes of Doc's attendance at the Carmel Synagogue in Greenham, "A moment or two after the beginning of the service the door opens and Dr. Friedmann comes in and tiptoes past the rows of seats with such an alarmed and guilty look on his face that one might almost take him for one of the schoolboys rather than one of the teachers."[211]

With regards to his observance of the dietary laws, Helmut Schmidt writes, "The delights of Carmel's kitchen were always limited but with the help of some London delicatessen shops Doc managed to maintain his own standards which at times deviated from those of a beth-din."[212]

Friedmann taught at Carmel until his retirement in 1961. After his retirement, he settled in Hampstead, London, and gave lectures on Jewish history at the Leo Baeck College. He returned briefly to Carmel in about 1966. He was then at the City Literary Institute, where he lectured until his death.[213] In this Institute, his acting abilities again came to the forefront. One of his students, Olga Noble, writes, "At times, as if by magic, his classroom – always well attended, since he was very popular – was transformed into a theatre hall and he himself into an actor when, in his presentation, a biblical, historical or mythical story became a colourful dramatic performance bringing to life long-dead protagonists."[214]

He died on 15 October 1976,[215] at the age of 79.

207. Carmel 1956, p.25.
208. Carmel Clarion, vol.1, no.1, (p.6, unnumbered).
209. Carmel Clarion, vol.1, no.3, (p.6, unnumbered).
210. 7 years, pp.31–32.
211. FMF, p.22.
212. Ibid., p.26; The Old Carmeli Year Book 1977, p.8.
213. FMF, pp. vi, 33.
214. Ibid., p.32.
215. Ibid., p. vi.

ROBIN MANFRED GILBERT

Gilbert was born on 13 October 1929[216] in the Willesden area of London[217] to Joseph and Carmel (née Epstein) Gilbert,[218] Joseph being a founder governor of Carmel College. David Stamler writes on Kopul's choice of the name "Carmel College," "As well as liking the alliteration, Kopul was not uninfluenced by the fact that the wife of the school's staunchest supporter, J. C. Gilbert, was called 'Carmel'. When asked if she was flattered by Kopul's choice, Mrs. Gilbert replied, 'Ask me in ten years time if I'm honoured'."[219]

He attended St. Christopher's School in Letchworth from April to July 1940, when he then went to the USA, presumably to escape wartime dangers. He returned to St. Christopher's in November 1943 and remained there until July 1947.[220]

Gilbert taught for a year at Carmel,[221] presumably 1949–1950. He then attended Balliol College Oxford University between the years 1950 and 1954, where in 1954 he took a Third Class Honours degree in Oriental Studies (Arabic and Turkish), (which became an M.A. in 1958).[222] In that same year (1954), he was appointed headmaster of the Selim School in Aden,[223] where he remained until about 1956. Whilst in Aden, he worked "under cover" to help with the emigration of the Jews from Aden.[224]

At that time, Gilbert began his long association with ORT, which extended for over forty years. His first activity was for the Ethiopian Jews when he organised a vocational training programme for them in the Gondar region of Ethiopia.[225] Also there he worked "under cover" to assist with their emigration.[226] Two years later he was sent to Morocco again to pioneer vocational training. Then in 1960 to Geneva as Director of the ORT Anières Institute for Teacher Training, where students were trained in fields such as electro-mechanics and industrial design. Two years later,

---

216. The Balliol College Register (Oxford University), third edition, 1900–1950, p.478.
217. General Register Office index, Births registered in October, November and December 1929, p.G-342.
218. Ibid., Marriages registered in January, February and March 1925, pp. E-174, G-209.
219. Memories of KR, p.101.
220. E-mail from Old Scholars of St. Christopher's School, 30 November 2012.
221. Jewish Chronicle, 6 August, 1954, p.5. He appears in the staff photograph taken at Greenham in 1950.
222. E-mail from Balliol College, Oxford, 28 November 2012.
223. Jewish Chronicle, 6 August, 1954, p.5.
224. E-mail from Brian Elias, 20 May 2013.
225. World ORT, obituary, 17 Jan 2006; Jewish Chronicle, obituary, 17 March 2006, p.68.
226. E-mail from Brian Elias, 20 May 2013.

Robin was back in Asia, this time in India, where under his leadership at the Sir Eli Kadoorie School in Mumbai (Bombay), boys were trained in mechanics, carpentry and draughtsmanship, whilst girls learned hairdressing and secretarial skills. From 1965 until he retired in June 1997 (with a gap of 6 years in about the middle of this period), he worked at various ORT administrative positions in Geneva and London, finally becoming the Consultant to the director-general.[227]

Gilbert died in Geneva on 11 January 2006, at the age of 76, and was buried in the Jewish cemetery there.[228] In his obituary he was described as

> a lovely man, a gentleman; highly educated, an intellectual who had a great interest in literature and the arts . . . No matter how busy he was, he was always kind and pleasant and was a highly trusted and capable moderator at major meetings. His exceptional fluency in French meant that he was also called upon, from time to time, to act as a translator, which role he executed, as he did with so much else, with tremendous skill.[229]

Robin was also praised by his long time friend Brian Elias:

> Robin truly had the capacity to make a difference to the lives of people around him, and more significantly, to the lives of hundreds of people he did not know at all. He was charming, good looking and highly intelligent with a good sense of humour, and was someone who took great interest in other people's lives. He cared enormously about justice and fairness. He was immensely cultured and loved reading and art. These interests remained with him throughout his life.[230]

ESRA SHERESHEVSKY

He was born on 4 May 1915 in Königsberg (now Kaliningrad), East Prussia, Germany, to Joseph Salomon and Rachel Shereshevsky,[231] and was the youngest of nine children. After the Nazis rose to power, his entire family went to Eretz Yisrael. However, before joining his parents and

---

227. World ORT, obituary, op. cit.; Jewish Chronicle, obituary, op. cit.
228. Ibid; ibid.
229. World ORT, obituary, op. cit.
230. E-mail Brian Elias, 20 May 2013.
231. British Certificate of Naturalisation dated 25 January 1952.

siblings, Esra spent two and a half years learning at the Telz Yeshiva in Lithuania.[232] In Eretz Yisrael he studied at the Hebrew University and the Mizrachi Teachers' College in Jerusalem.[233] His first degree was in physical training and his second in teaching. He also became a member of the Haganah and was distinguished as a marksman.[234]

At the beginning of 1946, Shereshevsky was sent by the Mizrachi World Organisation to Sydney Australia to conduct and develop the first Jewish Day School in Bondi[235] (forerunner of Moriah College) and he remained there until the beginning of 1950 when he tendered his resignation and went to England to take up a position in Carmel College.[236] He began there in June 1950,[237] and taught Jewish Studies to the various classes.[238] He noticed that the initial letters of the school motto B'chol Derochecha Daeihu were bet daled bet, which spelled "badad," and hence the school song has the line "da BADAD tamid yanchecha."[239] In January 1952, he became a British naturalised citizen.[240]

When Shereshevsky left Carmel in the summer of 1953, the school magazine "Badad" wrote about him:

> Once again [the earlier case was Neuschloss] Dropsie College, Philadelphia, has captured one of our most popular masters. This time it is Mr. Shereshevsky, the Head of our Hebrew Department. His true vocation is undoubtedly Hebrew Instruction. At one time, however, he endeavoured to show a P.T. class the correct way to jump a vaulting-box and broke his wrist in the process!
>
> Mr. Shereshevsky has inspired everyone with an eternal awe for the Dagesh, and an interest in the gems of Hebrew Literature.

232. Esra Shereshevsky, *The Sage of Leipzig* (Jerusalem: Rubin Mass, 1993), p.74.

233. Ibid.

234. Jewish Exponent (Philadelphia), obituary, 3 July 2008. However, this obituary gives no details from which Universities he received these degrees. Furthermore, the Register of Students 1955–56, of Dropsie College, whilst giving the degrees of other students, does not quote any degrees for Shereshevsky. All that it states after his name, is that he had studied at the Mizrachi Teachers' Training College in Jerusalem and at the Hebrew University.

235. Shereshevsky, *The Sage of Leipzig*, op. cit., p.74.

236. Jewish Exponent, op. cit.; Suzanne D. Rutland, *If you will it, it is no dream – The Moriah Story 1943–2003*, pp.35–36; e-mail from Phillip Nagley, 24 July 2012.

237. Rau letters, 16 June 1950.

238. Carmel College Senior School, sample school reports, spring 1951 – autumn 1952, forms 3 – 5, (name withheld).

239. Related to the author whilst at Carmel College.

240. British Certificate of Naturalisation dated 25 January 1952; London Gazette, 11 March 1952, p.1405.

We are indebted to him for instructing the Perek Yomi and we assure him that it will continue in the tradition he has established.[241]

Perek Yomi was a voluntary group at the school in which every day the pupils would study a chapter of Nach. The author heard that they had begun with the Book of Samuel.[242]

In his book "So Strange My Path," Abraham Carmel writes at some length on Esra:

> The staff [at Carmel] also included a most fascinating character from Galilee, living today in the United States. Nobody ever used his full name, a matter of at least twenty letters, and we all called him 'Sherry' for short. Like so many Israelis, Sherry was a born politician. Notwithstanding a singularly warm and generous nature, his greatest delight was the dangerous amusement of creating situations within the community. He was a great cat-lover. His room was a regular stray cats' home, and we, his colleagues, used to fancy that from his perpetual association with felines he was gradually developing both the outward features and the inward characteristics of that testy species. However that may have been, Sherry, having touched off a first-class row, would purr very much in the manner of the innumerable pussycats he had taken under his protection. And when challenged about his intriguings, he would display a broad, disarming grin that melted your wrath as the sun dissolves butter. With a wave of the hand he would simply utter the magic formula 'Nah, nah!' which was his final dismissal of all accusations."[243]

Even after leaving Carmel, Esra did not forget the school. Three years after he had left, the Carmel magazine reported, "We were pleased to see an old master Mr. Shereshevsky who came down and visited us this term. Mr. Shereshevsky taught Hebrew at Greenham."[244]

Following Carmel, he went to Dropsie College as a student[245] and was

---

241. Badad, p.3.
242. Unwritten recollections of author.
243. Abraham Carmel, *So Strange My Path*, p.158.
244. Carmel 1956, p.6.
245. The Dropsie College for Hebrew and Cognate Learning, Register 1956–1957 (Philadelphia, 1956), p.62, Students 1955–1956.

in 1957 awarded the degree of Ph.D. for a thesis entitled "Rashi as teacher: interpreter of text and molder of character."[246]

Shereshevsky was later a member of the faculty at Gratz College where he remained for many years. There he taught mostly Hebrew Language and Hebrew Literature, which included Bible and Classical Literature. He also taught the same subjects at the Jewish Community High School [JCHS] of Gratz College.[247]

He eventually became professor at Temple University where he chaired the Department of Near Eastern and Hebrew Studies,[248] and he was one of the first professors to establish Hebrew as a full course of study at an American University.[249] He authored several books including "Rashi: The Man and his World,"[250] and wrote more than 120 articles on Hebrew and Jewish education. He spoke twelve languages and published in six.[251]

In 2004, he returned to Israel, which since 1950, he had visited more than 100 times. He died in Jerusalem on 28 February 2008 at the age of 92.[252]

DR. MARTIN PURLEY

He was born on 21 March 1909 in Breslau in Germany (which is today Wroclav in Poland) to Salo and Rebecka Perle.[253]

Whilst still at kindergarten age, Purley learned to read at home. Since there was no Jewish school at the time in Breslau, he attended the Catholic Realschule (elementary school) between the years 1915 and 1918. When he was nine years old he transferred to the Koenig Wilhelm Gymnasium, where he matriculated in 1927. He also took part in the activities of the Ezra youth movement. For his higher education, he studied English, History, and Geography at Breslau University between 1927 and 1928, and at Cologne University between 1928 and 1929. At the same time, he studied religious subjects at the Jewish Theological Seminary, and was awarded a certificate at the Jewish Teachers Seminary in Cologne which qualified

---

246. E-mail from Pennsylvania University, 22 January 2013.
247. E-mail from Gratz College, 23 January 2013.
248. Shereshevsky, *The Sage of Leipzig*, op. cit., p.74.
249. Jewish Exponent, obituary, op. cit.
250. e.g., "Malmad" library catalogue.
251. Jewish Exponent, obituary, op. cit.
252. Ibid. His obituary in the "Jewish Exponent" states that whilst at Carmel he gained two additional degrees at Oxford University, a degree in law and a Ph.D. in Latin and Greek. Oxford University, however, has no record of him. (E-mails from Degree-conferrals Oxford University, 22 and 23 January 2013).
253. British Certificate of Naturalisation dated 27 July 1946.

Carmel College Teaching Staff at Greenham – circa 1950. Back row L to R: *Roberts, Friedmann, Stamler, Israel Cohen.* Front row L to R: *Robin Gilbert, Rapstoff, Landau, Ewart, Kopul, Nagley, Gita Cohen, Kenneth Burrows*

him to be a teacher for Hebrew classes. Between 1929 and 1930, he attended lectures at University College of London University, and also at Jews' College, London. After the summer of 1930, he returned to Breslau University where he continued his studies and in 1933 was awarded a doctoral degree for his thesis entitled, "Die Hyperbel und ihre Verwendung bei Shakespeare" (The hyperbola and its use by Shakespeare).[254]

Following the receipt of his doctorate, Purley taught between 1933 and 1937 at the Jewish Secondary School in Breslau. Came 1938 and he left Germany for England and for two years taught at the Aryeh House School in Brighton.[255] Alan Greenbat remembers him as his Hebrew teacher there.[256]

---

254. Curriculum Vitae of Martin Purley, published as the last page of his thesis; e-mail from Martin Purley's daughter Rebecca Kohn, 4 April 2013.
255. E-mail from Rebecca Kohn, op. cit.
256. E-mail from Alan Greenbat, 8 April 2013.

After the start of the Second World War, as with many Jews who had fled from Hitler and came to Britain, he was interned in the Isle of Man as an "enemy alien!" On this Alan Greenbat recollects, "I remember very clearly how one day in 1940, the police came, took him away, and he was – as far as I know – interned on the Isle of Man."[257]

Following his release, Purley served in the Pioneer Corps in the British Army for five years.[258] Even though he was in the Army, he did not forget his former pupils, as Alan Greenbat records, "When I had my bar mitzvah in 1942, I received a bar mitzvah gift from him in the form of a Hertz Siddur, but I had no means of knowing where he was, in order to thank him."[259] After D-day, he served as an interpreter to a large Prisoner of War camp, first in France and then in Belgium. At that period, during his free time, he taught and helped in Jewish orphanages in Antwerp and later in Brussels.[260]

After the war, Purley was in 1946 a Madrich (counselor) at the Sunshine Hostel for children from the Kindertransports. It was there that he met his wife, Ilse Wohlforth, who was the Housemother there, and they were married in the autumn of 1946.[261] Dorothea Shefer, whose parents had also, at some time, been warden and housemother of the Sunshine Hostel, remembers the Purleys and describes them as "very nice, kind, modest people and very observant Jews."[262]

A few months prior to getting married, he became a naturalised British citizen.[263] About that period he taught at the North West London Jewish Day School in Minster Road Hampstead, and in September 1947 he joined the staff of the North West London Jewish Grammar School in Willesden Lane, where he taught Geography and Modern Hebrew.[264] Also at that period he taught at the Warm Lane Hebrew Classes in Cricklewood Synagogue.[265]

In 1950 Purley joined the staff at Carmel.[266] He taught a whole variety

257. Ibid.
258. E-mail from Rebecca Kohn, op. cit.
259. E-mail from Alan Greenbat, op. cit.
260. E-mail from Rebecca Kohn, op. cit.
261. Ibid.; General Register Office index, Marriages registered in October, November and December 1946, pp.P-33, W-421.
262. E-mail from Dorothea Shefer, 7 April 2013.
263. British Certificate of Naturalisation dated 27 July 1946.; London Gazette, 20 September 1946, p.4758.
264. E-mail from Dr. Marcel Weinstock, 22 July 2013.
265. E-mail from Rebecca Kohn, op. cit.
266. Ibid.

of subjects in the Prep School at Crookham. These were Jewish Studies, Geography, History, Mathematics and French.[267] He was also the form master of class 3 of the Prep School.[268] An Old Carmeli, Emmanuel Grodzinski, writes that Martin Purley's "wife knew my mother from their schooldays in Switzerland, so whenever he went to London, he would go to the Grodzinski shop in Hendon, and bring me back fresh black bread and butter sandwiches."[269] (Butter was still rationed in those days![270])

After three years at Carmel, his family went in 1953 to live in Israel, and during the following thirty years, including well past his pension age, Purley taught English in Tel-Aviv at Zeitlin School, Talpiot School, and Yeshivat Hayishuv Hachadash.[271] His address in Tel-Aviv was in Frishman Street, and a number of his former pupils at Carmel, including Jeremy Rosen, David Shaw, and Emmanuel Grodzinski visited him there.[272] On his teaching English in Tel-Aviv, his daughter writes:

> Though employed for teaching English only (since coming on Aliyah), he was a real educator, very dedicated, and brought in the Sidra and the Haftarah of that week at the beginning of every lesson. In his words: 'I wanted my pupils to see the human problems as depicted in English Literature in comparison with those in the Bible, e.g. temptation and crime in Macbeth.' Even today I meet people who tell me they were pupils of his, how much they loved and respected him.[273]

He also served in the Israeli army. His only son was killed in the Yom Kippur War but despite this tragedy, his daughter writes that he and his wife "had a smile for everybody and their home was always full of visitors."[274]

He died on 9 June 1987 at the age of 78.[275]

---

267. Carmel College Prep School, sample school reports, spring 1951 – spring 1953, forms 1, 2 and 4, (name withheld).
268. Ibid., autumn 1952, form 3 (name withheld).
269. E-mail from Emanuel Grodzinski, 8 March 2013.
270. 1954: Housewives celebrate end of rationing (Internet).
271. E-mail from Rebecca Kohn, op. cit.
272. E-mails from Jeremy Rosen, 13 March 2013, David Shaw, 24 January 2013 and Emmanuel Grodzinski, 11 March 2013.
273. E-mail from Rebecca Kohn, op. cit.
274. Ibid.
275. Ibid.

MATHIAS LANDAU

He was born in Germany[276] to Edmund and Marianne Landau. His father was one of the most prominent mathematicians of his generation, and was likely a descendant of Rabbi Yechezkel Landau of Prague, who was known as the "Noda Be-Yehudah," and was one of the world's leading rabbis of his time, or alternatively, he was a descendant of Rabbi Yechezkel's brother.[277] Marianne was the daughter of Paul Ehrlich, who in 1908 shared the Nobel Prize for Medicine.[278]

Mathias' school education was at Schule Schloss Salem[279] in Germany, and he was there at the same time (1933) that Prince Philip, the husband of Queen Elizabeth, studied there.[280] Mathias was involved with the building of the bridge across the Bosphorus.[281]

A pupil has recollections of him, "Reputed to have fought in the Spanish Civil War, but this may be apocryphal. . . . [He] possibly qualified at Gottingen, but I'm a bit hazy about this. Wrote letters in dark blue ink on Royal Blue paper. Liked Lewis Carrol's symbolic logic."[282]

One of his pupils at Carmel was Michael Goitein and he writes about Mathias:

> At some point, late in my time at Carmel, Mr. Landau (designer of the angle tri-sector) was my math teacher. He was an accomplished mathematician who, during school holidays, would go to Cambridge and work on their computer, EDSAC (standing for Electronic Delay Storage Automatic Calculator). He may have been interested in solving problems in queuing theory; I seem to remember his telling me about the problem of traffic bunching up on a busy highway. EDSAC was developed at the University of Cambridge and put into operation

276. Telephone conversation between author and David Lewin, 20 September 2012. Lewin estimates that Landau was born between about 1910–1920.
277. M. Zelcer, "A.A. Fraenkel's Philosophy of Religion," Hakirah (Flatbush, New York), vol.12, Fall 2011, p.216, fn.15.
278. Sanford L. Segal, *Mathematics under the Nazis* (Princeton University Press, 2003), chap.8, p.454.
279. The school was established by the educator Kurt Hahn with support of Prince Maximilian of Baden in 1920 and from the beginning accepted girls and boys. Under the Nazi regime, Hahn (who was Jewish) was forced to emigrate to Scotland where he founded the British Salem School of Gordonstoun.
280. Telephone conversation between author and David Lewin, 28 November 2012.
281. Ibid., 20 September 2012; David, *An Eye – or is it I? – on myself*, (London, October 2009), p.143.
282. E-mail from an early pupil (requested anonymity), 27 September 2013.

in 1949. It was the first practical stored-program electronic computer in the world, using rack upon rack of vacuum-tubes, almost filling a whole room. These days it would be hard to find a computer with as little power as EDSAC but, if one could, it would easily fit into the palm of one's hand if not on the tip of one's finger. Mr. Landau sent me the programmer's guide to the machine – a very slim document indeed which I still have. He encouraged me to try writing a very short program for it which he offered to try out for me on his next visit to Cambridge. Oddly, although I have some notes about the program I wrote, I have no memory of whether it worked.[283]

Landau was an addicted smoker. On Shabbat one is forbidden to smoke and for him, being an observant Jew, this was a serious problem, but he found a solution! He would get hold of dozens of capped empty milk bottles and would then spend a hour or two on Friday afternoon smoking furiously and blowing the smoke into these bottles and then sealing them. During Shabbat he would inhale the smoke![284] Regarding his smoking, he argued that "incipient cancer caused smoking, rather than the other way round."[285]

Following his teaching at Carmel, he taught during the second half of the 1950s at Whittingehame College in Brighton. His teaching there included Maths for the sixth form.[286]

One of Mathius' activities was "skiing now and then."[287]

David Lewin reports that Mathias "moved to live in Germany. Immediately there came an endless stream of letters to my [David Lewin's] mother – not a day passed without at least one – often several letters from him. And these letters were accompanied by cuttings from newspapers, postcards and all manner of other enclosures which he wanted to share."[288]

283. Recollections – Michael Goitein.
284. Recollections – Jeremy Rosen, chap.1; Recollections – Michael Goitein, fn.13.
285. E-mail Eldon Smith, 21 September 2012.
286. Lewin, *An Eye – or is it I? . . . op. cit.*, p.142; e-mails from Eldon Smith, 21 and 23 September 2012.
287. E-mail Eldon Smith, 21 September 2012.
288. Lewin, *An Eye – or is it I? . . . op. cit.*, pp.142–43.

F. C. HOUGHTON-DODD

He taught Singing, Piano, and Music. A pupil writes about him:

> Delightful piano teacher. Was also Musical Director of the Newbury and District Amateur Operatic Society and took a couple of us down to watch the rehearsals of 'The Yeomen of the Guard.' He was also involved with the composer Gerald Finzi in the Newbury String Players which Finzi founded. He brought them to Carmel for a concert.[289]

JACOBSON

A pupil has recollections of him walking "around dormitory duty with a cane, wearing a green gown said to be from the University of Barcelona. Feared and not much liked."[290]

CYRIL ISRAEL RAPSTOFF

He was born on 28 May 1926.[291] At the end of the Second World War, he was in the Royal Artillery and was a member of Kibbutz Shmaryahu[292] which was then situated in Wiltshire. His wife to be, Jeanette (Netta) Samuel, was also a member of this Kibbutz and at the end of June 1945 they were married at the Cathedral Road Synagogue in Cardiff.[293] At this wedding, Cyril, his father, and the best man all appeared in khaki. Following the ceremony a luncheon was held at the Cardiff Jewish Club, and the Hatikvah was sung by the Kibbutz Shmaryahu choir. The couple were planning to settle in Eretz Yisrael as Chalutzim.[294]

In 1950 Rapstoff joined the staff at Carmel[295] where his teaching in 1950/51 included History and Hebrew Studies to the Prep School.[296] Joe Dwek remembers him as a smallish man with no sense of humour.[297]

---

289. E-mail from an early pupil (requested anonymity), 27 September 2013.
290. Ibid.
291. Information from Cyril Rapstoff's widow Netta (Jeanette), January 2014.
292. Kibbutz Shmaryahu was a communal farm in England where young people prepared for agricultural work in an Israeli Kibbutz.
293. Jewish Chronicle, 22 June 1945, p.3.
294. Ibid., 6 July 1945, p.12.
295. Telephone conversation between author and Netta Rapstoff, 11 December 2013.
296. Carmel College Prep School, sample school reports, summer 1950 and spring 1951, (names withheld).
297. E-mail from Joe Dwek, 9 August 2013.

The family then moved to Birmingham where Cyril was in charge of the senior class at the Birmingham Hebrew School.[298] Whilst living in Birmingham, he studied during the academic year 1959/60 at the City of Cardiff Trinity College and received a Diploma in Psychology of Childhood. From 1962 to 1965, he continued his studies part-time at this College for a Diploma in Education, and he was required to retake one paper in June 1966.[299] The family lived in Birmingham until at least the beginning of the 1970s.[300] During at least the beginning of the 1980s, the family was living in Leicester[301] and Cyril was teaching, possibly at the Leicester Polytechnic.[302] One of his interests was archaeology.[303]

He and his wife then went to live in Israel in 1985[304] and in November 1996 Cyril, aged 70, died at the Hadassah Mount Scopus Hospital in Jerusalem.[305]

KENNETH BURROWS

He was at Carmel at about the beginning of the 1950s.[306] Possibly he taught English.[307]

HOWEL PUGH ROBERTS

He was born on 7 November 1884 in the parish of Llangollen in Wales, in the county of Denbigh,[308] the first son of Morris Henry Roberts, who was a house furnisher. His schooling was at Llangollen County School between the years 1896 and 1900, which was followed by Grove Park

---

298. Jewish Chronicle, 21 December 1956, p.16.
299. E-mails from Birmingham University, 16 and 21 January 2014. Birmingham University accredited such qualifications, (e-mail Birmingham University, 20 January 2014).
300. Jewish Chronicle, 15 January 1971, p.26.
301. Ibid., 26 June 1981, p.32.
302. Telephone conversation between author and Netta Rapstoff, 16 January 2014.
303. Information from Netta Rapstoff, January 2014.
304. Telephone conversation between author and Netta Rapstoff, 9 March 2014.
305. Jewish Chronicle, 22 November 1996, p.54.
306. There is a photograph of him with a group of pupils who include Joe Dwek, Kreps, Seruya and Yudkin.
307. E-mail from Malcolm Shifrin, 23 February 2014.
308. The General Register Office index for Births registered in October, November and December 1884, p.R-448, states that his birth was registered in this quarter of 1884 at Corwen which spans the boundaries of the counties of Denbighshire and Merionethshire. However, an e-mail from Jesus College Oxford dated 25 April 2013, states "he was born on 7 November 1885 in the parish of Llangollen," but also notes "Confusingly, he twice gives the year of his birth as 1884 (not 1885)." The year 1884, as shown in his birth registration, is obviously the correct year.

School in Wrexham between the years 1900 and 1903. At his Grove Park School he was Prefect of Boarders and was in the first eleven for association football and cricket.[309]

In October 1902, Jesus College Oxford awarded Roberts a Welsh Foundation Scholarship and he passed the Responsions[310] in December of that year.[311] He was admitted to that College on 17 (or 19) October 1903. In 1905, he was placed in the Second Class Honours of Classical Moderations, and in 1907 in the Third Class honours of Literae Humaniores.[312] The degree of B.A. was conferred upon him on 9 November 1907 (and this became an M.A. on 16 June 1910).[313] Whilst at Jesus College, he was in the College's association football team.[314]

In 1907 Roberts joined the staff of Dolgellau Grammar School, in Wales. There he taught Latin and Greek to all the classes, and French, English Language, and English Literature to the lower years.[315] He was there until 1909 when he became a teacher at St. Bartholomew's Grammar School in Newbury. On him, the school magazine wrote, "A further master on the classical side of the school to help the Headmaster is required, owing to the fast-growing numbers, and this work is to be undertaken by Mr. H P Roberts, BA, formerly scholar of Jesus College, Oxford."[316] Just over three years later the magazine reported, "Mr. Roberts left us this term in order to go abroad. He took a great interest in the School and was a constant visitor at the nets and at practice games, both cricket and football."[317] One year later, the magazine wrote, "Mr. Roberts re-appeared among us for a short time last term, but he has again departed, this time permanently."[318] His going abroad was in 1912/13, when he attended

---

309. E-mails from degree conferrals Oxford University, 9 April 2013 and Jesus College Oxford, 25 April 2013.

310. "Responsions" are examinations taken prior to entering Oxford University.

311. E-mail from Jesus College, op. cit.

312. The four-year Classics course taken at Jesus College is known as Greats or Lit. Hum. (Literae Humaniores), and is divided into two parts. The first-part exam, Mods (short for Moderations), is taken after five terms (i.e., two-thirds of the way through the second year); the focus is on knowledge of the classical languages and their literature, though there are also opportunities to study philosophy, ancient history, archaeology, and linguistics. (Jesus College Oxford, Classics – Internet).

313. E-mails from degree conferrals Oxford University, op. cit., and Jesus College, op. cit.

314. E-mail from Jesus College, op. cit.

315. E-mail from Dolgellau School, 19 April 2013.

316. Newburian (magazine of St. Bartholomew's Grammar School, Newbury), July 1909; the various quotes from this magazine were reproduced in an e-mail from St. Bartholomew's Grammar School, dated 6 March 2013.

317. Ibid., December 1912.

318. Ibid., December 1913.

Université de Caen and in 1913 he received a baccalauréat ès lettres.[319]

In mid-1915 Roberts married Kathleen Butler,[320] who was learning to be an artist. The couple therefore moved to London, when she enrolled in the Slade School of Art, and he became a teacher at the Stationers' Company School.[321] He remained there until he retired in the summer of 1945. He taught Classics and English and in his later years there he was the Senior Classics and English Master and in charge of the Sixth Form, During his last seventeen years at the School, he acted as a Second Master, and for two years he was President of the Association of Old Boys.[322] When he left the school, one of his former pupils wrote on his recollection of his lessons:

> Instead of driving us to translate isolated and uninteresting sentences from Latin into English, he said that we were strong enough to read Ovid and Virgil, and read them as if they were real books. Then again, instead of ploughing through the interminable notes to a few plays of Shakespeare, he began to tell us of Marlowe and Donne and Ben Jonson. We were startled at first, and disturbed, for our routine had been broken. We felt like mental serfs, afraid of the offer of freedom. This did not last long, for something must have told us that we had the rare good fortune to be in the presence of a great teacher.[323]

In describing Roberts in his Obituary, it states:

> He had no trace of foppishness and happily and habitually wore his trousers at half mast; yet he had great dignity and his discipline in class was as absolute as it was effortless. His compelling bass voice was always to be heard in Prayers. His skill as a mentor and his profound scholarship was something apparent even to the junior schoolboy. A true Celt, he was deeply interested in poetry.[324]

---

319. E-mail from Jesus College, op. cit.
320. General Register Office index, Marriages registered in April, May and June 1915, pp.B-181, R-318.
321. Individual Decisions, West Berkshire, 14 Feb 2008, Acquisition and Disposal Policy West Berkshire Museum, Fine Art, p.12.
322. The Stationers (school magazine of Stationers' Company School, London), obituary, July 1964, pp.3–4.
323. Ibid., July 1945, p.92.
324. Ibid., obituary, July 1964, p.4.

In addition to his class teaching, he actively participated in a number of extra-curricular activities. He would referee school football matches[325] and act as a judge in swimming competitions.[326] In addition to his umpiring cricket matches,[327] he would be a member of the staff team in matches against the pupils[328] and he even played when he was over 50 years old.[329] In one match, "Mr. Roberts, who had been heard to whisper that he did not know how to catch, gave himself the lie by taking an excellent one from a high hit . . ."[330] and in a match during the following year he "batted well until he was dismissed by a loud shout."[331] In an athletic competition held in May 1929, there was a Tug-of-War between staff and pupils, in which the staff were defeated. Roberts was in the staff team, but injured his knee during the event.[332] In his early years at the school, he was also active in the school's Cadet Corps.[333]

An important society in the school was the Macaulay Club, in which pupils and sometimes staff would deliver papers on all manner of literary subjects. During the course of the years, he took a great interest in the welfare of this Club,[334] often being in the Chair at its meetings,[335] and furthermore, he himself delivered a number of papers on subjects such as "Keats"[336] and "The Poetry of G.M. Hopkins."[337] Whilst he was at the school there were some "lean years" for this Club and Roberts was heard to remark on this "Those science fellows, yes, very nice fellows most of them, but you don't need brains to get through Matric' on the Science side."[338]

He was also active in the Literary and Dramatic Society and arranged the production of Shakespeare's "Julius Caesar," which ran in the school for three nights in 1917.[339] His wife, who had trained in Art, assisted with the décor.[340] In the following year, he put on a production of "The Tem-

---

325. Ibid., e.g. March 1916, p.11; April 1919, p.8.
326. Ibid., e.g. July 1916, p.29; December 1919, p.59.
327. Ibid., e.g. July 1918, p.37.
328. Ibid., e.g. July 1930, p.51.
329. Ibid., July 1938, p.61.
330. Ibid., July 1931, p.36.
331. Ibid., July 1932, p.37.
332. Ibid., July 1929, p.47.
333. Ibid., December 1921, p.63.
334. Ibid., e.g. December 1922, p.50; December 1924, pp.54–55.
335. Ibid., e.g. July 1931, p.26.
336. Ibid., April 1921, p.2.
337. Ibid., December 1934, p.69.
338. Ibid., March 1932, p.2.
339. Ibid., July 1917, p.26; Special issue, July 1935, p.28.
340. Ibid., July 1917, p.26.

pest."[341] He was often in the Chair for the Society's debates.[342] One such debate was "That, in the opinion of this house, Wireless Broadcasting has very little educational value,"[343] and in the following year he chaired a debate "The pessimist is more desirable than the optimist."[344] On one occasion there was a brains-trust, in which he was on the panel. Pupils submitting question were presumably supposed to include their names and forms. One pupil, however, did not do so. His question was whether "it was true that a drowning man comes up three times and goes down four." The other members of the team did not seem to know, but Roberts answered "if the identity of the questioner could be discovered, the society could investigate the problem practically."[345]

After he left Stationers' Company School, he returned to "help with the French teaching" at St. Bartholomew's.[346] It seems that due to the "War Emergency," the school was short of staff. After just one year Roberts left, and the school magazine wrote, "We are very grateful to him for all he did to restore the French to its old standard: how successful he was can be gauged by the School Certificate results . . ."[347] He continued to live with his wife in Newbury,[348] in what an Old Carmeli described as "an attractive, quite old, cottage on Greenham Common."[349]

About 1950, Roberts joined the staff at Carmel, which was then situated near his home in Newbury, where he taught English, Latin, and Greek.[350] He would cycle into school each day.[351] Abraham Carmel describes Roberts in his book, "So Strange My Path":

> [He was] a grand old man of the scholastic world who had emerged from retirement to assist at Carmel in those critical early years. A Welsh Non-conformist, Roberts was a man of firm and noble principles. His mere presence in the school was in itself an invaluable asset, quite apart from his devoted teaching. . . . I heard Roberts saying 'I

---

341. Ibid., July 1918, p.32; Special issue, July 1935, p.28.
342. Ibid., e.g. March 1916, p.15; April 1924, p.13; March 1926, p.16.
343. Ibid., April 1924, p.13.
344. Ibid., April 1925, p.7.
345. Ibid., July 1943, p.28.
346. Newburian, December 1945.
347. Ibid., December 1946.
348. Ibid.
349. E-mail from George Mandell, 4 March 2013.
350. Carmel College Senior School, sample school reports, autumn 1951 – summer 1952, form 4, (name withheld); e-mail from George Mandell, op. cit. – in it he stated that Roberts name last appeared on the school reports in the summer of 1953.
351. E-mail from John Fischer, 11 October 2012.

once taught in a school where there was one Jewish boy – only one, mark you, but ever such a nice boy.' He paused to roll one of the home-made cigarettes which were the pride of his life. 'Well,' he went on, 'one day I was teaching either Roman or Greek history, I forgot which. Anyway, we had been dealing with empires, and at the end of the lesson this delightful young chap came up to me and said, 'Sir, my father has an empire.' 'Your father has an empire? What on earth do you mean, boy?' I asked him . . . It turned out he meant that his father owned a large emporium in Guildford or somewhere![352]

When he left Carmel in the summer of 1953, the magazine "Badad" wrote about him:

Mr. Roberts exerted a remarkable degree of patience and perseverance in his tutelage. He imparted his pearls of wisdom to indolent young gentlemen, with a vivacity and an activity that was surprising. If [name of pupil] did not absorb any of Virgil's genius, it was not the fault of Mr. Roberts who punctuated his discourse with a conditioned reflex of the leg, which should have penetrated anything.[353]

At that year's Annual Speech Day, a presentation was made to him.[354]

Carmel College moved from Greenham since they realised that the noise from the aeroplanes of the American Air Force would have made remaining there as intolerable. Roberts was also living there and an Old Carmeli, George Mandell writes:

One summer holiday, either 1953 or (less likely) 1954, I went on a cycling holiday with a friend who I think had left Carmel by then, Victor Sperber, and on our way home (to London, from Torquay) we called in on HPR [Roberts] and had tea with him and his wife. They were very unhappy, even embittered. The American aeroplanes that were now parked on the Common used to rev their engines up for hours on end, according to Roberts, making life completely miserable for people who lived close by. He claimed that the compensation he'd been offered (by the Americans? the British Government? I don't remember) wasn't nearly enough for him to move to an equivalent home elsewhere because, of course, the amount he'd get for his ex-

352. Abraham Carmel, *So Strange My Path*, p.157.
353. Badad, p.3.
354. Jewish Chronicle, 31 July 1953, p.9.

isting home would be very little, because of the aeroplanes and, in general, the US air base. There seemed to be no future for him and his wife except to stay put and suffer the noise. I suppose that's what happened but don't know because I had no more contact with him.[355]

The OCA Bulletin of May 1957 reports that he was accepted as an Associate Member of the Old Carmeli Association.[356]

Roberts died on 7 April 1964[357] at the age of 79.

ROMNEY COLES

He was born on 23 March 1907[358] in the West Ham Forest Gate area of London[359] to Edward Reginald and Holly Georgina (née Berry) Coles.[360]

His schooling began at Godwin Road Elementary School in West Ham.[361] Beginning in April 1918 he attended Bluecoat School in Barnstable, but he was only there for less than one term (until June 1918), when his family returned to London.[362] He then went to West Ham Secondary School.[363]

Coles matriculated in June 1924 and began his studies at King's College London University in October 1926, his subjects being Chemistry and Physics. In 1928 he passed the first part of his examinations and in 1929 was awarded the degree of B.Sc. in Chemistry with First Class Honours.[364] In the 1960s the College still had records of his work as an undergraduate in the chemistry laboratories, even to the extent of which elements he failed to identify in qualitative analysis![365]

A motor cycle accident in the late 1920s resulted in a badly broken leg with multiple fractures, and this caused one of his legs to be shorter than

355. E-mail from George Mandell, 4 March 2013.
356. Old Carmeli Association, Bulletin no.5, 13 May 1957, p.3.
357. The Stationer, op. cit., July 1964, p.3.
358. E-mail from Romney Coles' son Revel, 23 November 2012.
359. General Register Office index, Births registered in April, May and June 1907, p.C-116; British 1911 census.
360. E-mail from Revel Coles, op. cit.; General Register Office index, Marriages registered in April, May and June 1905, pp. B-27, C-70.
361. E-mail from King's College London University, 8 January 2013.
362. E-mail from North Devon Record Office, 11 January 2013.
363. E-mail from King's College, op. cit.
364. E-mail from Kings College, op. cit.; List of Graduates of London University up to 1931, p.615.
365. Unwritten recollections of the author who saw these records when he was studying at the same department of that College.

the other one. He then changed from motor cycles to motor cars, because a few years later he bought an Austin 10 car which he owned until 1955.[366]

In the summer of 1934, Coles married Kathleen Radmore in the Romsey area, which is situated in the county of Hampshire[367] and, for a short period soon after the opening of Carmel College, Kathleen was a teacher in the Prep School.

Coles first taught at Taunton School in Southampton which, when the Second World War began, was evacuated to Bournemouth. In the early years of the war, he served with the ARP.[368] In September 1943 he was appointed as the Head of Science at the Kings School in Canterbury (the school was then in Cornwall) where he remained until July 1948.[369] (This school is considered to be the oldest extant school in the world, with a history going back over 1,400 years; amongst its many buildings is a Synagogue.[370]) According to Jeremy Rosen, Coles was passed over for promotion at this school.[371]

In 1948, he moved to Ireland to set up a new preparatory school in Headfort House. It opened in May 1949 with Coles as its headmaster.[372] Half a century later, he was still remembered there as the person who "designed and constructed the heated trolley that is still in use for carrying delicious hot food and plates to the Dining Room."[373] (Unfortunately, Carmel did not have the luxury of even one heated trolley!) However, he was only there for about one year. The reason for this short stay was suggested by the present Headmaster Dermot Dix, "I believe he had been under the impression that the new school (founded in 1949) would be a secondary independent (or 'public') school; but a decision was made – I think by Lady Headfort, the prime mover in setting up the school in her family's mansion – to run the school as a prep or junior school (up to age 13)."[374]

In the summer term of 1950, he became the head of Chemistry at Carmel,[375] and at a later date the Senior Master. He taught Chemistry

---

366. E-mail from Revel Coles, op. cit.
367. General Register Office index, Marriage registered in July, August and September 1934, pp.C-268, R-88.
368. E-mail from Revel Coles, op. cit.
369. E-mail from Kings School Canterbury, 2 January 2013.
370. Wikipedia – The King's School Canterbury.
371. Recollections – Jeremy Rosen, chap.1.
372. E-mail from Headfort School, 7 January 2013; e-mail from Revel Coles, op. cit.
373. Headfort School, 50th anniversary, newsletter.
374. E-mail from Headfort School, op. cit.
375. Jewish Chronicle, 30 June 1950, p.17.

throughout the Senior School,[376] and in his early years at Carmel, whilst the school was still at Greenham, he also taught Physics.[377]

During the early 1950s there was a lot of friction between the governors and Kopul, with the governors being dissatisfied with Kopul. However, in contrast, writes Jeremy Rosen, "They were very impressed by Romney Coles and they felt that he should be the academic head of the school rather than Kopul. I never heard my father criticise Coles, so I assume he was not party to the intrigue."[378] However, George Mandell, has a different version:

> I can give you a personal recollection: at the time there was a sort of joke, or bon mot, going round the school which went: 'Everybody said that now either Coles will have to resign or Kopul will have to resign, but in the event it was the Governors who resigned.' The row had to do with a dispute between Kopul, on the one hand, and Romney Coles, the Senior Master, on the other. The dispute was brought before the Governors, which is the background to the bon mot.[379]

In fact it would seem that Coles had great respect for Kopul, to the extent that although Coles would always address all the pupils by their surnames there were two exceptions, the Rosen boys – he would never call them "Rosen" but "Rooky" or "Mickey"; he obviously felt that to call out "Rosen" would be disrespectful towards Kopul.[380]

David Waldman, who was one of Coles' pupils and went on to get a Major Open Scholarship at St. Catherine's College Oxford[381] described Coles as "the perfect English gentleman and the greatest teacher one could wish for. He transmitted his passion to those of us who were privileged to do A-level Chemistry."[382] On Romney Coles' lessons the author recollects:

> For his lessons, there were no exercise books, one had to have a loose leaf file and the writing in it had to be precisely as he wanted. In a

---

376. Carmel College Senior School, sample school reports, various terms between summer 1950 to spring 1961, classes up to scholarship sixth (names withheld).

377. Ibid., summer 1950 – spring 1952, forms 2 – 4 (name withheld).

378. Recollections – Jeremy Rosen, chap.1.

379. E-mail from George Mandell, 4 March 2013.

380. 7 years, p.51.

381. Carmel 1961, p.6.

382. Recollections – David Waldman.

heading, the third letter had to go through the margin. In later years, he seemed to slacken on this particular requirement.[383] He made us learn by heart the periodic table of elements. We worked out a method of combining the chemical symbols into words – a type of mnemonic and this made it easier to remember. It began libebcnof, namgalsipscle, kcasctivcrmni. (No this is not Polish or some Balkan language!) Even today I still remember the periodic table because of this mnemonic.[384]

Jonathan Isserlin likewise writes, "I can still quote the Periodic Table (and not Tom Lehrer's version[385]) almost perfectly!"[386]

The author recollects how "Mr. Coles would also talk about the famous chemist, T. W. Richards, once commenting that he might have died. In fact, he had died long before that time – in 1928 – which was about the year that Mr. Coles had graduated."[387] Another pupil of his, Henry Law, writes how Coles' methodology would interest pupils in Chemistry:

> Romney Coles made Chemistry interesting. Wherever possible he would allow the pupils to do practical work. We would prepare samples all the compounds on the syllabus and each of us had his own collection of labelled test tubes containing our samples. Some were very beautiful, such as the coloured crystals of ferrous ammonium sulphate and the various alums. Since boys like collecting things, this was good psychology. Where the materials were regarded as too dangerous – such as the manufacture of sulphuric acid by the Lead Chamber process, he would set up the experiments on his own demonstration bench or in the glass fume cupboard. He was also keen on digressing, and would spend up to a third of a two-hour session talking around and off the topic. This was a certain way of ensuring that we remembered what we needed to know.[388]

The Advanced Level Practical examination consisted of a qualitative and a quantitative analysis. Coles called this "spot and vol" – spot the elements

---

383. 7 years, p.50.
384. Ibid., p.57.
385. Tom Lehrer is a songwriter and pianist. Amongst his repertoire is his singing "The Element Song" accompanied by pictures of the elements. It can be seen on YouTube on the Internet.
386. Recollections – Jonathan Isserlin.
387. 7 years, p.57.
388. Recollections – Henry Law, Carmel College days, part 1, p.5.

(qualitative analysis) and the volume (or concentration) of a material (quantitative analysis), and would every few weeks make the class do these exercises.[389] Michael Goitein, one of Coles' first pupils describes how Coles "served up" this material:

> I remember the laboratory exercises even more vividly than his classroom teaching. They were intellectual fencing matches. We performed quantitative analyses to measure such things as the concentration or pH of various solutions; and, most enjoyable of all, we were challenged to determine the composition of an endless stream of unknown compounds and mixtures. It was a battle of wits of Mr. Coles dreaming up fiendishly difficult and tricky problems, and we amateur detectives tasked with unraveling the mysteries.[390]

Another recollection of Goitein's involving Coles was "eking caffeine from tea leaves, which required boiling the tea leaves in open water for what seemed like hours, and which cemented my dislike of tea for many decades."[391]

He had an original way for the pupils to remember the formula for sulphuric acid which was in rhyme form. Even chemists resort to poetry!

> Once there was a chemist,
> A chemist he is no more;
> For what he thought was H_2O [water],
> was H_2SO_4 [sulphuric acid].[392]

Although when the school was at Mongewell, his teaching was limited to the Senior School, whilst the school was in Greenham, Coles would also give science lessons to the Prep School, even to the children aged seven. David Shaw writes on this:

> I remember following Mr. Coles to the lab for Physics in his long flowing robes flapping like angels wings. All the staff wore robes and quite often Mortar boards. He took his class of 7 year olds very seriously. For our first lesson on electricity . . . yes electricity, I can still

---

389. 7 years, p.61.
390. Recollections – Michael Goitein.
391. Ibid.
392. 7 years, pp.50–51.

see him pouring iron filings on a sheet of cardboard under which he had placed a magnet and explaining the patterns made by the Field, North and South Poles, etc. In his lessons he would occasionally do 'Chemical Magic.' There could be a bang followed by a purple plume of smoke from an unsolicited place.[393]

Once he complained that his Jewish calendar had let him down! It was towards the late afternoon during Chanukah and his class was in the middle of an examination, when they were summoned to the hall for the lighting of Chanukah candles. His calendar had not mentioned that candles were to be lit at a particular time![394]

In addition to his class teaching, he was responsible for the external and internal examinations at Carmel.[395] Another pie which Coles had his finger in – or should one say his whole hand, since he made it his exclusive pie – was the bells which rung day and part of the night throughout Carmel.[396] Michael Goitein recollects, "Other than Mr. Coles no one, but no one, was allowed to touch this splendid apparatus under pain of a punishment too dreadful to be articulated."[397]

As with many other teachers at Carmel, Coles was also the author of a book. It was called "Chemistry Diagrams" and was first published in 1948,[398] before he arrived in Carmel. Michael Goitein briefly describes this book, "Over the years he had made wonderfully artistic and meticulous drawings of a large number of industrial and natural chemical processes – steel production, the extraction of quicklime from limestone, the formation of stalactites and stalagmites and so forth."[399] On this book, the author recollects, "This was one of the textbooks which every pupil had to purchase and from time to time, the boys were given prep (the equivalent of homework in a day school) to copy out a particular diagram. I can say from personal experience that it was a lot of work!"[400]

During the summer and winter terms of 1950, Romney Coles' wife, Kathleen, was also on the staff. She was the form teacher for the seven year olds, and would teach them almost every secular subject, namely,

---

393. Recollections – David Shaw.
394. 7 years, p.39.
395. Unwritten recollections of author.
396. Recollections – Michael Goitein.
397. Ibid.
398. "Copac" library catalogue.
399. Recollections – Michael Goitein.
400. 7 years, p.50.

English, Maths, Geography, and Nature Study.[401] During the Nature Study lessons, she would utilise the waterfall in the grounds, and the pond where frogs and pond life abounded. In her Maths lessons she would teach the pupils the rudiments, and in her English lessons make sure that the pupils could do joined writing.[402]

Coles remained at Carmel until he retired in December 1967[403] and at some subsequent period he was made a Vice-President of the Old Carmeli Association.[404] After his retirement, he and his wife moved to Cala Murada in Mallorca,[405] believing, as a number of English retirees did, that the lower cost of living and fine weather would facilitate a comfortable old age.[406] There, he utilised his skill with his hands and constructed a beautiful wooden front gate for his house.[407] However, about eight years after moving to Cala Murada the Coles came back to England[408] disenchanted, having found themselves living not in the idyllic place they had hoped for. They then made their home in Oxfordshire,[409] where they lived until Coles died on 21 February 1990,[410] at the age of almost 83.

D. A. KENT

He taught Maths to (at least) form 2 of the Senior School during the summer term 1950.[411]

L. YEOMANS

He taught Maths to (at least) form 3 of the Senior School during the summer term 1950.[412]

401. Carmel College Prep School, sample school reports, summer and autumn 1950, form 1, (name withheld).
402. Recollections – David Shaw.
403. The Old Carmeli, no.4, 1967–8, p.7.
404. The Old Carmeli Year Book 1977, p.2.
405. E-mail from Revel Coles, op. cit.
406. Recollections – Michael Goitein.
407. Recollections – David Shaw.
408. E-mail from Revel Coles, 5 December 2013.
409. Recollections – Michael Goitein.
410. E-mail from Revel Coles, op. cit.
411. Carmel College Senior School, sample school report, summer 1950, form 2 (name withheld).
412. Carmel College Senior School, sample school report, autumn 1950, form 3 (name withheld).

MRS. GITA SHAHAR (NÉE COHEN)

She was born in Manchester on 25 May 1921 as Gita Cohen and became Shahar when she married Tuvia Shahar in Jerusalem in 1954.[413] Her primary schooling was in Margate[414] where her father Rev. Moshe Cohen was the Minister of the Margate Hebrew Congregation.[415] She attended Furzedown Teacher's College in London where she received a diploma in teaching.[416]

Her first teaching position was in the 1940s in the Avigdor Primary School in Stamford Hill London.[417]

When Carmel College opened, she was a teacher to the children of staff who, although they had reached the age of compulsory schooling, had not yet reached the Carmel Prep School age. However, this was not found to be successful and was discontinued.[418] During the academic year 1950/51 she taught at the Prep School, Hebrew, English, and Arithmetic and for at least the spring term 1951, she was the form mistress of the lowest class of the Prep School.[419] She left Carmel, very likely after the spring term of 1951.[420]

She then moved to Israel and taught in the Kadima School of Languages in Tel-Aviv,[421] and in 1954 married Tuvia Shahar in Jerusalem.

In January 1956, the Shahars arrived in Sydney, and both Tuvia and Gita joined the staff of the Moriah College.[422] In 1957, she was listed as one of the seven full-time teachers at the College, teaching both Jewish and secular studies. Amongst her classes was, at least, class 3. In 1958, she stopped teaching secular studies "for health reasons" and at the end of that year she resigned from the staff of Moriah College in order to start a family.[423] In March 1962, the Shahars moved to Sydney when Tuvia took up the position of Director of Jewish Studies at Mount Scopus College

---

413. E-mail from Gita (Cohen) Shahar's son Ravi, 27 August 2013.
414. Telephone call between author and Gita (Cohen) Shahar's brother-in-law Ludwig Nelken, 26 August 2013.
415. Jewish Year Book (London): e.g. 1933, p.235; 1937, p.211; 1940, p.216.
416. E-mail from Ravi, op. cit.
417. Ibid.
418. Recollections – Jeremy Rosen.
419. Carmel College Prep School, sample school reports, autumn 1950 and spring 1951, form 1 (names withheld).
420. There was a new form master for form 1 in the summer term 1951.
421. E-mail from Ravi, op. cit.
422. Suzanne D. Rutland, *If you will it, it is no dream – The Moriah Story 1943–2003* (Caringbah, N.S.W.: Playright Pub., 2003), p.55; Jewish Chronicle, 17 July 1964, p.10.
423. E-mail from Harold Nagley Moriah Heritage Centre, 18 November 2013.

in Melbourne,[424] and Gita taught at the Lubavitch Primary School in Melbourne.[425]

After about a year they returned to England[426] and she was appointed Headmistress of the Bnos Yerushalayim Girl School in Stamford Hill.[427] Following this in the 1970s[428] until at least 1989 she did remedial general subjects at the Yesodey Hatorah Girls School in Stamford Hill. The secretary of this school writes, "[She] was liked by all. She was a very fine, unassuming person and a very righteous woman."[429] In the 1980s she was a teacher in the Princess May Primary School in Stoke Newington,[430]

> During her lifetime she would spend hours on the telephone talking to women about their problems, listening with a sympathetic ear.[431]

She died in London in November 2002, at the age of 81, and was buried in Jerusalem.[432]

EMIL SCHLESINGER

Schlesinger was born in the Salford area of Greater Manchester in the spring of 1925,[433] to Rev. Victor and Rosa Schlesinger.[434] His schooling was at Stand Grammar School, where he enrolled in about 1936. The school records show that he was in the Lower Fifth (4th year) in July 1940.[435] He introduced tennis into this school.[436] He was the secretary of the Music Club, and from 1941 to 1943 he was a sub-librarian in the school library. He was also the recipient of a number of prizes, namely the Hutchinson reading prize in 1942, and the Latin prize in 1943. He passed the Northern Universities Joint Board High School Certificate.[437] His

---

424. Rutland, op. cit, p.66; Jewish Chronicle, 17 July 1964, p.10.
425. E-mail from Ravi, op. cit.
426. Jewish Chronicle, 17 July 1964, p.10.
427. E-mail from Ravi, op. cit.
428. Ibid.
429. E-mail from Yesodey Hatorah Girls Finance Office, 24 February 2014.
430. E-mail from Ravi, op. cit. The Princess May Primary School's records do not go back that far. (E-mail Princess May Primary School, 14 November 2013).
431. E-mail from Ravi, op. cit.
432. Ibid.
433. General Register Office index, Births registered in April, May and June 1925, p.S-147.
434. Telephone conversation between author and Emil Schlesinger's nephew Avigdor, 6 September 2012.
435. E-mail from Harry Wilkinson, 22 March 2013.
436. Telephone conversations between author and Avigdor Schlesinger, 26 and 27 August 2012.
437. E-mail from Wilkinson, op. cit.

studies continued at Manchester University where, in 1950, he received a lower second B.A. degree in French.[438]

Schlesinger began to teach at Carmel in 1950, where he became the senior French master in the Senior School.[439] In 1951 he also taught French, Latin, and English at the Prep School.[440] "The Young Carmelonian" writes of his teaching, "During his lessons he has shown himself to be a most broad-minded man who can give and take a good joke, whilst maintaining a high standard of work. When we hear the cry 'Stop chewing," we know that we are in for trouble."[441]

In addition, he was a Form Master[442] and a House Master,[443] and at Mongewell he was the House Master of the Study Block.[444]

As to be expected, from the time that he joined the Carmel staff, he was greatly involved with tennis. In the summer of 1953, the magazine "Badad" wrote on this subject, "A last word of appreciation to Mr. Schlesinger who has devoted much of his time and all his patience to organising tennis during the past two years."[445] He played in a tennis match against the pupils, and, one does not have to guess who won![446] During his last year at the school, he coached boys in tennis. The Carmel magazine writes:

> Mr. Schlesinger has been taking coaching [for tennis] this season, and has been very successful. As he is leaving this term, I would like to take this opportunity of thanking him for his ceaseless efforts in the sphere of tennis during the last four years. He has overcome many difficulties which faced us, and it has been a great pleasure to have worked under him. I think that above all his other activities in the School, Mr. Schlesinger will be remembered as the genial and patient Tennis Master who could have a good laugh on the court as well as a good game.[447]

---

438. E-mails from Manchester University, 5 December 2012.
439. Carmel 1955, p.5; Carmel College Senior School, sample school reports, autumn 1951 – summer 1953, autumn 1954, forms 1 – 5 (names withheld).
440. Carmel College Prep School, sample school reports, spring and summer 1951, form 4 (name withheld).
441. The Young Carmelonian, p.16.
442. Carmel College Senior School, sample school reports, autumn 1951 – summer 1953, forms 4 – 5 (name withheld).
443. Ibid., autumn 1952 and spring 1953, form 5 (name withheld).
444. The Young Carmelonian, p.16; Carmel College Senior School, sample school reports, spring – summer 1954, lower sixth form (name withheld).
445. Badad, p.9.
446. Carmel 1954, p.48.
447. Carmel 1955, p.49.

He left Carmel for family reasons in the summer of 1955[448] and went to teach French and German in Stand Grammar School,[449] the school where he had been a pupil. The then Headmaster, Dr. Geoffrey Barnes, writes that "[Emil] had special responsibility for the welfare of the Jewish boys, [who then were 20–25 per cent of the school population[450]] a function which he carried out with considerable efficiency and diplomacy, in fact we owed our good relations with the Jewish community in the area largely to his diplomatic skills."[451] On this subject, the Old Standians remember him "having to corall the Jewish boys while we had our pagan assembly. I often wondered what they did in that room? Did they have their own assembly or just read books?"[452]

There were some pupils at this school who would rag him mercilessly, and from the reminiscences of one of them, it can be seen that in later life the consciences of this alumnus and his colleagues pricked them. On this the alumnus writes:

> I was in 6LA in 1978 and 7LA in 1979 and I feel I and the rest of the form owe an apology to Mr. Schlesinger (French) for making his life hell. We were based in the huts at the back of the gym near the playground and carried out some rotten tricks when "Slaz" [Schlesinger] used to come to take the register each morning. Crimes included:
>
> Unscrewing the door from its hinges but leaving it in situ. When Slaz pushed, it fell flat shattering the glass. Piling all the furniture up in the centre of the room and exiting by the fire door so that all Slaz found was an empty room. Emptying the dry powder fire extinguishers onto the floor and again exiting via the fire door so there was a mysterious lack of footprints. Stealing the wheels of David End's Marlboro mini. Smashing the windows in the old huts with a ping pong ball (honest!)
>
> I can't remember which incident got me suspended during my mock "A" levels but I am eternally grateful for the revision time. I would never have passed without the time off!
>
> And so to the song, this was made up by someone and sung to Slaz. . . . It is to the tune of the Floral Dance:

448. Ibid.
449. E-mail from Geoffrey Barnes, 10 December 2012.
450. Ibid., 18 December 2012.
451. Ibid., 10 December 2012.
452. Stand Grammar School, Contributions from Old Standians (Internet).

> We're in a class in a grammar school
> We're in class and the teacher's a fool
> We're in 6LA and every day
> We start the day in the same old way
> Slaz comes in, the light goes on
> And then we sing the same old song
> Allez Allez Allez Le Slaz
> Allez Le Slaz and Allez Le Slaz[453]

On a more pleasant note, they also remember him as one who "organised the photographic society."[454] Dr. Barnes writes, "One of Emil's chief interests was amateur photography, and he provided us with a number of photographs of school events. It was his custom to provide a portrait photograph of each departing headmaster. His own photograph of me hangs in my study."[455]

When there was a school reorganisation in the area, Emil was promoted to the position of Head of Modern Languages at Bury Sixth Form College, a new college situated in the Wellington Road of Bury.[456]

He was also a lover of Classical Music. When he retired he would lecture, accompanied by slides, to non-Jews on Israel.[457]

He died in 1998 at the age of 73.[458]

LANG

He was a Jewish teacher who taught whilst the school was at Crookham.[459]

INGRAM

He taught music whilst the school was at Crookham and famously wrote on one boy's report "a waste of parent's money and teacher's time."[460]

---

453. Ibid.
454. Ibid.
455. E-mail from Geoffrey Barnes, 18 December 2012.
456. Ibid.
457. Telephone conversations between author and Avigdor Schlesinger, 26 and 27 August 2012.
458. Ibid.
459. E-mail from Alan Gold, 20 July 2014.
460. Ibid.

MS. J. GILBERT ROBINSON

She taught Elocution in the Prep School[461] between 1951 and 1953, and in the Senior School[462] in 1950 and 1951. She also taught Poetry in the Prep School.[463]

HELMUT DAN (REINHARD) SCHMIDT

He was born on 9 March 1915 in Beuthen, which was then at the south-eastern tip of German Silesia,[464] to Anselm and Elfriede Schmidt, his mother having British nationality.[465] He grew up in Silesia, and [before or at the beginning of (?)] the Second World War, he moved to Eretz Yisrael, where he worked with the German political scientist Richard Koebner.[466] During the Second World War, he served in the Jewish Brigade in Italy and in the Middle East, where his activities included intelligence work. Decades later, this intelligence work was to extricate him from problems when he went to visit his sister in the United States. His name was that of a suspected war criminal and only after he was able to show that he had been fighting on the side of the Allies, did they realise that he was not the Helmut Schmidt they were looking for![467]

At some period Schmidt took up Israeli citizenship.[468] He was awarded the degree of M.A. in History from the Hebrew University in 1941.[469] He was in Israel when the State was declared and fought in the War of Independence.[470] According to the "Jewish Chronicle," in 1950 he was a member of the Department of Modern History at the Hebrew University in Jerusalem.[471] Soon after, he left Israel and joined the staff at

---

461. Carmel College Prep School, sample school reports, summer 1951, spring 1952, autumn 1952 – summer 1953, forms 1 – 4 (names withheld).
462. Carmel College Senior School, sample school reports: autumn 1950 and summer 1951, form 3 (name withheld).
463. Carmel College Prep School, sample school reports, autumn 1952 and summer 1953, form 4 (name withheld).
464. In 1945 the city was transferred to Poland as a result of the Potsdam Conference.
465. British Certificate of Naturalisation dated 14 June 1956.
466. Recollections – Michael Bharier, Carmel Memories, chap.4.
467. Ibid.
468. see British Certificate of Naturalisation, where nationality is given.
469. Verbal information from Mador Bogrim, Hebrew University Jerusalem, 27 January 2013.
470. Recollections – Michael Ellman.
471. Jewish Chronicle, 11 August 1950, p.24. However, his name does not appear in the list of the "Academic Staff of the Hebrew University for the season 1949/50," (The Hebrew University of Jerusalem 1925–1950, semi-jubilee volume, April 1950). Koebner's name does appear (p.189), and it is possible that Schmidt was some sort of assistant to Koebner. There is also no mention

Carmel. From October 1950 to May 1953, whilst at Carmel, he studied at St. Catherine's College of Oxford University and on 18 July 1953 had the degree of B.Litt. conferred upon him.[472] In June 1956, he became a naturalised British citizen.[473]

The subjects he taught at Carmel included Economics, Geography, French, and Modern Hebrew.[474] With regards to the range of subjects that Schmidt could teach, Jeremy Rosen wrote that "he could teach almost any subject so long as he had a day to read up on it before starting to teach. I recall he was able to help a Swedish student to pass his GCE exams by teaching himself Swedish from a simple Swedish grammar one step ahead of his pupil."[475]

Michael Bharier wrote of his lessons, "He always coloured his geography lessons with glimpses of the history and historical personalities of the places he discussed. He knew many languages and I remember his teaching the class about the Rosetta stone."[476]

In the course of his teaching Geography, Schmidt would arrange "field trips." One of his trips took place in June 1955, which turned out to be a glorious summer's day, something which is not predictable in England! A number of locations were visited and these included the Anglo-Saxon Dorchester Abbey, the Roman Villa of Chedworth in Gloucestershire, the "model village" of Bourton-on-the-Water, which is a replica of the original Bourton right down to the last detail, and a Jacobite House with its secret hiding place.[477] There is no report of any pupil utilising this hiding place to avoid returning to Carmel!

When writing historical articles, Schmidt's advice was "criticise the sources."[478] Other advice he gave was to "teach first, then go into industry or the professions later." Neil Alton, to his detriment, did not take this advice, and admitted afterwards that Schmidt was right.[479]

---

of Schmidt's name in the booklets giving the list of lectures for the years 5705 (1944/45), 5706 (1945/46), 5707 (1946/47) – these are the only booklets which can be traced – Koebner's name appears in each of these three booklets.

472. E-mail from Degree Conferral, Oxford University, 18 December 2012.

473. British Certificate of Naturalisation dated 14 June 1956; London Gazette, 17 August 1956, p.4727.

474. Unwritten recollections of author; Carmel College Senior School, sample school reports, various terms between spring 1954 to summer 1959, classes from form 2 upwards (names withheld).

475. Recollections – Jeremy Rosen, chap.1.

476. Recollections – Michael Bharier, Carmel Memories, chap.4.

477. Carmel 1955, p.15.

478. Recollections – Michael Ellman.

479. Recollections – Neil Alton.

He was also a form teacher and as Michael Bharier explains, his pupils had to be spick and span:

> He inspected us, from our hair to our shoes, every morning and ex-pected us to be as meticulously groomed as himself. In all the time I knew him, he wore only one substantial pair of maroon shoes. These, like the man, never seemed to age. He would award us 'penalty points,' which he would inscribe in a little book, if we failed to meet his stan-dards of dress. He became quite attached to the class and remained in charge of us for three years.[480]

Jeffrey Fisher recollects a rather unpleasant encounter between Schmidt and a green sticky plant!

> We also did things (not always very nice) to teachers. Dr. Schmidt was a gentle soul who always taught wearing a gown. He taught Ge-ography but more important for me, he introduced me to Economics (in the 1950s, Economics started to be taught at schools, not a par-ticularly good idea – Economics is more a university subject), which interested me enough to go on and study Economics at university and take up a career as an economist.
>
> In the grounds of Carmel were all kinds of plants, some more inter-esting than others. One particularly interesting one – whose name I do not know, either in Latin (though I did take O-Level Latin in order to later on get into Cambridge) or any other language – was a sticky green plant, that is, if you threw it at something, it would cling to that something because of its stickiness. On one particular day, we col-lected a whole lot of these plants into the classroom with the intention of throwing them at a teacher when he was not looking (I've no idea if Dr. Schmidt was chosen for this exercise or whether he just turned out as the "victim"). Dr. Schmidt turned his back to the class when writing on the board and every time he did this, a barrage of sticky green plants headed his way. It did not take long before the whole of his cloak was covered with these plants, from his neck downwards.
>
> Unfortunately, Dr. Schmidt once turned round sooner than ex-

---

480. Recollections – Michael Bharier, Carmel Memories, chap.4.

pected and saw a sticky green plant heading towards his face. I can't remember what his reaction was: as I said, he was a gentle soul.[481]

Schmidt would also take part in Carmel's extra-curricular activities, some of them musical. During 1954, he would hold Tuesday night concerts. During the spring term they were devoted to selections from, amongst others, Madame Butterfly, La Tosca, The Mikado, and The Barber of Seville. For the following term, the accent was on symphonic works, such as Beethoven's Seventh and Ninth (the Choral), Dvorak's New World, and Haydn's Ninety-Fourth. He also taught a number of pupils to play the recorder, and at the 1954 Purim party, he and one of the pupils played a duet.[482] But he did not limit his activities to music; at one period there was a Puppet Club under his patronage.[483] He also established a group called the "Horizon Society" whose aim was to try and expand the pupils' knowledge "beyond the normal horizons of the school curriculum, mostly in the area of great thinkers of the past."[484] His activities in this group included his acting as a "Mentor throughout the labyrinths of philosophic thought."[485] In November 1955, Schmidt established the "Carmel College Meteorological Station," which at the beginning had instruments to measure the air pressure, the maximum and minimum temperatures, and the quantity of rainfall."[486]

He had an interesting series of vehicles to transport him from place to place. Michael Bharier explains:

> In my first years at Carmel, he used to ride a small Lambretta scooter. He later graduated to a Messerschmitt car, a miniscule vehicle resembling the fuselage of a small plane without wings (which it, in fact, was), the driver sitting in front of the passenger. To get in or out, one had to raise the entire roof, a perspex bubble. He would undertake a journey in this car like a flight; 'Prepare for takeoff; no smoking please; fasten your seat belt'. It became a school joke to see Mr. Schmidt and his Messerschmitt.[487]

481. Recollections – Jeffrey Fisher.
482. Carmel 1954, p.43.
483. Ibid., p.9.
484. Recollections – Michael Bharier, Carmel Memories, chap.4.
485. Carmel 1959, p.32.
486. Carmel 1961, p.30.
487. Recollections – Michael Bharier, Carmel Memories, chap.4.

Photographs showing Schmidt at Carmel were often taken in his famous "bubble-car"[488] and on one Purim it "was lifted and precariously balanced over the waterfall between the lake and the river"![489]

Michael Bharier in his reminiscences of Schmidt writes:

> Over the years I discovered that he had been a profound influence on many others, not only students from the school. The late pianist, Peter Wallfisch, told me, in a very moving letter, how he had been encouraged early in his career in Israel (or was it Mandate Palestine then?), by Helmut Schmidt not only by his attendance at a recital but also by a very favorable press review he wrote. Schmidt told me that he had known Peter's wife, Anita Lasker, the cellist, when she was just a child as her counselor at a summer camp in Germany in the pre-war years.[490]

In 1959, he took a year's leave for a Research Scholarship to Princeton University.[491] Following his return to Carmel in 1960, the Carmel magazine wrote "We are glad to report that he [Schmidt] and his Messerschmitt have come back in time to help the Upper Sixth Economics set with their impending 'A' Levels."[492]

At the same time as he was teaching at Carmel, Schmidt would do research, which led to publications which included a book over 400 pages long, published in 1964, entitled "Imperialism; the Story and Significance of a Political Word, 1840–1960," which he authored together with Richard Koebner.[493] He also had several papers published in the Leo Baeck Institute Year Books. These included "Anti-Western and Anti-Jewish Tradition in German Historical Thought" and "Chief Rabbi Nathan Marcus Adler (1803–1890): Jewish Educator from Germany."[494] Papers of his also appeared in, amongst others, the journals "Judaism" and "History."[495]

His research was not limited to historical subjects and whilst at Carmel, Schmidt would utilise the pupils as "guinea pigs." Michael Ellman explains:

---

488. Reflections – Helmut Schmidt.
489. Recollections – Jeremy Rosen, chap.1.
490. Recollections – Michael Bharier, Carmel Memories, chap. 4.
491. Carmel 1959, p.6.
492. Carmel 1960, p.5.
493. "Copac" library catalogue.
494. Leo Baeck Institute Year Books. 1959, 1962 (Internet).
495. Biblioteka Džona Plamenca, Univerzitet Crne Gore (University of Montenegro) (Internet).

He once gave us a questionnaire on which, inter alia, we were asked to give our opinions about various nationalities (including Germans and Arabs). He used the results for an academic article about how children were prejudiced at an early age. I gave what turned out to be the politically correct answer to these questions, 'I have too little information to make a judgement,' and was the only one to do so.[496]

His article entitled "Bigotry in School Children" was published in March 1960 in the journal "Commentary" and the results showed that already from the age of seven, the boys had very strong feelings against certain groups and even after ten years at Carmel, they still had almost identical biases.[497]

In 1977, Jeremy Rosen, the then Headmaster of Carmel, wrote of him, "Mr. Schmidt still manages to get nearly everyone through various combinations of Economics and Politics."[498] He remained at Carmel for a total of several decades.

After he retired, he went to live in Basingstoke in Hampshire,[499] but he wintered regularly with his sister in Sarasota in Florida.[500] Schmidt died in September 1999 at the age of 84.[501]

HERMAN

He was a teacher at Crookham at about the beginning of the 1950s. He died during the course of the academic year and his place was taken by Nisbet.[502]

R. NISBET

He stood in for a teacher called Herman who had died during the year and he taught Latin, French, and English. Joe Dwek remembers him as "an unimposing, quiet School Master."[503]

---

496. Recollections – Michael Ellman.
497. Jewish Chronicle, 8 April 1960, p.25.
498. The Old Carmeli Year Book 1977, p.7.
499. By 1991 he was already living in Basingstoke (Old Carmeli Association Occupational Directory 1991).
500. E-mail from Michael Bharier, 30 June 2013.
501. Recollections – Michael Bharier, Carmel Memories, chap.4.
502. E-mails from Joe Dwek, 9 and 28 August 2013.
503. E-mails from Joe Dwek, 9 and 28 August 2013.

GILBERT PATRICK WARNER

He was born on 12 July 1914 in Sparkhill, Birmingham to John Henry Warner, a Clerk in Holy Orders, and Lilian Mary (née Bufton).[504] His son Dick reports that he was commonly known as "Paddy Warner,"[505] and this was because of his Irish ancestry. He studied in Bradford Grammar School between the years 1922 and 1932.[506] There he was a member of the School Chess Club; in 1930 he played in a match against the staff, and in 1932, he played on the 2nd board in a match against another school.[507]

He was admitted in 1933 to St. John's College, Cambridge. In 1935 he gained with First Class Honours the Classical Tripos part 1 in Latin and Greek, and in the following year, the English Tripos part 2 with Upper Second Class Honours. In 1936 he received the degree of B.A. (which in 1943 became an M.A.).[508]

During the Second World War, Warner served with the British Military Intelligence in Italy,[509] and was also based in Wales with the Education Corps.[510] In about 1945, he married Pamela Joan Fieldhouse,[511] but she died at the beginning of 1969 at the early age of 47.[512] He married again in the late 1970s to Kate Mullholland and she predeceased him.[513] From about 1946 he taught at various schools.[514]

He joined the staff at Carmel in January 1951,[515] where he taught English, Latin, and Greek, and was also a Form Master.[516] In addition to his class teaching, he was involved in a whole variety of extra-curricular activities.

As to be expected, as Head of the English department, Warner was very active in the school's Union Society, where he was its Vice-President (Kopul was the President). In the Spring term of 1956, he gave an

504. E-mail from the Library, St. John's College Cambridge, 4 January 2013.
505. E-mail from Dick, son of Gilbert Warner, 5 November 2013.
506. E-mail from Bradford Grammar School, 16 January 2013.
507. The Bradfordian (school magazine of Bradford School), March 1930, p.20; March 1932, p.17.
508. E-mail from St. John's College, op. cit.
509. E-mail from Dick Warner, 5 December 2013.
510. E-mail from Patrick, son of Gilbert Warner, 19 December 2013.
511. E-mail from Dick Warner, 17 December 2013.
512. General Register Office index, Deaths registered in January, February and March 1969, p.W-967.
513. E-mail from Dick Warner, 17 December 2013.
514. Ibid., 5 December 2013.
515. Rau letters, 12 January 1951.
516. Carmel College Senior School, sample school reports, spring 1951 – spring 1957, classes up to sixth form (names withheld).

"intriguing talk" to this Society on "Etymology" which "provoked much thought-searching study."[517] The Carmel magazine wrote that he "attended practically every meeting [of the Union Society] and spent much of his spare time organising the society and trying to persuade the committee to adopt some form of agenda."[518] Even the junior pupils merited his attention and he even managed to interest them in Greek philosophy by means of a talk which he gave to the Junior Union Society.[519]

In sporting activities he was a member of the team in staff versus pupils matches in both tennis and squash, winning in the first sport and losing in the second one.[520] He was also involved in cricket and in 1954 he wrote the pen-portraits of the players.[521] Warner was in charge of squash and on this the Carmel magazine wrote that he was "mainly responsible" for its "rise in popularity and standard." It then continued, "although he is unduly modest about his own playing ability his coaching has been invaluable to both the School team and beginners alike."[522] He was for several years the Housemaster of Gilbert House and in a summary of a year's activities, he gave his House an ethical lesson by telling them that they "should remember that it is by the efforts of the, perhaps undistinguished, majority that the Competition is – rightly – decided, not by individuals."[523]

His literary talents were illustrated in the Carmel magazine of 1954, where he contributed an article entitled "Portrait of a Carmelonian," who happened to be an Israeli who came to Carmel from Israel "speaking almost no English and quite startlingly unaware of what an English school is like." In describing this boy, Warner writes:

> And his knowledge is astonishing, most especially of history, history of almost any period from Pericles to Palmerston. To ask him a question in form is to invite disaster. Out it comes in a flood almost past damming and, sometimes, in a mixture of Hebrew and English and something that – like his writing – might be either. And woe betide you if you get a date wrong; it will not escape him. Perhaps it is good for us to have him there, a sort of walking conscience. . . .[524]

---

517. Carmel 1956, p.25.
518. Ibid., p.26.
519. Carmel 1954, p.40.
520. Ibid., pp.48, 49.
521. Ibid., pp.46–47.
522. Carmel 1955, p.50.
523. Carmel 1956, p.41.
524. Carmel 1954, p.11.

"The Young Carmelonian" summed up Warner as a "cool, calm, and collected, a most agreeable man, learned in Virgil, Cicero, and Horace. He is also an outstanding sportsman, and is famous as the owner of a succession of wonderful cars."[525]

Warner was one of the teachers that Abraham Carmel wrote about in his book "So Strange My Path":

> He [Warner] was a most indefatigable and painstaking teacher. No trouble was too much for him to take, and the boys, who were spoon-fed all the way from the Second to the Sixth Form, could command the personal time and attention of this departmental head almost at will. Warner was to be seen coaching some boy, practically a complete stranger to Latin, for a university entrance examination only a bare month ahead.[526]

He left Carmel in the summer of 1957 to work for the British Council as the first deputy headmaster of the General Wingate School in Addis Ababa, Ethiopia, and he was later promoted to the position of headmaster.[527] A presentation was made to him when he left Carmel which consisted of a beautiful six volume set of English poets,[528] and also a book on Ethiopia.[529] The following year, the Carmel magazine wrote, "Recent dispatches from a distant African kingdom have informed us that Mr. Warner, our former senior English and Classics Master, alternates his time between going on Safari hunts and teaching chess to the natives."[530]

Warner remained at this school in Ethiopia until 1961. Then for a year he was a lecturer at the University of Vienna in Austria.[531] The Warner family then moved to Waterford in the Republic of Ireland, but Gilbert Warner worked in Belfast, initially commuting there on a weekly basis in a feeble left-hand drive car. Later the family moved to Belfast. There he worked for a short period at the Belfast Academical Institution and then for about two years at the Belfast Royal Academy. Both these institutions were "solid protestant schools" and Gilbert was "shocked to his core to

---

525. The Young Carmelonian, p.15.
526. Abraham Carmel, *So Strange My Path*, pp.157–58.
527. E-mail from Dick Warner, 5 December 2013.
528. E-mail from Patrick Warner, 18 December 2013. This set of books is still in the family and in regular use.
529. Unwritten recollections of author.
530. Carmel 1958, p.5.
531. E-mail from Dick Warner, 5 December 2013.

be sounded out as to his sectarian affiliations before being employed."[532]

At the Belfast Royal Academy he worked on an "informal basis," which was quite common then. One of the former teachers remembers him there as a person who "kept pretty much to himself," adding that he was a "crossword enthusiast" who "set crosswords and was adept at solving the very difficult Ximenes crossword in the Observer." The car that he drove at that period was a Wartburg, an East German vehicle, which people "thought to be an eccentric choice."[533]

The Warner family were still in Belfast in November 1963 when President Kennedy was assassinated. They then moved to Wymondham in Norfolk where Gilbert Warner taught English and classics at the County Grammar School for about two years,[534] beginning in the Easter term 1964.[535] The family lived on one of the many nissen huts on the campus, which had been erected for a wartime Canadian military hospital.[536] In addition to his teaching, he took part in several extra-curricular activities, and was also the Senior Editor of the school's annual printed magazine which began in the year that he joined the staff.[537]

In March 1964, he accompanied five pupils of the school to Norwich where they took part in a Verse Speaking Festival, he and another teacher having prepared these pupils for this competition.[538] When he joined the school, he resuscitated the Chess Club which had been out of action for a couple of terms, and he also personally donated two chess books as a prize for a chess "knock-out" competition.[539]

In December 1965, Warner was the producer of the school play "Arms and the Man" by George Bernard Shaw. On this production, the School magazine wrote, "Mr. Warner is to be congratulated on mastering the limitations of the Tomlinson Hall stage. Even with the awkward business of drawing the curtains he acted on the principle of 'if you're stuck with it, make something of it'."[540] His son adds a comment on this production, "[It was on] a stage in the [school's nissen] huts and woe betide the tall

532. E-mail from Patrick Warner, 18 December 2013.
533. E-mails from Edward McCamley of Belfast Royal Academy, 28 and 29 January 2014.
534. E-mail from Patrick Warner, 18 December 2013.
535. The [Wymondham] County Grammar School Magazine, 1964, p.2.
536. E-mail from Patrick Warner, 18 December 2013.
537. The [Wymondham] County Grammar School Magazine: 1964, p.1, 1966, p.1. The 1965 issue has not been traced.
538. Ibid., 1964, pp.13–14.
539. Ibid., p.21.
540. Ibid., 1966, pp.11–13.

actor because the headroom was minimal."[541] One could add "woe betide Gilbert Warner" who himself was very tall indeed! But in the light of his own comment, maybe there was no need to say "woe betide," as can be seen from his comment, "I cannot pay them [the actors] a higher compliment than to say that, for the first time in my life when producing a play, I sat in the audience and watched it, leaving it all to them. When, in the intervals, I went backstage, it was only to find that I was in the way."[542]

Gilbert Warner's next place of employment was at Eversley College in Folkestone, Kent (which is in the south-east of England), where he held the position of its first Warden, and his wife was later the College Receptionist. When he took up residence there in September 1966, the building was in an almost uninhabitable state, with only his apartment habitable, if one can use that word, since he received his water in "rubber pipes slung through a hole in one window."[543] However, the grounds of Eversley College had a lawn and the Warner family played croquet on it, and it also had tennis courts.[544]

This institution did not have a permanent student body but was an "in-service" teacher training college of the Kent County Council and it ran numerous short courses throughout the year. Warner's first term there was the autumn term 1966, and he utilised it collecting staff and working out a programmer of future courses. During the first teaching term, which began in January 1967, on Friday afternoons, out went the builders and in came the students, and on Monday morning, the reverse took place! He was there until 1973, and during this period there were almost seventy courses each year; the vast majority of them were for teachers, but there were also a few for older pupils, and for Youth Service, and one must not forget that there were two for school caretakers.[545]

He wrote what "Google Books" describes as a "book" entitled "Founding Days at Eversley College" which was published by the Kent County Council in 1973.[546] In fact it is a brief article of just over two pages giving a very brief history of the place from the time it was built towards the beginning of the 20th century.[547]

---

541. E-mail from Patrick Warner, 18 December 2013.
542. The [Wymondham] County Grammar School Magazine, 1966, p.13.
543. G. P. Warner, "The Founding Days of Eversley College" (Kent County Council, 1973) [henceforth: Founding Days]. This paper can be found in the Folkestone Library.
544. E-mail from Patrick Warner, 18 December 2013.
545. Founding Days.
546. Google books (Internet).
547. Founding Days.

Following his retirement in about 1973, Warner moved permanently to the Republic of Ireland (Eire).[548] In fact one could call it a return to Ireland for the Warners, since former generations of the Warner family had lived there since Elizabethan times, and it was just Gilbert Warner's father who had moved to England in about 1900. Gilbert had always wanted to return to Ireland and on his first home leave from Ethiopia, he got a friend to book a family holiday in Waterford, which was a county in which his father had preached. There Gilbert bought a small cottage, and later a farmhouse at Dunnabrattin, and this became the family home and base.[549] One of his former pupils visited him there and described it and its furnishings, "[It was a] 300-year old thatched cottage beside the sea. Any space that was not filled with book-cases was adorned with curious African tribal objects such as masks, spears and shields, and the walls and furniture were stained brown from the smoke of the open fire."[550]

In the Republic of Ireland he continued to teach Classics part time at Newtown School in Waterford.[551] Several of that school's magazines[552] list him as a part time Latin teacher, and from this it would seem that he taught there from September 1976 to December 1984 or summer 1985.[553]

Roger Johnson, who was a teacher at that school for over forty years has recollections of Gilbert Warner there:

> Indeed I remember 'Paddy' [Gilbert Warner] well – he was a gentle and likeable man, who taught Latin as a part time teacher – only a few hours a week. He often managed to fit his classes either side of a lunch break, and then enjoyed the exceptionally good food served to pupils and staff alike! He had a wonderful sonorous voice and I would quite often find myself eating with him.[554]

One of his pupils at this school was Rachel Finnegan and she has many memories of Gilbert Warner:

---

548. E-mail from Patrick Warner, 18 December 2013.
549. Ibid., 19 December 2013.
550. E-mail from Dr. Rachel Finnegan, 8 January 2014.
551. E-mail from Dick Warner, 5 December 2013.
552. The magazines for 1977, 1979, 1981 and Autumn 1984. Although the 1977 magazine writes "Mr. A. Warner (Latin)," the change in initial is almost certainly due to a typographical error.
553. E-mail from Roger Johnson, 28 January 2014.
554. Ibid., 21 December 2013.

During my two final years at Newtown School Waterford (1979–81), I had the great privilege of being taught Latin by Mr. Gilbert Patrick (or Paddy) Warner. The school no longer had an official Latin teacher, but Mr. Warner, who had recently retired from Carmel College, agreed to give individual tuition to the few students wishing to take this subject. This was my first introduction to Latin, but very soon, through his careful tuition and guidance, I made sufficient progress to take Latin for the Leaving Certificate Examination. Inspired, though not particularly encouraged by him to proceed with Classical studies (he thought my employment opportunities would be limited), I went on to take a BA in Classics at Trinity College Dublin, followed by a PhD.

Looking back almost thirty-five years later, I recall Mr. Warner vividly. He was a very tall, slightly stooped gentleman with a slow, deliberate voice and a courteous English manner of the "old style." He reminded me of Mr. Chips. While he relaxed in an old armchair talking and smoking his pipe, I took notes, totally enthralled by his unending knowledge not only of Latin and Ancient History, but of English Literature, Politics, and of every other subject he chose to discuss. I particularly remember him for his playful sense of humour, and the way in which he managed to bring a joke or pun into almost everything he said. His method of teaching was truly inspired and inspiring.

He was also a very kind and generous man, and in my year off before going to university, taught me Beginners Greek twice a week at no charge.[555]

He wrote a number of articles and books, including one about the Comeragh Mountains in southern Ireland, celebrating his love of hillwalking.[556]

Warner died on 30 April 2003, at the age of 88, at his home at Dunnabrattin, Annestown, Co Waterford, Republic of Ireland.[557]

ARTHUR SAMUEL HOFFMAN

He was born in the East End of London on 14 October 1917. His schooling was at Grocers School, then known as Hackney Downs School, in

---

555. E-mail from Dr. Rachel Finnegan, op. cit.
556. E-mail from Dick Warner, 5 December 2013.
557. Ibid.

Hackney,[558] where he had been awarded a scholarship.[559] For his Jewish education he attended cheder at Egerton Road Synagogue in Stamford Hill.[560] The alumni of Grocers School had a club called the "Clove Club." Hoffman was a member of this club and did well with their rowing team on the River Lea.[561] He was also a keen swimmer and managed to achieve life-guard status.[562]

According to the "Jewish Chronicle," after leaving Grocer's school he went to London University where he received a teaching degree in 1939, and he also gained a rowing blue at the University.[563] To this, his son Jonathan added that whilst Arthur was at the university he captained the university rowing team, and whilst seated at 'Stroke' took London University to three Head of the River Championships in 1936, 1937, and 1938.[564]

At the outbreak of the Second World War, Hoffman joined the Royal Artillery and fought in the Middle East and Europe, rising to major. He was wounded in the siege of Tobruk, was mentioned in dispatches and received medals. He joined the Jewish Brigade when it was formed in September 1944, and when it entered Berchtesgaden, Hitler's Austrian mountain retreat, he ordered his men not to mistreat their German SS captives.[565]

His son Jonathan writes that after the war, from about 1945/46 to 1950 he was a teacher at Harrow School.[566] In the period after the war, when money and materials were tight, he would make furniture for members of his family. When one of his sons said he was a fine carpenter, Arthur instantly pulled him up saying "excuse me, a cabinet maker, please," and

---

558. E-mail from Jonathan, son of Arthur Hoffman, 28 October 2013.

559. Jewish Chronicle, 21 August 1998, obituary, p.17.

560. Ibid.

561. E-mail from Arthur Hoffman's brother Ronnie, 28 November 2013.

562. Ibid.

563. Jewish Chronicle, 21 August 1998, obituary, p.17.

564. Hesped (eulogy in honour of dead) for Arthur Hoffman delivered by his son Jonathan. However, London University has no record of Arthur, although they admit that their records might not be complete (e-mail from London University, 30 October 2013). Ronnie, however writes, "After Grocers he went to Shoreditch Technical College where he qualified as a teacher, later taking a job in a London junior school, where he remained slightly unsettled until WW2 [World War II]," (e-mail from Ronnie Hoffman, op. cit.).

565. Jewish Chronicle obituary, op. cit.; Bexhill Observer, 10 July 1998, obituary; Hesped, op. cit.; e-mail from Jonathan Hoffman, op. cit.

566. E-mail from Jonathan Hoffman, op. cit. However Harrow School has no record of him (e-mail from Archivist of Harrow School, 29 October 2013); when informed of Harrow School's reply, Jonathan then seemed to have had doubts whether he had taught at Harrow School (e-mail from Jonathan, 30 October 2013).

he would show his sons the art of creating secret dovetails.[567] It seems that he would have been a good woodwork teacher!

In 1951, he joined the staff of the Carmel Preparatory School where he remained until 1953. He taught a variety of subjects which included English, Maths, French, Hygiene, and P.E., and he also held the positions of House Master and Form Master.[568] For a period he was also Carmel's bursar.[569]

In his book, "So Strange My Path, "Abraham Carmel describes Hoffman:

> The beau idéal of the sergeant–major type – walrus moustache, parade-ground bellow, lively and pungent wit, and all the rest of the traditional characteristics. As an organiser and a disciplinarian he was superb, though a little more rough-and–ready perhaps, than the polished types normally to be found occupying the tutelary position he did. That, however, was wholly in keeping with the general character of the Preparatory School staff, which was altogether unlike that of the normal scholastic kind.[570]

One of Hoffman's pupils in the Prep School, which was then located at Crookham, was David Shaw, and he has recollections of him:

> We had a suggestion box at Crookham, when it was under the excellent headmastership of 6'4" Mr. Hoffman (Hoffy). He read the entries in the refectory once a week, and answered seriously. That was fine and we loved the entertainment. The practice was abandoned when questions became too numerous, repetitive, and plainly silly. For a few summer terms, we enjoyed playing 'rounders'. 'Hoffy' joined in and took no prisoners. We were little and he rejoiced in his powerful swing that sent the little ball miles.[571]

Hoffman would also use his power and try and run the school like an army! Abraham Carmel explains:

---

567. Hesped, op. cit.
568. Carmel College Prep School, sample school reports, spring 1951 – summer 1953, forms 1 – 4 (names withheld).
569. E-mail from Ronnie Hoffman, op. cit.
570. Abraham Carmel, *So Strange My Path*, pp.144–45, 155.
571. Recollections – David Shaw.

At precisely seven and a half minutes past nine,' he barked, 'you will proceed form by form to your form-rooms. At nine twelve point five you will gather your books and stand in the aisles between the desks with your feet eight inches apart. At nine seventeen your Form Masters will enter the form-rooms, and they will at this precise moment proceed to call your names. By nine twenty-three all relevant data will have been duly collected, and you will then have your first lesson, which will be lesson Number Two on the time-table.'

Here the fiery martinet paused to cast a baleful eye over his audience to make sure he had their full attention.

'After the break,' he continued, 'there will be fire-drill. Every boy will go to his dormitory by way of one of three routes. Those boys who are resident on the top floor will go by the back staircase, and those on the first floor by way of the central stairway. You will lie on your beds with your dressing-gowns over you while awaiting the sounding of the alarm. The bottom of the dressing-gown should cover approximately one-third of your ankle, and you should breathe regularly at the rate of two hundred per minute . . . Now does any boy not clearly understand?'

Since no one volunteered for further elucidation of these Orders of the Day, the operations were duly carried out, whereupon Hoffman announced that the evacuation of the school had taken 2.7 minutes, or five seconds less than in the previous term's exercise.[572]

His youngest brother Ronnie has two recollections of Arthur whilst he was at Carmel. The first is directly connected with Carmel and led to a catastrophic situation in the kashrut of the teachers' food, and arose by virtue of his position as the bursar. Ronnie elaborates:

One of his 'finds' was a local baker who could and did produce excellent bread and rolls to order. One standard was a white dinner roll which everyone on the staff particularly enjoyed with the evening meat meal. One day, when visiting the baker, Arthur complemented him on the excellence of the rolls, of their crisp crusts and of their startling white interior. He was told: 'Ah, there's a secret ingredient. I

---

572. Abraham Carmel, *So Strange My Path*, pp.155–56. Obviously this description by Abraham Carmel is to illustrate Hoffman's methods, and does not give an exact account of what occurred.

always add a few spoonfulls of powdered milk to the flour.' There was some hasty but quiet re-adjustment.[573]

The second recollection is not directly connected with Carmel but occurred whilst he was on the staff at Carmel. Again Ronnie elaborates:

> In common with his father and brothers, Arthur had an interest in cars. He was specially fond of unusual vehicles, and for several years owned and drove an old nineteen-thirties Lanchester which Daimler-like, had a pre-selector gear-change mechanism. Near to Carmel for many post-war years was a large US Air Force station and Arthur used occasionally to give lifts to American servicemen. One of them, watching the pre-selection process remarked: 'Hey! General Motors has just brought out the fluid flywheel, and you've got that here already!' to which Arthur's response was 'Already? This car is twenty years old!' It was a tale he loved to retell.[574]

He left Carmel probably in 1953.[575] He then went into (or, unsuccessfully, tried his hands on) a whole variety of jobs, such as selling fork-lift trucks and opening a speed reading centre.[576] Emmanuel Grodzinski recollects that from 1957 to 1959, Hoffman was in commerce and worked in Caxton Street, in the Westminster area of London.[577]

In 1981 he left London for Bexhill-on-Sea in East Sussex and bought a small hotel there. It made national headlines when both the AA and the RAC refused to list it because of this hotel's ban on smokers.[578] Ironically, Arthur himself was a heavy smoker, but he did give it up briefly when he opened his hotel![579]

He also had other interests, such as Bridge, which included writing a Bridge column in the local paper for many years, and founding a Bridge club in Bexhill.[580] Earlier in his life he played county cricket for Berkshire and on this, one of his obituaries adds he was "a lousy batsman but a very

---

573. E-mail from Ronnie Hoffman, op. cit.
574. Ibid.
575. He appears in the Carmel College Prep School photograph taken in 1953.
576. E-mail from Jonathan Hoffman, op. cit.
577. E-mail from Gary Borrow, 4 July 2013.
578. Jewish Chronicle obituary, op. cit.; Bexhill Observer obituary, op. cit.
579. E-mail from Jonathan Hoffman, op. cit.
580. Jewish Chronicle obituary, op. cit.; Bexhill Observer, obituary, op. cit.; Hesped, op. cit.

good wicket keeper."[581] He would also write "Letters to the Editor"[582] and on 4 June 1998, which was just a few weeks before he died, he wrote a letter to "The Times" of London which was published on 10 June. It was titled "Uses for economists" and stated,, 'Sir, Further to Mr. Eddie Kent's letter (June 3) my preferred definition of an economist is someone who knows more about money than the people who have got it."[583]

Hoffman died on 30 June 1998 in Bexhill-on-Sea at the age of 80.[584]

MORRIS (MOISHE) ELLMAN

He was born in the East End of London on 16 December 1904[585] to a family of Yiddish-speaking immigrants from Bessarabia and grew up there in the East End of London. He studied at Myrdle Street Central School, but left school at the age of 14 in order to attend the Etz Chaim Yeshiva, which was located in the East End. He studied there for six years.[586]

He then studied at Birkbeck College between 1927 and 1928, and matriculated in June 1928. He began at Queen Mary College, London University in October 1928. During the academic year 1928/29, he did his intermediate studies in English, Mathematics, and Latin. This was followed between 1929 and 1934 when he undertook studies for an Honours degree in Mathematics over the course of five years. In 1934 he was awarded a Third Class Honours degree.[587] Due to his poverty, he had to work his way through College and he did this by teaching in the Hebrew Classes on Sundays and weekday evenings.[588]

Following the receiving of his degree, Ellman started teaching in the Jewish Secondary School and was also head of the Stamford Hill Talmud Torah. In 1939 he took charge of the Hebrew Classes in Brighton.[589]

He was strongly anti-Nazi and was present at the "Battle of Cable Street" when the Fascists attempted a march through the predominantly

581. Bexhill Observer, obituary, op. cit.
582. Hesped, op. cit.
583. Letters to the Editor, The Times (London), 10 June 1998, p.21.
584. Jewish Chronicle obituary, op. cit.
585. General Register Office index, Births registered in January, February and March 1915, p.E-176, his surname is spelled Elman; e-mail from Queen Mary College, London University, 22 January 2013.
586. E-mail from Morris Ellman's son Michael, 13 May 2012; Jewish Chronicle, obituary, 26 August 1994, p.17.
587. E-mail from Queen Mary College, op. cit.
588. E-mail from Michael Ellman, op. cit.
589. Jewish Chronicle, obituary, op. cit.

Jewish East End. At the outbreak of the Second World War, Ellman volunteered to serve in the British army and served in the Royal Electrical
and Mechanical Engineers (REME).[590] After the war, in November 1945,
he became a teacher at the Hasmonean Grammar School.[591]

One of his main outside interests was classical music; he had many records and he also liked to attend concerts. He also liked reading books by
P. G. Wodehouse and solving the crossword puzzle in "The Times." He
was also a good swimmer and when he was young he played table tennis.[592]

Ellman joined the staff at Carmel in the spring term of 1951, where
he taught Mathematics up to the top form of the school.[593] He also gave
some Jewish Studies lessons.[594] At Greenham he lived with his family in
the Lodge at the entrance to the estate, and at Mongewell he lived with
his family in an apartment situated above the "long dorm" in the gymnasium building.[595]

The magazine "The Young Carmelonian" wrote that he is "one of the
most respected members of our staff. No boy has even been known to take
advantage of him, and get away with it! He can make an Einstein out of
the dullest wit, or at least he is expected to do so. In addition to his proper
subject, Mr. Ellman is a very skilful tutor of Bar Mitzvahs, and a Chazan
of repute."[596]

With regards to his maintaining discipline in class, his son Michael
writes, "The boys thought he was stern, strict, and short-tempered, and
he did not care much for being shouted at. However, he had learned to
discipline boys the hard way – when he began teaching he was unable to
keep discipline and soon realised that it was impossible to teach anything
unless the class was quiet and attentive."[597]

In December 1954, at the request of his wife, he left Carmel and returned to the Hasmonean as head of Maths.[598] An alumnus of that school
has a recollection of him from the academic year 1973/74:

---

590. E-mail from Michael Ellman, op. cit.
591. Ibid.; Jewish Chronicle, obituary, op. cit; booklet "The Hasmonean 1945–1970" (London),
  members of staff, p.22.
592. E-mail from Michael Ellman, op. cit.
593. Carmel College Senior School, sample school reports, spring 1951 – autumn 1954, form
  3 – upper sixth form, (name withheld)
594. Ibid., spring and summer 1952, form 4, (name withheld).
595. E-mail from Michael Ellman, op. cit.; Unwritten recollections of author.
596. The Young Carmelonian, p.16.
597. E-mail from Michael Ellman, op. cit.
598. Ibid.; Jewish Chronicle, obituary, op. cit.

I well remember a Maths lesson with Ellman when I was in L6 and Julian [Schamroth] in U6. This would have been in 73/4. We were all sitting in the 6th form block with Ellman standing in the corner of the classroom between the door and the window looking out on to the playground. Suddenly, a football crashed into the classroom breaking a window on the way. Ellman turned a dark shade of mauve and stood absolutely still while we all froze in delicious anticipation of a punch-up. Twenty seconds later Julian's face appears in the window on the door peering in to see what's going on. He can't see Ellman who's alongside the door in the corner of the classroom. Making his decision, Julian flings open the door, trapping Ellman in the angle behind it. We're all, as I said, totally frozen, waiting for the explosion. Seeing us all in this state, and not being able to see Ellman at all, Julian shouts out, in what were nearly his last words ever, 'Well, why are you all so quiet then?'

I don't quite remember what happened next, its all a bit of a blur, and it must have been the trauma of it all, but in my mind's eye it's like a Tom & Jerry cartoon with lots of noise and feathers flying and so on!

What I want to know, Julian, is – does it still hurt?[599]

Even when he reached the retirement age of 65, Ellman continued teaching there part-time.[600] When he finally retired from the Hasmonean, a reception to mark the occasion was held in May 1979. Philip Witriol describes it:

Y'day to reception to Moishe Ellman at Page Street, Hasmo Girls' School. Very enjoyable . . . The whole thing was very well done. Moishe [Ellman] was presented with an illuminated address by a distinguished OB, a Ph D mathematician and, of course, ex yeshiva bachur. Moishe spoke quite well, said he'd been setting himself a multiple choice question as to the reasons why he had gone on so long past retirement age. Of the five possible answers (loved teaching Maths so much, couldn't tear himself away from such a fine bunch of colleagues, needed the money, was dreading his retirement speech, and wanted to put it off as long as possible), had come to the conclusion that the last was the right answer. (I have forgotten the fifth choice).[601]

---

599. Hasmo Legends VII: "Woody" Woodthorpe Harrison – David Prager (Internet).
600. The Witriol Diaries, Part V (Hasmo Legends XXIV) (Internet).
601. Hasmonean – the final chapter, posted on May 28, 2011 by Philip Witriol (Internet).

Following his retirement, Ellman moved to Bournemouth, and often led the services and did the leining at the Jewish hotels there. He was able to do that until he was 80, when his voice deserted him.[602] He died on 11 May 1994,[603] at the age of 89.

D. COOPER

In the summer term 1951, Cooper took over from Gita Cohen and was form master of form 1 of the Prep School, and taught the various secular subjects to this form, namely, English, Arithmetic, History, Science, and Nature Study.[604] During the winter term 1952, he also taught Science to (at least) forms 3 and 4 of the Prep School.[605]

P. C. COLLINS

During the academic year 1951/52, he taught Science and Nature Study to (at least) the lowest classes of the Prep School.[606]

H. G. SUMNER (OR SAMUEL?)

He taught Art to various forms in the Senior School during the academic year 1951/52.[607]

JACOB (JACK) EPSTEIN

He was born on 8 December 1923[608] in the Middlesbrough area,[609] the son of Isidore Epstein, the then Rabbi of Middlesbrough, and Jessie (Sheinah) née Hurwitz.[610] His mother died aged 26 on 5 February 1924,

---

602. Ibid.; Jewish Chronicle, obituary, op. cit.

603. E-mail from Michael Ellman, 4 December 2013.

604. Carmel College Prep School, sample school reports, summer 1951 – summer 1952, form 1 (names withheld).

605. Carmel College Prep School, sample school reports, autumn 1952, form 3 and form 4 (names withheld).

606. Carmel College Prep School, sample school reports, autumn 1951 – summer 1952, form 1 and form 2 (names withheld).

607. Carmel College Senior School, sample school reports, autumn 1951 – summer 1952, form 2 and form 4 (names withheld).

608. Tombstone inscription in Bushey United Synagogue Cemetery London.

609. General Register Office index, Births registered in January, February and March 1924, p.E-351.

610. Tombstone inscription in Middlesbrough Jewish Cemetery.

just a few months after his birth.[611] During the following year his father married Gertrude Joseph.[612]

When he was about 4 years old, the family moved to London and his schooling included Willesden Secondary School. At the beginning of the Second World War the family was evacuated to Letchworth and he attended Letchworth Grammar School. There he was appointed as Head Boy.[613]

On 1 August 1947, Epstein was awarded the degree of B.Sc. in Chemistry at the University of London under their External Programme.[614] His subsidiary subject for this degree was Physics.[615] In 1949 he was awarded the Ministers' Diploma at Jews' College[616] and early that year he was appointed Youth Minister at Golders Green Synagogue.[617] Having a Minister's Diploma, he was in fact Reverend Jacob Epstein. Had the pupils at Carmel known this, they would have undoubtedly enjoyed themselves calling him "Reverend Epstein," but it seems they didn't know! Anthony Rau did however know, since in a letter home he wrote, "I might see Rev Epstein . . . he's the man who will come to teach here next term."[618] In October 1949, he registered with London University and studied at Jews' College, and on 1 August 1950 was awarded the degree of M.A. in Hebrew and Aramaic.[619]

During the following summer, Epstein was amongst a group of twenty-five teachers and headmasters to visit Israel to take part in the Teachers' Training Course sponsored by the Department for Education and Culture of the Jewish Agency.[620]

In the summer of 1951 he resigned his position of Youth Minister to accept a teaching appointment at Carmel,[621] where he joined the staff in the autumn of 1951. At first he taught Physics up to A-level, and also Chemistry and Jewish Studies.[622] At a later date, he taught Chemistry

---

611. Ibid.

612. General Register Office index, Marriages registered in April, May and June 1925, pp. E-307, J-552.

613. Telephone conversation between author and Jacob Epstein's sister Helen Botchko, 6 January 2013, and e-mails from Helen Botchko, 10 and 14 January 2013.

614. E-mail from London University, 11 January 2013.

615. Jacob Epstein – Curriculum Vitae.

616. Jewish Chronicle, 6 July 1951, p.8.

617. Jewish Chronicle, 3 June 1949, p.5; Jewish Chronicle, 6 July 1951, p.8.

618. Rau letters, 10 July 1951.

619. E-mail from London University, op. cit.

620. Jewish Chronicle, 6 July 1951, p.8.

621. Ibid.

622. Jacob Epstein – Curriculum Vitae; Carmel College Senior School, sample school reports,

throughout the school right up to scholarship level, his pupils having a very high rate of success in the public examinations. After Romney Coles retired in 1967, he became Head of the Chemistry Department. From 1959 to 1965 he was also a Housemaster.[623]

In addition to classroom teaching, Epstein would give some voluntary gemara shiurim, and he would sometimes do the leining at the last moment, should a pupil have failed to prepare it. He would also daily (yes! 7 days a week) conduct "Perek Yomi" (learning a chapter of Nach every day). When the end of Nach was reached, as is customary, he made a siyum, during which the participants read different extracts from the Nach.[624]

On his teaching of gemara, George Mandell writes, "He taught me a certain amount of Talmud himself, and it was thanks to him that I spent a few weeks at his brother-in-law's yeshiva near Montreux in 1954 or 1955. Although I did not continue with gemara in later life I'm glad to have had the experience."[625]

"The Young Carmelonian" wrote on him in 1954 that he "is a young master with a most profound knowledge, and his culture is as broad as the ocean. He is considered to be eternal, as time does not enter into his world. It is unusual to find a master who is an authority in Art and Science, but Mr. Epstein is the exception. He has never been heard to say an uncharitable word about any man."[626] His contact with the pupils was not limited to teaching, as one Old Carmeli recollects:

> One of my main recollections of him at Carmel, especially before the school moved from Newbury to Wallingford, is that his room was a kind of salon, where sixth-formers gathered on Friday and maybe other evenings and drank coffee and talked about art and religion and other grown-up sorts of things. It was his personality that attracted us and made the salon so popular.[627]

About the end of 1954 he contracted tuberculosis (TB) and was away from the school recuperating and convalescing over a very long period.[628]

---

various terms between autumn 1951 and summer 1959, classes up to sixth form (names withheld).

623. Jacob Epstein – Curriculum Vitae.
624. Unwritten recollections of author.
625. E-mail from George Mandell to Miriam Epstein (widow of Jack), 13 February 2006.
626. The Young Carmelonian, p.16.
627. E-mail from George Mandell to Miriam Epstein, 13 February 2006.
628. Carmel 1955, p.5.

When welcoming him back to Carmel, the Carmel magazine added, "We must add that, due undoubtedly to the inspiring Carmel atmosphere, Mr. Epstein has now passed his driving test."[629] Several years later, his car again came into the Carmel news via a Purim lark, in which some sixth form pupils "moved" his car to the end of the playing fields.[630]

On the subject of Purim, Joe Miller recollects, "Our chemistry teacher and housemaster at that time as we all slept in the Main Building was Jackie Epstein, he had a wardrobe full of ties and was more than willing to loan us his ties for the Purim fancy dress."[631]

He left Carmel in 1969 and was appointed as Head of the Chemistry department at St. Joseph's College in London, a Catholic school for boys, where, like in Carmel, he taught Chemistry throughout the school up to scholarship level. He remained there for just two years until 1971.[632]

In December 1971 Epstein went to live in Israel, and the following year he became a member of the staff at the Reali School, which is an independent co-educational High School in Haifa. There he taught Chemistry throughout the school preparing the pupils for University entrance examinations.[633]

He returned to England in September 1980 and for a year was an Academic Visitor at Imperial College London.[634] From September 1981 to the end of the 1987/88 academic year he taught Chemistry at Wimbledon College,[635] and from 1988 did part-time Chemistry teaching for Collingham Tutors.[636]

At that period, Epstein's activities were not limited to formal teaching at institutions. In 1981 he became a member of the "After Eight Society" and in their obituary for him, they wrote, "He soon became well established as a member to whom everyone warmed and who was highly respected for his erudition. He particularly enjoyed participating in the walks and rambles of the Society over the years, both for the physical challenge and the conviviality it provided which enlivened the trekking in the country hills."[637]

---

629. Carmel 1956, p.5.
630. Recollections – Jeremy Rosen, chap.1; Biography of KR, p.52.
631. Recollections – Joe Miller.
632. Jacob Epstein – Curriculum Vitae.
633. Ibid.
634. Ibid.
635. E-mail from Wimbledon College, 5 December 2013.
636. Jacob Epstein – Curriculum Vitae.
637. Obituary for Jack Epstein by the "After Eight Society."

Similarly, his widow relates on his physical activities on an incident which occurred soon after they were married:

> We went to the Lake District, and on the first day [Jack] decided that we must climb Mount Skiddaw, near Cockermouth, 'but we have no boots' – I protested. He was intent and off we went to the High Street, bought our boots, and immediately onto the foot of the mountain, and together we climbed it, some 930 metres."[638] Furthermore, in town he was always ready for a walk; "leave the car at home," he would say. I didn't and he often arrived at our destination before me.[639]

After he retired he would give shiurim in Tanach to a group of adults.[640] He spent his last years in the Sage Old Age Home in Golders Green.[641] On his period at the Sage, his nephew Yehoshua Cymerman, who was studying at Lakewood Yeshiva, recollects:

> I would go to visit him at Sage. Every time I would come I would receive a huge smile and before I left another appreciative smile. Despite the fact that he was very sick and weak, all he cared about was making sure that I felt good about coming. When I used to take him to Daven I was amazed by his sudden strength. He would refuse help whilst Davening and was focused throughout the Tefilah.[642]

Epstein died on 7 February 2006 at the age of 82, and was buried in the United Synagogue cemetery in Bushey.[643] At a meeting on his second yahrzeit, his widow Miriam said:

> Those of you here who knew Jack regarded him no doubt, as indeed he was – as a quiet, unassuming, self-effacing, and reticent person, who on close acquaintance revealed himself to be exceptionally learned and scholarly – not only in the world of Judaism and its vast sources of literature, but also in the areas of wider culture, whether the arts,

---

638. Miriam Epstein at SPNI (Society for the Protection of Nature in Israel) meeting held on 26 May 2009.
639. Ibid.
640. Telephone conversation between author and Helen Botchko, 10 January 2013, and e-mail from Helen Botchko, 14 January 2013.
641. Ibid.
642. Letter from Yehoshua Cymerman to Miriam Epstein, after the death of Jack.
643. United Synagogue burial records; Tombstone in Bushey United Synagogue Cemetery London.

or the sciences. I would say that in fact he was at home in Dante, Shakespeare, and Schopenhauer as he was with Rashi and Rambam.[644]

ABRAHAM CARMEL

He was born in Greenwich London as Kenneth Charles Cox in 1911 to wealthy Anglican parents, who died when he was quite young. At first he was a Protestant, but by the age of seventeen he was not happy with this and he began to search other religions such as Hinduism, Buddhism and Islam, but then came back to Christianity but to the Roman Catholic branch. His studies took him from 1934 onwards to several Catholic Colleges. The first was the Catholic College of Campion House in Middlesex, where he studied for four years. This was followed by St. Mary's College in Birmingham and then the Pontifical Bede College, which was normally situated in Rome, but because of the Second World War, had been evacuated to Lancashire. In July 1943, after nine years of preparation, he was ordained as Father Kenneth Charles Cox.[645] Whilst in this position, he was the founder of the "Open Door Youth Club" which was highly successful in combating juvenile delinquency.[646]

However, just a short period after his ordination, he already had his doubts about Catholicism. He therefore left the Catholic Church and joined the staff of the Anglican Public School Claysmore in Dorset. Whilst there, he finally decided that Judaism was the religion for him and he made contact with the London Beth Din, who demanded that he obtain employment in a Jewish environment. Thus in August 1951, he first arrived at Carmel College.[647]

It was in 1953 that the London Beth Din decided to accept him as a convert. He went through the required procedures and he also changed his name to Abraham Isaac Carmel.[648] In the latest edition of his book

644. Speech delivered by Miriam Epstein at second Yahrzeit of Jack, p.1.
645. Abraham Carmel, *So Strange My Path*, passim; Tradition: A Journal of Orthodox Jewish Thought,(New York: Rabbinical Council of America), vol.29, no.2, 1995, Book Review on "So Strange My Path"; Tradition, vol.23, no.2, Winter 1988, "My Chosen People," Abraham Isaac Carmel.
646. Canadian Jewish Chronicle, 18 April 1962, p.16.
647. *So Strange My Path*, passim. The various Carmel College publications refer to his University degrees. All state that he received the degree B.D. and some add the degree B.A. One of them writes that he received these degrees at Birmingham. However, Birmingham University has no record of him receiving a degree, nor have the various Catholic Colleges he studied in at that period. His book does not mention his receiving any University degree.
648. *So Strange My Path* – passim.

"So Strange My Path," he explains why he chose the surname "Carmel." "This I did, not primarily in honor of the school, much as I loved it, but in honor of Mount Carmel in Israel where Elijah the Prophet had demonstrated the truth of one G-d in the face of the false prophets of the pagan god Baal."[649]

In an interview that he gave a British national newspaper whilst he was at Carmel, he said:

> I decided I must cut myself off completely from my life up to the day I resigned as a priest. I am no longer in touch with my family or old friends. They have no idea where I am. I am afraid that if they knew, I should be given no peace. The Catholic Church would do all it could to persuade me to go back.[650]

At Carmel he was a Form Master and a House Master, and taught English, History, and Latin to the lower classes of the Senior School.[651] The author will never forget his first Latin lesson with him:

> He came into the class and started to give a lecture on the importance of the subject he was teaching without mentioning the word 'Latin'. Only after about five minutes did I know what subject he was talking about. He then wrote a number of sentences on the board and told the class to translate them into Latin. Those who had been in the prep school had already started Latin and could thus attempt the exercise. I, who had never learnt Latin just sat there and did nothing.[652]

In 1954, he was the "Consulting Editor" of a magazine for the junior classes which was aptly called "The Young Carmelonian." He wrote the Editorial which began:

> After many disappointments, frustrated efforts, and anxious moments, the Young Carmelonian has come to life. The need has long been felt, and we are most grateful to all those who have, by their encouragement and practical support, helped to realise our dream. The Juniors

---

649. Abraham Carmel, *So Strange My Path* (revised edition, 1993), p.243.
650. Anthony Brittenden, "Catholic Priest becomes a Jew," source not known, possibly the London newspaper "Daily Express" (?) in 1957(?).
651. 7 years, p.46.
652. Ibid.

themselves are deserving of the highest praise. In addition to their having contributed their own articles, they have raised most of the funds for publication. I have not met their equal in any school, or organisation anywhere.[653]

He also contributed an article to this magazine entitled "Out of the Ghetto" in which he summarised the history and visions of Carmel College.[654]

One of the many societies at Carmel was the Junior Union Society, and he was so much involved with this society, that the Carmel magazine wrote, "The Committee would like to thank Mr. Carmel who attended every meeting and helped the Society to no small extent."[655] In 1959 he even actively participated in "a very controversial debate . . . on the subject 'Is religion necessary in life?' . . . The motion was carried unanimously, partly due to a rousing speech from the floor by Mr. Carmel."[656] That year, the Society's Secretary described him as "the man behind the throne for all our activities."[657]

He also had a connection with the school's sports programme, by being the Housemaster of Alexander House in the academic years 1957/58 and 1958/59.[658] He was also a different sort of Housemaster, namely Housemaster for the dormitories on the first floor of the Main Building.[659]

In July 1957, he wrote a letter to Malcolm Shifrin ("Shif") in which he stated, "I am founding a new society for 'The Education of Jewish Girls in the Home.' Would you consent to becoming Vice-Pres?"[660]

In about October 1959, he went to Israel, on behalf of a number of Jewish businessmen to induce Frederick Grunwald "by moral persuasion and friendly advice" to return to England for a legal trial.[661] This resulted in his premature departure from the staff of Carmel, as Jeremy Rosen explains:

> Eventually, he left Carmel reluctantly. He got involved in some hare-brained scheme to bring Freddie Greenwood and another Jew-

653. The Young Carmelonian, p.5.
654. Ibid., pp.7, 9.
655. Carmel 1956, p.28, similar sentiments in Carmel 1958, p.28.
656. Carmel 1959, p.28.
657. Ibid., p.29.
658. Carmel: 1958, p.40, 1959, p.48.
659. 7 years, pp.96–98.
660. Letter from Abraham Carmel to Malcolm Shifrin (Shif), 4 July 1957.
661. Jewish Chronicle, 9 October 1959, p.11.

ish white-collar fugitive from the law for financial misdemeanors. Perhaps he meant well, trying to assuage anti-Jewish sentiment but Kopul felt he was courting publicity for his own ends. He asked him to leave Carmel to 'reassess his options'. . . . He always dreamed of returning to Carmel and years later contacted me [Headmaster Jeremy Rosen] about the possibility of returning to Carmel. I would not have objected but simply did not have the funds available.[662]

On his departure, the Carmel magazine wrote, "We are saying goodbye, temporarily . . . to Mr. Carmel who will be studying for a year in Israel."[663]

After leaving Carmel College, he spent a period in Israel studying Hebrew at an Ulpan, and he also studied at the Mercaz Harav Yeshivah [the Rabbi Kook Yeshivah], both of them situated in Jerusalem. For about six months from about September 1960, he taught English at the Reali Grammar School in Haifa, as well as instructing Israeli army and navy cadets.[664]

However, due to ill health, he then had to leave Israel, and he briefly returned to England. In an interview which he then gave to the "Jewish Chronicle," he stated that he had been particularly impressed by the Israeli youth whom he considered to be the best in the world. He described them as "virile, idealistic and healthy in every way," He felt that the standard of education in Israeli grammar schools was very high but this was not the case with the discipline. In Israel he had met with President Ben-Zvi, Ben-Gurion as well as with government and religious authorities.[665] It was also during this period that his spiritual autobiography entitled "So Strange My Path" was first published.[666]

He then went to the U.S.A. and in April of 1961, the "Jewish Chronicle" reported, "Mr. Carmel, who is on the staff of Carmel College, is on a three months tour of the United States to study systems of education."[667] In fact he had been made to leave Carmel nearly three years earlier!

On his lecturing in North America, he writes, "The Jewish Welfare Board made it possible for me to visit 375 communities in America and Canada to deliver lectures to capacity audiences. They also

662. Recollections – Jeremy Rosen, chap.1.
663. Carmel 1959, p.6.
664. Jewish Chronicle, 3 February 1961.
665. Ibid.
666. "Copac" and "Malmad" library catalogues.
667. Jewish Chronicle, 7 April 1961, p.16.

helped me visit fifty-five campuses where I was favorably received."[668]

Between 1962 and 1981 he was on the staff of the Yeshivah of Flatbush Joel Braverman High School where he taught English Literature.[669]

In the autumn of 1963, he enrolled in the Graduate School of Education at Yeshiva University in New York where he continued his studies until the spring of 1966. On 16 June that year he was awarded a Master's degree, majoring in General Jewish Education.[670]

Thirteen years after he converted, he celebrated his "bar mitzvah."[671] This took place in the Fifth Avenue Synagogue in New York where he was a member. After the service there was a celebratory Kiddush, at which the Rabbi of the Synagogue, Dr. Immanuel Jacobovitz (who was later the British Chief Rabbi) spoke.[672]

In the summers of 1980 and 1981 he enrolled in the Ferkauf Graduate School of Yeshiva University for the program "Jewish Education Administration and Supervision."[673] However, since he died in the spring of 1982, at the age of 71, a year after his retirement, it would seem that he did not finish this program. Carmel was buried in Israel.[674]

On his funeral, Jeffrey Ben-Zvi wrote that "his funeral was so large that traffic and bus lines had to be diverted for the crowd that assembled outside the Yeshivah of Flatbush High School. Such was the measure of the love his students and his adopted People had for him. A remarkable man."[675]

A plaque was erected to his memory at the Yeshivah of Flatbush which states, "An exemplary human being whose devotion to his fellow man and love for his devoted people, Israel and the Yeshiva of Flatbush, will be an everlasting inspiration to students and faculty alike."[676] Furthermore

---

668. Abraham Carmel, *So Strange My Path*, (revised edition, 1993), p.243. Due to the numerous audiences he addressed, this obviously did not take place during his "three months tour," but at some later date.

669. E-mail from Alumni Office, Yeshivah of Flatbush, 15 January 2014.

670. E-mail from Yeshiva University, 28 February 2014. Although the degree he was awarded was "Master of Science," this does not mean that it was in the field of science. All the Master degrees which were then awarded by this College were designated "Master of Science" (e-mail from Yeshiva University, 3 March 2014).

671. In fact a covert to Judaism takes his natural birth date as when he was born. This was therefore a "pseudo-bar mitzvah," perhaps based on the Talmudic statement that a person who converts to Judaism is like a new born baby (Talmud, Yevamot 22a).

672. Jewish Chronicle, 21 April 1967, p.25.

673. E-mail from Yeshiva University, 28 February 2014.

674. Tradition, op. cit., vol.23, no.2, Winter 1988, op. cit.

675. "A remarkable man," comments by Jeffrey S. Ben-Zvi on book "So Strange my Path," (Internet).

676. Photograph of plaque sent in e-mail from Joel Wolowelsky, 6 February 2014.

at every Yahrzeit of his, Carmel would be remembered at the Yeshivah of Flatbush and their Annual Freshman Seminar was named in his memory.[677]

FRANK ARVESCHOUG

He was born on 17 June 1915 in Low Fell, Gateshead, Durham.[678] He attended Morpeth Grammar School. and was admitted to Durham University's Armstrong College in Newcastle in the Michaelmas (Autumn) term of 1936. There he was a Pure Science student and passed (on his second attempt) his intermediate exams in Chemistry, Zoology, and Botany in the Easter (Spring) term of 1938, and in Maths in the Michaelmas term of 1938. He then passed his part 1 finals in the Easter term of 1939 and his part 2 finals in the Easter term a year later. He was awarded his B.Sc. pass degree in absentia on 26 June 1940.[679] A month and a half later on 7 August 1940, he joined the Army Education Corps.[680]

In 1947 he was awarded a Teaching Diploma from Manchester University, the diploma being awarded after a course of initial training in teaching.[681] His first teaching post was at Gosforth Grammar School between the years 1949 and 1951.[682]

This was followed by a position at Carmel where he taught Science and Biology between 1951 and 1953.[683] During this period, his family lived in a caravan.[684] When he left Carmel, the magazine "Badad" wrote about him:

> Mr. Arveschoug, the Biology Master, also taught Chemistry and Physics to the Junior forms and enthused his pupils with the dubious delights of seeing the skull beneath the skin. The 'lucus naturae' [freaks of nature], who were abundant in the School, helped him to

677. Yeshivah of Flatbush – Abraham Carmel, (Internet); e-mail from Abraham Levy, 5 February 2012.

678. General Register Office index, Births registered in July, August and September 1915, p.A-28; e-mail from Durham University, 9 December 2013.

679. E-mail from Durham University, op. cit.

680. Ibid.

681. E-mail from University of Manchester, 11 June 2013.

682. E-mail from Frank Arveschoug's son Roger, 25 September 2012.

683. Ibid.; Carmel College Senior School, sample school reports, autumn 1951 – summer 1953, forms 2 – 3 (name withheld).

684. Telephone conversation between author and Roger Arveschoug, 24 September 2012.

formulate his views on euthanasia and vivisection. We are sorry to see him go.[685]

On occasion, he gave First Aid to staff and pupils alike. It was on a Sunday afternoon in November 1951, that a chemical which was "bubbling furiously" splattered into Romney Coles' eye; this was dealt with by Arveschoug, who at the time was teaching biology in the next room.[686] On another occasion he "gave an opinion on a boy's broken bone (having fallen down some stairs)."[687]

After he left Carmel, he became the senior Biology master and also did general teaching at Malton Grammar School in North Yorkshire from September 1953 until July 1957.[688] This was followed by a post of Biology teacher at Hammond's Grammar School, in Swaffham, Norfolk where he remained until he died on 4 September 1975,[689] at the age of 60.

DR. ALEXANDER TOBIAS

He was born on 4 April 1916 in Birmingham,[690] to Joe and Gertrude (née Goodman) Tobias, his father being a tailor, and at a later date was the President of the New Synagogue in Birmingham for twenty-six years.[691] Alexander's schooling was first at Birmingham Hebrew School and Talmud Torah between the years 1921 and 1927, and this was followed by his studying at the King Edward's Five Ways School in Birmingham between 14 September 1927 and 29 July 1929.[692]

Tobias then went to Manchester Yeshiva which was followed by Jews' College, London,[693] and on 1 August 1940, he was awarded the degree of B.A. in Hebrew with First Class Honours from London University.[694] In 1945 he received the degree of Ph.D., also from London University, for

---

685. Badad, p.3.

686. Rau letters, 21 November 1951.

687. Ibid., 25 October 1952.

688. Staff at Malton Grammar School, (Internet).

689. E-mail from Roger Arveschoug, op. cit.; telephone conversation between author and Roger Arveschoug, op. cit.

690. General Register Office index, Births registered in April, May and June 1916, p.T-167; Record card of Alec Tobias at King Edward's Five Ways School, Birmingham (his name is given on this card as Alec rather than Alexander).

691. Tobias Record Card, op. cit.; Jewish Chronicle, 21 December 1945, p.14; Jewish Chronicle, 14 August 1959, p.9.

692. Tobias Record Card, op. cit.; Jewish Chronicle, 21 December 1945, p.14.

693. Jewish Chronicle, obituary, 10 January 1997, page 21.

694. E-mail from Transcripts Office, London University, 11 October 2013.

a thesis entitled "The development of the Rabbinate in Central Europe during the years 1348 – 1648."[695]

In May 1941 he was appointed Acting Minister at the Edgware District (United) Synagogue[696] (deputizing for the Reverend Saul Amias who was an Honorary Chaplain to the Forces) where he remained until the end of the War. From 1945 to 1951 he was the Minister at Brixton Synagogue.[697] When he took up this position in Brixton, Tobias stated that "one of the primary functions of the pulpit is to educate." Consequently, he chose to give a series of educational talks rather than traditional sermons.[698] At that period he would also participate in the Jewish Youth Study Group Schools.[699]

In the first edition of Abraham Carmel's book "So Strange my Path," it states that Tobias then had a "nervous breakdown."[700] In later editions however, Tobias' name in Abraham Carmel's book was changed to "Dr. Antonius London"![701]

He joined the staff at Carmel in October 1951 with a verbal contract which he did not fully understand. Otherwise he might not have joined the school! He wrote that when he arrived at Carmel in 1951 "several men introduced themselves with titles . . . so I found more chiefs than Indians."[702]

Throughout his period at Carmel, Tobias taught almost entirely in the Prep School, a fact that he did not know when he took up his position.[703] The subjects he taught were Torah, Ivrit, English, and History and he was also a form master.[704]

When he began at Carmel, the Prep School was in Crookham, whilst the Senior School was three and a half miles away in Greenham and to

---

695. Senate House Libraries, University of London, Catalogue of University of London theses.

696. Jewish Year Book 1950, p.458; Jewish Chronicle, 21 December 1945, p.14.

697. Jewish Year Book 1952, Who's who, p.468. The Jewish Year Book of 1951 (p.102) lists him as the Minister of Brixton Synagogue, whereas the 1952 Jewish Year Book (p.92) states that the position was vacant.

698. Jewish Chronicle, obituary, op. cit.

699. E-mail from Noach (miTelshestone) Hall, 23 June 2014.

700. Abraham Carmel, So Strange My Path, p.158; Jeremy Rosen also states that he had a nervous breakdown (Recollections – Jeremy Rosen, chap.1).

701. Ibid., third printing 1977. Rumour has it that the reason for the change was because of legal action.

702. Reflections – Alexander Tobias.

703. Ibid.

704. Carmel College Prep School, sample school reports, autumn 1951 – summer 1953, forms 1 – 4 (names withheld).

get between the two locations at night he sometimes took a bus and sometimes walked.[705]

He would also show films to the Prep School boys. On Jacob Fachler's first Sunday at Carmel, someone took him to the Prep School to see the film which was then being shown. It was "Great Expectations" and Jacob reported that he then "had nightmares for days."[706]

Tobias admitted that he "took no part in the sports activities of the school and was often reminded of this failing," but he then immediately added, "My glory lay elsewhere."[707]

He was an expert leiner and even knew the entire Torah by heart. Sometimes boys would test him by beginning a verse and ask him to finish it, but one could never catch him out![708] His proficiency was not limited to leining. Jacob Fachler writes that Tobias "was the most amazing shofar blower. He also knew the precise tunes for all the High Holydays with different nuances for Ne'ila on Yom Kippur – he taped all this for me at the time."[709]

Tobias would like to pinch boy's cheeks and utter nonsensical expressions such as "malabush" or "maladendo."[710] Anton Dell reports that he received this cheek pinching treatment if he got anything wrong whilst he was receiving his bar mitzvah lessons from Tobias.[711]

Whilst at Carmel, he would calculate the times for the beginning and end of Shabbat and Festivals, which would then be the "official" times for London and would appear in the media.[712] It is reported that he was also consulted by the Greenwich Observatory.[713]

Of Tobias, Abraham Carmel wrote, "If a day comes when Toby gets married or is offered a university post, the Common Room at Carmel will become very dull and drab."[714] Indeed it was in December 1963 that he left Carmel to take up new roots in New York. He travelled on the Queen Mary boarding the ship on a Friday. That Shabbat, the Shul on the ship had no problem to find someone to read from the Torah.[715] Toby (as he was popularly known!) was on the ship!

---

705. Reflections – Alexander Tobias.
706. Recollections – Jacob Fachler.
707. Reflections – Alexander Tobias.
708. 7 years, p.31.
709. Recollections – Jacob Fachler.
710. Recollections – Jeremy Rosen, chap.1.
711. Recollections – Anton Dell.
712. Unwritten recollections of author.
713. Jewish Chronicle, obituary, op. cit.
714. Abraham Carmel, *So Strange My Path*, p.159.
715. Reflections – Alexander Tobias.

He had originally intended his sojourn in New York to be just temporary, but it turned into a permanent residency. He wrote that he "held no position for five months until I took up a modest post in manuscript cataloguing at the Jewish Theological Seminary from which I retired somewhat early."[716] He had hoped to hear from some Old Boys he had taught at Carmel but he commented that "neither the American nor British Postal services have broken down under the strain of replies."[717] However, he was in regular contact with Jonathan Finlay, who wrote just before Tobias died, "Toby calls or writes every couple of weeks: still an incredibly vibrant, if somewhat eccentric, intellect; we talk music, film, opera, politics and history."[718]

He died in New York on 11 December 1996 at the age of 80.[719] His Obituary in the "Jewish Chronicle" states:

From the Rambam to Rembrandt, from Rashi to Rigoletto, Toby would fascinate young and old alike with a wealth of information and insight – always with accuracy and modesty. . . . A query about a reference in the Talmud would produce an immediate response of chapter and page. A remark about a Beethoven concert would evoke a critical comment on the pace of the conductor's performance.[720]

JOHN SWINDALE NANSON SEWELL

He was born in Stockport on 20 July 1904,[721] and was the great-nephew of Anna Sewell,[722] the author of "Black Beauty." Not only was his great-aunt an author, he himself was the author of several books written from 1928 onwards, including "Grays School Days" and "Black and White."[723] Before the Second World War, Sewell ran his own private school.[724]

In March 1938 he was granted a commission as Pilot Officer of the Ulster Bomber Squadron of the R.A.F. in the Auxiliary Air Force General

716. The Jewish Chronicle Obituary states that he retired in 1981.
717. Reflections – Alexander Tobias.
718. Communication from Old Carmeli Association to fellow Old Carmelis, February 1997.
719. Ibid.; Jewish Chronicle, obituary, op. cit.
720. Jewish Chronicle, obituary, op. cit.
721. General Register Office index, Births registered in July, August and September 1904, p.S-500; Farnborough Grammar School, Philip Fouracre remembers Dr. J.S.N. Sewell (Internet).
722. Philip Fouracre, op. cit.
723. "Copac" library catalogue.
724. Philip Fouracre, op. cit.

Duties Branch.[725] In February 1940 the Air Ministry sent out a notification with the names of those in the Auxiliary Air Force General Duties Branch who had been "Transferred to the Administrative and Special Duties Branch in their present rank and seniority" on 29 August 1939. (This was an Intelligence Branch mainly for pilots who could no longer fly.[726]) Amongst the names was Sewell's.[727]

He studied at Trinity College Dublin, where he was awarded the degree of B.A. in the autumn of 1939 and an M.A. in the autumn of 1942.[728]

Sewell came to Carmel in about the spring term of 1952. In addition to being the master-in-charge of the Prep School, he would teach his pupils English, Maths, and Latin.[729] The magazine "The Young Carmelonian" wrote of him that he had "raised the standard of studies in the Junior [Prep] School to a wonderful degree, and the effects of his training are very evident. Dr. Sewell is known outside the teaching profession for his outstanding literary gifts."[730]

A pupil of his writes, "He was very strict . . . He loved marking errors with his red Bic biro . . . I seem to remember that he was a heavy smoker . . . He gave me the nickname Monkey as I was a rather cheeky chap as an 8 year old and loved to climb ropes. I don't recall him ever striking a boy – unlike every other Carmel male teacher I ever knew."[731] Another of his pupils commented that he "was an older and more frail version of Coles. Always be-gowned and remote."[732]

In both 1954[733] and 1955, Sewell composed a poem for the Prep School magazine "Alpha." The latter poem occupied three pages of the magazine

---

725. London Gazette, 24 June 1938, p.4085. His name appears in "The Air Force List" of November 1939, under the heading "Officers serving on the Active List of the R.A.F., General Duties Branch – Pilot Officers, 1939, pp.305, (index) cxxxv.

726. Wikipedia – RAF Intelligence.

727. London Gazette, 2 February 1940, pp.656, 659, 660. After Sewell's name is stated in brackets, "since promoted."

728. E-mail from T.C.D., 9 July 2012. According to the school magazine of Farnborough Grammar School, (The Story of Al-fa 1957, p.57) he was also awarded a Ph.D. from T.C.D. However T.C.D. has no record of him receiving such a degree there, (e-mail from T.C.D., 9 July 2012). Al-fa also states that he was awarded the degree of B.es L. from the Sorbonne. However, a search by the French National Archives of the archives of the University of Paris (Sorbonne) could find no record of him (e-mail from Service de Archives, 15 May 2013).

729. Carmel College Prep School, sample school reports, spring 1952 – summer 1953, forms 1, 3 and 4 (names withheld).

730. The Young Carmelonian, p.15.

731. E-mail from David Sheldon, 4 July 2012.

732. E-mail from Jeremy Rosen, 4 July 2012.

733. Alpha 1954, p.20.

and was entitled "Joe or Killing By Kindness, (A Cautionary Tale)." It began:

> A little boy called Johnny Low
> Once had a little dog called Joe,
> And Johnny's Dad and Mum had seen
> That Joe was trained and very clean. . . .[734]

He left Carmel in 1955 or 1956[735] and he then began to teach Mathematics at Farnborough Grammar School in Hampshire.[736] There he was also editor of the school magazine "Beta" which was for the "lower forms and younger pupils."[737] An alumnus remembers Sewell "with his Grundig tape recorder and recording his own plays."[738] Another alumnus, Ian Johnson, writes about him, "I never had any trouble with him but he certainly was not an easy character. During one lesson we were apparently misbehaving so he said, more or less, 'Gentlemen, unless you apologise, I shall not return' and stalked off. We didn't, so he didn't. Nice free period."[739] He left this school suddenly no later than 1964 and "his departure was not recorded," unlike the case of his contemporaries.[740]

He died in Basingstoke towards the end of 1988,[741] at the age of 84.

MURRAY ROSTON

He was born in London on 10 December 1928[742] to Hyman (Chaim Lejzor) and Matilda Rosenstein.[743] In September 1940, his father officially changed his name and the name of the members of his immediate family from Rosenstein (Rozensztajn) to Roston.[744]

Murray's elder brother, Jerrold, was drowned at a Jewish Youth Study

---

734. Alpha 1955, pp.17–20.
735. Carmel 1956, p.5; there is no mention of his leaving Carmel College in the Prep School magazine.
736. Farnborough Grammar School, FGS Staff 1957–1968 plus a few earlier ones.
737. Farnborough Grammar School, Beta, the Junior Magazine of Farnborough Grammar School (Internet).
738. Ibid., Chris Hicks (Memories) 1952 to 1959 (Internet).
739. Ibid., Ian Johnson (Memories) 1954 – 1963 (Internet).
740. Ibid., Philip Fouracre remembers Dr. J.S.N. Sewell (Internet).
741. Ibid.
742. General Register Office index, Births registered in January, February and March 1929, p.R-106; Wikipedia – Murray Roston.
743. London Gazette, 1 October 1940, p.5811.
744. Ibid.

Group School at Finhant Switzerland, in August 1947 aged 20.[745] In his memory, amongst the trophies awarded at Carmel, was the Jerrold Roston Cup.[746]

Murray attended the City of London School from April 1940. When he joined, it was not situated in the "City of London," since due to the Second World War, it had already been evacuated to Marlborough in Wiltshire, and it only returned to London in May 1944. He was a prefect there and he left the school in July 1947. He participated in many of the sporting activities; he played in the school's Fives Team, and for his House in rugger, hockey, cricket, fives, soccer, athletics, and swimming, and was awarded House Colours. He was also Editor of the school magazine from 1946 to 1947, and in 1947 acted the part of Macduff when the school put on a performance of Shakespeare's Macbeth.[747]

Following his schooling, he won an Open Classics Scholarship to Queen's College Cambridge University,[748] and in 1949, he was admitted to this College.[749] He took Part 1 of the Tripos in Greek and Latin, and then changed for Part 2 of the Tripos to English Literature.[750] In 1952 he was awarded a B.A. (which became an M.A, in 1956).[751]

He was also one of the founders of the Wembley Bachad[752] and took an active part in the work of the Jewish Youth Study Groups.[753]

In July 1952 Roston joined the staff at Carmel[754] where he taught English. He also gave some lessons in Jewish Studies including Ivrit.[755] In the academic year 1954/55 he taught Latin to a pupil in the Upper Sixth.[756] He also conducted the "Perek Yomi" during the illness of Jack Epstein.[757]

In addition to his class teaching, he took part in the Union Society activities. In November 1953, he gave a talk on Plato "in which he dealt with

---

745. Memories of KR, pp.20–21; Jewish Chronicle, 15 August 1947, p.13.
746. Recollections – Jeremy Rosen, chap.1.
747. E-mail from City of London School, 22 January 2013.
748. Wikipedia – Murray Roston.
749. E-mail from Queen's College, Cambridge, 10 September 2012.
750. E-mail from Murray Roston, 18 January 2013.
751. E-mail from Queen's College, op. cit.
752. "Bachad" was a religious Zionist youth movement whose members prepared themselves for Aliya.
753. Jewish Chronicle, 19 October 1956, p.6.
754. Rau letters, postmarked 3 July 1952.
755. Carmel College Senior School, sample school reports, summer 1953, form 3; autumn 1955, form 5; spring 1956, form lower 5 (name withheld); 7 years, p.53.
756. Ibid., autumn 1954, summer 1955, and autumn 1956, upper sixth form (names withheld); it is likely that he taught these pupils Latin since they needed it to get into University.
757. Carmel 1955, p.6.

the more personal characteristics and beliefs of these Greek philosophers, and in particular their religion and its relation to Judaism."[758]

Whilst still in Greenham, Roston would organise occasional play readings. This was followed up in Mongewell, when towards the end of the spring term 1954, he founded the school's Dramatic Society. This Society immediately began its activities and during that very same term it broadcast the plays "Journey's End" by Robert Cedric Sheriff and "The Housemaster" by Ian Hay.[759]

He also took part in the sports activities of the school and played in both the tennis and squash matches between the staff and the pupils.[760]

In the spring of 1956, Roston married Faith Lehrman[761] and a few months later, at the end of the summer term 1956, he left Carmel to live in Israel.[762]

Whilst at Carmel, he had continued his research and in 1955/56 was awarded the degree of M.A. by London University, and in 1960/61 the degree of Ph.D. for a thesis entitled "The use in English drama of themes from the Old Testament and its Apocrypha."[763]

In Israel he became a Lecturer in the English department of Bar-Ilan University, and at that time he was the only member of the staff from Britain.[764] At a later date, he became Professor of English there. He also taught on a number of occasions as visiting professor at Stanford University California, as well as the University of Virginia. In 1999, he was appointed to the permanent faculty at UCLA (University of California Los Angeles) as Adjunct Professor, and subsequently taught there every third year whilst retaining his position at the Bar-Ilan University.[765] He wrote a number of books which include, "Biblical Drama in England," "Sixteenth Century English Literature," and "The Search for Selfhood in Modern Literature."[766]

As of 2013, he was living in Kiryat Ono in Israel.[767]

---

758. Carmel 1954, p.40.
759. Ibid., p.43.
760. Ibid., pp.48, 49.
761. General Register Office index, Marriages registered in April, May and June 1956, pp.L-214, R-98; Carmel 1956, p.4.
762. Carmel 1956, p.4.
763. Senate House Libraries, University of London, Catalogue of University of London theses.
764. Jewish Chronicle, 19 October 1956, p.6.
765. Wikipedia – Murray Roston.
766. "Malmad" library catalogue.
767. Israel online telephone directory.

MENDEL BLOCH

He was born on 27 March 1904[768] in the district of Crickhowell which spans the boundaries of the counties Breconshire and Monmouthshire in Wales,[769] to Gustav (Getzel) Bloch and Annie Bloch (née Gudkowsky).[770] In 1922, he gained the Ebbw Vale Scholarship and Monmouthshire County Exhibition which were both tenable at Cardiff University for three years.[771] On 21 July 1925, he was awarded the degree of B.A. in Hebrew and History at this University. Five years later on 22 July 1930, the same University awarded him an M.A. for a "Critical translation of the Ikharim of Joseph Albo with a consideration of his philosophic system and a general summary of teaching and disputations of Jewish theologians in regards to the question of what constitutes the articles of fundamentals of the Jewish faith."[772]

In the summer of 1925, Bloch married Gertrude Swift but they were later divorced.[773] From 1926 to 1935, he was the Minister of the Portsmouth and Southsea Hebrew Congregation.[774] During this period he was also the President of several Portsmouth Jewish Societies, which included the Zionist Council and the Social and Literary Society.[775] According to his daughter-in-law, "he was known as the sporting Reverend due to his fondness for sport."[776]

In April 1935, Bloch was inducted as the Minister of Borough Synagogue,[777] a synagogue whose history goes back to the beginning of the 19th century, and which was situated in Walworth in South-East London.[778] He remained there until 1939.[779] Also there he did not limit himself to the pulpit, but was involved in a variety of communal activities which included being Vice-President of the Union of Young Israel Societies, Chairman of

---

768. E-mail from Mendel Bloch's daughter-in-law Elaine Bloch-Jaffe, 14 August 2012.
769. General Register Office index, Births registered in April. May and June 1904, p.B-54.
770. E-mail from Elaine Bloch-Jaffe, op. cit.
771. Jewish Chronicle, 13 October 1922, p.21.
772. E-mail from Cardiff University, 5 February 2013.
773. E-mail from Elaine Bloch-Jaffe, op. cit.
774. E-mail from Robert Cooper, archivist of Portsmouth Hebrew Congregation, 17 August 2012; Jewish Year Book 1940, p.365.
775. Jewish Year Book 1930, pp.217–18, 317.
776. E-mail from Elaine Bloch-Jaffe, op. cit.
777. Jewish Chronicle, 13 April 1935, p.34.
778. JCR-UK Jewish Communities and Records, Borough Synagogue (Internet).
779. The 1939 Jewish Year Book, p.375, writes that at that date he was Minister of Borough Synagogue, and the 1940 edition, p.365, writes that he was a former Minister of that Synagogue.

the Aftercare Committee of the Borough Jewish Schools, and Director of the Cultural Activities of the British Maccabi Association.[780]

Whilst in the British Armed Forces, he was in the Royal Army Educational Corps and in August 1947 was promoted to Lieutenant (Education Officer).[781]

After his discharge from the Armed Forces, he became a teacher at the Hasmonean School in London in September 1948,[782] where he taught English "with a good sense of humour."[783] A story related about him was that during a discussion in the Hasmonean staff room, a question was asked "as to whether a Jew could watch opera or ballet. 'Certainly not ballet,' said MB [Bloch], 'Al tistakel lakankan'."[784] (the music-hall dance "Can-Can" is a pun on the word "Kankan"!).

Bloch also participated in the Hasmonean Summer Holiday camp. One of the teachers at the Hasmonean at the time, Bernie Hechsher, reports that one of the dormitories at this Summer Camp had planned a midnight feast. In order to stop it, Bloch decided to sleep on the floor of that dormitory that night. In addition, that night they were using the ropes of the fire escape. Bloch was annoyed at these goings on. However, by breakfast time the next morning, he had composed a rhyme of these activities, in order to show that there were no bad feelings.[785] He remained at the Hasmonean until September 1952.[786]

That same month he joined the staff of Carmel.[787] At first he taught in the Prep School; the subjects he taught included Hebrew, English, and Maths.[788] In 1954, the magazine "The Young Carmelonian" wrote on him, that he is "the valuable teacher of our Preparatory School, and his genial and patient manner is much appreciated by his young pupils. Mr. Bloch's knowledge of football is envied by boys and masters alike."[789] His extra-curricular activities included being in charge of the "Debating and

---

780. e.g., Jewish Year Book 1939, p.375.
781. Supplement to London Gazette, 12 September 1947, p.4282.
782. Booklet "The Hasmonean 1945–1970" (brought out to mark the 25th anniversary of the Hasmonean Grammar School), members of staff, p.22.
783. Telephone conversations between author and Bernie Hechsher on 17 August 2012.
784. Joseph Witriol's writings – "Hasmonean the Final Chapter," 28 January 1979 (Internet). The quote comes from Pirkei Avot (chap.4 mishna 20) and means "don't look at the container."
785. Telephone conversations with Bernie Hechsher, op. cit.
786. "The Hasmonean," op. cit., p.22.
787. The Old Carmeli, no.3, p.7, Retrospect.
788. Carmel College Prep School, sample school reports, autumn 1952 – summer 1953, form 3 (name withheld).
789. The Young Carmelonian, p.16.

Dramatic Society," where on occasion he was "in the Chair" in a debate.[790] In 1956, he contributed an article to the Prep School magazine "Alpha" on the English poet Walter de la Mere, with examples of his poetry.[791] For a short period in the latter part of the 1950s, he was the Master-in-Charge of the Prep School,[792] but as Alex Tobias wrote "nobody ever held it for long!"[793] Joe Miller has reminiscences of Mendel Bloch from when he was in the Prep School:

> I can remember my first housemaster Mr. Bloch who also taught us English classes, getting us during one class every week to write letters home to our parents and families. He even assisted with ideas for content and [I] now realise the importance of keeping in touch with people on a regular basis and possibly for no ulterior motive. When the letters were all completed, he actually took the envelopes, making sure they were addressed correctly and that they promptly reached the post box.[794]

About the academic year 1957/58, Mendel Bloch transferred to the Senior School.[795] However, even before that period, he would arrange for the Senior School "some useful and enjoyable [football] matches."[796] In the Senior School he taught English, Chumash,[797] and Modern Hebrew.[798] As with the Prep School, in addition to his class teaching, he took part in extra-curricular activities which included organising "various literary competitions among the junior forms."[799] From the academic year 1957/58 he was the Housemaster of Montefiore,[800] and it was in that year that they won the inter-house cup for the first time.[801] In consequence, in 1959, he wrote, "The achievements of Montefiore House are very gratifying

790. Alpha 1954, pp.5–6.
791. Alpha 1956, pp.13–14.
792. Booklet "Carmel College 1948–1957," undated (c.1958).
793. Reflections – Alexander Tobias.
794. Recollections – Joe Miller.
795. Can be derived from: Carmel 1958, pp.6, 42.
796. Carmel 1955, p.44.
797. Telephone conversation between author and Nigel Simons, 26 December 2012; Carmel College Senior School, sample school reports: autumn 1958 – summer 1959, form 5 (name withheld).
798. Carmel College Senior School, sample school report, spring 1958, form 5 (name withheld).
799. Carmel 1958, p.6.
800. Ibid., p.42.
801. Carmel 1959, p.49.

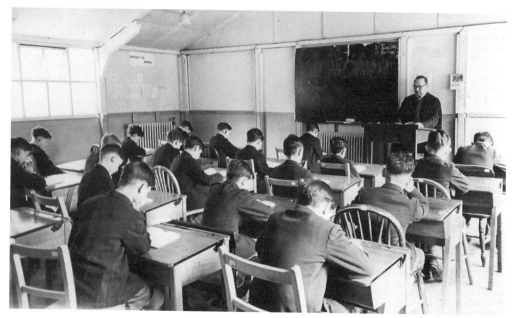

Mendel Bloch Giving a Lesson in Mongewell in 1956

. . . It is probably a good thing for the honours to go round but 'what we have, we hold' and we will not relinquish our supremacy without a keen struggle."[802]

Bloch also taught Bar Mitzvahs. Geoffrey Paradise who was taught his by Bloch added how "he used to warble away in his mellifluous bass voice."[803] On this question of "Bloch and Bar Mitzvahs," Jacob Fachler wrote that "when I arrived in April 1957, Mr. Bloch heard that a new boy knew the Torah reading trope (leining) – so he promptly appointed me his deputy Bar Mitzvah tutor. I was teaching BM [Bar Mitzvah] to boys who were 18 months older than me."[804]

His sister-in-law was Dora Bloch. She was the 75-year-old woman who was in hospital in Entebbe as the result of choking on some food, at the time of the rescue of the Israeli hostages in Entebbe in 1976, and she was then brutally murdered there.[805] After her murder, Mendel Bloch said, "I

802. Ibid., p.50.
803. Recollections – Geoffrey Paradise.
804. Recollections – Jacob Fachler.
805. Dora Bloch (1901–1976) – Find a Grave Memorial (Internet).

have heard of one Frenchwoman among the hostages who said that Mrs. Bloch did a wonderful job of comforting other hostages."[806]

After he retired in the 1970s, his family paid for him to continue living in a staff house on the Carmel campus for a number of years.[807] However, when at about the age of 80, he got very ill, his son and daughter-in-law took him to Australia to live with them.[808] He died there on 30 June 1985,[809] at the age of 81.

Alex Tobias who worked with him for many years in the Prep School wrote about him:

> In the religious area the person with whom I most associated was the avuncular Mr. Mendel Bloch. He was devoted to the college. I was so happy when he spent a Pesach with me in Brooklyn in 1965. I did not see him after that, but I daily mourn the sad fate which was his and which has hurt me deeply. He possessed humour albeit with a habit of repeating puns. Had he found a Sullivan he would have made a good Gilbert.[810]

GEORGE L. BUTCHER

He taught Art to various forms in the Senior School in 1953.[811] A pupil recollects him always wearing a bow tie.[812]

MRS. ELIZABETH JOYCE GLOVER

She was born on 29 May 1927[813] in Llanelli, Carmarthenshire, in Wales as Elizabeth Joyce Rawlings, and she became a Glover when she married Roy Arthur Glover in about the autumn of 1949, in Llanelli.[814] The archives of

806. "Who is Dora Bloch?" Spartanburg Herald, South Carolina, 15 July 1976, p.A7.
807. E-mail from Jeremy Rosen, 29 January 2013.
808. E-mail from Elaine Bloch-Jaffe, op. cit.
809. Jewish Chronicle, 12 July 1985, p.20.
810. Reflections – Alex Tobias.
811. Carmel College Senior School, sample school reports, spring 1953 – summer 1953, form 3 and form 5 (names withheld).
812. E-mail from an early pupil (requested anonymity), 27 September 2013. The school photographs for 1953 also show him wearing a bow tie.
813. E-mail from Sidney Gold, 9 October 2013.
814. Ibid., 3 October 2013.

the Carmarthenshire County Council have records of the admission of an Elizabeth Rawlings to one of their schools.[815]

She joined the staff of the Prep School in Carmel about the begriming of 1953 and was teacher of the lowest class in the Prep School for many years. She taught these pupils many of the secular subjects, namely, English, Arithmetic, Science, and Art, and she was the form mistress of year 1.[816] She also taught Science to the higher classes of the Prep School.[817]

In 1991 she was living in Emmer Green in Reading[818] and she died towards the end of 1998, at the age of 71, predeceasing her husband by about three years.[819]

MICHAEL GEORGE COX

He was born on 15 October 1925[820] in the Edmonton area of London.[821] From 1936, his schooling was at the Royal Liberty School in Romford, but he left after the fifth form without taking the matriculation. According to his lifelong friend John Gray, Cox was not particularly academic but he was more interested in Art than in any other subject. He was also active behind the scenes in school plays and he developed an interest in musical drama.[822]

After leaving school, he worked in a London insurance office for about two to three years until about 1945/46. He was then called up for National Service and joined the Fleet Air Arm[823] of the Royal Navy and he was posted to India and Ceylon. There he was active in organising a Music

---

815. E-mail from Archive Service of Carmarthenshire County Council, 14 February 2014. However, before further details could be obtained from them, a fungus infestation was discovered in the room where their archives were kept, (ibid., 4 March 2014) and the room was immediately closed off and it remains so!

816. Carmel College Prep School, sample school report, spring 1953, form 1 (name withheld).

817. Carmel College Prep School, sample school reports: spring 1953, form 3; summer 1953, form 4 (name withheld).

818. Old Carmeli Association, Occupational Directory, 1991.

819. E-mail from Sidney Gold, 9 October 2013.

820. E-mail from University College London Records Office, 10 January 2013; Order of service of funeral of Michael George Cox.

821. General Register Office index, Births registered in October, November and December 1925, p.C-226.

822. Notes by John Gray on life of Michael Cox, received April 2014.

823. The "Fleet Air Arm" is the branch of the British Royal Navy responsible for the operation of naval aircraft.

Appreciation Group and he listened to a great deal of recorded classical music. He was also interested in Indian music and Oriental Art.[824]

Following demobilisation, between October 1947 and June 1950, he attended the Slade School of Fine Art in London, studying for a Diploma in Fine Art. His course included classes in Fine Art Anatomy, Perspective, and the History of Art and Design.[825] Following the receiving of his diploma from the Slade School, he took an Art Teacher's Diploma at the Institute of Education of London University.[826]

When Alban Berg's opera "Wozzeck" gave its first performance in the Covent Garden Royal Opera House, Michael Cox was involved in the décor.[827]

He joined the staff at Carmel in October 1953 (which corresponded with the school's removal to Mongewell), to teach arts and crafts. A brick building just inside the inner gate of the Carmel campus was designated as the arts and crafts room. However, at that stage this room was not yet ready for use. So instead of arts and crafts, Cox organised walks during his scheduled lesson periods. The pupils used their feet instead of their hands! However, a few weeks later, a temporary room was found for art in the North Court.[828]

Cox would display the best paintings on the wall of the Art room.[829] Amongst the subjects that Cox would suggest, and even give the class to paint, were Biblical themes.[830]

The art activities were not limited to painting as Jeremy Rosen writes, "[Cox] would send us up onto the Ridgeway[831] to pick up chunks of chalk to carve (I guess the art budget at Carmel was limited at that time)."[832]

Another item in Cox's curriculum was handwriting.[833] Legible handwriting is an "essential commodity" in today's world. The time which is wasted in trying to read illegible handwriting cannot be measured! Henry Law writes that at that period he was in the fifth form when his writing

---

824. Notes by John Gray, op. cit.
825. E-mail from University College London University Records Office, op. cit.
826. Ibid., 27 February 2013.
827. Notes by John Gray, op. cit.
828. Unwritten recollections of author.
829. 7 years, p.48.
830. E-mail from Jeremy Rosen, 29 May 2012; 7 years, p.48.
831. The Ridgeway, which is situated just south of Wallingford, is a National Trail, thought to be the oldest road in Britain and it follows one of the banks of the River Thames as far as Goring-on-Thames (Wikipedia – The Ridgeway).
832. E-mail from Jeremy Rosen, op. cit.
833. Carmel College Senior School, sample school reports, autumn 1954 – summer 1955, form 2 (names withheld).

improved, "I think this was due to the encouragement of Mr. Cox, who promoted the Italic style. All that was necessary was to buy a pen with a broad nib . . . . After a bit of practice, it was easy to produce attractive looking and legible writing."[834]

From the start of his being on the staff at Carmel, he did not limit his activities to the class periods. On his very first Purim, the school hall was decorated under his guidance, and likewise at the half term.[835] He was also responsible for the "Art and Layout" of the 1954 Carmel Magazine.[836]

In addition, as soon as he joined the school, he founded an Art Club, which organised a visit to the Flemish Exhibition at the Royal Academy situated at Burlington House in Piccadilly, London.[837] The following year he took some pupils to the Gaugin exhibition held at the Tate Gallery in London and acted as their guide.[838]

He did not only train his pupils to use their hands, he also trained them to use their ears. He would give voluntary tuition in musical apprecia- tion[839] and in the academic year 1953/4, most of the school went on a visit organised by him to the Royal Festival Hall.[840]

On occasion, he would try to open the eyes of older pupils to unpleas- ant activities going on in the world. With this aim in mind, Anthony Rau relates in a letter written home in October 1953, how Cox took him to Oxford to see the Japanese film, "Rashamon" which was X-rated (adults only). This film, produced in 1950, depicts the retelling of a rape and murder from several different points of view, each claiming a different version of who committed the murder.[841] Rau commented, "It was very good."[842] Another one of his pupils at Carmel was Gabriel Chanan and he also has recollections of Michael Cox:

> I found him to be a superb art teacher. My personal development owed a lot to him (art was my main subject at that time). He did not impose styles but helped each pupil to find the style that suited him. Mine was rather traditional. He was particularly good at showing you how to work out what you were really seeing rather than what your

834. Recollections – Henry Law, Carmel College days, part 2, p.11.
835. Carmel 1954, p.42.
836. Ibid., p.4.
837. Ibid., p.42.
838. Recollections – Henry Law, Carmel College days, part 2, p.11.
839. Carmel 1957, p.5.
840. Carmel 1954, p.43.
841. Cinema / Chicago, Rashamon (internet).
842. Rau letters, 23 October 1953.

preconceptions might tell you were seeing. This was a lesson that had applications far beyond visual arts. I always found him sympathetic, understanding and encouraging.[843]

Although he was non-Jewish, Cox would sit at the masters' table on Shabbat wearing a capel![844] John Gray writes that "he liked the ethos of the school, and he was one of the gentile teachers who adopted Jewish customs – for example, he would not eat bare headed in the dining-room, he would never knowingly take any food in his rooms that was not kosher."[845]

After leaving Carmel towards the end of the 1950s, he joined the staff of the Quintin Kynaston School in St. John's Wood in London, as principal teacher of the Art department.[846] He remained there until his retirement.[847] Gabriel Chanan reports that he visited him at this school and that he saw him a few times at concerts at the Royal Festival Hall.[848]

Pupils at the Quintin Kynaston School who were taught by Michael Cox, have the highest of praise for him. Brian Ash writes, "Mr. Cox was truly the 'Mr. Chips' of his day. His encouragement and patience gave me the confidence in my abilities to pursue my subsequent career." Another of his pupils at this school,[849] Michael Shine writes:

> Michael Cox, the Art master. I wholeheartedly echo Brian Ash's comments regarding this talented artist and genuinely very nice man, Michael Cox. He was one of the masters at the school who encouraged the boys, in his case to be self expressive. I can't say he turned me into an artist, but his classes were an oasis of tranquility in a desert of madness. With more teachers like him, some of us may have achieved more of our potential.[850]

In 1960, he, together with a handful of people, thought that Little Missenden (a village in Buckinghamshire), would be a good place for an annual Festival, which they accordingly established. Cox continued with this work for about forty years. (This was unpaid work and all the people organising

---

843. E-mail from Gabriel Chanan, 4 April 2013.
844. 7 years, p.32.
845. Notes by John Gray, op. cit.
846. E-mail from Gabriel Chanan, op. cit.
847. Notes by John Gray, op. cit.
848. E-mail from Gabriel Chanan, op. cit.
849. Friends Reunited, Teacher memory, Quintin Kynaston School, (Internet).
850. Ibid. According to his profile in Friends Reunited, Michael Shine now lives in Israel.

this annual Festival did this in their spare time.[851]) The contents of these Festivals include Concerts, Poetry and Drama, and Exhibitions. For the third Festival held in 1962, Michael Cox dramatised and produced the play St. Christopher, basing it on a text from Caxton's "Golden Legend." That year's Festival also contained an Exhibition of design for furniture and fabrics which had been chosen by Michael Cox. He eventually became the co-Artistic Director of this Festival.[852]

It was in the year 2002, as a result of ill-health, that he had to step down from his work for the Festival. Alan Hedges, the Director of this Festival writes, "Even then he didn't stand down entirely, though. He used to spend several months on a warm Greek island every summer, and I was instructed to send him drafts of the brochure each year so he could give me his comments – which he always did!"[853]

Cox died on 4 March 2013 aged 88,[854] and at his funeral Alan Hedges gave a eulogy which included:

> I found him very congenial – a kindred spirit. Michael had a dry wit, a mischievous grin and infectious enthusiasm.
>
> He was very much his own man – I never remember him doing anything just because it was fashionable or 'expected'. He had high standards – he believed in doing things properly, but he had his own values, and his own sense of what was 'proper'. He was frank about what he thought, and he didn't suffer fools gladly.[855]

ROBERT GAVRON

He was born[856] on 13 September 1930, the son of Nathan and Leah Gavron.[857] His schooling was at Leighton Park School in Reading between the years 1944 and 1948. The archivist of that school writes, "He was clearly academically gifted, and made many contributions to the life of the school. He was a member of the Debating Society, the Musical Soci-

851. E-mail from Alan Hedges, 2 March 2014.
852. 54th Little Missenden Festival, News (Internet); booklet. "Little Missenden Festival, Ten Years 1960–1969."
853. 54th Little Missenden Festival, News (Internet).
854. Order of service of funeral of Michael George Cox.
855. 54th Little Missenden Festival, News (Internet).
856. His forename on his birth registration is given as Israel and not Robert (General Register Office index, Births registered in October, November and December 1930, p.C-345). This is likewise the case with his marriage registration.
857. The Peerage, Robert Gavron, Baron Gavron (Internet); Who's Who 2002, p.784.

ety and the Science Society. He played for the school's soccer team and was awarded 2nd XI cricket colours. He did Higher Certificate exams in Latin, French, Greek and Roman History, and European History."[858]

He was then admitted to St Peter's Hall (now St Peter's College) Oxford University on 17 October 1950. He passed the B.A. in Jurisprudence in 1953 and was placed in the First Class. The B.A. was conferred on him on 20 November 1954 (and this became an M.A. on 1 November 1958).[859]

Gavron joined the staff at Carmel in October 1953[860] for just one academic year[861] where he taught History, English, French, and P.E. and was also a Form Master.[862] Despite the short period that he was at Carmel, he participated in many extra-curricular activities. In the field of sports, he was involved in cricket, squash, and tennis,[863] and also in rowing and riding.[864] He took a great interest in and worked on behalf of the Union Society[865] and was the Chairman of the Carmel magazine committee.[866]

Even after he left Carmel, he still took an interest in its activities. In the summer of 1957, he brought students to Carmel to play a cricket match against them,[867] and during the academic year 1966/67, he came to Carmel on a Sunday morning and delivered a lecture entitled "Business Studies."[868]

In 1955, a year after he left Carmel, Gavron married Hannah Fyvel,[869] and he also became a barrister[870] and was admitted to the Bar by the Middle Temple. Also that year, he entered the printing industry, where he later became a printing millionaire. Amongst many other positions which he held, he was the Director of the Royal Opera House between 1992 and 1998. He was a philanthropist and in 1990 was invested a Commander of the British Empire (C.B.E.).[871] In 1996, he was elected an Honorary

---

858. E-mail from Leighton Park School, 24 February 2014.
859. E-mail from degree-conferrals, Oxford University, 17 October 2013.
860. Carmel 1954, p.9.
861. Carmel 1955, p.5.
862. Carmel College Senior School, sample school reports, spring and summer 1954, form 1 (name withheld).
863. Carmel. 1954, pp.47, 48, 49.
864. The Young Carmelonian, p.16.
865. Carmel, 1954, p.41.
866. Ibid., p. 4.
867. Carmel 1957, p.34.
868. Conversation between author and Nigel Simons, 28 May 2014.
869. General Register Office index, Marriages registered in July, August and September 1955, pp.F-492, G-12; Carmel 1955, p.5.
870. Carmel 1955, p.5.
871. The Peerage, Robert Gavron; Wikipedia – Baron Gavron; Who's Who 2002, p.784.

Fellow of the Royal Society of Literature.[872] In August 1999, the "London Gazette" announced on its cover page:

> The Queen has been pleased by Letters Patent under the Great Seal of the Realm dated in the forenoon of 6th August 1999 to confer the dignity of a Barony of the United Kingdom for life upon Robert Gavron, Esquire, C.B.E., by the name, style and title of Baron Gavron, of Highgate in the London Borough of Camden.[873]

A few months later on 8 November 1999, was the formal ceremony in the House of Lords, when Gavron "was introduced between the Lord McIntosh of Haringey and the Baroness Blackstone, the Gentleman Usher of the Black Rod and Garter King of Arms preceding; and made and subscribed to the solemn affirmation pursuant to statute."[874]

It was announced in the House of Lords that on his third day there, Lord Gavron would make his maiden speech. But that did not happen! When nearly two weeks later he did make it, he began:

> My Lords, I should like to start with an apology. Many noble Lords may think that I have already made my maiden speech. My name was indeed put down on my third day in this House by a noble Lord who is also a longstanding and dear friend. He did not consult me. He saw a suitable opportunity for me and felt confident that without any preparation I could 'wing' it. I failed. I could not do so; I was not quite up to it.[875]

He would periodically submit questions to the House and would speak at Parliamentary debates on a whole variety of subjects. One of them was the subject of "Roadworks" where he stated:

> On a typical day in autumn, on my four-mile journey through Camden from my home to my office, I pass 15 holes in the road, including one that is 30 yards long and one that is 50 yards long, which are controlled by traffic lights. At 10 o'clock in the morning, I have never

872. Royal Society of Literature, Current RSL Fellows, Honorary Fellows (internet); Wikipedia – Robert Gavron, Baron Gavron.
873. London Gazette, 18 August 1999, p.8907.
874. House of Lords, Minutes and Order Paper – Minutes of Proceedings, 8 November 1999.
875. House of Lords debates, 23 November 1999, c.376.

seen more than three of the 15 holes — that is, 20 per cent — with anyone working in them.[876]

As of 2013 he was a Member of the House of Lords.

GEOFFREY ARTHUR ROSE

He was born on 9 April 1926 in New Southgate, the son of Rev. R. N. Rose.[877] His schooling was at Kingswood School, where he was a pupil between 1936 and 1944. At least during his last four years at this school, he was active in many extra-curricular activities. In sports he was a member of the second XV rugger team; he was part of the Swords Club team, where in his final year he was its captain; he was a member of the Chess Club, and was also on the Athletics Committee. In the school's dramatic performances, he played the part of Mrs. Yeo in the Senior Literary Association's production of "Strife." To the school's Scientific Society, he gave a talk on "Television." He was a member of the School's chapel committee, and was also a School Prefect, later an Upper House Prefect, and finally a Senior Prefect.[878]

Early in 1944, Rose was awarded a scholarship to Queen's College Oxford University,[879] where he began on 12 October 1944 to study medicine as a Styring Scholar. He passed his B.A. through a combination of his studies towards the Bachelor of Medicine Degree and the War Decree. He left the College in the summer of 1946 and his B.A. was conferred to him at a ceremony on 22 November 1947. He went on to be awarded the degrees of Bachelor of Medicine and Bachelor of Surgery in 1949, and the degree of Doctor of Medicine in 1958.[880]

For his National Service, he was in the Medical Branch of the Royal Air Force and on 1 May 1951 was appointed to the commission of Flying Officer.[881]

Whilst he was studying for his Doctor of Medicine degree, he joined the Carmel staff in the autumn term of 1953[882] to teach Biology, travelling

---

876. Ibid., 16 November 2004, c.1291.
877. E-mail from St. John's and the Queen's College Oxford, 1 March 2013.
878. E-mail from Kingswood School, 11 March 2013.
879. Ibid.
880. E-mail from Degree Conferrals, Oxford University, 27 February 2013,; e-mail from St. John's, op. cit.
881. London Gazette, 5 June 1951, p.3117.
882. Carmel 1954, p.9.

in from Oxford for one and a half days each week.[883] Although almost
all teachers had their examination papers duplicated by the school office,
Rose, at least on one occasion, would go round the classes and write the
questions on the blackboard.[884]

In addition to teaching Biology, as soon as he came to the school, he became active in the school societies. During the first term that he was at the
school, the Carmel magazine reported that "an extremely interesting and
controversial talk on 'Medicine and Ethics' [was] given by Mr. Rose [to the
Union Society], which covered such subjects as euthanasia, birth control
and sterilisation. It provoked a keen discussion, in which Mr. Rose's views
were hotly debated."[885] Also during that year, he gave a lecture to the Science Society entitled "Medicine in Russia," and "with the aid of numerous
photographs shown on the epidiascope, he gave a survey of the conditions
which Russian medical students encountered, and he went on to outline
the system of medical aid there."[886] He also spoke to the Biology Society
on "Nutrition," "Reproduction," "Pre-Historic Animals," and "Creatures
Under the Sea."[887] In addition to lecturing to existing societies, he also
founded a Junior Biology Society.[888] When Rose left at the end of the
summer term 1955, the Carmel magazine wrote that "his work on behalf
of the [Biology] society has been selfless and invaluable, and we wish him
every success in the future."[889]

In 1959, he was appointed lecturer at the London School of Hygiene
and Tropical Medicine and during the subsequent years he progressed
up the academic ladder. In 1977 he became Professor of Epidemiology, a
position he retained until he retired in 1991. He was also Honorary Consultant Physician and medical registrar and senior registrar at St. Mary's
Hospital Paddington, and between 1970 and 1977 was the Professor of
Clinical Epidemiology there. He had become interested in epidemiology[890] whilst he had been the senior registrar. He was able to work at these
positions, even though in 1967 he was involved in a serious road accident
which left him impaired for life. In 1991 he was awarded a C.B.E. Follow-

---

883. Ministry of Education, Report by H. M. Inspectors on Carmel College, issued 8 June 1955,
    p.15.
884. Unwritten recollections of author.
885. Carmel 1954, p.40.
886. Ibid., p.42.
887. Ibid.
888. Ibid., p.9.
889. Carmel 1955, p.13.
890. Epidemiology is the study of the patterns, causes, and effects of health and disease condi-
    tions in defined populations (Wikipedia – Epidemiology).

ing his retirement he acted as Research Advisor to the Royal College of General Practitioners.[891]

Rose died on 12 November 1993, at the age of 67. His obituary states:

> He had a broad knowledge and quick intellect combined, unusually, with modesty and tolerance of other people's views. . . . Geoffrey Rose's public and research career was marked by wisdom, wit, and generosity and was guided by his profound religious beliefs. He set us an example. When he retired he abandoned epidemiology and threw away his reprints and his slides. He turned his full attention to his wife, Ceridwen, and his family and his friends.[892]

CHARLES JAMES COLQUHOUN

He was born in the Berwick area[893] in the county of Northumberland, on 1 October 1883.[894] On his fourth birthday his family moved to New-castle-on-Tyne and his early schooling was at a private school run by the Misses Richards. He was then awarded a scholarship to Dame Allan's School in Newcastle-on-Tyne,[895] where he studied between the years 1894 and 1899. In 1898, he passed Cambridge Junior Locals with Hon-ours and Distinction in Maths.[896]

At the age of 16, he began at the University of Durham in the Mich-aelmas (Autumn) Term 1899 as a student at its Armstrong College, the College of Physical Science in Newcastle-on-Tyne. He was a "Newcas-tle-upon-Tyne Corporation Exhibitioner," which was a form of schol-arship which allowed ten students from Newcastle free access to "Day Classes" in each academic year. The lectures he attended during all three years of his studies were in Maths, Physics, and Chemistry, and in addi-tion, Geology in the first two years. He passed his first year exams for the Associateship of Science (which is below the level of a full degree) in Maths, Physics, and Chemistry in June 1900, and then passed his finals for the Associateship in just Maths and Physics in June 1901. He received his

891. British Medical Journal (London), vol.307, 27 November 1993, obituary, G.A. Rose; The Independent, 16 November 1993, obituary, Professor Geoffrey Rose.

892. British Medical Journal, obituary, op. cit.

893. General Register Office index, Births registered in October, November and December 1883, p.C-107. He was registered as James Charles Colquhoun.

894. E-mail from Wallingford Museum, 22 October 2013.

895. Unidentified magazine article "Charles Colquhoun – 100 Not Out!," dated 1984(?), p.13.

896. E-mail from Wallingford Museum, op. cit.

Associateship on 28 September 1901. He then stayed on to do his B.Sc., towards which his A.Sc. counted, passing his finals in Maths and Physics in June 1902, but he only received his degree of B.Sc. on 30 September 1905.[897]

The announcement of his B.Sc, came when he lay desperately ill with a serious lung infection, that his doctor said, "Oh well, it's just in time to put on his tombstone!"[898] Despite his doctor's very pessimistic prognosis, he recovered!

Colquhoun then began his teaching career at Lichfield Grammar School and he was there for just two terms in 1903. This was followed by possibly five terms at Bradford-on-Avon Secondary School. He then returned as a teacher to the school he had studied at – Dame Allan's School – where he taught for the two years 1905 to 1907.[899] During this period he was studying for his M.Sc. exams which he passed in June 1906, but he only received his degree on 28 September 1907.[900]

For health reasons, on his doctor's advice, he then went on a long sea-voyage and his doctor arranged with a sea-captain to sign Colquhoun on as a purser for a trip to the Baltic, where he visited Finland and St. Petersburg. Eighty years later, he could still recall peasants in a horse-drawn bus grouped around the only one of their number who could read, listening to his account of the news from a daily paper.[901]

Following this, he began his longest period of full-time employment at a particular school. This was at Wallingford Grammar School where he taught Maths from 16 September 1910 until he retired in July 1950. The only break in this forty-year period was when he left on 25 July 1915 to join the army that August; he returned to this school after the War on 23 January 1919.[902]

At first, his eyesight had kept him from the army, but before long his

897. E-mail from Durham University Library, 29 October 2013; e-mail from Newcastle University, 7 November 2013. The reason for the lapse of time between passing the degree examinations and the actual receiving of the degree at Durham University is explained by the University as follows, "You do indeed have to attend a ceremony to receive your degree, or you can take it in absentia at a ceremony. By that process, you become a graduate; until then you are merely a graduand with permission to supplicate for your degree. As well as passing your exams, you do have to meet some other criteria before receiving your degree, such as having fulfilled the residence requirements and having cleared all your debts with the university, and having returned all your library books!" (e-mail from Durham University Library, 30 October 2013).
898. Unidentified magazine article, op. cit.
899. E-mail from Wallingford Museum, op. cit.
900. E-mail from Durham University Library, op. cit.
901. Unidentified magazine article, op. cit.
902. E-mail from Wallingford Museum, op. cit.

Carmel College Senior School Teaching Staff – circa 1957

Maths was being put to good effect as musketry instructor. For this he was trained at Bisley (a large village in Surrey which is noted for its rifle shooting ranges[903]), where he obtained a first class in the Lewis gun, and he became Company Sergeant Major Instructor of Musketry. This even came in useful in his Maths teaching since during his lessons he would

903. Wikipedia – Bisley, Surrey.

lapse into war-time reminiscences about gunnery in order to illustrate a point in maths![904]

As with most other schools, there is an Old Boys Association, and Colquhoun was involved in 1912 in setting up one for Wallingford Grammar School, and he acted as their auditor. He also played the accompaniment for songs at the Old Boys dinner.[905]

He would relate how once on 1 April, pupils at Wallingford Grammar School gathered for an assembly, where he played the hymns. 'What hymn shall we have," he asked, '"Let's have hymn 639, sir', came a united answer from a group of sixth formers. The 'Head' accordingly announced the hymn – only to find that the last hymn in the book was number 638!!!"[906] April Fool!

He also took a keen interest in cricket at that school and on one occasion the school cricket team set off in a horse-drawn brake to play King Alfred's School at Wantage. He had offered any pupil who would score a century in that match (to score a century was uncommon!), a golden half-sovereign. Indeed one of the players did so, and at the following Monday morning's assembly, the player was duly presented with this gold coin.[907]

His qualifications and interests were by no means limited to Maths and Science. In 1932, he received the Music diploma L.R.A.M. as an external student of the Royal Academy of Music. He was awarded it for piano teaching and this involved having "to perform to a fairly high standard and answer questions on teaching methods."[908]

Colquhoun was a teacher of piano at Carmel for seventeen years[909] beginning in October 1953,[910] which was well past the age when others retire! In addition to his teaching piano, during the course of his first year at Carmel, he also gave a most interesting talk on the "Appreciation of Piano Music."[911]

One of the major music pupils of piano at Carmel was Michael Bharier and he wrote at length about Colquhoun:

904. Unidentified magazine article, op. cit.
905. E-mail from Wallingford Museum, op. cit.
906. Wallingford magazine, October 1975, Mini-Profile 'Coe'.
907. Unidentified magazine article, op. cit.
908. E-mail from Royal Academy of Music, 14 October 2013.
909. Unidentified magazine article, op. cit.
910. Carmel 1954, p.9.
911. Ibid., p.43.

Upon arrival at Carmel I was introduced to Charles Colquhoun, the piano teacher. He was an elderly man who had lived in Wallingford for many years. He had been a Mathematics teacher at the local high school but also had a distinguished musical pedigree.

He had studied piano with Adelina de Lara, one of the last pupils of Clara Schumann. Some of his scores were covered with her notes and comments, which came in very useful when making decisions about performance. She had told him about casual visits from Johannes Brahms, who would pat her on the shoulders and praise her playing. He had also studied with Frank Merrick, a pupil of the prominent piano pedagogue Theodore Leschetizky (himself a student of Czerny who had studied with Beethoven). For composition he had studied with Gustav Holst. He recounted that one day he came in and found Holst scratching his head trying to assemble a clarinet in pieces and how he helped him put it together.

From my personal perspective it turned out he had been born and raised in northeast England, first Berwick-upon-Tweed then New-castle, my own birthplace. He would try to make me feel at home by using colloquial Geordie expressions and talking about the colorful Cullercoats fisher wives. He lived with his wife and an unmarried daughter in Flint Cottage, the oldest house in Wallingford [which is adjacent to Flint House, today the town museum]. He taught genera-tions of piano students there and later at Carmel.

During the war some Jewish children had been evacuated from London to his home. Their father was a friend of Kopul (Dr. Lip-pmann, I think) and this is how he was introduced to the school when it moved to Wallingford.

His wife Isabel [née Brooker, who he married in the autumn of 1927 in Bournemouth[912]] was also a musician and she taught singing at the school. She was the driver in the family, in more ways than one. She was very warm and welcoming. One cold snowy wintry night, after I had left the school, my sister and a friend were stranded in Wallingford. They knocked on the door of Flint Cottage, and Rose identified herself as my sister. Mrs. Colquhoun brought them in, fed them a warm drink, then drove them where they had to be nearby.

---

912. General Register Office index, Marriages registered in October, November and December 1927, pp.B-125, C-207.

CJC's [Colquhoun] piano techniques were somewhat outdated, I did not have the patience to practice properly and he was not a disciplinarian. Consequently my own technique did not progress very well, something with which I still struggle.

His musical tastes were firmly rooted in the three B's, Bach, Beethoven, and Brahms, with a special interest in 19th century German romantic piano, particularly Schumann and Brahms, although he did play some Chopin. He viewed Debussy as a talented but personally distasteful man and did acknowledge that Stravinsky had revolutionised music. He loved the music of Elgar – 'reminds me of the time when everything in the garden was green' – but did not like the works of Vaughan Williams – 'too much of the midnight oil, my boy, if you know what I mean.' Later he told me he admired the symphonies of Shostakovich but he had little time for other 20th-century music, especially the second Viennese school.

His memories were telescoped at times. One day he asked me, 'Isn't it sad about Enrique Granados? He was so young.' – as if it had just happened. He went on to tell me that he had drowned when his liner was sunk by a German U-boat. This had happened in 1916. Another time he recognised a piece I was learning for an AB exam and told me another student had done the same piece a few years before. 'Let me see if I can find that,' he said. He came back with the AB booklet a few days later, from 1929! He said another time that he felt a lot of people who had never been to Russia spoke as if they were experts on the place. He told me he had been there. 'Now when I was in St. Petersburg the people were wonderful.' This was in the 1950's. It hadn't been called St. Petersburg since 1905!

I may not have acquired great piano technique but I learned a lot about music and musicianship in my lengthy talks with him. I also learned a lot about menshlichkeit. He was a true mensch. He was about as honest and straight a man as I have ever known.[913]

Even though he was 87 years old when he finally left Carmel, he was still too young to retire! He went to teach for a few years part-time at Moulsford Preparatory School.[914]

Colquhoun died at the age of 101 in 1985.[915]

---

913. Recollections – Michael Bharier, chap. 3.5.
914. Unidentified magazine article, op. cit.
915. Recollections – Michael Bharier, chap. 3.5.

MEIR GERTNER

He was born on 9 January 1905 in Rozavlea in Transylvania, to Izac (Yizhak) and Sheindel Gertner, both his parents being Roumanian citizens,[916] and they were both Chasidim. From his earliest years he studied in Cheders and Yeshivot, but at the same time was secretly studying secular literature, such as history and poetry. He wore a large black capel, and apart from the area of his long peyot, his head was shaven. By the time of his Bar Mitzvah he was already a talmid chacham (scholar in Jewish studies), and following his Bar Mitzvah, he left the Cheder in Rozavlea and entered the Yeshiva of Wisho, which was presided over by a son of the Vishnitzer Rebbe.[917]

At the age of 20, he moved to Hamburg, where he immediately cut off his peyot and grew a magnificent mane of hair. Three years after his arrival in Hamburg, he passed his "abitur," (the equivalent of the British A-levels). When Hitler came to power, he was studying Semitics, History and Literature at the University of Hamburg, but because he was not an Aryan, they refused to give him a doctorate.[918]

Gertner went to Eretz Yisrael in 1938. During the War of Independence, he was in Jerusalem where he joined the Haganah and was also employed as a teacher by the Keren Hayesod. He then taught at the Teachers Training College at Ramat Rachel near Jerusalem, became Deputy Head of the Keren Kayemet Schools, gave advanced Hebrew courses on the radio, and published a "beginner's course in Hebrew." However, all this did not give him satisfaction and his brother Levi, suggested that he take a sabbatical year or two in England.[919]

Towards the end of 1952, he got married in Jerusalem to Thea (Leah) Bott (née Shmelzon), a divorcee who had come from Germany.[920] Just over a year later in January 1954, taking his brother's advice, he came to England and joined the staff at Carmel[921] where he taught Bible, Modern

---

916. British Certificate of Naturalisation dated 11 December 1961.
917. *Meir Gertner – An Anthology* , ed. A.H. Friedlander and Fred S. Worms, (London: B'nai B'rith, 1978), [henceforth: Gertner], Biographical Sketch, pp.11–13.
918. Ibid., pp.13–16.
919. Ibid., pp. 16–18. An article in the "Jewish Chronicle" (16 July 1954, p.30) which appeared soon after he joined the staff at Carmel, makes mention of certain additional facts whilst he was in Israel, which do not appear in his "Biographical Sketch"; these are that he continued his studies at the Hebrew University and this was followed by him being a lecturer at the "Peoples' University" which had been founded by the Central European Olim, where he lectured on Hebrew language, literature and Tanach, and that later he became an Israeli Army education officer and was also in charge of teachers' training courses.
920. Hatzofe (Tel-Aviv), 14 September 1952, p.3.
921. Carmel 1954, p.9.

Hebrew, and Hebrew Literature. But everything did not go smoothly, as can be seen in his biography, "There were frequent clashes [between him and Kopul]. Teaching Bible is a highly subjective undertaking. Kopul interfered frequently and Meir felt dispirited by his lack of authority in framing the syllabus."[922]

Throughout the time that he was at Carmel, he never lived on the school campus, but (at least at first), in Wallingford.[923] Henry Law summed up Gertner and his teaching, "The teaching of Modern Hebrew was a catastrophe. The teacher was Meir Gertner, an Israeli on a short fuse who could not teach or keep order and would knock the boys about." Law, however, added that away from the class, Gertner could be quite different, "Years later I met him on a train and we had a perfectly friendly conversation."[924]

One of Gertner's pronouncements was, "You are not judged on what you can do; you are judged on what you do do. If my grandmother had wings, she would be a jet bomber," with him pronouncing the second "b" in bomBer."[925]

The author recollects regarding Gertner, "If he saw a boy writing something in his lessons, he would take it and tear it to pieces. I was once calculating and making Jewish calendars in an exercise book for the next umpteen years and I was working on it in one of his lessons. He took the book and was about to tear out the page I was then working on. The class begged him not to and miracle of miracles, he didn't!"[926] One boy was less fortunate. For some reason, Gertner opened the lid of a desk and the top layer inside the desk were a boy's chemistry notes. Gertner took them out and tore them to shreds.[927]

In addition to his teaching, he took part in the activities of the Union Society. The author recollects, "In a debate on the need for reform in the English language, the speakers were teachers. One of them was Mr. Gertner, whose mother tongue was not English. He commented that one needed 'vowels' in English. He brought as an example the word 'reading.' One could pronounce it as both 'reding' with a short 'e' or 'reeeding' with a long 'e'."[928]

---

922. Gertner, Biographical Sketch, p.18.
923. 7 years, p.48.
924. Recollections – Henry Law, Carmel College days, part 1, p.7.
925. 7 years, p.48.
926. Ibid.
927. Unwritten recollections of author.
928. 7 years, p.70.

In the same year that he came to Carmel he was involved with the Carmel magazine. There were a number of pages of material in Hebrew, and he was the editor of the "Hebrew Section."[929] For the following year's magazine, he translated into Hebrew an extract from Yeats' "The King's Threshold."[930]

Gertner left Carmel in 1956 and moved to Oxford in order to study for a doctorate.[931] In October 1956, he was admitted to St. Catherine's College at Oxford University, to read for the degree of Doctor of Philosophy in Oriental Studies, and he was awarded this degree in 1962.[932] The title of his thesis was "Midrash in the Dead Sea Scrolls"; he had written it under the supervision of Professor Godfrey Rolles Driver, the Professor of Semitic Philology at Oxford.[933]

In 1958, someone drew his attention to a vacancy for a Lecturer in Modern Hebrew at the School of Oriental and African Studies in London, to replace Isidor Wartski who was retiring. Gertner received this position and was there until he retired in 1972; during that period he was promoted to the grade of a Reader.[934] His biographer writes on his teaching there:

> His classes were invariably crowded, there was standing room only. Meir taught in depth; he would open the book they were going to study say – a chapter in the Bible; he would rarely get beyond the first sentence. His tremendous range of knowledge, his phenomenal memory, would cause him to examine each word individually. He would quote the views of dozens of commentators. He would analyse the origin of the word and find Hebrew, Greek, or Latin synonyms. He would explain the transition of the meaning of the words as used in the Bible and as applied to Modern Hebrew. He would hold his audiences spellbound.[935]

From about 1960 onwards, he would publish numerous papers in several different languages, and since many of them were in journals which were hard to find, after his death a book entitled "Meir Gertner: an Anthology"

---

929. Carmel 1954, p.4.
930. Carmel 1955, pp.34–35.
931. Gertner, Biographical Sketch, p.18.
932. E-mail from Degree Conferrals Oxford University, 13 May 2013.
933. Gertner, Meir at Oxford, p.28.
934. Ibid.
935. Ibid., Biographical Sketch, pp.18–19.

which contained a selection of his writings was published.[936] Examples of these papers were "'Prophetic motifs and pagan masks in poetical mirrors' by Tchernichowsky . . ."; "The Pessach Haggadah: A Torah Tale with Tree-like Rings"; and "Midrashim in the New Testament."[937]

It was also during this period, namely in December 1961, that he became naturalised as a British citizen.[938]

Whilst at the School of Oriental and African Studies, he was invited to also lecture at Jews' College, but answered "I am not your man." Instead he lectured at Leo Baeck College for ten years.[939]

Coinciding with his retirement, Oxford University set up a Centre for Postgraduate Hebrew Studies, and he was appointed the first holder of the Hertz Fellowship, which had been established in memory of Chief Rabbi Hertz. Gertner held this fellowship until his death.[940] He died on 23 August 1976 at the age of 71, and was buried in the United Synagogue cemetery in Bushey.[941]

CHARLES STEPHENSON MARSHALL

He was born on 25 July 1929 in Bradford, Yorkshire and between the years 1940 and 1947 attended Grange High School for Boys. This was followed by his National Service for two years as an Army Physical Training Instructor.[942]

Between the years 1949 and 1952, Marshall attended Loughborough Training College in order to obtain his initial teaching qualification.[943] There he was in the Department for Training of Teachers. He was then awarded a Teacher's Certificate by the University of Nottingham. Between the years 1951 and 1952, he continued at Loughborough College, this time at their Department of Physical Education, and in 1952 received both a Supplementary Teacher's Certificate in Physical Education from the University of Nottingham and also the Diploma of Loughborough

936. AJR (Association for Jewish Refugees) Information, vol XXXIII, no.10, October 1978, p.11.
937. Gertner, p.6.
938. British Certificate of Naturalisation dated 11 December 1961; London Gazette. 23 January 1962, p.602.
939. Gertner, Biographical Sketch, p.19.
940. Ibid., Meir at Oxford, pp.28–29.
941. Tombstone inscription in Bushey United Synagogue Cemetery London.
942. E-mail from Charles Marshall, 1 January 2013.
943. E-mail from Institute of Education, London University, 24 July 2013.

College in Physical Education. His first post was at Liverpool Blue Coat School as a Teacher of Physical Education between 1952 and 1954.[944]

In the summer term of 1954 he joined the staff at Carmel[945] as the head of the department of Physical Education of the Senior School,[946] and he also taught Physical Education at the Prep School.[947]

David Saville reports that Marshall "once wrote on the gym floor, '3 press-ups, 2 vaults and 4 rope-climbs' and Izzy Gletzer said 'My word sir, what a wonderful vocabulary you've got'."[948]

Needless to say, that as the P.E. teacher, he was actively involved in the various sports played at the school. During his first year at Carmel, he added basketball to the list of Carmel sports, and the Carmel magazine writes that "a great debt of gratitude is owed to Mr. Marshall for introducing and encouraging the game and for refereeing our matches."[949] When there were squash matches between the pupils and the staff, he would play in the staff team.[950] He would also coach the boys in squash "from which many boys benefited greatly."[951] With "apparently boundless energy" he would coach boys in rowing and this "led to a large number of younger boys taking up rowing."[952] A few years later the Carmel magazine wrote, "But all our success [in rowing] of this and previous years is due to Mr. C. S. Marshall, the master-in-charge, for his friendship and encouragement, which have made us feel that he is more of a friend than a master. All credit is due to him."[953] That same year, similar sentiments appeared in connection with athletics, "This great improvement in our school athletics is in great part due to our sports master, Mr. Marshall, who has worked tirelessly to instill enthusiasm into the boys and to help them to derive every possible benefit from his great technical knowledge."[954]

For the academic year 1955/56 and also the following year, he was the Housemaster of Alexander House and in his summary of the activities of that House for the first year of his Housemastership, he was frank in his comments, "The juniors have, generally speaking, disappointed us a

---

944. E-mail from Charles Marshall, op. cit.
945. Carmel 1954, p.9.
946. E-mail from Charles Marshall, op. cit.
947. Alpha 1954, cover page.
948. Recollections – David Saville.
949. Carmel 1955, p.48. Actually basketball was played whilst the school was in Greenham.
950. Ibid., p.49.
951. Carmel 1956, p.38.
952. Carmel 1957, p.31.
953. Carmel 1960, p.33.
954. Ibid., p.38.

Charles Marshall Giving a Lesson in the Gymnasium in Mongewell in 1956

little. Perhaps they have rested too much upon the laurels which they won and deserved last year. Their contemporaries in other houses have now overtaken and left them far behind."[955] The Carmel magazine, each year included "Pen-Portraits" of the boys who participated in various sports and some of them were written by Marshall.[956]

In the summer of 1957, he married Joyce Bragg in the Worth Valley area, which is in the West Riding of Yorkshire.[957] He left Carmel in 1969[958] and at some later date was made a Vice President of the Old Carmeli Association.[959]

Between 1970 and 1977 he was the Deputy Head at Hamilton Lodge School for Deaf Children in Brighton.[960] This school would use lip read-

---

955. Carmel 1956, p.40.
956. e.g., Carmel: 1957, pp.32, 33; 1959, p.44.
957. General Register Office index, Marriages registered in July, August and September 1957, pp.B-147, M-378; Carmel 1958, p.4.
958. E-mail from Charles Marshall, op. cit.
959. The Old Carmeli Year Book 1977, p.2.
960. E-mail from Charles Marshall, op. cit.

ing and listening as opposed to sign language. As to be expected Charles Marshall was also involved with Physical Education at that school, and this is confirmed by Mike Arthurs who taught History at that school at that period and who recollects that he "was a P.E. teacher and was particularly known for gymnastic training."[961] In a later communication, Arthurs further recollects that when Marshall began at Hamilton Lodge, he "had no previous knowledge of the Deaf. He trained on the job," adding that his sport's activities at this school included "football, cricket, swimming, gymnastics, and activities in the hall."[962]

Between October 1971 and July 1972, he attended the Institute of Education of London University and in July 1972 was awarded a Diploma in the Teaching of Deaf and Partially Hearing Children.[963] The Department he studied at in this Institute was that of Child Development. His next post was between 1977 and 1989 as the teacher in the Charge Unit for Hearing Impaired Pupils at the Belle Vue Boys' Grammar School in Bradford, the city in which he was born and had his schooling. Between 1982 and 1985 he studied at the University of Leeds School of Education.[964] This University awarded him in 1984 a Diploma in the education of children with special needs (learning difficulties), and two years later the degree of Master of Education.[965]

As of June 2013, he was living in Cullingworth, which is near Bradford in Yorkshire.[966]

WILLIAM GAGEN

He was born on 18 November 1920[967] in the West Ham area of London[968] to William and Maud (née Burdfield) Gagen.[969] It has been suggested that he studied in Canada.[970] At the beginning of 1941, he married Margery E. Harfield in the Abingdon district.[971]

961. E-mails from Hamilton Lodge School, 18 and 19 July 2013.
962. Ibid., 23 September 2013.
963. E-mail from Institute of Education, 24 July 2013.
964. E-mail from Charles Marshall, op. cit.
965. E-mail from Leeds University, 15 July 2013.
966. E-mail from Charles Marshall, 29 June 2013.
967. E-mail from Sidney Gold, 23 May 2014.
968. General Register Office index, Births registered in October, November and December 1920, p.G-1.
969. General Register Office index, Marriages registered in October, November and December 1919, pp.B-175, G-1.
970. E-mail from Jeffrey Gandz, 21 May 2013.
971. General Register Office index, Marriages registered in January, February and March 1941,

He was elected a Fellow of the Royal Geographical Society on 14 July 1952. At that period he was a teacher at St. Mary's Preparatory School in Reigate, Surrey.[972] He was removed from the Fellowship at the end of 1967, probably because he failed to keep up his subscriptions.[973]

Gagen joined the staff at Carmel in the summer term of 1954.[974] He taught Geography[975] and Mathematics in the Senior School,[976] and he also taught in the Prep School.[977] Whilst at Carmel, he and his family lived in a caravan which he had brought to the school and which he parked in the corner of the field near to the Main Building. His wife worked in the linen room of the school.[978] His son Nigel became a pupil in the Prep School in the summer term 1954,[979] and that term received the first prize for secular subjects in Form III.[980]

In addition to teaching in the Prep School, he ran a "Model Aeroplane Club." In the course of his running this club, he designed a model aeroplane, and each of four boys then built it under his guidance.[981] Another club which he ran in the Prep School was a "Stamp Club." On it, he wrote, "All members would be well advised not to collect stamps from all over the world, but to limit their collection to specific countries or themes. In this way an attractive collection can be obtained in a short time at a reasonable cost."[982]

Gagen left Carmel after the Spring term of 1957.[983] In praising his Maths teaching, Jeffrey Gandz wrote, "He was the only person who ever taught Mathematics in a way that I could understand!"[984] Of his Geography lessons, Alan Gold recollects, "I remember some of his lessons including one where the book we were using had some fulsome description of the countryside and he went on 'now we go all soppy and sentimental.'

---

pp.G-1, H-72.

972. E-mail from Royal Geographical Society, 17 December 2012. However, St. Mary's School could find no record of him (telephone conversation between author and St. Mary's School, 17 April 2013).

973. E-mail from Royal Geographical Society, op. cit.

974. Carmel 1954, p.9.

975. E-mail from Alan Gold, 20 July 2014.

976. 7 years, p.48; Recollections – Jeffrey Gandz.

977. Alpha 1954, p.2.

978. 7 years, p.48.

979. Alpha 1954, p.4.

980. Alpha 1955, p.4.

981. Alpha 1954, p.6.

982. Alpha 1956, p.6.

983. Carmel 1957, p.5.

984. Recollections – Jeffrey Gandz.

I found this extremely funny and went into fits of uncontrollable laughter."[985]

He then became a teacher at the William Farr Church of England School in Welton,[986] a village in Lincolnshire. The school had a bungalow and Gagen lived there.[987] A person who was a pupil at that school in 1978, recollects that there was then an elderly teacher there called Gagen.[988]

He was also for about thirty years the clerk to the Welton Parish Council,[989] and in 1974 he was instrumental in the twinning between Welton and Monce en Belin,[990] a rural village in north-west France.

Gaggen lived in the school bungalow until he died[991] in the spring of 1999, which was just a few months after the death of his wife.[992]

ARTHUR JOSEPH HEALEY

He was born on 8 July 1914 and was educated at the Nelson School in Wigton, Cumberland.[993] He became the Head Boy and according to the then Headmaster "[he] is doing his job splendidly in every way." He was also Captain of both Rugger XV and Cricket XI and on this the headmaster believed that "he would gain some recognition even in Oxford."[994]

Following his schooling, in 1933 he joined St. Edmund Hall, Oxford University as a commoner and studied there until 1936. He received the degree of B.A. in Modern History with Second Class Honours on 15 October 1936, and in the following year received a diploma in Education.[995]

---

985. E-mail from Alan Gold, 20 July 2014.
986. E-mail from Marlene Chapman, Councillor on Welton-by-Lincoln Parish Council, 12 June 2014; telephone conversation between author and Marlene Chapman, 17 June 2014.
987. E-mail from Marlene Chapman, op. cit.; telephone conversation between author and Marlene Chapman, op. cit. This conflicts with the records of the Royal Geographical Society which state that in 1963 he was living in Scampton (e-mail from Royal Geographical Society, op. cit.), which is a village adjacent to Welton .
988. Telephone conversation between author and Mrs. Blakey of the William Farr School, 17 June 2014.
989. Telephone conversation between author and Malcolm Parish, former Chairman of Welton-by-Lincoln Parish Council, 22 June 2014.
990. E-mail from Marlene Chapman, op. cit.; telephone conversation between author and Marlene Chapman, op. cit.
991. Telephone conversation between author and Marlene Chapman, op. cit.
992. E-mail from Sidney Gold, 23 May 2014.
993. Application form from Arthur Healey to St. Edmund Hall, Oxford, 7 February 1933.
994. Letter from Headmaster of Nelson School to St. Edmund Hall, Oxford, 8 February 1933.
995. E-mail from Degree Conferrals, Oxford University, 18 December 2012; e-mail from St. Edmund Hall, Oxford, 13 December 2012.

Whilst at St. Edmund Hall, he obtained in 1934 colours in cricket and rugby, and in football in 1935.[996]

In 1938, Healey was living in Gloucester.[997] A year later in the spring of 1939, he married Margaret Dixon in Wigton, a small market town outside the Lake District.[998]

Between 1940 and 1943 he was in the RAF and stationed at Uxbridge (which is situated in the London area), and Wigtown in Scotland.[999] In July 1950, he was appointed to the commission of Pilot Officer in the Training Branch of the Royal Air Force Volunteer Reserve.[1000] About two years later, he was promoted to a Flying Officer.[1001] Of his service in the Armed Forces, he told his pupils at Carmel that he had to take orders from people younger than him![1002]

Healey joined the staff at Carmel in the summer term of 1954[1003] to teach History.[1004] For some unknown reason, he was known at Carmel as "Tim Healey," when his name was in fact "Arthur Joseph"! However, Alan Gold does offer the following suggestion, "Tim Healy was an Irish politician who would have been well known when our AJH [Healey] was growing up."[1005]

Of Healey's lessons, Jeremy Rosen wrote that he taught "from a well-used set of notes, so that year by year you knew exactly what he would teach and when compared to some teachers, this was a major recommendation."[1006] He also taught English from the first to the fourth forms,[1007] and Latin at least to the first form.[1008]

In addition to his class teaching, the Carmel magazine wrote of him on his first football season at the school how he "deserves much credit for the encouragement and help that he has given to the team."[1009] Even more so,

---

996. E-mail from St. Edmund Hall, Oxford, op. cit.

997. Ibid.

998. General Register Office index, Marriages registered in April, May and June 1939, pp.D-340, H-118.

999. E-mail from St. Edmund Hall, Oxford, op. cit.

1000. London Gazette supplement, 12 September 1950, p.4579.

1001. London Gazette supplement, 16 September 1952, p.4917.

1002. Information from Nigel Simons, 12 August 2012.

1003. Carmel 1954, p.9.

1004. Carmel College Senior School, sample school reports, autumn 1954 and autumn 1955, forms 2 – 3 (name withheld).

1005. E-mail from Alan Gold, 20 July 2014

1006. Recollections – Jeremy Rosen, chap.2.

1007. Carmel College Senior School, sample school reports, summer 1954 – summer 1957, forms 1 – 4 (name withheld).

1008. Ibid., summer – autumn 1954, form 1 (name withheld).

1009. Carmel 1955, p.44.

were his activities (even from the term he arrived), with cricket,[1010] and again here the Carmel magazine wrote of his "untiring efforts in raising the standard of play,"[1011] including the coaching of pupils in cricket.[1012] On occasion he would write the "cricket pen portraits" in the Carmel magazine.[1013] He was also the Housemaster of Montefiore[1014] but, as the saying goes "a change is as good as a rest," and thus at a later date he transferred to be Housemaster of Alexander.[1015]

The pupils at Carmel had heard that Healey had played as a member of a team in County cricket matches. However, an Old Carmeli, Matthew Engel, who was Editor of "Wisden Cricketers' Almanack"[1016] states this is incorrect and that Healey's name never appeared in "Wisden."[1017] Alan Gold offers an explanation which answers this apparent contradiction, "Re his being a county cricketer, I remember him saying that he played for Leicestershire 2nd XI and thus was never a first class cricketer and his name would not have appeared in Wisden."[1018]

Healey's attitude to sports versus lessons can be seen from an alleged conversation between him and a pupil, Geoffrey Levy, who was great at sports, "'Are you coming out to cricket practice now' and Geoff said, 'Well actually I have O Levels and a special assignment in English and I am very behind in my Maths prep.' Healey then replied, 'You boys have got the wrong attitude to sport'."[1019]

His wife Margaret became a matron in the Prep School in the academic year 1955/56.[1020] His son Peter was one of the first non-Jewish pupils at Carmel, joining in 1956 aged 7 and he remained there until 1967.[1021]

Healey left Carmel in about 1973 and retired, (his wife continuing at Carmel for a few more years),[1022] and he died at the beginning of 1977 in Oxfordshire,[1023] at the age of 62.

1010. Carmel 1954, p.47.
1011. Carmel 1955, p.53; similar wording in subsequent years.
1012. Carmel 1960, p.37.
1013. E.g., Carmel 1959, pp.42–43.
1014. Carmel: 1956, p.42, 1957, p.39.
1015. Carmel 1960, p.42.
1016. It is often referred to simply as Wisden. It is a cricket reference book published annually in the United Kingdom and is considered the world's most famous sports reference book.
1017. E-mail Matthew Engel, 14 September 2012.
1018. E-mail from Alan Gold, 20 July 2014.
1019. Recollections – David Saville.
1020. Alpha 1956, page after frontispiece.
1021. Old Carmeli Association, Occupational Directory 1991, list of members at beginning of book.
1022. E-mail from Jeremy Rosen, 23 December 2012.
1023. E-mail from Sidney Gold, 18 November 2013.

LAURENCE HENRY TONKS

He was born on 2 August 1895,[1024] in Chipping Norton, which is a market town in the Cotswold Hills in Oxfordshire.[1025]

He attended Leeds University where he was awarded in 1921, both the degrees of B.Sc. with honours and M.Sc. in Geology.[1026] On 27 January 1937, he was elected as a member of "The Geological Society."[1027]

In 1931, Tonks was the joint author of the book "The Geology of Manchester and the South-East Lancashire Coalfield." A few years earlier in 1926, he had contributed to a book on the geology of Carlisle, Longtown and Silloth District, and in 1948 he contributed to a book on the geology of Southport and Formby.[1028] Indeed he was professional geologist with more than twenty years experience in his field,[1029] and he even merited a Parliamentary mention in 1942, "Copy of a Treasury Minute dated 14th May 1942, granting a retired allowance to Mr. Laurence Henry Tonks, a Senior Geologist on the Staff of the Geological Society of Great Britain, under Section 2 of the Superannuation Act, 1887."[1030]

Following his retirement from geology, he went into teaching, and between 1942 and 1951, he taught Mathematics at Boston Grammar School. The secretary of the "Old Bostonian Association" writes of him, "He was a tall well-built man, who was popular with the pupils but his bulk generated good behavior." At the same period, he was treasurer of the British Legion.[1031]

Tonks joined the staff at Carmel in September 1954,[1032] but was only there for one year. That year his teaching included Mathematics to the first[1033] and second years,[1034] Physics[1035] and Chemistry to the third year, and General Science in the fourth year.[1036] During that year the author

---

1024. Ibid.
1025. General Register Office index, Births registered in July, August and September 1895, p.T-552.
1026. E-mail from Leeds University, 13 September 2012.
1027. E-mail from Geological Society, 25 June 2012.
1028. "Copac" library catalogue.
1029. Inspectors' Report, p.15.
1030. Journals of the House of Commons, (H. M. Stationery Office), vol. 197, Session 1941–42, 19 May 1942, p.104.
1031. E-mail from Boston Grammar School, 11 September 2012.
1032. Carmel 1955, p.5.
1033. Carmel College Senior School, sample school report, autumn 1954, form 1, (name withheld).
1034. Ibid., autumn 1954 – spring 1955, form 2, (name withheld).
1035. 7 years, p.49.
1036. Inspectors' Report, p.15.

was in the third form and received instruction from Tonks, and on these lessons the author writes, "He [Tonks] began his first lesson by explaining to us the difference between Chemistry and Physics. In Physics, he told us we measure how big an object is and how much it weighs. In Chemistry, we want to know what will happen to the object if we add something to it."[1037] Michael Bharier also has recollections of his lessons with Tonks:

> The Maths teacher was Mr. Tonks. He spent much of his time talking about his stamp collection, which he would bring in in little metal boxes, tobacco boxes, I think. . . . One more thing about Tonks – when writing on the blackboard with his back to the class, he would see who was talking through the reflection in his spectacles (I witnessed that). He was also reputed to be able to hit that person by flinging a piece of chalk over his shoulder – a bit apocryphal but amusing.[1038]

Jeffrey Fisher also has recollections of Tonks' stamp collection and of his throwing things at pupils:

> Mr. Tonks was a Maths teacher, a big burly gentleman with a head of white hair. I can't remember how good a Maths teacher he was (though he could have contributed in some way to my taking Maths at A-level) but I do remember that he was a stamp collector. It is quite possible that his stamp collection was more important to him than his teaching of Maths because on some occasions, he would come into the classroom, announce that he was not in the mood to teach Maths that day, and ask those in the class who collected stamps (I don't think I was one of them) to take out their albums (do school kids still collect stamps today?) and swap stamps with him. I am not aware if there are those who say that their Maths education was hindered by swapping stamps with Mr. Tonks instead of learning Algebra or Geometry.
>
> Mr. Tonks story is linked with the good old days of corporal punishment. All of us who were at school in the 1950s will surely remember heavy objects being thrown across the classroom by a teacher who wanted to "attract the attention" of a particular pupil: the object most often thrown was the board rubber. In one particular lesson, Mr. Tonks wanted to test his throwing skills but did not have a board

---

1037. 7 years, p.49.
1038. E-mail from Michael Bharier, 22 June 2013.

rubber at hand. The nearest heavy object was a chumash which he picked up and threw at someone at the back of the class: I cannot remember if the chumash reached its target. Mr. Tonks, affable as he was, was not Jewish. But what can a teacher do if a board rubber is not handy and you need to carry out a disciplinary mission?![1039]

Whilst in Carmel, he would participate in the activities of the Haber Society.[1040] When he left in the summer of 1955, the Carmel magazine wrote, "We extend our best wishes to Mr. Tonks, who came to us for only a year, and is, to our regret, leaving us this term."[1041]

He died about the beginning of 1973 in the Dorchester area,[1042] at the age of 77.

DR. DIRK BIJL

He was born probably in Holland. He studied Physics at Leiden University, and during the period when the Nazis occupied Holland he was studying for his doctorate. He already had a job as an assistant at a laboratory in Leiden, which was connected with the University. The Nazis had allowed it to stay open (even though they had closed all the Dutch Universities), because it housed a school for instrument makers who were, in their training, dependent on the scientists.[1043]

In the building where he lived, a young Jewish child, aged 2 or 3, was hidden, and when the Nazis made a surprise search of that building, Dirk Bijl smuggled him out in his rucksack and took him to a safe house. This child and his parents both survived the war.[1044] When the Nazis scrambled radio transmissions from England to prevent the Dutch from listening to them, Dirk Bijl constructed an aerial to put in front of the radio to block the scrambling and thus enable the listener to hear the programme. He also made these aerials for his relatives and friends.[1045]

On another occasion Bijl had a narrow escape from the Nazis. It was in about the summer of 1943 that the Nazis were picking up employable men to be sent away for forced labour. Dirk was on a train which suddenly stopped a few miles before Haarlem station and it was whispered that the

1039. Recollections – Jeffrey Fisher.
1040. Carmel 1955, p.13.
1041. Ibid., p.5.
1042. E-mail from Sidney Gold, 18 November 2013.
1043. Alida's Memoirs, chap.4, (Internet).
1044. Ibid.
1045. Ibid., chap.5. (Internet).

Nazis were at this station to take men for forced labour. Dirk together with hundreds of other men got off the train and walked home. Following this incident, every day for several weeks, Dirk would alight from this train at the station before Haarlem, and cycle home on the bicycle which his fiancée, Alida Johanna Lursen, brought daily to this station.[1046]

He came to England after the Second World War after having received a British Council scholarship to do research in Oxford University. The subject of his research was microwaves, and a report on the progress of his research was sent to the British Council after their requesting it. He also received a three year Fellowship at that University from the Pressed Steel Company. However, he was worried that he might not be able to find accommodation in Oxford and might as a result have to cut short his three year Fellowship.[1047] There is no record of his becoming a naturalised British citizen.

Bijl came to Carmel in the autumn term 1954. Although he was only there for one term, the Carmel magazine writes of him that he "managed to create a deep impression on his pupils in the short time he was here."[1048] That autumn term, the upper sixth (the top form of the school) was taught physics by him.[1049] At the same time he was doing research at the Clarendon Laboratories in Oxford.[1050]

One Friday, when he must have been working late at the school, he turned up in the dining hall during the Shabbat meal and sat at the staff table wearing his academic gown, obviously not realising that academic gowns were not worn by staff on Shabbat![1051]

After that term at Carmel he went on to be a lecturer in Natural Philosophy at St. Andrews University,[1052] and in 1959 he was appointed as a Reader.[1053] At a later date he became Professor of Solid State Physics at Bradford Institute of Technology.[1054]

Bijl died on 13 July 2004 in Bradford.[1055]

1046. Ibid., chap.4.
1047. Archives in Royal Society, Simon Papers 1906–1956, correspondence with Dr. Dirk Bijl.
1048. Carmel 1955, p.5.
1049. Carmel College Senior School, sample school report, autumn 1954, upper sixth form (name withheld).
1050. Rau letters, 1 October 1954.
1051. Unwritten recollections of author.
1052. Carmel 1955, p.5.
1053. Education & Training, vol. 7, iss.10, pp.438–442, (it was quoted that this item was to be found in this paper).
1054. Bulletin of the Institute of Physics and the Physical Society, vol.16, no.10, October 1965, p.426.
1055. Alida's Memoirs, "Welcome," (Internet).

MRS. MARGARET FLORENCE WHITFIELD

She was born on 8 July 1908[1056] in Shercock in the County of Cavan, her father being the Sergeant in the Royal Irish Constabulary.[1057] (Her daughter Julie strongly decried the suggestion that her mother was a French-Canadian![1058]) After the partition of Ireland, this area became part of the Republic of Ireland. Then her family, being Protestant, moved to County Fermanagh, which is in Northern Ireland.[1059] Her maiden name was Huddie and she became a Whitfield in the summer of 1940 when she married Trevor Drought Warburton Whitfield,[1060] who was later the Director of Education of Berkshire.[1061]

Her secondary education was at the Methodist College in Belfast.[1062] Following that, in 1928 she became a "Schol" of Trinity College Dublin (T.C.D.) having passed special examinations to be a Scholar of T.C.D,[1063] and there she studied Modern Languages, namely French and German. After one year at the University, she decided at the same time to study for a Law degree and in the winter of 1931 was simultaneously awarded degrees in Modern Literature and in Legal and Political Science both of them Class I. In addition she received a large gold medal for each of these two degrees.[1064] These medals were awarded for the best Class I in that subject and she was the only woman to have ever been awarded two large gold medals.[1065]

Immediately after graduation, Mrs. Whitfield moved to London and worked for Notleys, a large advertising agency. On the outbreak of the Second World War, she joined the BBC as a Foreign Language Monitor. She worked there until 1943 (the year she gave birth to her son John), listening to all kinds of wireless broadcasts in both French and German, making as rapid translation as the then technology would allow, and then passing on the information to the relevant government departments.[1066]

1056. E-mail from Margaret Whitfield's daughter Julie Ferguson, 10 December 2012.
1057. Ibid., 3 December 2012.
1058. Ibid.
1059. Ibid.
1060. General Register Office index, Marriages registered in April, May and June 1940, pp.H-205, W-456.
1061. E-mail from Berkshire Record Office, 21 November 2012.
1062. E-mail from Julie Ferguson, op. cit.
1063. E-mail from Trinity College Dublin (TCD), 22 November 2012.
1064. Trinity College [Dublin] Record Volume, 1951, pp.194, 291; e-mail from Julie Ferguson, op. cit.
1065. E-mail from Julie Ferguson, op. cit.
1066. Ibid.

She joined the staff at Carmel in the academic year 1954/55, but the Carmel magazine of that year forget to mention it and in the following year they were most apologetic!

> With shame, confusion, and sincere regret, the Senior Editor reports his unpardonable failure in the last magazine to record the arrival on our staff of Mrs. Whitfield, to teach German and French part-time. This belated acknowledgement at least allows him to pay tribute to the scholarship, conscientiousness and charm which have by now endeared her to the whole school.[1067]

The author has many positive reminiscences on Mrs. Whitfield:

> A more conscientious and hard working teacher it would be harder to find. For every prep night, without exception, she would set a written exercise to be done and she would meticulously mark it herself. One year, her prep night for French was on Sunday, and since she didn't come in on that day, she would write the prep exercise on the blackboard at the end of the previous week.
>
> She insisted that there were two French preps each week for her classes. At one period, it was decided that on two evenings a week, there would be extra-curricular activities instead of prep and this of course meant cutting down the number of preps. She was accordingly only given one. She told us that she had gone and asked for a second one but they wouldn't give it to her.
>
> When she was ill, we didn't get a free period. She would telephone the school and tell them which exercise we should do during her lesson. On one occasion the message did not reach us till the end of the lesson and so we didn't do it. That was no excuse with her – we had to do it in our own time. On the last few days of term, almost all the teachers stopped giving us lessons – but not Mrs. Whitfield. I believe it was already the last day of term when she gave us a French dictation.
>
> From the third form onwards she was our only French teacher. At first we were learning from a book 'En Route.' The class below us, who were also using this book had almost caught up with us – they were very excited about this. They never actually caught up since Mrs.

1067. Carmel 1956, p.5.

Whitfield changed over to Whitmarsh's French textbook. Thus everything we did that was connected with French had a 'Whit' in it![1068]

One of the difficulties in a French dictation (or, as she would always call it, "la dictée") was to get the right accents on the various vowels. With her, it was easy if you knew what to look for, as Geoffrey Paradise explains. "Mrs. Whitfield, with her very useful habit of twitching up her right eyebrow whenever there was an E acute accent in dictation."[1069] David Saville had a slightly different version of this "Mrs. Whitfield – in French 'Dictee' she used to scratch her nose on the left side for 'aigu' and the other side for 'grave' – I can't remember what she did for 'circomflex'."[1070] Another slightly different version by Spencer Batiste stated that "There was Mrs. Whitfield who in pronouncing French dictation had the useful ability to make her mouth reflect the direction of the respective accents."[1071] Clearly according to all versions, Mrs. Whitfield's facial contortions informed her pupils of the correct French accents,[1072] but very likely this was done unconsciously.

In addition to her pupils' reminiscences at Carmel, her daughter Julie also has reminisces of her mother's period at Carmel:

> She loved the teaching. She had an inflexible rule that if she set prep, then it should be marked by, and returned at, the next lesson. She used proper red ink in a fountain pen to mark the exercise books, and worked assiduously through them, with the help of copious cups of black tea, until the work was complete. . . .
>
> She always said that the authorities at Carmel were her best employers, ever. She was treated with unfailing courtesy and flexibility. When she was appointed, she thought that as a non-Jewish woman she was perhaps not their ideal candidate, but she was welcomed most kindly and stayed for over 20 years. She said that learning German was never that popular among the boys, and that it would have been better to have introduced Spanish far earlier.
>
> No pressure was ever put on her to take any 'domestic' responsibility within the school. As a mother of two young children, she

---

1068. 7 years, p.51.
1069. Recollections – Geoffrey Paradise.
1070. Recollections – David Saville.
1071. Recollections – Spencer Batiste.
1072. This is also referred to by Jeffrey Gandz in his Recollections.

was most unusual in her social circle in the 50s and 60s in that she worked at all, and she always appreciated that Carmel allowed her the departmental and teaching responsibilities, but timetabled her a weekday afternoon off as well as Saturdays and Sundays. As children, we were allowed to use the school swimming pool in the holidays. I vividly remember the tiny old pool, often green with algae, which we used before the grand opening of the swish new one.[1073]

One of her pupils, Neil Alton, describes Mrs. Whitfield, "Deep blue eyes – alternately sweet and steely."[1074] He also had the greatest of praise for her, "She was simply superb. As a teacher, lover of French literature, conveyer of French (and her own) humour, and tolerant above and beyond the call of duty of us."[1075]

For some reason Jacob Fachler assumed that she was "a motor racing enthusiast,"[1076] but her daughter strongly refuted this. "If you were to make a list of the ten things my mother was least interested in, a candidate for inclusion on the list would be motor racing!"[1077] However, although not a "motor racing enthusiast," she was "a demon bridge player."[1078] There is no smoke without fire, and one might well ask how she got this "motor racing" reputation. Alan Gold has an answer, "Mrs. Whitfield might not have liked motor racing in general but she frequently talked about the driver Mike Hawthorn who was killed in a crash. How do I know? Mike was famed for wearing a spotted bow tie and was known in France as Le Papillon (the Butterfly). Whenever this word came up she would shake her head and say 'poor Mike Hawthorn'."[1079]

Her daughter relates that "after retirement in about 1973, she and my father continued to walk, travel, particularly in France, where she was often pleased by the regular compliments she received on the unusual excellence of her spoken French, most especially on her correct use of the subjunctive!"[1080] She died on 29 April 1982 at the age of 73.[1081]

1073. E-mail from Julie Ferguson, op. cit.
1074. Recollections – Neil Alton.
1075. E-mail from Neil Alton, 15 January 2013.
1076. Recollections – Jacob Fachler.
1077. e-mail from Julie Ferguson, 3 December 2012.
1078. Ibid.
1079. E-mail from Alan Gold, 20 July 2014.
1080. Email from Julie Ferguson, 3 December 2012
1081. Ibid., 10 December 2012.

JULYAN FRANCIS BUNNEY

He was born on 23 April 1925[1082] in the Truro area in Cornwall[1083] to Edgar Opie and Winifred Bunney, his father's occupation being a grocer's traveler. He first attended Bosvigo (Elementary) Council School in Truro, and then, between 22 September 1936 and 23 July 1943, Truro School as a day-scholar. In June 1940 and in December 1940, he passed the Oxford & Cambridge School Certificate Examination and received an exemption from Matriculation. A few years later in July 1942 and in July 1943 he passed the London High School Certificate Examinations.[1084] During his last two years at the school he was a member of the 1st Rugby XV, and was also a prefect.[1085]

Between October 1943 and June 1946 he studied at Exeter University where he was awarded the degree of B.Sc. (General).[1086] His area of study was Radio Bursar: Physics and Pure and Advanced Mathematics, and in mid-1947, he received a College Diploma in Education from the same University, a diploma which was instituted originally "for those wishing to teach in Senior and Central Schools."[1087]

Bunney was in the Royal Navy where he was promoted to a Temporary Sub-Lieutenant (Special Branch) in September 1946.[1088] According to the December 1945 edition of the Truro school magazine, whilst he was still studying at Exeter University, he joined the Radar Branch of the RNVR (Royal Navy Volunteer Reserve); other pupils did similarly whilst still at Exeter University.[1089] Henry law writes, that Bunney had been involved in radio and also in instruction and training, adding that "he certainly knew a lot about that side of the subject."[1090]

In 1947, following his National Service, he joined the staff of Caterham House Boys School where he taught Science and Mathematics. He also assisted in the school's sports programme in tennis and rugger.[1091] On his appointment, the school magazine wrote, "As an Old Boy of Truro

---

1082. Record Card of Julyan Bunney from Truro School.
1083. General Register Office index, Births registered in April, May and June 1925, p.B-160.
1084. Record Card of Julyan Bunney from Truro School.
1085. E-mail from Truro School, 10 January 2013.
1086. At that period the degrees of those studying at Exeter University were the London University external degrees.
1087. E-mail from Exeter University, 1 October 2012.
1088. London Gazette, 15 November 1946, p.5625.
1089. E-mail from Truro School, 11 January 2013.
1090. Recollections – Henry Law, Carmel College days, part 1, p.5.
1091. Caterham House Boys School magazine, 1949, School notes.

School . . . Mr. Bunney will be acquainted with some of the problems and opportunities of a school of this type."[1092] He was at that school for two years.[1093] In the summer of 1949 he married Rowena Jessop in Truro,[1094] the city where he had been born.

His next job was Physics master at Lord William Grammar School in Thame Oxfordshire. He began there during the academic year 1949/50, and he remained for about five years until he joined Carmel. Due to his teaching, many of his students there went on to pursue careers in Science.[1095] In addition to his teaching duties he was also a rugby coach. An Old Tamensian (as the alumni were called after the town "Thame") reminisces on him:

> He immediately commanded respect without ever raising his voice. His quietly authoritative manner was never challenged in class, and he was equally in control whether coaching or refereeing rugby. It mattered not that head boy [name of boy] was the school's outstanding rugby player; athlete and a favourite of headmaster [name of headmaster]. When he backchatted referee Bunney in a house match he was ordered off the field.[1096]

On his rugby activities there, another Old Tamensian recollects, "That particular match stands in my memory also because it was the last match that Mr. Julyan Bunney, an inspirational teacher and rugby coach was in charge, as he had been poached by Carmel College."[1097]

This was followed by his service at Carmel,[1098] where he joined the staff in the academic year 1954/55.[1099] At Carmel he taught Physics,[1100] and when he began at Carmel, General Science and Mathematics as well.[1101]

He would teach Physics right up to the third year sixth form. It was in this form that the pupils took the Scholarship level Physics paper. As to

1092. Ibid., 1947, School notes.
1093. Ibid., 1949, School notes.
1094. General Register Office index. Marriages registered in July, August and September 1949, pp.B-200, J-248.
1095. E-mail from Lord William School, 21 January 2013.
1096. Ibid., 22 January 2013.
1097. Old Tamensians Links, Cliff Nixey, (Internet).
1098. Telephone conversation between author and Julyan Bunney, 13 March 2012.
1099. Carmel 1955, p.5.
1100. Carmel College Senior School, sample school reports, summer 1955 – spring 1957, classes up to scholarship Sixth (names withheld).
1101. Unwritten recollections of author; Carmel College Senior School, sample school report, autumn 1955, form 3 (name withheld).

be expected, the questions in this paper were not easy and according to Ian Rabinowitz, it was not Bunney who solved them but the pupils in the class.[1102] A similar comment was made but more cautiously by Henry Law, "I might be wrong, but my impression with Julyan Bunney was that he was not as bright as the best of the pupils and at times would defer to them gracefully." However, Law then adds, "Or perhaps it was just his way of showing respect to the pupils. Either way it was creditable."[1103]

In the 1950s, calculations were often performed using a slide-rule, so much so that Henry Law wrote that "a slide rule was essential equipment even for O-level science."[1104] Whereas Romney Coles was a devotee of slide-rules and said that he had forgotten the last time he had used logarithms, Bunney, for some unknown reason, was dead against them, although the author did see him using one surreptitiously.[1105]

He had consideration for all his pupils. There were pupils in his A-level class who were studying Biology instead of Mathematics and as a consequence knew no Calculus. At A-level it is preferable to use Calculus, but out of consideration for the Biology students, he avoided using it, although this did sometimes result in giving slightly different answers in mathematical problems.[1106]

He was also involved in the sporting activities of the school and from the academic year 1959/60 onwards, was Housemaster of Gilbert House. The house captain praised him for "his encouragement both on and off the field" and how the House felt "a deep sense of pride in being privileged to have him" as the housemaster.[1107]

When one boy said to Bunney that those pupils whose dormitory was at Nuneham Murren (the farm house) worked hard, he replied that since they had moved there, the shares in the tobacco companies had soared.[1108] Indeed it was a smokers' paradise.

After leaving Carmel, in the early 1960s he became Deputy Headmaster at the Royal Latin School in Buckinghamshire, where he remained until he retired in the early 1980s. Another former deputy head of that school, Andy Cooper, writes of him, "Mr. B was a teacher of Physics, a stern man by outward demeanour but, a fair, generous man who lived by

1102. Conversation between author and Ian Rabinowitz, 1 March 2012.
1103. Recollections – Henry Law, Carmel College days, part 1, pp.4–5.
1104. Ibid., p.6.
1105. 7 years, p.61.
1106. Ibid., p.62.
1107. Carmel 1960, p.43.
1108. 7 years, p.104.

the highest of personal moral standards and expected the same from staff and students."[1109]

As of 2013, he was living in Cumnor, which is near Oxford.[1110]

HARRY ERNEST GEORGE

He was born on 28 June 1895[1111] in the West Ham area of Essex,[1112] to Alfred George who was a schoolmaster at Linden Road County School.[1113] By 1901 his family was living in Gloucester.[1114] His schooling was at Crypt Grammar School in Gloucester (a school whose history stretches back to the sixteenth century[1115]), where he enrolled on 7 September 1907.[1116] This was followed by his studying at Merton College, Oxford University, between the years 1914 and 1915 and between the years 1919 and 1921. He attended Merton as a "Mathematical Postmaster"[1117] and received a Second Class Honours degree in Physics in 1921. His M.A. was awarded in 1930.[1118] He also gained another degree. This was from London University where he became an external student, his mode of study being through distance learning. According to his University record, he registered for the statistics examination in February 1923. In November 1931 he passed the intermediate examination, and he was awarded the degree B.Sc. Special with First Class Honours on 1 August 1938.[1119]

His university studies at Oxford had been interrupted due to the First World War and he served as a second lieutenant in the Royal Garrison Artillery in Egypt, France, and Salonika.[1120] The War Office had in August 1917 published the names of those in the Officers' Cadet Unit of the Royal Garrison Artillery, who had been promoted to the rank of second lieutenant. This list contained over 60 names, one of them being Harry

---

1109. E-mail from Andy Cooper, 15 January 2013.

1110. Ibid.

1111. Merton College Register 1900–1964 (Oxford), p.102.

1112. General Register Office index, Births registered in July, August and September 1895, p.G-205.

1113. E-mail from Crypt School, 26 February 2014, quoting from admissions register for 1906–1908, entry no. 1719.

1114. British Census 1901.

1115. The Crypt School (Internet).

1116. E-mail from Crypt School, op. cit.

1117. "Postmaster" is the Merton name for a Scholar, i.e., a student holding a financial award based on academic ability.

1118. Merton College Register, op. cit .

1119. E-mails from London University, 18 and 19 December 2013.

1120. Merton College Register, op. cit.

Ernest George.[1121] During that war, he fought on the same front, but on the other side, of his "enemy," another Carmel teacher, Dr. Friedmann![1122]

In 1923 he was on the staff at Mill Hill School in London.[1123] It was in his room that a pupil at that school, Cecil Goyder, made the first two-way radio communication between Britain and New Zealand.[1124] From 1923 to 1944, he was a Physics master at Nottingham High School.[1125]

He then left to take up the post of Headmaster of Ramsey Grammar School on the Isle of Man, beginning in September 1944.[1126] The school magazine extended him a "hearty welcome" and added, "We all hope that he will settle down and feel quite happy in his new surroundings."[1127] In a book on the history of this school, the author, Miss Louisa Williamson, who had been a History mistress at that school throughout the entire period when he was the Headmaster, wrote that Harry George had been "chosen out of well over a hundred applicants" but she summed him up critically:

> He was the exact opposite of his predecessor in the classroom, the school and community. A sincere man, no doubt, but an authoritarian with the trappings and manner of a caricature schoolmaster who alienated many inside and outside the school who cherished those who had created what was felt to be good. Two years after appointment he was to find the School more than doubled in size with the adoption of four years free, compulsory secondary education.[1128]

Whilst he was headmaster, the school began its "annual Gilbert and Sullivan productions."[1129] He retired from this school in 1955 and "no doubt

---

1121. Supplement to the London Gazette, 16 August 1917, p.8444.

1122. FMF, pp.26–27; The Old Carmeli Year Book 1977, p.9.

1123. E-mail from Mill Hill School, 26 November 2012.

1124. This was related to the author by Harry George whilst he was at Carmel, although a book on the history of Mill Hill School does not mention him in connection with Goyder. (Roderick Braithwaite, "Strikingly Alive" The History of the Mill Hill School Foundation 1807–2007 (Phillimore: Chichester, 2006), p.159.

1125. E-mail from Nottingham High School, 27 November 2012.

1126. Y Feeagh (The Raven) (magazine of Ramsey Grammar School, Isle of Man), no.36, July 1944.

1127. Y Feeagh (The Raven), no.37, December 1944, Random Notes.

1128. Miss L. E. Williamson, A Short History of Ramsey Grammar School, (about 1972), p.14.

1129. Whether it was he who introduced "Gilbert and Sullivan" productions to the school, or, as a result of someone else introducing them to the school he became interested in "Gilbert and Sullivan," is not known.

many able Sixth Formers benefitted from his teaching at a time when there was an urgent demand for mathematicians."[1130]

He then joined the staff at Carmel in the academic year 1955/56[1131] where he taught Mathematics[1132] and Physics.[1133] Towards the beginning of 1959, he had an eye operation, which meant he was out of the school for the subsequent half a year. However, during this period he did not neglect his pupils. The author was at the time studying for A-level Mathematics and recollects, "After his operation, Mr. George went through all the past papers for about the previous twenty years and wrote out all the answers for us. We then went through all the answers by ourselves to learn how to answer this type of question. It was fortunate that the examiners set the same type of question year in and year out."[1134] If he thought that the examiners had set an unfair question, he would comment on this, when he wrote out the answers. He also marked G.C.E. papers in Mathematics.[1135]

In addition to his teaching, he brought Gilbert and Sullivan into the school.[1136] He was so well liked by his pupils, that whilst recuperating from his eye operation they put their "meager pocket money together over time and bought him a set of Gilbert and Sullivan LPs [Long Playing gramophone records]."[1137] Moshe Benaim writes, "there was Mr. George, from whom I learned a great deal about Gilbert and Sullivan, if not about Physics."[1138]

He left Carmel in the summer of 1960,[1139] when he was aged 65, and died in about May 1987 in the Worcester area,[1140] at the age of almost 92.

RONALD LEWIS EVANS

He was born on 5 February 1918 in Monmouthshire Wales, his father being a men's outfitter. He attended Ebbw Vale County School between

---

1130. Miss L. E. Williamson, *A Short History of Ramsey Grammar School*, (about 1972), pp.15–16.
1131. Carmel 1956, p.4.
1132. 7 years, p.58; Carmel College Senior School, sample school reports, autumn 1956 – spring 1959, forms 4 – 5, (name withheld).
1133. 7 years, p.55.
1134. 7 years, p.60.
1135. Unwritten recollections of author.
1136. Carmel 1956, p.4.
1137. Recollections – David Shaw.
1138. Recollections – Moshe Benaim.
1139. Carmel 1960, p.5.
1140. E-mail from Sidney Gold, 18 November 2013.

1929 and 1932, and this was followed between the years 1932 and 1937 at the Grammar School in Abergavenny in Monmouthshire.[1141]

He was admitted to Emmanuel College Cambridge to study Mathematics on 1 October 1937, and a month later on 3 November he matriculated. In 1939 he received Third Class Honours in Part 1 of the Tripos. He was awarded his degree (on his second attempt) in 1940 under the wartime regulations of the University which permitted students to graduate without having completed the necessary nine terms (the formula was to "allow" them up to three "military terms" instead). However, just two "military terms" were used to complete his requirements, since he was at the University for six whole terms, and nineteen days of the Michaelmas Term 1939.[1142] There is a letter in his University file which indicates that he hoped to come back to the University after the War to train as a teacher, but there is no record that he did so.[1143] In 1944 his degree became an M.A. His other activities at the university were hockey and choral singing.[1144]

In the summer of 1948, Evans married Kathleen Mary Bown in Hinckley,[1145] a market town in Leicestershire where Kathleen had been born and schooled.

A few months later, in the autumn term 1948, he joined the staff at St. Bartholomew's School in Newbury (a school whose history goes back to 1466[1146]), where he taught Mathematics to the sixth form and where he remained until December 1955. He was also at various dates during this period the form master of Forms Vc and IVc.[1147]

He then joined the staff at Carmel[1148] to teach Mathematics up to and including the sixth forms.[1149] It is reported that in 1952, whilst he was teaching at St. Bartholomew's School, Kopul had approached him to establish a Maths department at Carmel's Greenham campus. However, since at that period, Kopul knew the school would have to relocated,

1141. Record card of Ronald Evans at Emmanuel College.

1142. E-mail from Emmanuel College, Cambridge, 8 January 2013; Record Card, op. cit.

1143. E-mail from Emmanuel College, op. cit.

1144. Record Card, op. cit.

1145. General Register Office index, Marriages registered in July, August and September 1948, pp. B-164, E-489.

1146. Wikipedia – St. Bartholomew's School.

1147. E-mail from St. Bartholomew's School Newbury, 5 February 2013, quoting from the school magazine Newburian.

1148. Carmel 1955, p.5.

1149. Unwritten recollections of author; Carmel College Senior School, sample school reports, autumn 1955 – summer 1956, forms 3 and 5 (names withheld).

Ronald Evans asked Kopul to approach him again when he knew where Carmel would be located.[1150]

On his teaching capabilities, Michael Bharier writes, "Mr. Evans brought me to such a high level in Maths that I found first year Maths in university very elementary."[1151] On a lighter note, David Saville wrote, "Mr. Evans the Maths teacher – he used to teach Maths in the loggia . . . and the first five minutes were always taken up with their [the boys at his lesson] reciting the Birkat Hamazon, following the 'Aruchat Eser' [ten o'clock snack], as they had been to Miss Aron's tuck-shop a few minutes earlier."[1152]

Soon after he came to Carmel, he introduced hockey as one of Carmel's sports. Jeremy Rosen records that he was an "international hockey referee."[1153] The author's recollection of Ronald Evans and hockey is that "even bad weather wouldn't deter him. Once it started snowing whilst we were playing and it was getting heavier but he went on. I kept asking myself when was he going to stop and let us go inside? Finally, even he came to the decision that we needed to stop."[1154]

He, together with his wife were also involved with tennis at Carmel. The Carmel magazine writes on this, "I would like to thank Mr. and Mrs. R. Evans for the expert coaching which they have afforded to the junior boys and the enthusiasm that they have installed into them."[1155] On various occasions he would be a member of the School cricket team.[1156]

He was on the staff of Carmel until it closed in 1997 and was indeed the longest serving member of staff[1157] – a period of 42 years. After Romney Coles had retired in 1967, he became Senior Master,[1158] and for part of the period between the resignation of David Stamler as Headmaster and the taking up of the position by Jeremy Rosen, Ronald Evans functioned as the acting Headmaster.[1159]

In addition to his activities at Carmel, he was a Member of a working party which produced texts for a School Mathematics Project, and

---

1150. This was reported in an addition made to a Wikipedia article on Carmel College (Oxford-shire), on 3 September 2013, by an unknown person without giving a citation.
1151. Recollections – Michael Bharier, chap.2.
1152. Recollections – David Saville.
1153. Recollections – Jeremy Rosen, chap.2.
1154. 7 years, p.49.
1155. Carmel 1960, p.39; similar comments in Carmel 1961, p.37.
1156. Carmel 1961, p.38.
1157. Recollections – Jeremy Rosen, chap.1.
1158. Ibid., chap.2.
1159. AJR (Association of Jewish Refugees) Information, vol. XXVI, no.7, July 1971, p.3.

an Associate Fellow of the Institute of Mathematics and its Applications. His non-mathematical interests were being a member of the local church choir and umpiring hockey.[1160]

Evans died on 20 April 2012, at the age of 94, and although he was not Jewish, a death notice appeared in the "Social and Personal" announcements of the "Jewish Chronicle."[1161]

WILLIAM FRANCIS WARREN

He was born on 28 June 1930[1162] and studied at Bexhill Grammar School for boys between 1941 and 1949.[1163]

In October 1950, he began studying for a B.A. at Christ Church College Oxford University and in 1954 received a Second Class degree in Biochemistry with Pharmacology as a supplementary subject. His B.A. degree was in fact conferred on 21 November 1953, since one could have it conferred after successfully completing Part 1 of the Honour School. In October 1954, he was admitted as a student for the degree of Doctor of Philosophy by the Biological Sciences Board. He then went on to do his D.Phil. degree in Biochemistry, which was conferred upon him on 1 November 1958, the subject of his thesis being "Particulate preparations from barley seedlings."[1164]

Whilst studying for his doctorate, Warren joined the staff at Carmel as a part-time Biology master for the academic year 1955/56.[1165] Of his activities, the Carmel magazine writes:

> He has been extremely active in his realm and the fruits of his labours may be seen in the form of various of his pupils stealthily crawling around the grounds, magnifying glass in one hand and notebook in the other. Although no species of animal previously thought to be extinct appears to have been found, some of our seniors have had unintentional swims whilst studying aquatic plants.[1166]

1160. Record Card, op. cit.
1161. Jewish Chronicle, 4 May 2012, p.27. The announcement incorrectly states that he was also a master at Carmel whilst it was at Newbury.
1162. E-mail from Christ Church College Oxford, 10 April 2013.
1163. E-mail from William Warren, 22 May 2013.
1164. E-mails from Oxford University, 5 March 2013 and Christ Church College, Oxford, 6 March 2013.
1165. Carmel College Senior School, sample school reports: autumn 1955 – summer 1956, form 3; autumn 1955, form 5 (name withheld).
1166. Carmel 1956, p.5.

Having completed his doctoral degree, he went for the Michaelmas (autumn) term of 1958, to teach at the Stowe School in Buckingham.[1167] During the following two years he was employed as an Assistant Lecturer and Post-Doctoral Researcher in the Old Radcliffe Infirmary at Oxford.[1168] In January 1961, he finally left Oxford and during that year took a number of temporary teaching posts. During the Lent (spring) term 1961, he was in charge of Chemistry (replacing a teacher who had been given a schoolmaster studentship at Oxford for one term) at Lancing School in West Sussex. Of Warren, the school magazine writes that "he brought with him a boundless enthusiasm for scouting and all things chemical."[1169] During the following term, he taught at Westminster School in a similar position.[1170]

In the autumn term 1961,[1171] he began to teach Botany, Biology, and Chemistry at the King Edward's School for Boys in Birmingham, but he felt that he "was not considered as a true member of any of these departments."[1172] He left that school at the end of the summer term 1962,[1173] and the school magazine commented that although he was there for only a year he "has given invaluable help and assistance to both the Juniors and the Seniors."[1174]

He was then appointed as Head of Science and House Tutor at Bembridge School which was situated on the Isle of Wight.[1175] He remained there until 1972, and then went on to teach as Head of Chemistry at Cheltenham (Pate's) Grammar School, where he remained until he retired in 1987.[1176]

As of May 2013 he was living in Cheltenham.[1177]

1167. E-mail from Stowe School, 10 July 2013.
1168. E-mail from William Warren, op. cit.
1169. E-mail from Lancing School, 21 March 2013.
1170. E-mail from Westminster School, 11 March 2013.
1171. King Edward's School Chronicle (Birmingham), vol. LXXVI, no.338, March 1962 (incorrectly dated July 1962), pp.4, 32.
1172. E-mail from William Warren, op. cit.
1173. King Edward's School Chronicle, vol. LXXVI, no.339, July 1962, p.45.
1174. Ibid., p.74.
1175. E-mail from William Warren, op. cit.; his teaching at Bembridge is also mentioned in the e-mail from Christ Church College, op. cit.
1176. E-mail from William Warren, op. cit.; in 1973, the Pate's school magazine, "The Patesian," referred to Warren's arrival at the school as the Head of Chemistry (e-mail from Pate's School, 16 July 2013).
1177. E-mail from William Warren, op. cit.

WILLIAM CHARLES PHELPS

He was born in Aston (an area within the city of Birmingham)[1178] on 16 June 1908, and his schooling was at the Central Secondary School in Birmingham. He then studied at Birmingham University, beginning in the academic year 1926/27. In his first year he studied Latin, English, French, and Pure Maths; in the following year (1927/28) he studied Latin, French, Philosophy, and History, and in his final year (1928/29) he studied Latin, French, and German. In 1929 he was awarded the degree of B.A. In the academic year 1930/31, he started an M.A. in French but there is no record of him completing this.[1179]

After graduating, Phelps spent a period of time in 1929 in teaching practice at the King Edward Camp Hill Boys' School in Birmingham. This was followed by his teaching in St. Austell in Cornwall and in London. During the Second World War he was with the Royal Air Force.[1180] Charles Marshall recollects that he worked at Bletchley Park with the code cracking teams.[1181]

In January 1948, Phelps returned to the King Edward Camp Hill School, where he taught French throughout the school. When he left this school at the end of the Easter term of 1955, the school magazine wrote about him:

> [He] brought to the teaching of French a deep interest in the boys with whom he came in contact and that they appreciated his interest was soon reflected in his great and widespread popularity amongst the boys of the School. There is little doubt that . . . his personality impressed itself on the School and he will be remembered with affection by many to whom he sought to impart some of his own love of French.[1182]

After leaving Camp Hill School, he took up an appointment under the Gateshead Education Committee at the Camp School in Hexham Nor-

---

1178. General Register Office index, Births registered in July, August and September 1908, p.P-439.
1179. E-mail from Birmingham University, 24 April 2013.
1180. Camp Hill Chronicle (Birmingham), Summer 1955.
1181. E-mail from Charles Marshall, 18 March 2013. The "Roll of Honour" which gives the names of those who worked in Bletchley Park during the Second World War, does not include William Phelps; however, Bletchley Park admits that their list is incomplete.
1182. Camp Hill Chronicle, Summer 1955.

William Phelps – 1956

thumberland.[1183] But he was only there for one term since in the following term, namely in September 1955, he joined the staff at Carmel where he was appointed as Senior French master (in place of Emil Schlesinger).[1184] He also taught Latin.[1185] In addition he was the form master of the lower fifth,[1186] and also a House master.[1187] The Carmel magazine writes, "Mr. Phelps started to have French singing groups, but overcome either by the French or by the singing (or possibly by the groups) appears to have temporarily resigned the project."[1188]

On him, Michael Goitein writes, "Mr. Phelps, a pleasant man who smoked like a chimney. What was extraordinary, and gave me a lifelong insight into addiction, was that he would set his alarm for the middle of the night to wake himself up in order to have a cigarette!"[1189]

He left Carmel in the summer of 1956, after having been there just one year. The author explains why he left so quickly and suddenly:

> Rabbi Rosen told us that in one of his lessons, he [Phelps] made some comment which some boys took to be anti-Semitic. These boys com-

---

1183. Ibid.
1184. Carmel 1956, p.5; Carmel College Senior School, sample school reports, autumn 1955 – summer 1956, form 5 (name withheld).
1185. 7 years, p.55.
1186. Carmel College Senior School, sample school reports, autumn 1955 – summer 1956, form 5 (name withheld).
1187. Ibid., summer 1956, form 3 (name withheld).
1188. Carmel 1956, p.5.
1189. Recollections – Michael Goitein.

plained to Rabbi Rosen and he as a consequence had to speak to Mr. Phelps about it. Mr. Phelps felt offended and left. Afterwards he was obviously sorry that he had been so precipitous in leaving, since he wrote to some boys saying how wonderful Carmel was. Rabbi Rosen added that had they not already found another Latin teacher, he was sure that he would have come back.[1190]

Michael Bharier also commented on Phelps' abrupt leaving of Carmel:

I think there were cultural biases about Jews at the time in the UK, not necessarily ill-intentioned, but biases nonetheless. These could easily have been interpreted as anti-Semitism. I came across it a few times myself, even at university level. Innocent seeming questions about the appearances of Jews or one time about Jews' sexuality. Really a product of ignorance rather than hostility.[1191]

Charles Marshall recollects that after leaving Carmel he returned to teach again in Northumberland,[1192] possibly, although there is no material to support it, he returned to the Camp School in Hexham.

He died in the 1960s, very likely in the autumn of 1966 in Birmingham.[1193]

ERNEST ALFRED GRAY

He was born on 17 September 1908 in Sculcoates which is in the East Riding of Yorkshire, to Alfred and Amy Gray.[1194]

His schooling included Glenalmond College in Perth, Scotland (a college which was founded by the British Prime Minister Gladstone[1195]), where he studied from the Lent term of 1923 to Christmas 1925.[1196] At

---

1190. 7 years, p.55.

1191. E-mail from Michael Bharier, 28 November 2012.

1192. E-mail from Charles Marshall, op. cit.

1193. Ibid; the General Register Office index, Deaths registered in October, November, December 1966, p.P-607 records the death of a William C. Phelps aged 58 in Birmingham, which was the place where his family lived.

1194. General Register Office index, Births registered in October, November and December 1908, p.G-207; e-mail from Trinity College, Cambridge, 4 December 2012; History of the Gray Family, Person Page – 87, (Internet).

1195. Glenalmond College (Perth), Glenalmond's History (Internet).

1196. The Glenalmond Register, 1847–1954, p.176.

this school he was in the "New Wing" House,[1197] and in a "Dramatic Play on the Trojan War" he acted the part of the "Greek servant."[1198] He then continued at the Royal Veterinary College of London University where he began on 10 January 1927,[1199] and he graduated from that College on 12 July 1932.[1200]

During the following years he was at various places all over England. In April 1937, it was the Harper Adams Agricultural College in Newport Salop, and in July of that same year, at the East Anglian Institute of Agriculture in Chelmsford. In March 1941 he was at the Veterinary Laboratories in Finchley Road, London, and just over two years later he was at the Agriculture Department of King's College, Newcastle-on-Tyne. In July 1945 he was at the School of Agriculture at Cambridge.[1201]

On 1 November 1946, he was admitted "as a Research Student, with membership of Trinity College [Cambridge University]. He was approved for the Master of Science [M.Sc.] degree and was admitted to the Faculty of Biology. . . . He submitted a thesis entitled 'The association of bacteria and ciliate protozoa in a chalk stream,' and graduated on 22 May 1950."[1202] In addition he was a Member of two professional bodies, namely the "Royal College of Veterinary Surgeons"[1203] and the "Institute of Biology."[1204]

During his lifetime, he wrote books on a whole variety of subjects which had some connection with medicine. His first books, published in the late 1930s and 1940s, were three books, each on the diary of John Knyveton, a surgeon from the mid-18th century. However, these three diaries are believed to be fictitious![1205] His next publication, which was first published in 1946, was "Diseases of Poultry" and in later years many editions of it were brought out.[1206] In 1952 he published a biographical book on the 18th century surgeon John Hunter[1207] and in November 1954 delivered a lecture before the Cambridge University History of Medicine Society

---

1197. The Glenalmond Chronicle, no. CCLXVIII, April 1923, pp.1.
1198. Ibid., p.13.
1199. E-mail from Royal Veterinary College, 4 December 2012.
1200. E-mail from Royal College of Veterinary Surgeons, 6 December 2012 with Record Card of Ernest Gray.
1201. Record Card of Ernest Gray at Royal Veterinary College.
1202. E-mail from Cambridge University Library, 4 December 2012.
1203. Cover of Ernest Gray's book "Diseases of Poultry."
1204. Carmel College, Roll and Calendar 1958–59, Staff, p.1.
1205. Wikipedia – Fake Memoirs.
1206. "Copac" library catalogue.
1207. Ibid.

on the profound and far-reaching influence of John Hunter on veterinary medicine.[1208] Gray also wrote juvenile fiction and whilst at Carmel wrote a book entitled "Roman Eagle, Celtic Hawk,"[1209] a book which was set in the earliest years of Roman Britain.[1210] A few years later, whilst still at Carmel, he wrote another juvenile literature book entitled "The Dog that Marched to Moscow," which tells the story of a junior surgeon who was caught up in Napoleon's fateful march on Moscow in 1812. A review on this book states "the title [of this book] is utterly misleading, for, although there is a little poodle in the story who does march to Moscow, he is really quite unimportant." However the reviewer concludes that "the book is very easy and quick to read, hard to put down. . . ."[1211]

Due to ill health, Gray had to retire from being a veterinary surgeon[1212] and he came to teach Biology[1213] at Carmel in the academic year 1956/57. The Carmel magazine writes of him that as soon as he came he "created a new enthusiasm for Biology and associated subjects, after the previous keenness had been allowed to wane."[1214] That same year he displayed "some very interesting biological specimens in the loggia. They have included exhibits on the 'Fauna of England', birds, and the history of the discovery of the blood system."[1215]

David Shaw also has a recollection of Gray showing the pupils biological specimens which were even older, "On one occasion he produced a skull. We called it 'Wallace'. He pronounced to the class 'Do you know this skull is 3,000 years old!!' followed by a simultaneous outburst of 'happy birthday to you'."[1216]

The samples he showed the boys were not always static, since Neil Alton writes about Gray "making a dissected frog's legs leap, to our horror and fascination."[1217]

From his first year at the school he was active in the "Junior Biology Society." The Carmel magazine reports, "Great thanks are due to our new Senior member, Mr. Gray, for giving so much of his valuable time in

---

1208. Medical History, vol.1, iss.1, January 1957, fn. on p.38.
1209. "Copac" library catalogue.
1210. We Dig Vindolanda," Roman Britain novels (Internet).
1211. Montreal Gazette, 27 June 1959, p.12.
1212. Recollections – Geoffrey Paradise.
1213. Carmel College Senior School, sample school reports, autumn 1956 – summer 1959, forms 4 – 5 (names withheld).
1214. Carmel 1957, p.5.
1215. Ibid., p.6.
1216. Recollections – David Shaw.
1217. Recollections – Neil Alton.

the interests of the Society and generally keeping it running."[1218] It was during his period at the School that this Society brought out a magazine and it included a section "Book Reviews" which reviewed Gray's book "Roman Eagle and Celtic Hawk." It wrote, "Many boys are unaware that this book which is in the school library has been written by one of our masters. Strongly written and full of interest, we recommend our readers to get this book and enjoy a first rate story."[1219]

He left Carmel at the end of the summer term of 1960.[1220]

After leaving Carmel, Gray wrote further books.[1221] In 1983 he published a book on the life of the physician scientist, Dr. Arthur Hill Hassall, who lived in the 19th century, and amongst other things worked in the fields of botany, human histology, and sanitary reform. On this book, the reviewer wrote, "Dr. Ernest Gray has rendered a great service in producing this fine portrait, warts and all, of a Great Victorian whose achievements in many fields have until now not been sufficiently recognised."[1222]

He died in about September 1989 in the Cambridge area,[1223] at the age of 81.

MEYER BEYR BERNARD STEINBERG

He was born on 27 December 1927 in London[1224] to Solomon and Amelia Steinberg.[1225] Between the years 1935 and 1939 he attended a London County Council Elementary School and this was followed by Raine's Foundation Grammar School between the years 1939 and 1946.[1226]

His University studies began at Birkbeck College, London and on 3 October 1950 he transferred to Queen Mary College, London, where he studied for a B.A. General degree. During both his first and second years, 1950 to 1952, his subjects were English, French, and German. On 1 August 1952, he was awarded a B.A. General degree, second division.[1227]

1218. Carmel 1957, p.27.
1219. Junior Biology Society magazine, 1958 (p.6, pages unnumbered).
1220. Carmel 1960, p.5.
1221. "Copac" library catalogue.
1222. Journal of the Royal Society of Medicine (London), vol.76, November 1983, book review, p.990.
1223. E-mail from Sidney Gold, 18 November 2013.
1224. E-mail from Chief Rabbi's Office, 13 September 2012.
1225. General Register Office index, Marriages registered in April, May and June 1925, pp. K-1, S-373.
1226. E-mail from Queen Mary College, London University, 2 October 2013.
1227. Ibid.; e-mail from Transcripts, London University, 7 October 2013. London University

He then went to King's College London on 14 October 1952, where he studied for a Postgraduate Certificate in Education, which he received in July 1953.[1228] This was followed by his military service in the Royal Air Force.[1229] On 27 December 1954 he married Sheindel Hananeli at Philpot Street Synagogue in the East End of London.[1230]

Steinberg joined the staff at Carmel in the autumn term of 1956, and at the same time his wife reinforced the office staff. That year the Carmel magazine wrote that he had "achieved great popularity as a teacher of French and Hebrew."[1231]

In addition to his class teaching of French,[1232] he was active in the school's "French Club" where he was its President. On this Club, the Carmel magazine reported that he "introduced a new mathematical puzzle, which contributed to the knowledge of French numerals as much as to the popularity of the boys who have been successful at it."[1233]

Both Steinberg and Mrs. Whitfield were teaching French at the same time for O-level, and when it came to the French dictation in the summer of 1958, each class wanted their own teacher to give it. The author heard that Coles was not very pleased with that arrangement, but in the end Mrs. Whitfield gave it in the hall and Steinberg in the library. A pupil who was seated in the hall but by the library door, said that he had the advantage of hearing the dictation an extra time![1234]

When Steinberg left Carmel at the end of the summer term 1958, the Carmel magazine wrote that he "is the source of the musical sounds which reverberate throughout the main building in a foreign tongue on Saturday nights in the winter terms."[1235]

Immediately following Carmel, he joined the Hasmonean staff in September 1958 where he taught French and Geography. He remained there until August 1963.[1236]

Michael Goldman, who was one of Steinberg's pupils at the Hasmonean

---

did not give Honours for its B.A. General degree; instead it divided the successful candidates, in decreasing order of merit, to first division, second division, etc.

1228. E-mail from King's College, London University, 7 October 2013; e-mail from Queen Mary College, op. cit.

1229. E-mail from Bernard Steinberg's son Edmond, 3 June 2013.

1230. E-mail from Chief Rabbi's Office, op. cit.

1231. Carmel 1957, p.5.

1232. Carmel College, sample school reports, autumn 1956 – spring 1958, forms 3 – 5 (name withheld).

1233. Carmel 1957, p.27.

1234. Unwritten recollections of author.

1235. Carmel 1958, p.6.

1236. Booklet "The Hasmonean 1945–1970," members of staff, p.22.

recalls, "Mr. Steinberg – Geography – First Class Teacher."[1237] On a lighter note, Adrian Reiss who was an Old Carmeli who had moved over to the Hasmonean, records an encounter there with Steinberg:

> On one occasion I managed to leave Willie [William Stanton, the Headmaster] speechless. Someone in [class] 5B had brought a large tape-recorder to school. Our form-master at that time was Bernie Steinberg, the French master. Bernie asked the tape-owner if he was recording lessons? I called out 'there's nothing in the lessons worth recording'. To which Bernie replied 'go to Mr. Stanton and tell him what you've just said.' I did so, and Willie said to me 'if there's nothing worth recording in the lessons, then there's no point in your attending them.' This was a reference to the table outside his study, a punishment table for seating students like myself. I knew that table well. I had an inspiration. 'No sir. We attend lessons for their educational values, but record things for their entertainment values.' He didn't have an answer to that, and so sent me back to Bernie's class, unpunished.[1238]

In 1962/63 he was awarded the degree of M.A. in Education for his thesis "Provisions for Jewish schooling in Great Britain, 1939–1960" and in 1968 he received the degree of Ph.D. for a thesis entitled "The emergence of contemporary Jewish educational systems: a comparative study, with special reference to Israel and the U.S.A." Both degrees were awarded by London University and he was registered with the Institute of Education of that university.[1239]

In 1964, Steinberg had considered going to Dropsie College in Philadelphia,[1240] but instead, about that year, he became the Headmaster of the Kerem School (a Jewish Primary School in Hampstead Garden Suburb, London, established in 1948[1241]) where he remained until 1968.[1242]

During July of that year[1243] he moved to South Africa and became the religious leader of the Grahamstone Hebrew Congregation in Cape Province. At the same time, he was the adviser to Jewish students and the head of the Hillel House at Rhodes University. He held these posi-

---

1237. Hasmo Legends XVI, 1959, (Internet).
1238. Hasmo Legends XIX. (Internet).
1239. Senate House Libraries, University of London, Catalogue of University of London theses.
1240. E-mail from Queen Mary College, op. cit.
1241. Find a Jewish School, Kerem School, (Internet).
1242. E-mail from Edmond Steinberg, op. cit.
1243. AJR (Association of Jewish Refugees) Information, vol.XXIV, no.11, November 1969, p.4.

tions until 1970.[1244] During his first year at Rhodes University, he was mainly responsible for the establishment of a degree (at this University) in modern Jewish studies, officially designated as "Post-Biblical Studies (Judaica)."[1245] In August and September 1969, he delivered seven lectures at this University on the subject of "Paths to Modern Jewry 1648 – 1948" which were then published in a book.[1246]

In 1970 Steinberg was appointed a Lecturer in the Department of Sociology of Rhodes University in Cape Province, where he remained until 1973.[1247] He then became a Lecturer in the Faculty of Education at the University of Cape Town. Three years later in 1977 he was promoted to a Senior Lecturer and in 1980 received an associate professorship there. He took early retirement from the Faculty of Education in 1987.[1248]

He was then appointed associate professor in Jewish Civilization in the Department of Hebrew and Jewish Studies of the University of Cape Town (a Department which includes the Kaplan Centre for Jewish Studies and Research[1249]), and was acting head of this department between 1990 and 1992.[1250]

In June and July 1992, he worked on the archives in the Parkes Library at Southampton University in England. It would seem that his work was on the papers of Rabbi Dr. Solomon Schonfeld, which are stored in this library and comprise about one thousand boxes.[1251]

During his lifetime, Bernard Steinberg had a number of papers published in learned Jewish journals on Sociology and on Education. Examples of such papers are "Jewish education in the United States: a study in religio-ethnic response," "Social Change and Jewish Education in Great Britain," "Modern Orthodox and Ultra-Orthodox School Pupils in Johannesburg," and "Macro- and Micro-Perspectives on Jewish Schooling."[1252]

His son Edmond writes on his father:

> Professor Steinberg was a quintessential academic and educator. He published extensively in academic journals (including The Jewish

1244. E-mail from Edmond Steinberg, op. cit.
1245. AJR (Association of Jewish Refugees) Information, op. cit.
1246. "Copac" library catalogue.
1247. E-mail from Edmond Steinberg, op. cit.
1248. Zionist Record, (Johannesburg), 20 August 1993, Obituary for Meyer [Bernard] Steinberg.
1249. University of Cape Town, Department of Hebrew & Jewish Studies, (Internet).
1250. Zionist Record, op. cit.
1251. Parkes Library [University of Southampton] Newsletter, no.2, Spring 1993.
1252. "Rambi" – Bernard Steinberg. ("Rambi" is a catalogue of papers on all branches of Jewish Studies which appear in numerous Journals.)

Journal of Sociology and other journals in the U.K. and U.S.A.) on his areas of specialisation, viz. comparative Jewish education with focus on the education systems in the U.S.A., England and Israel, and also the domain of language education. Beyond his formal academic activities, Professor Steinberg was a prolific public speaker, in particular presenting talks on Jewish themes to various Jewish communities in southern Africa, often on the topic of Jewish education. He also participated in the University of Cape Town's extra-curricular programmes of non-academic courses, often lecturing on the topic of modern Jewish literature, which was a particular passion he held. Professor Steinberg was a prominent figure in the Cape Town Jewish community, and in particular, his local community, the Claremont Hebrew Congregation. In his later years he served as a counselor for Lifeline. In his personal time, he was an enthusiastic philatelist, and he enjoyed walks and gardening.[1253]

He died on 28 June 1993,[1254] at the age of 65.

KATHLEEN MARY EVANS

She was born on 7 November 1924 in Hinckley Leicestershire,[1255] as Kathleen Mary Bown, and she became an Evans when she married Ronald Lewis Evans in the summer of 1948.[1256] Her schooling was in Hinckley.[1257]

Between 1942 and 1945, she studied at the Chelsea College of Physical Education where she received her diploma.[1258] Whilst there, she was in the 2nd VI tennis team[1259] and also in the 2nd XI hockey team.[1260] In June 1944, at the Annual General Meeting of the Student Christian Movement, she was elected as Secretary for the year 1944–1945.[1261] The Chelsea College magazine for September 1945 wrote of her holding this

1253. E-mail from Edmond Steinberg, 3 June 2013.
1254. Ibid.
1255. Telephone conversation between author and Kathleen Mary Evans, 20 January 2013.
1256. General Register Office index, Marriages registered in July, August and September 1948, pp.B-164, E-489.
1257. Telephone conversation between author and Kathleen Mary Evans, 20 January 2013.
1258. Ibid.
1259. Chelsea College of Physical Education, Old Students' Association Magazine, [henceforth: CCPE OSA Magazine], no.XXV, September 1943 pp.18–19. (Material from these magazines was extracted by Dr. Ida M. Webb [letters to author from Dr. Webb 11 February 2013 and 10 March 2013.] Dr. Webb had received a doctorate on her study of the history of this College.)
1260. Ibid., no.XXVI, September 1944, p.15.
1261. Ibid., pp.6–7.

Carmel College Preparatory School – circa 1956–57

office, "Sincere thanks to the retiring officers K. M. Bown . . . for unfailing co-operation."[1262]

She then went to teach sports and Mathematics at the Uttoxeter High School for Girls in Staffordshire.[1263] The Chelsea College magazine for December 1946 magazine reported that she "is moving to a Formation College in Worcester"[1264] and a year later the magazine reported that she is "happy working at Drake Hall Emergency Training College," which was situated near Stafford.[1265] At that period, she became engaged to Ronald Evans.[1266] Mrs.Evans then went to teach in St. Bartholomew's

---

1262. Ibid., no.XXVII, September 1945, p.8.
1263. Telephone conversations between author and Kathleen Mary Evans, 20 and 31 January 2013. The CCPE OSA Magazine, no.XXVII, September 1945, p.22, gives this school in Utto-exeter as one of her addresses.
1264. CCPE OSA Magazine, no.XXVIII, December 1946, p.37.
1265. Ibid., no.XXIX, December 1947, p.40.
1266. Ibid.

Preparatory School in Berkshire.[1267] The Chelsea College magazine for December 1948, reporting on alumni, wrote that she "has been supervising all subjects in school practice with students." It continued that she would be getting married on 6 August and would live in Newbury where she intends to devote her time to housework. Her fiancé [Ronald] works in a school in Berkshire [St. Bartholomew's High School]."[1268] On the birth of her daughter Marilyn, she gave up teaching except for evening work.[1269] The November 1952 magazine reported that she "has been taking some keep fit and dancing classes and is returning to part-time teaching next term."[1270] A year later, the magazine wrote that "she has been working full time at school recently and has Open Day this term in which each form gives a P.T. and Dancing display. . . . The hockey club she formed last season got to the top five in the Berks tournament."[1271] Jeremy Rosen writes that she became an "England selector" in hockey.[1272]

She was also a member of the Chartered Society of Physiotherapy.[1273]

Mrs. Evans joined the staff at Carmel in the academic year 1956/57, to teach junior Mathematics.[1274]

In addition to her classroom teaching activities, she was very much involved with tennis at Carmel. The Carmel magazine wrote on this, "Our warmest thanks go to Mrs. Evans for all the time and trouble taken in coaching us and our success is largely due to her."[1275] However, not every pupil could succeed in tennis, and one who did not was Michael Bharier who writes, "I was one of the kids that no one wanted on their team. I remember Mrs. Evans making a group of younger kids watch while I served at tennis, as an example of how not to serve."[1276]

She remained at Carmel until it closed in 1997, and like her husband,

---

1267. Telephone conversations between author and Kathleen Mary Evans, 20 and 31 January 2013 (according to a non-clear recollection by her).
1268. CCPE OSA Magazine, no.XXX, December 1948, p.38.
1269. Ibid., no.XXXII, November 1950, p.39.
1270. Ibid., no.XXXIV, November 1952, p.40.
1271. Ibid., no.XXXV, November 1953, p.47.
1272. Recollections – Jeremy Rosen, chap.2.
1273. Carmel College Prospectus, undated (about 1959); Telephone conversation between author and Kathleen Mary Evans, 20 January 2013. The records of the Chartered Society of Physiotherapy from the 1940s and 1950 are no longer extant (e-mail from Chartered Society of Physiotherapy, 1 March 2013).
1274. Carmel 1957, p.4.
1275. Carmel 1961, p.37.
1276. Recollections – Michael Bharier, chap.2, Life at Carmel.

was on the staff for over 40 years.[1277] As of 2013, Mrs.Evans was living in Shillingford, Oxford.

REV. BERNARD SIMPSON WARD

He was born in the spring of 1921 in the Liverpool area[1278] and during the Second World War was a radio operator with the R.A.F.[1279] On 5 July 1947, he was awarded by the University of Liverpool the degree of B.A. in General Studies.[1280] In the following year, he was admitted to Fitzwilliam College Cambridge University where he studied Theology and Religious Studies and in 1950 was awarded the degree of B.A.[1281] (which a few years later became an M.A.).

Following a period of officiating in a church in the North of England, in September 1951 he became a part-time pastor at Evangelical Free Church in Exeter. In addition to his day-to-day church functions, he was a member of various evangelical church organisations and regularly attended inter-church conferences.[1282]

To supplement his income, he tried his hand at market gardening, but his family reported that this was not successful since he was unable to "discriminate reliably between 'seed and weed'."[1283] He therefore in June 1952 took up being a part-time postman. Being in a rural district, his postal deliveries involved him tramping down farm lanes and over fields, a total daily distance of seven miles, in order to arrive at many of the addressees. He thus left home every morning before five o'clock, dressed in his postman's uniform, and when he had finished his postman's round in the middle of the morning, he would change into his clerical grey and clergyman's collar.[1284] Due to the often unfavorable British climatic conditions, he would often return from his postal rounds very cold and wet and as a result would sit for some time with his feet in a bowl of hot water. One day, when his daughter was about two or three years old, she asked her mother, "Please can I put my feet in a bowl of hot water like a postman?"[1285]

1277. Recollections – Jeremy Rosen, chap.1.
1278. General Register Office index, Births registered in April, May and June 1921, p.W-397.
1279. "Minister is Part-time Postman," Exeter Express & Echo, 5 March 1954.
1280. E-mail from University of Liverpool, 6 December 2013.
1281. E-mail from Fitzwilliam College Cambridge, 8 January 2013.
1282. Exeter Express & Echo, op. cit.
1283. E-mail from Rev. Bernard Ward's daughter Margaret Harding, 18 June 2012.
1284. Exeter Express & Echo, op. cit.
1285. E-mail from Margaret Harding, op. cit.

He then started teaching in Bramdean Prep School in Exeter where one of his pupils asked him, "Excuse me Sir, aren't you our postman?" During the first term at that school he had to teach all subjects. Therefore each night his wife tutored him from text books about the next day's lessons. One of the subjects that he had to teach was Art and since neither he nor his wife knew anything about Art, he would ask a pupil to bring out his painting to the front of the class and tell the other boys about it.[1286]

In 1957, he moved to the village of Brightwell-cum-Sotwell (which is situated a few miles from Wallingford) and became the pastor of the Free Church there.[1287] In the spring term of 1957 he joined the staff in Carmel to teach Latin[1288] and one of his first assignments was to get the then lower fifth form through the O-level. He was introduced as Mr. Ward and only later did the pupils learn that he was also a Reverend. (For the first term of that academic year, the school had found a person (whose hobby was to grow strawberries) to come to teach this class Latin.)[1289] At a later date Rev. Ward also taught Scripture to the few Christian pupils at the school.[1290]

Michael Bharier recalls that Ward "privately expressed strong anti-Papist sentiments to me when the new pope was crowned in 1958. He said that all the ceremony was very impressive but that the world had forgotten how the Pope had endorsed Mussolini's invasion of Ethiopia in the 1930's, and how Mussolini had rewarded him." Bharier then added, "At that moment I was impressed with Ward's humanity."[1291]

The textbook then used for teaching Latin was Kennedy's Latin Primer, an old fashioned boringly set out textbook. In the course of his teaching, Ward would make his pupils memorise pages of this Primer, for example, verb declensions, which he would then test them on; the questions he asked would include "tucked away" lines on these pages. At one stage he wanted to use the "set books" alternative for the O-level, but the class objected and he thus gave up this idea.[1292]

Henry Law was awarded an Open Scholarship to Oxford in Science, but at that period one could not enter Oxford University unless one had

---

1286. Ibid.
1287. E-mail from Neville Burt, Elder of a Wallingford Church and a former Pastor of Brightwell Free Church, 15 June 2012.
1288. Carmel College Senior School, sample school report, autumn 1957, form 5, (name withheld).
1289. 7 years, p.56.
1290. E-mail from Margaret Harding, op. cit.
1291. E-mail from Michael Bharier, 29 May 2012.
1292. Unwritten recollections of author.

Rev. Bernard Ward – 1957

passed Latin O-level or the University's equivalent. Law had not passed Latin but with the coaching of Ward, he overcame this obstacle and could thus enter the University [1293]

Jacob Fachler wrote of Ward, "[He] looked like Mr. Punch and was the worst disciplinarian in the history of the school."[1294] According to his family, Rev. Ward himself said that "his beaky nose was partly attributable to fact he broke it by walking into a lamppost during WW2 [World War II] blackout."[1295]

He was the ideal candidate for ragging, and indeed did he get it! On one occasion, the class brought in a boy from a lower class into Ward's lesson and gave him the fictitious name of "John Oberman." They informed Ward that he had been sent up a class by the Head Latin teacher because he was so good at Latin. Ward swallowed all this and even gave him some work to test his Latin proficiency! When this came to Kopul's ears he was not amused, and as a result "John Oberman" was unable to sit down in comfort for some time afterwards![1296]

There was a further ragging which again resulted in painful conse-quences to the perpetrator. This time the crime was making some wise crack about boy scouts in Ward's class. David Stamler who was in an

1293. E-mail from Henry Law, 17 June 2012.
1294. Recollections – Jacob Fachler.
1295. E-mail from Margaret Harding, op. cit.
1296. Reflections – the author.

adjoining room heard this wisecrack and summoned the whole class to his study, where he called the perpetrator by name to step forward, told him to take off his glasses, gave him a very hard slap across his cheek, saying that if he could bully Rev. Ward, then he could bully him. Stamler then gave the class a warning not to continue this ragging of Rev. Ward. However, the class did not change their ways![1297]

In 1965 he left Brightwell-cum-Sotwell[1298] and was later a pastor in Wales. He died on 18 December 2005,[1299] at the age of 84.

HERMANN WALTER (NAPHTALI JOSEPH) EHRMANN

He was born on 22 April 1926[1300] in Mainz Germany, his father being Dr. Ludwig Ehrmann, a respected doctor and a lay leader of the Mainz Orthodox Community. Hermann attended the Orthodox Jewish Primary School in Mainz and in 1936 the family went to Eretz Yisrael,[1301] where Hermann attended the Ma'aleh Central School in Jerusalem from 1936 to 1939.[1302] However, due to financial considerations, in 1939 the family moved to Melbourne, Australia,[1303] where he attended the Melbourne High School. The school records show that he was in Como House and that in 1941 he was in Form 3A. However, during 1942 he was at a different school, the Taylor College, but in the following year he returned to the Melbourne High School where he was in Form 5C1.[1304] Following some preliminary examinations in a number of subjects which included Hebrew, German, English, Economics, and Maths, and then some further examinations, he matriculated in May 1949.[1305]

Ehrmann began his studies for a B.A. at Melbourne University and in November 1949 passed the first year examinations in German and Philosophy.[1306] At the same time he worked as a part-time Hebrew teacher on Sundays for the United Jewish Education Board.[1307] However, he then

---

1297. E-mail from Michael Bharier, 29 May 2012; 7 years, p.56.
1298. E-mail from Neville Burt, op. cit.
1299. E-mail from Margaret Harding, op. cit.
1300. Record Card of Hermann Ehrmann at Melbourne University.
1301. E-mail from Hermann Ehrmann's sister-in-law Susie Ehrmann, 27 November 2012.
1302. Ibid., 12 December 2012.
1303. Ibid., 27 November 2012.
1304. E-mail from Melbourne High School, 12 December 2012.
1305. Record Card of Hermann Ehrmann, op. cit.
1306. Ibid.
1307. E-mail from Susie Ehrmann, 12 December 2012; Scope (Mount Scopus College magazine, Melbourne), 1964, Obituaries, p.15.

won a scholarship to Queensland University where he completed his B.A. with distinction on 29 April 1954, and two months later, on 23 June, he was awarded a Certificate of Education from the same University.[1308] He also qualified for the Certificate of the Senior Teachers' College in Brisbane. Presumably, it was during this period that for two years he was the Headmaster of Brisbane's United Hebrew Education Board.[1309]

In the 1950s, he went to England, and in 1955 he was awarded the degree of M.A. by Sheffield University for his thesis entitled "The works of August, Graf von Platen-Hallermunde, in relationship to some aspects of romanticism in Germany."[1310]

Ehrmann joined the staff at Carmel in the summer term 1956,[1311] where he was a teacher in the Prep School.[1312] He also involved himself with the Prep School's Chess Club. The magazine "Alpha" reports, "With the advent of Mr. Ehrmann, who is a keen chess player, it is hoped that the Chess Club will regain its former strength and prestige and that there will be a revival of the Chess Ladder and inter-Form and inter-House competitions."[1313] In addition, Ehrmann was the Housemaster of the study-block,[1314] which the Carmel magazine described as a "luckless task."[1315] He was only in Carmel for one year, leaving after the spring term of 1957.[1316]

Prior to his return to Melbourne, in June 1959, he taught in American High Schools, which had been established in Europe for the children of American troops stationed there. In 1960 he joined the staff of the Mount Scopus College, which is in Melbourne, where he taught English, History, and Jewish History to the first three forms of the senior school. The College magazine "Scope" commented that "all those who passed through his classes realised the intensity of feeling he had for his work."[1317]

However, Ehrmann was not happy in Australia, and therefore at the

---

1308. E-mail from Queensland University, 24 January 2013; Scope, op. cit.

1309. Scope, op. cit.

1310. University of Sheffield website, StarPlus, the library catalogue – Hermann Walter Ehrmann.

1311. Carmel 1956, p.5.

1312. Alpha 1956, opposite p.1.

1313. Ibid., p.6.

1314. The study block was a dormitory block, with 2 pupils in each room, which was a temporary war-time structure, where many 6th formers lived.

1315. Carmel 1956, p.5.

1316. Carmel 1957, p.5.

1317. Scope, op. cit.

end of 1963, he moved back to Germany[1318] where very soon after, in May 1964, he died in Mainz at the very early age of 38.[1319]

RAPHAEL JAMES LOEWE

He was born on 16 April 1919 in Calcutta in India to Herbert James Loewe and Ethel Victoria (née Hyamson),[1320] and was the fourth generation of a family to devote their life to Jewish scholarship.[1321]

His schooling was first in Oxford where, between the years 1927 and 1932, he attended the Dragon School.[1322] This was a school which was started in 1877 by a group of Oxford University dons for their own children.[1323] Loewe's schooling was followed between the years 1932 and 1937 at The Leys School in Cambridge and there he was awarded the Greek Testament Prize.[1324]

In 1938 he was admitted to St. John's College at Cambridge University as a Major Scholar in Classics, where in 1940 he gained a First in Part I of the Classical Tripos,[1325] and in 1942 was awarded the degree of B.A. (which became an M.A. in 1946). In 1949 Oxford University awarded him an M.A.[1326] by incorporation.[1327]

In 1940, during the Second World War, Loewe enlisted and, after spells in the Pioneer Corps and the Suffolk Regiment, he became an officer in the Royal Armoured Corps.[1328] In 1943 he was awarded the Military Cross[1329] for the North African Campaign[1330] whose citation stated "This officer has always acted with the utmost courage in battle and stopped at nothing to serve his Regiment and the British Army."[1331] In Italy in 1944, he carried wounded men from a minefield, and when asked afterwards if

---

1318. E-mail from Susie Ehrmann, 27 November 2012; Scope, op. cit.
1319. Note written on Record Card of Hermann Ehrmann, op. cit.; e-mail from Susie Ehrmann, 27 November 2012.
1320. E-mail from St. John's College Cambridge, 28 January 2013.
1321. The Telegraph, 26 June 2011 (online edition), obituary to Raphael Loewe.
1322. E-mail from St. John's College, op. cit.
1323. Dragon School, Oxford (Internet).
1324. E-mail from The Leys School, 17 January 2013.
1325. E-mail from Caius College Cambridge, 24 January 2013.
1326. E-mail from St. John's College, op. cit.
1327. A person who has been awarded a degree by Cambridge, Oxford, or Dublin can be awarded the same degree by one of these three universities without further examination; this is known as degree by incorporation.
1328. The Eagle 2012, St. John's College Cambridge, p.179.
1329. London Gazette, supplement, 6 July 1943, p.3087.
1330. Record card of Raphael Loewe at Brown University.
1331. The Telegraph, op. cit.

he wanted anything he answered "a cup of tea would be nice."[1332] It was obviously because of his army record, when the pupils at Carmel assembled in the main hall on Remembrance Sunday for the two minutes of silence, it was Loewe who presided over it.[1333]

After the war he carried on postgraduate research in Balliol College, Oxford between 1948 and 1949.[1334] This was followed by his being appointed as an Assistant Lecturer in the Department of Hebrew at the University of Leeds on 1 January 1949. He was promoted to a full Lecturer on 1 October of that year. On 30 September 1954 he resigned from this post.[1335] During this period, namely towards the beginning of 1952, he married Chloe Klatzkin in London.[1336]

After resigning from his post at Leeds University, he immediately took up the S.A. Cook bye-fellowship at Caius College Cambridge which he held for three years[1337] and it "was awarded for study in "Old or New Testament; Rabbinics or Patristics; Philosophy of Religion; or Comparative Study of Religion."[1338] One of his obituaries speculates that he gave up his secure post at Leeds University because "he thought that he would find a more permanent post in his home university [Cambridge] but nothing was at that time available and there followed a period in which he had no academic appointment."[1339] Therefore, maybe he had no other option but to join the staff at Carmel; in his application form for Brown University and in the various obituaries for him, Carmel College is not even mentioned!

It was in the academic year 1957/58 that Loewe joined the staff at Carmel.[1340] His teaching of Tanach at Carmel was not in the traditional Jewish way but by critical studies as done in non-Jewish universities, by bringing down such things as the Nash papyrus or Ugaritic texts to support the ideas brought in his lessons.[1341] But he also gave "non-problematic" lessons, and on this Jacob Fachler wrote that he "taught me the

1332. Ibid.
1333. 7 years, p.52.
1334. E-mail from St. John's College, op. cit.
1335. E-mail from Leeds University, 12 February 2013.
1336. General Register Office index, Marriages registered in January, February and March 1952, pp.K-306, L-363; Record Card of Raphael Loewe, op. cit.
1337. Record Card of Raphael Loewe, op. cit.
1338. E-mail from Caius College, op. cit.
1339. The Eagle, op. cit., p.180.
1340. Carmel 1958, p.4.
1341. 7 years, p.54.

fundamentals of Hebrew grammar that stayed with me for the rest of my life."[1342]

In order that his class should remember a particular Hebrew grammatical rule regarding five verbs which all began with the letter "aleph," he told them the following sentence, "The groom *said* to his bride, I am *willing* to *eat* anything you *bake* even though I *perish.*"[1343] It is possible that the pupils remember this sentence, but what the grammatical rule was, is a different matter![1344]

With regards to him, Henry Law writes, "Raphael Loewe had previously won my respect with a reply to an officious boy who complained that someone else in the class was not wearing a kipah. 'Oh, shut up, I'm not G-d's policeman'."[1345] Jeffrey Fisher also has recollections of Loewe's lessons:

> Raphael Loewe taught us Nach (or Jewish studies in general). Raphael Loewe won the George Cross (the 2nd highest honour after the Victoria Cross) for bravery during the 2nd World War. As a result of his injuries, he used a walking stick. All this came together in his Nach lessons when he was teaching us about famous battles. He would enact these battles before us at the front of the classroom. He would charge from one side of the classroom to the other, walking stick raised like a spear, to give us a better understanding of the way the battle proceeded. I cannot recall which battles he was teaching us, nor what age class he was teaching at the time. But it is easy to imagine that this was a fun thing for young schoolboys to see.[1346]

In addition to teaching Hebrew, Loewe would teach the classical languages Latin and Greek. One of his main pupils was David Saville, who in his reminiscences writes the following about Loewe:

> I was particularly close to him since he taught me Latin, Greek, and Hebrew 14 times a week as I was being prepared for a scholarship at Cambridge University, which didn't happen. In fact when Loewe joined the staff I was Editor of the School Magazine and I wrote 'We

---

1342. Recollections – Jacob Fachler.
1343. Unwritten recollections of author.
1344. For the Hebrew grammar specialists, the literature states "for these 5, aleph quiesces in Qal Imperfect."
1345. Recollections – Henry Law, Carmel College days, part 2, p.32.
1346. Recollections – Jeffrey Fisher.

welcome Mr. Loewe – he teaches Hebrew, Classics, and Saville.[1347] He once came up to Dr. Tobias – Toby, Toby I have got something new. He replied 'If it's more than 2,000 years old, I don't want to hear it'.[1348]

At the Carmel Monday morning assemblies, a teacher would often give a lecture. On one occasion it was Loewe who spoke, and his subject was the excavations at Hazor. During his lecture "he was talking about one of the rooms at Hazor and said its size was about the size of the 'staff lavatories.' This size estimation became the talk and amusement of some of the boys. Of all the rooms in the school he could choose for this comparison, he had to choose the 'staff lavatories'."[1349]

Loewe left Carmel in 1961.[1350] That same year, he became a lecturer at Leo Baeck College to help train Reform clergy.[1351] For the academic year 1963/64, he took temporary leave in order to be a Visiting Professor of Jewish Studies at Brown University which is in Providence, Rhode Island, where he lectured on "The History of Jewish Thought and Institutions" and delivered a specialised seminar in Biblical Studies.[1352] He also gave some public lectures entitled "Jewish Philosophy and Jewish Mysticism in Counterpoise" and "Holiness in Judaism: Society, Season and Situation."[1353] In a newspaper interview he said that "his only misgivings of America, and it is a humorous one at that, is . . . [his] dislike of American envelopes, 'They all taste,' he said."[1354]

About 1965 he returned to be a lecturer at University College London University (where he had first been a lecturer in 1961–1962[1355]) and he went up the scale until he became the Goldsmid Professor of Hebrew, where he remained until he retired in 1984.[1356]

During his lifetime, Loewe published extensively. His works included the translation of medieval Jewish compositions such as Isaac ibn Sahula's animal fables – "Meshal Haqadmoni," and the poems and Targumim

---

1347. Carmel 1958, p.4.

1348. Recollections – David Saville, p.2.

1349. 7 years, p.52.

1350. E-mail from David Saville, 17 April 2013.

1351. The Telegraph, op. cit.; Raphael Loewe's record card, op. cit.

1352. "Students Of Judaism Should Know Foundations Of Their History," Rhode Island Herald, 6 March 1964.

1353. E-mail from Brown University, 15 January 2013.

1354. Rhode Island Herald, op. cit.

1355. Record card of Raphael Loewe, op. cit.

1356. The Guardian, 4 August 2011 (online edition), obituary of Raphael Loewe.

in the Barcelona Haggadah. He also wrote some historical works which included "Cambridge Jewry: the first 100 years – Gown and Tallith."[1357]

He translated from Aramaic to English two liturgical poems which are recited on Shavuot, "Akdamut Millin" and "Yatziv Pitgam"; the translations appear in the Routledge Machzor.[1358]

He died on 27 May 2011 at the age of 92.[1359]

JOSHUA JOSEPH GABAY

He was born in Gibraltar on 24 July 1932, the eldest son of a managing director. His schooling was at the Gibraltar Grammar School. He continued his education in England, where in October 1953, he was admitted to Pembroke College, Oxford University, where he studied until 1956. On 28 July 1956, he obtained the Third Class Honours degree of B.A. in Modern Languages – Spanish and French – (which became an M.A. on 3 May 1962). He also obtained a certificate in public administration in 1957.[1360]

Gabay joined the staff at Carmel in the academic year 1957/58 to teach French. However the Carmel magazine humorously made his French teaching a secondary activity! "Mr. Gabay, the Gibraltar centre-forward, has earned a name for himself in the realms of cricket (He also teaches French)."[1361]

He was also a good squash player and together with Charles Marshall, was often included in the school's squash team in outside fixtures.[1362] On the 1959/60 football season, the Carmel magazine wrote, "Mr. Gabay has worked ceaselessly, and if at times he was disappointed, his keenness has always urged us to try to justify his efforts."[1363] That year, and also the following year, he wrote up the Football Pen Portraits for the Carmel magazine.[1364]

In the academic year 1960/61, he took over being the Housemaster of Montefiore House. In his report of the House's sporting activities of that

1357. "Copac" and "Malmad" library catalogues.
1358. Service of the Synagogue, Pentecost, fourteenth edition (London: Routledge & Kegan Paul, 1954), pp.205, 210–11.
1359. The Telegraph, op. cit.; The Guardian, op. cit.
1360. E-mails from Pembroke College Oxford, 6 December 2012, and Degree Conferrals, Oxford University, 18 December 2012.
1361. Carmel 1958, p.4., bracketed words in original.
1362. Carmel 1960, p.38.
1363. Ibid., p.35.
1364. Ibid., pp.35–36; Carmel 1961 pp.34–35.

year, Gabay wrote that "Montefiore's record during the year has not been studded with any major victories or sensational awards. Still, its redeeming feature has been the exemplary enthusiasm shown by most members in whatever field of action they have been engaged."[1365]

Not only in sports! He also participated in the cultural activities of Carmel. When Abraham Carmel left, Gabay took over the position of Vice-President of the Junior Union Society and "played a vital part in the smooth running of the society."[1366] Lest the fact that he was a French teacher be forgotten, in the summer term of 1960, he put on a production in French of an adaption of "Nous les Gosses," with the actors being from the junior part of the Senior School.[1367]

In the summer of 1970, David Stamler unexpectedly resigned from being Headmaster of Carmel. At the time Gabay was master in charge of the Preparatory School, and he claimed that the Chairman of the Governors had promised that he would be appointed Headmaster of Carmel College. However, there were a lot of local politics, with divisions amongst the Governors, the staff, the parents, and even the pupils as to whether Gabay or Jeremy Rosen should be appointed as the new Headmaster. By the casting vote of the Chairman of the Governors, Jeremy Rosen was appointed. This did not end all the fighting. Gabay would not co-operate with Jeremy. It reached such a state, that Jeremy said to the Chairman of the Governors that either he goes or Gabay goes. The Chairman ruled that Gabay must go.[1368] So go he went!

After leaving Carmel, he first went to Iran to take up the position of Director of Education for the ORT Iran School Network which he held for about three years. In Iran he met and married Manijeh Yerushalmi in 1974. His next position was between 1975 and 1980 when he was Education Consultant for the Private Rad Foundation in New York, France, and Switzerland. In 1981, he returned to Gibraltar where he became a private tutor and private company director, and his tutoring continued periodically till he died.[1369]

Gabay was actively involved with Gibraltarian communal activities. His first position was that of Chairman of the Gibraltar Heritage Trust which

---

1365. Carmel 1961, p.44.
1366. Carmel 1960, p.27.
1367. Ibid., p.29.
1368. Recollections – Jeremy Rosen, chap.2.
1369. E-mail from Joshua Gabay's widow Manijeh, 28 January 2013. It is not clear whether the obituary sent with this e-mail was written by her, or she enclosed it with her e-mail. It will therefore be referred to as "obituary," without any given author.

he held for two years beginning in 1989.[1370] (The aims of this Trust are to preserve, record and enhance the unique flavour and atmosphere of Gibraltar.[1371]) In 1996 he was elected to the House of Assembly (which is the Gibraltar Parliament) as a member of the Opposition Party, the Gibraltar Socialist Labour Party,[1372] where he was described as "a first class parliamentarian and debater,"[1373] and he remained there until the year 2000.[1374] During this period, Gabay was the opposition education spokesman and on one occasion "he accused the Chief Minister of being more interested in the surface of things than substance, implying the continued reliance on income from tobacco."[1375] His obituary states that these "apposite quips . . . were enjoyed by all."[1376] He also represented Gibraltar at various Commonwealth Parliamentary Association Conferences abroad.[1377] In 2000 he became a member of the Chief Minister's Advisory Council on External Affairs.[1378]

In summing up his manifold activities, his obituary states, "He was well liked and much admired in the community. In addition, his conscientious nature and outstanding intellect and charisma made him an excellent teacher. He dedicated a lifetime to his accomplishments in the field of education and he touched the lives of many pupils who still remember him with great affection and respect."[1379]

Gabay died on 20 March 2010,[1380] at the age of 77.

VIOLA COMPTON

Viola Compton was born on 26 November 1886 in Fulham, London. She was a British film actress who starred in a large number of films especially in the 1930s. These included the comedies "Third Time Lucky," "Excess Baggage," and "Man in the Mirror."[1381] Her surname at birth was MacKenzie, but the family, who had a number of actors, such as her actress sister

1370. Ibid.
1371. Gibraltar Heritage Trust (Internet).
1372. Gibraltar Parliament , Eighth House of Assembly (1886–2000) (Internet); (Gibraltar) 1996 General Election Results (Internet).
1373. Gibraltar Chronicle, 23 March 2010 (online edition), obituary of Joshua Gabay.
1374. E-mail from Manijeh Gabay, op. cit.
1375. This week's news by Panorama News Weekly, Gibraltar, 7 June 1999, (Internet).
1376. Obituary, op. cit.
1377. Ibid.
1378. Ibid.
1379. Ibid.
1380. Ibid.
1381. Wikipedia – Viola Compton.

Fay and her grandfather the Shakespearean actor Henry, used Compton as their stage surname. Viola's brother Compton MacKenzie was a writer and a Scottish Nationalist.[1382]

When one does not know a particular person, it can lead to an embarrassing situation. This indeed occurred between Viola Compton and Charles Colquhoun the piano teacher. Michael Bharier explains:

> Kopul had engaged a new elocution teacher to try to improve our diction. Colquhoun ran into her in the staff lounge. He did not know her name. Upon finding out what she did, he said that she must surely have known a lot of actors and actresses. She said she had. He then said (he told me) 'There is one actress I cannot abide, Fay Compton.' The elocution teacher was Viola Compton, Fay Compton's sister! He told me he tried to apologize when he found out and that she was very sweet about it, but he was upset about his faux pas.[1383]

She taught Elocution in Carmel for the academic year 1957/58, coming in one day each week to give these lessons to the various classes. The author writes about her lessons:

> Even though it was just one lesson per week, she wrote on every boy's report. By the fifth form, the report consisted of a separate page for each subject and under the dotted line for the teacher's signature was written 'subject master.' She had dutifully gone through every report, crossed out the word 'master' and written 'mistress.'[1384] I am sure she didn't know the names of all the boys she was writing reports for. There was one boy who always had a music lesson at the time of his elocution period and therefore Miss Compton never saw him throughout the term. Yet he still received a report from her! Maybe it was by mental telepathy![1385]

It wasn't easy or even pleasant for a lady then aged over 70 to teach a class of boys, especially since "the classes ragged her to such an extent that she

---

1382. Wikipedia – Compton MacKenzie.
1383. Recollections – Michael Bharier, chap 3.5, Carmel Memories, Music at Carmel, a personal recollection.
1384. Carmel College Senior School, sample school report, autumn 1957, form 5 (name withheld).
1385. 7 years, p.60.

refused to come back for the following year. At some later 'social' in the school, Rabbi Rosen recited some poem he had made up about her.[1386]

She died on 7 April 1971 in Birchington-on-Sea,[1387] at the age of 84.

FREDERICK NELSON

He was born on 15 June 1934 in Manchester,[1388] and he attended Wood-heys Primary School in Sale. This was followed by Sale Grammar School where he studied from September 1945 to July 1952. Throughout the years he was there, there was in general a considerable variation from term to term in his end of term class positions. In 1949 he passed the School Certificate. Both in 1951 and 1952 he passed the Advanced Level Certificate in the subjects E., F. and G. (probably English, French, and Geography). In both of those years he passed Scholarship level English Literature.[1389] His son Paul adds that he had an interest in bird watching and he used to read a lot.[1390]

In December 1951 he sat for an Oxford Scholarship and obtained entrance as a Commoner to St. John's College. However, before going there, he did his National Service between 1952 and 1954.[1391] He then took up his University place and he studied there between the years 1954 and 1957. On 17 October 1957 he received a Second Class Honours degree of B.A. in English Language and Literature (which became an M.A. in December 1961).[1392] At the University he was in the Oxford 2nd Eight rowing team,[1393] and from time to time in the 1st team.[1394]

As soon as he graduated, he joined the staff at Carmel in September 1957 replacing Gilbert Warner. Whilst at Oxford, Nelson had met Gillian King and when he came to Carmel they were engaged and, as a consequence, there were regular telephone calls linking Carmel to Oxford! On his initial activities at Carmel, the Carmel magazine wrote, "Mr. Nelson has successfully combined his duties of senior English Master with

1386. Ibid.
1387. Wikipedia – Viola Compton.
1388. E-mail from Paul, son of Frederick Nelson , 27 February 2013.
1389. Frederick Nelson's record card at Sale Grammar School.
1390. E-mail from Paul Nelson, 27 February 2013.
1391. note added to Frederick Nelson's record card at Sale Grammar School.
1392. E-mail from Degree Conferrals Oxford University, 18 December 2012.
1393. E-mail from Paul Nelson, 27 February 2013.
1394. Ibid., 22 April 2013.

Housemaster and is an authority on Oxford night life!"[1395] In the summer of 1958, they were married – in Oxford.[1396]

In his first term at Carmel, he succeeded (as far as the author recollects), in getting a group of seven boys (which included the author) through O-level English Literature in one term, a course which normally takes one year. For this exam, there were two set books to learn, Shakespeare's "Richard II" and Bernard Shaw's "The Devil's Disciple."[1397]

At the end of that term the long dorm had a party at which, for the first part, a number of members of staff attended. The author continues, "The last staff member to leave was Mr. Nelson and before he left, he sang one of his undergraduate songs on 'wooing a poor young maid' and which ended, 'Now I am a bachelor living with my son. . . .'"[1398]

Henry Law also has reminiscences of Nelson:

> A pleasant bonus for the Scholarship level year came about through the introduction of a 'General Paper'. The intention was to ensure that science students had a wider cultural background with a knowledge of politics and the arts. A newly qualified young English teacher, Mr. Nelson, an Oxford graduate, was assigned to the task. There was a good relationship because the age gap between us was small. He stirred up our interest in a range of topics, including the philosophy of design and product design.[1399]

He was the Director of the Carmel "Dramatic Society" which put on a number of dramatic performances during his tenure at Carmel.[1400] In 1960, he was the Producer of a four-act play, "The Dybbuk." His wife, Gillian, was very much involved in the technical side of the production, which included her being part of the team for "wardrobe" and "make-up." She also utilised her sewing and secretarial skills by making the stage curtains and typing the programmes.[1401]

Both he and his wife did not limit their dramatic skills just to Carmel.

1395. Carmel 1958, p.4.
1396. General Register Office index. Marriages registered in July, August and September 1958, pp.K-280, N-475.
1397. 7 years, p.116.
1398. Ibid., p.100.
1399. Recollections – Henry Law, Carmel College days, part 2, p.22.
1400. Carmel 1959, p.29.
1401. Carmel College Dramatic Society presents the Dybbuk by S. Ansky, duplicated programme.

Whilst in Carmel, they were in an amateur dramatic society in Benson,[1402] which got a few mentions in the local papers.[1403]

In 1960, a political "Liberal Society" was established at Carmel by some senior boys in the school and Nelson was associated with it. The Society brought out some newspapers and he contributed an article. The author recollects:

> In one of the editions, the guest column was written by Mr. Nelson. He wrote about a debate which took place in the Oxford University Union at which the Prime Minister was the proposer and he informed the chairman that if the motion wasn't carried he would walk out the meeting. As a result the Chairman *changed the method of voting* and then said that the motion had been carried, even though many of those present thought that it had not. Mr. Nelson concluded that the fact that the honour of a Prime Minister would be wounded were he to be beaten by University students, was completely contrary to Liberal principles.[1404]

He left Carmel in 1962[1405] and took a position of English master at the King's School Chester (a school which was founded in 1541 by King Henry VIII following the dissolution of St Werburgh's Abbey, which then became Chester Cathedral[1406]). About 1965, he became Head of English at that school. In addition to his class teaching, he produced and directed a number of school plays and also took part in a number of performances. In the school's sporting activities, for about twenty years, he looked after the 2nd Eight rowing team. He remained at this school until he took early retirement for family reasons in 1990.[1407]

At a later date he entered a nursing home.[1408] Nelson died on 10 May 2013,[1409] at the age of nearly 79.

1402. Benson is a village about one and a half miles north of Wallingford.
1403. E-mail from Paul Nelson, 27 February 2013.
1404. 7 years, pp.71–72.
1405. Carmel 1962, p.8.
1406. The King's School Chester, A rich, royal history, (Internet).
1407. E-mail from Paul Nelson, 27 February 2013.
1408. Ibid.
1409. Ibid., 13 May 2013.

YEHUDA OFIR

He was born on 25 December 1933 in Haifa, Israel. He first attended Yavne Elementary School in Haifa and this was followed by Midreshet Noam in Pardes Hana. At that period he was a member of the Bnei Akiva youth movement.[1410] He then attended evening classes at the Haifa Legal and Economic High School Faculty of Law, whilst working at an English law office.[1411]

He wanted to study law in England and join Gray's Inn. However, the Inn informed him that there was a difficulty – he had never learned "hic haec hoc," or, "translated" into English, he had not passed the compulsory requirement of O-level Latin (as was also the case with many non-British students).[1412]

He was admitted to Leeds University in October 1953.[1413] After he began at the University, he upgraded his degree course and this required him to pass his matriculation,[1414] which he did that December.[1415] During his first session at the University (1953/54) he studied non-degree Law; the courses included Roman Law, the English Legal system, and the Law of Contract. In his second year his course included Land Law, Legal History, and Equity, and in his third and final year, included Jurisprudence and Sale of Goods.[1416] In June 1956 he was successful in his degree examination, but since a period of three years from matriculation was required before one could graduate, his degree could not be conferred until December 1956.[1417] However, since at that time he was working in France, he didn't graduate until 1958,[1418] when he attended the degree ceremony.[1419]

Leeds University had exempted Ofir from their Latin requirement,[1420] and when he passed in June 1954 their exam in Roman Law, Gray's Inn also exempted him from this requirement; on 19 January 1955, he was admitted as a student to this Inn (or, in their flowery lan-

1410. E-mail from Gerti, widow of Yehuda Ofir, 3 August 2013.
1411. E-mail from Gray's Inn, 25 October 2013.
1412. Ibid.
1413. E-mails from Leeds University, 19 November 2013 and 11 December 2013.
1414. E-mail from Leeds Alumni, 6 December 2013.
1415. Letter from Registrar, Leeds University to Yehuda Ofir, 22 June 1956.
1416. Leeds University, Record Card for Yehuda Ofir.
1417. Letter from Registrar, Leeds University to Yehuda Ofir, op. cit.
1418. E-mail from Leeds Alumni, op. cit.
1419. Letter from Yehuda Ofir to Registrar, Leeds University, 20 June 1958.
1420. E-mail from Gray's Inn, op. cit.

guage, "was admitted to the Honorable Society of Gray's Inn").[1421]

In order to be admitted to the Bar, one not only has to use one's brains to pass examinations, one also has to use one's stomach! That is, that one's has to eat a certain number of dinners at Gray's Inn, and accordingly, Ofir was occupied in arranging the "dining dates."[1422]

He joined the staff at Carmel during the academic year 1958/59, where he taught Hebrew and Gemara and he also organised the singing of Hebrew folk songs.[1423] On Purim, he walked into the dining hall during the Purim meal, all dressed up, to the delight of everybody.[1424] As with many of the teachers at Carmel, Ofir had a transport vehicle, but as David Saville reports, he had a unique distinction, "[He] broke the then record of driving from Carmel to Marble Arch in 59 minutes, in his Dauphine."[1425] Neil Myeroff recollects something even more unusual than David Saville's recollection of Ofir, "He used to ask us (believe it or not) to punch him in the stomach to show what strong muscles he had there! How do I remember such things!!!"[1426] It seems that dining at Gray's Inn had strengthened his stomach!

In November 1959, it was reported in the "Jewish Chronicle" that he had been successful in the Bar final examinations.[1427] He was called to the Bar on 24 November 1959,[1428] and he then left Carmel.[1429] A few days later his visa to remain in England expired and it is very possible that the British authorities would not renew it and so he left England.[1430]

He first returned to France, where he became (or continued as) the Legal Adviser to the Paris branch of the Zim Shipping Company. He was only there until 1961, when he returned to Israel, and completed his Israeli law internship at a law firm. He then became the Legal Adviser at the Corporate head office of Maritime Fruit Carriers Ltd. He would also work pro bono as a legal adviser for a health services organisation.[1431]

Ofir died in Haifa on 9 December 1975 at the early age of nearly 42.[1432]

1421. Ibid.
1422. Ibid.
1423. Carmel 1959, p.4; Carmel College Senior School, sample school reports, autumn 1958 and summer 1959, form 5 (name withheld).
1424. Unwritten recollections of author.
1425. Recollections – David Saville.
1426. E-mail from Neil Myeroff, 25 April 2013.
1427. Jewish Chronicle, 20 November 1959, p.39.
1428. E-mail from Gray's Inn, op. cit.
1429. Carmel 1960, p.5.
1430. E-mail from Gray's Inn, op. cit.
1431. E-mail from Gerti, op. cit.
1432. Ibid.

HYAM ZOUNDELL MACCOBY

He was born on 20 March 1924 in Sunderland, the son of Ephraim Myer, a mathematics tutor, who taught him Biblical Hebrew and Talmudic Aramaic, from the age of four.[1433] His grandfather, whom he was named after, was the Kamenitzer Maggid.[1434]

His schooling was at Bede College Boys' School in Sunderland. He then received a Domus Exhibition to Balliol College in Oxford University, and he began studying Classics there in 1942. However, after two terms, his studies were interrupted, in June 1943, by his war-time service. Since he was short in stature, he was sent to Catterick as a Royal Signaller, and then from 1944 to 1946 he served in the "Signals: Bletchley Special Unit" which was based at the Decoding Centre at Bletchley Park, where he worked mainly on the night shifts translating decoded messages for dispatch.[1435] Following the war, he received, as with all the others who served there, a "Certificate of Service."[1436] (According to the "Roll of Honour" of Bletchley Park, he was there between the years 1942 and 1945, as a translator with the rank of Army Sergeant.[1437]) He then returned to Balliol, and presumably, he changed his courses from Classics to English. In 1951 he was awarded a Second Class Honours degree in English Language and Literature (which became an M.A. in 1952).[1438]

At the beginning of 1950 he married Cynthia Davies in the Llanelly area,[1439] who was a B.A. graduate of Somerville, a woman's College of Oxford University.[1440] For many years[1441] he was a teacher of English at Chiswick School, in West London.[1442]

1433. The Guardian, 31 July 2004, (online edition), obituary of Hyam Maccoby.

1434. Wikipedia – Hyam Maccoby.

1435. World War II, Jewish Personnel at Bletchley Park, Jewish Virtual Library (Internet); Balliol College Register, 1942–3, p.422.

1436. Certificate of Service at Bletchley Park to Hyam Zandell (sic) Maccoby.

1437. The "Roll of Honour" gives the names of those who worked in Bletchley Park during the Second World War. One of the sources of the information of names which appear on this Roll of Honour are "names found in the various publications about the work of Bletchley Park." Maccoby's name appear on this list.

1438. E-mails from Balliol College, Oxford, 5 December 2012; Balliol College Register, op. cit.; e-mail from Degree Conferrals Oxford University, 18 December 2012.

1439. General Register Office index, Marriages registered in January, February and March 1950, pp.D-269, M-300; E-mail from Balliol College, op. cit.

1440. Balliol College Register, op. cit.

1441. His obituary in the Guardian states "for some 20 years" but he started at Carmel before 20 years were up; Chiswick School's records do not go back that far (e-mail from Chiswick School, 6 December 2012). Indeed it is not clear which years he was at Chiswick School.

1442. The Guardian, obituary, op. cit.

In the academic year 1958/59 he joined the staff at Carmel. The Carmel magazine wrote, "We extend a cordial welcome to . . . Mr. Maccoby, who not only teaches English[1443] and Hebrew, but is also actively concerned with the Union Society and Chess Club."[1444] He was also the Form master of 5A.[1445] In the summer of 1959, the committee of the Union Society recorded their debt to him for his organisational talents which were of great assistance.[1446] He left Carmel at the end of the summer term 1962. The Carmel magazine noted, "It is with regret that we take leave of our chess master Mr. Maccoby . . . with many thanks for his efforts on our behalf."[1447]

In 1975, he was appointed librarian and tutor at Leo Baeck College,[1448] where he remained until 1995.[1449] Three years later, he joined the Centre for Jewish Studies at Leeds University, as visiting professor, and at a later date research professor.[1450]

From mainly the late 1980s, he became a prolific writer. His books, many of them dealing with the beginnings of Christianity included "The Day G-d Laughed, Sayings Fables and Entertainments of the Jewish Sages"; "Judaism in the First Century"; "Judas Iscariot and the Myth of Jewish Evil"; "The Mythmaker, Paul and the Invention of Christianity"; and "Jesus the Pharisee."[1451]

He died on 2 May 2004,[1452] at the age of 80.

JOHN PETER CLAVER TOALSTER

He was born on 24 December 1929 in Hull[1453] in the East Riding of Yorkshire. He was a believing Catholic and it is likely that his names "Peter Claver" are named after a Saint who lived from the 16th to 17th centuries

1443. Carmel College Senior School, sample school reports, autumn 1958 – summer 1959, form 5 (name withheld).
1444. Carmel 1959, p.4.
1445. Carmel College Senior School, sample school report, summer 1959, form 5A (name withheld).
1446. Carmel 1959, p.28.
1447. Carmel 1962, p.40; there were similar sentiments for his activities in the Union Society, ibid., p.25.
1448. The Guardian, obituary, op. cit.
1449. Jewish Chronicle, 14 May 2004, obituary, p.30.
1450. The Guardian, obituary, op. cit.
1451. "Copac" library catalogue.
1452. The Guardian, obituary, op. cit.
1453. E-mail from John Toalster, 14 November 2012.

and was a Spanish Jesuit priest who worked amongst the slaves in Columbia.[1454]

Toalster attended St. Bede's Grammar School in Bradford (which is a Catholic Grammar School opened in 1900 and named after the Venerable Bede[1455]), between the years 1940 and 1948 and in his final year at that school he was the school captain. He was also the captain of swimming, and committee member of the school debating society.[1456]

Toalster was admitted to Merton College of Oxford University on 19 October 1948. In 1952, he passed the B.A. in Literae Humaniores and was placed in the Third Class. On 16 July 1955 the degree of B.A. (and also M.A.) were conferred upon him.[1457] The subjects which he had studied for his B.A. were Latin and Greek languages and literatures, philosophy and ancient history.[1458] He also took part in extra-curricular activities as the College representative on the Bridge Club and Opera Club.[1459]

His university studies were followed by a period of two years in National Service.[1460] This included being from May to December 1953 at the Institute of Army Education. There he worked on the classifying and summarising of thousands of historical documents which covered 150 years of the history of a military academy Toalster was described as carrying out his work "most meticulously" and that he showed "real initiative."[1461] During the last six months of 1954 he was employed in teaching mathematics, geography, and map-reading up to Army second class standard, and English up to G.C.E. standard. He was praised as having a "pleasant easy manner . . . maintaining good classroom discipline" and that "his lessons are invariably well thought out and carefully planned."[1462]

His first civil teaching positions were only for a short period and they were at three Primary Schools in the West Riding of Yorkshire.[1463] This was followed by his being employed at Hulme Grammar School in Oldham, and he was there from September 1955 until July 1957. Apart from

---

1454. Wikipedia – Peter Claver.
1455. St Bede's Catholic Grammar School (Internet).
1456. Hulme Grammar School Oldham, Staff Application Form of John Toalster.
1457. E-mail from Degree Conferrals, Oxford University, 31 October 2013.
1458. E-mail from John Toalster, op. cit.
1459. Hulme Grammar School Oldham, Staff Application Form of John Toalster.
1460. E-mail from John Toalster, op. cit.
1461. Testimonial from HQ Scottish Command (Education Branch) for John Toalster, 15 February 1955.
1462. Testimonial from No. 4 Army Education Centre, Chilwell Notts for John Toalster, 8 March 1955.
1463. Letter from Headmaster of Hulme Grammar School to Chief Education Officer of West Riding of Yorkshire, dated 1 March 1956.

his teaching Latin, he also assisted with Games, probably junior football and cricket.[1464] Ian Holt, writes about him, "I remember JCPT [Toalster] well, because he started at Hulme at the same time as I started as an 11 yr old pupil – September 1955. He was the Junior Classics Master, teaching mainly Latin to boys up to GCE O-level . . . He only stayed at Hulme for a relatively short period – until 1957 I seem to remember."[1465]

Toalster joined the staff at Carmel in 1958[1466] and on him, the Carmel magazine wrote, "Mr. Toalster has taken on the onerous task of Study Block Housemaster, and besides teaching Classics, has given scooter lessons to members of the staff and has popularised the music of Bach amongst the boys."[1467] He was also in the following year the Housemaster of Gilbert.[1468]

Although he was a religious Catholic, Henry Law reports that "[Toalster] never made any attempt to push his Catholic faith on his Jewish pupils."[1469] On the contrary, as can be seen from a recollection of David Saville who attended many of Toalster's lessons, "He said to me once 'I am fed up with all this Latin and Greek, let's go to the library and learn a 'Blatt Gemara'."[1470]

Toalster looks back at the "kindness, good nature, generosity of my colleagues [at Carmel] . . . from all of whom I received help in my efforts to learn Hebrew, including even an elementary introduction to Talmudic studies; and not forgetting several hilarious moments with . . . [Raphael Loewe] spent in the composition of scurrilous Latin and Greek verse."[1471]

He left Carmel at the end of the spring term 1960[1472] and then went globe-trotting where he taught in a number of universities all over the world including those located in St. Gallen in Switzerland, Munich in Germany, Nicosia in Cyprus, and Karachi in Pakistan.[1473] During this period, namely in 1967, he married Marion English, who came from St. Albans.[1474]

Between the years 1974 and 1977 he studied Turkish philology, In-

---

1464. E-mail from Ian Holt, Lead Archivist, Hulme Grammar School, 12 November 2013.
1465. Ibid., 4 November 2013.
1466. E-mail from John Toalster, op. cit.
1467. Carmel 1958, p.4.
1468. Carmel 1959, p.49; Carmel College, Roll and Calendar 1958–59, staff, p.1.
1469. Recollections – Henry Law, Carmel College days, part 2, p.30.
1470. Recollections – David Saville.
1471. E-mail from John Toalster, op. cit.
1472. Carmel 1960, p.4.
1473. E-mail from John Toalster, op. cit.
1474. Ibid.

do-European philology, and Greek Literature for his doctorate at the Justus-von-Liebig Universität, Giessen in Germany, and in 1977 was awarded the degree of Dr. Phil.[1475] The title of his thesis was "Die uighurische Xuan-Zang-Biographie : 4. Kapitel mit Übersetzung und Kommentar," and a copy is to be found in some British libraries.[1476]

His listed areas of expertise were many and included the following: Philologies: Classical, Turkish, Indo-European, Germanic, Romance, and Semitic.[1477]

As of November 2013 Toalster was living in Giessen in Germany.[1478]

DENNIS FRANK MILLS

He was born on 18 July 1925 in Bloxwich in Walsall.[1479] Henry Law recollects that Dennis Mills had talked about being brought up in Brighton at some period of his childhood.[1480]

At the outbreak of the Second World War, Mills joined the South Staffs regiment and volunteered for the Army Commandos. He trained, amongst other places, in Achnacarry[1481] and he took part in the D-Day landings in No. 6 Commando. They, together with Lord Lovat's brigade (the one with the piper[1482]), came ashore at the Sword beach.[1483] Joseph Tate remembers that Dennis Mills would wear his green tie with the Commando emblems.[1484]

At the Summer Exhibition of the Royal Academy held in 1951, he exhibited one of his productions. He was listed as a sculptor and he showed a piece titled "Embryonic Kitten – grain study in course pine." At the

---

1475. Ibid.
1476. "Copac" library catalogue.
1477. getCited, Dr. John Peter Claver Toalster (Internet).
1478. E-mail from John Toalster, 1 November 2013.
1479. E-mail from Dennis Mills' widow Janet, 16 June 2013.
1480. E-mail from Henry Law, 4 March 2013.
1481. Achnacarry is located in the Lochaber region of Highland Scotland. In 1942, a Commando Basic Training Centre was established at Achnacarry Castle. Achnacarry is located in the Lochaber region of Highland Scotland. In 1942, a Commando Basic Training Centre was established at Achnacarry. Castle.
1482. Lord Lovat instructed his personal piper, to pipe the commandos ashore at Sword Beach in defiance of specific orders not to allow such an action in battle. When his piper demurred, citing the regulations, Lord Lovat replied: "Ah, but that's the *English* War Office. You and I are both Scottish, and that doesn't apply," (Wikipedia – Simon Fraser, 15th Lord Lovat).
1483. E-mail from Janet Mills, op. cit. Sword beach is on the Normandy coast, about 9 miles from Caen.
1484. E-mail form Joseph Tate, 17 March 2013.

time he was living in Southwick in Sussex (which is three miles from Brighton).[1485]

According to Michael Bharier, the original contact between Dennis Mills and Carmel College came via Wellesley Tudor-Pole. Tudor-Pole was a mystic and Kopul came to know of him through Israel Sieff. Michael recollects:

> I do remember that Kopul told us that Tudor Pole had some sixth sense urge to go into a small shop somewhere. In that shop he found a beautiful artwork, I think it was a sculpture of a horse. He was impressed enough with this to inquire who had done it. It turned out that the artist was a young man in difficulties and Tudor Pole helped him out in some way. The young man was Dennis Mills. I don't remember any more detail than that.[1486]

According to this account, presumably Tudor Pole then told Kopul about Dennis Mills.

Mills joined the staff at Carmel in the academic year 1958/59 as the Arts and Crafts master,[1487] and he lived in the attic which was situated on the top floor of the Main Building. This room was more than just his bedroom, but became, according to the Carmel magazine "the meeting place of school art enthusiasts." It further added that "the sudden wave of enthusiasm in the sphere of canoe-building and modeling is due [to him]."[1488] Henry Law elaborates:

> A new art master had arrived, Dennis Mills. He had been to sea and was keen on boat building. He got the boys to build kayaks by constructing a wooden frame and stretching canvas over. He also arranged for the rowing boats to be renovated, with plywood decks being fitted over the open sections fore and aft. These strengthened and stiffened the hulls and reduced the amount of water they took on board. I got involved in this, including the final painting, which was completed only just in time for a race.[1489]

1485. Angela Jarman, *Royal Academy Exhibitors 1905–1970*, volume III (Hilmarton Manor Press: Calne, Wiltshire, 1981), p.158.
1486. Two e-mails from Michael Bharier, 7 March 2013.
1487. Carmel 1959, p.4.
1488. Ibid.
1489. Recollections – Henry Law, Carmel College days, part 2, p.31.

Henry Law also recollects, "Kopul showing us a piece he [Dennis Mills] had made from a small tree stem – it was a weasel or seal, and he had exploited the natural shape of the timber and its grain to capture the sinuosity of the animal."[1490]

In 1961, Mills used his artistic skills to design the cover of the Carmel magazine with an abstract drawing entitled "Pipe Dream."[1491] That year, he succeeded in putting the Carmel boats into a polythene bag![1492] He left Carmel about 1964.[1493]

In the early 1990s, Henry Law would sometimes see Dennis Mills in Brighton.[1494] He died on 28 March 1997 of thyroid cancer,[1495] at the age of 72.

RABBI MAURICE (MOSHE ISAAC) YOUNG

He was born on 29 February 1936 in Liverpool. Of his birth-date, he writes, "Leap-Year Baby – picture appeared in the Press, and haven't left the Press since!"[1496]

Rabbi Young attended the Liverpool Institute High School, where he began in September 1947. According to the "Green Book" of that school, in the academic year 1949/50, he was in the Lower Fifth, in the following year the Upper Fifth, and the next year in a form designated as RA.[1497] These letters RA stood for "Remove A" and it was generally made up of boys who had taken O levels already in the Upper Fifth and included the boys who wished to leave school at the end of that year,[1498] as was the case of Moshe Young.

He left the school in 1952 and enrolled in the Liverpool Talmudical College (Yeshiva) where he studied until 1959,[1499] and from there he received Semicha from the Principal of the Yeshiva, Rabbi Zalman Plitnick, who was also the Communal Rabbi of Liverpool (and was the successor to Rabbi Unterman who became Chief Rabbi of Israel). On Rabbi Young's leaving the Yeshiva, a reception was held, and he was presented with a set

---

1490. E-mail from Henry Law, 4 March 2013.
1491. Carmel 1961, cover and p.2 (unnumbered).
1492. Ibid., p.5.
1493. E-mail from Peter Rhodes, 4 March 2013.
1494. E-mail from Henry Law, op. cit.
1495. E-mail from Janet Mills, op. cit.
1496. E-mail from Rabbi Moshe Young, 17 December 2012.
1497. Liverpool Institute Green Books, 1949, 1950, 1951.
1498. E-mail from Iain Taylor (alumni of Liverpool Institute), 24 January 2013.
1499. E-mail from Rabbi Moshe Young, op. cit.

of Chumashim. It was pointed out that he had pursued the whole of his Jewish Studies in Liverpool.[1500] He was the last full-time student at that Yeshiva.[1501]

In September 1959 he joined the staff at Carmel to teach Jewish Studies.[1502] On this he writes, "I was recommended to Rabbi Rosen by my good friend the late Dr. Alexander Tobias (Toby) zl, whom I had earlier met at a Summer School holiday."[1503]

At Carmel, Rabbi Young had eating problems. He was particular to wait a full six hours between meat and milk. However, at Carmel, lunch was almost always meaty and the supper was usually milky, but the time lapse between these meals was only about five and a half hours.[1504] On Sundays his timetabling was such that he could eat the lunch meaty meal with the Prep School who ate at an earlier hour. The downside was that on Sundays, for the second time that same day, the supper meal was sometimes meaty![1505]

During his first year at Carmel, he had a "bachelor flat" which was in fact just one room, with no water amenities, on the top floor of the Main Building. (Most of the other rooms on that floor had similar "no amenities" and were studies, each room for two to three sixth formers.)[1506]

In the summer of the following year he got married to Doreen Pearlman[1507] and the Young family moved to Oxford. On his sojourn in the University City, Rabbi Young writes that it "was an experience it itself being able to mix with dons and students."[1508]

Being in Oxford meant he had to commute to Carmel every day and he was not accident free, as Joe Miller recollects, "I recall playing football as a back and talking to a teacher, Rabbi Young. The conversation will remain with me forever, as he told me he had recently had a car accident. When I asked what had happened, he just told me 'that he didn't know as he was not looking!' A classic comment."[1509]

1500. Jewish Chronicle, 2 October 1959, p.47.

1501. Henry Lachs, who was President of the Yeshiva, informed the author of this fact.

1502. Carmel 1960, p.4.

1503. E-mail from Rabbi Moshe Young, op. cit.

1504. There are opinions that it is sufficient to wait until the beginning of the sixth hour. Also the custom of many Anglo Jews is to wait just three hours.

1505. Unwritten recollections of author.

1506. E-mail from Rabbi Moshe Young, op. cit.

1507. General Register Office index, Marriage registered July, August and September 1960, pp.P-26, Y-494; Jewish Chronicle, 15 April 1960, p.7. The wedding took place in Sunderland, the city where Doreen lived.

1508. E-mail from Rabbi Moshe Young, op. cit.

1509. Recollections – Joe Miller.

On the members of staff at Carmel, Rabbi Young was highly complimentary, "I must say that the Staff members at the school were the most versatile and intellectually stimulating that I have ever come across in a staff room."[1510]

He left Carmel in 1962 and in January 1963 became a teacher at the Hasmonean Grammar School for Boys where he remained until December 1969.[1511] During this period he became an external student at London University, and in 1967 received a B.A. Honours degree in "Classical, Mediaeval, and Modern Hebrew."[1512]

Between 1970 and 1971, he was the Director in the outreach programme, "The Society for the Promotion of Jewish Learning."[1513] This was followed by his being Principal of the Manchester Jewish High School for Girls between the years 1971 and 1980.[1514] For most of that period, the author was Director of Jewish Studies at the King David High School in Liverpool, and had had accepted his Jewish orientated syllabus for O-level Scripture Knowledge. However, the examiner setting and marking the papers was non-Jewish, and accordingly did not have a Torah-orientated approach to Tanach. Although the phrasing of the exam questions was acceptable, one could see from his reports that his marking of the pupils' scripts did not accord with Jewish tradition. One of the schools who took this exam was Rabbi Young's school in Manchester, and on this the author wrote:

> [Rabbi Young] was dissatisfied with this examiner's report and he wrote to the examiners pointing out that 'the accepted method of Bible Study is to read into the text both Midrashic and classic Rabbinic commentaries.' My discussions at the time with other Jewish educationists confirmed the point made by Rabbi Young. . . . I understand that because of the examiner's method of marking the scripts, Rabbi Young then stopped entering his pupils for this examination.[1515]

1510. E-mail from Rabbi Moshe Young, op. cit.
1511. Booklet "The Hasmonean 1945–1970" (brought out to mark the 25th anniversary of the Hasmonean Grammar School), members of staff, p.22.
1512. E-mail from Rabbi Moshe Young, op. cit.
1513. Ibid.
1514. Ibid.
1515. Chaim Simons. *My Fight for Yiddishkeit: Reminiscences of a Director of Jewish Studies*, (Kiryat Arba, Israel, 2005), p.74.

Whilst he was in Manchester he received in 1974 a Diploma in Management in Education from the Manchester Polytechnic.[1516]

In 1980, Rabbi Young went southwards to London and took a similar position at the Hasmonean High School for Girls, but this only lasted for one year. It was then northwards to Tyne and Wear to become for three years a teacher at the Gateshead Teacher Training College (Seminary). Then in 1985, it was back to his original position at the Manchester Jewish High School, where he remained until 1996.[1517]

In 1996 he emigrated to the "New World" or in Yiddish terminology the "Goldener Medinah." He arrived in Lakewood and he became a teacher in two Teacher Training Seminaries – in Boro Park and in Lakewood. In both of them he taught Nach, and in Boro Park he also taught Hashkafah, and in Lakewood he also taught Educational Psychology.[1518]

Rabbi Young made a visit back to the "Old World" in 2001, to be one of the Guests of Honour at a Jewish educational conference held in Bournemouth. Amongst his activities at this conference, was being a member on the panel of a Brains Trust. The topics at this Brains Trust were very practical in Jewish education, and included "The Purpose of Secular Studies," "Learning Kodesh through Loshon Hakodesh," "Directing Teenagers Without Causing Rebellion," "the Advisability of Playing Sports in Schools and Yeshivas," and "Monitoring Teachers."[1519]

In addition to his teaching activities, he also utilised his pen (or probably today his computer!) to write columns in the Orthodox Jewish newspaper "Hamodia," and to write books.[1520] The books he authored were "Apples from the Tree," a 400-page tome which contained "seventy-two eye-opening essays" which focused on "matters relating to the home, school, Jewish life, education, and psychology,"[1521] and a further book entitled "Whose Love is Greater?" a book which explains how to train a child to face challenges which will occur later in life.[1522]

As of December 2012, he was living in Lakewood, New Jersey.[1523]

1516. E-mail from Rabbi Moshe Young, op. cit.
1517. Ibid.
1518. Ibid.
1519. Dei'ah veDibur, Information & Insight, News, 14 March 2001, (Internet).
1520. E-mail from Rabbi Moshe Young, op. cit.
1521. JewishStore.com, *Apples from the Tree* (Internet).
1522. Feldheim.com, *Whose Love is Greater* (Internet).
1523. E-mail from Rabbi Moshe Young, op. cit.

YISRAEL (EDWARD) ALEXANDER

He was born in Berlin on 21 July 1921 to Rabbi Dr. Eliezer (Siegfried) and Ada (Adelaide) Alexander. His father had a Synagogue in one of the western residential areas of Berlin and he also served as the Rabbi of a Jewish hospital.[1524]

Alexander's schooling first consisted of four years at a "volksschule" (elementary school) and this was followed by attending the Lessing Gymnasium (High-School).[1525] Because of the Nazis policies regarding Jews studying in German public schools, he transferred to the Adas Yisroel School, which was an Orthodox Jewish School in Berlin.[1526]

He was a member of a Zionist Youth Movement and after Kristallnacht he was sent to Buchenwald (which at that time was a political camp), for "re-education." He was there for about four weeks and his discharge from Buchenwald was conditioned on him and his friends leaving Germany.[1527] He came to England on the kindertransport shortly before the start of the Second World War and there he joined a Bachad Hachshara centre.[1528] As an "enemy alien" in England he was deported to the Isle of Man where he remained for about five months.[1529]

At the Bachad Hachshara centre he met his future wife Chaya (Klara) Windholz and they were married on 20 August 1944 at the Hachshara in Buckingham.[1530]

Soon after the end of the War, in July 1945, Alexander and his wife went to Eretz Yisrael. Since they were members of a collective Zionist farm destined for Kibbutz Tirat Tzvi (in the Bet Shean valley) and his wife was pregnant, they received legal certificates and even travelled "first class" on board a passenger cruiser. They were on this kibbutz for about three years. Since his wife was voted as a member of this kibbutz, but he was

---

1524. E-mail from Yisrael Alexander's son David, 28 April 2013. The information in the various e-mails from David were taken from Yisrael Alexander's unpublished biography. Yisrael's parents perished in the Holocaust.

1525. The school was named after the German poet Gotthold Ephraim Lessing. Even though Lessing was not Jewish, under the Nazis the name of the school had to be changed to "German high school for boys."

1526. E-mail from David Alexander, 28 April 2013.

1527. Ibid., 14 January 2014.

1528. Ibid., 28 April 2013. These Bachad Hachshara centres aimed to prepare the youth to work on a kibbutz by learning agricultural techniques.

1529. E-mail from David Alexander, 14 January 2014.

1530. Ibid., 28 April 2013, 11 March 2014; General Register Office index, Marriage registered July, August and September 1944, pp.A-8, W-351.

denied this, they moved to Ra'anana,[1531] where he remained for the rest of his life,[1532] with the exception of the short period he taught at Carmel.

His first teaching position in Israel was from September 1947 until the summer of 1955 and was at the Yavneh Elementary School in Ra'anana where he taught a variety of subjects which included Jewish Studies, agriculture, music, and English. Then, for a period of three years, he was the Headmaster of the Shabazi school, a small all-Yemenite school in Ein Yaacov, an area of Even Yehudah.[1533] Yafah Dorani recollects how Yisrael Alexander helped her establish a branch of the religious youth group Bnei Akivah in the area. He allowed her to go around the classes in the school to notify the pupils, and he gave her tables and chairs which were no longer in use, and he also wished her success with her venture.[1534] In 1958 he taught English and music part time in a number of schools in the Kfar Sava area.[1535]

He came to Carmel to teach Jewish Studies for three years between September 1959[1536] and July 1962.[1537] He lived with his family at Nuneham Murren (known as the farm), where there were the dormitories for some of the sixth formers and he was the Housemaster there.[1538] He also organised a singing group to which he taught many Hebrew songs,[1539] and also a group where he taught the theory of "Ta'amei Hamikra" (musical notes on the books of the Tanach).[1540]

On his return to Israel, Alexander taught music for three years at the Bar-Ilan School in Kfar Sava and was also the choir master there. He then became the Headmaster of this school, where he remained for thirteen years.[1541]

In his function as Headmaster, his son David (who was also a pupil at Carmel), writes that "he was a revolutionary person, daring to implement his educational vision particularly enhancing tradition of the various different Jewish communities. Much of his pioneering work would years

1531. E-mail from David Alexander, 14 January 2014.
1532. Ibid., 28 April 2013.
1533. Ibid., 15 January 2014.
1534. Ohr bachatzer ha'achorit – story of Yafah Dorani (Internet).
1535. E-mail from David Alexander, 15 January 2014.
1536. Carmel 1960, p.4.
1537. Carmel 1962, p.8.
1538. Carmel 1960, p.4.
1539. 7 years, p.76; Yisrael Alexander, Notes on Song-Sheet no.1/2, and 8 songs headed "Shiru Lashem Shir Chadash," undated (September 1959).
1540. 7 years, p.75.
1541. E-mail from David Alexander, 15 January 2014.

later become standard tradition in the State Religious Schools."[1542] On his headmastership, David also writes, "I attended lately a reunion of his former pupils at Bar Ilan School in Kfar Sava. Decades after graduation they speak of him with glittering eyes and recreate endless incidents which reflect his special personality as an educator. And you should remember we talk about elementary school (!) not a high school or an academic institution."[1543]

From 1979 to 1985, Alexander held a senior position in the Ministry of Education.[1544] He retired in 1985, but from 1989 onwards he taught Jewish Studies at non-religious schools on a voluntary basis.[1545] In addition he would guide groups of tourists in Israel, coach Bar Mitzvah boys (mostly of non-orthodox background), and eagerly participate in activities which were bound to Education.[1546]

He died on 13 January 2005,[1547] at the age of 83.

BEAGLEY

He joined the staff at Carmel in the autumn of 1959 and was Housemaster of the top floor of the Main Building. "The first night [of term] he called a meeting of those sleeping in the Main Building. He gave a very stern lecture including, 'I will beat anyone who doesn't listen to the prefects'." After just half a term, his employment was abruptly terminated.[1548]

KANT RISHI

He came from India and joined Carmel in the autumn of 1959. Jeremy Rosen writes of him, "And there was the equally distinguished, scholarly Dr. Kant Rishi. An Indian, he too was an academic moonlighting. He looked and acted as if he had been part of the Raj. He was one of the gentler more dignified teachers we had at Carmel. He did not last long."[1549] Rabbi Young has a different version of Rishi's academic degrees, "the only thing I can remember about him was that he told me about his academic

---

1542. Ibid., 28 April 2013.
1543. Ibid., 15 January 2014.
1544. Ibid.
1545. Ibid.
1546. Ibid., 24 April 2013.
1547. Ibid.
1548. 7 years, p.104.
1549. Recollections – Jeremy Rosen, chap.1.

achievement. He said that he had a B.A. degree from Bombay, failed!!!"[1550] Needless to say, Rishi could well have been saying this in jest![1551] After the speedy departure of Beagley, Kant Rishi became the Housemaster of the top floor of the Main Building.[1552]

MRS. ISABELLA BROWN BENNETT CRASTON

She was born on 17 June 1922[1553] in Sunderland County Durham as Isabella Brown Bennett Archibald,[1554] the daughter of William and Isabella B. (née Bennett) Archibald.[1555] She became a Craston when she married John Leslie Craston in the autumn of 1950 in the Sunderland area.[1556]

Between the years 1927 and 1935 her primary schooling was at High Southwick Board School in Sunderland. Her grammar school education was between 1935 and 1942 at The Bede Collegiate Grammar School in Sunderland. During the Second World War she was evacuated to Richmond, Yorkshire, returning to her family in Sunderland towards the end of the war. From 1945 to 1948, she studied at Langham Towers Teacher Training College in Sunderland and in 1948 obtained her teaching qualification.[1557]

Her brother William comments that at that period they were not keen in her area to employ women teachers.[1558] Possibly for this reason, Mrs. Craston then moved to Malvern in Worcestershire for her first teaching job. Whilst she was working, she met her future husband John Craston, who later secured a job at Harwell Atomic Research Establishment and in the early 1960s, they moved to Abingdon.[1559]

Her next teaching job was at the Carmel College Prep School from

---

1550. E-mail from Rabbi Moshe Young, dated 30 April 2013.

1551. There is indeed a joke that if an Indian person wished to impress a potential employer with his performance at university, but had failed to pass his degree course, he would have his business cards printed with the legend: *BA Calcutta (Failed)*.

1552. 7 years, p.104.

1553. E-mail from Sidney Gold, 7 May 2014.

1554. General Register Office index, Births registered in July, August and September 1922, p.A-24.

1555. General Register Office index, Marriages registered in July, August and September 1919, pp.A-27, B-97.

1556. General Register Office index, Marriages registered in October, November and December 1950, pp.A-20, C-222.

1557. E-mail from Councillor William Archibald (brother of Isabella) via his daughter Irene Arnold, 17 June 2014.

1558. Telephone conversation between Councillor William Archibald and the author, 19 May 2014.

1559. E-mail from Councillor William Archibald, op. cit.

about 1960, and during the academic year 1960/61, she was the form mistress of form 3 of the Prep School.[1560] According to Tony Barr-Taylor, who was a teacher at Carmel at that period, Isabella Craston was very astute, very alert and very well read, and she was particularly good at teaching English. She did not take part in the sporting activities of the school but was active in the dramatic performances. He also added that she smoked![1561]

One of her pupils at Carmel was David "Buster" Rosen and he also has recollections of her teaching of English. "English in particular came to life with her booming voice and grand gestures. I looked forward eagerly to these lessons which made literature, places and people so vibrant and exciting. I have some recall of her wearing bright colours as well; but again it could be just the drama of her personality that created these impressions."[1562]

From at least 1965 onwards she was living in Brightwell-cum-Sotwell,[1563] a village situated about two miles from Wallingford. There the Crastons "bought a plot of land and designed and built themselves a particularly distinctive house, that was extremely modern and much talked about."[1564]

About the late 1970s, she directed the village production of the Gilbert and Sullivan comic opera "Trial by Jury."[1565] Her brother William elaborates that she "had a life long love of music and drama. She took part in many amateur dramatic performances, playing many roles and receiving good reviews!"[1566]

In June 2002 she died aged 80, at the Reading hospital.[1567] Her husband died eleven years later in November 2013, in a nursing home in Abingdon.[1568]

1560. Carmel College Prep School, sample school reports, autumn 1960 and spring 1961, form 3 (name withheld).
1561. Telephone conversation between Tony Barr-Taylor and the author, 19 May 2014.
1562. E-mail from David Rosen, 29 May 2014.
1563. E-mail from Sidney Gold, 7 May 2014.
1564. E-mail from Councillor William Archibald, op. cit.; telephone conversation between author and Councillor William Archibald, 18 June 2014.
1565. Telephone conversation between author and Eric Dore, Chairman of the Brightwell-cum-Sotwell Web Group, 19 May 2014.
1566. E-mail from Councillor William Archibald, op. cit.
1567. Ibid.
1568. Oxford Mail, 11 December 2013 (online edition).

HUGH CROSTHWAITE

He was born on 2 February 1923 in Welton le Marsh which is near Spilsbury in Lincolnshire, to Joseph Nixon Crosthwaite, a Clerk in Holy Orders, and Mabel Eveline (née Camm).[1569] At the age of nine, he won a scholarship to the choir school, St. Michael's College, Tenbury,[1570] which he joined in 1932. In 1934 he was appointed as a chorister. In the summer of 1935 he left for Stamford School with a scholarship of £35,[1571] where he studied until 1941.[1572] Midway through the autumn term of 1940 he was appointed as a School Prefect and he also achieved the rank of Sergeant in the School's Officer Training Corp.[1573]

He was admitted in 1941 to St. John's College, Cambridge University.[1574] In 1943, in Part 1 of the Classical Tripos he received a lower second, and in Part 2 in 1944, he again received a lower second. In 1945, he received a B.A. Honours degree, (which in 1966 became an M.A.)[1575] He also played in the University Orchestra.[1576]

Crosthwaite joined the staff at Carmel in the summer term 1960 to teach Latin, where he replaced John Toalster.[1577] During his first term at Carmel, he produced a one-act play in Latin entitled "Miles et Senex" which was acted by the Junior forms.[1578] The following year, he participated in the "dressing-up" part of a dramatic performance. The Carmel magazine explains, "Mr. Crosthwaite had a professional touch with the make-up and even succeeded in making the cast look presentable under the searching glare of David Duke's most efficient lighting."[1579]

After he had retired from teaching, when not doing research, he continued his exercises in music – the piano, organ, and bassoon – and at walking and climbing in the English Lake District and the Swiss Alps. At that period he was living in Birmingham.[1580]

In 1992, at the suggestion of Alfred de Grazia,[1581] Hugh Crosthwaite

---

1569. E-mail from St. John's College Cambridge, 15 January 2013.
1570. Grazian Archive (archives of Alfred de Grazia), Immanuel Velikovsky, (Internet).
1571. E-mail from Hereford Cathedral, 15 January 2013.
1572. E-mail from Stamford School, 16 January 2013.
1573. Ibid., 17 January 2013.
1574. E-mail from Cambridge Alumni Relations Office, 15 January 2013.
1575. E-mail from St. John's College, op. cit.
1576. Grazian Archive, op. cit.
1577. Carmel 1960, p.4.
1578. Ibid., p.29.
1579. Carmel 1961, p.28.
1580. Grazian Archive, op. cit.
1581. Alfred de Grazia (born 1919 in Chicago) is a political scientist and author who has defended

published a book called "Ka: a handbook of mythology, sacred practices, electrical phenomena, and their linguistic connections in the ancient Mediterranean world."[1582] Five years later, he published a follow-up book called "A Fire not Blown . . ." in which he "tried to develop some of the ideas" he had put forward in his previous book "Ka" and apply the "electrical interpretation of ancient myths and cosmology to a particular area of the ancient Mediterranean world."[1583]

He died on 3 August 2008[1584] at the age of 85.

RABBI SYDNEY BENZION LEPERER

He was born on 4 August 1922[1585] in the Hackney area of London.[1586] He attended the Jews' Free School and was there during the Second World War when it was evacuated to Soham, a small town in Cambridgeshire. In an "Evacuation News Sheet" brought out by the school in December 1939, there is the comment that S. Leperer was going to sit his Matriculation examination in the following January.[1587] Frank Rose recollects Leperer at Soham and writes:

> One of the older boys at Soham was Sidney Leperer (known as Pepper). . . . He intended to become a Rabbi and was studying Latin on his own because this was necessary for university entrance. Sidney had two very valuable exercise books filled with history notes for the period we were studying – 1485–1688 and 1688–1815. I spent many nights copying out the notes by the oil lamp and then passing the original notes onto two other boys who were also studying for the Matriculation. We learned the notes off by heart.[1588]

---

the catastrophism theory of Immanuel Velikovsky (Wikipedia – Alfred de Grazia).

1582. Hugh Crosthwaite, *Ka: a handbook of mythology, sacred practices, electrical phenomena, and their linguistic connections in the ancient Mediterranean world* (Princeton, New Jersey: Merton Publications, 1992), Introduction by Alfred de Grazia, p.4.

1583. Hugh Crosthwaite, *A Fire not Blown* (Princeton, New Jersey: Merton Publications, 1997), Preface.

1584. E-mail from St. John's College, op. cit.

1585. Jewish Chronicle, obituary, 15 December 1995, p.27.

1586. General Register Office index, Births registered in July, August, September 1922, p.L-289.

1587. Jews' Free School magazine, Central School, Evacuation News Sheet, Issue no.1, December 1939, (Internet).

1588. From the East End to Soham, memoirs collected by Michael Rouse, memoirs of Frank Rose (Internet).

In the late 1940s, he taught at the Hebrew Classes of the New West End Synagogue. One of his pupils was Noach Hall, and Rev. Leperer was his first Chumash teacher.[1589] Noach recollects these Chumash lessons:

> Sometime between 1947 and 1949, I graduated to the 'top class' which was considered real 'learning in depth' and where my first introduction to *Chumash* began. Our teacher was The Reverend Sidney Leperer. . . . I recall that Rev. Leperer was an accomplished teacher, knew how to enthuse and smile whilst doing so and equally to tolerate zero nonsense during the class time. His quite speedy reaction to inattention was physical! In two strides he was at ones side and used his unique 'attention getting torture' to remedy this lack of courtesy extremely rapidly. Using thumb and forefinger of both of his hands, he took the hair at the side of the ears and twisted it – fast – explaining whilst so doing that a bicycle ride might bring us back to our task in hand – learning the Posuk [verse] of the moment in the Chumash! The pain was short lived and the experience uncomfortable, but it certainly achieved his objective.[1590]

Rabbi Leperer was registered with the University of London for a programme of study under the academic direction of Birkbeck College, and on 1 August 1947, was awarded the degree of B.A. in History – Branch II with upper Second Class Honours.[1591]

In September 1949, his engagement to Miriam Jacobs was announced[1592] and the wedding took place in the following spring in Birmingham,[1593] the city where Miriam lived.

He was appointed Minister of the Walthamstow and Leyton Synagogue in mid-1951.[1594] This was followed two years later by his appointment as assistant minister at Hampstead Garden Suburb Synagogue.

In April 1956, he was appointed minister at North Finchley and Woodside Park District Synagogue, a position which he held for a period of

---

1589. Noach [Hall] miTelshestone, "Some thoughts on The New West End," Mosaic, Magazine of the New West End Synagogue, London, Rosh Hashanah 5771/2010, p.37.

1590. E-mail from Noach Hall, 28 February 2013.

1591. E-mail from transcripts office University of London, 4 July 2013.

1592. Jewish Chronicle, 2 September 1949, p.7.

1593. General Register Office index, Marriages registered in April, May, and June 1950, pp.J-173, L-257.

1594. Jewish Chronicle, 15 June 1951, pp.3, 19.

four and a half years.[1595] On his activities at this Synagogue, Rev. Michael Plaskow writes:

> [Rabbi Leperer] was one of the teachers for the Adult Education Group and played a great part in its progress. The review of the weekly sidra during the Shabbat service was one of many innovations. This proved to be quite popular and as a result, a further series of talks was introduced covering such subjects as prayer, etc. An Adult Study Group in Rabbinics was held at different homes in the locality. Furthermore, another Study Group was formed to cater for youth aged 16 to 19 years. Yet another outstanding achievement was the establishment of our Yavneh Kindergarten in 1959 which is still going strong today.[1596]

Rabbi Leperer had studied at Gateshead Yeshiva, Etz Chaim Yeshivah in London, and Jews' College[1597] where in mid-1956 he received a Rabbinical Diploma.[1598]

In September 1960 he joined the staff of Carmel to teach Jewish Studies and History, and the Carmel Magazine added that he had "quickly established himself as the Tuck Shop's leading customer for tobacco."[1599] On Shabbat, he would give an "intermediate" level Gemara shiur.[1600]

A few months prior to his coming to Carmel, the sanatorium which had occupied a wing of the gymnasium building had moved to its new premises. Rabbi Leperer and his wife lived in this wing. At that period the gymnasium building was about to collapse and as a result there was no squash and basketball, whose venue had been the gymnasium.[1601] However, the Leperer's were told that that wing was still safe![1602]

In mid-1969, Rabbi Leperer took on the job of a chaplain to Jewish students at Oxford University.[1603] However just a year and a half later he resigned due to the tragic death of his only son,[1604] and he was appointed

---

1595. Jewish Chronicle: 26 August 1960, p.6; 15 December 1995, Obituary, p.27.
1596. E-mail from Michael Plaskow, 3 March 2013.
1597. Jewish Chronicle, 15 December 1995, op. cit.
1598. Jewish Chronicle: 1 June 1956, p.5: 15 December 1995, op. cit.
1599. Carmel 1961, p.4.
1600. E-mail from Nigel Simons, 21 May 2012.
1601. Carmel 1961, p.42.
1602. Related by the Leperers (whilst they were still living there) to the author.
1603. Jewish Chronicle: 21 February 1969, p.19, 14 March 1969, p.28, 15 December 1995, op. cit.
1604. Jewish Chronicle: 2 October 1970, p.19, 15 December 1995, op. cit.

Minister of the Hove Hebrew Congregation.[1605] In 1974 he was appointed lecturer and later senior lecturer in Jewish History at Jews' College.[1606]

He had continued with his studies, and in 1977 he was awarded the degree of Ph.D. by London University for a thesis entitled "Abraham Tang as a precursor of the Haskalah in England."[1607] In 1994 he became the Acting Principal of Jews' College.[1608]

Rabbi Leperer died on 5 December 1995 at the age of 73.[1609] At the time of his death, he was involved in the preparation of a new translation of "Megilat Sefer, The Autobiography of Rabbi Jacob Emden," and it was completed by Rabbi Meir Wise, and then published.[1610]

In describing him, his obituary states:

> He will be best remembered for his outstanding contribution as a teacher, whether at Carmel College, Jews' College, or Jewish Youth Study Groups. It was a role for which he was ideally suited, as he possessed humour, patience, a love of learning and an even greater love for humanity. He combined these qualities with genuine humility and absolute integrity, which made him a rare and special person, who will long be cherished by all who knew and loved him.[1611]

GERALD THOMAS

He was born on 7 February 1938 in Maesteg in Wales.[1612] Between the years 1948 and 1955, he was a pupil at Maesteg Grammar school.[1613] From October 1955 to June 1958, he was a student at University College Swansea, University of Wales, where he studied Applied Mathematics, and in July 1958 was awarded the degree of B.Sc.[1614] From 1958 to 1960 he was a Maths teacher at Reeds School in Cobham.[1615]

In the summer of 1960 he married Maureen Harwood in the Deptford

---

1605. Jewish Chronicle: 11 December 1970, p.11, 15 December 1995, op. cit.

1606. Jewish Chronicle, 15 December 1995, op. cit.

1607. Senate House Libraries, University of London, Catalogue of University of London theses.

1608. Jewish Chronicle, 15 December 1995, op. cit.

1609. Ibid.

1610. ShafTec Enterprises, New Title: Megilat Sefer by Rabbi Jacob Emden in English, (Internet).

1611. Jewish Chronicle , 15 December 1995, op. cit.

1612. Canadian Obituaries, Gerald Thomas, (Internet).

1613. Curriculum Vitae of Gerald Thomas, received from his family by letter on 14 July 2013.

1614. E-mail from Swansea University, 18 July 2013.

1615. Curriculum Vitae of Gerald Thomas, op. cit.

area.[1616] He became a member of the staff at Carmel during the 1960/61 academic year to teach Maths. Cricket was also a specialty with him as the Carmel magazine writes, "[He] also 'guests' very successfully for the 1st XI [cricket team]."[1617] In a game against Henley Police Cricket Club, Thomas excelled in both batting and bowling by scoring 47 of Carmel's 113 runs, and taking 5 wickets for just 5 runs.[1618] He, together with Gabay, was a housemaster of Montefiore House. The school house captain of Montefiore, in his annual report thanked these two masters "for being so helpful and untiring as our House masters; we cannot easily forget their support, especially during the soccer matches when they did all but score the goals for us."[1619] He was on the staff at Carmel until about 1968.[1620]

It was in the Carmel swimming pool that his daughter learned to swim and she later went on to represent Canada in international events.[1621] Carmel College should thus get some credit for this!

Between 1968 and 1969, he studied at London University where he received an Education Diploma.[1622]

In 1969, Thomas emigrated to Canada with his wife and three children,[1623] and from then until he retired in 1994, he was a High School teacher in Maths in Ontario in the Hamilton School System.[1624] He was also involved at this school with cricket, rugby, soccer, swimming and water polo.[1625]

As soon as he arrived in Canada, Thomas became very much involved with aquatic sports, and in the course of the following decade he held many positions in these aquatic activities, which included the following: From 1970, he officiated at swim meets at McMaster University, so much so, that he was described as a "fixture" at this University. Between 1979 and 1988, he was a member of the Swim Ontario Board of Directors, being its President for three of these years. In 1989, he was one of the founding members of the Ontario Aquatic Hall of Fame and remained

1616. General Register Office index, Marriages registered in July, August and September 1960, pp.H-114, T-314.
1617. Carmel 1961, p.4.
1618. Ibid., p.38.
1619. Ibid., p.44.
1620. E-mail from Peter Rhodes, 4 March 2013.
1621. E-mail from Charles Marshall, 4 July 2013.
1622. Curriculum Vitae of Gerald Thomas, op. cit.
1623. Canadian Obituaries, Gerald Thomas, (Internet).
1624. Curriculum Vitae of Gerald Thomas, op. cit.; Canadian Obituaries, Gerald Thomas (Internet).
1625. Curriculum Vitae of Gerald Thomas, op. cit.

one of its directors until 1994.[1626] He was also president of the Canadian Amateur Swimming Association. He culminated his involvement in swimming as the head official at the 1992 Olympic Games held in Barcelona Spain.[1627] In 1993, he received the Elizabeth Collins Ralph Award for his outstanding contribution to swim officiating.[1628]

In 1994, Thomas retired from teaching and then, together with his wife, travelled the world.[1629] Just a month before he died, he and his wife visited England and whilst there, they had lunch with Charles Marshall, with whom they had remained in contact.[1630] On 5 June 2013, Thomas died suddenly at the age of 75. His family asked that instead of sending flowers, people should send a donation to the Canadian Diabetics Association.[1631]

MARTIN PHILIP COOMBE

He was born towards the end of 1936 in the Watford area,[1632] which is near London, to Harry and Frances (née Carter) Coombe.[1633]

He studied at Sheffield University, beginning, it would seem, in 1956, in the Faculty of Pure Science. In June 1957, he took his intermediate B.Sc. examinations receiving 54 in Zoology, 56 in Botany, and 49 in Physiology, which gave him an average mark of 53. In his second year he received 62 in Zoology and in June 1959, he was awarded a lower Second Class degree.[1634]

Coombe joined Carmel in the academic year 1960/61 as a Biology teacher. In addition, he was the Housemaster of the M and S dormitory block.[1635] He introduced compulsory showers for all the boys after getting up each morning.[1636] He also participated actively in the sporting activities of the school, by being a Housemaster of Alexander House[1637] and would on various occasions play in the school's cricket team.[1638]

1626. Gerry Thomas passes Away, Biography from Ontario Aquatic Hall of Fame (Internet).
1627. Canadian Obituaries, Gerald Thomas (Internet).
1628. Ontario Swimming Officials' Association, Honour Roll (Internet).
1629. Canadian Obituaries, Gerald Thomas (Internet).
1630. E-mail from Charles Marshall, op. cit.
1631. Canadian Obituaries, Gerald Thomas (Internet).
1632. General Register Office index, Births registered in January, February and March 1937, p.C-188.
1633. General Register Office index, Marriages registered in July, August and September 1935, pp.C-221, C-283.
1634. E-mail from Sheffield University, 4 July 2013.
1635. Carmel 1961, p.4. This was the 2 story dormitory block.
1636. E-mail from Roger Goldner, 9 March 2013.
1637. Carmel 1961, p.42.
1638. Ibid., p.38.

In his religious observance, Coombe was a Seventh Day Adventist.[1639] This is a Protestant Christian sect, which observes their Sabbath from Friday sunset to Saturday sunset.[1640] On this, David Frome writes that "whereas the other non-Jewish staff would assist or be assigned duties over the Sabbath, he was obviously off somewhere doing his own thing so was never around at that time."[1641]

The year Coombe came to Carmel, three papers were delivered by pupils to the Haber Society, two of them being on biological topics. On this, the Carmel magazine reported, "[It] is no coincidence but a direct result of the new enthusiasm in that department created by Mr. Coombe."[1642]

Peter Rhodes comments on Coombe's driving ability, "He was a keen rally driver and had an Austin Healey Sprite. He once picked me up from Reading Station on a Sunday morning and drove me to Carmel in 12.5 minutes. As we entered the back drive he said to me 'only on a Sunday'."[1643] David Frome also recollects that he drove an Austin Healey Sprite, and added, "A really cool car! When he said that he was 'going to town over the litter' some bright spark piped up 'I didn't know you were that bad a driver, Sir.' He laughed with the rest of us. A great guy."[1644] David Uri still remembers the way Coombe dressed, "[He] always wore check sports jackets under his gown and favoured cavalry trill trousers and brown brogue shoes."[1645]

Coombe left Carmel in about 1966.[1646] In 1991, he was living in Leighton Buzzard in Bedfordshire,[1647] and appeared on the electoral roll of that place in 2002.[1648] Following his retirement from teaching, he was between March 2005 and April 2008 a director of Clare Court (Poole) Management Co. Ltd., a company which managed real estate, and which is situated in Dorset.[1649]

1639. Telephone conversation between author and Nigel Simons, 29 November 2012.
1640. Wikipedia – Seventh-day Adventist Church.
1641. E-mail from David Frome, 4 March 2013.
1642. Carmel 1961, p.28.
1643. E-mail from Peter Rhodes, 4 March 2013.
1644. E-mail from David Frome, 4 March 2013.
1645. E-mail from David Uri, 5 March 2013.
1646. E-mail from Peter Rhodes, 4 March 2013.
1647. Old Carmeli Association, Occupational Directory, 1991.
1648. 192.com (Internet).
1649. Dellam Corporate Information Limited – Clare Court (Poole) Management (Internet).

DR. PAUL F. HOWARTH

He joined the staff in the academic year 1960/61 as a Physics teacher, and according to the Carmel magazine this was soon after receiving his Ph.D.[1650] In addition he was the form master of form 4A.[1651]

In the summer term of 1961, a Broadcasting Club was set up in the school and Howarth gave "much support in many different ways. He helped both on the technical side and in the compiling of programmes."[1652]

Peter Rhodes has "red" recollections of him, "He was very keen on the colour red and so we would use it as much as possible in our diagrams. I once went a bit far as to demonstrate light refraction in water I had someone machine gunning (with red tracer) a fish. He did maintain that one day electricity would be transmitted like radio waves and to a certain extent this is beginning to happen with Israeli technology.[1653]

He was in favour of nuclear disarmament, and worked on the Blue Streak Missile programme.[1654] Harold Berwin recollects that Howarth would relate to his pupils "classified tales of the Blue Streak missile programme."[1655]

1650. Carmel 1961, p.4. However, the University which awarded him the Ph.D. has not been traced.
1651. Telephone conversation between author and Nigel Simons on 29 November 2012.
1652. Carmel 1961, p.31.
1653. E-mail from Peter Rhodes, 4 March 2013.
1654. Telephone conversation between author and Nigel Simons on 29 November 2012.
1655. E-mail from Harold Berwin, 8 October 2012.

Bibliography
(of Sections 1 and 2)

Some items in the bibliography could be put under more than one of the headings given below. In such a case, the choice of where to put them has been purely arbitrary.

JEWISH RELIGIOUS BOOKS

Babylonian Talmud.

Mechilta to Shemot.

Pirkei Avot.

Service of the Synagogue, Pentecost, fourteenth edition, (London: Routledge & Kegan Paul, 1954), Shulchan Aruch commentaries.

Tanach.

BOOKS (INCLUDING THOSE ON THE INTERNET)

Alida's Memoirs, the memoirs of Alida Bijl-Lursen on the period of the Nazi occupation of Holland, published on the Internet by her granddaughter Jenny Radcliffe.

Barfield, Samuel. *Thatcham, Berks and its Manors*, vol.1 (Oxford: James Parker, 1901).

Bawdwen, Rev. William. *A Translation of the Record called Domesday so far as relates to the counties of Middlesex, Hertford, Buckingham, Oxford and Gloucester* (Doncaster, 1812).

Bernstein, Avraham. *Yeshivat Mir – Hazericha b'paatei kedem* (Bnei Brak, 1999–2001) vol.3.

Braham, John Randall Daniel. *Night Fighter* (New York: Norton, 1962).

Braithwaite, Roderick. *"Strikingly Alive" The History of the Mill Hill School Foundation 1807–2007* (Phillimore: Chichester, 2006).

Buckeridge, Anthony. *Jenning's Diary* (London: Collins, 1953).

———. *Jennings Goes to School* (London: Collins, 1953).

———. *Our Friend Jennings*, first edition 1955 (London: Collins. reprinted edition 1973).

Carmel, Abraham. *So Strange My Path* (1st edition New York: MBY Foundation, 1960; Third printing, New York: Bloch Publishing Company, 1977; Revised edition, New York: Bloch Publishing Company, 1993).

Coleridge, Samuel Taylor. *The Rime of the Ancient Mariner*.

Dildy, Douglas C. *Raid Dambusters, Operation Chastise 1943* (Oxford: Osprey Publishing, 2010).

Domesday Book: Open Domesday, Berkshire (Internet).

Encyclopedia Britannica, 11th edition (Cambridge: University Press, 1910).

Fisher, Stuart. *British River Navigations: Inland Cuts, Fens, Dikes, Channels and Non-tidal Rivers* (London: Adlard Coles Nautical, 2013).

Gilbert, Martin. *The Boys* (London: Phoenix, 1997).

Gray, Edward William. *The History and Antiquities of Newbury and its Environs* (Speenhamland Berkshire: Hall and Marsh: 1839).

Greenham: a common inheritance, Ten thousand years of History, Victorian Pleasures and Country Life (Internet).

Greenham and Crookham Common: A Timeline (Internet).

In memory of F.M. Friedmann (Oxford, 1978).

Jarman, Angela. *Royal Academy Exhibitors 1905–1970*, volume III (Calne Wiltshire: Hilmarton Manor Press, 1981).

Lewin, David. *An Eye – or is it I? – on Myself* (London, October 2009).

Lewis, Theodore. *"Remembrances of Mir Yeshiva,"* Introductory section of Bar Mitzvah Sermons at Touro Synagogue (Brooklyn, New York, c.1989).

Meir Gertner – An Anthology. ed. A.H. Friedlander and Fred Worms (London: B'nai B'rith, 1978).

Memories of Kopul Rosen, ed. Cyril Domb (London, 1970).

Murray's Berkshire Architectural Guide, ed. John Betjeman and John Piper (London: John Murray, 1949).

"My Name is Aaron," (compiled by Harold Nagley's student Nerada Stern, 1983).

Ohr Bachatzer Ha'Achorit, story of Yafah Dorani (Internet).

Pedgley, Berenice and David. *Crowmarsh, A history of Crowmarsh Gifford, Newnham Murren, Mongewell and North Stoke* (Crowmarsh: Crowmarsh History Group, 1990).

Report by H.M. Inspectors on Carmel College, issued 8 June 1955 (Ministry of Education. UK).

Rosen, Jeremy. *Kopul Rosen 1913–1962*, (2011).

Rutland, Suzanne D. *If you will it, it is no dream – The Moriah Story 1943–2003* (Caringbah, N.S.W.: Playright Pub., 2003).

Segal, Sanford L. *Mathematics under the Nazis* (Princeton, New Jersey: Princeton University Press, 2003).

Shereshevsky, Esra. *The Sage of Leipzig* (Jerusalem: Rubin Mass, 1993).

Simons, Chaim. *My Fight for Yiddishkeit: Reminiscences of a Director of Jewish Studies* (Kiryat Arba, Israel, 2005).

———. *Seven Years at Carmel College: Reminiscences of a Pupil 1953–1960* (Kiryat Arba, Israel, 2006).

Warner, G. P. *The Founding Days of Eversley College* (Kent County Council, 1973).

Williamson, Miss L. E. *A Short History of Ramsey Grammar School* (about 1972).

NEWSPAPERS, JOURNALS, PERIODICALS, YEAR-BOOKS, ETC.

The Air Force List – November 1939 (London: H.M. Stationery Office).

AJR (Association of Jewish Refugees) Journal (London: Association of Jewish Refugees in Great Britain).

Al-fa (the Magazine of Farnborough Grammar School).
Antiques Trade Gazette (London).
Auction Catalogue, sale of the Crookham House Estate (1939).
Auction Catalogue, sale of Greenham Lodge (1938).
The Balliol College Register (Oxford University), third edition, 1900–1950
Beta (the Junior Magazine of Farnborough Grammar School).
Bexhill Observer.
Biblioteka Džona Plamenca, Universitet Crne Gore (University of Montenegro).
The Bradfordian (the magazine of Bradford School).
British Medical Journal (London: British Medical Association).
Bulletin of the Institute of Physics and the Physical Society (London: Institute of
    Physics and Physical Society).
Camp Hill Chronicle (Birmingham).
Canadian Jewish Chronicle.
Catalogue of University of London theses (Senate House Libraries, University of
    London).
Caterham House Boys School magazine (Caterham, Surrey).
Chelsea College of Physical Education, Old Students' Association Magazine.
The County Grammar School Magazine (Wymondham School, Norfolk).
Dei'ah veDibur (Internet).
The Dropsie College for Hebrew and Cognate Learning, Register.
The Eagle (St. John's College Cambridge).
Education & Training (Bradford: MCB University Press).
Evening Standard (London).
Exeter Express & Echo.
54th Little Missenden Festival.
Foreign Affairs (New York: Council on Foreign Relations).
General Register Office Index (births, marriages and deaths).
Gibraltar Chronicle (online edition).
The Glenalmond Chronicle (magazine of Glenalmond College, Perth, Scotland).
The Glenalmond Register, 1847–1954 (Edinburgh: Old Glenalmond Club).
The Guardian (online edition).
Hakirah: the Flatbush Journal of Jewish Law and Thought, (Flatbush, New York).
The Hasmonean 1945–1970 (brought out to mark the 25th anniversary of the
    Hasmonean Grammar School, London).
Hatzofe (Tel-Aviv).
Headfort School – The First 50 Years (brought out to mark the 50th anniversary of
    Headford School, Kells, Ireland).
The Hebrew University of Jerusalem 1925–1950, semi-jubilee volume, April 1950.
House of Lords debates.
House of Lords, Minutes and Order Paper – Minutes of Proceedings.
Individual Decisions, West Berkshire. 14 Feb 2008, Acquisition and Disposal Policy
    West Berkshire Museum.
Jerusalem Post.
Jewish Chronicle (London).
Jewish Exponent (Philadelphia).
Jewish Observer and Middle East Review (London).
Jewish Year Book (London: The Jewish Chronicle).

Jews' Free School magazine, Central School, Evacuation News Sheet, December 1939.
Journal of the Royal Society of Medicine (London: Royal Society of Medicine).
Journals of the House of Commons, (London: H. M. Stationery Office),
King Edward's School Chronicle (the magazine of King Edward's School, Birmingham).
Leo Baeck Institute Year Book (Oxford University Press. Oxford Journals), (Internet).
List of Graduates of London University up to 1931 (Senate House Library, University
    of London).
Little Missenden Festival, Ten Years 1960–1969.
Liverpool Institute Green Books (Liverpool Institute).
London Gazette (London: The Stationery Office).
Masmid, magazine of Yeshiva University, New York.
Medical History (History of Medicine Society, Cambridge University).
Merton College Register 1900–1964 (Basil Blackwell: Oxford, 1964).
Montreal Gazette.
Mosaic, magazine of the New West End Synagogue, London.
Newburian (the magazine of St. Bartholomew's Grammar School, Newbury).
The New Yorker (New York).
Oxford Mail (online edition).
Panorama News weekly, Gibraltar (Internet).
Parkes Library [University of Southampton] Newsletter, no.2, Spring 1993.
The Peerage (Internet).
Rhode Island Herald (Providence, Rhode Island).
Scope (the magazine of Mount Scopus College, Melbourne).
Spartanburg Herald Journal (South Carolina).
The Sphere (published by London Illustrated Newspapers, Ltd.).
The Stationers (the magazine of Stationers' Company School, London).
The Telegraph (online edition).
The Times (London).
The Times Educational Supplement (London).
Tradition: A Journal of Orthodox Jewish Thought (New York: Rabbinical Council of
    America).
Trinity College Record Volume (Dublin: Hodges, Figgis & Co. Ltd, 1951).
Who's Who 2002, (London: A & C. Black).
World ORT News Update
Y Feeagh (The Raven) (the magazine of Ramsey Grammar School, Isle of Man).
Zionist Record (Johannesburg).

BOOKS AND BOOKLETS PUBLISHED BY CARMEL COLLEGE

Beshir Vekol Todah (Carmel College Publications, no.1, first edition, 1955).
Carmel College 1948–1957.
Carmel College Library, A Brief Guide, 1960.
Carmel College Library, A Brief Guide, second edition, 1962.
Carmel College Provisional Prospectus, undated (about April 1948) – reproduced in
    "Reflections."
Carmel College Prospectus, undated (about 1951).
Carmel College Prospectus, undated (about 1956).
Carmel College Prospectus, undated (about 1959).
Carmel College, published as a tribute to Kopul Rosen, undated (1962).

Carmel College, Roll and Calendar, 1958–59.
Introduction to Carmel College, Brochure brought out on occasion of gala performance
of "The Diary of Anne Frank" (1959).
Rosen, Kopul. An Appraisal of Carmel College, 1961.

CARMEL COLLEGE MAGAZINES

Alpha (1954 – 1956).
Badad.
Carmel (annual summer magazine 1954–1962).
Carmel College Preparatory School magazine (1958–1959).
Carmel Clarion.
Carmel Fanfare.
Junior Biology Society Magazine.
The Phoenix.
The Young Carmelonian.

MATERIAL PUBLISHED BY OLD CARMELI ASSOCIATION

The Old Carmeli (magazine of Old Carmeli Association).
Old Carmeli Association Bulletin.
Old Carmeli Association, Occupational Directory 1991.
The Old Carmeli Year Book 1977.
Reflections: Carmel College 1948–1988. (Wallingford: Old Carmeli Association, 1989).
Rules and Constitution of The Old Carmeli Association, (1953).

CARMEL COLLEGE AUDIO-VISUAL MATERIAL

Cine camera short extracts of Carmel Sports Days – filmed by Batiste and Koppel
families.
Extracts from tape recordings of speeches made by Kopul Rosen on various Carmel
ceremonial occasions.
Foundation for a Vision – film produced by Pearl and Dean in 1965 (includes scenes
from Kopul era).
Gramophone record of Carmel Boys' Choir, about 1957.
Recording of the 1960 Speech Day.
Tape Recording made by Kopul Rosen, early 1962

ARCHIVAL MATERIAL

RECOLLECTIONS OF OLD CARMELIS OF KOPUL ERA

E-MAILS RECEIVED FROM OLD CARMELIS OF KOPUL ERA AND OUTSIDE SOURCES

INTERNET

Index of Names
associated with Carmel College

ACADEMIC STAFF

NON-ACADEMIC STAFF

PUPILS

GOVERNORS, DONORS AND POTENTIAL DONORS

Grounds of Carmel including bridge

Front view of Main Building

East wing of Main Building

Interior of Main Building

The room which was Kopul Rosen's study

Grounds of Carmel overlooking (what were!) the tennis courts

View of rear of Main Building

Grounds of Carmei